Home Cooking

CONTENTS

COOKING WITH STYLE

America's Best Homemade Recipes!

CONTENTS

OVER 1200 FAMILY-PROVEN RECIPES!

EXCLUSIVELY DISTRIBUTED BY:

P.S.I. & ASSOCIATES, INC.

13322 SW 128TH ST.
MIAMI, FL 33186
(305) 255-7959

Address all correspondance to the address above.

ISBN# 155993-174-4

27978

Appetizers
APPEALING

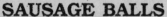

SAUSAGE BALLS
Makes 4 dozen

1 pound hot sausage, at room
   temperature
10 ounces extra-sharp Cracker
   Barrel cheese, grated
3 cups Bisquick mix

Mix Bisquick and grated cheese;
add sausage. Blend well. Shape into
small balls. Freeze on cookie sheet.
Store in a plastic bag in the freezer.
Place frozen balls on greased cookie
sheet. Bake at 300 degrees for 35-45
minutes. Serve hot.

Marcella Swigert, Monroe City, Mo.

CHINESE
ROLL-UPS WITH HOT
MUSTARD SAUCE
Makes 10

1 pound ground beef
1 can water chestnuts, chopped
2 tablespoons chopped onion
1 package onion and mushroom
   soup mix
1 tablespoon beef bouillon
1 can bean sprouts, drained
3 packages crescent rolls
1/4 cup prepared mustard
1/4 cup mayonnaise
1 clove garlic, chopped
1/4 teaspoon hot sauce
2 teaspoons horseradish

Brown ground beef. Add next 5
ingredients. Simmer for 5 minutes.
Remove from heat. Place 1 tablespoon meat mixture in center of each
crescent triangle. Pull corners over
meat mixture; pinch together to seal.

Place on baking sheet. Bake at 350
degrees for 15 minutes, or until
browned. Combine remaining ingredients; mix well. Refrigerate until
serving time. Serve hot mustard sauce
over roll-ups while still warm. May
be frozen for use later.

Marcella Swigert, Monroe City, Mo.

MUSHROOM
MUNCHIES

1/4 cup vegetable oil
1/4 cup vinegar with lemon
1 tablespoon sugar
1/2 teaspoon onion powder
1/4 teaspoon garlic powder
Pinch of oregano
1 (10-ounce) can whole mushrooms, drained

Mix ingredients together in small
bowl. Add mushrooms and marinate
for 1 hour. Toothpicks will assist with
serving or snacking of the whole
mushrooms.

**Millicent Corkum, St. John's, Newfound-
land, Canada**

FANCY DOGS
Serves 12

1 (6-ounce) jar mustard
1 (6-ounce) jar currant jelly
1 pound hot dogs, cut diagonally

Combine mustard and jelly in fondue pot; mix well. Heat to boiling
point. Add cut hot dogs. Heat until
warm. Place over fondue flame, stirring occasionally.

Marcella Swigert, Monroe City, Mo.

NUTTY BLEU
CHEESE DIP
Makes 2 cups

1 cup mayonnaise
1 (8-ounce) container sour cream
1/4 cup (1 ounce) bleu cheese,
   crumbled
1 tablespoon finely chopped onion
2 teaspoons instant beef bouillon
1/2 to 3/4 cup walnuts, coarsely
   chopped
Assorted fresh vegetables

In medium bowl, combine mayonnaise, sour cream, bleu cheese, onion,
and bouillon; mix well. Stir in nuts;
cover and chill. Stir before serving.
Garnish as desired. Serve with vegetables. Refrigerate leftovers.

Agnes Ward, Erie, Pa.

QUICK PEANUTTY
POPCORN BALLS
Makes 8 (2-1/2-inch) balls

1/2 cup light corn syrup
1/4 cup sugar
3/4 cup peanut butter
2 quarts plain popped corn

In a saucepan mix corn syrup and
sugar. Cook over medium heat; stir
constantly until mixture comes to a
boil and sugar is completely dissolved.
Remove from heat. Stir in peanut
butter until smooth. Immediately pour
mixture over popcorn in large bowl.
Stir until well-coated. Grease hands
and shape into 8 (2-1/2-inch) balls.

Vickie Vogt, Kewaskum, Wis.

BRAUNSCHWEIGER BALL

1 (8-ounce) package cream cheese, softened
1 pound braunschweiger, at room temperature
1/4 cup mayonnaise
1/4 teaspoon garlic salt
2 tablespoons dill pickle juice
1/2-3/4 cup chopped dill pickle
1/4 cup (or more) chopped onion
3 drops Tabasco sauce
1 tablespoon Worcestershire sauce
1/2 cup salted peanuts, chopped

Combine half the cream cheese with the remaining ingredients, except peanuts; mix well. Spread in a mold. Chill for several hours. Unmold. Frost with remaining cream cheese. Garnish with chopped peanuts. Snack with assorted crackers or slices of party loaf bread.

Marcella Swigert, Monroe City, Mo.

DILL WEED DIP

2/3 cup real mayonnaise
2/3 cup sour cream
1 tablespoon dried onion
1 tablespoon dried parsley
2 teaspoons dill weed
1 teaspoon Lawry's seasoning salt
Dash pepper
2 drops Tabasco sauce
1/2 teaspoon Worcestershire sauce
1/2 teaspoon Accent

Mix together and let set at least 2 hours before serving. Fresh vegetables and bread cubes are great to serve with the dip.

Loriann Johnson, Gobles, Mich.

SAVORY CHEESE BITES
Makes 7 dozen

1 cup water
1/8 teaspoon salt
4 eggs
1/2 cup butter
1 cup flour
1 cup shredded Swiss cheese

Combine water, butter, and salt in a pan; bring to a boil. Stir until butter melts. Add flour; stir vigorously until mixture leaves sides of pan to form a smooth ball. Remove from heat. Add eggs, one at a time; stir until well-blended. Return to heat and beat mixture until smooth. Remove from heat; stir in cheese. Drop batter by heaping teaspoonfuls onto a greased baking sheet. Bake 400 degrees for 20 minutes, or until puffed and golden brown.

Vickie Vogt, Kewaskum, Wis.

SAUSAGE TEMPTERS IN APPLESAUCE
Makes 4 dozen

1   pound pork sausage
2   cups applesauce
1   ounce cinnamon red candies
2   drops red food coloring

Form sausage in ¾-inch balls. Brown and cook meatballs in a skillet. Turn them so they brown evenly. Place a toothpick in each ball. Heat applesauce, candies and food coloring until candies dissolve. Place sausage balls in sauce, toothpick side up. Serve hot.

Note: A chafing dish would be ideal in which to keep sausages hot while serving.

Carmen Bickert, Dubuque, Iowa

SALMON LOG

1 (1-pound) can salmon
1 (8-ounce) package cream cheese, softened
1 tablespoon lemon juice
2 tablespoons grated onion
1 teaspoon prepared horseradish
1/4 teaspoon salt
1 teaspoon liquid smoke seasoning
1/2 cup chopped walnuts
3 tablespoons snipped parsley

Drain and flake salmon, removing skin and bones. Combine salmon with the next 6 ingredients; mix well. Chill several hours. Combine walnuts and parsley. Shape salmon mixture into 8x2-inch log, or use a fish mold. Roll in nut mixture. Chill well. Serve with crisp crackers.

Brenda Peery, Tannersville, Va.

CRAB PUFFS

1   cup water
1   stick margarine
1   cup flour
4   eggs

Bring water to boil and add margarine, return to boil. Add flour all at once. Remove from heat and beat in 1 egg at a time. Then add all the following ingredients:
3   scallions, chopped
1   teaspoon dry mustard
1   (6½-ounce) can crabmeat
1   teaspoon Worcestershire sauce
½   cup sharp cheddar cheese, grated

Drop on cookie sheet by spoonfuls. Bake at 400 degrees for 15 minutes. Turn oven down to 350 degrees and bake 10 additional minutes.

These can also be frozen.

Rosie E. O'Connell, Greensburg, Pa.

FAVORITE SPOON BREAD

Serves 8

1 1/3 teaspoons sugar
1 1/2 teaspoons salt
1 cup cornmeal, sifted
1 1/3 cups water, boiling (cool 5 minutes)
1/4 cup butter *or* margarine
3 eggs, lightly beaten
1 1/4 cups milk
1 teaspoon baking powder

Preheat oven to 350 degrees. Mix together sugar, salt and cornmeal. Pour water over meal mixture, stirring constantly. Mix in butter; let stand until cooled; add eggs, milk and baking powder, blending well.

Pour into buttered pan (2-quart). Place in shallow pan of hot water. Bake in a 350-degree oven for 35 minutes, or until crusty. Spoon out; serve.

This spoon bread has a light texture, soft center, and crusty top. Most delicious!

Jeanie Blass, Richmond, Va.

NO–KNEAD ROLLS

Makes 2 dozen

1/2 cup scalded milk
3 tablespoons shortening
3 tablespoons sugar
2 teaspoons salt
1/2 cup water
1 cake yeast *or* 1 package active dry yeast
1 egg
3 cups all-purpose flour
Melted shortening

Blend together milk, 3 tablespoons shortening, sugar, and salt. Cool to lukewarm by adding water. Add yeast, and mix well. Add egg. Add flour, gradually, mixing until dough is well-blended. Place in greased bowl. Brush top with melted shortening and allow to rise until light. Knead dough a few times to make smooth ball. Form into desired shapes and bake in 400-degree oven for 15-25 minutes or until golden brown. Easy and very tasty.

Agnes Ward, Erie, Pa.

POPPY SEED BREAD

1 package Duncan Hines Yellow Cake Mix
1 package toasted coconut instant pudding (Royal brand)
1/4 cup (scant) poppy seeds
4 eggs
1 cup hot water
1/2 cup Crisco oil

Mix well; pour into 2 well-greased loaf pans 9x5-1/2x2 1/2-inches. Bake at 350 degrees for 40-50 minutes. This is a very moist bread!

This is very delicious spread with Philadelphia Cream Cheese, plus makes a nice bread to serve along with fruit salad!

Alberta Wiley, Zionsville, Ind.

CHOCOLATE FUDGE MUFFINS

1 cup butter or margarine
4 squares semisweet chocolate
1-1/2 cups white sugar
1 cup flour
1/4 teaspoon salt
4 eggs, beaten
1 teaspoon vanilla

In a saucepan over low heat, combine margarine and chocolate. Melt, stirring frequently, so the chocolate does not burn or stick.

In a bowl, combine sugar, flour and salt. Stir in chocolate mixture. Beat eggs, then add them to batter with the vanilla. Stir until eggs are well-blended, but do not beat the mixture. Line muffin tins with paper liners. Fill each one about two-thirds full. Bake at 300 degrees for 30–40 minutes. Check to see if muffins are done by inserting a toothpick in one near the center of the muffin. If the toothpick does not come out clean, bake for another 5 minutes. Let muffins cool 5 minutes before removing them from the pan. These taste much like brownies. Keep any leftovers in a covered container, then rewarm them.

Lillian Smith, Montreal, Quebec, Canada

CRANBERRY BANANA NUT BREAD

2 cups flour
3 teaspoons baking powder
1/2 teaspoon salt
1/2 teaspoon cinnamon
1 cup fresh cranberries, ground
1 teaspoon grated orange rind
1 cup mashed very ripe bananas (3 large)
1/2 cup milk
4 tablespoons butter
1 cup sugar
1 egg
1 cup chopped pecans

Sift together flour, baking powder, salt and cinnamon. Blend orange rind with ground cranberries. In 2-quart bowl, blend bananas and milk. Cream butter and sugar together; blend in egg. Sift dry ingredients alternately with banana mixture, stirring until just blended. Stir in cranberry mixture and pecans. Bake in 9x5x3-inch pan at 350 degrees for 1 hour and 15 minutes. Store at least 24 hours before slicing.

Jenni Lien, Stoughton, Wis.

BUTTERMILK CORN BREAD

3/4 cup Lysine cornmeal
1 cup white flour
3 tablespoons sugar
1 teaspoon soda
3/4 teaspoon salt
1 cup buttermilk
1 egg, beaten
2 tablespoons melted margarine

Preheat oven to 400 degrees. Stir together cornmeal, flour, sugar and salt. Set aside.

Dissolve soda in buttermilk. Add beaten egg and melted margarine; stir until mixed, then add to dry ingredients and mix well. Turn into greased 9x9-inch pan, or into greased muffin pan. Bake 20 minutes, or until golden and done.

These are delicious and healthful eating.

Irene Adney, Eureka Springs, Ark.

CHEESE DIP
Makes 3-1/2 cups

2 cups sour cream
1-1/2 cups shredded Cheddar
  cheese
1/4 cup sliced pimiento-stuffed
  olives
1/2 teaspoon salt
1/4 teaspoon sage

Blend sour cream with remaining ingredients. Serve chilled. Especially good with saltine crackers!

Lucy Dowd, Sequim, Wash.

FRUIT DIP
Make 3 cups

2 cups sour cream
1/4 cup drained crushed pineapple
2/3 cup chopped red apples
1/2 teaspoon curry powder
1/2 teaspoon garlic salt
Apple slices for garnish

Blend sour cream with apple, pineapple, curry powder, and garlic salt. Place in bowl and chill. Garnish with sliced apples around outer edge of bowl.

Good with corn chips or shredded wheat wafers.

Lucy Dowd, Sequim, Wash.

FRESH MUSHROOM DIP

1-8 ounce package cream cheese, softened
2 tablespoons snipped ripe olives
2 tablespoons snipped parsley
3/4 teaspoon seasoned salt
4 drops bottled hot pepper sauce
1/2 cup sour cream
1/2 pound fresh mushrooms, finely chopped

Combine cream cheese and seasonings; fold in sour cream and chill. Stir in mushrooms just before serving.

Marcella Swigert, Monroe City, MO

DIPPETY DOO DIP

1 squeeze tube of hickory smoked cheese
1 cup sour cream
1 can bean with bacon soup (undiluted)
2 or 3 minced green onions (use all)

Combine all ingredients and warm over double boiler or in Microwave. Mix well. Serve with tortilla chips.
You can't eat just one!

Mary Bruesehoff, Spokane, WA

SNACKIN DIPS FOR CHIPS
Serves 4

1 can (6 1/2 ounce) chunk tuna
1 envelope instant onion soup mix
1 cup dairy sour cream
1 tablespoon prepared horseradish
Parsley for garnish
Potato chips - celery sticks - cherry tomatoes

Drain tuna. Combine tuna with soup mix, sour cream, and horseradish. Garnish with parsley. Arrange potato chips, celery sticks, and tomatoes on platter.   **Agnes Ward, Erie, PA**

LOW CAL CLAM DIP
Makes 2 cups

1-8 ounce can minced clams
1-1/2 cups cottage cheese
1/2 teaspoon seasoned salt
2 teaspoons lemon juice
1 teaspoon Worcestershire sauce
1 tablespoon minced green onions
Assorted crisp vegetable dippers

In blender container, combine clams with liquid, cottage cheese seasoned salt, lemon juice, and Worcestershire sauce. Cover and whirl around until smooth. Stir in green onions. Cover and chill at least two hours to blend flavors. Serve with cauliflower, broccoli, and strips of carrots, zucchini, and cucumbers.

Agnes Ward, Erie, PA

BLUE CHEESE DIP

3 ounces blue cheese, crumbled
1/2 cup sour cream
1/2 cup mayonnaise
Dash of paprika
Dash of garlic powder
Assorted vegetables, cut in strips

Mix together all ingredients except vegetables and chill 2 hours to blend flavors. Serve with vegetables.

Charlotte Adams, Detroit, MI

RAW VEGETABLE DIP
Yield - 2-1/2 cups

2 cups applesauce
1/2 pint dairy sour cream
2 tablespoons minced onion
1 teaspoon Worcestershire sauce
1/2 teaspoon salt

Slowly cook applesauce abut 5 minutes to evaporate some of the liquid; chill. Combine the applesauce, sour cream, onion, Worcestershire sauce and salt. Mix well. Use as a dip for fresh, raw vegetables of your choice.

Agnes Ward, Erie, PA

CHEESE BALL

8 ounce cream cheese
6 ounce blue cheese, crumbled
6 ounce jar Old English cheese
2 tablespoons mayonnaise
Dash of garlic salt
2 tablespoons finely chopped onion
6 ounce chopped walnuts

Mix all three (3) cheeses together with an electric mixer. Add mayonnaise, garlic salt, onion, and walnuts to cheese mixture. Shape into a ball and wrap with plastic wrap. Refrigerate twenty-four (24) hours before serving. When ready to serve, sprinkle paprika.

Joanie Lopez, Beckley, WV

Serve chicken wings and sauce with steamed rice.
Mrs. Betty L. Herrick, Nokomis, Fla.

CHEESE-COCONUT BALLS
Makes about 30

2 packages (3 ounces each) Roquefort cheese
1 package (4 ounces) shredded cheddar cheese
1 package (8 ounces) cream cheese, softened
1 package (3 1/2 ounces) flaked coconut

Mash cheeses and combine them thoroughly with electric mixer. Chill for at least one hour. Shape into 1-inch balls and roll in coconut. Serve with fresh apple slices.

Mrs. Agnes Ward, Erie, Pa.

PINEAPPLE CHICKEN WINGS
Serves 4

12 chicken wings
3 tablespoons butter
1 small onion, sliced
8 1/2-ounce can pineapple chunks, drained, juice reserved
Orange juice
1/4 cup soy sauce
2 tablespoons brown sugar
1 tablespoon vinegar
1 teaspoon ground ginger
1/2 teaspoon salt
1/2 teaspoon ground mace
1/2 teaspoon hot pepper sauce
1/4 teaspoon dry mustard
1 1/2 tablespoons cornstarch

Fold chicken wing tips under to form triangles. Melt butter in large skillet; add wings and onion. Cook until wings are brown on both sides, about 10 minutes. Measure reserved pineapple syrup and add enough orange juice to make 1 1/4 cups liquid. Blend in soy sauce, sugar, vinegar, ginger, salt, mace, hot pepper sauce and mustard. Pour over chicken.

Cover and simmer 30 minutes, or until chicken is tender, basting top pieces once or twice. Remove chicken to hot plate. Add a small amount of water to cornstarch, blending to dissolve. Add slowly to the hot liquid in pan, stirring, and bring to boil to thicken. Return chicken to skillet, along with pineapple chunks.

BROILED CHICKEN LIVER ROLL-UPS

2 cans water chestnuts
1 pound chicken livers
1/2 pound bacon (cut each slice into thirds)
1 bottle soy sauce
1/2 cup brown sugar

Drain water chestnuts and slice each into 3 pieces. Wrap each water chestnut with a small piece of chicken liver and bacon piece. Secure with a toothpick and marinate in soy sauce for at least 4 hours.

Just before serving, remove roll-ups from soy sauce and roll each in brown sugar. Place on broiler rack and broil for about 10 minutes, or until crisp. Serve at once.

TASTY CHICKEN BASKETS
Makes 40-50 baskets

Baskets (directions follow)
Filling:
2 cups chopped cooked chicken meat
5 slices bacon, fried and crumbled
3 tablespoons diced, pared apple
1/2 teaspoon salt
1/8 teaspoon pepper
1/4 cup mayonnaise
1/4 cup finely chopped pecans
4-ounce can mushrooms, chopped

Combine and mix all filling ingredients. Cover and refrigerate for 2 hours. Makes 2 1/2 cups filling, enough for 40-50 baskets.
To make Baskets:
Cut 90-100 rounds from regular sliced bread using a 1 1/2-inch round cookie cutter. Spread half the rounds with softened butter.

Cut a small hole from the centers of remaining bread rounds, "doughnut" fashion. Place each "doughnut" atop a buttered round, and fill center with chicken filling, mounding high. Garnish with sprigs of parsley.

Louise Beckner

ROLLED SANDWICHES
Makes 25-30 sandwiches

1 loaf of bread, sliced into lengthwise slices
Filling:
1/4 pound (1 stick) butter, softened
4 ounces cream cheese
1/4 teaspoon paprika
1/4 teaspoon salt
1 tablespoon mayonnaise
3/4 cup minced nuts, raisins, dates and/or figs

Slice crusts from long pieces of bread. Combine *Filling* ingredients well. Spread on bread slices. Roll up from narrow ends. (Before rolling, strips of sweet pickles or olives may be placed over filling for colorful variations.) Press end of roll firmly and wrap each roll tightly in plastic wrap. Store in refrigerator overnight.

Before serving, slice each roll into 1/4-inch slices. Arrange on serving plate.

Note: Instead of the nuts-and-dried-fruit filling, you can use one of the following: 1 1/2 cups tuna salad, crab, shrimp, salmon, finely chopped raw vegetables, grated cheddar cheese, chicken, turkey or ham filling.

Sue Hammer

SHRIMP PUFFERS
Makes 60 appetizers

8 tablespoons softened butter or margarine
2 eggs, separated
3 cups shredded sharp cheddar cheese
15 slices white bread (thin-sliced)
60 cooked shrimp, shelled and deveined

Blend butter, cheese and egg yolk until smooth. Beat egg whites until stiff; fold into cheese mixture.

Trim crusts from thinly sliced bread; cut each piece in quarters diagonally. Top each slice with a shrimp and 1 teaspoon of the cheese mixture. Bake in a preheated 350-degree oven on lightly greased cookie sheets for about 15 minutes, or until puffy and golden.

7

CANAPE PUFFS
Makes about 25 puffs

1/2 cup water
1/4 cup (1/2 stick) butter
1/2 cup flour
2 eggs

Heat water and butter to boiling; reduce heat and stir in flour all at once. Stir about 1 minute until mixture forms ball around spoon. Remove from heat and beat in eggs, one at a time, until mixture is smooth.

Place by rounded teaspoonsful onto ungreased cookie sheets. Bake in a preheated 400-degree oven for about 25 minutes or until golden. Remove and cool on racks.

Slice off tops; remove any doughy insides. Fill with any sandwich filling; chill until serving time.

Blanche Towner

EGG & HAM HORS D'OEUVRES
Makes 20 appetizers

5 hard-cooked eggs
1 teaspoon minced chives
Salt and paprika
1-2 drops hot pepper sauce
Mayonnaise
1/2 pound boiled ham

Separate yolks and whites of eggs. Force yolks through a sieve; add chives, seasonings and mayonnaise to moisten. Beat to a smooth paste. Chop egg whites and ham together and mix with yolks. Form into 1-inch balls and garnish with additional mayonnaise.

Mrs. Agnes Ward, Erie, Penn.

BLUE CHEESE MUSHROOMS

1 pound mushrooms (1-1 1/2 inches in diameter)
1/4 cup green onion slices
2 tablespoons butter or margarine
1 cup (4 ounces) crumbled blue cheese
1 small package (3 ounces) cream cheese, softened
Remove stems from mushrooms;

chop stems. Saute stems and green onion in margarine until soft. Combine with cheeses, mixing well. Stuff mixture into mushroom caps. Place on a broiler pan rack and broil for 2-3 minutes or until golden brown. Serve hot.

Mrs. Agnes Ward, Erie, Penn.

SWEET AND SOUR MEATBALLS

1 pound lean ground beef
1 envelope dry onion-soup mix
1 egg
Combine beef, soup mix and egg and form into tiny meatballs. Brown in skillet; discard all but 1 tablespoon fat.

Sauce:
8-ounce can tomato sauce
16-ounce can whole-berry cranberry sauce

Combine ingredients for sauce with reserved tablespoon of fat from meat in saucepan. Heat; add meatballs. Cover and simmer for about an hour. Serve with toothpicks.

Bonnie La Roche, Bensalem, Penn.

PEPPERONI BALLS

1 package hot roll mix
1/4 pound mozzarella cheese, cut in cubes
1/4-1/2 lb. pepperoni, thinly sliced

Prepare roll mix according to package directions, but *omitting egg* and using *1 cup water*. Dough does *not* need to rise. Place one cheese cube on one pepperoni slice. Pinch off a piece of dough and shape carefully around cheese and pepperoni, forming a ball. Repeat until all ingredients are used.

Fry in deep hot oil for about 5 minutes, or until golden brown, turning once. Drain on paper towels and serve warm.

BLUE CHEESE BITES
Makes 40 appetizers

1 package (10-count) refrigerated biscuits

1/4 cup margarine
3 tablespoons crumbled blue cheese or grated Parmesan cheese

Cut each biscuit into four pieces. Arrange pieces on two greased 8x1 1/2-inch round baking pans. Melt margarine; add cheese and stir to blend. Drizzle cheese mixture over biscuits. Bake in 400-degree oven for 12-15 minutes.

Mrs. Robert T. Shaffer, Middleburg, Penn.

CHICKEN WINGS

1 pound chicken wings
1/4 pound (1 stick) butter
1/4 teaspoon garlic powder
2 tablespoons parsley
1 cup fine, dry bread crumbs
1/2 cup Parmesan cheese
1 teaspoon salt
1/4 teaspoon pepper

Cut off tips from chicken wings and discard; split remaining portion of wing at joint to form two pieces. Melt butter, mixing in garlic powder. Combine bread crumbs, Parmesan cheese and seasonings. Dip chicken wing portions in seasoned butter, then roll in crumbs. Bake on a greased baking sheet (use one with edges) in a preheated 325-degree oven for about 50 minutes.

These can be frozen and baked later.

Nancy Lesky, LaCrosse, Wis.

DEVILED EGGS

4 hard-cooked eggs
1/3 cup grated Parmesan cheese
1 teaspoon prepared mustard
Pepper
Skim milk
Paprika

Halve the eggs lengthwise; remove yolks and mash. Add the cheese, mustard, few grains pepper, and enough milk to moisten well. Beat until fluffy and refill the egg whites. May want to garnish with paprika for added color. (65 calories per egg half)

Shari Crider, Stoughton, Wis.

HAM BALLS
Makes approximately 48 appetizers

4 cups ground lean ham
1/2 cup finely chopped onion
1/4 teaspoon pepper
2 eggs
1 cup plain bread crumbs

Combine and mix all ingredients. Shape into 1-inch balls. Place in a shallow pan and bake at 400 degrees for 25 minutes.

Sour Cream Gravy:
2 tablespoons shortening
2 tablespoons flour
1/4 teaspoon dill seed
1/4 teaspoon marjoram
1/2 cup water
1 1/2 cups sour cream

Melt shortening; add flour and seasonings. Cook until it bubbles. Add water and sour cream, stirring constantly. Cook until thick. Makes 2 cups sauce.

Serve *Ham Balls* with *Sour Cream Gravy;* provide toothpicks for dipping.

Edna Peavy

DEVILED TURKEY BONBONS

1 cup cooked, finely chopped turkey
1 cup finely chopped nuts
1 tablespoon chopped onion
2 tablespoons chopped pimiento
1/4 teaspoon salt
Hot pepper sauce to taste
1/4 cup cream of mushroom soup.

Combine turkey and 1/2 cup nuts. Add remaining ingredients except remaining nuts; mix well. Shape into small balls and roll in remaining chopped nuts. Chill until serving time.

SIMPLE HORS D'OEUVRES

It's true that these tempting tidbits have a French name, may be very elaborate, and are usually met in hotels, but that's no reason for not serving them simply, in the home, for a little variety.

Try a bit of pink, moist salmon on a piece of rye toast . . . some ripe olives . . . celery, stuffed with cream cheese flavored with mayonnaise, salt and paprika, or filled with a mixture of equal parts cream cheese and Roquefort cheese which has been seasoned with Worcestershire sauce . . . slices of salami. . . . All these are as truly and delightfully "hors d'oeuvres" as the most elaborate arrangement of caviar and egg.

CHEESE SURPRISE APPETIZERS

2 cups grated sharp cheddar cheese
1/2 cup softened butter
1 cup flour
1 small jar green, pimiento-stuffed olives

Mix cheese, butter and flour to form dough. Shape into small balls about 1 inch in diameter. Flatten ball with hands; place one olive in center, wrap dough around it, sealing edges completely. Freeze until just before ready to serve. (These *must* be frozen.)

When ready to serve, place frozen appetizers on baking sheet and immediately place in 375-degree oven. Bake about 10 minutes, or until golden. Cheese will puff up and melt.

Eleonora R. Scholl, Glendale, Wis.

ASPARAGUS ROLLS
Makes 20 appetizers

20 slices bread
1 package frozen asparagus
1 5-ounce jar processed pimiento cheese spread

Trim crusts from bread slices; spread each with cheese. Cook asparagus until just tender. Chill. Lay one piece asparagus diagonally across slice of bread. Turn opposite corners over asparagus, overlapping. Press firmly to seal. Wrap several sandwiches together in waxed paper. Place in covered container and chill for several hours.

Dorrie Fortner

MEATBALL APPETIZERS
Makes about 8 dozen tiny meatballs and 2 cups sauce

1 1/2 pounds ground beef
2 eggs
1/4 cup milk
1 cup plain bread crumbs
1/4 cup chopped onion
1 1/2 teaspoons chopped parsley
1 1/2 teaspoons salt
1/8 teaspoon pepper
3 tablespoons oil
10-ounce bottle chili sauce
1/2 cup grape jelly
1 tablespoon instant coffee

Combine meat, eggs, milk, crumbs, onion, parsley, salt and pepper and mix well. Shape into tiny meatballs and brown well on all sides in skillet in hot oil. Remove meatballs from pan. Drain excess drippings, leaving just 2-3 tablespoons. Add chili sauce, jelly and instant coffee to pan drippings and simmer, stirring occasionally, until jelly melts (about 4 minutes). Add meatballs and simmer 10 more minutes. Serve on toothpicks.

Meatballs can be browned, refrigerated, then cooked with sauce just before serving.

Dorrie Fortner

ANTIPASTO

2 cans tuna fish, undrained
1 can anchovies, undrained
1 small jar stuffed olives, drained
1 small bottle cocktail onions, drained
1 medium can mushrooms, cut up and drained
1 jar sweet pickled cauliflower, drained and cut in small pieces
1 small jar tiny sweet pickles, drained and cut in small pieces
1 No. 2 can green beans, drained
1 cup carrots, cooked crisp, cut in small rings
1 bottle chili sauce
1 bottle catsup

Mix all ingredients. Add a little salad oil if not moist enough. Marinate in refrigerator for at least one day. Eat with crackers. Makes a delicious hors d'oeuvre.

Mrs. Dena Little, Bened, Ill.

RYE CRACKERS

2 cups rye flour
2 cups wheat flour
Salt to taste
1/4 teaspoon baking soda
1/2 cup vegetable oil
1 cup (or more) water
1 tablespoon caraway seeds

Mix together. Roll out thinly on floured surface. Cut into desired shapes. Bake on cookie sheets at 275 degrees for about 30 minutes.

Fay Duman, Eugene, OR

DILL CRACKERS

2/3 cup Wesson oil
1 envelope ranch-style dry salad dressing
1 teaspoon dill
1/2 teaspoon lemon pepper
1/4 teaspoon garlic salt
10 ounce package oyster crackers

Mix all together, except crackers. Coat crackers with mixture, tossing until well coated, about 5 or 6 minutes.

Edna Askins, Greenville, TX

NUT BALLS

1 stick butter
1 cup pecans
1 teaspoon vanilla
2 tablespoons sugar
1 cup flour

Mix all ingredients and roll into tiny balls and bake at 250 degrees for one hour. Cool slightly and roll in confectioners' sugar. Roll in sugar again about half-hour later.

Karin Shea Fedders, Dameron, MD

TUNA SPREAD

1 can tuna (water packed), drained

10

---

1 (8-ounce) package cream cheese, softened
1 small onion, finely chopped
Salt and pepper to taste

Blend all ingredients until smooth. Serve with crackers. This can be rolled into a log and used for all types of festive entertaining.

Mrs. John J. Jenkins, Steubenville, OH

NUTS, BOLTS AND SCREWS

1 pound pecans
1 large box Cherrios
1 medium box stick pretzels
1 tablespoon Worcestershire sauce
1 box Wheat Chex
2 tablespoons salt
1 tablespoon garlic salt
1 pound oleo or butter
8 8

Melt butter in large roaster. Pour in all cereals, nuts and pretzels and seasonings. set oven at 200 degrees. Stir every 15 minutes for 1 hour.

Sue Hibbard, Rochester, NY

WHEAT GERM CRUNCHIES
Makes 3-1/2 dozen

1/2 cup all-purpose flour
1/2 teaspoon soda
2 teaspoons baking powder
1/4 teaspoon salt
1 cup brown sugar, firmly packed
1/2 cup shortening
1 egg, beaten
1/2 teaspoon vanilla
1/2 cup coconut
1/2 cup uncooked oatmeal
1 cup wheat germ
1-1/2 cups corn or wheat flakes

Sift flour, soda, baking powder and salt. Cream shortening and sugar. Add egg and vanilla. Add dry ingredients and wheat germ. Mix well. Stir in coconut, oatmeal and cornflakes just enough to mix. Drop by teaspoons on greased cookie sheet or roll into walnut-sized balls with fingers and place on greased cookie

---

sheet. Bake 15 minutes at 350 degrees.

Barbara Beauregard-Smith, Northfield, South Australia, Australia

TAFFY APPLES

1 large can crushed pineapple (save drained juice)
2-1/2 cups miniature marshmallows
1 egg
1 tablespoon flour.
12 ounces Cool Whip
3/4 cup cocktail or Spanish peanuts
1-1/2 tablespoons vinegar
1/2 cup sugar
4-6 apples, unpeeled and chopped

Combine drained pineapple and marshmallows; refrigerate overnight. Beat pineapple juice, egg, flour, vinegar and sugar; heat until thick, stirring constantly. Cool and refrigerate overnight, separate from pineapple.

Next day: Mix sauce and Cool Whip; add peanuts, marshmallow mixture and apples; stir. Refrigerate at least 2 hours before serving.

Debbie Jones, Walnutport, PA

CELERY PINWHEELS

1 medium stalk celery
1 (3-ounce) package cream cheese
2 tablespoons crumbled Roquefort cheese
Mayonnaise
Worcestershire sauce

Clean celery and separate branches. Blend together the softened cream cheese with the Roquefort cheese. Add mayonnaise to make the mixture of spreading consistency and season with a dash of Worcestershire sauce. Fill the branches of celery with cheese mixture. Press branches back into the original form of the stalk. Roll in waxed paper and chill overnight in refrigerator. Just before serving, slice celery crosswise forming pinwheels. Arrange pinwheels on crisp lettuce for serving.

Marcella Swigert, Monroe City, MO

Beverages

REFRESHING

ICED TEA A LA MODE
Serves 3

2 cups double-strength cold tea
1 pint vanilla ice cream

Blend tea and ice cream until smooth and pour into a tall glass.

PEANUT BUTTER SHAKE
Makes 4 cups

2 cups milk
1 pint vanilla ice cream
1/4 cup creamy peanut butter

Combine all ingredients in container of electric blender; process until smooth. Serve at once.

Bertha Fowler, Woodruff, S.C.

HIGH-CALCIUM BANANA SHAKE
Serves 6

2 cups non-fat milk
1/4 cup non-fat dry milk
1 tablespoon vanilla extract
2 tablespoons fructose
1 banana
1 cup ice cubes

Place all ingredients in a blender and blend until smooth. Serve immediately, preferably in a chilled glass. (90 calories per shake)

SWEET CHERRY SODA
Serves 2

1/3 cup ruby-red cherry sauce
2 scoops vanilla ice cream
Club soda
2 whole sweet cherries

In a blender container, combine cherry sauce and ice cream. Cover and process until smooth. Pour half of mixture into each of 2 tall glasses. Fill glasses with club soda. Garnish each serving with a whole cherry.

Annie Cmehil, New Castle, Ind.

SPICED PEACH PUNCH
Serves 12 (Hot drink)

1 (46 ounce) can peach nectar
1 (20 ounce) can orange juice
1/2 cup brown sugar, firmly packed
3 (3 inch) pieces stick cinnamon, broken
1/2 teaspoon whole cloves
2 tablespoons lime juice

Combine peach nectar, orange juice, and brown sugar in a large saucepan. Tie cinnamon sticks and cloves in a cheesecloth bag and drop into saucepan.

Heat slowly, stirring constantly, until sugar dissolves; simmer 10 minutes. Stir in lime juice; ladle into mugs. You may garnish with cinnamon sticks. Serve warm.

Mrs. C. Michele Mastindill, Calhan, Colo.

CRANBERRY COCKTAIL PUNCH
Serves 30

2 (32 ounce) bottles cranberry juice cocktail, chilled
2 cups orange juice, chilled
1 cup pineapple juice, chilled
1/2 cup sugar
1/2 cup lemon juice, chilled
1 (28 ounce) bottle ginger ale, chilled
1 tray ice cubes
Lemon slices for garnish

In large punch bowl, stir first 5 ingredients until sugar is dissolved. Add remaining ingredients, except lemon slices, which should be added just before serving.

Leona Teodori, Warren, Mich.

CAFE SWISS MOCHA

1/4 cup powdered non-fat dairy creamer or non-fat dry milk
1/4 cup instant coffee
1/3 cup sugar
2 tablespoons cocoa

Shake in jar to mix. Use 1 level tablespoon, to 6 ounces boiling water. Put 1 heaping teaspoon into 1 cup cold water; heat in microwave for 1 minute, 15 seconds; let sit a moment; stir.

Ann Stuzee, Lincoln, Neb.

PACIFIC FRUIT PUNCH

1 large can orange juice
1 large can apriocot nectar
1 large can pineapple juice
1 quart ginger ale
1 cup fresh strawberries
1 quart orange sherbet, soften in refrigerator

Combine juices and ginger ale in punchbowl. Add sherbet, strawberries, and ice. Garnish individual glasses with pineapple spears and small umbrellas.

SPICED TEA MIX
Makes ¾ cup

⅔ cup Tang Orange Flavored Breakfast Beverage Crystals
3 tablespoons instant tea
1 teaspoon nutmeg
1 teaspoon allspice

Combine all ingredients and blend well. Store in tightly covered jar. For 1 serving, combine ½ cup *each*, water and apple juice in saucepan, and bring just to a boil. Pour over 1 well-rounded teaspoon Tea Mix in mug and stir until dissolved. Serve hot or over ice. For 1 quart, combine 2 cups each water and apple juice, and bring just to a boil. Add ⅓ cup mix; stir until dissolved. Serve hot or over ice.

Diane Cole, Cleveland, Ohio

ICED TEA SODA
Serves 8

4 cups double-strength cold tea
1/2 cup light corn syrup
1 pint vanilla ice cream
Carbonated water

Blend tea and corn syrup. Fill a tall glass half-full with mixture. Add a scoop of ice cream, then fill the glass to the top with carbonated water.

LOW-CAL SPICED TEA MIX
Makes 48 servings

1 cup lemon-flavored instant tea, sweetened with NutraSweet
1 tablespoon Tang, sweetened with NutraSweet
1 tablespoon apple pie spice
1 (1 1/2-ounce) package lemonade drink mix, sweetened with NutraSweet

Combine all ingredients in a bowl and mix well. Store mixture in airtight container. For each serving, place 1 1/4–1 1/2 teaspoons mix in cup. Add 3/4 cup hot water. Stir well. (3 calories per serving)

Brenda Peery, Tannersville, Va.

HOLIDAY PUNCH
Serves 50

3 cups sugar
3 cups water
4 cups cranberry juice cocktail
3 cups lemon juice
2 cups orange juice
2 cups unsweetened pineapple juice
2 quarts ginger ale

Combine sugar and water in saucepan; stir over heat until sugar dissolves. Bring to boiling point; let boil, without stirring, for about 7 minutes. Cool; add fruit juices. When ready to serve pour over ice; add ginger ale. Garnish with sprigs of mint.

Jennie Lien, Stoughton, Wis.

CITRUS ICED TEA A LA MODE
Serves 5

3 cups double-strength cold tea
1/2 cup chilled orange juice
1 pint vanilla ice cream

Blend ingredients until smooth and pour into a tall glass.

PINEAPPLE-ORANGE PUNCH
Makes 5 quarts

½ gallon orange sherbet
1 (46-ounce) can pineapple juice, chilled
1 (33½-ounce) bottle ginger ale, chilled
3 cups orange-flavored drink, chilled
3 cups lemon-lime carbonated beverage, chilled

Place sherbet in a large punch bowl; add remaining ingredients and stir well. Chunks of orange sherbet will remain in punch.

Sharon Case, Chicago, Ill.

HOT CHOCO-MALLOW MIX
Makes 6 cups

4 cups dry non-fat dry milk
1 cup dry non-dairy creamer
¾ cup sugar
¾ cup cocoa
1 cup colored, miniature marshmallows

Stir together dry non-fat milk, non-dairy creamer, sugar and cocoa in large bowl. Stir in marshmallows.

Spoon mix into glass jar with tight-fitting lid. Use smaller containers, if desired. Attach instruction label: For each serving combine ¼ cup mix and 6 ounces boiling water in mug. Stir and serve.

Sally Simpson, Detroit, Mich.

COFFEE EGGNOG

2 eggs, separated
1/3 cup sugar
1/3 cup instant coffee
Dash salt
1 teaspoon vanilla extract
2 cups milk, chilled
3/4 cup water
1 cup heavy cream, whipped
Shaved unsweetened chocolate

In small bowl, beat egg whites at high speed until soft peaks form. Gradually, beat in sugar until stiff peaks form. In large bowl, beat egg yolks until lemon colored. Gradually beat in coffee, salt, vanilla, milk, and 3/4 cup water. Stir in egg-white mixture and whipped cream; mix well. Serve well chilled, with chocolate shavings sprinkled over each serving.

Alpha Wilson, Roswell, N.M.

EGGNOG
Makes 6 large glasses

4 eggs
4 cups milk
4 tablespoons lemon juice
1/2 cup cream
1/8 teaspoon nutmeg
1/8 teaspoon salt
1/3 cup sugar

Beat eggs until thick and lemon colored. Add sugar, salt, nutmeg, and lemon juice; add ice cold milk and cream. Beat with mixer until frothy.

Betty Klopfenstein, Waterman, Ill.

FRIENDSHIP TEA

1 pound 2 ounce jar Tang
3/4 to 1 cup instant tea
2 tablespoons cinnamon
1 pound package dry lemonade
2-1/2 cups sugar

Mix together; store in closed container. To use: add 2 spoonfuls of mixture to one cup of hot water.

Marcella Swigert, Monroe City, MO

SPICED TEA

1 cup instant tea
2 cups Tang
1/3 cup lemonade mix (crystals)
2 tablespoons sugar
1 teaspoon cinnamon
1 teaspoon ground cloves

Mix thoroughly. Keep in airtight container. Use 1 rounded teaspoonful per cup hot water.

Florence Kloss, Lebanon, Ore.

SPICED TEA

1-1/2 cups instant tea
1 cup Tang
1 (3-ounce) package lemonade mix
2-1/2 cups sugar
1 teaspoon cloves
2 teaspoons cinnamon

Mix all ingredients. Use 2 teaspoonfuls to one cup hot water.

Dovie Lucy, McLoud, Okla.

NEW ENGLAND SWEET CIDER PUNCH

3 oranges
1 lemon
1/4 cup maraschino cherries
1 quart cider

Extract juices from oranges and lemon; add to cider together with cherries. Chill thoroughly before serving.

Lucy Dowd, Sequim, WA

FRUIT SMASH PUNCH
Makes 1 gallon

2 cups hot water
1 package raspberry gelatin
1 package cherry gelatin
6 cups cold water

1-1/2 cups lime or lemon juice
5 cups fresh or frozen orange juice
1/2 to 1 cup sugar
5 or 6 ripe bananas
1 quart chilled ginger ale

Make gelatin in usual manner; add cold water and fruit juices; stir in sugar. Just before serving, mash or whip bananas until smooth and creamy. Beat into mixture. Add ginger ale, the last minute.

Marcella Swigert, Monroe City, Mo.

PEACH PICK ME UP
Makes 3-1/2 cups

2 containers (8-ounce each) peach yogurt
6 ounces frozen apple juice concentrate
1/2 teaspoon almond extract
3 ice cubes

Place all ingredients in blender container; cover. Blend on high speed until ice is reduced to small pieces and mixture is well combined. Serve immediately in tall chilled glasses.

Mrs. Peggy Fowler Revels, Woodruff, SC

CHOCOLATE TOFU NUTRITIONAL SHAKE
Serves 4

3 cups milk
1 cup Silken Tofu, drained
2 bananas, broken into chunks
4 tablespoons instant cocoa mix powder
2 tablespoon honey
1 tablespoon wheat germ

Combine ingredients in blender, 1/2 at a time; whirl until smooth and creamy. Serve cold. Wonderful as a complete protein breakfast drink or for snack any time.

Any fresh fruit in season such as berries, cantaloupe or papaya can be substituted for the chocolate flavor.

Pour into tall glasses, sprinkle with nutmeg.

Hyacinth Rizzo, Snyder, NY

EASY PARTY PUNCH

3-ounce package raspberry gelatin
3-ounce package cherry gelatin
3 cups boiling water
5 cups cold water
3 cups pineapple juice
12 ounces frozen orange juice
2 pints pineapple or lemon sherbet

Dissolve gelatins in boiling water; add next 3 ingredients. Stir in one tray ice cubes until melted. Spoon in sherbet. Serve immediately or let stand at room temperature.

Barbara Brittain, San Diego, CA

GOOD LUCK PUNCH
Makes 1 gallon

1 quart fresh rhubarb
Water to cover
3 cups sugar
2 cups water
Juice of 6 lemons
1 cup pineapple juice
1 quart gingerale

Cut rhubarb into 1-inch pieces; cover with water and cook until soft, about 12-15 minutes. Drain through cheesecloth. Should be about 3 quarts of juice. Dissolve sugar in the 2 cups water and cook 10 minutes to make a syrup.

Combine all juices, except ginger ale, pouring over chunk of ice in punch bowl. Just before serving, add ginger ale.

PARTY PINK PUNCH

1 (46-ounce) can pineapple juice
1 large bottle lemon lime pop
1 small can pink lemonade, frozen
1 can water
2 large bottles strawberry pop
Sugar, if desired
Raspberry sherbet

Mix first six ingredients. Drop spoonfuls of sherbet on top before serving. Delicious!

Barbara Brittain, San Diego, Calif.

AUTUMN PUNCH
Makes 7-1/2 quarts

1-1/2 cups honey
3/4 cup lemon juice
6 whole cardamom seeds
3 (3-inch) sticks cinnamon
1 teaspoon whole allspice
2 teaspoons whole cloves
1-1/2 quarts cranberry juice
5 cups apple juice
5 cups apricot nectar
3 quarts ginger ale
Crushed ice

Combine first 6 ingredients in a saucepan; bring to a boil; reduce heat; simmer 10 minutes. Strain and discard spices. Chill. Combine chilled mixture with remaining juices and ginger ale. Serve over ice.

Mrs. Bruce Fowler, Woodruff, S.C.

RHUBARB PUNCH

1 quart diced rhubarb
1 quart water
3/4 - 1 cup sugar
1/4 cup lemon juice

Cook rhubarb in water until very tender. Let drain through cloth-lined colander or strainer. Add sugar; stir to dissolve. Add lemon juice. Chill to serve.

This recipe makes a delicious soft pink punch.

May Ann Kooker, Bluffton, OH

SHERBERT PUNCH

3 (2-liter) bottles 7-Up, chilled
1/2 gallon orange or raspberry
    sherbet

Soften sherbet. Add by large scoops to punch bowl. Pour chilled 7-Up over the sherbet and serve.

Sue Thomas, Casa Grande, Ariz.

SPICY CALIFORNIA PUNCH

4 cups unsweetened grapefruit juice
4 cups orange juice
2 cups honey
1/4 cup lime juice
1 teaspoon allspice
1 teaspoon nutmeg

In a 3-quart container, combine 4 cups each of both grapefruit juice and orange juice, then add honey, lime juice, and spices. Let stand at room temperature for 1 hour to allow flavors to blend. Chill. To serve, pour over ice in a punch bowl or several pitchers.

Agnes Ward, Erie, Pa.

TROPICAL FRUIT SMOOTHIE
Makes 5 cups

1 (15-ounce) can cream of coconut
1 medium banana
1 (8-ounce) can juice packed
    crushed pineapple
1 cup orange– juice
1 tablespoon bottled lemon juice
2 cups ice cubes

In blender, combine all ingredients, except ice; blend well. Gradually add ice; blend until smooth. Serve immediately; refrigerate leftovers.

Peggy Fowler Revels, Woodruff, S.C.

COFFEE COOLER

4 quarts strong coffee, cold
1 cup sugar
2 quarts vanilla ice cream
1 tablespoon vanilla
1 quart whole milk

Combine coffee, milk, and vanilla. Add sugar and stir until dissolved. Chill thoroughly and pour over ice cream that has been spooned into a punch bowl. Serves about 50 small punch cups.

Sue Thomas, Casa Grande, Ariz.

14

ZESTY FRUIT REFRESHER

1 cup cranberry cocktail juice
1 cup prune juice (Welch's)
2 cups apple juice

Mix all the above juices and place in refrigerator. When ready to serve, place 1/2 cup fruit juice mixture into glass tumbler and fill rest of glass with ginger ale.

M. Powell Hamilton, Ontario, Canada

FRUIT LOW-BALL
Serves 6

1 (10-ounce) package frozen peaches
1/4 cup firmly-packed light brown sugar
1/4 teaspoon cinnamon
1 quart buttermilk
1 medium orange

Thaw peaches. Combine peaches, sugar, and cinnamon in blender. Whirl at medium speed until smooth. Add buttermilk; whirl again.

To serve, pour into six 8-ounce glasses. Slice orange very thin; garnish each glass edge with an orange wheel. Top with dash of cinnamon. Very zesty and refreshing with the buttermilk!

Judie Betz, Lomita, CA

ORANGE-TOMATO COCKTAIL
Serves 6

1-1/2 cups chilled tomato juice
1 cup chilled orange juice
1 tablespoon lemon juice
1/2 teaspoon salt
1 slice onion

Blend all ingredients in blender about 30 seconds or until thoroughly mixed. Add 4 ice cubes, one at a time, and blend until mixed.

Agnes Ward, Erie, PA

PINEAPPLE SLUSH
Makes 3 cups

1 (5-1/4 ounce) can pineapple tidbits, undrained
1 medium banana, chilled
1/4 cup milk
2 cups pineapple sherbet

Combine all ingredients in container of electric blender; process until smooth.

Edna Askins, Greenville, Texas

MOCHA
Serves 8-10

2/3 cup instant cocoa mix
1/2 cup instant coffee
8 cups boiling water
Sweetened whipped cream or Cool Whip

Mix cocoa and coffee in pot or pitcher. Pour in boiling water and stir. Serve hot and topped with Cool Whip or whipped cream.

Betty Klopfenstein, Waterman, Ill.

CHOCOLATE-PEANUT-BUTTER MILK SHAKE
Makes 2 cups

2 tablespoons powdered chocolate drink mix
3 tablespoons crunchy peanut butter
1 cup milk, chilled
1 teaspoon honey
Dash cinnamon
Dash nutmeg
8 ice cubes

Place all ingredients in blender. Cover and process until frothy. Pour into vacuum containers.

Annie Emchil, New Castle, Ind.

MELON SHAKE
1 serving

1/2 cup watermelon, cantaloupe or honeydew melon balls
2 large scoops vanilla ice cream (about 1 cup)
1/4 cup milk

Place melon balls in blender. Add ice cream and milk. Cover and blend until smooth. Serve immediately.

Phyllis Beaty, Rossville, Ga.

LO-CALORIE BANANA MILK SHAKE

6 ounces skimmed milk
1/2 teaspoon vanilla
1 banana, sliced frozen
1/2 teaspoon Sprinkle Sweet or sweetener

Put milk in blender. Add vanilla and frozen banana, a little at a time. If a thicker shake is desired, add ice cubes until desired thickness.

Betty Klopfenstein, Waterman, IL

SPICY MILK TEA
Serves 4

6 whole cloves
4 thin slices fresh ginger or 1/2 teaspoon ground ginger
2 cinnamon sticks
4 cups water
4 teaspoons jasmine tea
1 cup milk or half-and-half
Honey
Cardamom, optional
Mint sprigs for garnish

Bring water to boil. Add cinnamon, cloves, and ginger. Cover; simmer 10 minutes. Add tea and steep for a few minutes. Add milk. Bring to boil again. Remove from heat. Strain into a teapot. Serve with a sprinkle of cardamom and a bit of honey. Garnish with mint.

For 1 serving:
Boil 1 cup water. Add 1/2 cinnamon stick, 3 cloves, 2 slices fresh ginger, and 1 teaspoon tea.

Arlene Ranney, Eureka, Calif.

Breads
TO MAKE

QUICK MIX (LIKE BISQUICK)
Makes 13 cups

8-1/2 cups all-purpose flour
3 tablespoons baking powder
1 tablespoon salt
2 teaspoons cream of tartar
1 teaspoon baking soda
1-1/2 cups instant nonfat dry milk
2-1/4 cups vegetable shortening

In a large bowl, sift together dry ingredients. Blend well. With pastry blender, cut in shortening until evenly distributed. Mixture will resemble cornmeal in texture. Put in a large airtight container. Label. Store in a cool, dry place. Use within 4 months.

This works with every Bisquick recipe I've ever tried — even when I used to live at a low altitude!

Michele Martindill, Calhan, Colo.

MUFFINS
Makes 1 dozen

1-1/2 cups biscuit mix
1/2 cup sugar
1 tablespoon poppy seeds
3/4 cup raisins, chopped
1 egg, beaten
3/4 cup sour cream
1 teaspoon vanilla

Combine biscuit mix, sugar, and poppy seeds; make a well in center of mixture. Add remaining ingredients. Stir until just moistened. Spoon into greased muffin pans, filling half full. Bake at 400 degrees for 20 minutes or until they test done.

Kit Rollins, Cedarburg, WI

INDIAN FRIED BISCUITS

2 cups flour
3 tablespoons baking powder
1/2 teaspoon salt
2 tablespoons sugar
2/3 or 3/4 cup milk

Mix dry ingredients; add milk and mix well. Pat out on floured flat surface to 1/4-inch thickness. Slice into 2x3-inch or 3x4-inch pieces. Fry in 1/2 inch hot oil, browning each side. Serve warm.

Edna Askins, Greenville, Texas

BRAN APPLESAUCE MUFFINS

1-1/4 cups whole-wheat flour
3/4 cup 100% bran cereal
1/2 cup sugar
1 teaspoon baking soda
1 teaspoon cinnamon
1/2 teaspoon salt
1/2 teaspoon nutmeg
1 cup applesauce
1/2 cup oil
1 teaspoon vanilla
2 eggs

Topping:
1 tablespoon sugar
1/2 teaspoon cinnamon

Heat oven to 400 degrees. Grease 12 muffin cups. Lightly spoon flour into measuring cup; level off. In large bowl, combine all muffin ingredients, stirring just until dry ingredients are moistened. Fill muffin cups two-thirds full. Combine topping ingredients; sprinkle over top of each muffin. Bake at 400 degrees for 15-20 minutes or until toothpick inserted comes out clean. Remove from pan immediately. Serve warm.

Cheryl Santefort, South Holland, Ill.

CRANBERRY BANANA BREAD

2 cups fresh cranberries
1 cup sugar
1 cup water
1/3 cup shortening
2/3 cup sugar
2 eggs
1¾ cups all-purpose flour
2 teaspoons baking powder
1/2 teaspoon salt
1/4 teaspoon baking soda
1 cup mashed banana
1/2 cup coarsely chopped walnuts

Combine cranberries, 1 cup sugar and water; cook over medium heat about 5 minutes, or until cranberries begin to pop. Drain and set aside. Cream shortening; gradually add ⅔ cup sugar, beating until light and fluffy. Add eggs, 1 at a time, beating well after each. Combine dry ingredients; add to creamed mixture alternately with banana, mixing well after each addition. Fold in cranberries and walnuts. Line a greased 9 x 5 x 3-inch loaf pan. Spoon batter into pan. Bake at 350 degrees for 60 minutes, or until bread tests done. Cool 10 minutes in pan; remove from pan.

Mrs. Albert H. Foley, Lemoyne, Pa.

CHEDDAR SCONES
Makes 6

1½ cups all-purpose flour, unsifted
¼ cup chilled unsalted butter *or* vegetable shortening
2 cups (6 ounces) coarsely shredded sharp cheddar cheese
⅛ teaspoon salt
½ cup milk

Preheat oven to 450 degrees. Sift flour into shallow bowl. Cut in shortening until mixture resembles coarse meal. Mix in cheese and salt. Gradually stir in just enough milk to form stiff dough. Turn dough onto well-floured work surface. Roll out to ⅝-inch thickness. Cut into rounds using lightly floured, scalloped (3-inch) round cookie cutter. Arrange 1 inch apart on ungreased baking sheet. Reroll any remaining scraps and cut out additional rounds. Bake about 15 minutes, or until puffed and light brown. Serve hot.

SIX-WEEK BRAN MUFFINS
Makes 5-1/2 dozen

1 cup shortening
2-1/2 cups sugar
4 eggs
5 cups all-purpose flour
5 teaspoons baking soda
1/2 teaspoon salt
1 quart buttermilk
6 cups bran cereal, such as Kellogg's All-Bran®, not bran flakes
2 cups boiling water

Cream sugar and shortening together. Add eggs and mix, 1 at a time. Sift dry ingredients together and add alternately with buttermilk to shortening mixture. Add cereal and boiling water until blended. Fill muffin tins three-fourths full and bake at 400 degrees for 20–25 minutes. Batter can be stored in tightly covered bowl in refrigerator for 6–10 weeks.

Great to have on hand for busy morning breakfasts.

Marsha Miller, Hilliard, Ohio

RYE BREAD

2 packages yeast
1 cup lukewarm water
1/2 cup brown sugar
1 cup flour
3/4 cup molasses
Grated rind of 1 orange (optional)
1 tablespoon anise seed
1 tablespoon salt
3 or 4 tablespoons melted butter
2 cups rye flour
4 cups white flour

Dissolve yeast in warm water. Add brown sugar and 1 cup flour; mix and let rise. Heat 2 cups milk until lukewarm. Add remaining ingredients.

Mix with spoon and let rise in large mixing bowl. Stir down and add enough flour to make a soft dough. Turn onto floured surface and knead. Divide into 4 parts and knead each. Shape into loaves and put in greased bread pans. Let rise until even with pan tops. Bake at 400 degrees for 10 minutes; reduce to 325 degrees and bake 45 minutes. Turn out onto racks; butter crusts.

Marcella Swigert, Monroe City, Mo.

BUBBLE BREAD

3 loaves frozen bread dough
1 package butterscotch pudding (not instant)
1/2 cup butter over 2 bundt pans
1 cup pecans
1/4 cup cinnamon-sugar
1/4 cup Karo syrup
1 cup brown sugar

Thaw and shape dough into 1-inch balls. Sprinkle pudding mix, pecans, cinnamon-sugar, and brown sugar evenly over bottoms of the two bundt pans. Drizzle butter and Karo over mixture, and top with dough balls.

Let rise over night at room temperature. Bake at 350 degrees for 30-35 minutes. This is a wonderful bread for breakfast guests, as it can be prepared the evening before and popped into the oven to serve piping hot for breakfast.

Karen Pfeifer, Flagstaff, Ariz.

CARROT BREAD

2 eggs
1 cup sugar
⅔ cup oil
1½ cups flour
¾ teaspoon soda
1 teaspoon cinnamon
1 teaspoon nutmeg
½ teaspoon salt
1½ cups raw carrots, grated
1 cup walnuts
¾ cup raisins

Beat eggs; add sugar and oil. Sift together flour, soda, cinnamon, nutmeg and salt; add to egg mixture. Beat well. Add carrots, nuts and raisins. Grease 5 soup cans or 1 (9 x 5-inch) loaf pan. Fill cans half full. Bake at 350 degrees for 45–50 minutes for soup cans, or 1 hour for loaf pan.

Shari Crider, Stoughton, Wis.

SPOON BREAD

1 package yeast
1/4 cup water
1/4 cup sugar
1/3 cup shortening
1/2 cup cold water
1 egg, slightly beaten
1 teaspoon salt
Pinch alum
3/4 cup scalded milk
3-1/2 cups flour

Dissolve yeast in warm water. Set aside. Combine sugar, salt, alum and shortening in scalded milk. Stir until shortening is melted. Cool with 1/2 cup water. Pour this and egg into yeast; add flour and mix. Cover, let rise 45 to 60 minutes. Spoon down. Let rise again 45 minutes. Spoon into greased muffin pans. Let rise. Bake at 400 degrees 15 to 20 minutes.

Betty Ireton, Kingston, OH

BUTTERHORNS
Makes 3 dozen

1 cup milk
1/2 cup margarine
1/2 cup sugar
1/2 teaspoon salt
1 package yeast
3 eggs, beaten
4 1/2 cups flour
Melted butter

Heat milk to scalding; add margarine, sugar and salt. Cool to lukewarm. Add yeast; stir until dissolved. Add eggs, then flour; mix to a smooth, soft dough. Knead lightly on floured surface. Place dough in a greased bowl; cover. Let rise in warm place until doubled in bulk. Divide dough into thirds. Roll each third on lightly floured surface to size of 9-inch pie pan. Cut each round in 12 wedges; roll each triangle, starting with wide end and rolling to center. Arrange on greased baking sheet; brush lightly with melted butter. Cover; let rise until light. Bake in 350-degree oven for 15 minutes.

Very tender and good!

Mrs. George Franks, Millerton, Pa.

PECAN LOAF

2 cups flour
4 teaspoons baking powder
1 teaspoon salt
3 tablespoons margarine
2 tablespoons butter *or* other shortening
1 egg, plus 1 egg yolk
1 cup milk
1/2 cup pecans, chopped

Mix and sift flour, baking powder and salt. Cut in margarine and other shortening. Add beaten egg, egg yolk and milk, then pecans. Sugar may be added, as desired, if a sweeter bread is preferred (2 teaspoons). Turn into a buttered 10-inch loaf pan. Let stand 20 minutes. Then bake in 350-degree oven for 50 minutes.

This is really an unusual and delicious recipe!

Suzan L. Wiener, Spring Hill, Fla.

DATE NUT BREAD

1-3/4 cups milk, scalded
1/4 cup warm water
1 cake compressed yeast
1 cup brown sugar
1 cup chopped dates (or chopped raw prunes)
2 teaspoons salt
1/2 cup melted shortening
1/2 cup chopped walnuts
2 eggs, well-beaten
6 cups flour

Sift flour and measure. Soften yeast in warm water. Combine milk, salt, sugar, and shortening. Cool to lukewarm. Add yeast, nuts, eggs, dates, and flour. Mix thoroughly. Turn onto lightly floured board. Knead until smooth. Cover with warm damp cloth. Let rise until double in bulk. Form in loaves. Place in well-greased loaf pans. Cover with warm damp cloth. Let stand 30 minutes. Bake in moderate oven of 350 degrees for 50 minutes.

Mrs. E. O'Brien, Richmond, Va.

QUICK BUTTERMILK BREAD STICKS
Makes 8

These taste so good and freeze well, so I usually double the recipe (To double buttermilk use ¾ cup.)

1 cup flour, spooned lightly into cup
¼ teaspoon salt
½ teaspoon soda
2½ tablespoons butter *or* margarine
6 tablespoons buttermilk (I use ⅓ cup plus 1 tablespoon)
Milk for glaze
Sesame *or* poppy seeds, if desired

Preheat oven to 450 degrees. Lightly grease a baking sheet.

Into a medium bowl measure flour, salt and soda; mix with pastry blender. Cut in butter until like fine crumbs.

Add buttermilk; mix gently until combined. On a lightly floured surface (I use a pastry cloth on the counter) knead until a smooth ball—less than 1 minute. Cut into 8 parts; roll each into a 6-inch bread stick. To simplify glazing, place bread sticks close together on baking sheet; rub tops with milk; sprinkle with seeds, if using, then rearrange so they are at least 1 inch apart. Bake until beginning to brown, about 12 minutes. Serve warm with butter. Freeze leftovers.

COCONUT MUFFINS

2 cups flour
1/2 teaspoon salt
4 teaspoons baking powder
1/4 cup sugar
3 tablespoons margarine, melted
1 egg, beaten
1 cup milk
1 cup coconut

Sift dry ingredients together. Combine milk, egg and melted margarine; add to dry ingredients. Add coconut and mix gently. Fill paper-lined muffin cups two-thirds full and bake at 450 degrees for 15 minutes.

Jodie McCoy, Tulsa, Okla.

STRAWBERRY BREAD

1-1/2 cups sifted flour
1/2 teaspoon baking soda
1/2 teaspoon salt
1 cup sugar
1 teaspoon orange extract
1 (10-ounce) package frozen strawberries, thawed
2 eggs, beaten
2/3 cup oil *or* melted butter
1/2 cup chopped walnuts

Sift dry ingredients into large bowl. Make a well in the center. Mix rest of ingredients and pour into the dry well. Stir just until blended. Pour into a 9x5-inch greased and lightly floured loaf pan and bake at 350 degrees for 1 hour. Can be served warm or cold.

Agnes Ward, Erie, Pa.

BANANA NUT BREAD

An old-time favorite, this is also an economical bread to bake. You can usually pick up overripe bananas in the store for a substantial savings. This bread can be spread with cream-cheese fillings, peanut butter (a favorite of children), or many other spreads.

1/2 cup shortening
1-1/3 cups sugar
2 large, ripe mashed bananas
2 tablespoons milk
2 eggs
1-3/4 cups flour
1/2 teaspoon soda
1-1/2 teaspoons baking powder
1 teaspoon salt
1 teaspoon nutmeg
1 cup chopped nuts

Cream together shortening and sugar; add mashed bananas and milk, and mix well. Add eggs and blend well. Mix together flour, soda, baking powder, salt and nutmeg, and add to mixture. Fold in nuts and bake at 350 degrees for 45 minutes, or until tested done. Cool on racks.

ORANGE MUFFINS
Makes 6

1 cup all-purpose flour
2 teaspoons baking powder
1/8 teaspoon salt
1-1/2 tablespoons melted butter or margarine
1 egg, beaten
1/2 cup milk
1/3 cup firmly packed brown sugar
Grated rind and juice of 1 orange

Combine flour, baking powder and salt. Add butter, egg, milk and sugar, stirring until just moistened. Blend in orange juice and rind.

Spoon batter into muffin cups in pans, filling two-thirds full. Bake at 400 degrees for 17–20 minutes, or until brown and tested done.

BUTTER CRUMB DUMPLINGS
Serves 8

2 cups sifted flour
4 teaspoons baking powder
1 tablespoon poppy seeds
1 teaspoon celery salt
1 teaspoon poultry seasoning
2 teaspoons dried onion flakes
1/4 cup oil
3/4 cup plus 2 tablespoons milk
1/4 cup melted butter or margarine
2 cups soft bread crumbs

Mix first six ingredients together. Mix and blend in oil and milk. Stir butter into crumbs. Drop dough by tablespoonfuls in 12 equal portions into buttered crumbs and roll to cover with crumbs. Place on top of hot meatballs and gravy.

Bake, uncovered, at 400 degrees for 20-25 minutes, until dumplings are golden. If extra sauce is desired, simmer 1 can cream of chicken soup with 1/4 teaspoon poultry seasoning and 1 teaspoon onion flakes. Stir in 1/2 cup sour cream and reheat.

Ann Gumperz, Santa Rosa, Calif.

FRESH FRUIT OAT MUFFINS
Makes 20

2 cups whole-wheat flour
1 cup rolled oats
1/2 cup unprocessed wheat bran
1/2 cup brown sugar (packed)
1-1/2 teaspoons baking soda
1 teaspoon salt
2 eggs
1-1/2 cups buttermilk
1/4 cup vegetable oil
3 cups finely chopped peaches (or 2 cups fresh Bartlett pears, nectarines or plums)
3 teaspoons orange juice
1-1/2 teaspoons cinnamon

Combine all ingredients in bowl. Blend. Spoon batter into 2-1/2-inch non-stick muffin cups. Bake in 400-degree oven for 20 minutes, or until pick inserted in center comes out dry. Serve warm. Muffins can be frozen.

Kit Rollins, Cedarburg, Wis.

GLAZED LEMON BREAD

1/3 cup melted butter or margarine
1 cup sugar
2 eggs
1/4 teaspoon almond extract
1 1/2 cups sifted all-purpose flour
1 teaspoon salt
1 teaspoon baking powder
1/2 cup milk
1 tablespoon lemon peel
1/2 cup chopped nuts

Blend together well the butter and 1 cup sugar. Beat in eggs; add extract. Sift dry ingredients; add to egg mixture alternately with milk. Blend just to mix. Fold in peel and nuts; turn into a greased (8 1/2)x(4 1/2)x(2 3/4)-inch glass loaf pan. Bake 70 minutes at 325 degrees. If you use a metal pan, bake at 350 degrees. I have also used 2 mini-loaf pans, and baked until loaves tested done in center.

Glazed Topping:

Mix 1/4 cup sugar (not powdered) with 3 tablespoons fresh lemon juice. Spoon over bread immediately, as it comes from oven.

Hazel Hullinger, Decatur, Ill.

SHORTBREAD

1/2 pound (2 sticks) butter
1/4 pound (1/2 cup) shortening
1 cup sugar
1 teaspoon nutmeg
1 egg
6 cups flour
3/4 teaspoon soda
1/2 teaspoon cream of tartar

Mix butter and shortening until soft. Mix with sugar and egg. Beat well. Mix flour, soda, cream of tartar, and nutmeg. Combine mixtures. Sprinkle sugar on pastry board and rolling pin. Toss dough onto board. Roll thin and cut in shapes. Bake on greased baking sheets. Bake in moderate 350-degree oven for 10 minutes.

Suzan L. Wiener, Spring Hill, Fla.

COTTAGE CHEESE BREAD

1 cup cottage cheese
2 eggs, beaten
1 cup sugar
3/4 cup milk
1 teaspoon vanilla
2-3/4 cups flour
2-1/2 teaspoons baking powder
1/2 cup raisins
1/2 cup walnuts
10 chopped cherries

Mix first 7 ingredients in order given; add raisins and walnuts. Pour into greased loaf pan. Decorate top with chopped cherries and sprinkle with sugar. Bake at 350 degrees for about 1 hour.

Sheila Symonowicz, Loganville, Pa.

BANANA-POPPY SEED MUFFINS
Makes 12

2 ripe, medium bananas *or* 1 cup
1 egg
3/4 cup sugar
1/4 cup vegetable oil
2 teaspoons grated orange peel
2 cups flour
1-1/2 tablespoons poppy seeds
2 teaspoons baking powder
1/2 teaspoon salt
Citrus Glaze (recipe follows)

Purée bananas in blender. In a bowl mix bananas, egg, sugar, oil and orange peel until blended. Combine flour, poppy seeds, baking powder and salt. Stir banana mixture into dry mixture until moistened. Spoon batter into 12 greased muffin cups.

Bake at 375 degrees for 20 minutes. Remove from pan; cool. Top with glaze.

Citrus Glaze:
1-1/4 cups confectioners' sugar
1/4 cup orange juice
1 teaspoon grated orange peel
1 teaspoon vanilla

Combine ingredients and mix until smooth. Top each muffin with glaze.

Vickie Vogt, Kewaskum, Wis.

BROWN BREAD

1-1/2 cups all-purpose flour
1-1/2 cups rye flour
1 cup yellow cornmeal
1 teaspoon baking soda
1 teaspoon salt
1/2 cup raisins
1/2 cup walnuts
2 cups buttermilk
1/2 cup dark molasses

Mix flours, cornmeal, baking soda and salt together. Add raisins and nuts. Slowly add buttermilk and molasses alternately to dry ingredients; beat after each addition.

Pour into buttered 9-inch loaf pan. Bake at 375 degrees for 50 minutes, or until tested done.

Let stand in pan on wire rack for 5 minutes. Loosen sides with knife and turn out on rack.

Brush with butter while still warm. Cool before slicing.

CHEESE QUICK BREAD

2 cups all-purpose flour
4 teaspoons baking powder
1/4 teaspoon salt
1/4 cup butter
1 cup grated cheddar cheese
2 eggs
1/4 cup white sugar
1 cup milk

In a large bowl, sift together flour, baking powder, and salt; cut in the butter until particles are the size of small peas. Stir in the cheese. In small bowl beat eggs until foamy; beat in sugar, then milk. Pour egg mixture into flour mixture; stir only until evenly moistened. Transfer dough to a greased 9x5-inch loaf pan. Bake in a 350-degree oven for 50 minutes, or until toothpick inserted in center comes out clean. Remove from pan and serve hot or cold. This is a moist, tasty bread and makes great ham sandwiches.

Lillian Smith, Montreal, Quebec, Canada

PEPPERONI 'N CHEESE CRESCENTS
Serves 8

1 (8-ounce) can Pillsbury Crescent
  dinner rolls
24 slices pepperoni
2 slices mozzarella cheese
1 egg white

Separate dough into 8 triangles. Place 3 slices of pepperoni, slightly overlapping, on each triangle. Top each with 1/4 slice cheese. Roll up, starting at shortest side of triangle and roll to opposite point. Place point-side down on ungreased cookie sheet. Curve into crescent shape. Brush with egg white. Bake at 375 degrees for 10-15 minutes or until golden brown.

Helen Harios, Ethel, Miss.

CINNAMON SWEET ROLLS
Makes 2 dozen

1 yellow cake mix
2 packages dry yeast
5 cups flour
2-1/2 cups *hot* water
4 tablespoons butter
Brown sugar
Cinnamon
Nuts (optional)

Topping:
1 stick margarine, melted
4 tablespoons brown sugar
3 tablespoons light corn syrup

Mix first 3 ingredients thoroughly. Add hot water and mix well. Let rise to double in size. Cut in half; roll to rectangular shape. Melt butter and spread over rolled dough. Sprinkle with brown sugar, cinnamon, and nuts. Roll like a jelly roll; cut in 1-1/2-inch pieces. Place on greased cookie sheet. Repeat with remaining dough. Cover and let rise to double in size.

Mix together topping ingredients and spread over top of rolls, just prior to baking. Bake at 375 degrees for 25 minutes. Be sure cookie sheet has sides.

Harold L. Bird, Muskegon, Mich.

FEATHER DUMPLINGS

2 cups flour
1 teaspoon salt
4 teaspoons baking powder
1/4 teaspoon salt
Mix and add:
1 egg, beaten
2 tablespoons butter, melted
2/3 cup milk

Mix well (stiff dough). Drop by teaspoonfuls into boiling, salted water or broth. Cover and simmer for 18-20 minutes. Dumplings are light as air; handle with care.

Ann Sterzer, Lincoln, Neb.

PUMPKIN-PECAN–RAISIN BREAD

3 cups flour
2 teaspoons baking powder
1¼ teaspoons salt
1 teaspoon baking soda
1 teaspoon cinnamon
½ teaspoon nutmeg
2 eggs
1 (16-ounce) can pumpkin
1 cup packed light brown sugar
½ cup maple syrup
¼ cup Crisco oil
½ cup raisins
½ cup chopped pecans

In large bowl mix the first 6 ingredients. In another bowl combine the next 5 ingredients. Grease a 9 x 5-inch loaf pan. Stir liquid ingredients into dry ingredients and stir until moistened. Add raisins and nuts, then spoon into loaf pan.

Bake for 1¼ hours in a 350-degree oven. Cool bread on a wire rack in the pan for 10 minutes. Then remove and let completely cool on rack.

This is a most delicious bread for the holidays and is also a tradition in my family.

Esther M. Garback, Gloversville, N.Y.

BUTTERHORN ROLLS

5 cups flour
2 packages yeast
1 cup warm tap water
2 tablespoons sugar
3 eggs, beaten
1/2 cup margarine or butter
1 teaspoon salt
1/2 cup sugar

Dissolve yeast and 2 tablespoons sugar in warm tap water. Cream 1/2 cup sugar and 1/2 cup butter or margarine with 3 well-beaten eggs. (I use the mixer.) Add yeast mixture and 1/2 cup flour and salt. Beat until smooth. Add rest of flour and mix by spoon. Place in greased bowl and cover. Set in refrigerator overnight.

Next day, divide in 4 parts. Roll each portion to about 1/4-inch thickness, like a pie in a circle. Brush top with Crisco oil and cut into pie-shaped wedges, about 8 or 9 pieces. Roll up beginning with wide end to form crescent roll. Let rise on greased cookie sheet for 3 to 4 hours. Bake at 400 degrees for about 5 to 7 minutes, until golden brown.

Eula Wilson, Bethel, Ohio

PUMPKIN BANANA NUT BREAD
Makes 2 loaves

1 cup solid-pack pumpkin
½ cup (1 medium) ripe banana, mashed
1 cup brown sugar, firmly packed
½ cup vegetable oil
2 eggs
2¼ cups all-purpose flour
1 teaspoon baking powder
½ teaspoon baking soda
1 teaspoon ground cinnamon
½ teaspoon ground ginger
¼ teaspoon salt
1½ cups nuts, chopped

In large mixer bowl, combine pumpkin, banana, sugar and oil; mix

well. Beat in eggs, 1 at a time. In medium bowl, combine flour, baking powder, baking soda, cinnamon, ginger and salt; beat into pumpkin mixture. Stir in nuts. Pour into 2 greased 7½ x 3½ x 2½-inch loaf pans. Bake in preheated 450-degree oven for 50–60 minutes, or until toothpick inserted in center comes out clean. Cool 5 minutes in pans. Remove and cool completely before slicing.

Note: Bread may be frozen.

Diane Votaw, Decatur, Ind.

CHERRY MUFFINS

6 ounces *or* 3/4 cup biscuit mix
1/2 cup sugar
3/4 cup whole milk
2 tablespoons margarine
1 egg
1/2 cup cottage cheese
1 cup tart cherries, water-packed

Blend milk, margarine and egg, and stir into combined dry ingredients. Fold in cherries and cottage cheese. Spoon into 12 medium-size muffin tins until two-thirds full. Bake at 425 degrees for 20–25 minutes.

These muffins are really unusual and very delicious.

Suzan L. Wiener, Spring Hill, Fla.

COUNTRY HAM MUFFINS
Makes 12

1 (12-ounce) package corn muffin mix
4 ounces cooked ham, cut into ½-inch cubes
¼ teaspoon maple extract

Heat oven to 400 degrees. Grease 12 (2½-inch) muffin-pan cups. Prepare muffin mix according to package directions, adding the ham with dry ingredients and the maple extract with liquid ingredients. Spoon batter into prepared muffin-pan cups. Bake 15 minutes, or until golden brown. Serve warm.

MINCEMEAT MUFFINS

Makes 12

2 cups all-purpose flour
1 cup chopped pecans, toasted
⅓ cup granulated sugar
2 teaspoons baking powder
1 teaspoon grated orange peel
½ teaspoon salt
¼ teaspoon freshly grated nutmeg
⅓ cup milk
2 large eggs
1¼ cups prepared mincemeat

Heat oven to 400 degrees. Grease 12 (2½-inch) muffin-pan cups. In large bowl stir flour, pecans, sugar, baking powder, orange peel, salt and nutmeg to mix well. In small bowl, using wire whisk or fork, thoroughly beat milk and eggs; add to flour mixture along with mincemeat, stirring until just blended. Spoon batter into prepared muffin-pan cups; bake 15 minutes until golden.

Marcella Swigert, Monroe City, Mo.

PUMPKIN ROLLS

Makes 15 rolls

1 (16-ounce) package hot roll mix
⅓ cup warm water (105–115 degrees)
1 cup canned *or* cooked, mashed pumpkin
1 egg
2 tablespoons sugar

Filling:
2 tablespoons butter *or* margarine, melted
½ cup sugar
1½ teaspoons pumpkin pie spice
⅓ cup raisins

Glaze:
1 cup sifted confectioners' sugar

1 tablespoon plus 1 teaspoon milk
¼ teaspoon vanilla extract

Dissolve yeast packet from hot roll mix package in warm water; let stand 5 minutes. Combine pumpkin, egg and 2 tablespoons sugar; mix well. Add yeast; stir in flour packet from hot roll mix package to make a stiff dough. Place dough in a well-greased bowl, turning to grease top. Cover; let rise in a warm place (85 degrees) 45 minutes, or until doubled in bulk. Turn dough out onto a floured surface; knead 12 times. Roll dough into a 15 x 12-inch rectangle. Spread with melted butter. Combine ½ cup sugar and pumpkin pie spice; sprinkle over butter. Top with raisins. Beginning at long side, roll up jelly-roll fashion; press edges and ends together securely. Cut into 1-inch slices; place rolls, cut side down, in a greased 13 x 9 x 2-inch baking pan. Cover; let rise in a warm place (85 degrees) free from drafts, about 30 minutes, or until doubled in bulk. Bake at 375 degrees for 20 minutes, or until golden. Combine glaze ingredients until smooth; drizzle over warm rolls.

Helen P. Webb, Hillsborough County, Fla.

MONKEY BREAD

2 (10-ounce) packages canned biscuits
1/2 cup sugar
2 teaspoons cinnamon
3/4 cup brown sugar
1 stick margarine
1/2-3/4 cup chopped nuts

Mix sugar and cinnamon together. Cut each biscuit into fourths and roll each small piece in cinnamon-sugar mixture. Place in greased bundt pan. Sprinkle in nuts as you add the biscuit pieces. Combine brown sugar and margarine; heat until margarine is melted and sugar is dissolved. Pour over top of biscuit pieces. Bake in 325-degree oven for 30 minutes or until done. Cool slightly and invert on plate. So easy to make and enjoyed by all ages.

Mary M. West, Columbia, Ind.

LOW-CHOLESTEROL COTTAGE CHEESE BREAD

1 cup cottage cheese
2 eggs, beaten
1 cup sugar
3/4 cup milk
1 teaspoon vanilla
2-3/4 cups flour
2-1/2 cups baking powder
1/2 cup raisins
1/2 cup nuts, chopped

Mix in order given; add raisins and chopped nuts. Pour into greased loaf pan. Bake at 350 degrees for 60 minutes. Decorate top of loaf with chopped cherries and sprinkle with sugar before baking.

Sheila Symonowicz, Loganville, Pa.

BUTTERNUT-NUT RAISIN BREAD

Makes 3 loaves

3 1/2 cups unbleached flour
2 teaspoons soda
1 cup raisins
1 cup vegetable oil
2 cups sugar
4 eggs
1 1/2 cups cooked butternut squash, mashed
1/2 cup honey
1 cup water
1 1/2 teaspoons ground nutmeg
1 1/2 teaspoons ground cinnamon
1 teaspoon ground mace
1 1/2 teaspoons salt

Combine flour, soda and raisins; stir well and set aside. Combine oil, sugar and eggs in large mixing bowl; beat well. Stir in squash, honey, water, spices and salt. Add flour mixture; stir just until all ingredients are moistened. Pour batter into 3 greased 9 x 5 x 3-inch loaf pans. Bake at 350 degrees for 1 hour. Cool.

Note: Batter may be baked in 3 greased 1-pound coffee cans. Bake at 350 degrees for 1 hour and 20 minutes.

Sandra Russell, Gainesville, Fla.

RAISIN BREAD

2 cups flour
4 teaspoons baking powder
2 tablespoons shortening
1/2 cup sugar
1/4 cup raisins
1/2 cup currants
Dash of nutmeg
1 egg
1/2 cup milk

Mix dry ingredients; cut in the shortening. Add raisins and currants. Beat whole egg and add milk to it. Combine the 2 mixtures as in baking powder biscuits; put in a greased pan and bake in a moderate 350-degree oven for 40-45 minutes.

Lucy Dowd, Sequim, Wash.

DILLY BREAD

Wonderful with pork or beef slices, or a tuna-salad mixture.

1 package dry yeast
1/4 cup warm water
1 cup creamed cottage cheese
1 tablespoon butter or margarine
2 tablespoons sugar
1 tablespoon minced onion
2 teaspoons dill seed
1 teaspoon salt
1/4 teaspoon soda
1 egg
2–2-1/2 cups all-purpose flour

Dissolve yeast in warm water; set aside. Heat cottage cheese and margarine to lukewarm. Combine yeast and cottage cheese mixtures in bowl, and add sugar, onion, dill seed, salt, soda, and egg. Add flour until stiff dough forms. Cover; let rise until double. Turn into greased 1-1/2-quart casserole or 8-inch cake pan. Let rise in pan 30–40 minutes, or until light.

Bake at 350 degrees approximately 50 minutes. Brush with butter. Cool completely before slicing.

Brown breads long ago were steamed and served only with baked beans. This bread is also delicious when sliced for sandwiches.

GINGER MUFFINS

1 cup shortening
1 cup sugar
1 cup waffle syrup (may use part molasses)
3 eggs
1 cup buttermilk
1-3/4 teaspoons soda
3 teaspoons ginger
2 teaspoons cinnamon
1 teaspoon nutmeg
1/2 teaspoon salt
3 cups flour

Cream shortening and sugar. Add eggs, one at a time. Add syrup, then milk with soda dissolved in it. Then add flour and spices. Bake at 375 degrees for 10–12 minutes.

Diantha Susan Hibbard, Rochester, N.Y.

YAM DINNER ROLLS

⅔ cup warm water
1 package yeast
1½ tablespoons sugar
1½ teaspoons salt
1 tablespoon shortening, softened
1 (No. 2) can yams, drained and mashed
3½ cups all-purpose flour, sifted
¾ cup raisins (optional)

Measure water into large mixing bowl. Stir in sugar and salt. Add yeast and dissolve. Add shortening and yams; mix until thoroughly blended. Combine flour and raisins; add to yeast mixture in 2 additions, mixing until blended after each addition. Turn onto floured surface and knead until dough is smooth and elastic. Place in greased bowl; cover and let rise in warm place until double in bulk. Punch down and let rise a second time. Roll out to ¼-inch thickness and cut with floured 2-inch round cutter or shape into rolls. Place on greased baking sheets. Cover and let rise. Bake in hot oven of 425 degrees for 12 minutes.

Fay Duman, Eugene, Ore.

CORN BREAD LOAF

1 cup flour
3/4 cup yellow cornmeal
1/4 cup white sugar
1/2 teaspoon salt
4 teaspoons baking powder
2 eggs
1-1/4 cups milk
1/4 cup melted butter or shortening

In mixing bowl, mix together all dry ingredients. In a small bowl, beat eggs; add milk and melted butter. Add liquid to dry ingredients, mixing just until blended. Pour into a greased 8-1/2x4-1/2x2-1/2-inch loaf pan. Bake in 350-degree oven for 40 to 45 minutes or until golden brown and tester inserted in the center comes out clean. Cool for 5 minutes in the pan, then turn out onto rack. Serve warm with butter. This is a moist even-textured corn bread, and it is an "easy-to-slice" loaf.

Lillian Smith, Montreal, Quebec Canada

NO-KNEAD POTATO ROLLS
Makes 2 dozen

1 cup scalded milk
3 tablespoons shortening
1 tablespoon sugar
2 teaspoons salt
1 package compressed or granular yeast
2 eggs
1 cup leftover mashed potatoes
4 cups enriched flour

Combine scalded milk, shortening, sugar, and salt. Cool to lukewarm, adding yeast that has been dissolved according to package directions. Stir in eggs and mashed potatoes; blend well. Add flour, a cup at a time. Cover and let stand 15 minutes. Shape dough into walnut-size balls, and place them on a greased baking sheet. In a warm place, allow rolls to rise, about an hour, until double in size. Bake in 400-degree oven for 15-20 minutes.

Mae Gianocca, Half Moon Bay, Calif.

SWEDISH RYE BREAD
Makes 2 loaves

3 cups milk, scalded
1 package dry yeast
1/2 cup granulated sugar
3 tablespoons brown sugar
3/4 cup dark corn syrup
2 cups rye flour
3-1/2 cups all-purpose flour, or
   enough to make a stiff dough

Dissolve yeast in 1/4 cup milk. Add yeast, brown and white sugars, corn syrup, and rye flour to the scalded milk; beat well. Add white flour; mix well; cover, and let rise overnight.

Shape into 2 loaves and place on a buttered cookie sheet. Cover with towel; let rise until double in bulk. Preheat oven to 350 degrees and bake bread 1 hour, or until loaf sounds hollow when tapped with finger.

Agnes Ward, Erie, PA

HEALTH BREAD

3 packages dry yeast
2 cups warm water
1/2 cup sugar

Dissolve yeast in warm water; add sugar and set aside.

Mix together:
2 cups hot water
1 cup shortening
1 cup molasses
2 cups All Bran
2 cups oatmeal
2 cups rye or cracked wheat flour
2-1/2 teaspoons salt
1/2 cup wheat germ

When cool, add yeast mixture and stir well. Add enough white flour to handle dough easily. Knead; let double in bulk. Put into bread pans; let rise again. Bake at 350 degrees for 1 hour.

VITAMIN-RICH BREAD
Makes 1 loaf

1 cup seedless raisins
1/2 cup white raisins
2 teaspoons baking soda
1 tablespoon melted butter or
   margarine
1-1/2 cups orange juice or apple
   juice (heated)
2 eggs
1 cup sugar
1-1/4 cups sifted flour
1/4 teaspoon salt
2 cups bran flakes

Combine raisins, white raisins, baking soda, butter, and heated orange or apple juice in a bowl. Let stand for 10 minutes. Beat eggs and sugar together well. Stir in flour and salt. Combine with raisin mixture and bran flakes; beat only until well-blended. Turn into greased 9-inch loaf pan and bake at 350 degrees for about 1 hour. Cool 5 minutes in pan before turning out onto rack. Store 24 hours for easier slicing.

Agnes Ward, Erie, Pa.

THRIFTY THREE-GRAIN BREAD
Serves 12

1 cup cornmeal, yellow or white
1 cup rye flour
1 cup graham flour
2 teaspoons baking soda
1 teaspoon salt
1/4 teaspoon allspice
1/8 teaspoon ginger
3/4 cup molasses
1-3/4 cups sour milk
1/4 cup light cream

Place dry ingredients in a large mixing bowl; mix well. In separate bowl stir together molasses, sour milk, and cream. Pour liquid into dry mixture; stir only until well moistened. Pour batter into greased 9-inch loaf pan; bake at 350 degrees for 1 hour and 15 minutes. Cool thoroughly before slicing.

Gwen Campbell, Sterling, Va.

IRISH SODA BREAD

4 cups flour
1 teaspoon salt
1 teaspoon baking soda
4 tablespoons caraway seeds
2 cups buttermilk
2 cups raisins

Mix dry ingredients and seeds; add liquid and stir to blend, just until all ingredients are moistened. Add more buttermilk, if needed. Mix in raisins. Place dough in greased 9 x 5 x 3 inch loaf pan. Bake at 425 degrees for approximately 45 minutes, until toothpick inserted in center comes out clean. If loaf is browning too fast, place sheet of aluminum foil on top. Remove from pan and cool on a wire rack.

Note: This bread has a hard crust, but a moist interior.

Carme Venella, Laurel Springs, NJ.

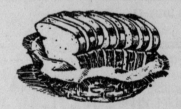

PEANUT BUTTER BREAD

3/4 cup sugar
1/2 cup peanut butter
1 teaspoon vanilla
1-3/4 cups milk
2-1/4 cups flour
4 teaspoons baking powder
1/2 teaspoon salt

Cream together sugar, peanut butter, and vanilla. Add milk and mix well. Combine flour, baking powder, and salt. Add to creamed mixture and beat well. Place in a greased loaf pan and bake at 350 degrees for 45-50 minutes, or until golden brown. Allow to cool for 10 minutes before removing from pan. This is a very moist loaf with a rich peanut taste.

Lillian Smith, Quebec, Canada

CALIFORNIA PRUNE-NUT BREAD

1 cup chopped dried prunes
2 teaspoons shredded orange peel
1 cup orange juice
2 cups sifted flour
3/4 cup sugar
3 teaspoons baking powder
1/2 teaspoon salt
1/2 teaspoon cinnamon
2 beaten eggs
2 tablespoons salad oil
1/2 cup chopped walnuts

Combine prunes, orange peel and juice; let stand 30 minutes. Sift together dry ingredients. Combine eggs, oil and prune mixture; add to dry ingredients, mix well. Add nuts; turn into greased 9 x 5 x 3-inch loaf pan. Bake in 350 degree oven for 50 to 60 minutes. Remove from pan and cool.

Judie Betz, Lomita, CA

CHOCOLATE NUTBREAD

6 cups sifted flour
1 teaspoon salt
2 cups sugar
6 teaspoons baking powder
1/2 cup cocoa
2 eggs
2 cups rich milk
1 tablespoon butter, melted and cooled
1 cup chopped pecans
1 cup ground pecans

Combine flour, salt, sugar, baking powder, and cocoa; sift together into mixing bowl. Beat eggs with milk. Add liquid to the dry ingredients and blend. Add butter, chopped nuts, and ground nuts; mix thoroughly. Divide dough evenly between 2 greased loaf pans. Let stand in a warm place for 30 minutes. Bake in a 325 degree oven for 1 to 1-1/4 hours or until tested done. Turn out on a rack to cool. Let stand for 24 hours before slicing.

CHERRY NUT BREAD

2-1/2 cups flour
1 cup sugar
2 teaspoons baking powder
1/2 teaspoon salt
1/2 cup shortening
12-14 chopped maraschino cherries
3/4 cup chopped nuts
2 eggs beaten
1/2 cup milk
1/4 cup maraschino cherry juice

Sift dry ingredients together. Cut in shortening, then add cherries and nuts. Combine liquid ingredients; add liquid to dry ingredients. Stir only until flour is moistened. Pour into greased 9x5x3 inch loaf pan. Bake at 350 degrees 50-60 minutes.

Dorothy Pelster, Hastings, Neb.

MAPLE-NUT BREAD

2 cups sifted flour
3 teaspoons baking powder
1 teaspoon salt
1/2 cup brown sugar
1/4 cup shortening
2 eggs
1/2 cup milk
1/4 cup maple flavored syrup
1/2 teaspoon maple extract
3/4 cup chopped nuts

Sift together flour, baking powder and salt. Add sugar, shortening, eggs, milk, syrup and maple extract. Stir until blended; beat 2 minutes on low speed of mixer. Stir in nuts; pour into a well greased 8-1/2 x 4-1/2-inch loaf pan. Bake 1 hour at 350 degrees.

Mrs. Betty Slavin, Omaha, NE

POLISH DARK RYE BREAD WITH CARAWAY

2 cups scalded milk
2 tablespoons sugar
1 package dry yeast
4 cups rye flour
2 tablespoons caraway seeds (optional)
2 tablespoons butter
1 teaspoon salt
1/2 cup lukewarm water
2-1/2 cups whole wheat flour

Pour scalded milk over butter, sugar, and salt in large bowl. Stir and cool. Dissolve yeast in lukewarm water. Add softened yeast, 3 cups rye flour to milk; mix and beat well. Beat in remaining rye flour. Cover and let rise in warm place until double. Turn out onto well-floured board and knead in whole wheat flour and caraway seeds. Knead until dough is smooth and elastic. Divide in half and shape into round or oblong loaves. Place in well-greased pans. Cover and let rise in warm place until double.

Bake at 450 degrees for 15 minutes. Reduce heat to 350 degrees and bake 35-40 minutes more.

Marie Micco, Somerville, MA

ALL AMERICAN CORNBREAD

Serves 12

2 cups biscuit mix
1 cup butter
1 cup half and half
1 cup yellow cornmeal
1/2 teaspoon baking soda
1/2 teaspoon salt
3/4 cup sugar
2 eggs, slightly beaten

Scald half and half with butter; add to thoroughly mixed dry ingredients. Mix in eggs. Pour into greased and floured 13x9x2-inch pan. Bake at 350 degrees for 30 minutes. Allow to stand for several minutes before cutting.

Marcella Swigert, Monroe City, Mo.

Brunch
BUFFET

BREAKFAST SANDWICH

4 eggs, hard-cooked and finely
   chopped
4 bacon slices, browned crisp and
   chopped
1/4 cup mayonnaise
1 cup Swiss cheese, grated
1 teaspoon tarragon
1-1/4 teaspoons mustard
8 slices bread

Mix together all ingredients, except bread. Spread mixture evenly between 8 slices bread, forming 4 sandwiches. Spread melted butter on outside surfaces of top and bottom of sandwiches. Brown on both sides in heavy skillet or on a microwave browner for 30 seconds; flip over and cook 1-1/2 minutes on the second side.

Mildred Sherrer, Bay City, Texas

ALL-TIME FAVORITE PANCAKES

1-1/4 cups flour
2 teaspoons baking powder
1/2 teaspoon soda
1/2 teaspoon salt
1 egg, beaten
1 cup buttermilk
2 tablespoons salad oil

Blend egg, milk, and oil. Measure flour after stirring. Blend dry ingredients together. Add to liquids; beat with rotary beater until all flour is moistened. Grease heated griddle, if necessary, and pour batter from pitcher or tip of large spoon in pools slightly apart. Turn pancakes as soon as they are puffed and full of bubbles, but before bubbles break. Turn and brown on other side. Serve at once with blueberry sauce or syrup.

Suzan Wiener, Spring Hill, Fla.

SAUSAGE SCRAPPLE
Serves 9

This is a shortcut version of a country cooking favorite. Serve fried slices for breakfast, brunch or dinner, plain or with maple syrup or ketchup.

½ pound well-seasoned
    bulk pork sausage
1½ cups water
⅓ cup yellow cornmeal
⅓ cup water
½ teaspoon salt
¼ teaspoon crumbled
    sage (optional)

Spray a large saucepan with pan release; add sausage and 1½ cups water. Heat to boiling; stir to crumble sausage; reduce heat; simmer about 20 minutes.

Meanwhile, in a small bowl stir together cornmeal, ⅓ cup water, salt and sage if using; set aside. Line an 8-inch square pan with foil long enough to also cover contents when pulled over.

Drain cooked sausage in a strainer, reserving broth. Spoon grease from broth; return 1 cup stock to saucepan. Vigorously stir in moistened cornmeal; bring to boiling, stirring. Cover; cook over low heat about 10 minutes, stirring occasionally. Stir in sausage; return to boiling. Pour into prepared pan; spread until smooth on top. Refrigerate; when cold cover closely with foil. Freeze, if desired, in meal-size units.

To serve, cut into squares; flour lightly. It can be fried in a skillet glazed with butter, or until crisp in deep fat. Serve hot with maple syrup or ketchup.

Note: Scrapple is usually poured into a loaf pan then sliced to fry. My friend, Anne Beaven, discovered and shared this wonderful timesaving idea of spreading scrapple in a shallow pan—no messy slicing, just cut into squares.

SUNDAY OVEN OMELETTE
Serves 4

2 tablespoons butter
7 eggs
1/4 teaspoon salt
1/3 cup dairy sour cream
1/4 cup milk
3/4 cup diced ham
1/2 cup shredded cheddar cheese

Melt butter in 9x9x2-inch glass baking dish. Whip eggs; add remaining ingredients and whip again. Pour into baking dish. Bake at 350 degrees for 40-45 minutes; test with a knife for doneness.

Angie Biggin, Lyons, Ill.

SCRAPPLE

1½ pounds pork sausage
4 cups water
1 teaspoon salt
2 teaspoons sage

1 cup yellow cornmeal
1 cup cold water

In a large saucepan, break sausage into small pieces. Add 4 cups water, stirring to separate meat. Bring to a boil. Reduce heat; simmer 20 minutes. Drain meat, reserving 3 cups broth. Add salt and sage. Bring again to a boil. Combine cornmeal and 1 cup cold water; gradually add to broth, stirring constantly. Cover and cook over low heat for 10 minutes. Stir occasionally. Add sausage. Pour into 1¼ x 5 x 3-inch loaf pan. Refrigerate overnight. Slice and fry. Very good served with eggs.

Helen Harlos, Ethel, Miss.

HAM WAFFLES
Serves 6

1 cup 100% Bran cereal
2 cups milk
2 cups sifted flour
1 tablespoon baking powder
¾ teaspoon salt
½ cup shortening
2 eggs, separated
1 cup diced ham

Soak cereal in milk for 5 minutes. Sift together flour, baking powder, and salt. Cut in shortening until it is as fine as meal. Add to soaked cereal along with beaten egg yolks and diced ham. Blend thoroughly. Beat egg whites until stiff and fold them into the cereal batter. Bake in a hot waffle iron until golden brown.

Mrs. Robert T. Shaffer, Middleburg, Pa.

¼ teaspoon salt
2 cups milk

Fit pastry into dish; crimp dough edges; brush with white of the separated egg. Spread sausage over crust; arrange apples in a single layer over sausage. Sprinkle with walnuts; add cheese; spread evenly. Beat egg yolk with whole eggs, coriander, dry mustard and salt; add milk. Pour over cheese/apple mixture; bake at 375 degrees for 45–50 minutes until custard is set.

Gwen Campbell, Sterling, Va.

BELGIAN DESSERT WAFFLES
Makes 6 waffles

1 package Pillsbury yellow cake mix
1-1/2 cups milk or light cream
4 eggs
1/2 teaspoon salt

Preheat waffle iron at medium heat. Lightly oil the waffle grid surface to prevent sticking. In large mixing bowl, combine cake mix, milk, eggs, and salt. Blend and beat as directed on package. Batter will be thick. Pour about 1 cup batter for a 9-inch waffle in preheated waffle iron. Bake until waffle is golden brown, about 2-4 minutes. Waffles will become more crisp upon cooling. Cool waffles on a wire rack. Stack sections of waffles with whipped cream and fresh, canned, or frozen fruit. Drain liquid from fruit, if necessary.

Annie Cmehil, New Castle, Ind.

THE CALCIUM CRUNCH BREAKFAST TREAT
Serves 4

2 cups plain, non-fat yogurt
3 cups melon, cut in cubes
3 cups berries
1/2 cup Grapenuts cereal

Place 1/2 cup of yogurt in a cereal bowl. Sprinkle 2 tablespoons of grapenuts on top of yogurt. Top with 1-1/2 cups of fruit. (175 calories per serving)

COUNTRY SAUSAGE QUICHE
Serves 8–10

Ready-made crust for 12-inch quiche pan
1 egg, separated
1¼ pounds pork sausage, cooked and crumbled
2 Golden Delicious apples, peeled and thinly sliced
¼ cup walnuts, chopped
2 cups cheddar cheese, shredded
3 eggs
¼ teaspoon coriander
¼ teaspoon dry mustard

P.D.Q. COFFEE CAKE

1 compressed yeast cake
2-1/2 cups lukewarm milk
1/2 cup shortening (part butter adds flavor)
1/2 cup sugar
1 egg
2 teaspoons salt
5 cups flour
1 stick butter or margarine, melted
Cinnamon and sugar mixture

Crumble yeast cake into a bowl and add milk. Stir until dissolved. In separate bowl combine shortening, sugar, egg, and salt. Combine the two mixtures. Add 1 cup of flour at a time to combined yeast mixture; beat after each addition. Beat dough until smooth and blended. Cover bowl and let rise until double. Punch dough down by giving it a stir with a spoon. Divide dough into 3 layer cake pans. Melt 1 stick of butter or margarine. Drizzle on top of cakes. Sprinkle mixture of sugar and cinnamon over cakes. Let rise again. Bake 20 minutes in a 450-degree oven.

Jane Williams, Columbus, Ohio

APPLE SCHMARREN

¼ cup flour
2 teaspoons sugar
⅜ teaspoon salt
⅔ cup milk
2 eggs
1 medium tart apple, peeled and thinly sliced
1½ teaspoons raisins, optional
Cinnamon and confectioners' sugar
3 tablespoons butter

Combine first 3 ingredients. Whisk in milk and eggs. Peel the apple; slice into batter. Add raisins; fry batter in the butter. I use an 8-inch non-stick fry pan. It should be nicely browned on all sides, so don't stir too often. Serve with cinnamon and confectioners' sugar sprinkled over the top.

Linda Taylor, Gravois Mills, Mo.

PUMPKIN PANCAKES
Makes 16

2 cups biscuit mix
2 tablespoons brown sugar
2 teaspoons cinnamon
1 teaspoon allspice
1½ cups milk
½ cup canned pumpkin
2 tablespoons vegetable oil
2 eggs
1 teaspoon vanilla extract

Combine biscuit mix, brown sugar, allspice and cinnamon. Add milk, pumpkin, oil, eggs and vanilla. Beat until smooth. Cook on lightly greased and heated griddle. This is a moist and tender pancake!

Vickie Vogt, Kewaskim, Wis.

HAM & EGGS CASSEROLE
Serves 6

3 cups cooked ham, diced
5 hard-cooked eggs, sliced
1 (6-ounce) can button mushrooms, drained
1 (10-1/2-ounce) can cream of onion soup
1/2 cup milk
1 teaspoon prepared mustard
2 cups Swiss cheese, grated
1 tablespoon Worcestershire sauce
1/2 teaspoon liquid hot sauce
1 cup dry bread crumbs
4 tablespoons butter or margarine, melted
2 tablespoons parsley, chopped

Grease a 2-quart casserole. Make alternate layers of ham, eggs, and mushrooms; start and finish with ham. In a saucepan combine soup, milk, and mustard. Add cheese, Worcestershire sauce, and hot sauce; heat until cheese melts, stirring constantly. Pour over layered mixture in casserole. Mix crumbs and butter; sprinkle over top. Bake at 325 degrees for 25 minutes until hot and crumbs are golden; scatter parsley over individual servings.

Gwen Campbell, Sterling, Va.

FRENCH TOAST
Serves 2

1 egg white
1 tablespoon skim milk
1 teaspoon sugar
1 tablespoon butter, melted
2 slices bread

Mix all ingredients, except bread. Soak bread in mixture. Cook on lightly oiled griddle over low heat. Turn frequently to brown evenly. Serve with sugar and cinnamon mixed together, maple syrup, honey or jam. (90 calories per slice)

Edna Askins, Greenville, Texas

CINNAMON TOAST COFFEE CAKE
Serves 10-12

2 cups flour
1 cup sugar
2 teaspoons baking powder
1 teaspoon salt
1 cup milk
2 tablespoons melted butter
1 teaspoon vanilla
1/4 teaspoon cinnamon
1/4 teaspoon nutmeg
1/2 cup seedless raisins

Topping:
1/2 cup melted butter
1/2 cup sugar
1-1/2 tablespoons cinnamon

Combine dry ingredients; stir in milk, 2 tablespoons butter, and vanilla until batter is smooth. Add raisins. Spread evenly into well-greased and lightly floured 15x10x1-inch jelly roll pan or sheet cake pan. Bake at 350 degrees for 20-25 minutes until lightly browned. While coffee cake is baking, combine 1/2 cup sugar and cinnamon. Remove cake from oven after 10 minutes of baking; drizzle 1/2 cup melted butter evenly over top of hot cake; sprinkle with sugar-cinnamon topping mixture and return to oven. Bake 10-15 minutes more. Serve warm.

Dee L. Getchell, Old Lyme, Conn.

CHOCOLATE LOVER'S BREAKFAST BREAD

Makes 2 loaves

3 cups flour
3 eggs
2 cups sugar
1 cup oil
1 teaspoon vanilla
1 teaspoon *each* ground cinnamon, baking soda and baking powder
½ cup sour cream
2 cups shredded zucchini
1 cup semisweet chocolate bits

Combine flour, eggs, sugar, oil, vanilla, cinnamon, baking soda, baking powder and sour cream in mixer bowl. Beat at medium speed for 2 minutes, or until well-blended. Stir in zucchini and chocolate bits. Pour batter into 2 well-greased (8 x 4-inch) loaf pans and bake at 350 degrees for 1 hour and 15 minutes.

HEATH BAR COFFEE CAKE

2 cups flour
1/4 cup brown sugar
1/4 pound butter or margarine
6 chilled Heath candy bars
1 egg
1 cup milk
1 teaspoon vanilla
1 teaspoon baking soda
1-1/2 teaspoons salt
1-1/2 cups nuts, chopped

Grease and flour a 9x13-inch pan. Mix together flour, sugar, soda, salt, and butter to the consistency of pie dough (reserve 1 cup for topping).

Beat together egg, vanilla, and milk; add to first mixture. Pour into prepared pan. Break up Heath bars into small pieces, using a rolling pin. Add Heath bars and chopped nuts to reserved cup of first mixture; sprinkle on top of cake. Bake at 350 degrees for 40 minutes.

Agnes Ward, Erie, Pa.

SAUSAGE CORN BREAD APPLE PIE

Serves 8

1 pound pork sausage
1 tablespoon vegetable oil
1 egg, beaten
1 1/2 cups buttermilk
1 3/4 cups corn bread mix
1 can apple pie filling
1/8 teaspoon cinnamon
1 tablespoon sugar

Cook sausage over medium heat until browned; stir to crumble; drain well and set aside. Place oil in a 10-inch cast-iron skillet or heavy 10-inch baking pan. Heat at 400 degrees for 5 minutes, or until hot. Combine egg, buttermilk and corn bread mix in a large mixing bowl; stir until mixture is smooth. Stir in crumbled sausage; pour into skillet. Bake at 400 degrees for 25–30 minutes. Place sugar, cinnamon and pie filling in a small saucepan. Cook over low heat, stirring constantly, until heated. Spread over corn bread. Serve hot. This is a good brunch main dish or for breakfast.

Leota Baxter, Ingalls, Kan.

CHOCOLATE CHIP STREUSEL COFFEE CAKE

Streusel:
1/2 cup brown sugar
1/2 cup flour
1/4 cup margarine
1/4 cup chopped walnuts
1 cup chocolate chips

Cake:
1 (8-ounce) package cream cheese
1-1/2 cups sugar
3/4 cups margarine
3 eggs
3/4 teaspoon vanilla
2-1/2 cups flour
1-1/2 teaspoons baking powder
3/4 teaspoon baking soda
1/4 teaspoon salt
3/4 cup milk

For streusel, combine brown sugar and flour. Cut in margarine until mixture resembles coarse crumbs. Stir in walnuts and chocolate chips. Set aside. Grease and flour a 13x9x2-inch pan. Combine cream cheese, sugar, and margarine, mixing at medium speed until well-blended. Blend in eggs and vanilla. Add combined dry ingredients alternately with milk, mixing well after each addition. Spoon batter into prepared pan. Sprinkle with crumb mixture. Bake at 350 degrees for 40 minutes. Cool.

Great for large crowds! If you like cheese filling, you'll love it!

Mrs. George Franks, Millerton, Pa.

NO-FRY DOUGHNUTS

Makes 1½–2 dozen

2 packages yeast
1½ cups lukewarm milk (scalded then cooled)
½ cup sugar
1 teaspoon nutmeg
2 eggs
4½ cups flour
¼ cup warm water
1 teaspoon salt
¼ teaspoon cinnamon
⅓ cup shortening
¼ cup margarine, melted Cinnamon and sugar

In large mixer bowl, dissolve yeast in warm water. Add milk, sugar, salt, spices, eggs, shortening and 2 cups flour. Blend ½ minute on top speed, scraping bowl occasionally. Stir in remaining flour, until smooth, scraping sides of bowl. Cover. Let rise in warm place until double, 50–60 minutes. Turn dough onto well-floured, cloth-covered board; roll around lightly to coat with flour (dough will be soft to handle). Roll dough to about ½-inch thickness. Cut with a 2½-inch doughnut cutter. Place 2 inches apart on baking sheet; brush doughnuts with melted margarine. Cover; let rise until double, about 20 minutes. Heat oven to 425 degrees. Bake 8–10 minutes, or until golden brown. Immediately brush with melted margarine and shake in sugar and cinnamon or use doughnut glaze.

Sharon Crider, Evansville, Wis.

29

BREAKFAST EGG DISH

Serves 6

8 slices bread
1/2 cup melted butter
1 cup grated Cheddar cheese
Bacon or ham bits
Chopped green pepper
Sliced mushrooms, optional
2 cups milk
1/4 teaspoon salt
1/8 teaspoon pepper

Cut crust off the slices of bread and cube bread. Put in a 9x13 inch buttered pan. Pour the melted butter over the bread cubes; sprinkle on bacon bits, green pepper, and mushrooms.

Separate the eggs. Beat the yolks with the milk, salt, and pepper; pour over ingredients in the pan. Beat egg whites until stiff. Seal above mixture with egg whites. Cover and keep in the refrigerator overnight.

Bake at 325 degrees for 40-45 minutes.

EGG 'N' CHIPS

Serves 6

6 hard-boiled eggs, chopped
2 tablespoons chopped green pepper
1/2 teaspoon salt
2/3 cup mayonnaise or salad dressing
1-1/2 cups diced celery
3/4 cup coarsely chopped walnuts
1 teaspoon minced onion
1/4 teaspoon pepper
1 cup grated Cheddar cheese
1 cup crushed potato chips

Combine eggs, celery, walnuts, green pepper, onion, salt, pepper and salad dressing or mayonnaise. Toss lightly, but thoroughly, so ingredients are evenly moistened. Use additional salad dressing if needed. Place in a greased 1-1/2 - quart baking dish. Sprinkle with cheese and top with crushed chips. Bake at 375 degrees for about 25 minutes or until thoroughly heated and cheese has melted.

Shirley Anne Crist, Marion, IN

FOOLPROOF SCRAMBLED EGGS

Serves 3-4

6 eggs
1/3 cup light cream
3/4 teaspoon salt
1/8 teaspoon pepper
1/2 teaspoon Worcestershire sauce

Beat eggs; beat in cream and seasonings. Cook in upper part of double boiler, over hot water, until just set, stirring often. Serve at once with toast.

Agnes Ward, Erie, PA

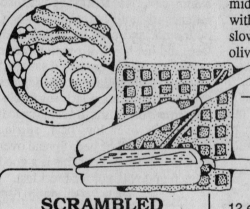

SCRAMBLED BAGEL ROYALE

Serves 2

2 bagels
1-1/2 tablespoons butter or margarine
4 eggs
2 tablespoons milk
3 tablespoons chopped onion
1/4 cup lox pieces or smoked salmon
2 ounces cream cheese
2 slices tomato garnish

Slice bagels in half horizontally. Lightly spread with one tablespoon of butter or margarine; toast lightly. Over medium high heat, saute chopped onion in remaining half tablespoon of butter or margarine until translucent. Beat eggs with milk; add to onions. Stir eggs. When eggs are almost set, add lox pieces and cream cheese that has been cut into small chunks; scramble in pan until cheese begins to melt.

Spoon mixture over bagels. Garnish with tomato slices.

TOLEDO HAM AND EGGS

Serves 6

1 cup chopped, cooked ham
1 tablespoon olive oil
2 cups cooked peas
2 canned pimentos, chopped
1/4 cup chopped green olives
Salt and pepper, if desired
6 eggs
2 tablespoons olive oil

Saute ham in olive oil for 2-3 minutes. Combine with peas, pimento, and olives. Heat well; add salt and pepper if desired. Put in the middle of a hot platter and surround with the eggs, which have been slowly cooked in the 2 tablespoons of olive oil.

Agnes Ward, Erie, PA

TUNA STUFFED EGGS

Makes 24 halves

12 eggs
6 slices bacon
1 - 3-1/4 to 3-1/2 - ounce can tuna, drained and finely flaked
3/4 cup mayonnaise
1 tablespoon lemon juice
1/2 teaspoon hot pepper sauce
1/2 teaspoon salt

In 4-quart saucepan, place eggs and enough water to come one inch above tops of eggs over high heat; heat to boiling. Remove saucepan from heat; cover tightly and let eggs stand in hot water 15 minutes; drain.

Meanwhile, in 10-inch skillet, cook bacon until browned, remove to paper towel to drain. Crumble bacon, set aside.

Peel and slice eggs lengthwise in half. Remove yolks and place in medium bowl. With fork, finely mash yolks. Stir in tuna, mayonnaise, lemon juice, hot pepper sauce and salt until smooth. Pile egg yolk mixture into egg whites center. Sprinkle with bacon. Cover and refrigerate.

Dorothy K. Garms, Anaheim, CA

SAUSAGE NOODLE BAKE

1 (10-1/2-ounce) can cream of
  chicken soup
1/2 cup milk
1-1/2 cups shredded cheddar
  cheese
1 pound pork sausage, cooked and
  crumbled
1 (12-ounce) package wide noodles
1 medium green pepper, chopped
1 medium onion, chopped
Buttered cracker crumbs

Preheat oven to 350 degrees. Generously butter a 2-quart casserole dish. Combine soup and milk, blending well. Heat over medium heat stirring occasionally. Add 1 cup of the cheddar cheese and stir until melted. Cook noodles according to directions. Add cooked sausage, drained noodles, green pepper, and onions to cooked noodles. Mix well. Pour soup/milk/cheese sauce over all and mix well. Pour into buttered casserole dish. Top with cracker crumbs and remaining 1/2 cup cheese. Cover and bake for 20 minutes. Uncover and bake for an additional 15 minutes until top is golden and bubbly.

Serve this delicious casserole with a crisp green salad. I guarantee your family will love it and it will quickly become a family favorite.

Phyliss Dixon, Fairbanks, Alaska

BANANA DATE COFFEE CAKE
Serves 8-10

1/3 cup mashed bananas
1/2 cup butter, softened
3 large eggs
1 teaspoon vanilla
1-1/4 teaspoons water
3 cups flour
1 teaspoon baking soda
2 teaspoons baking powder
1-1/2 cups chopped dates

Topping:
1/3 cup chopped dates
1/3 cup chopped nuts
1/3 cup flaked coconut

Beat together mashed bananas and butter until creamy. Add eggs, vanilla, and water; beat well. Blend in flour, baking soda, and baking powder, and beat well; stir in 1-1/2 cups chopped dates. Spoon batter into a greased and floured 9x13-inch baking pan. Combine topping ingredients and sprinkle over batter. Bake in a 350-degree oven for 20-25 minutes, or until knife inserted comes out clean. Cool on rack.

Mrs. D. Garms, Anaheim, Calif.

BRUNCH PIE
Serves 6

3 tablespoons margarine
2 (15-ounce) cans corned beef hash
3 eggs
1/2 cup chopped onion
1 cup grated cheddar cheese
1 (16-ounce) can mixed vegetables,
  drained
1/2 cup evaporated milk
1 tablespoon flour
1/2 teaspoon dry mustard
Dash garlic powder

Coat a 9-inch pie pan with margarine. Mix hash and 1 beaten egg; press into plate to form crust. Bake at 375 degrees for 10 minutes. Sauté onion in 3 tablespoons margarine. Layer cheese, sautéed onion, and vegetables all into crust. Beat together remaining eggs, evaporated milk, flour, mustard, and garlic powder. Pour over mixture in crust. Bake at 350 degrees for 30-40 minutes, until filling is set. Let stand 10 minutes before cutting.

Mrs. Albert H. Foley, Lemoyne, Pa.

CINNAMON RAISIN BATTER BREAD

1 package active dry yeast
1-1/2 cups warm water (105-115
  degrees)
2 tablespoons honey
2 tablespoons butter
1 teaspoon salt
3 cups flour, divided
1 tablespoon cinnamon
1 cup raisins

In a large bowl, dissolve yeast in warm water. Stir in honey. Add butter, salt, and 2 cups of the flour. Beat with electric mixer on low speed until blended. Beat 1 minute on high speed. Stir in remaining flour with a wooden spoon. Cover and let rise in a warm place until doubled in size. Punch down by stirring with a heavy spoon. Add cinnamon and raisins. Spoon batter into a loaf pan. Let rise again until batter reaches the top of the pan (not over!). Bake in preheated 350-degree oven for about 40 minutes or until loaf sounds hollow when lightly tapped. Cool on wire rack.

This batter bread is a wonderful treat for breakfast or in the "munchkin's" lunch sack as a peanut-butter-and-jelly sandwich.

Phyliss Dixon, Fairbanks, Alaska

BLUEBERRY COFFEE CAKE
Serves 10-12

2 cups sifted cake flour
1 teaspoon baking powder
1 teaspoon baking soda
1 cup sugar
2 sticks (1/2 pound) margarine
2 eggs
1 cup cultured sour cream
1 teaspoon vanilla
1 can blueberry pie filling

Preheat oven to 375 degrees. Sift flour, baking powder, soda, and sugar together into a large bowl. Cut in margarine as you would for pie crust. Beat together eggs, sour cream, vanilla, and combine with flour mixture, blending well. Spread half the batter in a greased 13x9x2-inch baking pan. Spoon pie filling over batter and spread evenly. Spread remaining batter over blueberry filling. Sprinkle with the following topping:

Blend together as for pie crust 1/4 cup cake flour, 3 tablespoons margarine, and 1/4 cup sugar. Sprinkle over top of batter in pan. Bake in a moderately hot oven of 375 degrees for 40 minutes, or until lightly browned. Serve warm or cold.

Trenda Leigh, Richmond, Va.

OMELET SUPREME
Serves 3

3 slices bacon, cut into small pieces
2 small potatoes, peeled and sliced
8 fresh spinach leaves, stems removed, sliced into 1/4 inch slices
6 eggs, lightly beaten with fork
1/2 cup yogurt
Salt and pepper to taste

In skillet, heat bacon; add potatoes; fry until bacon is crisp, and potatoes lightly browned. Add spinach; remove mixture to bowl. In shallow bowl, mix eggs, yogurt, salt, and pepper; pour into skillet. Distribute potato mixture evenly over eggs; cook over low heat without stirring. As eggs set on bottom, lift edges; let uncooked mixture run underneath. When omelet is set, fold with fork. Serve immediately.

June Harding, Ferndale, Mich.

OLD FASHIONED BREAD OMELET

Combine and soak for 10 minutes:
2 cups bread cubes
1 cup milk

Preheat oven to 325 degrees.
Combine in bowl:

5 eggs, beaten
1/2 cup grated cheese
1 cup alfalfa sprouts, chopped
1 small onion, finely chopped
1 tablespoon parsley flakes
1 teaspoon garlic powder
Salt and pepper to taste
Bread and milk mixture

Heat in skillet:
1/4-1/2 cup bacon pieces until done

Pour in egg mixture and cook over medium heat without stirring, about 5 minutes. When browned underneath, place pan in oven for 10 minutes to finish cooking the top. Turn out onto hot platter. Omelet can be folded in half.

Christine Nofziger, Elmworth, Alberta, Canada

BROCCOLI OVEN OMELET
Serves 6

9 eggs
1 (10 ounce) package frozen chopped broccoli, thawed and drained
1/3 cup finely chopped onion
1/4 cup grated Parmesan cheese
2 tablespoons milk
1/2 teaspoon salt
1/2 teaspoon dried basil
1/4 teaspoon garlic powder
1 medium tomato, cut into 6 slices
1/4 cup grated Parmesan cheese

Beat eggs with whisk in bowl until light and fluffy. Stir in broccoli, onion, 1/4 cup Parmesan cheese, milk, salt, basil, and garlic powder. Pour into ungreased 11x7x2 inch baking dish. Arrange tomato slices on top. Sprinkle with 1/4 cup Parmesan cheese. Bake uncovered in 325 degree oven until set, 25-30 minutes.

Great for holiday brunch, also as vegetable side dish.

Cheryl Santefort, Thornton, Ill.

QUICHE LORRAINE

1 (9-inch) pie crust
1 tablespoon soft butter
12 bacon slices
4 eggs
2 cups whipping cream
3/4 teaspoon salt
1/8 teaspoon nutmeg
1/4 pound natural Swiss cheese, shredded (1 cup)

Spread crust with soft butter; beat eggs, cream, salt, and nutmeg with wire whisk; stir in cheese and pour egg mixture into crust. Fry bacon until crisp and brown. Drain on paper towels and crumble; sprinkle in pie crust. Bake 15 minutes at 400 degrees; turn oven to 325 degrees and bake 35 minutes. Quiche is done when knife inserted in center comes out clean. Let stand 10 minutes before serving.

1933 Queen Dorothy Edwards Conlon

GARDEN MEDLEY
Serves 6

1/4 cup butter or margarine
2 cups cauliflower
1/4 cup chopped onion
2 cups sliced zucchini
1/2 cup halved cherry tomatoes
1/4 teaspoon salt
1/4 teaspoon thyme leaves, crushed
2 tablespoons grated Parmesan cheese, if desired

In large skillet, melt butter. Add cauliflower and onion; sauté 2-3 minutes. Add zucchini; cover and cook over medium heat, stirring occasionally, 3-5 minutes, or until vegetables are crisp-tender. Stir in tomatoes, salt, and thyme; cook 1-2 minutes until thoroughly heated. Spoon into serving dish; sprinkle with Parmesan cheese. (100 calories per serving)

Mrs. Sherwin Dick, Inman, Neb.

QUICK AND EASY BUCKWHEAT PANCAKES

1/2 cup bread crumbs
2-1/2 cups scalded milk
2 cups buckwheat flour
1/2 teaspoon salt
1/2 yeast cake
2 tablespoons molasses
1/4 teaspoon baking soda

Add bread crumbs and salt to scalded milk. Cool. When lukewarm add yeast and stir until yeast is dissolved. Add buckwheat flour and stir until smooth. Put in warm place overnight. In the morning add molasses and soda mixed with a little lukewarm water. Beat smooth. Bake on hot griddle.

These pancakes are delicious and more healthful than the regular kind. Your family will love them!

Suzan L. Wiener, Spring Hill, Fla.

SELF-FILLED CUPCAKES

1 package Deluxe Devil's Food
  cake mix
1 (8-ounce) package cream cheese
1 egg
1/2 teaspoon salt
1/3 cup sugar
2 (8-ounce) package semisweet
  chocolate chips

Mix cake according to package directions. Place individual baking liners in muffin pan. Fill cup two-thirds full. Cream the cheese with the sugar. Beat in egg and salt; stir in chocolate chips. Drop rounded teaspoonfuls of mixture in cake batter. Bake as cake directs.

Dovie Lucy, McLoud, Okla.

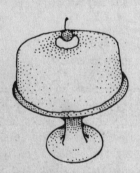

FRUIT UPSIDE-DOWN CAKE
(Electric Fry Pan)

1/2 cup butter
1/2 cup packed brown sugar
1 (20-ounce) can sliced pineapple,
  drained
1 (25-ounce) jar pitted prunes,
  drained
1 (15-ounce) can apricot halves,
  drained
12 pecan halves
1 (18-1/2-ounce) package yellow
  cake mix
2 eggs
1 cup water
2 teaspoons grated lemon rind
Pecan halves

In preheated 12-inch electric skillet, melt butter; coat pan with melted butter by rotating pan to cover sides and bottom. Sprinkle in brown sugar to cover bottom evenly. Arrange the fruit over brown sugar. Prepare cake according to directions *but* use 2 eggs, 1 cup water, and lemon rind; beat smoothly. Spoon batter over fruit, spreading carefully to edges. Cover tightly and set temperature at 300 degrees. Cook, covered, for 40 minutes; do not remove lid until finished. Loosen cake with sharp knife and unmold while hot onto serving dish. Serve warm with whipped cream.

Agnes Ward, Erie, Pa.

PRINCESS CAKE

Cake:
1 (16-ounce) package white cake
  mix
1 (3-3/4-ounce) package strawberry
  pudding mix
3 eggs
1 cup water
1 cup vegetable oil
1/2 cup sour cream
1/2 cup chopped nuts

Frosting:
2-1/4 cups cold milk
2 (1-1/2-ounce) packages powdered
  whipped topping
1-1/2 (3-3/4-ounce) packages
  strawberry pudding mix

Preheat oven to 350 degrees. Grease and flour a 10-inch tube pan. Blend all cake ingredients, except nuts, in a large bowl; beat 2 minutes at medium speed. Stir in nuts. Turn batter into prepared pan and bake 40-50 minutes, or until tested done. Cool 15 minutes in pan, then remove to rack to finish cooling. Split cooled cake crosswise into 2 layers. Whip all frosting ingredients until mixture thickens (about 5 minutes)). Spread frosting between cake layers as well as on the top and sides. Decorate the cake lavishly with 3-4 cups sliced strawberries.

Agnes Ward, Erie, Pa.

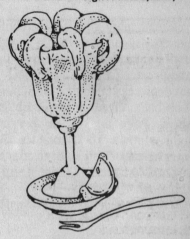

OLD FASHIONED FUDGE CAKE

1 cup white sugar
1 egg
1-1/2 cups white flour
1 teaspoon baking soda
1/4 teaspoon baking powder
1/4 teaspoon salt
1 cup sour milk (to sour, add 1
  teaspoon vinegar)
3 tablespoons butter
4 level tablespoons cocoa
1 teaspoon vanilla

Melt butter and cocoa together over low heat, beat until smooth. In large mixer bowl, beat together sugar, egg and vanilla. Sift dry ingredients and add alternately with milk. Beat smooth. Add warm cocoa mix slowly to batter as you mix on low speed. Beat until smooth and creamy. Pour into prepared 9-inch layer cake pans or 9x13-inch pan. Bake in preheated 350 degree oven for 25 minutes for layers, or 30 minutes for flat cake. Test middle with toothpick for doneness. Cool on rack. Ice with favorite frosting.

Pearle M. Goodwin, South Ryegate, Vt.

35

RUSSIAN TEA CAKES
Makes 36

1 cup margarine, softened
1/4 cup confectioners' sugar
1 teaspoon vanilla extract
2 cups flour
1/2 cup toasted pecans, chopped
Confectioners' sugar

Cream margarine, 1/4 cup confectioners' sugar and vanilla together until light and fluffy. Mix in the flour and pecans. Chill 2 hours. Pinch off small pieces of dough and roll into 1-inch balls. Place on greased baking sheet. Bake at 375 degrees until lightly brown, 10-12 minutes. Cool on wire rack. Roll in confectioners' sugar before serving. Store in airtight container.

Edith Ruth Muldoon, Baldwin, N.Y.

2 cups sugar. Beat in egg yolks. Then beat in 1 cup apricot nectar, lemon rind, and vanilla. In another bowl, stir together flour, baking powder, and salt. Beat into the creamed mixture, then fold in egg whites, gently but thoroughly. Turn batter into greased and floured angel food or tube cake pan. Bake at 350 degrees for 1 to 1-1/4 hours, or until toothpick inserted in center comes out clean. Just before cake finishes baking, heat remaining 1/3 cup sugar with remaining 1/3 cup apricot nectar, just to a boil (stir to dissolve sugar). When cake is done, transfer to rack and slowly pour hot apricot syrup over all. Let cake remain in pan until cool.

Sharon McClatchey, Muskogee, Okla.

PUMPKIN POUND CAKE
Serves 12

3 cups sifted flour
4 teaspoons baking powder
1/4 teaspoon baking soda
1/2 teaspoon salt
1 cup butter or margarine
1 cup sugar
1 cup brown sugar, packed
2 eggs
1 cup canned or mashed, cooked pumpkin
1 teaspoon lemon extract
1/2 cup milk
1 cup chopped walnuts
Sifted powdered sugar

Sift together flour, baking powder, baking soda and salt; set aside. Cream together butter, sugar and brown sugar in mixing bowl until light and fluffy, using electric mixer at medium speed. Add eggs, one at a time, beating well after each addition. Blend in pumpkin and lemon extract (total beating time 10 minutes). Add dry ingredients alternately with milk to creamed mixture, beating well after each addition, using electric mixer at low speed. Stir in walnuts. Pour batter into greased 10-inch tube pan. Bake in 325 degree oven 1 hour and 20 minutes, or until cake tester inserted in center comes out clean or top springs back when lightly touched with finger. Cool in pan on rack 10 minutes. Remove from pan; cool on rack. Sprinkle with powdered sugar.

Barbara Beauregard - Smith, Northfield, S. A., Australia

GLAZED APRICOT CAKE
Serves 16-20

4 eggs, separated
2 sticks (1 cup) butter, softened
2-1/3 cups sugar, divided
1-1/3 cups apricot nectar, divided
Grated rind of 1 lemon
1-1/2 teaspoons vanilla extract
2-1/2 cups plus 1 tablespoon flour
2-1/2 teaspoons baking powder
1/4 teaspoon salt

Beat egg whites until stiff. Set aside. In a large bowl, cream butter with

LEMON PUDDING CAKE
Serves 6

2 eggs, separated
1 teaspoon grated lemon peel
1/4 cup lemon juice
2/3 cup milk
1 cup sugar
1/4 cup all-purpose flour
1/4 teaspoon salt

Heat oven to 350 degrees. Beat egg whites until stiff peaks form; set aside. Beat egg yolks. Blend in lemon peel, juice and milk. Add sugar, flour and salt; beat until smooth. Fold into whites. Pour into ungreased 1-quart casserole. Place casserole in pan of very hot water (1 inch deep). Bake 45–50 minutes. Serve warm or cool and, if desired, with whipped cream.

"500" CAKE

1/2 cup butter
1 cup sugar
2 eggs
1/2 cup sour cream
1 cup mashed bananas
2 cups flour
1/2 teaspoon salt
1 teaspoon baking soda
1 teaspoon baking powder
1/2 cup chopped dates
1/2 cup chopped nuts
1 teaspoon vanilla

Cream butter and sugar. Add eggs. Add sour cream and mashed bananas alternately with sifted dry ingredients. Fold in nuts and dates which have been dusted with a little of the flour. Add vanilla. Pour into greased cake pans or cupcake tins. Bake at 350 degrees for 30 minutes.
Note: Buttermilk may be used instead of sour cream.

Leah Maria Daub, Milwaukee, Wis.

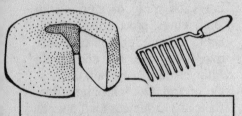

SOUR CREAM CAKE

1/2 cup chopped pecans
1/2 cup sugar
1 teaspoon cinnamon
4 eggs
1 package yellow cake mix
1 package instant vanilla pudding mix
1/2 cup oil
1 cup sour cream

Combine pecans, sugar, and cinnamon; set aside. Combine remaining ingredients; beat for 4 minutes. Spoon half the batter into well-greased and floured bundt or spring pan. Sprinkle half of the pecan mixture over batter, then add remaining batter and remaining pecan mixture over top. Bake in a preheated 350-degree oven for 1 hour. Cake may be glazed with thin icing or dusted with confectioners' sugar.

Leota M. Baxter, Ingalls, Kan.

APPLE CAKE WITH TOPPING

3 cups flour
2 cups sugar
1-1/2 teaspoons
1 teaspoon salt
3/4 cup cooking oil
2 eggs, beaten
1 teaspoon vanilla
1 cup chopped walnuts
3 cups chopped apples (unpeeled)

Mix oil, sugar, and eggs. Add dry ingredients and vanilla by hand. Add nuts and apples. Bake at 350 degrees for 1 hour in a well-greased tube or bundt pan. Remove from oven and pour topping over cake. Return cake to oven and bake 15 minutes more. Slide knife around cake to loosen.

Topping:
1 cup light brown sugar
1 stick butter or margarine
1/4 cup orange juice

Cook over low heat for 3 minutes after the mixture starts boiling. Pour over cake as directed above.

Trenda Leigh, Richmond, Va.

POPPY SEED CAKE
Serves 10-12

1 (18-1/2-ounce) package yellow cake mix
1 (3-3/4-ounce) package instant vanilla pudding mix
4 eggs
1 cup sour cream
1/2 cup (1 stick) melted butter
1/2 cup cream sherry
1/3 cup poppy seeds

Preheat oven to 350 degrees. Grease bundt cake pan and flour lightly, shaking out excess. Combine all ingredients in large bowl and beat 5 minutes with electric mixer. Pour batter into pan. Bake until tester in center comes out clean, about 1 hour. Let cool completely in pan. Invert onto platter and serve. Garnish each serving with sliced fruit.

Frances Falk, W. Palm Beach, Fla.

ORANGE PEANUT– BUTTER CAKE
Serves 12

2 oranges
1 (18-ounce) package yellow cake mix with pudding
1-1/4 cups water
3 eggs
1/2 cup peanut butter
1 teaspoon ground cinnamon
1/3 cup packed brown sugar

Grate peeling from oranges; reserve. Peel oranges and cut into bite–size pieces; drain well. In large bowl, combine cake mix, water, eggs, peanut butter, and cinnamon; mix according to package directions. Stir in orange peel and pieces. Pour batter into greased and floured 13x9x2-inch cake pan. Sprinkle brown sugar over top of batter. Bake at 350 degrees for 35-40 minutes or until done. Serve warm or cool.

Kit Rollins, Cedarburg, Wis.

PRALINE CHEESECAKE
Serves 12

Crust:
1-1/2 cups graham cracker crumbs
6 tablespoons butter, melted
1/4 cup sugar
2 tablespoons pecans, finely chopped

Filling:
1-1/2 pounds cream cheese
1 cup dark brown sugar
2 tablespoons flour
3 eggs
1/2 teaspoon vanilla
1/4 cup pecans, finely chopped

Combine all crust ingredients. Press on bottom and up sides of 9-inch springform pan.

For filling beat together cheese and sugar until creamy. Add flour, then eggs. Blend in vanilla and pecans. Pour into crust. Bake at 350 degrees for 50 minutes. Allow to cool. Chill in refrigerator before serving.

Lisa Varner, Baton Rouge, La.

PEACHES AND CREAM CHEESECAKE

1-1/2 cups flour
1 teaspoon salt
2 eggs
1 cup milk
2 teaspoons baking powder
2 small packages regular vanilla pudding
1 (20-ounce) can drained peaches, reserve juice
2 (8-ounce) packages cream cheese
1 cup sugar
6 tablespoons peach juice
1 teaspoon cinnamon
2 tablespoons sugar

Combine first six ingredients and beat 2 minutes at medium speed. Pour into greased 9x13-inch pan. Arrange peaches over top of batter. Combine cheese, sugar, and peach juice; beat for 2 minutes. Spoon over peaches. Mix sugar and cinnamon together and sprinkle over the top. Bake at 350 degrees for 30-35 minutes.

Kit Rollins, Cedarburg, Wis.

BLUEBERRY SNACK-CAKE
Serves 9

1/4 cup butter or margarine
1 cup sugar
1 egg
1-1/2 cups flour
2 teaspoons baking powder
1/2 cup milk
1/2 teaspoon almond flavoring
1 cup fresh or frozen blueberries

Topping:
1/2 teaspoon cinnamon
2 tablespoons sugar
2 tablespoons melted butter

Cream butter and sugar; add egg and beat well. Mix flour and baking powder together and add to creamed mixture alternately with milk mixed with almond flavoring. Beat until smooth. Fold in blueberries. Pour into greased 8x8x2-inch pan. Mix together cinnamon, sugar and melted butter; sprinkle over top. Bake at 350 degrees for 25-30 minutes, or until it tests done.

GERMAN CHOCOLATE UPSIDE-DOWN CAKE

1 cup coconut
1 cup chopped pecans
1 oackage German Chocolate cake mix

Mix these two ingredients and put into a greased 9x13-inch pan. Mix 1 package German chocolate cake mix according to directions and pour on top of coconut pecan mixture.

In saucepan put 1 stick margarine and 1 (8-ounce) package cream cheese, softened. Heat until mixture is warm enough to stir in 1-pound box confectioners' sugar. Spoon over top of cake mix. Bake at 350 degrees for 35-40 minutes. Do not cut until cooled.

Hazel C. Jackson, Glade Spring, Va.

RASPBERRY CREAM COFFEE CAKE
Serves 8-10

1 (3-ounce) package cream cheese
1/4 cup butter or margarine
2 cups packaged biscuit mix
1/4 cup milk
1/2 cup raspberry preserves
1 cup sifted confectioners' sugar
1 to 2 tablespoons milk
1/2 teaspoon vanilla

In medium mixing bowl cut the cream cheese and butter into biscuit mix until crumbly. Stir in 1/4 cup milk. Turn onto a lightly floured surface. Knead 8 to 10 strokes. On waxed paper, roll dough to a 12x8-inch rectangle. Invert onto a greased baking sheet. Remove paper. Spread preserves down center of dough. Make 2-1/2-inch long cuts at 1-inch intervals on long sides. Fold strips over the filling. Bake in a 375 degree oven about 20 minutes or until golden brown. Let coffee cake cool 5 minutes before frosting.

In small mixing bowl stir together sugar, the 1 to 2 tablespoons milk, and vanilla. Drizzle over slightly cooled coffee cake. Serve warm.

EASIEST CHERRY CAKE
Serves 12

1 (14-ounce) can crushed pineapple
2 (20-ounce) cans cherry pie filling
1 box white or yellow cake mix
Nuts, coconut, or whipped topping
1 1/4 sticks margarine

Spray 9x13-inch cake pan with non-stick spray or grease with shortening. Spread crushed pineapple in pan. Sprinkle cake mix over pineapple and cherry pie filling. Add 1/2 cups nuts or coconut on top. Dot with margarine. Bake at 350 degrees for 1 hour or until golden brown. Top with whipped topping, if desired.

STRAWBERRY CAKE

1 box white cake mix
1 box strawberry gelatin
1 cup strawberries, mashed
1 cup Crisco oil
4 eggs, beaten
1/2 cup sweet milk
1/2 cup coconut
1/2 cup nuts, finely chopped

Combine all ingredients; beat. Bake at 300 degrees until cake springs back when touched.

Frosting:
1 (1-pound) box powdered sugar
1 stick margarine, melted (8 tablespoons)
1/4 cup mashed drained strawberries
1/4 cup coconut

ZUCCHINI PINEAPPLE CAKE

3 eggs
2 cups sugar
2 teaspoons vanilla
1 cup cooking oil
2 cups zucchini, peeled and grated
3 cups flour
1 teaspoon baking powder
1/2 cup raisins
1 teaspoon salt
1 teaspoon nuts
1 cup crushed pineapple, drained

Beat eggs until fluffy; add sugar, vanilla, oil, and zucchini. Blend well. Add dry ingredients and mix well. Stir in pineapple, raisins, and nuts.

Bake in one large greased and floured loaf pan or two small loaf pans. Bake in 325-degree oven for 1 hour. Cool in pan on wire rack. When cool wrap in foil to store.

Mrs. L. Mayer, Richmond, VA.

HAZELNUT CHEESECAKE

1-1/2 pounds cream cheese, at room temperature
1 cup sugar
3 eggs
1 cup hazelnuts, finely chopped
1 teaspoon vanilla extract
1 cup heavy cream
2 tablespoons rum
Bread crumbs

Preheat oven to 375 degrees. In bowl of electric mixer, combine cream cheese, sugar, eggs, hazelnuts, vanilla extract, heavy cream, and rum. Butter a 10x3-inch deep layer-cake or springform pan and coat with bread crumbs. Pour batter into pan. Put pan with the cheesecake batter into a deep pan. Fill outside pan with water until water reaches halfway up sides of cheesecake pan. Bake for 45 minutes. Cool and serve.

Irene Donner, Jamestown, N.Y.

ELEGANT APPLE CHEESECAKE

2 (8-ounce) packages cream cheese, softened
1 (16-ounce) carton cream-style cottage cheese
1-1/2 cups sugar
4 eggs
3 tablespoons cornstarch
1-1/2 tablespoons lemon juice
1 tablespoon vanilla
1/4 pound butter, melted and cooled
2 cups dairy sour cream
1 (21-ounce) can apple pie filling

Lightly butter a 9-inch springform pan. In a large mixing bowl, combine cheeses; beat until light and fluffy. Add sugar; blend well. Add eggs, one at a time, beating well after each addition. Add cornstarch, lemon juice, vanilla, and butter; blend until smooth. Blend in sour cream. Pour batter into prepared pan. Bake at 325 degrees for 1 hour and 10 minutes, or until center is set. Turn oven off. Let cheesecake stand in oven, with the door closed, for 2 hours. Cool completely. Chill 6 hours. Spoon apple pie filling over the top.

Gwen Campbell, Sterling, Va.

APRICOT NECTAR CAKE

1 (46-ounce) can apricot nectar
7 tablespoons cornstarch
1-1/2 cups sugar
1 large angel food cake

Combine the first three ingredients and cook over medium heat until mixture becomes clear and bubbly. Watch closely, stirring constantly. Take off heat and pour over a large angel food cake, which has been torn into small pieces and placed in a greased 9x13 glass baking dish. Cover and allow it to chill 24 hours in refrigerator. Serve with a scoop of whipped topping. This is a quick and easy cake that is absolutely delicious!!

Denise Winchell, Pleasant Hill, Ill.

CRANBERRY CAKE

3 cups sifted flour
1-1/2 cups sugar
1 teaspoon soda
1 teaspoon salt
1 cup mayonnaise
1 cup chopped nuts
3/4 cup whole cranberry sauce
2 tablespoons orange peel
1/3 cup orange juice

Sift dry ingredients. Add remaining ingredients. Pour into greased 9x13-inch pan. Bake at 350 degrees for 45 minutes.

Icing:
2 tablespoons butter
2 cups sifted confectioners' sugar
1/4 cup whole cranberry sauce

Combine ingredients and spread on hot cake.

Sharon McClatchey, Muskogee, Okla.

ORANGE HONEY CAKE

2 cups sifted cake flour
3-1/2 teaspoons baking powder
3/4 teaspoon salt
1/2 cup butter or shortening
1/2 cup sugar
2/3 cup honey
2 egg yolks
1/2 cup orange juice
2 egg whites, stiffly beaten

Sift flour; measure; add baking powder and salt; sift 3 times. Cream butter thoroughly; add sugar gradually; cream until light and fluffy. Add honey; blend. Add egg yolks and beat thoroughly. Add flour alternately with orange juice, a small amount at a time, beating well after each addition until smooth. Fold in egg whites. Bake in 2 greased 9-inch layer pans in 350-degree oven for 30-35 minutes.

Agnes Ward, Erie, Pa.

39

CHUNKY CHOCOLATE CUPCAKES
Makes 1 dozen

1 cup sifted flour
1 cup sugar
1-1/2 teaspoons baking powder
1/2 teaspoon salt
2 eggs
1/4 cup cooking oil
1 teaspoon vanilla
1/4 cup milk
1-1/2 ounces unsweetened chocolate, chopped
Creamy Orange Frosting (recipe follows)

Sift together flour, sugar, baking powder and salt into bowl. Combine eggs, oil, vanilla, and milk in small bowl. Beat well. Combine egg mixture with dry ingredients; beat until blended. Stir in chocolate. Spoon batter into paper-lined 2-1/2-inch muffin-pan cups, filling two-thirds full. Bake in 400-degree oven 20-25 minutes or until cupcakes test done. Remove from pans, and cool on racks. Frost with Creamy Orange Frosting.

Creamy Orange Frosting:
Combine 2-1/2 cups sifted confectioners' sugar, 3 tablespoons soft butter or margarine, 1 teaspoon grated orange rind, and 2 tablespoons orange juice. Beat until smooth.

Barbara Beauregard-Smith, South Australia

LEMON-BLUEBERRY CAKE

1 (17-ounce) package lemon cake mix
1 cup sour cream or plain yogurt
4 eggs
1 can blueberries in heavy syrup

Mix cake mix, eggs, and sour cream together in large mixing bowl. Mix first on low speed of electric mixer and then on high speed until smooth and creamy. Drain blueberries; rinse, then drain again. Fold blueberries into cake mixture. Pour into greased and floured tube or bundt pan and bake in preheated 350-degree oven for 35-45 minutes until top springs back when lightly touched. Bake 15 minutes more before removing from oven. When cool, sprinkle with powdered sugar. Serve with a sauce, if desired.

Agnes Ward, Erie, Pa.

WALNUT POUND CAKE

3-1/2 cups flour
1 pound margarine or butter, softened
1/4 teaspoon salt
1 pound confectioners' sugar
6 eggs, unbeaten
1 teaspoon vanilla
1 teaspoon fresh lemon juice
1-1/2 cups walnuts, chopped

Cream butter and sugar until soft. Add salt, vanilla, juice, flour, and eggs. Beat at medium speed for a full 10 minutes until mixture is light and creamy.

Grease a round 10-inch tube pan. Add nuts to batter and blend well. Pour batter into pan. Bake at 350 degrees for 1-1/2 hours. Cake will crack and should be lightly brown. Freezes well.

Vivian Nikanow, Chicago, Ill.

GLAZED FRESH APPLE CAKE

2 cups sugar
1 cup butter or margarine
1 teaspoon soda
1/2 teaspoon salt
3 cups diced apples
1/2 cup chopped nuts
1/2 cup raisins
3 cups flour
3 eggs, well beaten
1-1/2 teaspoons vanilla
1 teaspoon cinnamon

Cream sugar and oil. Add eggs and beat well. Add dry ingredients and vanilla; beat. Add by hand apples, nuts, and raisins. Bake in tube pan at 350 degrees for 1 hour and 20 minutes.

Glaze:
1/2 stick margarine
1/2 cup brown sugar
2 tablespoons milk

Combine all ingredients in small saucepan and cook over medium heat 3 minutes. Cool and drizzle over warm cake.

Mrs. P. B. Brothers, Richmond, Va.

CRANBERRY-SAUCE CAKE

3 cups flour
2 teaspoons baking soda
1 cup mayonnaise
1 (16-ounce) can whole cranberry sauce, reserving 1/4 cup
1/2 cup orange juice
1 tablespoon grated orange rind
1 cup sugar
1 teaspoon salt
1 cup chopped nuts

Grease 9-inch tube pan. Line bottom with waxed paper. Mix dry ingredients into large bowl. Add other ingredients, except 1/4 cup reserved cranberry sauce, and mix well. Bake in 350-degree oven for 1-1/4 hours. Remove from pan and cool completely before icing.

Icing:
Mix 3 tablespoons soft butter with 2 cups confectioners' sugar and 1/4 cup reserved cranberry sauce. Beat until creamy and spread on cake.

LEMON CRACKLE CAKE

20 soda crackers (2" squares)
3/4 cup brown sugar
1 cup flour
1 teaspoon baking soda
1/2 cup butter or oleo
1 cup coconut

Crush crackers in bowl; add brown sugar, flour and soda. Work in butter; add coconut. Pat 3/4 of mixture into greased and floured 8 or 9-inch baking pan. Carefully spread on filling; cover with rest of crumb mixture. Bake at 350 degrees for 30 to 35 minutes or until slightly brown.

Lemon Filling:

1 cup sugar
2 tablespoons cornstarch
1 cup cold water
2 eggs, beaten
Juice of 2 lemons or 1/2 cup lemon juice
1/4 cup butter
1 teaspoons vanilla

In sauce pan, combine sugar and cornstarch. Gradually stir in water. Add remaining ingredients. Cook over medium heat until thickened. Cool before adding to cake.

Mrs. Stanley M. Lewis, Sussex, WI

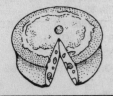

ORANGE - KISS ME CAKE

Serves 12

1-6 ounce can (3/4 cup) frozen orange juice concentrate, (thawed)
2 cups flour
1 cup sugar
1 teaspoon baking soda
1 teaspoon salt
1/2 cup shortening
1/2 cup milk
2 eggs
1 cup raisins
1/3 cup chopped walnuts

Grease and flour bottom of 13 x 9 inch pan. Combine 1/2 cup orange juice concentrate with remaining ingredients in large mixer bowl. Blend at lowest speed of mixer for 30 seconds. Beat 3 minutes at medium speed. Pour into pan. Bake at 350 degrees for 40-45 minutes. Drizzle remaining orange juice concentrate over warm cake; sprinkle with sugar-nut topping (recipe follows).

Sugar-Nut Topping:

1/3 cup sugar
1/4 cup chopped walnuts
1 teaspoon cinnamon

Combine all ingredients in small bowl.

Barbara Nowakowski, N. Tonawanda, NY

CREAM CHEESE TOPPED PINEAPPLE CAKE

2 eggs
2 cups sugar
2 cups all-purpose flour
1 (20-ounce) can crushed pineapple packed in own juice, undrained
1/2 cup chopped pecans
2 teaspoons baking soda
1 teaspoon vanilla

Preheat oven to 350 degrees. Lightly grease 9 x 13-inch baking pan. Beat eggs in large bowl until light and fluffy. Add sugar and beat until thick. Stir in flour, pineapple, pecans, baking soda, and vanilla; mix thoroughly. Pour into pan and bake until tester inserted in center comes out clean. Bake 40-45 minutes. Let cake cool in pan on rack.

Cream Cheese Frosting:

2 cups powdered sugar

1 (8-ounce) cream cheese (room temperature)
1/4 cup (1/2 stick) butter (room temperature)
1 teaspoon vanilla
Additional chopped pecans for garnish

Combine powdered sugar, cream cheese, butter, and vanilla; mix until fluffy. Spread over cooled cake and sprinkle with chopped nuts. Cut into squares to serve.

This is a quick and easy cake to make and is delicious!

Lois Conway, Coloma, WI

PINEAPPLE UPSIDE DOWN CAKE

1/2 cup packed brown sugar
1/4 cup butter
1 - can sliced pineapple (drained - reserve 1 tablespoon juice)
Maraschino cherries, halved
1 - 16 ounce container frozen pancake batter, thawed
1/4 cup granulated sugar

Heat oven to 350 degrees. Melt butter and put in glass pie plate. Add brown sugar and stir till smooth. Cut pineapple slices in half and arrange pineapple and cherries on sugar mixture in a decorative manner. Open top of pancake batter container completely. Add granulated sugar and reserve pineapple juice. Stir well. Pour over pineapple. Bake 30-35 minutes until golden brown and toothpick inserted in center comes out clean. Cool 5 minutes. Loosen edges of cake with small knife. Invert cake on serving platter.

This is a delicious and unusual way to make an upside-down cake. If pineapple is arranged pinwheel fashion, with a half-cherry in each curve, you get a lot more fruit on your cake.

Helen Weissinger, Levittown, PA

MISSISSIPPI MUD CAKE

2 cups sugar
1 cup soft margarine
4 eggs
1-1/2 cups flour
1/3 cup cocoa
2 teaspoons vanilla
1/4 teaspoon salt
1 cup chopped nuts
1 bag small marshmallows

Mix sugar, margarine, and eggs until well blended. Add dry ingredients to above mixture; add vanilla and chopped nuts. Grease and flour an oblong pan, bake at 300 degrees for 30 minutes. Remove from oven and spread marshmallows on top; return to oven for 10 minutes or until marshmallows have melted (watch closely).

Icing:

1 stick margarine
1 box powdered sugar
1/2 cup evaporated milk
1/3 cup cocoa
1 teaspoon vanilla
1 cup chopped nuts

Mix all ingredients together; spread on cake when cool.

Marie Mitchell, Conroe, TX

ALMOND JOY CAKE

2 cups flour
2 cups sugar
1 teaspoon soda
1 stick margarine
3 tablespoons cocoa
1/2 cup shortening
1 cup water
2 beaten eggs
1 teaspoon vanilla
1/2 cup buttermilk

Combine sugar, flour, and soda. Boil together margarine, cocoa, shortening, and water. Pour over flour mixture. Add eggs, buttermilk, and vanilla; mix. Bake in greased and floured 13 x 9-inch pan. Cool.

Filling:

1 can evaporated milk
1 jar marshmallow creme
1 cup sugar
2 cans Angel Flake coconut

Heat milk, marshmallow creme, and sugar until creme and sugar melt. Stir in coconut. Pour over cake.

Icing:

3 tablespoons cocoa
1 stick margarine
6 tablespoons milk
1 package confectioners' sugar
1 cup toasted, whole almonds
1 teaspoon vanilla

Boil cocoa, margarine, and milk. Pour over sugar and stir until smooth. Add almonds and vanilla. Spread over filling.

Suzanne Dawson, Cypress, TX

KAHLUA CHEESE CAKE

Serves 12-14

Chocolate crumb crust (recipe follows)
1-1/2 cups semi-sweet chocolate pieces
1/4 cup Kahlua
2 tablespoons butter
2 large eggs, beaten
1/3 cup granulated sugar
1/4 teaspoon salt
1 cup sour cream
2 (8-ounce) packages cream cheese, softened, cut in pieces
Whipped cream and chocolate leaves (optional)

Prepare chocolate crumb crust. Preheat oven to 350 degrees. In small saucepan, over medium heat, melt chocolate with Kahlua and butter; stir until smooth. Set aside. In bowl, combine eggs, sugar, and salt. Add sour cream; blend well. Add cream cheese to egg mixture; beat until smooth. Gradually blend in chocolate mixture. Turn into prepared crust. Bake 40 minutes or until filling is barely set in center. Remove from oven and let stand at room temperature for 1 hour. Then refrigerate several hours or overnight. Garnish, if desired.

Chocolate Crumb Crust: Combine 1-1/3 cups chocolate wafer crumbs, 1/4 cup softened butter, and 1 tablespoon granulated sugar. Press firmly into bottom of 9-inch spring form pan.

Mae Gianocca, Half Moon Bay, Calif.

ZUCCHINI FRUITCAKE

2 eggs
1 cup cooking oil
2 cups sugar
1 teaspoon vanilla
3 cups flour
1 teaspoon baking soda
1 teaspoon salt
1/2 teaspoon baking powder
3 teaspoons cinnamon
1-1/2 teaspoons nutmeg
2 teaspoons allspice
3 cups grated zucchini
1 cup walnuts
1 cup light raisins
1 cup mixed candied fruit
1/2 cup currants

Beat eggs with oil; stir in sugar and vanilla. Sift together flour, soda, salt, baking powder, cinnamon, nutmeg, and allspice. Add to egg-sugar mixture. Stir in zucchini, nuts, raisins, candied fruit, and currants. Turn into two greased 9 x 5-inch loaf pans. Bake in 350-degree oven for one hour and 20 minutes or until done. Cool in pan on rack for 15 minutes, then turn out onto wire rack to complete cooling. When cool, wrap in foil and store in airtight container.

Mrs. P. B. Brothers, Richmond, VA

CHOCOLATE CHERRY UPSIDE-DOWN CAKE

2-1/4 cups flour
1-1/2 cups sugar
3/4 cup cocoa
1-1/2 teaspoons baking soda
3/4 teaspoon salt
1-1/2 cups water
1/2 cup cooking oil
1/4 cup vinegar
1-1/2 teaspoons vanilla
1 can cherry pie filling

Spread pie filling in a greased 9x13-inch pan. In a large bowl mix flour, sugar, cocoa, soda, and salt. In another bowl, mix water, oil, vinegar, and vanilla. Add liquid mixture to dry mixture and stir just to moisten. Pour batter over cherries. Bake 350 degrees for 35 minutes. Cool 10 minutes in the pan. Invert on large platter. Serve with ice cream or whipped topping.

Helen Keillor, Berwyn,
Alta Toh OEH, Canada

CHOCOLATE CHIP CAKE

2 cups all purpose flour
1 cup packed brown sugar
1/2 cup granulated sugar
3 teaspoons baking powder
1 teaspoon salt
1/2 teaspoon baking soda
1/2 cup shortening
1-1/4 cups milk
3 eggs
1/2 cup semi-sweet chocolate chips finely chopped or
1/2 cup miniature semi-sweet chocolate chips
1-1/2 teaspoons vanilla

Heat oven to 350 degrees. Grease and flour oblong pan, 13 x 9 x 2 inches or 2 round layer pans, 8 or 9 inch x 1-1/2 inches. Beat all ingredients in large mixer bowl on low speed, scraping bowl constantly, 30 seconds. Beat on high speed, scraping bowl occasionally, 3 minutes.

Pour into pans. Bake in a 350 degree oven for 40-50 minutes. Bake until wooden pick inserted in center comes out clean. While cake is cooling, prepare Chocolate Butter Frosting.

CHOCOLATE ECLAIR CAKE

Serves 15

1 cup flour
1 stick (1/2 cup) butter or margarine
1/4 teaspoon salt
1 cup water
4 eggs (best at room temperature)
2 packages instant French vanilla pudding
2-1/2 cups cold milk
8 ounces cream cheese, softened
12 ounces (large container) Cool Whip or other whipped topping
3 ounces chocolate chips (1/2 of 6-ounce bag)
2 tablespoons butter or margarine
1 cup confectioners' sugar
3 to 4 tablespoons milk

Bring water and butter to a boil until all butter is melted. All at once add flour and salt; beat until mixture forms a ball that leaves the sides of saucepan; cool slightly. Add eggs one at a time, beating thoroughly after each addition. Spread pastry mixture into ungreased jelly roll pan (15 x 10 x 1-inch). Bake at 400 degrees for 35 minutes. Remove from oven; pierce bubbles with fork while hot. Cool completely.

Mix instant pudding with milk; add softened cream cheese, beat together thoroughly. Spread whipped topping over pudding mixture. Melt chocolate chips and butter over low heat, mix to add confectioners' sugar and milk, alternately until thin glaze forms. Pour or drizzle chocolate glaze over whipped topping. Refrigerate at least 1 hour or longer. Cut into squares to serve.

CHOCOLATE SUNDAE CAKE

1 package devil's food cake mix
1 cup brown sugar
1/3 cup cocoa
2 cups water
2 cups miniature marshmallows
1 cup pecans, chopped

Combine brown sugar, cocoa, and water. Mix well. Pour into a 13x9-inch pan. Place marshmallows evenly on top.

Make cake batter following package directions. Pour into pan. Top with nuts. Bake at 350 degrees for 30 minutes. Cool in pan on wire rack. Cut into bars or squares to serve.

Mrs. P. B. Brothers, Richmond, Va.

COOKIES 'N CREAM CAKE

1 package white cake mix
1-1/4 cups water
1/3 cup oil
3 egg whites
1 cup crushed, creme-filled chocolate sandwich cookies
10 whole cookies

Frosting:

3 cups powdered sugar
3/4 cup shortening
1 teaspoon vanilla
2 egg whites

Heat oven to 350 degrees. Grease and flour 2 round cake pans. In large bowl, combine all cake ingredients, except cookies. Mix at low speed until moistened. Beat 2 minutes at high speed. Stir in crushed creme-filled chocolate cookies. Bake at 350 degrees for 25-35 minutes or until it tests done. Cool layers.

In small bowl combine 1/2 cup of the powdered sugar, shortening, vanilla, and egg whites. Blend well. Beat in remaining sugar until frosting is smooth. Fill and frost cake. Arrange whole cookies on end and on top of frosted cake.

Suzanne Dawson, Cypress, TX

43

BANANA CAKE

8 servings

1/2 cup butter or margarine
1-3/4 cups sugar
2 eggs
1 cup sour cream
2-1/2 cups cake flour
2 large, well-ripened bananas, mashed
1 teaspoon baking powder
1 teaspoon salt
1 teaspoon soda
1 teaspoon vanilla

Topping:

1-1/4 cups firmly-packed brown sugar
1/4 cup butter or margarine, softened
1/2 cup chopped nuts

Cream together the shortening and sugar until light. Beat in eggs, one at a time, until thoroughly blended, then add the mashed bananas and blend well.

Sift together cake flour, baking powder, salt, and soda. Fold flour mixture into shortening, sugar, egg, banana mixture alternately with the sour cream; beginning and ending with dry ingredients. Pour batter into a greased and floured rectangular pan 12 x 8 x 12 inches. Spread topping which has been mixed into crumbs, over top. Bake at 325 degrees, 45-50 minutes, or until cake tests done. DO NOT OVERBAKE. Cool on wire rack in pan. Cut in squares to serve.

P.B. Brothers, Richmond, VA

BANANA CRUNCH CAKE

5 tablespoons oleo, melted
1 package coconut-pecan frosting mix
1 cup rolled oats
1 cup sour cream
2 eggs
2 large bananas
1 package cake mix (white or yellow)

Preheat oven to 350 degrees. Grease and flour 10-inch tube pan. In large bowl, mix frosting mix, oats and melted oleo. Set aside.

In another bowl, blend next three ingredients until smooth. Blend in cake mix. Pour 1/3 of batter (2 cups) into prepared pan. Sprinkle 1-1/4 cups crumb mixture over batter. Repeat twice with batter and crumbs, ending with crumb mixture. The last crumb mixture will only be 1/2 cup on top. Bake 50 to 60 minutes until toothpick inserted in center comes out clean. Cool upright in pan 15 minutes. Remove from pan and turn cake so crumb mixture is on top.

Louise Walker, Dallas, TX

BLUEBERRY PICNIC CAKE

Serves 8

1 egg
2/3 cup sugar
2 cups cake flour, sifted
2 teaspoons baking powder
1/4 teaspoon cinnamon
1/4 teaspoon cloves
1/4 teaspoon salt
1/3 cup milk
3 tablespoons butter or margarine, melted
1-1/4 teaspoons vanilla extract
1 cup fresh blueberries
2 tablespoons sugar

In a mixing bowl, beat egg; gradually add sugar; beat until light and fluffy. Sift together flour, baking powder, spices, and salt. Add to egg mixture, alternating with the milk; mix thoroughly. Add melted butter and vanilla; gently fold in blueberries. Pour cake batter into a lightly greased 11 x 7 x 1-1/2-inch baking dish; smooth top. Sprinkle top with 2 tablespoons sugar. Bake at 350 degrees for 30-35 minutes. Cool cake and leave in pan; cover and carry to picnic.

Gwen Campbell, Sterling, VA

COCONUT DATE CAKE

1/2 cup sugar
2 eggs
1 teaspoon salt
1/4 cup oil
2 teaspoons baking powder
1/2 cup milk
2 cups flour
1 cup chopped nuts
1 box chopped dates
1/2 teaspoon almond extract
1 teaspoon cinnamon

Mix sugar and eggs. Add other ingredients as listed; mix well. Grease and flour tube cake pan. Bake in a 350 degree oven for approximately 30-35 minutes. Serve with whipped topping. Also delicious served with canned fruit.

Verda Earp, Chouteau, OK

CARROT CAKE

2 cups sifted flour
2 cups sugar
2 teaspoons baking powder
1 teaspoon soda
1 teaspoon salt
2 teaspoons cinnamon
1/2 teaspoon nutmeg
1-1/4 cups oil
4 eggs
3 cups shredded carrots

Preheat oven to 350 degrees. Grease and flour a 10-inch tube pan. Mix flour, sugar, baking powder, soda, salt, cinnamon and nutmeg thoroughly in mixer bowl. Add carrots and eggs. Beat 3 minutes at medium speed on mixer. Pour batter into pan. Bake 1 hour or until cake surface springs back when touched lightly. Cool 10 minutes in pan. Remove from pan and complete cooling on rack.

Glaze:

3-ounce package cream cheese
1-2/3 cups confectioners' sugar
1/8 teaspoon salt
1 teaspoon vanilla

Beat cream cheese, confectioners' sugar, salt and vanilla together until creamy. Spread on cooled cake.

Eva Tilley, Seal Beach, CA

CHOCOLATE ANGEL FOOD CAKE

1/4 cup cocoa
1 cup cake flour
1-3/4 cups sugar
1-1/2 cups egg whites
3/4 teaspoon salt
1-1/2 teaspoons cream of tartar
1 teaspoon vanilla
1/4 teaspoon almond extract

Sift cocoa, cake flour, and 3/4 cup sugar together four times. Beat egg whites and salt until foamy. Sprinkle cream of tartar over egg whites; continue beating until stiff, but not dry. *Fold* in remaining sugar, one tablespoon at a time. Add vanilla and almond extract. *Fold* in dry ingredients, a little at a time. Pour into ungreased 10 inch tube pan. Bake 60-70 minutes at 325 degrees. Frost, if desired, although it is delicious plain.

Mrs. Melvin Habiger, Spearville, Kan.

OLD-FASHIONED TRIPLE FUDGE CAKE

1 package devil's food cake mix
1/2 cup chopped nuts
1/2 cup semi-sweet chocolate pieces
1 (12 ounce) jar thick fudge ice cream topping
Ice cream, whipped topping, or whipped cream

Mix cake as directed on package. Stir in nuts; spread batter in a greased and floured 13 x 9 x 2 inch pan. Sprinkle chocolate-pieces evenly over batter; bake as directed on package. Immediately after baking, poke deep holes through top of hot cake (still in pan), space holes about 1 inch apart. Spoon fudge topping evenly over cake. Topping will melt into holes. Serve when completely cool. Top with ice cream or whipped cream.

Pauline Dean, Uxbridge, Mass.

OREO COOKIE CAKE

1 pound oreo cookies
1 cup melted margarine
8 ounce soft cream cheese
2 - 8 ounce containers whipped topping
1 cup powdered sugar
1 large package instant chocolate pudding

Crush cookies and (set aside 1/2 cup). Mix crumbs with butter, and press into 9 ix 13 pan. Refrigerate 1 hour. Mix cream cheese, sugar, 1 carton whipped topping. Spread over cookie crust. Refrigerate 1 hour. Prepare pudding mix by directions on package. Spread over cheese mixture. Refrigerate 1 hour. Top with whipped topping, sprinkle with rest of cookie crumbs. Garnish with maraschino cherries.

Lowela C. McDaniel, Roanoke, VA

TURTLE CAKE

1 package German chocolate cake mix
1 (14-ounce) package caramels
1/2 cup evaporated milk
6 tablespoons margarine
1 cup chopped pecans
1 cup chocolate chips

Prepare cake mix according to directions. Pour 1/2 batter into greased and floured 9 x 13 inch pan. Set other batter aside. Bake at 350 degrees for 18 minutes. Melt caramels and milk together, then stir in pecans. Sprinkle baked part of cake with chocolate chips, and pour caramel mix over that. Pour remaining batter over top. Return pan to oven and bake 20 minutes. Cut into squares to serve.

Cheryl Santefort, Thornton, IL

BUTTERMILK COFFEE CAKE
9 Servings

2 cups sifted flour

1 cup sugar
1/2 teaspoon ground cinnamon
1/4 teaspoon baking powder
1/4 teaspoon salt
1/2 cup butter or margarine
1 teaspoon ground cinnamon
1/2 teaspoon baking soda
3/4 cup buttermilk
1 teaspoon vanilla

Sift together flour, sugar, 1/2 teaspoon cinnamon, baking powder and salt into bowl. Cut in butter with pastry blender or two knives until mixture is crumbly. Reserve 1/2 cup crumb mixture. Combine reserved crumbs with 1 teaspoon cinnamon; set aside. Dissolve baking soda in buttermilk. Add buttermilk mixture and vanilla to remaining crumb mixture, stirring just enough to moisten. Spread batter in greased 8 inch square pan. Sprinkle with reserved crumbs. Bake in 375 degree oven 35 minutes or until done. Cut into squares and serve warm. If you love cinnamon you will love this coffee cake.

Barbara Beauregard-Smith, Northfield, Australia

BLUEBERRY COFFEE CAKE

2 cups flour
1 cup sugar
3 teaspoons baking powder
1/4 teaspoon salt
1/2 cup butter or margarine
2 eggs, beaten
1 cup milk
1-1/2 cups blueberries
1/2 cup coconut
1/2 cup chopped nuts

Mix flour, sugar, baking powder, and salt; cut in butter until mixture resembles cornmeal. Combine beaten eggs and milk; stir in dry ingredients. Stir only until dry mixture is well moistened. Do not overmix! Fold in blueberries. Grease a 9 x 12-inch pan and pour cake batter into pan. Sprinkle with coconut and chopped nuts. Bake in a 350 degree oven for 25-30 minutes. "Great for breakfast."

Agnes Ward, Erie, PA

QUICK COFFEE-CHOCOLATE CAKE

1 package yellow cake mix
1/2 cup brewed coffee
1 teaspoon flavoring

Prepare cake mix according to package directions, using coffee as part of the liquid and add vanilla. Bake according to package directions.

Topping:
3 tablespoons butter or margarine, room temperature
1/2 box confectioners' sugar
1 square unsweetened chocolate, room temperature
Brewed coffee
1 teaspoon vanilla flavoring
1 teaspoon chocolate flavoring (optional)

In a saucepan, brown the butter or margarine. Add chocolate and stir until melted. Pour over confectioners' sugar in bowl and mix, adding enough coffee until spreading consistency. Add flavoring and spread on cake.

Alice McNamara, Eucha, OK

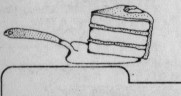

SNICKERDOODLE COFFEE CAKE

1 cup flour
1 cup sugar
1 teaspoon baking powder
1/2 teaspoon salt
1 tablespoon ground cinnamon
1/2 cup milk
1/4 cup melted margarine
1 egg

Mix together the flour, sugar, baking powder, salt, cinnamon, milk, margarine and egg. Pour into a greased and floured 8 or 9 inch square pan. Sprinkle top heavily with sugar (this gives a crusty top). Bake at 400 degrees for 25 minutes. Best when served warm.

Karen Krugman, Tampa, FL

ORANGE BUTTERSCOTCH COFFEE CAKE

Batter:
1/2 cup butter or margarine
1 cup granulated sugar
1 egg
1 teaspoon vanilla
1-1/2 cups sifted all-purpose flour
1-1/2 teaspoons baking powder
1/2 teaspoon cinnamon
1/2 teaspoon salt
1 cup milk
3/4 cup uncooked oats

Topping:
1/4 cup firmly packed brown sugar
1 tablespoon all-purpose flour
1 tablespoon butter or margarine, melted
2 teaspoons grated orange peel

Beat together butter and sugar until light and fluffy; add egg and vanilla; blend well. Sift together flour, baking powder, cinnamon and salt; add to creamed mixture alternately with milk; stir in oats. Pour batter into greased and floured 8 inch square baking pan. Combine all topping ingredients and sprinkle evenly over batter. Bake in preheated 350 degree oven for 40 to 45 minutes. Cool in pan 15 minutes before serving.

ALMOND POUND CAKE

3 cups sugar
2 sticks (1/2 pound) butter or margarine
1/2 cup shortening
5 large eggs
1/4 teaspoon salt
3 cups flour
1 small can evaporated milk (3/4 cup) plus water to make 1 cup liquid
2 teaspoons almond extract

Cream sugar and shortening. Add eggs and salt, cream well. Add remaining ingredients. Pour into a very lightly greased 12 cup bundt pan. Put into cold oven; set temperature at 320

degrees. Bake 1 hour and 30 minutes. Cool 15 minutes and remove from pan.

Leah M. Daub, Milwaukee, WIS

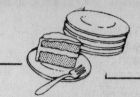

CHERRY NUT BROWNIE CAKE

1/2 cup maraschino cherries
3/4 cup flour, spooned lightly into cup
1/2 teaspoon baking powder
1/4 teaspoon salt
1/2 cup butter or margarine, softened
1 cup sugar
2 large eggs
2 envelopes Choc-bake (or 2 squares unsweetened chocolate, melted)
1 teaspoon vanilla
1/2 cup chopped walnuts or pecans

Quarter cherries with scissors; place on paper towel to drain; set aside. Measure flour, baking powder and salt into small bowl; whisk to blend; set aside.

In large bowl, beat butter or margarine briefly; beat in sugar. Beat in eggs one at a time; beat in chocolate and vanilla. By hand or on lowest mixer speed, beat in dry ingredients. Stir in cherries and nuts. Spread in greased and floured or foil-lined 8-inch squares pan. Bake at 350 degrees until firm in center, about 35 minutes. Cool on rack. Ice as directed below. Freeze leftovers in serving size units.

Chocolate Icing:
Looks and tastes like fudge icing.
2 tablespoons cocoa
2 tablespoons water
2 tablespoons butter or margarine
1 teaspoon maraschino cherry juice
1-1/8 cups unsifted confectioners' sugar (1/8 cup is 2 tablespoons)

Measure cocoa, water, butter and cherry juice into medium saucepan. Heat, stirring, just until smooth. Remove from heat; whisk in sugar. Icing should be just thin enough to pour. Add a little more sugar if necessary. Pour over cool cake; spread to edges. Allow icing to set before cutting cake.

PINEAPPLE BANANA CAKE

3 cups sifted all-purpose flour
1 teaspoon baking soda
1 teaspoon cinnamon
1 teaspoon salt
2 cups sugar
1-1/2 teaspoons vanilla
3 eggs
2 cups diced ripe bananas

Measure the dry ingredients and sift together. Dice the bananas and measure the quantity. Add bananas to the dry ingredients along with oil, eggs, vanilla, crushed pineapple, and juice. Stir to blend, but DO NOT BEAT. Pour into a greased 9-inch tube pan. Bake at 350 degrees for 1 hour and 15 minutes. Set aside to cool without removing from pan.

This cake is served without any kind of frosting. This is a real moist cake, keeps well, and is delicious.

Judy Smith, Indianapolis, IN

PETER'S PUMPKIN CAKE

1/2 cup shortening
1 cup brown sugar
1/2 cup white sugar
1 egg
3/4 cup cooked or canned pumpkin
2 cups flour
3 teaspoons baking powder
1/2 teaspoon cinnamon
1/2 teaspoon nutmeg
1/2 teaspoon ginger
1/2 teaspoon salt
2/3 cup chopped nuts
1/2 teaspoon soda
1/2 cup sour milk

Cream shortening and sugars together. Beat egg and add to the pumpkin. Mix with creamed sugar and shortening. Sift flour, baking powder, spices, and salt together. Mix nuts in flour mixture. Add soda to sour milk; add to creamed mixture. Bake in greased, floured loaf pan in 350 degree oven for 45 minutes.

Agnes Ward, Erie, Pa.

PUMPKIN FIG CAKE

Filling:
1 (8 ounce) package dried figs finely chopped. (about 1 cup)
1/2 cup toasted almonds, chopped
1/2 cup sugar
1/4 cup water
2 tablespoons lemon juice
1/2 teaspoon grated lemon peel
1/2 teaspoon nutmeg

Cake:
1/2 cup butter or margarine
1 cup brown sugar, firmly packed
3 large eggs
1/2 cup white sugar
2-1/2 cups all-purpose flour
1 teaspoon baking powder
1 teaspoon soda
1/2 teaspoon nutmeg
1 teaspoon salt
1 cup canned pumpkin
1/2 cup dairy sour cream
1 teaspoon grated lemon peel
1 teaspoon vanilla
1/2 cup toasted almonds, chopped

Combine filling ingredients in small saucepan. Simmer over medium-low heat until liquid is absorbed, about 10 minutes. Cool.

To make cake, cream together butter and sugars in large mixing bowl. Add eggs, one at a time, beating well after each addition. In a smaller bowl, stir together flour, baking soda, nutmeg, baking powder, and salt. Add to butter-sugar mixture, alternately with pumpkin. Stir in sour cream, lemon peel, and vanilla.

Sprinkle the bottom of a well-greased 12-cup bundt pan with almonds. Spoon half cake batter over nuts. Distribute fig filling evenly over batter. Top filling with remaining batter. Bake in a 350 degree oven for about 50 minutes, until cake tests done. Cool in pan on wire rack, 15 minutes. Turn cake out of pan and cool thoroughly on wire rack.

Mrs. P. B. Brothers, Richmond, Va.

PUMPKIN PIE CAKE

Crust:
1 box (2-layer size) white or yellow cake mix (reserve 1 cup)
1/2 cup margarine, very soft
1 egg

Mix together and press into 13x9-inch baking pan.

Filling:
1 large can (1 pound, 13 ounces) pumpkin
3 eggs
2/3 cup evaporated milk
2 teaspoons cinnamon
1 cup sugar

Mix ingredients together and pour over crust.

Topping:
1 cup reserved cake mix
1/2 cup sugar
1/4 cup margarine, softened
1 cup chopped walnuts or pecans (optional)

Mix cake mix, sugar, and margarine together until crumbly. Sprinkle over filling. Sprinkle nuts on top (optional). Bake at 350 degrees for 1 hour and 15 minutes. Serve warm with whipped topping.

Ruby Goreoski, Albany, Ore.

YELLOW SQUASH CAKE

1 box yellow cake mix
1 (3-1/2 ounce) package vanilla instant pudding
1/4 cup oil
4 eggs
3 cups yellow squash (grated)
1/2 teaspoon salt
1 teaspoon cinnamon
1/4 teaspoon nutmeg
1/4 teaspoon allspice
1 cup walnuts (chopped)

Mix all ingredients together for 4 minutes. Bake in 2 loaf pans or a greased and floured angel food cake pan. Bake at 350 degrees for 55 minutes or until toothpick comes out clean. Frost with your favorite frosting, if desired.

Helen Taugher, Micholson, Pa.

PINEAPPLE UPSIDE-DOWN CAKE

Serves 6-8

1/4 cup butter
2/3 cup light brown sugar, packed
6-7 pineapples slices, drained
6-7 maraschino cherries, drained
2 eggs, separated
3/4 cup granulated sugar
1/4 cup boiling pineapple juice
3/4 cup sifted cake flour
1/2 teaspoon baking powder
1/8 teaspoon salt
1/2 teaspoon vanilla

Melt butter in a 10-1/2-inch oven-proof skillet. Remove from heat. Sprinkle brown sugar over melted butter. Arrange pineapple over this mixture with a cherry in each pineapple center. Beat egg yolks until light, adding granulated sugar gradually. Stir in hot juice. Sift in dry ingredients; mix well. Add vanilla. Fold in stiffly beaten egg whites. Pour cake batter over pineapple mixture. Bake in 325-degree oven for 30 to 35 minutes. Let cool 3 to 5 minutes before inverting on cake plate. Serve warm or cold, with or without whipped cream or whipped topping.

Mrs. E. O'Brien, Richmond, Va.

LOVELY LUAU CAKE

3/4 cup butter or margarine
1-1/2 cups sugar
1 teaspoon lemon extract
1-1/4 teaspoons vanilla extract
3 cups cake flour, sifted
1/4 teaspoon salt
4 teaspoons baking powder
1/4 cup flaked coconut, toasted
1 cup unsweetened pineapple juice
5 large egg whites, stiffly beaten
Luau Whipped Cream Icing (recipe
   follows)

Cream butter; gradually add sugar; cream until light and fluffy. Add extracts. Sift together flour, salt, and baking powder; add toasted coconut. Add to creamed mixture alternately with pineapple juice. Fold in stiffly beaten egg whites. Turn into 3 greased and floured 9-inch cake pans. Bake at 350 degrees for 25-30 minutes. When cool, frost.

Luau Whipped Cream Icing:
1 teaspoon unflavored gelatin
2 tablespoons cold water
3 tablespoons sugar
1 teaspoon vanilla extract
1 pint whipping cream

Soften gelatin in cold water for 5 minutes; dissolve over hot water. Whip cream until stiff; beat in sugar and vanilla. Add cooled gelatin; beat mixture until it forms peaks. Spread between layers and on cake.

Gwen Campbell, Sterling, Va.

LEMON SURPRISE CAKE

1 box Duncan Hines Butter Cake Mix
1 (6-ounce) box lemon gelatin (dry)
2 cups hot water
1 (4-ounce) box French vanilla
   instant pudding; dry
1 (12-ounce) container Cool Whip
1 large (15-ounce) can crushed
   pineapple, drained

Bake cake mix according to directions. While still warm, mix gelatin with hot water; cool gelatin liquid until lukewarm. Punch holes into cake with fork, and pour gelatin over top of cake. Let cool completely.

Drain pineapple (save juice) and mix with instant pudding. Add Cool Whip and mix well. If too stiff, add a little pineapple juice. Nuts can be added. Spread on cooled cake. Refrigerate.

Leota L. Arnold, Vincennes, Ind.

CHOCOLATE PEANUT BUTTER CAKE

2-1/4 cups flour
1 cup peanut butter
1/2 cup butter or margarine, softened
2 cups brown sugar, packed
1 cup milk
3 eggs
1 teaspoon baking powder
1/2 teaspoon baking soda
1 teaspoon vanilla
1 (6-ounce) package chocolate chips

In large mixing bowl, combine flour, peanut butter, margarine and brown sugar until crumbly, using mixer's low speed. Measure 1 cup crumbs for topping. To remaining crumbs, add milk, eggs, baking powder, baking soda, and vanilla. Blend until moistened. Beat 3 minutes on medium speed, scraping bowl often.

Generously grease and flour 9x13-inch pan. Pour batter into pan and sprinkle with reserved crumbs. Sprinkle with chocolate chips. Bake at 350 degrees for 35-40 minutes.

This is my grandchildren's *favorite* cake!!

Dorothy Sorensen, Muskego, Wis.

DANISH CREAM-CHEESE CAKE

Makes 1 cake

1 package (8-roll size) crescent roll dough
1 large package (8 ounces) cream cheese, softened
1 egg beaten
1 1/2 tablespoons flour
1/2 cup sugar
1 teaspoon vanilla
1/2 cup chopped nuts
1/2 cup sugar
1 teaspoon cinnamon
Additional nuts for garnish
Confectioners' sugar

Unroll crescent roll dough onto a greased cookie sheet. Pinch perforations between individual rolls to seal dough. Combine cream cheese, egg, flour, sugar and vanilla, and beat until fluffy. Spread filling over dough. Combine 1/2 cup nuts, the sugar and cinnamon, and sprinkle over cheese mixture. Fold dough around filling. Sprinkle with additional nuts.

Bake in a preheated 350-degree oven for 30 minutes, or until browned. Cool. Sprinkle with confectioners' sugar.

This is easy and quick, and delicious with morning coffee.

Mrs. Doris Szabo, Fonda, N.Y.

48

CRANBERRY SWIRL CAKE

Makes one 10-inch tube or bundt cake

1/4 cup butter
1 cup sugar
2 eggs
2 cups flour
1 teaspoon baking powder
1 teaspoon baking soda
1/2 teaspoon salt
1 cup sour cream
1 teaspoon vanilla
1 cup whole-berry cranberry sauce
1/3 cup chopped nuts
Glaze: 3/4 cup confectioners' sugar
1/2 teaspoon vanilla
Warm water

Cream butter and sugar until fluffy. Add eggs and blend well. Sift dry ingredients together and add to creamed mixture alternately with sour cream which has been mixed with vanilla. Mix well.

Pour half the batter into a greased 10-inch tube or bundt pan. Top with 1/2 cup cranberry sauce, and pour remaining batter over sauce. Top with remaining cranberry sauce, and swirl through batter with a knife. Sprinkle nuts on top.

Bake in preheated 350-degree oven for about 50 minutes, or until done. Cool cake.

Make *Glaze* by mixing sugar and vanilla with enough warm water to make a glaze consistency. Top cooled cake with *Glaze*.

Judy Haffner, Auke Bay, Alaska

BLACK BOTTOM CUPCAKES

Part 1:
8 ounces cream cheese, softened
1 egg
1/3 cup granulated sugar
1/8 teaspoon salt
Large handful of chocolate chips

Part 2:
1-1/2 cups plus 1 tablespoon all-purpose flour
1 cup granulated sugar
1/4 cup cocoa powder
1/2 teaspoon salt
1 cup warm water
1 teaspoon soda mixed with 1 tablespoon white vinegar
1/2 cup salad oil
1 teaspoon vanilla

Mix Part 1 ingredients together, adding chocolate chips last; set aside. Mix Part 2 ingredients together. Fill paper-lined muffin cups half-full of Part 2 and top each with 1 tablespoon of Part 1. Bake at 350 degrees for 20-25 minutes, until toothpick comes out clean.

These cupcakes are wonderful treats for all ages!

Sandra J. Stevenson, Matthews, N.C.

PUMPKIN FRUIT CAKE

1 package (15 ounces) seedless raisins
1/2 cup self-rising flour*
1-1/2 pounds mixed candied fruit
2 cups chopped walnuts
2 teaspoons cinnamon
2 teaspoons nutmeg
1 teaspoon ginger
1 cup melted margarine
3 cups mashed, cooked pumpkin
3 eggs, well beaten
3/4 cup sugar

Preheat oven to 325 degrees. Combine first four ingredients in a bowl. Combine remaining ingredients and mix well. Add fruit mixture and mix until well blended. Spoon into greased 10-inch tube pan or two 9-inch bread pans. Bake for 2-1/2 hours, or until done.

*Can use 1/2 cup all-purpose flour, adding 1/4 teaspoon salt, 1 teaspoon baking powder, and 1/2 teaspoon soda.

Judy Haffner, Auke Bay, Alaska

BROWNIES IN A CONE

Makes 12

12 flat-bottom ice-cream cones
1 (21- or 23-ounce) box brownie mix
1 (6-ounce) package chocolate chips
3/4 stick butter (or 6 tablespoons)
Candy sprinkles

Preheat oven to 350 degrees. Place cones in muffin tins or on baking sheet. Prepare brownie mix according to package directions. Spoon batter into cones, three-fourths full. Bake for 30-35 minutes, or until tops are cracked and have risen above the rims of the cones. Remove the cones from oven and cool to room temperature.

Frosting:

Melt chips and butter. Stir until smooth. Dip tops of brownies into chocolate. If not well-covered, dip again. Stand the cones upright and sprinkle tops with candy sprinkles. Let cones stand at room temperature until the chocolate hardens.

Vickie Vogt, Kewaskum, Wis.

RIBBON CAKE

3 eggs
2 cups sugar
3 cups flour
2 teaspoons cream of tartar
1 teaspoon vanilla
2/3 cup butter
1 cup milk
1 teaspoon soda
1/2 teaspoon salt
1 tablespoon molasses
1/2 cup raisins
1/2 cup sliced citron
1 teaspoon cinnamon
1/2 teaspoon cloves
1/2 teaspoon allspice
1/2 teaspoon nutmeg
1 tablespoon flour
Jelly
Confectioners' sugar

Cream butter, add sugar, stir until well blended. Add eggs, beat thoroughly. Mix salt, soda and cream of tartar with flour. Add vanilla to mix. Add dry and liquid ingredients alternately to first mixture. Mix smooth. Grease and flour three layer cake pans. Pour cake mixture into two of them. To remaining cake mixture add molasses, raisins, sliced citron, cinnamon, cloves, allspice, nutmeg, and flour; mix well. Pour into third cake pan. Bake 25 minutes in moderate 350 degree oven. Turn out of pans and cool. Put layers together with jelly. Dust top layer with confectioners' sugar.

Susan Wiener, Spring Hill, Fla.

CARDAMOM POUND CAKE

1 pound butter
1 pound brown sugar
6 eggs
2 teaspoons vanilla
4 cups sifted all-purpose flour
1 teaspoon baking powder
1-1/2 teaspoons ground cardamom
2 cups cut dates
2 cups diced candied cherries
Powdered sugar

Have ingredients at room temperature. Cream butter; add sugar gradually; beat in eggs one at a time; mix well. Add vanilla. Blend in sifted dry ingredients. Stir in dates and cherries. Pour into greased and floured 10-inch tube pan. Bake at 300 degrees about 1 hour and 45 minutes. Cool in pan 10 minutes before removing. Cool completely, wrap and store in refrigerator at least a week before serving. Sprinkle with powdered sugar before serving.   Kit Rollins, Cedarburg, Wisc.

PUMPKIN SPICE CAKE

Serves 16

2¼ cups cake flour, sifted
1½ teaspoons ground cinnamon
¾ teaspoon ground nutmeg
1 cup pumpkin
Non-calorie liquid sweetener equal to ½ cup sugar
1 (1¼-ounce) envelope low-calorie dessert topping mix, whipped
1 tablespoon baking powder
¾ teaspoon ground cloves
7 eggs, separated
½ cup cooking oil
½ teaspoon finely shredded orange peel
½ teaspoon cream of tartar

Sift together flour, baking powder, spices and ¼ teaspoon salt. Combine egg yolks, pumpkin, cooking oil, sweetener and orange peel; beat until

smooth. Wash beaters; beat egg whites and cream of tartar to stiff peaks. Fold pumpkin mixture into whites. Sprinkle ¼ dry ingredients atop. Fold in dry ingredients, adding ¼ at a time. Turn into an ungreased 9-inch tube pan. Bake in 325-degree oven for 45 minutes. Invert in pan; cool. Remove from pan; serve with topping.
Diane Votaw, Decatur, Ind.

SWEET APPLE CIDER CAKE

4 cups all-purpose flour
3 teaspoons baking soda
¼ teaspoon salt
1 teaspoon cinnamon
¼ teaspoon allspice
⅛ teaspoon cloves
1 cup currants
½ cup vegetable shortening
½ cup brown sugar, firmly packed
½ cup granulated sugar
4 eggs, separated
2 cups sweet apple cider

Mix and sift dry ingredients; add currants. Cream shortening and sugars. Add egg yolks; beat thoroughly. Add flour mixture alternately with cider; fold in stiffly beaten egg whites. Turn into greased loaf pan; bake at 350 degrees for 1 hour. Dust top with confectioners' sugar.
Gwen Campbell, Sterling, Va.

SOUR CREAM TOPPED CHOCOLATE TORTE

1 package fudge brownie mix
2 teaspoons vanilla extract
1/3 cup chopped cashew nuts
2 tablespoons chopped walnuts
Raspberry jam
Coconut for garnish
Chocolate frosting (recipe follows)

Prepare the package of fudge brownie mix according to box directions. Add vanilla extract, walnuts and cashews; mix well. Spread in

well-greased 15x10x1-inch baking pan. Bake in preheated hot 400 degree oven 10-12 minutes. Cool; cut crosswise into 3 equal parts. Put layers together with a thin layer of raspberry jam and chocolate frosting. Spread remaining frosting on top. Sprinkle with coconut for garnish.

Chocolate Frosting:
1 (4 ounce) package sweet cooking chocolate
1/2 cup sour cream

Melt cooking chocolate over hot water. Add sour cream and blend well. Use immediately.
Marie Fusaro, Manasquan, N.J.

CARROT-ZUCCHINI CUPCAKES

Makes 18

1 1/2 cups all-purpose flour, unsifted
1 cup sugar
1 teaspoon baking powder
1 teaspoon ground cinnamon
1/2 teaspoon salt
1/2 teaspoon baking soda
3/4 cup vegetable oil
2 large eggs
1 teaspoon vanilla extract
1 cup coarsely shredded carrots
1 cup coarsely shredded zucchini
1/2 cup golden raisins
Cream Cheese Frosting (recipe follows)

Preheat oven to 350 degrees. Line 18 muffin-pan cups with fluted paper liners. In large bowl, combine flour, sugar, baking powder, cinnamon, salt and baking soda.

In cup or small bowl, beat together oil, eggs and vanilla. Stir oil mixture into flour mixture just until mixed. Fold in carrots, zucchini and raisins. Spoon into cups. Bake for 20–25 minutes. Cool cupcakes on wire rack. Prepare Cream Cheese Frosting. Frost cupcakes and sprinkle with nuts.

Cream Cheese Frosting:
In a small bowl, using electric mixer, cream 3 ounces cream cheese, softened, with 1 1/2 cups sifted confectioners' sugar and 1 teaspoon vanilla extract; beat until fluffy.
Mrs. K.W. Kenney, Richmond, Va.

PEANUT BUTTER CAKE

1 package butter cake mix
1/2 cup smooth peanut butter
1 stick soft butter or margarine
2/3 cup water
4 eggs

Mix as directed on cake mix package, adding peanut butter to water. Bake according to directions on package. When cool frost with Peanut Butter Frosting (recipe follows).

Peanut Butter Frosting:
1 box confectioners' sugar
1 cup peanut butter
1/2 cup butter
1/4–1/3 cup cream or milk

Mix all ingredients until smooth and fluffy. If frosting is too thin, add additional confectioners' sugar.

Leota Baxter, Ingalls, Kan.

GAIL'S RICH CHOCOLATE CAKE

4 (1-ounce) squares unsweetened chocolate, melted
3/4 cup butter or margarine, melted
2 cups sugar
4 eggs, beaten
2 cups sifted flour
1 teaspoon vanilla
1/2 teaspoon baking powder
1 cup buttermilk

Grease and flour 2 (9-inch) layer cake pans. Preheat oven to 350 degrees. Mix chocolate and butter (or melt together). Gradually add sugar to eggs; beat well. Blend in chocolate mixture and vanilla. Stir in blended dry ingredients, alternately with buttermilk. Bake at 350 degrees, for 30-35 minutes or until cake tests done.

Chocolate Cream Cheese Frosting:
1 (3-ounce) package cream cheese, softened
1-1/2 teaspoons milk
1/4 cup unsweetened cocoa
2-1/2 cups sifted confectioners'

sugar
1 teaspoon vanilla

Blend cream cheese and milk. Add combined confectioners' sugar and cocoa to make a frosting of spreading consistency. Add more milk, if needed. Add vanilla. This cake freezes very well, even frosted.

Gail Scharenbroch, Charlevoix, Mich.

STRAWBERRY SHORTCUT CAKE

1-1/2 cups miniature marshmallows
2 cups or 2 (10-ounce) packages frozen sliced strawberries (completely thawed and drained), reserve syrup
1 (3-ounce) package strawberry gelatin
2-1/4 cups all-purpose flour
1-1/2 cups sugar
1/2 cup solid shortening or margarine
3 teaspoons baking powder
1/2 teaspoon salt
1 cup milk
1 teaspoon vanilla
3 eggs

Generously grease bottom only of 9x13-inch baking pan. Sprinkle marshmallows evenly over bottom of pan. Combine thawed berries, gelatin, and syrup from berries; stir thoroughly. Set aside.

Combine rest of ingredients, beating about 3 minutes until thoroughly mixed. Pour batter evenly over marshmallows in prepared pan. Spoon strawberry mixture over batter.

Bake at 350 degrees for 45-50 minutes. Serve with whipped cream.

Dorothy Sorensen, Muskego, Wis.

CHOCOLATE-CHERRY UPSIDE-DOWN CAKE

1   (21-ounce) can cherry pie filling
2¼ cups all-purpose flour

1½ cups sugar
¾   cup unsweetened cocoa powder
1½ teaspoons baking soda
¾   teaspoon salt
1½ cups water
¼   cup cooking oil
¼   cup vinegar
1½ teaspoons vanilla

Spread cherry pie filling evenly over bottom of greased 13 x 9 x 2-inch pan. In large bowl, stir flour with sugar, cocoa, soda and salt.

In another bowl, combine water, oil, vinegar and vanilla. Add liquid to dry mixture, all at once. Stir just to moisten. Pour batter evenly in pan over cherry filling.

Bake in preheated 350-degree oven for 30–35 minutes. Cool 10 minutes in pan; invert onto plate and cool.

Corena J. Bennington, Whitestown, Ind.

CHOCOLATE DREAMS
Makes 24

1 package (18.5 ounce) chocolate cake mix
1 cup water
1/3 cup buttermilk
1/2 teaspoon vanilla
2 eggs
1 package (8 ounce) cream cheese, softened
1/2 cup sugar
1 egg
1/2 teaspoon salt
1 package (6 ounce) semi-sweet chocolate pieces
1/2 cup chopped pecans

Preheat oven to 350 degrees. In large bowl, combine cake mix, water, buttermilk and vanilla. Mix until well blended. Add 2 eggs, one at a time, beating after each addition until well blended and smooth. Spoon mixture into greased paper lined muffin tins, filling each cup half full.

In medium bowl, beat together cream cheese and sugar until light and fluffy; beat in 1 egg and salt. Stir in chocolate pieces. Drop 1 tablespoon cheese mixture on each cupcake; sprinkle with nuts. Bake 25-30 minutes or until done.

Bobbie Mae Cooley, Bowen, Ill.

APPLESAUCE CUPCAKES
Makes 1 dozen

1/2 cup shortening
1 egg
1/3 cup sugar
1-3/4 cups sifted cake flour
1 teaspoon baking soda
1/4 teaspoon salt
1 teaspoon cinnamon
1/4 teaspoon cloves
1/4 teaspoon allspice
1/4 teaspoon ginger
1 cup unsweetened applesauce
1/2 teaspoon lemon juice
1 teaspoon vanilla
1/3 cup raisins

Preheat oven to 375 degrees. Cream shortening until fluffy. Beat egg and sugar until lemon-colored. Add to shortening and blend well. Sift together all dry ingredients; add to shortening mixture, alternately with applesauce, blending well after each addition. Stir in lemon juice, vanilla, and raisins. Line 2 small cupcake pans with paper baking cups. Pour batter into paper liners. Fill liners two-thirds full and bake 15 to 20 minutes. If paper cups are not used, grease the cupcake pans very lightly.

Suzan L. Wiener, Spring Hill, Fla.

CRANBERRY-PECAN UPSIDE-DOWN CAKE

1½ cups cranberries
½ cup chopped pecans
½ cup butterscotch topping
⅓ cup margarine
⅔ cup sugar
1 egg
½ teaspoon vanilla
1 cup flour
1½ teaspoons baking powder
½ teaspoon salt
½ cup milk

Arrange cranberries and nuts in the bottom of a greased 8-inch square pan. Pour topping over. Cream margarine and sugar until light and fluffy. Blend in egg and vanilla. Add combined dry ingredients to creamed mixture alternately with milk, mixing well after each addition. Pour batter over topping mixture. Bake at 350 degrees for 45 minutes, or until toothpick inserted comes out clean. Immediately invert onto serving platter. Serve warm, topped with whipped cream or ice cream.

Shari Crider, Stoughton, Wis.

DOUBLE CHOCOLATE SNACK CAKES

1 2/3 cups all-purpose flour
1 cup packed brown sugar
1/4 cup Hershey's cocoa
1 teaspoon baking soda
1/2 teaspoon salt
1 cup water
1/3 cup vegetable oil
1 teaspoon vinegar
3/4 teaspoon vanilla
1/2 cup Hershey chocolate chips

Heat oven to 350 degrees. Grease and flour 8x8x2-inch square pan *or* 12-cup muffin pan. Combine dry ingredients. Add water, oil, vinegar and vanilla. Beat until smooth. Pour into pan or muffin tin. Sprinkle chocolate chips on top. Bake 35–40 minutes for cake *or* bake 25–30 minutes for cupcakes.

Delicious, easy and economical!
Carol Johnson, Mableton, Ga.

DATE NUT CAKE WITH WHIPPED CREAM
Serves 6

2 large eggs
3/4 cup sugar
1/4 cup evaporated milk
1 (8-ounce) package dates, pitted
1 cup coarsely chopped nuts
3 tablespoons flour
1 teaspoon baking powder
1/2 teaspoon salt
1 cup heavy cream
Maraschino cherries for garnish

In medium bowl of electric mixer, combine eggs, sugar, and evaporated milk; beat well. Fold in dates and nuts until well-combined. Mix together flour, baking powder, and salt; mix into date batter thoroughly. Pour into well-greased 8x12-inch baking pan. Bake at 325 degrees for 20 to 25 minutes, until puffed and slightly browned on top. Remove and cool completely on wire rack. Cake will fall slightly. Just before serving time, whip cream until stiff peaks form. Cut cake into bite-size pieces and layer in serving dish with whipped cream. Garnish with maraschino cherries.

Leona Teodori, Warren, Mich.

APPLE WALNUT CAKE
Serves 12–15

1 (21-ounce) can apple pie filling
1 cup sugar
2 cups flour
1 teaspoon salt
1½ teaspoons soda
2 eggs, beaten
1 teaspoon vanilla
⅔ cup cooking oil
¾ cup chopped walnuts

Topping:
½ cup sour cream
1 cup sugar
½ teaspoon salt

Preheat oven to 350 degrees. Spread pie filling in bottom of 9 x 13-inch pan. Combine sugar, flour, salt and soda. Sprinkle sugar mixture over pie filling. In bowl combine eggs, vanilla and oil. Mix well. Add ½ cup nuts. Pour over ingredients in pan. Bake at 350 degrees for 40–50 minutes until cake springs back from light touch. Cool on rack for about 20 minutes. Pierce warm cake with a fork.

Combine topping ingredients and stir over medium heat until boiling. Pour over cake and sprinkle with remaining nuts.

Leota Baxter, Ingalls, Kan.

PRUNE SPICE CAKE

1½ cups flour
1 teaspoon baking powder
½ teaspoon soda
½ teaspoon cinnamon
¼ teaspoon ginger
¼ teaspoon salt
¾ cup sugar
¼ cup brown sugar
½ cup oil
1 egg
1 small jar baby prunes
1 teaspoon vanilla
½ cup cold water
½ cup raisins
½ cup nuts, chopped

Sift together the flour, baking powder, soda, cinnamon, salt and ginger. Set aside. Mix together the sugars, oil, egg, prunes and vanilla. Add mixture to dry ingredients. Stir in the cold water and beat 1 minute at medium speed. Stir in the raisins and nuts. Pour into loaf pan which has been greased and floured. Bake 30 minutes at 350 degrees. Let cool in pan. Remove from pan and glaze with ½ cup confectioners' sugar, 1 tablespoon cream and ¼ teaspoon vanilla.

Margaret Hamfeldt, Louisville, Ky.

JAVA SPICE CAKE

2 cups hot, strong coffee
1 cup finely chopped prunes
¾ cup raisins
1 cup finely chopped pecans
2¾ cups cake flour
1 tablespoon baking powder
½ teaspoon baking soda
½ teaspoon ground allspice
½ teaspoon ground pepper
6 tablespoons butter, room temperature
1½ cups sugar
3 eggs
Coffee Frosting (recipe follows)

Coffee Frosting:

½ cup butter, room temperature
6 ounces cream cheese, room temperature
3 tablespoons instant coffee powder, dissolved in 6 tablespoons hot coffee
7–8 cups sifted confectioners' sugar
3–4 drops angostura bitters

Preheat oven to 350 degrees. Grease 3 (9-inch) round cake pans. Dust with flour. In small bowl, pour hot coffee over prunes and raisins. In another bowl, mix pecans with ¼ cup flour. Sift together remaining flour, baking powder, baking soda, allspice and pepper. In a large bowl, cream butter with sugar. Add eggs. Beat until light and fluffy. Add flour mixture alternately with prune-coffee mixture, stirring well after each addition. Fold in flour-coated pecans. Pour into prepared pans. Bake 30–40 minutes, or until top springs back when touched lightly. Turn out onto rack. Cool completely. Prepare Coffee Frosting. Put layers together with about half the frosting. Cover sides and top with remaining frosting. Garnish with pecan halves.

Frosting:

Cream butter and cream cheese until smooth. Add dissolved coffee. Beat until blended. Add confectioners' sugar. Continue to beat until light and fluffy. Stir in bitters. If needed, add more confectioners' sugar to bring to spreading consistency.

Laura Hicks, Troy, Mont.

MOM'S APPLE CAKE

2 cups sugar
4 eggs
1 cup salad oil
3 cups flour
1 teaspoon baking soda
½ teaspoon salt
1 teaspoon ground cinnamon
1 teaspoon vanilla extract
2 cups diced apples
1 cup dark, seedless raisins
1 cup nuts (optional)
Apple Glaze (recipe follows)

Preheat oven to 350 degrees. With mixer beat sugar and eggs for 5 minutes. Slowly beat in salad oil. Beat in flour, soda, salt, cinnamon and extract. With spoon stir in apples, raisins and nuts. Bake 1 hour and 10 minutes, or until done. Remove cake from pan.

Apple Glaze:

1⅓ cups confectioners' sugar
2 tablespoons apple juice
Nuts

Mix well; sprinkle with nuts and spoon over cake, letting some run down the sides.

APRICOT-APPLE-SAUCE CAKE
Serves 12-15

1 cup all-purpose flour
3/4 cup whole-wheat flour
2 teaspoons ground allspice
1 teaspoon baking soda
1/2 cup sugar
1/2 cup shortening
1 cup applesauce
2 eggs
3/4 cup diced, dried apricots
1/2 cup chopped nuts (pecans, walnuts, or almonds)
Confectioners' sugar

Preheat oven to 350 degrees. Grease a 12-cup bundt pan or tube pan. Combine flours, allspice, and baking soda; set aside. In a large bowl, with mixer at low speed, cream sugar and shortening; beat in applesauce and eggs until fluffy. Add flour mixture; beat at medium speed for 2 minutes, scraping bowl occasionally. Stir in apricots and nuts. Pour batter into pan and bake 30-40 minutes until top springs back when lightly touched with finger. Cool cake in pan 10 minutes; invert onto serving platter and dust lightly with confectioners' sugar.

Leota Baxter, Ingalls, Kan.

JELLY BEAN CONFETTI CAKE

2 cups all-purpose flour
3/4 cup miniature jelly beans, cut in half (not licorice)
1 cup sugar
1 cup butter or margarine, softened
1 (8-ounce) package cream cheese, softened
1 teaspoon vanilla
3 eggs
1-1/2 teaspoons baking powder
1/4 teaspoon salt
Confectioners' sugar

Heat oven to 325 degrees. Generously grease and flour 12-cup fluted tube pan or angel-cake pan. Lightly spoon flour into measuring cup. Level off. In small bowl, toss jelly beans with 2 tablespoons of the flour. Set aside.

In large bowl, beat sugar, butter, cream cheese, and vanilla until well blended. Add eggs one at a time, beating well after each addition. Add remaining flour, baking powder, and salt. Blend well. Spoon 1 cup of batter evenly over bottom of prepared pan. Stir jelly beans into remaining batter; spoon into baking pan. Bake in a 325 degree oven for 50 to 60 minutes, or until toothpick inserted in center of cake comes out clean. Cool upright in pan 10 minutes. Invert on serving plate. Cool completely. Sprinkle with confectioners' sugar.

MOCK CRAB CAKES

2 cups zucchini squash, peeled and grated
1 cup seasoned bread crumbs
1 teaspoon Old Bay seasoning
1 egg, well beaten
1 tablespoon mayonnaise
Butter flavored Crisco

Mix all ingredients together. Form mixture into individual serving patties, then roll in bread crumbs. Fry patties in butter flavored Crisco until crispy and golden brown.
Peggy Fowler Revels, Woodruff, S.C.

APPLE CAKE WITH NUT TOPPING

3/4 cup cooking oil
2 cups sugar
2 eggs, beaten
3 cups flour
1-1/2 teaspoons soda
1 teaspoon salt
1 teaspoon vanilla
1 cup chopped walnuts
3 cups chopped apples (with peelings)

Mix oil, sugar, and eggs and blend well. Add dry ingredients and vanilla by hand. Blend in nuts and apples. Spoon batter into a well-greased tube or bundt pan. Bake at 350 degrees for 1 hour. Remove from oven and pour topping over cake. Return cake to oven and bake 15 minutes more. Cool on wire rack. Slide knife around cake to loosen.

Topping:
1 cup light brown sugar
1 stick butter or margarine
1/4 cup orange juice
Cook over low heat for 3 minutes after the mixture starts boiling. Pour over cake and continue as directed.
Mrs. P. B. Brothers, Richmond, Va.

SOUR CREAM DEVILS FOOD CAKE

2 cups sour cream
2 teaspoons soda
4 eggs
1 teaspoon vanilla
2 cups sugar
2 cups flour
6 tablespoons cocoa

Beat sour cream, soda, eggs, and vanilla until foamy; add sugar, flour, and cocoa that has been sifted together. Pour into a greased and floured pan. Bake at 350 degrees for 30 minutes. Frost with your favorite frosting.

Mildred Sherrer, Bay City, Texas

CREAM CHEESE POUND CAKE

3/4 cup butter or margarine
1 (8-ounce) package cream cheese, room temperature
1-1/2 cups sugar
1-1/2 teaspoons vanilla
4 eggs
1-3/4 cups flour
1-1/2 teaspoons baking powder

Cream butter and cream cheese until light; add sugar gradually, beating constantly. Add vanilla. Beat in eggs, one at a time. Combine flour and baking powder; add to creamed mixture, beating well. Pour into greased 9x5-inch loaf pan. Bake at 350 degrees for 1 hour and 15 minutes or until wooden pick inserted in center comes out clean. Cool in pan 10 minutes. Turn onto a cake rack to cool completely.
Suzanne Dawson, Cypress, Tex.

RHUBARB CAKE

1-1/2 cups brown sugar
1/2 cup shortening
1 egg
1 teaspoon vanilla
2 cups flour
1 teaspoon soda
1/2 teaspoon salt
1 cup buttermilk or sour cream
1-3/4 cups chopped rhubarb, may use frozen
1/2 cup chocolate chips

Topping:
1/2 cup brown sugar
1 teaspoon cinnamon
1/2 cup chopped nuts
1/2 cup chocolate chips

Cream 1-1/2 cups brown sugar, 1/2 cup shortening; add egg and vanilla. Combine flour, soda, and salt together. Add flour mixture, alternating with buttermilk, beating after each addition. Stir in rhubarb and chocolate chips. Pour into greased 9x13-inch pan. Combine topping and sprinkle over cake mixture. Bake at 350 degrees for 45 minutes.

This is a delicious cake. Serve with ice cream, whipped cream, or just plain. You will get raving reviews.
Roselyn Finan, Fort Wayne, Ind.

PRALINE CHEESE CAKE

1 cup graham cracker crumbs
3 tablespoons sugar
3 tablespoons melted butter
3 (8 ounce) packages cream cheese
1-1/4 cups dark brown sugar, firmly packed
3 eggs
2 tablespoons flour
1/2 cup chopped pecans
1-1/2 teaspoons vanilla
Maple syrup

Mix crumbs, sugar and butter, and press into 9-inch springform pan. Bake at 350 degrees for 10 minutes. Cool. Beat cream cheese and brown sugar until fluffy. Beat in eggs, one at a time. Sift in flour, add pecans and vanilla. Pour mixture into pan. Bake at 350 degrees for 55 minutes or until set. Cool in pan, remove to serving plate, and brush with maple syrup and garnish with chopped pecans. Chill for at least 3 hours.

Patricia Habiger, Spearville, Kan.

GOLDEN CARROT CAKE

2 cups sugar
1-1/2 cups salad oil
3 eggs
1 teaspoon vanilla
3 cups flour
1 teaspoon soda
1/2 teaspoon salt
1 teaspoon cinnamon
1 cup crushed pineapple
2 cups raw carrots, finely grated
1 cup nuts, chopped

Mix together sugar, salad oil, eggs, and vanilla. Add combined flour, soda, salt, and cinnamon. Mix well. Add pineapple, grated carrots, and nuts, mixing well. Place into a 13x9-inch pan and bake in a 350-degree oven for 1 hour and 15 minutes or until tested done. Frost with a cream cheese icing. **Note:** Use as a dessert, snack, or coffee cake.

Agnes Ward, Erie, Pa.

ONE-STEP COCOA CAKE
Serves 12

2-1/2 cups all-purpose flour
1-3/4 cups sugar
1/2 cup cocoa
2 teaspoons baking soda
1/2 teaspoon salt
1 cup milk
2/3 cup softened butter or margarine
2 teaspoons vanilla
3 eggs
1/4 cup sliced almonds

Heat oven to 350 degrees. Grease and flour 13x9-inch pan. In large bowl, combine all ingredients, except almonds. Beat 1 minute at low speed; beat 3 minutes at highest speed. Pour into prepared pan; sprinkle almonds over top. Bake at 350 degrees for 35-45 minutes, or until center tests done. Cool; cut into squares.

Agnes Ward, Erie, Pa.

PINEAPPLE CRUSH CAKE

1 package Duncan Hines Pineapple Cake or Lemon Cake
1 (8-ounce) package cream cheese
1 (4-ounce) box instant vanilla pudding
2 cups chilled milk
1 (4-ounce) can crushed pineapple, drained
1 (8-ounce) carton Cool Whip or La Creme whipped topping

Make cake according to directions on package. Bake in a 9x13x2-inch pan which has been greased and lined with waxed paper. Let cake cool and place in refrigerator for several hours. Split the cake, making 2 layers. Cooling makes it easier to split.

Filling:
Beat cream cheese until fluffy; add to this the package of instant vanilla pudding and 2 cups cold milk. Mix or beat mixture in a small bowl, 2 minutes on medium speed. Spread on

cooled half of cake. Spoon over filling mixture one (4-ounce) can of crushed (drained) pineapple. Top with the other half of the cake. Spread whipped topping over sides and top of cake.

Store in refrigerator overnight. It is especially nice since you can make it the day before you plan to serve it.

May Folden, San Jose, Calif.

CARROT CAKE

2/3 cup fructose
3/4 cup cooking oil
2 eggs
1 1/2 cups cake flour
1/2 teaspoon salt
1/2 teaspoon cinnamon
1 teaspoon baking powder
1 teaspoon baking soda
1 cup cooked carrots

Mix all ingredients together with electric beater. Bake in a greased and floured 8x8-inch pan, at 375 degrees for approximately 45 minutes.

TUTTI-FRUTTI CREAM CAKE

3 cups cake flour, sifted
4 teaspoons baking powder
1 teaspoon baking soda
1/4 teaspoon salt
3/4 cup shortening
1-1/2 cups sugar
2 tablespoons sour cream
1/4 cup flaked coconut
1/4 cup maraschino cherries, sliced
1/4 cup crushed pineapple, drained
1/4 cup mashed bananas
4 eggs
1-1/2 cups milk

Sift first 4 ingredients; cream shortening with dry ingredients. Add sugar, sour cream, coconut, cherries, pineapple, and mashed bananas. Beat in one egg at a time; mix thoroughly. Add flour alternately with milk; beat until smooth. Turn into a well-greased tube pan; bake at 350 degrees for 1 hour. When cool, dust with confectioners' sugar across top of cake.

Gwen Campbell, Sterling, Va.

55

FRUITED APPLESAUCE CAKE

Serves 10-12

1/2 cup margarine
1 cup brown sugar, firmly packed
1 cup canned applesauce
2-1/4 cups cake flour
1/2 teaspoon salt
1/2 teaspoon baking soda
1 teaspoon baking powder
1/2 teaspoon cloves, powdered
1/2 teaspoon cinnamon
1/2 teaspoon nutmeg
1/2 cup seedless raisins, washed
    and drained
1/2 cup dried currants
1/4 cup ground nuts

Cream together margarine and brown sugar until light and fluffy. Add applesauce; mix well. Sift together dry ingredients; add to applesauce mixture, mix well.

Add raisins, currants and nuts, mix until well incorporated. Turn into 9 x 5x3-inch loaf pan with paper cut to fit bottom. Bake at 325 degrees for 1 hour or until tested done. Cool 10 minutes; remove from pan and finish cooling on rack. Remove paper.

Agnes Ward, Erie, Pa.

LEMON PECAN CAKE

Serves 16

2 cups butter
4 cups brown sugar, firmly packed
6 eggs, separated
4 cups flour
1 teaspoon baking powder
3 tablespoons lemon extract
1 pound pecans, chopped
1/2 pound candied cherries,
    chopped
1/2 pound candied pineapple,
    chopped

Cream butter and sugar; beat in egg yolks one at a time. Sift 2 cups flour and baking powder together; add to creamed mixture alternately with lemon extract, beating well. Dredge pecans and fruits in remaining flour in large bowl. Pour batter over fruit mixture. Stir well. Fold in

stiffly-beaten egg whites. Cover; let stand overnight. Spoon batter into greased and floured 10-inch tube pan. Bake tube cake in 275 degree oven for 2 hours. Remove cake from pan. Cool, cover and age for 24 hours.

Agnes Ward, Erie, Pa.

SOUR MILK GINGERBREAD

Serves 8-10

1-1/2 cups flour
1/2 teaspoon soda
1/2 teaspoon baking powder
1/4 teaspoon salt
1 tablespoon ginger
1/4 teaspoon ground cloves
2 teaspoons cinnamon
1/3 cup shortening
1/2 cup brown sugar, firmly packed
1 egg, beaten
1/2 cup light molasses
1 cup buttermilk

Sift together first 7 ingredients. Cream shortening by beating until soft and smooth. Gradually add sugar, beating thoroughly after each addition. Continue beating until light and fluffy. Add egg and beat until mixture looks light and fluffy again. Add molasses and beat thoroughly. Add flour and milk alternately to molasses mixture by adding 1/3 of the flour and 1/2 of the milk at a time, beginning and ending with flour. Stir after each addition until well blended. Pour into well-greased and floured 9-inch square cake pan. Bake at 350 degrees for 20-25 minutes or until done. Serve plain, with lemon sauce, or with whipped cream.

Lemon Sauce:

1/2 cup sugar
Few grains salt
1 tablespoon cornstarch
1 cup boiling water
2 tablespoons butter
1-1/2 tablespoons lemon juice
Dash of nutmeg

Mix sugar, salt and cornstarch in saucepan. Add water gradually, stirring as you add. Let mixture come to boil and boil for 5 minutes, stirring constantly to prevent lumping. Remove from heat. Add butter, lemon

juice and nutmeg. Stir until well blended. Makes 1 cup.

Betty Lyke, Flower Mound, Texas

EASY COCONUT CAKE

1 box white cake mix
2 packages frozen coconut
2 (8-ounce) cartons sour cream
2 cups sugar
1 (8-ounce) container Cool Whip

Mix cake mix according to directions on box. Bake in 2 (8- or 9-inch) round cake pans; split into 4 layers. Mix packages of coconut with sour cream and sugar. (Set aside 1/2 cup of this mixture for later use.) Spread the rest of the mixture thickly between layers. Mix the 1/2-cup mixture with the whipped topping. Spread on top and sides.

Refrigerate 3 days in an airtight container before cutting. This is delicious and a super-great dessert than can be made ahead of time.

Joni Bowen, Belen, Miss.

SPICED APPLE RING

Serves 6–8

1 (20-ounce) can apple
    pie filling
1 (9-ounce) package
    yellow cake mix
Cinnamon
Brown sugar
Chopped nuts (optional)

Spread apple pie filling on bottom of a round microwave-Bundt cake pan. Sprinkle a little cinnamon on the pie filling.

Prepare cake mix according to package directions. Pour cake batter over pie filling. Microwave on HIGH power for 9–10 minutes, turning 1/4 turn every 2–3 minutes until done.

Invert immediately on a large plate. Sprinkle with cinnamon, brown sugar, and chopped nuts. Cool slightly and served topped with whipped cream or Cool Whip. This is a very quick and easy microwave cake.

Kayleen Avers, Hastings, Neb.

CAROL'S GERMAN CHOCOLATE-CARAMEL CAKE

1 package German chocolate cake mix
1 can Eagle Brand sweetened condensed milk
1 (12.25-ounce) jar caramel ice-cream topping
1 small container Cool Whip
¼ cup chopped pecans

Bake a German chocolate cake as directed in a 9 x 13-inch pan. While still warm poke holes, with a wooden spoon handle, about every 1–2 inches apart. Pour and spread on sweetened condensed milk. Spoon on caramel ice-cream topping. When cool spread on container of Cool Whip and sprinkle with ¼ cup chopped pecans. Store in refrigerator before serving. Very rich!

Jody Piercy, Fort Morgan, Colo.

WHITE SPONGE CAKE

6 egg whites
1/2 teaspoon cream of tartar
2 cups sifted cake flour
2 cups sugar
2 teaspoons baking powder
1 cup hot milk
3/4 teaspoon almond extract
1 teaspoon vanilla

Beat egg whites until foamy; add cream of tartar and beat until stiff. Sift together cake flour, sugar, and baking powder. Add hot milk to dry ingredients and mix well. Blend in almond extract and vanilla. Fold beaten egg whites into mixture. Bake in ungreased 13x9x2-inch pan at 375 degrees for 25 minutes. *Do not* invert pan while cooling.

If you do not have cake flour, remove 2 tablespoons from each cup of flour.

Betty Slavin, Omaha, Neb.

GOLDEN DOLLAR ANGEL CAKE

1/2 cup sifted cake flour
3/4 cup sifted sugar
6 egg whites
3/4 teaspoon cream of tartar
1/4 teaspoon salt
1/2 teaspoon vanilla
1/4 teaspoon almond extract
3/4 cup sifted cake flour
1 teaspoon baking powder
6 egg yolks
3/4 cup sugar
1/4 teaspoon salt
1/2 teaspoon vanilla
1/2 teaspoon lemon extract
1/4 cup boiling water

Sift flour and sugar, separately, 4 times; set aside. Beat egg whites until frothy; add cream of tartar and salt, then beat until mixture stands in peaks. Add sugar gradually while continuing to beat. Add flavorings, and fold in flour. Pour into an ungreased tube pan and let stand while preparing the second mixture.

Sift flour and baking powder together. Beat egg yolks until they reach a lemon color and are fluffy. Add sugar and salt, beating continuously. Add flavorings. Fold in flour mixture alternately with hot water. Pour slowly over batter in pan. Bake in a preheated oven at 350 degrees for 30-35 minutes. Invert pan until cool. Frost and serve.

Julie Habiger, Spearville, Kan.

SIMPLE PINEAPPLE CAKE

1 large can crushed pineapple
1 can angel flake coconut
1 (19-ounce) box yellow cake mix
1 stick margarine or butter

In an 11x7-inch baking dish, combine pineapple, juice, and all other ingredients. Place coconut and dry cake mix on top and spread evenly. Cut butter in thin slices and place over mix. Bake at 425 degrees for 40 minutes, or until top is brown and crunchy. Let cool before cutting into squares and serve upside down.

Suzan L. Wiener, Spring Hill, Fla.

MAPLE POUND CAKE

1 cup white sugar
3/4 cup light brown sugar
4 large eggs
1 teaspoon vanilla
1/2 teaspoon lemon extract
1/2 teaspoon maple extract
1 cup margarine
1 cup milk
1/2 teaspoon baking powder
1/2 teaspoon baking soda
1/2 teaspoon allspice
3 cups white flour

In large mixer bowl, combine sugars, margarine, eggs and extracts. Beat well until light and fluffy. Sift together dry ingredients and add alternately with milk. Beat smooth. Pour into non-stick or greased and floured large tube pan and bake in preheated 325 degree oven for one hour. Test with toothpick for doneness. Bake until toothpick comes out clean. Cool in pan for a few minutes, then turn out on rack. Serve plain or with whipped topping.

Pearle M. Goodwin, South Ryegate, Vt.

APPLE CAKE

1-1/2 cups flour, sifted
1/2 teaspoon salt
3 teaspoons baking powder
2 tablespoons shortening
1/2 cup milk
1/2 cup sugar
4 small apples
1 teaspoon cinnamon

Sift and mix together flour, salt, and baking powder. Cut in shortening; add milk and sugar. Place dough on floured board and roll out to 1/2-inch thickness. Place in shallow greased pan. Pare and slice apples. Press apple slices into dough and sprinkle with cinnamon. Bake for 30 minutes at 350 degrees.

Suzan L. Wiener, Spring Hill, Fla.

COOKIE CRUST CRUNCH CAKE

(Makes 2 loaf cakes)

2-1/4 cups vanilla wafer crumbs
1-1/4 cups pecans, finely chopped
1/2 cup sugar
1/2 stick butter or margarine
1 (18-1/4-ounce) box yellow cake mix
3 large eggs
1 stick butter or margarine, softened
1 tablespoon orange extract
2/3 cup water

Combine vanilla wafer crumbs, pecans, and sugar in bowl. Add 1/4 cup butter; cut in until crumbs are fine. Divide evenly into 2 greased 9x5x3-inch loaf pans. In a large mixer bowl, combine cake mix, eggs, 1/2 cup butter, orange extract, and water. Mix cake as directed on package; divide batter evenly into pans. Bake at 350 degrees for 60 minutes or until tested done in center of cake. Cool in pans on rack 5 minutes; loosen cake from pans; turn upside down on rack; cool completely. These loaves freeze nicely.

Gwen Campbell, Sterling, Va.

ANGEL RIPPLE CAKE

(from prepared mix)
Serves 12-16

1 package angel food cake mix
1 tablespoon ground cinnamon

Cinnamon Cream Sauce:
3/4 cup whipping cream
1/2 cup milk
1/3 cup confectioner's sugar
1 teaspoon vanilla
1/2 teaspoon ground cinnamon

Preheat oven to 375-degrees. Mix cake as directed on package. Spoon 1/4 of batter into an ungreased 10-inch tube pan and spread evenly. With a fine small sieve, sprinkle 1/3 of cinnamon over batter. Repeat layering 2 or 3 times ending with cake batter. Bake and cool as directed.

For sauce, mix cream and milk in a chilled bowl. Beat with chilled beaters until thick. Blend in confectioner's sugar, vanilla and cinnamon. Serve sauce over cake slices.

EASTER RING CAKE

2 cups sifted flour
1-1/4 cups sugar
3 teaspoons baking powder
1 teaspoon baking soda
1/2 teaspoon salt
1/2 cup shortening
2/3 cup orange juice
1 cup sugar
2 eggs
1/4 cup sweet orange marmalade
Lemon Butter Fluff Icing (recipe follows)

Sift together flour, sugar, baking powder, soda, and salt; blend in shortening and 2/3 cup orange juice. Beat 2 minutes at medium speed of electric mixer. Blend in remaining orange juice with eggs, beat at medium speed 2 minutes. Fold in orange marmalade and turn into greased and lightly floured 9 inch tube pan. Bake in a 350 degree oven for 50-55 minutes or until tests done. Cool completely before removing from pan. Frost with Lemon Butter Fluff Icing, and decorate with flowers.

Lemon Butter Fluff Icing:

1 (3-ounce) package cream cheese
2 tablespoons cream
1/2 cup soft butter
4 cups powdered sugar
1 tablespoon lemon juice
2-3 teaspoons grated lemon rind
1 teaspoon vanilla

Soften cream cheese to room temperature; blend in cream and butter. Beat until soft and smooth. Gradually blend in powdered sugar, lemon juice, rind, and vanilla. Beat until light and fluffy. Tint mixture a delicate color, if desired.

NOTE: A bouquet of real spring flowers placed in center of this ring cake is a delightful touch.

Leona Teodori, Warren, Mich.

ANGEL CAKE DELIGHT

Serves 24

1 (20-ounce) can crushed pineapple
1 large angel food cake
8 cups prepared Dream Whip (may substitute Cool Whip)
2 envelopes Knox unflavored gelatin
3 tablespoons lemon juice
1 cup white granulated sugar
1 cup coconut

Pour four tablespoons cold water over gelatin. Stir and add 1 cup boiling water. Add pineapple, lemon juice, and sugar. Let stand until chilled. Prepare Dream Whip, or use Cool Whip. Mix with gelatin mixture. Add coconut. Pinch cake in fine pieces. Prepare cake, alternating with a layer of cake crumbs and a layer of Dream Whip mixture—ending with Dream Whip mixture. Chill. This cake keeps very well when prepared and stored in a lid-covered cake tray.

Great recipe for a party, a family gathering, or anytime!

–Faye Wilson, Maysville, Ky.

ORANGE PEANUT BUTTER CAKE

2 oranges
1 package yellow cake mix (with or without pudding)
1-1/4 cups water
3 eggs
1/2 cup peanut butter (smooth or chunky)
1 teaspoon ground cinnamon
1/3 cup packed brown sugar

Grate peel from oranges; reserve. Peel oranges and cut into bite size pieces; drain well. In large bowl, combine cake mix, water, eggs, peanut butter, and cinnamon; beat according to package directions. Stir in orange pieces and peel. Pour batter into a greased and floured 13x9 inch cake pan. Sprinkle brown sugar over top. Bake 350 degrees for 35-40 minutes. Serve warm.

Mrs. Kit Rollins, Cedarburg, Wis.

58

CREAM-FILLED RASPBERRY ROLL

3 eggs
1 cup granulated sugar
1/3 cup water
1 teaspoon vanilla
1 cup cake flour or 3/4 cup all-
    purpose flour
1 teaspoon baking powder
1/4 teaspoon salt
1/2 cup raspberry jelly, plus 1/3 cup
    for top of cake
Fluffy White Frosting (recipe fol-
    lows)
Coconut
1 tablespoon raspberry gelatin
    powder

Heat oven to 375 degrees. Line jelly roll pan, 15x10x1-inch, with waxed paper; grease. Beat eggs in small mixer bowl on high speed until very thick and lemon colored, 3-5 minutes. Pour eggs into large mixing bowl; gradually beat in granulated sugar. On low speed, blend in water and vanilla. Gradually add flour, baking powder, and salt, beating just until batter is smooth. Pour into pan, spreading batter to corners. Bake until wooden pick inserted into center comes out clean, 12-15 minutes. Loosen cake from edges of pan; immediately invert onto towel gener-ously sprinkled with powdered sugar. Carefully remove wax paper; trim stiff edges of cake, if necessary. While hot, roll cake and towel from narrow end. Cool on wire rack at least 30 minutes.

Unroll cake; remove towel. Beat jelly with fork just enough to soften; spread over cake. Carefully spread a layer of Fluffy White Frosting over jelly; roll up. Place coconut in a small jar (about 2/3 cup) with 1 tablespoon gelatin powder and shake to color coconut. Spread about 1/3 cup jelly over rolled up jelly roll and sprinkle coconut on top.

Fluffy White Frosting:

1/2 cup sugar
1/2 stick butter or margarine
1/2 cup shortening
1-1/2 tablespoons flour
1/3 cup warm milk (barely heated)

1 teaspoon vanilla

Cream sugar, butter, and shorten-ing. Add flour, and gradually add milk and vanilla. Beat until thick. Has consistency of whipped cream.
Geneva Cullop, Ceres, Va.

COCONUT POUND CAKE

1 cup butter, softened
3 cups sugar
6 large eggs
3 cups all-purpose flour
1/4 teaspoon soda
1/4 teaspoon salt
8 ounces sour cream
1 cup frozen coconut, thawed
1 teaspoon vanilla
1 teaspoon coconut extract

Cream butter and add sugar. Beat until mix is light and fluffy. Add eggs, one at a time, beating well after each addition. Mix together flour, soda, salt; add flour mixture alternately with sour cream to creamed mixture, be-ginning and ending with flour. Stir in coconut and flavorings last. Grease and flour 10-inch tube pan. Bake at 350 degrees for 1 hour and 15 min-utes. Remove from pan; cool com-pletely; dust with powdered sugar. If you like pound cake you will love this!!

Renee Dennis Wells, Columbia, S.C.

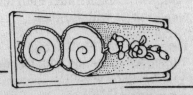

PINK AND PRETTY VALENTINE CAKE
(Serves 20)

1 cup sugar
3/4 cup butter or margarine, sof-
    tened
2-1/3 cups cake flour
3/4 cup milk
2-1/2 teaspoons baking powder
1 teaspoon vanilla
3 eggs
1/2 teaspoon salt
Buttercream Frosting (recipe
    follows)
Chocolate Hearts (recipe follows)

1 cup raspberry preserves
3 tablespoons orange juice
Red food coloring

Preheat oven to 350 degrees. Grease and flour 10-inch springform pan. In large bowl, with mixer at high speed, beat sugar and butter until fluffy. At low speed, beat in flour, milk, baking powder, vanilla, eggs, and 1/2 teaspoon salt until blended. Beat 1 minute at medium speed. Spoon batter into pan. Bake 45 minutes or until toothpick inserted in center comes out clean. Cool in pan on rack 10 minutes. Remove side of pan. Cool completely.

Prepare Buttercream Frosting and Chocolate Hearts. Place raspberry preserves in bowl. Stir in orange juice.

Remove cake from pan bottom. Cut into 3 layers. Place 1 layer on cake plate. Spread with half of rasp-berry mixture. Top with another layer. Spread with remaining raspberry mixture. Top with remaining layer. Spread top and side of cake with about 2 cups frosting. Add coloring to remaining buttercream to tint pink. Place about 1/2 cup of pink butter-cream in decorating bag with small writing tube. Use to pipe lattice on top of cake. Use remaining butter-cream to pipe border around top and bottom of cake and decorate side. Attach chocolate hearts. Refrigerate.

Buttercream Frosting:

3 cups confectioners' sugar
1-1/2 cups butter or margarine,
    softened
4 egg yolks

In large bowl with mixer at low speed, beat sugar and softened butter until mixed. At high speed beat until fluffy. At medium speed beat in 4 egg yolks.

Chocolate Hearts:

1/4 cup semi-sweet chocolate
    pieces, melted

Spread chocolate pieces, melted, into 4x3-inch rectangle on waxed paper-lined cookie sheet. Refrigerate until firm. With heart-shaped cookie cutter, cut chocolate into hearts. Re-frigerate.

GOOEY BUTTER CAKE

1/4 cup sugar
1/4 cup Crisco
1/4 teaspoon salt
1 egg
1 (6-ounce) cake of yeast
1/2 cup warm milk
2-1/2 cups all-purpose flour
1 tablespoon vanilla

Prepare a sweet dough by mixing sugar with Crisco and salt. Add egg and beat with electric mixer one minute until well blended. Dissolve yeast in warm milk. Add flour, then milk/yeast mixture, and vanilla to sweet dough batter. Mix 3 minutes with dough hooks or with hands. Turn dough onto floured board and knead for one minute. Place in a lightly-greased bowl; cover with a towel and let rise in a warm place for 1 hour.

M. Lanff, Philadelphia, Pa.

GOOEY BUTTER CAKE

1 yellow cake mix
4 eggs
1 stick butter, melted
1 pound box powdered sugar
1 (8-ounce) package cream cheese

Mix together the cake mix, 2 eggs, and butter. Spread batter into a 9 x 13 inch greased and floured pan. Batter will be thick. Blend remaining 2 eggs, powdered sugar, and cream cheese. Pour over batter. Bake at 350 degrees for 35 minutes or until top has a brown glaze and pulls from the sides of the pan.

Betty Ireton, Kingston, OH

APPLESAUCE CAKE

1-1/4 cups shortening (Crisco)
3 cups brown sugar
3 eggs
2-1/4 cups applesauce
4-1/2 cups sifted flour

1 teaspoon salt
2-1/4 teaspoons cinnamon
1 teaspoon ground cloves
2-1/4 teaspoons baking soda

Cream shortening, sugar, and eggs. Dissolve soda into the applesauce; add to egg mixture. Sift flour, salt, cinnamon, and cloves; add to egg mixture. Pour into tube pan; bake at 350 degrees for one hour. Let cool five minutes; invert on rack. No icing is needed.

Karin Shea Fedders, Dameron, MD

APPLE POUND CAKE

2 cups unsifted flour
1 teaspoon soda
1 teaspoon salt
1/2 teaspoon nutmeg
2 cups sugar
2 teaspoons vanilla
1 cup chopped pecans or walnuts
1/2 teaspoon cinnamon
1-1/2 cups corn oil
3 eggs
2 cups finely chopped apples
1/2 cup raisins

Preheat oven to 325 degrees. Combine flour, soda, salt, cinnamon, and nutmeg in a large bowl. With electric mixer at medium speed, beat together the oil, sugar, eggs, and vanilla until thoroughly combined. Gradually beat in the flour mixture until smooth. Fold in apples, pecans (or walnuts), and raisins. Turn into greased and floured 10-inch tube pan or bundt pan. Bake at 325 degrees for 1 hour and 15 minutes or until cake tester inserted in center comes out clean. Cool cake in pan on wire rack for 10 minutes, then remove from pan to cool completely. Store in air-tight container.

Mrs. H. W. Walker, Richmond, VA

MAPLE-FLAVORED GINGERBREAD

Serves 16

2-1/2 cups all-purpose flour
1-1/2 teaspoons soda
1 teaspoon ground cinnamon
1 teaspoon ground ginger
1/2 teaspoon ground cloves
1/2 teaspoon salt
1/2 cup shortening
1/2 cup sugar
1 egg
1/2 cup molasses
1/2 cup maple-flavored syrup
1 cup hot water
Whipped cream

Combine flour, soda, spices, and salt; set aside. Cream shortening and sugar until light and fluffy. Add egg, beating well. Gradually beat in molasses and syrup. Add dry ingredients alternately with hot water, beating well after each addition. Pour batter into greased 13 x 9 x 2 inch pan. Bake at 350 degrees for 30 minutes or until done. Cool thoroughly in pan. Serve with whipped cream.

Barbara Beauregard-Smith, Northfield, S. A. Australia

ONE-BOWL CHOCOLATE CAKE

Sift into large bowl:
3-1/2 cups flour
2 cups sugar
5 tablespoons cocoa
1 teaspoon cinnamon
2 teaspoons baking soda
1 teaspoon salt

To these 6 ingredients add:
1 cup cooking oil
2 teaspoons vinegar
2 teaspoons vanilla
2 cups water

Beat well. Pour into ungreased 9 x 13 inch pan. Bake at 350 degrees for 35-45 minutes. This is a very moist cake, easy to make, and no eggs needed.

Tom McNiel, Constantine, MI

NO-COOK FROSTING

1/4 teaspoon salt
2 egg whites
1/4 cup sugar
3/4 cup Karo syrup, red or blue label
1-1/4 teaspoons vanilla

Beat salt and egg whites until mixture peaks. Add sugar, 1 tablespoon at a time, beating until smooth and glossy. Continue beating and add Karo syrup gradually, until frosting peaks. Fold in vanilla. Add vegetable coloring, if desired; frost top and sides of two 9 inch layers.

Mrs. Olen Begly, West Salem, Ohio

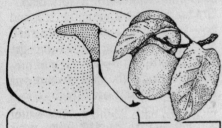

APPLE BUTTER CAKE

1/2 cup shortening
1 cup sugar
3 eggs
1 cup apple butter
2-1/2 cups sifted cake flour
3 teaspoons baking powder
1/2 teaspoon baking soda
1/2 teaspoon salt
1/2 teaspoon cinnamon
1/4 teaspoon nutmeg
1/2 cup apple butter
1 cup sour milk

Cream together shortening and sugar. Beat in eggs, one at a time; beat until light and fluffy. Stir in 1 cup apple butter. Sift together flour, baking powder, soda, salt, cinnamon, and nutmeg. Add dry ingredients . to creamed mixture, alternately with sour milk. Turn into 2 greased and floured 9 inch cake pans. Bake at 350 degrees for 30-35 minutes. Cool thoroughly. Spread bottom layer of cake with 1/4 cup of remaining apple butter. Top with frosting. Cover with top cake layer. Frost top and sides with any marshmallow frosting. Swirl remaining apple butter on top for marbled effect.

Leah Daub, Milwaukee, Wis.

DUTCH APPLE CAKE
Makes 1 13 x 9-inch cake

1 (18-1/2 ounce) package spice cake mix
1/2 cup butter or margarine, melted
2 eggs
1 (21 ounce) can apple pie filling
3/4 cup brown sugar, firmly packed
1 teaspoon cinnamon
1/4 cup butter or margarine, softened
1/2 cup chopped nuts

In large bowl, combine dry cake mix, melted butter, and eggs. Blend well. Spread on bottom of 13 x 9 inch baking pan. Spoon pie filling evenly over batter. In small bowl combine brown sugar and cinnamon; cut in softened butter; stir in nuts. Sprinkle over pie filling. Bake at 350 degrees for 50 minutes or until cake springs back when lightly touched.

Agnes Ward, Erie, Pa.

APPLESAUCE CAKE

1 stick (1/2 cup) butter or margarine, softened
1 cup sugar
1 large egg
1-1/2 cups applesauce
2 cups all-purpose flour
2 teaspoons baking soda
1 teaspoon cinnamon
1 teaspoon nutmeg
1/4 teaspoon ground cloves
1 cup chopped, pitted dates
1/2 cup chopped walnuts

In a large bowl cream the butter, add the sugar, a little at a time. Beat the mixture until light and fluffy. Beat in the egg and add the applesauce. Into a bowl sift together the flour, soda, and spices, gently stir the mixture into the applesauce mixture with the dates and walnuts. Transfer the batter into a well greased baking pan, 12 x 8 x 2 inches, and bake in a preheated oven 350 degrees for approximately 45 minutes. Let the cake cool in pan on a rack. Frost if desired.

Very moist cake. Raisins may be used instead of dates.

Paula L. Walton, Fort Pierce, FL

APPLESAUCE LAYER CAKE

2 eggs
1-1/2 cups sugar
1-1/2 cups applesauce
1/2 cup butter or shortening
1 teaspoon soda
1 teaspoon salt
1 teaspoon cinnamon
1 teaspoon nutmeg
1/2 cup nut meats
2 cups flour
1 cup raisins (if desired)

Cream together the shortening and sugar. Add eggs, applesauce; and then sift the flour, soda, salt, and spices together. Add to creamed mixture; stir in raisins.

Grease (2) 8-inch round cake pans or use typing paper cut to fit inside pans. Pour batter into pans and bake at 325 degrees for 40 minutes or until cake tests done.

This cake is especially tasty with a mocha or caramel frosting.

Betty Slavin, Omaha, NE

SAUCY APPLE SWIRL CAKE
Serves 16

1/4 cup sugar
1 teaspoon cinnamon
1 package yellow cake mix (Pillsbury Plus best)
1 (15 ounce) jar (1-1/2 cups) applesauce
3 eggs

Heat oven to 350 degrees. Grease and flour 12-cup fluted pan or 10-inch tube pan. In small bowl, combine sugar and cinnamon; set aside. In large bowl, blend cake mix, applesauce, and eggs until moistened. Beat 2 minutes at high speed. Pour 1/2 of batter into prepared pan. Sprinkle with sugar mix. Cover with remaining batter. Bake 35-45 minutes until toothpick comes out of center clean. Cool upright in pan 25 minutes; turn onto serving plate. Cool completely. Dust with powdered sugar.

Judie Betz, Lomita, Calif.

OATMEAL CAKE

1 cup quick oatmeal
1 1/4 cups boiling water
1 stick butter or margarine
2 eggs, beater
1 cup white sugar
1 cup brown sugar
1 1/2 cups flour
1 teaspoon soda
1 teaspoon cinnamon
1/2 teaspoon salt
1 teaspoon vanilla

Stir together the oatmeal, boiling water and butter until butter melts. Let cool. Add the eggs and beat, then add sugar and beat mixture again. Sift together the flour, soda, cinnamon and salt and add to cake mixture with the vanilla. Beat all well.

Pour into greased and floured 9x 13" pan. Bake at 350-degrees for about 32 minutes.

When done and still hot, spread with the following topping. Mix together in heavy pan 3/4 cup brown sugar, 3/4 cup pecan pieces (or other chopped nuts), 6 tablespoons butter and 1/2 cup condensed milk (1/2 cup coconut, optional). Cream and cook until thick (but not too long).Evenly place mixture on cake. Place cake under broiler until topping becomes bubbly.

Karen Shea Fedders, Dameron, Md.

$100 CHOCOLATE CAKE

1/2 cup butter
2 cups sugar
4 ounces semi-sweet chocolate, melted
2 eggs, beaten
2 cups sifted cake flour
1/4 teaspoon salt
2 teaspoons baking powder
1-1/2 cups sweet milk
1 teaspoon vanilla
1 cup chopped nuts

Cream butter and sugar. Add melted chocolate. Add beaten eggs. Add flour, salt, baking powder mixture, and vanilla, alternately with milk. Beat with hand beater, not mixer, after addition. Put in 2 (9-inch) cake pans. Bake in 350 degree oven for 45 minutes. Batter is thin.

Frosting:

1/2 cup butter
2 ounces semi-sweet chocolate, melted
1 egg, beaten
1/4 teaspoon salt
1 teaspoon lemon juice
1 teaspoon vanilla
1-1/2 cups confectioners' sugar
1 cup chopped nuts

Mix first 6 ingredients, then stir in confectioners' sugar. Beat until thick enough to spread. (Beat by hand.) Sprinkle chopped nuts on top.

Sandra Russell, Gainesville, Fla.

ORANGE KISS ME CAKE

1 (6-ounce) can frozen orange juice, (3/4 cup thawed)
2 cups flour
1 cup sugar
1 teaspoon soda
1 teaspoon salt
1/2 cup shortening
1/2 cup milk
2 eggs
1 cup raisins
1/3 cup chopped walnuts

Preheat oven to 350 degrees. Grease and flour bottom of 9x13-inch pan. Combine 1/2 cup orange juice with remaining ingredients in large bowl. Blend at lowest speed of mixer for 30 seconds. Beat 3 minutes at medium speed. Bake 40-45 minutes. Drizzle remaining orange juice over warm cake and sprinkle with topping (recipe follows).

Topping:

1/3 cup sugar
1/4 cup chopped walnuts
1 teaspoon cinnamon
Combine in a bowl.

Susan Kirch, Dexter, N.Y.

SUNSHINE CAKE

7 egg yolks
1 teaspoon lemon extract
1-1/2 cups powdered sugar
10 egg whites
1 teaspoon cream of tartar
1 cup cake flour
1/4 teaspoon salt

Preheat oven to 325 degrees. Line bottom of a 10-inch tube pan with wax paper; cut to fit. Beat egg yolks; add lemon extract and 1 cup of the powdered sugar. Beat until thick and pale; set aside. Beat egg whites until foamy; add the cream of tartar, and beat until whites form soft peaks. Gradually, add remaining 1/2 cup powdered sugar and beat until stiff. Stir a fourth of the whites into the yolk mixture. Spoon remaining whites on top of the yolk mixture and sift flour and salt over them. Carefully fold until blended. Spoon into pan and bake for 50-60 minutes, until a toothpick comes out clean. Invert pan on a rack and let cake cool completely before removing from the pan. Frost with your favorite icing.

Lucille Roehr, Hammond, Ind.

NO-BAKE PEPPERMINT ICE CREAM CAKE

10-inch angel food cake
6 chocolate peppermint patties
1/2 cup nuts
1/8 teaspoon peppermint extract
1 quart vanilla ice cream

Cut cake in 4 layers. Chop patties and nuts. Soften ice cream slightly. Stir in candy, nuts, and extract. Spread thick layer of ice cream mixture between cake layers and rebuild the cake. Cover top with ice cream mixture. Keep in freezer; no thawing necessary.

Sally Jonas, Lafayette, Ind.

CARROT CAKE

1/2 cup oil
1 cup sugar
2 eggs, well beaten
1/2 cup grated carrots, packed
1/2 cup crushed pineapple
1-1/2 cups sifted flour
1/2 teaspoon salt
1/2 teaspoon baking soda
1/2 teaspoon baking powder
1/2 teaspoon cinnamon
1 teaspoon vanilla
1/2 cup chopped walnuts

Combine oil and sugar; add well-beaten eggs, carrots, and crushed pineapple. Mix just to combine. Sift flour, salt, baking soda, baking powder, and cinnamon. Stir into oil mixture. Add vanilla and nuts. Mix to combine. Pour batter into a greased and floured 9x13-inch pan. Bake at 350 degrees for 30 minutes or until done. Cool.

Icing:

1 (3 ounce) cream cheese
3 ounces margarine
1-1/2 cups powdered sugar
1 teaspoon walnuts, chopped fine
1 teaspoon crushed pineapple

Mix together cream cheese, margarine, and powdered sugar. Beat until light and fluffy. Add nuts and pineapple. Ice cooled cake.

Leona Teodori, Warren, Mich.

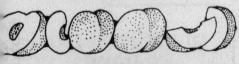

NO-FUSS FRUITCAKE

3/4 cup brown sugar
1/2 cup margarine or butter
1 egg
2-1/2 cups all-purpose flour
1 teaspoon baking soda
1/4 teaspoon *each* nutmeg and cloves
1/2 teaspoon cinnamon
1/4 cup orange or pineapple juice
1 cup applesauce, unsweetened or diced
2 cups chopped candied fruit
1 cup *each* raisins and chopped walnuts

In large bowl cream sugar and margarine or butter; add egg; beat well. Mix flour with spices and soda; stir into creamed mixture alternately with applesauce and juice. Fold in fruits, raisins, and nuts. Pour into two greased, floured 7-1/2 x 3-1/2 x 2 inch loaf pans. Bake for 1 hour at 325 degrees or until tests done with toothpick. Remove from pans; cool. Lightly glaze tops with mixture of confectioners' sugar and enough fruit juice or water to spread thinly. When glaze is set, press halved candied cherries over the top. Wrap in foil; store in cool place or freeze until needed.

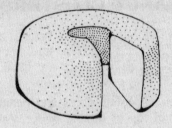

GRAPEFRUIT CHIFFON CAKE

2 cups all-purpose flour
1-1/2 cups sugar
3 teaspoons baking powder
1/2 teaspoon salt
1/2 cup oil
6 egg yolks
3 teaspoons grated grapefruit peel
2/3 cup grapefruit juice
6-7 egg whites
1/4 teaspoon cream of tartar

In a small mixer bowl stir together flour, sugar, baking powder, and salt. Make a well in center; in order add oil, egg yolks, peel, and juice. Beat smooth with an electric mixer. Wash beaters and in large bowl beat egg whites with the cream of tartar until stiff.

Gradually pour flour mixture (it will be thick) in a thin stream over surface and fold in gently. Bake in a 10-inch ungreased tube pan for 55 minutes at 350 degrees or until it tests done when lightly touched with the finger the cake springs back. Invert. Cool completely on cake cooling rack, loosen edges, and remove to cake plate. Glaze with the following:

2 cups sifted powdered sugar
3 teaspoons grapefruit peel, grated
1 teaspoon vanilla
2-3 tablespoons grapefruit juice

Mix all ingredients together using enough grapefruit juice to make it spread easily and drizzle down the sides when spread on top of cake.

Judy Smith, Indianapolis, IN

1 package yellow cake mix
1-6 ounce package instant vanilla pudding mix
1-1/4 cups cold milk
1-8 ounce package cream cheese
1-8 or 9 ounce container frozen whipped topping
1-20 ounce can crushed pineapple, well drained
1/2 cup chopped pecans
1/2 cup flaked coconut
1/2 cup Maraschino cherries, drained and chopped

Prepare cake according to directions on package. Pour into greased 10 x 15 jelly roll pan. Bake in preheated oven 350 degrees 15-20 minutes, or until done. Cool in pan.

Blend pudding mix with milk, beat in cream cheese (room temperature); then fold in frozen whipped topping. Spread on cooled cake. Sprinkle drained pineapple over pudding, then cherries, nuts, and coconut. Refrigerate until ready to cut. Can be made a day ahead. This not only makes a big beautiful cake but is very delicious. I've taken this to a lot of potlucks and someone always wants the recipe.

Roselyn Finan, Fort Wayne, IN

Candies
& CONFECTIONS

MARSHMALLOW WALNUT FUDGE
Makes 64 1-inch squares

1/2 pound (2 sticks) butter
8 squares (8 ounces) unsweetened chocolate
1 cup coarsely chopped walnuts
1 pound sifted confectioners' sugar
1 teaspoon vanilla extract
32 marshmallows

Combine butter and chocolate in saucepan. Melt over low heat. Pour into a large bowl and add nuts, sugar and vanilla. Knead until blended well, then pat into a greased 8-inch square pan. Cut marshmallows in half crosswise. Place marshmallows cut side down at 1-inch intervals so marshmallow will be in the center of each piece. Cut between the marshmallows into 1-inch squares.

YUMMY CANDY SQUARES
Yield: 16

2 cups chocolate or butterscotch chips
2/3 cup sweetened condensed milk
1 teaspoon vanilla
1/8 teaspoon salt
3/4 cup oatmeal
1/3 cup chopped nuts
1/4 cup flaked or shredded coconut

Melt chocolate or butterscotch chips over hot water; blend in remaining ingredients. Mix thoroughly. Spread into an 8-inch square pan. Chill until firm. Cut into squares.

Agnes Ward, Erie, Pa.

PEANUT CLUSTERS

2 cups chocolate chips
1 cup peanut butter
2 cups Spanish peanuts

Melt chocolate chips and peanut butter in top of double boiler. Add peanuts; stir and drop by teaspoons on waxed paper.

These are very good, and so simple and easy to make.

Elaine Dodd, Pasco, Wash.

NUT CARAMELS
Makes 5 dozen

1/4 cup butter or margarine
1 cup evaporated milk
1 cup sugar
1 cup dark corn syrup
Dash salt
1/4 teaspoon vanilla
1 cup pecans, coarsely broken

Heat butter and evaporated milk in small saucepan, cook sugar, corn syrup and salt over medium heat until it reaches firm-ball stage, 244 degrees on candy thermometer, stirring often. Slowly stir in milk so sugar mixture does not stop boiling. Cook, stirring constantly, until mixture reaches firm-ball stage again. Remove pan from heat and stir in vanilla and pecans. Mix well. Pour into well-buttered 8-inch square pan. When firm, turn out onto cutting board or wax paper. Cut into 1-inch squares and wrap each in plastic wrap.

Leona Teodori, Warren, Mich.

PECAN PRALINES
Makes 36

1 cup sugar
1 cup firmly packed brown sugar
1/3 cup evaporated milk
1/2 stick butter or margarine, softened
1-1/2 cups pecans or small can coconut

Combine sugars and evaporated milk in heavy saucepan; cook over medium heat. Stir in butter and pecans; cook until candy reaches soft-ball stage. Cool for 2 minutes. Beat until thick, but glossy. Drop by tablespoons onto waxed paper. Cool thoroughly.

Marcella Swigert, Monroe City, Mo.

QUICK PENUCHE CANDY

1/2 cup margarine
1/4 cup milk
1 cup packed brown sugar
1-3/4 to 2 cups sifted powdered sugar
1 cup chopped pecans

Melt margarine, add brown sugar and cook over low heat 2 minutes. Add milk and continue cooking until mixture boils. Remove from heat and let cool at room temperature. Gradually add powdered sugar until like a fudge consistency. Add nuts and spread in buttered 8-inch square pan. Cool.

Jodie McCoy, Tulsa, Okla.

PEANUT BUTTER BALLS

1/2 cup honey
1 cup peanut butter
1 cup powdered sugar
Corn flakes, crushed

Blend honey, peanut butter and powdered sugar until smooth. Roll into small balls, roll in crushed corn flakes. Refrigerate one hour or until cold.

Agnes Russell, Concord, N.H.

DOUBLE PEANUT CLUSTERS

1/2 cup peanut butter, smooth or crunchy
12-ounce package chocolate chips
2 cups dry-roasted peanuts, coarsely chopped.

Melt chocolate chips and peanut butter in top of double boiler or in saucepan over low heat or hot water. Stir in peanuts. Drop by teaspoonsful into foil baking cups or onto foil or waxed paper. Chill and store clusters in refrigerator.

Rich and delicious!

Cynthia Cardwell, Sterling, Ill.

EASY MARSHMALLOW FUDGE

2/3 cup evaporated milk
1 1/2 cups sugar
1/2 teaspoon salt
32 marshmallows (1/2 pound)
12-ounce package semisweet chocolate chips
1 teaspoon vanilla extract
1/2 teaspoon peppermint extract

Combine evaporated milk, sugar, salt and marshmallows in a saucepan. Cook over low heat, stirring constantly, until marshmallows melt. Blend in chocolate chips; stir until smooth. Add both extracts. Pour into a buttered 8-inch square pan. Chill. Cut into squares.

Patty Ross, Trenton, Ohio

WHITE FUDGE
Makes 1-1/2 pounds

2 cups granulated sugar
1/2 cup sour cream
1/3 cup white corn syrup
2 tablespoons butter
1/4 teaspoon salt
2 tablespoons vanilla, rum or brandy flavoring
1/4 cup quartered candied red cherries
1 cup chopped walnuts

In heavy 2-quart saucepan, combine sugar, sour cream, syrup, butter and salt. Bring to boil slowly, stirring until sugar dissolves. Boil, without stirring, over medium heat to 236 degrees, or until a little mixture dropped in cold water forms a soft ball.

Remove from heat and let stand 15 minutes. Do not stir. Add flavoring and beat until mixture starts to lose its gloss, about 8 minutes. Stir in cherries and nuts quickly. Pour into greased 8x8-inch pan. Cool and cut into squares.

Betty Burt, Winnemucca, Nev.

CHOCOLATE CARAMEL LOLLIPOPS
Makes 20

100   small chocolate caramels
16   cups rice cereal, toasted in oven
¾   cup water
20   wooden lollipop sticks
20   (5-ounce) paper cups

In double boiler top, combine caramels with water. Cook over hot water, stirring occasionally, until caramels melt. In a bowl combine caramel mixture and cereal. Using a wooden spoon, stir until cereal is well-coated. Spoon mixture into paper cups. Insert 1 lollipop stick into center of each cup. Refrigerate for 30 minutes to an hour. Remove lollipops from paper cups before serving.

Shari Crider, Stoughton, Wis.

CINNAMON FILBERTS

2 cups (1/2 pound) shelled filberts 1 egg white
1/2 cup sugar
1 teaspoon ground cinnamon
1/4 cup (1/2 stick) butter or margarine

Put nuts on shallow baking pan and toast in preheated slow oven (325 degrees) for 10 minutes. Beat egg whites until foamy; add sugar and cinnamon gradually and beat until stiff. Add nuts and mix well. Melt butter in same baking pan you used for toasting nuts and spread nut mixture over butter. Bake for 30 minutes, stirring every 10 minutes. Store in airtight container.

OLD-FASHIONED TAFFY PULL
Makes 1½ pounds

2   cups light molasses
1   cup dark brown sugar, firmly packed
2   tablespoons butter
⅓   cup water
1   tablespoon apple cider vinegar
  Pinch of baking soda

Cook all ingredients together in a heavy saucepan over medium heat. Stir constantly until sugar is dissolved, until mixture reaches the hard-ball stage (260 degrees on candy thermometer) and a small bit makes a hard ball when dropped into cold water. Pour onto a buttered cookie sheet. Cool. When cool enough to handle, rub butter on your hands and pull the candy, small portions at a time, until it is light golden in color and candy has a satiny finish. Pull into long strips ¾ inch in diameter and cut into 1-inch pieces with scissors. When cooled, wrap each piece in waxed paper.

You may add lemon, maple, almond or vanilla extract for variety, or divide the recipe and flavor each section with a different extract.

Diantha Susan Hibbard, Rochester, N.Y.

OLD-FASHIONED PEANUT BRITTLE
Serves 24

Quick-cooking in microwave in 9 minutes.

1 cup raw peanuts
1 cup sugar
½ cup light corn syrup
⅛ teaspoon salt
1 teaspoon baking soda
1 teaspoon vanilla
1 teaspoon butter

In a 1½-quart casserole, stir together peanuts, sugar, syrup and salt. Cook 8 minutes on HIGH, stirring well after 4 minutes. Add butter and vanilla. Cook 1 minute longer on HIGH. Add baking soda and quickly stir until light and foamy. Immediately pour onto lightly buttered baking sheet. Spread out thin. When cool, break into pieces. Store in airtight container.

Katherine W. Frierson, Deland, Fla.

CHOCOLATE MARSHMALLOW FUDGE

4-1/2 cups sugar
2 tablespoons butter
1 (1-2/3 cups) tall can evaporated milk
Pinch of salt
12 ounces semi-sweet chocolate chips
12 ounces German Sweet Chocolate
1 pint marshmallow creme
2 cups pecans or walnuts

Heat first 4 ingredients to a rolling boil. Place remaining 4 ingredients in large bowl. Pour boiling syrup over ingredients in bowl, stir until chocolate is all melted and pour into 9x13-inch pan.

It is easier to remove from pan if pan is buttered and lined with foil first. Let stand few hours before cutting. Where German Sweet Chocolate is not available, 3 to 4 squares of unsweetened chocolate may be used.

Katherine Frierson, Deland, Fla.

COCONUT TREATS

1 cup sugar
1/2 cup water
1 1/2 cups corn syrup
1 14-ounce package shredded coconut
1/2 teaspoon vanilla
Melted chocolate

Combine sugar with water and syrup; stir over heat to dissolve sugar. Cook without stirring to 236 degrees (soft-ball stage) on candy thermometer. Remove from heat; add coconut and vanilla. Cool. With teaspoon, shape into small balls and dip in melted chocolate.

PEANUT BUTTER CUPS

1/2 cup butter or margarine
1 pound powdered sugar
2 cups creamy peanut butter
3 cups Rice Krispies, crushed
2 cups (12 ounces) chocolate chips
4 tablespoons shortening

Mix butter, powdered sugar, peanut butter and Rice Krispies together well, (may need to use hands). Melt chips with shortening. Roll candy into small balls and dip in chocolate. Chill until chocolate hardens.

Judy Haffner, Auke Bay, Alaska

LOLLIPOPS

Combine over low heat:
2 cups sugar
2/3 cup light corn syrup
1/2 cup water

Cook without stirring to just past the crack stage (to 310 degrees on thermometer). Remove syrup from heat. Stir in a few drops of food coloring, all one color, or many if you want to divide candy into small pans. Flavor with 1 teaspoon vanilla or fruit flavors, peppermint, etc. Pour syrup by the tablespoonfuls onto a greased sheet. Press stick into each one.

Karin Shea Fedders, Dameron, Md.

MRS. MARTIN'S QUICK PEANUT CANDY
Makes 1 1/4 pounds

1/2 cup light corn syrup
1/2 cup sugar
1/2 cup peanut butter
4 cups crispy rice cereal
1 cup peanuts

Grease a large baking sheet. In a 3-quart saucepan, mix syrup and sugar. Stirring constantly, bring to a boil over medium heat; boil 1 minute. Remove from heat. Stir in peanut butter. Add cereal and peanuts. Quickly stir until well-coated. Spoon onto greased baking sheet. With greased hands, pat evenly to 1/2-inch thickness. Cool and then break into pieces.

Agnes Ward, Erie, Penn.

CANDIED CHERRY-PECAN SLICES
Makes 144

1 cup butter *or* margarine, softened
1 cup confectioners' sugar
1 egg
1½ teaspoons vanilla
2¼ cups flour
Dash of salt
2 cups candied cherries, halved
1 cup pecans

In small mixer bowl, cream butter until fluffy. Gradually add sugar, beating until light. Beat in egg and vanilla. Stir in flour and salt; mix well. Stir in cherries and pecans. Cover airtight and chill 1 hour. Divide dough into thirds. On lightly floured pastry cloth or other surface, with floured hands, shape each piece of dough into 12-inch roll. Wrap each roll in waxed paper; chill at least 3 hours, or until firm. Cut in ¼-inch slices (serrated knife). Place slices about 1 inch apart on ungreased cookie sheets. Bake in preheated 350-degree oven for 12–15 minutes, or until light brown at edges. Cool on racks. Store airtight in cool, dry place.

Diantha Susan Hibbard, Rochester, N.Y.

CLASSIC CHRISTMAS CANDY CANES

1 cup water
3 cups sugar
1-1/2 tablespoons heavy cream
1-1/2 teaspoons white vinegar
1/4 teaspoon salt
2 tablespoons butter or margarine
4-5 drops peppermint extract
3-4 drops red food coloring

Combine sugar, cream, vinegar, salt and butter in mixing bowl; cream as for a cake. Boil water; remove from heat; stir creamed mixture into hot water. Clip on candy thermometer; boil to crack stage (258 degrees). Remove from heat; pour mixture onto lightly-buttered baking sheet placed over cooling rack. Cool; add flavoring; work candy with spatula. Divide mixture into portions; leave one portion white; tint the second with red food coloring. Pull each portion separately into a rope 1/2 inch in diameter; twist the two together to form one rope. Cut into 4 to 5-inch lengths; curl one end over to form the candy cane shape.

Mrs. Gwen Campbell, Sterling, Va.

SOUR CREAM FUDGE

2 cups sugar
2 tablespoons white corn syrup
2 tablespoons butter
3/4 - 1 cup sour cream (depending upon consistency, thin dairy sour cream with milk until consistency of thick whipping cream).
1 teaspoon vanilla
1/2 cup walnuts

Mix sugar, corn syrup, butter and sour cream well. Cook over medium heat until soft ball stage. Cool. Add vanilla. Cool to room temperature. Beat until thick. Add nuts. Pour at once into buttered platter. Do not spread. Top will be glossy and uneven. Cut into 3/4-inch squares when firm.

Phyllis Lien, Stoughton, Wis.

HELEN'S SUNFLOWER BRITTLE

2 cups sugar
1 cup light corn syrup
1/2 cup water
Pinch of salt
1 cup raw sunflower seeds
1 tablespoon butter
1 teaspoon vanilla
1 teaspoon baking soda

Butter two cookie sheets well.
Mix sugar, corn syrup, water and salt in saucepan and bring to boil at 212 degrees F. on a candy thermometer. Add sunflower seeds; cook to 275 degrees F. Stir in butter and cook to 300 degrees F.

Remove from heat; add vanilla and mix well; add baking soda. Stir well. Pour onto buttered cookie sheets and spread into thin, even layer. Let cool, then break into pieces.

Mrs. Helen Beebe, St. Charles, Ill.

MOM'S CREAM CHEESE MINTS
Makes 7 dozen

4 ounces cream cheese, softened
2 cups confectioners' sugar
Peppermint extract, about 1/4 teaspoon or to taste
Wintergreen extract, about 1/4 teaspoon or to taste
Red food coloring
Green food coloring
Granulated sugar

Mix cream cheese and confectioners' sugar by hand until smooth and doughy. Divide mixture in half; add a few drops of peppermint extract to one half and a few drops of wintergreen extract to other half. Taste and adjust flavor. Blend green food coloring (several drops at a time) into peppermint mixture until soft green; blend red food coloring (several drops at a time) into wintergreen mixture until pastel pink. Pinch off small pieces of dough; roll into balls and dip into granulated sugar. Refrigerate, covered.

Marcella Swigert, Monroe City, Mo.

CATHEDRAL WINDOW CANDY

2 tablespoons butter
1 cup chocolate chips
1 beaten egg
1 cup confectioners' sugar
3 cups colored miniature marshmallows

Place butter and chocolate chips in medium, heat-resistant bowl. Heat, uncovered, in microwave oven for 4 minutes, or until melted. Combine egg and sugar; add slowly to chocolate mixture. Stir in marshmallows to coat well. Pour onto waxed paper. Shape into 18-inch log. Refrigerate. Slice before serving.

Sue Hammer

MILLION-DOLLAR FUDGE
Makes 2½ pounds

2 cups granulated sugar
  Pinch of salt
1 tablespoon butter
1 (5½-ounce) can evaporated milk, undiluted
1 (6-ounce) package semisweet chocolate bits
6 ounces sweet baking chocolate, cut into small pieces
1 (8-ounce) jar marshmallow creme
1 cup coarsely broken walnuts *or* pecans

Butter an 8-inch square pan; set aside.

Into a 2-quart heavy saucepan place sugar, salt, butter and evaporated milk. Stirring constantly, cook over medium-high heat until mixture comes to a full boil. Boil 5 minutes, stirring constantly.

Remove from heat. Add chocolate and marshmallow creme; stir vigorously and speedily until chocolate is melted and mixture is uniform in color. At once, stir in the nuts and pour into prepared pan. When cool, cut into desired size squares. Store in airtight container.

Nora Leigh, Richmond, Va.

PEANUT BUTTER BONBONS

Makes about 100

2 cups peanut butter
1/2 cup butter or margarine
1 pound sifted confectioners' sugar
3 cups crisp rice cereal
2 (6 ounce) packages butterscotch pieces (2 cups)
2 (6 ounce) packages semi-sweet chocolate pieces (2 cups)

In saucepan, melt peanut butter and butter. In large bowl, combine sugar and cereal. Pour peanut butter mixture over cereal mixture. Blend together with hands. Form into 1/2-inch balls. Chill until firm. Melt butterscotch pieces and chocolate pieces in separate double boilers. Dip half the candies in each coating. Swirl tops with back of teaspoon. Place on waxed paper-lined baking sheet. Chill.

Bea Comas, Portland, Maine

PECAN PRALINES

Makes 1½ dozen

1   (3½-ounce) package butterscotch pudding and pie filling mix
1   cup sugar
½   cup firmly packed brown sugar
½   cup evaporated milk
1   tablespoon margarine *or* butter
1½ cups pecan halves

In a large saucepan combine pudding mix, sugar, brown sugar, milk and margarine or butter. Cook over low heat, stirring constantly, until sugar dissolves and mixture comes to a boil. Continue cooking and stirring until mixture reaches the soft-ball stage (235 degrees) on candy thermometer, or until a small amount dropped into cold water forms a soft ball. Remove from heat; add nuts. Beat until mixture begins to thicken. Drop by tablespoonfuls onto waxed paper, making each praline about 3 inches in diameter. Cool until firm.

Leota Baxter, Ingalls, Kan.

OLD-FASHIONED TAFFY

Makes about 40 1-inch pieces

2 1/2 cups sugar
1/2 cup water
1/4 cup vinegar
1/8 teaspoon salt
1 tablespoon butter
1 teaspoon vanilla

Combine sugar, water, vinegar, salt and butter in a small Dutch oven. Cook without stirring over medium heat until mixture reaches 270 degrees (soft crack stage). Remove from heat at once and add vanilla.

Pour onto a greased 15x10x1-inch pan. Cool until it can be handled; then butter hands and pull candy until it is light in color and difficult to pull. Divide candy in half and pull each half into a rope 1 inch in diameter. Cut into 1-inch pieces; wrap each piece individually in waxed paper.

MYSTERY DROPS

Makes 30 candies

2 cups granulated sugar
2/3 cup milk
3/4 cup finely-ground soda crackers (30 crackers)
1/2 cup finely-chopped pecans
1 teaspoon vanilla
7 tablespoons peanut butter, smooth or crunchy

Combine sugar and milk in 2-quart heavy saucepan. Bring to boil, stirring until sugar is dissolved. Boil 3 minutes. Remove from heat. Add remaining ingredients, mixing quickly. Beat until mixture is thick enough to drop from teaspoon onto waxed paper.

Mrs. W. T. Gore, Aztec, N.M.

GLAZED NUTS

1 cup brown sugar
1-1/2 cups white sugar
1/2 cup sour cream
1 teaspoon vanilla
2 cups whole pecan halves *or* walnut halves

Combine both sugars and sour cream. Cook over medium heat until sugar is dissolved. While stirring cook to 238 degrees exactly on a candy thermometer. Remove from heat. Add vanilla and nuts. Turn onto waxed paper; separate with fork. Allow to dry before serving.

Brenda Peery, Tannersville, Va.

PINEAPPLE PENUCHE

1 cup white sugar
1/2 cup light brown sugar
1/4 cup heavy cream
1/2 cup well-drained crushed pineapple
1 tablespoon butter (no substitutes)
1 teaspoon vanilla
1/2 cup chopped pecans

Place butter, sugars, cream and pineapple in large stainless steel or enamel kettle. Bring to a boil over medium heat, stirring constantly. Boil to soft ball stage. Remove from heat and beat hard with wooden spoon. Add vanilla and nuts and beat well, until mixture is getting quite thick. Pour out onto buttered platter, spreading if needed, to edges. Allow to cool. Cut with sharp knife into bite-sized pieces.

Pearle Goodwin, South Ryegate, Vt.

FESTIVE MINTS

Makes about 9 dozen

1 1-pound package confectioners' sugar
1/2 cup (1 stick) margarine, softened
2 tablespoons evaporated milk
4-5 drops peppermint extract
Few drops food coloring

Combine all ingredients in a large bowl; beat at high speed until well-blended. Knead until smooth. Shape the mints in rubber candy molds. Place on cookie sheets which have been covered with paper towels and cover mints with additional layer of paper towels. Leave overnight to harden.

PEANUT BUTTER FUDGE

3 cups granulated or brown sugar
1/2 cup milk
2 tablespoons margarine
3 tablespoons marshmallow fluff
3 tablespoons peanut butter
1 teaspoon vanilla

Bring sugar, milk, and margarine to a boil; let boil for 3 minutes. Then take off stove; add marshmallow fluff, peanut butter, and vanilla. Beat with spoon for a few minutes. Poor into greased pan. Let set; cut into squares.

Zenana Warren, Bloomville, Ohio

PEANUT CREAM CANDY

Makes about 4 dozen

1 cup firmly-packed brown sugar
1 cup granulated sugar
1 cup dairy sour cream
Dash salt
1 cup creamy peanut butter
1 teaspoon vanilla

Combine sugars, sour cream and salt in saucepan and mix well. Cook over medium heat, stirring until mixture reaches soft ball stage (236 degrees) or until small amount forms a soft ball when dropped in cold water. Cool to lukewarm. Stir in peanut butter and vanilla. Mix well. Drop by teaspoonfuls onto greased baking sheets. Cool.

Judy Haffner, Auke Bay, Alaska

MARTHA WASHINGTON FUDGE

1 cup butter, softened
2 pounds confectioners' sugar
1 (14-ounce) can sweetened condensed milk
1 (7-ounce) can flaked coconut
2 cups chopped nuts
1 pound semisweet chocolate bits
4 ounces melted paraffin
1 teaspoon vanilla extract

Beat butter until creamy. Gradually mix in sugar, then blend in milk. Stir in coconut and nuts. Let stand for a while and then shape into balls. Melt chocolate and paraffin in top of double boiler over simmering water, just until smooth. Stir in vanilla. Keep warm. One by one, spear coconut balls on a toothpick and dip into chocolate mixture. Place on waxed-paper-covered baking sheet until coating hardens.

Store in airtight container.

Mrs. J.B. Blass, Richmond, Va.

PEANUT BUTTER BARK CLUSTERS

1-1/2 pounds almond bark
1-1/2 cups peanut butter
1-1/2 cups mini marshmallows
2 cups Rice Krispies
1-1/2 cups peanuts

Melt bark and add peanut butter; stir and set aside. Mix marshmallows, cereal and nuts and pour bark mixture over, stirring until well coated. Drop by teaspoons on waxed paper and cool.

A. M. Everett, Stoughton, Wis.

FIESTA FUDGE

Yield: 3 pounds

2-1/2 cups sugar
3/4 cup margarine
2/3 cup evaporated milk
1/2 teaspoon salt
1-1/2 cups peanut butter
1 jar (7 ounces) marshmallow creme
1 teaspoon vanilla
1-1/2 cups plain M & M candies

Combine sugar, margarine, milk, and salt in saucepan. Bring to full rolling boil over high heat, stirring constantly. Continue boiling over medium heat for 5 minutes, stirring constantly.

Remove from heat. Stir in peanut butter until melted. Stir in marshmallow creme and vanilla until well blended. Fold in candies and immediately spread in 13x9-inch pan. Cool at room temperature.

Melba Bellefeuille, Libertyville, Ill.

HOMEMADE CHOCOLATES

1 cup sweetened condensed milk
1/4 pound soft margarine
2-1/2 pounds powdered sugar
Flavoring to taste (such as: vanilla, rum, lemon, etc.)
12 ounces semi-sweet chocolate bits
4 ounces sweet or unsweetened chocolate
1/2 block paraffin wax
Toothpicks

Blend well sweetened condensed milk, margarine, sugar and flavoring. Shape into tiny balls; chill or freeze.

In double boiler, blend semi-sweet chocolate, sweet or unsweetened chocolate and wax. Blend well.

Impale each candy with a toothpick and dip quickly into chocolate, push from toothpick onto waxed paper and dribble a bit of chocolate over hole.

Agnes Russell, Concord, N.H.

BROWN SUGAR CANDY

Makes 1½ pounds

2	cups pecans (small or broken pieces)
½	cup butter
⅔	cup firmly packed brown sugar
1	(14-ounce) can sweetened condensed milk
1	teaspoon vanilla

Place pecans on large glass plate and microwave on HIGH (100 percent) power for 8 minutes, stirring every 2 minutes. Set aside. In an 8-cup measure, microwave butter on HIGH for 1 minute. Stir in brown sugar and milk until blended. Microwave on HIGH 7 minutes, stirring every 2 minutes. Beat with wooden spoon until stiff, about 5 minutes. Stir in vanilla and roasted pecans. Spread in lightly buttered 8-inch square glass dish. Chill until firm. Cut into squares.

Jen Lien, Stoughton, Wis.

WHITE CHOCOLATE CREAM FUDGE

Makes 6 dozen pieces

3 cups sugar
1 cup evaporated milk
¾ stick butter
1 (1-pint) jar marshmallow creme
12 ounces white chocolate, cut in small pieces
1 cup chopped pecans
1 (4-ounce) jar candied cherries

Bring sugar, milk and butter to a boil over low heat, stirring constantly. Cook to 237 degrees. Remove from heat; add marshmallow creme, white chocolate, nuts and cherries. Stir until marshmallow creme and chocolate are melted. Pour into a 13 x 9 x 2-inch buttered baking dish. Cool before cutting.

Joy B. Shamway, Freeport, Ill.

ORANGE PUFFS

Makes 4 dozen candies

2 3/4 cups sugar
1/2 cup orange juice
1/2 cup water
1 tablespoon grated orange rind
1/2 teaspoon grated lemon rind
2 egg whites, stiffly beaten
1/8 teaspoon salt

Combine sugar, orange juice, water, orange and lemon rinds. Stir over low heat until sugar dissolves. Cook to light crack stage (260 degrees on a candy thermometer). Gradually pour syrup over egg whites, beating constantly until mixture holds shape. Add salt. Drop from teaspoon onto waxed paper.

Blanche Towner

VANILLA CREAMS

2 cups white sugar
2 tablespoons butter
1/4 teaspoon cream of tartar
1 cup undiluted canned milk
1-1/2 teaspoons vanilla
1 cup finely chopped walnuts

Combine sugar and cream of tartar and stir until no lumps remain. Add butter and milk and place in large enamel kettle. Bring to boil, stirring enough to keep mixture from sticking to kettle. Using candy thermometer, cook to medium soft ball stage. Remove from heat and beat in vanilla. Beat vigorously until quite thick. Fold in nuts. Drop by teaspoonfuls onto buttered cookie sheet. Let harden.

Pearle Goodwin, South Ryegate, Vt.

PROFESSIONAL PEANUT BRITTLE

1-1/2 cups white sugar
1/2 cup light brown sugar
1 cup light Karo syrup
3 cups raw Spanish peanuts
1/2 teaspoon soda
Dash salt
1 teaspoon vanilla

Blend together in saucepan sugar, brown sugar and light syrup. Boil to 236 degrees, using candy thermometer. Add peanuts and cook to 300 degrees. Remove from heat. Mix soda, salt and vanilla together, add to mixture and stir well. Pour out onto marble slab, stretch out into thin sheet or use two lightly buttered cookie sheets. When cold, break into pieces and store in tight container.

This is a perfect peanut brittle and you'll never have a failure. Keeps for a long period with no quality loss.

Fay Duman, Eugene, Ore.

QUICK FUDGE SQUARES

2 squares (2 ounces) unsweetened chocolate
1/3 cup butter
2/3 cup sugar
1/4 cup light corn syrup
1/2 teaspoon salt
1 1/2 teaspoons vanilla extract
1/2 cup chopped nuts
2 cups uncooked oats

Melt chocolate and butter in top of double boiler over boiling water. Add remaining ingredients, except nuts and blend thoroughly.

Pack firmly into a greased 8-inch square pan. Sprinkle chopped nuts on top. Bake at 425 degrees for 12 minutes. When cool, turn out of pan and cut into small squares.

Lou Roehr, Hammond, Ind.

PENUCHE FUDGE

4 tablespoons butter
1-1/2 cups half-and-half
2 cups brown sugar
3 cups white sugar
2 teaspoons vanilla
1-1/2 cups walnuts, chopped

Melt butter, making sure it coats bottom and sides of saucepan. Pour half-and-half into pan; bring to boil. Add brown and white sugar and stir until dissolved. Stirring constantly, cook until mixture reaches soft ball stage. Remove from heat. Place pan in two inches of cold water. Add vanilla and walnuts. Beat with wooden spoon until thick. Pour into buttered fudge pan. Score while warm. Cut into squares when fully cooled.

Agnes Russell, Concord, N.H.

PECAN CANDY CLUSTERS

Makes about 24

1/2 cup sugar
1/2 cup evaporated milk
1 tablespoon corn syrup
1 cup semisweet chocolate chips
1 cup diced pecans
1/2 teaspoon vanilla

Put sugar, milk and syrup in a 2-quart pot. Stir over medium heat until bubbly all over top. Boil and stir 2 minutes more. Remove from heat. Stir in chocolate chips and vanilla, until chips are melted. Add nuts. Mix well. Drop by teaspoonsful onto waxed paper. Chill to set.

Kathrine Van Boxtel, Downey, Calif.

FUDGE NOUGATS

Makes 40 pieces

2 cups sugar
1/2 cup butter
1 cup evaporated milk
1 cup semisweet chocolate chips
3/4 cup all-purpose flour
1 cup finely crushed graham
   crackers
3/4 cup chopped nuts
1 teaspoon vanilla

Combine sugar, butter, and evaporated milk in a saucepan. Bring to a full rolling boil, stirring constantly. Boil for 10 minutes, stirring occasionally. Stir in chocolate chips, flour, crumbs, nuts and vanilla. Spread in a well-greased 12x8- or 12x9-inch pan. Cool. Cut into squares.

**Mrs. Dorothy Trunnels
Angels Camp, Calif.**

SEA FOAM CANDY

2   cups sugar
2   cups water
⅛   teaspoon salt
¼   teaspoon cream of
    tartar
2   egg whites, stiffly
    beaten
1   teaspoon vanilla
    Food coloring (optional)

Combine first 4 ingredients. Cover and boil for 5 minutes. Uncover and boil, without stirring, to soft-ball stage. Pour slowly over 2 stiffly beaten egg whites, mixing as you pour. (You may need help with this.)

Add 1 teaspoon vanilla and beat until it holds shape when dropped from a spoon. Add food coloring, if you like. Drop by tablespoon onto waxed paper placed on a cookie sheet.

Jean Baker, Chula Vista, Calif.

BABY RUTH
SQUARES

1   cup corn syrup

1   cup sugar
1½   cups salted peanuts
6   cups Rice Krispies
1   heaping cup peanut
     butter

Topping:
1   cup sugar
¼   cup milk
1   cup chocolate chips
2   tablespoons butter

Cook corn syrup and sugar until it boils. Remove from heat and stir in peanut butter, peanuts and cereal. Press into 9 x 13-inch pan. Cook topping ingredients, except chocolate chips, to full boil. Remove from heat and stir in chips. Spread on top of cereal mixture. Cut into small squares.

Cheryl Santefort, Thornton, Ill.

BEST
PEANUT BUTTER
BALLS

Makes 3 dozen

1   cup peanut butter
¼   cup margarine
2¼   cups sifted confection-
     ers' sugar
1½   cups rice cereal
6   ounces semisweet
     chocolate bits
2   tablespoons butter

Melt peanut butter and margarine over low heat, stirring to prevent scorching. Mix together sugar and cereal in a large bowl. Add peanut butter mixture and mix well. Form into small balls with a teaspoon or fingers. Place in freezer. Melt chocolate with butter in a double boiler. Dip frozen balls into chocolate to cover and place on waxed paper. Store in refrigerator.

Lucy Dowd, Sequim, Wash.

CHOCOLATE-DIPPED
APRICOTS

6-ounce package semisweet
   chocolate chips
2 tablespoons shortening
8 ounces dried apricots, halved

In top of double boiler over hot water, stir chocolate and shortening until melted and smooth. Keep warm.

Insert toothpicks into apricot halves; dip in chocolate. Allow excess to drip off back into pot. Place on waxed paper and remove toothpicks.

Let dry at room temperature for about 30 minutes or until chocolate is firm. Store in refrigerator or in a cool, dry place, packed loosely between sheets of waxed paper.

MINCEMEAT
CANDIES

Makes 6 dozen

1 (9 ounce) package condensed
   mincemeat, finely crumbled
1/4 cup orange juice
1/4 cup light corn syrup
1/4 cup butter or margarine, melted
1/2 cup corn flake crumbs
1/2 cup chopped walnuts
1/2 cup finely-chopped dried apricots
1 cup finely-chopped walnuts for
   coating

In large bowl, mix all ingredients except walnuts for coating until well blended. Chill thoroughly. Shape into 1-inch balls, roll in remaining nuts. Place on wax paper- lined baking sheet. Refrigerate until firm. Store in tight container.

Melba Bellefeuille, Libertyville, Ill.

APRICOT CANDIES

3/4 cup dried apricots
1/2 cup nut meats
3/4 cup fresh coconut, grated
1 tablespoon lemon juice
1/4 teaspoon salt
1 teaspoon vanilla
1 teaspoon lemon rind, grated
1 teaspoon orange rind, grated

Wash apricots and put them in food chopper with nut meats. Add coconut, lemon juice, grated orange and lemon rind. Mix and knead well. Roll out onto sugared board to about 1/4 inch thickness. Cut in squares and roll in confectioners' sugar.

Susan Wiener, Spring Hill, Fla.

71

BUTTER MINTS

3 cups sugar
1/4 pound (1 stick) butter
1 cup hot water
Dash of salt
Few drops of mint flavoring
Few drops of food coloring

Stir sugar with butter and hot water; add salt; bring to a boil in saucepan. Cover and wait for 3 minutes. Remove lid and wash down sides of pan with a brush dipped in water. Cook without stirring to 248 degrees.

Pour candy onto a buttered slab and allow to cool. Add a few drops of flavoring and food coloring. Pull candy until it loses its gloss. Stretch into a rope and cut into pieces. Wrap individual pieces in waxed paper or plastic wrap so they do not stick together.

Store candy in an airtight can.

HOLIDAY MINTS

3 egg whites
6 cups confectioners' sugar
Red and green food coloring
1/2 teaspoon peppermint extract
1/2 teaspoon spearmint extract

Beat egg whites until stiff, adding sugar gradually. Divide candy into 2 portions. Tint half green and half red. Add peppermint extract to red mixture and spearmint extract to green mixture. Roll candy between 2 pieces of waxed paper. Cut with small round cookie cutter. Let dry overnight.

Barbara Beauregard - Smith, Northfield, S. A., Australia

WALNUT CREAMS

1-1/2 cups granulated sugar
1-1/2 cups light brown sugar
1 cup milk
1/8 teaspoon salt
1 cup walnuts, chopped
1/2 teaspoon almond extract

Put sugar and milk into large saucepan; stir until sugar is dissolved. Boil until soft ball is formed when mixture is tested in cold water. Let stand until lukewarm. Beat vigorously. When it begins to get creamy, add nuts and extract. Pour into buttered pan. When hard, cut into squares with a knife which has been dipped in boiling water.

Susan Wiener, Spring Hill, Fla.

PEPPERMINT PATTIES
Makes 80 patties

2-1/4 cups sugar
1/2 cup water
1/4 cup light corn syrup
1 egg white, stiffly beaten
4 drops peppermint oil
1 (12-ounce) package chocolate chips, melted

Combine sugar, water, and corn syrup in small saucepan; bring to gentle boil and cook, covered, for 6 minutes. Uncover and boil to 225-238 degrees on candy thermometer, without stirring. Cool until just warm, then beat with wooden spoon until mixture gets cloudy. Add beaten egg white, a little at a time. Add oil of peppermint and beat until milky white. Cool, then shape into 1-1/2-inch patties and dip in melted chocolate.

Agnes Ward, Erie, Pa.

CHOCOLATE PEANUT BARS
Makes about 2 dozen

1/2 cup light corn syrup
1/4 cup brown sugar
Dash of salt
1 cup peanut butter
1 teaspoon vanilla
2 cups crispy rice cereal
1 cup cornflakes, slightly crushed
1 6-ounce package chocolate chips
Combine corn syrup, sugar and salt in a saucepan; bring to a full boil and then stir in peanut butter. Remove from heat and stir in remaining ingre-

dients. Press into a greased 9-inch square pan. Chill for 1 hour. Cut in squares. Store in the refrigerator.

Amelia M. Brown, Pittsburgh, Penn.

TOASTED ALMOND BALLS
About 6-1/2 dozen

1 cup semi-sweet chocolate chips
1 cup butterscotch chips
3/4 cup powdered sugar
1/2 cup cultured sour cream
1-1/2 teaspoons grated orange rind
1/4 teaspoon salt
2 cups vanilla wafer crumbs
3/4 cup finely-chopped toasted almonds

Melt chocolate and butterscotch chips at low heat. Mix in sugar, sour cream, orange rind, salt and crumbs; chill. Shape into 3/4-inch balls; roll in almonds.

Barbara Beauregard - Smith, Northfield, S. A., Australia

CHOCOLATE MARSHMALLOW CREME CANDY
Makes 4-1/2 pounds

3-1/2 sticks margarine
1 (15-ounce) can evaporated milk
5 cups granulated sugar
1-pound package Hershey's kisses
1 regular-size jar marshmallow creme
1 pound pecans (optional)

Melt margarine, add sugar and milk; bring to a boil. Boil for 5 minutes. Take off heat and add Hershey's kisses, marshmallow creme, and pecans. Spread waxed paper on cookie sheets and drop mixture by teaspoonfuls onto paper.

Stacie Adamson, Gallatin, Tenn.

Casseroles
CREATIVE

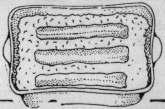

NO-FUSS SHORTCUT PAELLA
Serves 6

2 cups cooked chicken, cut into 1-inch pieces
1-1/2 cups chicken broth
10 ounces shrimp, shelled
1 (8-1/2-ounce) can peas, drained
2 cups rice
1 (3-ounce) can mushrooms, sliced and drained
1 envelope onion soup mix
1 teaspoon paprika

Combine chicken, chicken broth, shrimp, peas, rice, mushrooms, onion soup mix and paprika. Pour into 3-quart casserole; bake at 350 degrees, covered, for 1-1/4 hours until rice is tender.

Gwen Campbell, Sterling, Va.

MARDI GRAS MAGIC
Serves 6

1 pound red beans
1 pound smoked sausage, cut into bite-size pieces (kielbasa is fine)
1-2 stalks celery, chopped
1 onion, chopped
1 garlic clove, crushed
1 teaspoon sugar
1 teaspoon salt
1 bay leaf
8-10 cups water
1-1/2 cups uncooked rice (white, wild,or brown rice)

Rinse beans. In a large pot combine beans, sausage, celery, onion, garlic, sugar, salt, bay leaf, and 8-10 cups water. Bring to boil and stir frequently so mixture does not stick.

Reduce heat to low and cook, covered, until beans are tender, 1-1/2-2 hours. Add uncooked rice and cook until tender, about 15-20 minutes.

Ruby Walsh, West Chicago, Ill.

MACARONI HOT DISH
Serves 6

2 cups warm, cooked macaroni
1-1/2 cups grated cheese
1-1/2 cups bread crumbs
1 green pepper, diced
3 eggs, beaten
1 onion, diced
2 tablespoons margarine, melted
Pepper and salt to taste
1-1/2 cups milk
1 can mushroom soup

Mix all ingredients, except mushroom soup, and place in pan set in hot water. Bake at 350 degrees for 45 minutes. Cut in squares and then pour over undiluted mushroom soup which has been heated.

Suzan L. Wiener, Spring Hill, Fla.

HEARTY CASSEROLE
Serves 6–8

1 (11-ounce) can cheddar cheese soup
1 (1-pound) can julienne carrots, drained (reserve 1/3 cup liquid)
3/4 teaspoon crushed rosemary
1/4 teaspoon pepper
1 (9-1/4-ounce) can tuna, drained and flaked
1 (15-ounce) can macaroni and cheese
1/4 cup minced parsley
1 (3-1/2-ounce) can french-fried onion rings

Heat oven to 375 degrees. Mix soup with reserved liquid from carrots. Stir in rosemary and pepper. Spread tuna in oblong baking dish, 11-1/2 x 7-1/2 x 1-1/2-inch. Layer with macaroni and cheese, carrots and parsley. Pour cheese soup mixture over layers. Bake, uncovered, for 30–35 minutes, or until bubbly. Top with onion rings and bake 5 minutes longer.

Suzan L. Wiener, Spring Hill, Fla.

GRITS CASSEROLE
Serves 10-12

1 pound sausage
1/2 cup chopped green peppers
1 cup chopped onion
1 cup chopped celery
1 cup grits, uncooked
4 cups water
1 teaspoon salt
1 can cream of chicken soup
1 cup grated cheese

Preheat oven to 375 degrees. Brown sausage. Add peppers, onion, celery, and sauté. Cook grits in 4 cups water with 1 teaspoon salt. Combine cooked grits with sausage, peppers, onion, and celery. Pour mixture into 2-quart buttered casserole. Spread soup on top and sprinkle with cheese. Bake 30 minutes.

Renee Wells, Columbia, S.C.

RANCHO SAUSAGE SUPPER
Serves 6

1	pound pork sausage
1	cup chopped onions
1	green pepper, chopped
2	cups stewed tomatoes
2	cups dairy sour cream
1	cup uncooked elbow macaroni
1	teaspoon chili powder
1	teaspoon salt
1	tablespoon sugar

In a large skillet fry sausage until pink color disappears. Drain. Add onions and green pepper; cook slowly for 5 minutes. Stir in tomatoes, sour cream, macaroni, chili powder, salt and sugar. Cover. Simmer 30 minutes, stirring frequently, until macaroni is done. Serve hot.

Serve with a green salad and hard rolls.

Betty M. Burt, Winnemucca, Nev.

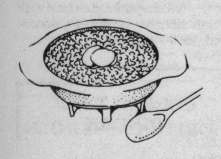

BEEF-ONION RING CASSEROLE
Serves 4–6

1-1/2–2 pounds ground chuck
Salt and pepper
1 can condensed cheddar cheese soup
1 can condensed cream of mushroom soup
1 package frozen Tater Tots
1 package frozen onion rings

Press raw meat into bottom of casserole; season with salt and pep-per. Combine the 2 soups and spread half over meat. Add Tater Tots. Pour rest of soup over Tater Tots. Top with onion rings. If canned onion rings are used, stir them into last half of soup mixture. Bake at 350 degrees for 1–1-1/2 hours.

Leota Baxter, Ingalls, Kan.

JIFFY MINESTRONE
Serves 8

4	cups coarsely chopped cabbage (½ medium-size head)
1	medium onion, coarsely chopped
¼	cup parsley, chopped
1	clove garlic, chopped
1	teaspoon salt
1	teaspoon oregano
¼	teaspoon pepper
3	tablespoons oil
5	cups beef broth
1	(16-ounce) can toma-toes *or* 2 cups chopped fresh
¼	pound spaghetti, broken up
1	medium zucchini, sliced
1	(16-ounce) can red kidney beans

In Dutch oven, over medium heat, sauté cabbage, onion, parsley, garlic, salt, oregano and pepper in oil, stir-ring often, 5 minutes, or until cabbage is crisp-tender. Add broth and toma-toes; bring to boil. Stir in spaghetti, zucchini and beans. Cook, stirring oc-casionally, for 10 minutes, or until spaghetti is of desired doneness. (200 calories per serving)

Nadia Boreiko, Dearborn, Mich.

ZUCCHINI AND CHICKEN SKILLET

2	medium zucchini, sliced
2	tablespoons shortening
½	cup tomatoes, drained
2	pounds chicken
1	can cream of celery soup
1	teaspoon paprika
1	teaspoon basil
	Salt and pepper to taste

In skillet brown chicken in shorten-ing. Pour off excess fat. Add soup, tomatoes and seasonings. Cover. Cook on low heat for 30 minutes. Add zuc-chini. Cook about 15 minutes longer.

Shella Symonowicz, Loganville, Pa.

SMOKED SAUSAGE AND SAUERKRAUT
Serves 4

1 pound smoked sausage
1 can sauerkraut
1 tablespoon cooking oil
1/2 pint water
1 potato, grated
1 carrot, grated
Pinch salt
1/3 cup sugar
2 onions, chopped

Heat oil in skillet and fry chopped onions; add sauerkraut and simmer for 2 minutes. Add water and sau-sage; cook until done. Add grated potato, salt, sugar, and grated carrot. Cook 4-5 additional minutes.

Lucy Dowd, Sequim, Wash.

PIZZA RICE PIE
Serves 4-5

2-2/3 cups cooked rice
1/3 cup minced onion
2 eggs, beaten
2 tablespoons melted butter or
    margarine
1 (8-ounce) can tomato sauce with
    cheese
1/4 teaspoon oregano
1/4 teaspoon basil
1 cup shredded mozzarella cheese
1 (4-1/2-ounce) package sliced
    pepperoni or salami
1/2 cup sliced stuffed olives

Mix together rice, onion, eggs, and melted butter. Line a 12-inch pizza pan with rice mixture and bake 12 minutes at 350 degrees, or until set. Spread tomato sauce with cheese over rice crust. Sprinkle with spices and cheese. Top with pepperoni and olives. Bake at 350 degrees for 20-25 minutes. After removing from oven, allow to stand a few minutes before serving.

Sharon McClatchey, Muskogee, Okla.

SAUCY PIZZA SURPRISE
Serves 6

3 cups cooked rice
2 cups (8 ounces)
    cheese, shredded
½ teaspoon basil
2 eggs, beaten
2 (8-ounce) cans tomato
    sauce
½ teaspoon oregano
½ teaspoon garlic powder

Combine rice, eggs and 1 cup cheese. Press firmly into 2 (9-inch) pans. Spread evenly. Bake at 450 degrees for 20 minutes. Combine tomato sauce and seasonings. Spread evenly over rice crust. Top with remaining cheese. Bake 10 minutes longer. *Note:* Other ingredients, such as cooked sausage, green pepper, mushrooms, etc., may be added before baking.

This pizza is great. A good way to use leftover rice, which makes a crust like deep-dish.

Leota L. Arnold, Vincennes, Ind.

CHICKEN-BROCCOLI BAKE
Serves 4–5

1 (10-ounce) package broccoli cuts
2 cups chopped, cooked chicken
4 ounces medium noodles
1 cup sour cream
1 (10 3/4-ounce) can cream of
    chicken soup
2 tablespoons chopped pimiento
1 tablespoon minced onion
1 teaspoon salt
1/2 teaspoon Worcestershire sauce
1 tablespoon melted butter
1/2 cup soft bread crumbs
1 cup grated Swiss cheese

Prepare broccoli as directed on package; drain. Cook noodles and drain. Combine chicken, sour cream, soup, pimiento, onion, salt and Worcestershire sauce. Add butter to bread crumbs and mix well. Place noodles in greased, shallow 2-quart baking dish. Sprinkle with 1/3 of the cheese. Add broccoli. Sprinkle with 1/2 of the remaining cheese. Pour on the chicken mixture. Sprinkle with rest of cheese, and then with bread crumbs. Bake at 350 degrees for 1 hour.

Pauline Dean, Uxbridge, Mass.

BEEFY CASSEROLE
Serves 4

1 large eggplant
1 medium onion, chopped
2 tablespoons butter
1 pound ground beef
Salt and pepper to taste
1 bay leaf

Peel eggplant and cut into slices 1 or 1 1/2 inches thick. Cook in boiling, salted water for 10–15 minutes, or just until tender. Drain. Sauté onion in butter until soft; add beef and seasonings. Cook until meat is nicely browned. Place slices of eggplant in a greased baking dish. Remove bay leaf and add meat/onion mixture to eggplant. Cover with thin slices of cheese. Bake at 400 degrees for 20 minutes, or until cheese is melted.

Leota Baxter, Ingalls, Kan.

TOWN AND COUNTRY CASSEROLE

1 package French's Real Cheese
    Scalloped Potatoes
1 pound smoked kielbasa or Polish
    sausage, cut in 1/4-inch slices
1 cup thinly sliced carrots
1 tablespoon freeze-dried chives
1 cup soft bread crumbs
1 tablespoon butter or margarine
1 tablespoon parsley flakes

Follow microwave method on package, except *increase* water to 3 cups and add carrots; microwave, covered, for 15 minutes. Add seasoning mix, milk, sausage, and chives. Microwave, covered, for 3-5 minutes. Combine crumbs, butter and parsley flakes; sprinkle casserole with crumb mixture; microwave, uncovered, for 5-7 minutes.

CORNED BEEF QUICHE

1 (9-inch) pie shell, unbaked
1 (15-ounce) can corned beef hash
1 small onion, finely shredded
1 cup Swiss cheese, shredded
2 teaspoons flour
1/4 teaspoon salt
Dash allspice
2 eggs, slightly beaten
1-1/4 cups milk

Pre-bake pie shell at 375 degrees for 7 minutes; remove from oven; set aside. Reduce oven temperature to 325 degrees. Crumble corned beef hash into pie shell; sprinkle onion over meat; top with Swiss cheese. Combine remaining ingredients; pour over hash and cheese. Bake 35-40 minutes, or until set. Cool 20 minutes before serving.

Gwen Campbell, Sterling, Va.

PORK CHOP CASSEROLE
Serves 4

6 pork chops
1 teaspoon salt
1/8 teaspoon pepper
4 medium apples, peeled and sliced
1 cup water
4 medium sweet potatoes, peeled and sliced
1 teaspoon Worcestershire sauce
1 medium onion, chopped

Wipe chops; brown them in a little fat in frying pan. Place chops in a large casserole; sprinkle with half the salt and pepper. Place apples and sweet potatoes in layers on chops and sprinkle with remaining salt and pepper. Sauté onion in the same frying pan where chops were browned. Add water and Worcestershire sauce. Mix and pour over chops, apples and potatoes. Cover and bake 1-1/2 hours in a moderate 375-degree oven.

Lucy Dowd, Sequim, Wash.

LEMON DILLED BEEF

2 1/2 pounds stewing beef
1/2 cup butter
2 1/2 cups chopped celery
1 1/2 cups chopped onion
1 cup chopped green pepper
1/3 cup lemon juice
2 cups beef stock
3 cloves garlic, finely chopped
1 1/2 teaspoons dill weed
Salt to taste
1 1/2 cups sour cream
3 tablespoons butter, softened
3 tablespoons flour
1 medium package noodles

Lightly brown beef in butter. Add vegetables, liquid and seasoning. Cover and simmer on low for 2 hours. Add sour cream and simmer, uncovered, for 30 minutes. Combine flour and butter; add by spoonfuls to bubbling mixture. Simmer 10 minutes and serve on prepared noodles.

Patricia Anderson, Fremont, Neb.

DELI REUBEN CASSEROLE
Serves 6.

3 cups sauerkraut, drained
1-1/2 cups tomatoes, drained
2 tablespoons Thousand Island dressing
2 tablespoons butter or margarine
3 packages corned beef, shredded
1 (10-ounce) can refrigerated flaky biscuits
3 rye crackers, crushed
1/4 teaspoon caraway seeds

Spread sauerkraut in a 13x9x2-inch baking dish; arrange tomatoes on top; spread with dressing; dot with butter. Place shredded corned beef and cheese over all. Separate each biscuit into halves; arrange over casserole. Sprinkle with the rye crackers and caraway seeds. Bake at 350 degrees, 12 minutes, or until biscuits are flaky and golden.

Gwen Campbell, Sterling, Va.

HAM & NOODLE BAKE

2 cups cooked ham, cubed
1/4 cup onion, chopped
1/8 teaspoon thyme leaves, crushed
2 tablespoons margarine
1 (10-3/4-ounce) can cream of chicken soup
3/4 cup water
2 cups cooked noodles (5 ounces)
1 cup canned, cut green beans, drained
1/2 cup shredded cheddar cheese

In saucepan, brown ham, cook onion with thyme in margarine until tender. Stir in remaining ingredients, except cheese. Pour into 2-quart casserole. Bake at 350 degrees for 30 minutes. Top with cheese; bake until cheese melts, 8 minutes longer. If refrigerated before cooking, bake 45 minutes longer.

This is made quickly and is nice for a company dinner.

Mrs. Albert Foley, Lemoyne, Pa.

CHICKEN AND BROCCOLI RICE CASSEROLE
Serves 6

1/2 cup chopped onions
1/2 cup sliced mushrooms
1 tablespoon butter
2 cups hot, cooked rice
2 cups cubed chicken breast
2 cups chopped, fresh broccoli (steamed) or
1 (10-ounce) package frozen broccoli, thawed
1 (10-3/4-ounce) can cream of mushroom soup, condensed
1/2 cup (2 ounces) shredded cheddar cheese

Simmer onions and mushrooms in large skillet with butter until tender. Stir in rice, chicken, broccoli, and soup. Pour into buttered 1-1/2-quart baking dish. Top with cheese. Bake at 350 degrees for 20-25 minutes.

My husband is fussy about casseroles, but he *loves* this one.

Dorothy Sorenson, Muskego, Wis.

CHICKEN CASSEROLE SUPREME

3 cups cooked chicken, deboned
1 (6-ounce) package Uncle Ben's rice, cooked
1 can cream of celery soup, undiluted
1 can cream of chicken soup, undiluted
1 can French-style green beans, drained
1 medium jar pimientos, sliced
1 cup mayonnaise
1 small can water chestnuts. sliced
Salt and pepper to taste

Mix all ingredients together and pour into 3-quart casserole. Bake 25–30 minutes at 350 degrees.

Mrs. A. Curtis, Rector, Ark.

LAZY BEEF CASSEROLE
Serves 4

1 pound lean beef chuck, cut into 1-1/2-inch cubes
1/2 cup red wine
1 (10-1/2-ounce) can consomme, undiluted
1/4 cup all-purpose flour
Freshly ground black pepper, to taste
1 medium onion, chopped
1/4 cup fine dry bread crumbs
1/4 teaspoon rosemary

Put meat in a casserole with the wine, consomme, pepper, rosemary, and onion. Mix flour and bread crumbs and stir into the liquid. Cover and bake at 300 degrees, about 3 hours. Serve with rice or noodles. (206 calories per serving)

Ronnie J. Heroux, Uxbridge, Mass.

EASY BEEF GOULASH
Serves 4

1 to 2 tablespoons vegetable oil
1 pound ground beef (chuck)
3 cups uncooked medium egg noodles
2 cups water
1 (8-ounce) can tomato sauce
1 envelope dry onion soup mix

Heat oil in a medium-size skillet over medium heat. Add ground beef and cook until lightly browned, stirring occasionally with a fork to break up meat. Drain off any excess fat. Sprinkle uncooked noodles over meat. Combine water, tomato sauce, and onion soup mix. Pour over noodles in skillet. Do not stir. Cover and bring to a boil. Reduce heat to moderately low and simmer about 30 minutes, or until noodles are tender. Stir and serve.
Note: You may have to add a small amount of water if the noodles seem to be sticking. This is very easy and quick for those hectic days.

Doris L. Rayman, Somerset, Pa.

GERMAN POTATO CASSEROLE

6 medium-size potatoes, peeled and sliced
1 pound hot pork sausage, cooked and drained
8 ounces sour cream
2 teaspoons dry onion soup mix
2 teaspoons lemon juice
1 can cream of mushroom soup
2 teaspoons Dijon mustard
1 can sauerkraut, washed and drained
1 cup buttered bread crumbs
Salt and pepper to taste

Peel, wash, and slice potatoes. Boil in salted water until tender. Mix sour cream, dry onion soup mix, mushroom soup, lemon juice, and mustard. Heat sauerkraut in 2 tablespoons sausage drippings. Alternate layers of potatoes, cream mixture, and sauerkraut. Put bread crumbs on top and bake in 350-degree oven until hot and bubbly, about 20-25 minutes.

Ruby Walsh, West Chicago, Ill.

INDIAN CASSEROLE

1 can hominy, drained
1 pound ground beef
1/2 cup chopped onion
1/2 cup chopped green pepper
1-3/4 cups canned tomatoes
1/2 teaspoon salt
1/4 teaspoon pepper
1 cup grated cheese

Brown beef, salt, onions, and green pepper. Add tomatoes and hominy. Pour into buttered casserole and bake at 350 degrees for 40 minutes. Remove from oven and sprinkle cheese on top. Return to oven and bake 15 minutes.

Note: I tried this recipe and cooked it in an electric skillet. I cooked it on low until thick, then placed slices of cheese over the top and put lid of skillet on until cheese melted. I served it with French bread and a cottage cheese and peach salad.

Corena J. Bennington, Whitestown, Ind.

MOCK OYSTER CASSEROLE
Serves 6

1 large eggplant
1 cup cracker crumbs (approx. 25 soda crackers, crushed)
2 eggs
1/2 cup milk
3 tablespoons butter
1/4 cup chopped celery
1/4 cup chopped green pepper
1/4 cup chopped onion
1 (11 ounce) can mushroom soup
Tabasco sauce to taste

Peel eggplant and cut into cubes. Boil eggplant for 3 minutes in salt water; set aside. Place 1/3 of the crushed crumbs in a buttered 2 quart casserole dish; add 1/2 the eggplant. Repeat layering the cracker crumbs and eggplant. Beat eggs slightly, add 1/2 cup milk, mushroom soup, peppers, onions, celery and Tabasco sauce, mixing well. Pour slowly over eggplant mixture. Dot with butter. Cover and bake at 375 degrees for 30 minutes. Uncover and add more milk if needed. Bake 15 minutes more uncovered, until golden brown.

Rose McBride, Kent, OH

RICE OLÉ
Serves 3-4

2 slices bacon
1/3 cup chopped onion
1/4 cup finely chopped green pepper
1-1/2 cups water
2 envelopes Lipton Tomato Cup-a-Soup
1 cup uncooked instant rice
1/2 teaspoon garlic salt

In skillet cook bacon until crisp; drain, reserving 2 tablespoons drippings. Crumble bacon; set aside. Add onion and green pepper to skillet; cook until tender. Add water and bring to boil. Stir in Cup-a-Soup, uncooked rice, garlic salt, and crumbled bacon; cover and remove from heat. Let stand for 5 minutes.
Agnes Ward, Erie, Pa.

YELLOW SQUASH CASSEROLE

6-8 Servings

2 pounds yellow squash, sliced (6 cups)
1/4 cup chopped onion
1 can cream of chicken soup
1 cup sour cream
1 cup shredded carrots
1 (8-ounce) package herb-seasoned stuffing mix
1/2 cup melted margarine

Cook squash and onion in boiling, salted water for 5 minutes; drain. Mix soup and sour cream. Stir in the carrots; fold in squash and onion. Combine stuffing mix and margarine. Spread half stuffing mixture in lightly buttered 12 x 7-1/2-inch baking dish; spoon vegetable mixture over stuffing. Sprinkle remaining stuffing mixture over vegetables. Bake in preheated 350 degree oven for 25-30 minutes, until heated thoroughly.

Iona Hodges, Springdale, Ark.

PINTO BEAN CASSEROLE

Serves 4-6

1 to 1-1/2 pounds ground beef
1/2 cup chopped onion
1/2 cup chopped green pepper
1 clove garlic, minced
1 (15-ounce) can tomato sauce
2 teaspoons chili powder
1 teaspoon salt
1 cup cooked rice
1 (15-ounce) can pinto beans
1-1/2 cups grated Cheddar cheese

Brown beef, onion, green pepper, and garlic. Blend in tomato sauce, chili powder, and salt. In greased 2-quart casserole, layer part of meat sauce, beans, half of cheese, and remainder of meat sauce. Top with other half cheese. Bake 350 degrees for 15-20 minutes. Let stand a few minutes before serving.

Rolls or garlic toast and salad with this casserole make a complete meal.

Mrs. Hobert Howell, Waco, TX

YAM AND CRANBERRY CASSEROLE

Serves 8

1 (40 ounce) can yams, drained
3 cups fresh, whole cranberries
1-1/2 cups sugar
1 small orange, sliced
1/2 cup pecan halves
1/4 cup orange juice or brandy
3/4 teaspoon cinnamon
1/4 teaspoon nutmeg
1/4 teaspoon mace

Combine cranberries, sugar, orange slices, pecans, orange juice, and spices in 2-quart casserole. Bake uncovered at 375 degrees for 30 minutes. Stir yams into cranberry mixture. Bake until heated through—about 15 minutes.

Nice to serve with your holiday turkey.

Helen Weissinger, Levittown, Pa.

CABBAGE CASSEROLE

1 medium onion, chopped
3 tablespoons butter
1/2 pound ground beef
1 teaspoon salt
1/8 teaspoon pepper
6 cups chopped cabbage
1 can tomato soup

Sauté meat and onion. Place 3 cups cabbage in 2 quart casserole; cover with meat mixture; top with remaining cabbage. Pour soup over top. Bake 350 degrees for 1 hour.

Sandy Marqueling, Fort Wayne, Ind.

GREEN TOMATO CASSEROLE

4 large green tomatoes, sliced
Salt and pepper to taste
3/4 cup Cheddar cheese, grated
1 tablespoon butter

Preheat oven to 400 degrees. Butter casserole dish. Lay 1/3 of tomato slices on bottom. Sprinkle with salt and pepper and 1/4 cup of cheese. Repeat with remaining slices. Top with 1/2 cup of cheese and dot with butter. Bake covered 40 to 60 minutes. Brown under broiler if desired.

This is a simple way to use green tomatoes and it tastes great.

Lillian Smith, Montreal, Canada

ROUND-UP BEAN CASSEROLE

1 pound ground beef
1 can red (kidney) beans
1 can butter beans
1 can pork and beans
1/2 cup catsup
3/4 cup brown sugar
1 teaspoon mustard
2 tablespoons vinegar
Chopped onion and bell pepper (optional)

Brown beef; season with salt and pepper. (Add onion and bell pepper at this time.) Combine with remaining ingredients. Put into casserole dish. Bake about 1 hour at 350 degrees.

This is also good cooked in a slow pot. It is simple to prepare, and with a salad makes a quick meal.

Mavis McBride, Conway, AR

SPINACH CASSEROLE

1 package frozen spinach
1 (8 ounce) package cream cheese
1 can cream of mushroom soup
1 can French onion rings
6 tablespoons butter or margarine
Cracker crumbs

Cook spinach according to package directions. Heat soup and cream cheese to soften. Mix with spinach; add onion rings. Pour into casserole. Melt butter; add enough cracker crumbs to absorb butter. Spread buttered crumbs on top and bake at 350 degrees for 20 minutes.

G. G. Crabtree, Lansing, MI

MACARONI LOAF

2 cups cooked macaroni
1/2 cup bread crumbs
1/2 cup grated cheese
3 tablespoons butter
1/2 tablespoon chopped parsley
1/2 tablespoon chopped onion
1/2 teaspoon salt
1/2 cup milk
1 egg, beaten

Place a layer of cooked macaroni into a greased baking dish. Sprinkle bread crumbs, grated cheese, parsley, onions, salt, and butter between each layer. Repeat until all ingredients are used. Pour egg and milk over mixture. Bake in 350 degree oven for 30 minutes or until it is set.

Joy B. Shamway, Freeport, IL

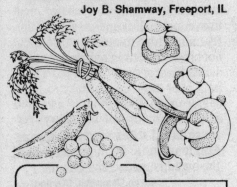

ORIENTAL RICE CASSEROLE

6-8 servings

1 pound ground beef
1 cup chopped celery
1 cup chopped onions
4 ounce can mushrooms
8 ounce can water chestnuts, sliced
8 ounce can bamboo shoots, drained
1/3 cup soy sauce
1 can cream of mushroom soup
2 beef bouillon cubes
2 cups hot water
3/4 cup rice

Brown beef, celery and onions. Drain off excess fat. Mix in mushrooms, water chestnuts, bamboo shoots and soy sauce. Dissolve bouillon cubes in hot water, stir in mushroom soup. Add to beef mixture. Stir in rice, place in 13 x 9 inch baking pan. Bake uncovered for 1 hour in a 350 degree oven. Delicious!

Sharon Crider, Evansville, WI

TOSTADO CASSEROLE

Serves 6

1 pound ground beef
15-ounce can (2 cups) tomato sauce
1 envelope taco seasoning mix
2-1/2 cups corn chips
15-1/2 - ounce can refried beans
2 ounces (1/2 cup) shredded Cheddar cheese

In skillet, brown ground beef. Add 1-1/2 cups of tomato sauce and seasoning mix, stirring to mix well. Line bottom of 11 x 8 x 2-inch baking dish with 2 cups corn chips. Crush remaining corn chips; set aside. Spoon meat mixture over corn chips in baking dish. Combine remaining tomato sauce and refried beans; spread over ground beef mixture. Bake at 375 degrees for 25 minutes. Sprinkle with shredded cheese and crushed corn chips. Bake 5 minutes more.

Sharon Sisson, Longview, WA

POT LUCK CASSEROLE

8 ounces noodles
1-1/2 pounds hamburger
1 onion, chopped
1 teaspoon salt
Pepper
2 (8 ounce) packages cream cheese
1 cup cottage cheese
1/4 cup sour cream
1/3 cup chopped green pepper
1/3 cup chopped green onion

Cook noodles. Simmer hamburger, onion, salt, pepper and tomato sauce. Cream in blender the cottage cheese, cream cheese and sour cream. Add chopped peppers and green onions. Layer noodles, meat and cheese sauce. Top with grated cheese and bake at 350 degrees for 30-40 minutes.

Fay Duman, Eugene, OR

HAMBURGER CASSEROLE

Serves 4

1 pound lean ground beef
1 (26 1/4 ounce) can of Franco-American Spaghetti
1 medium onion, chopped
1 medium green pepper, chopped

Saute onions and green pepper in 2 tablespoons margarine until nearly done, remove from pan and drain. Saute ground beef until brown; drain grease. Add spaghetti from can. Slightly chop while mixing. Add peppers and onions. Mix well. Pour into 1-1/2 quart casserole. Bake 375 degrees for 30-45 minutes.

Optional additions:
Mushrooms, sliced
Black and or green olives, sliced
1 small can green beans

Serve with Parmesan cheese, garlic bread and tossed salad.

Mrs. Joseph Erhardt, Lake Worth, FL

HAMBURGER MACARONI CASSEROLE

2 cups macaroni
1 pound ground beef
1 can condensed tomato soup
1 can condensed mushroom soup
1 medium green pepper
1/4 cup colby cheese, cubed
1/4 cup chopped pimiento, optional
1 (3-ounce) can French fried (Durkee) onions

Cook macaroni; drain. Brown the ground beef; drain. Add soups, green pepper, pimiento, macaroni, and the ground beef. Place half the mixture in a greased 2-quart casserole. Sprinkle with half the cheese and onions. Top with remaining macaroni mixture and cheese. Bake at 350 degrees for 25 minutes. Sprinkle with remaining onions, bake 5 additional minutes.

Connie Lawhun, Brunswick, OH

CREAMY CHIPPED BEEF CASSEROLE

2 packages chipped beef
1/2 package (16-ounce) frozen hash brown's (thawed)
1 can cream of mushroom soup
1 cup evaporated milk
2 tablespoon Crisco
1 can Durkee French fried onion rings

Snip beef in bite size pieces. Brown in Crisco until edges curl; drain. Mix milk and soup. Add beef, hash brown's and 1/2 can onion rings. Place in 2-quart casserole dish; bake covered for 30 minutes in 350 degree oven. Remove lid; crumble remainder of onion rings over top. return to oven for 5 to 10 minutes.
NOTE: Also good with hamburger or leftover ham.

Audria Moylan, Keokuk, IA

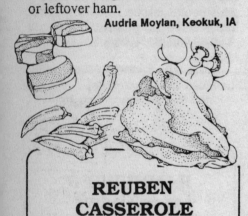

REUBEN CASSEROLE

5 cups herb seasoned croutons
1 cup hot water
1 (8-ounce) package Swiss cheese (sliced), set aside 2 slices
6-9 slices of canned corn beef
1/2 cup melted margarine
2 cups sauerkraut (drained)
1 teaspoon caraway seeds (if desired)

In a large bowl, put in croutons and margarine; toss gently. Add hot water, sauerkraut, and caraway seeds. Set aside 1 cup of mixture. Grease casserole dish. Layer crouton mixture, corn beef, and cheese slices. End up with the 1 cup of crouton mixture. Cover and bake in a 350 degree oven for 20 minutes. Top with the 2 cheese slices and bake uncovered 10 minutes until cheese melts.

Edna Mae Seelos, Niles, IL

DRESSING CASSEROLE

Serves 12

2 cups diced celery
1 clove garlic
12 cups toasted bread cubes
4 cups cubed corn bread
1/2 teaspoon pepper
4 cups turkey or chicken broth
1-1/2 cups chopped onion
1/2 cup butter
1 tablespoon sage
2 tablespoons salt
1 (13 ounce) can evaporated milk
2 eggs, slightly beaten

Cook celery, onion, and garlic in butter until light brown. Crumble bread cubes and corn bread in large bowl. Add sage, salt, and pepper. Stir celery mixture into bread cubes. Add evaporated milk, broth, and eggs. Mix well. Pour into greased 9 x 13" pan. Bake at 325 degrees for 35 to 40 minutes.

This is a good way to use up leftover corn bread. Recipe can easily be cut in half and baked in an 8 x 8" pan for smaller families. Bouillon may be substituted for the broth.

Terry Knower, Holmen, WI

NIGHT BEFORE CASSEROLE

Serves 10

2 cups macaroni, cooked
2 cups chicken, turkey, *or* tuna (if using chicken or turkey, it should be cooked)
2 cans mushroom soup
1/2 pound American cheese, cut into fine pieces
3 eggs, hard-cooked, cut into small pieces
2 cups milk
Chopped pimiento and green pepper to taste

Mix all ingredients together and refrigerate overnight or for at least 6-12 hours. Remove from refrigerator and bake for 1 hour in 350 degree oven.

Diantha Susan Hibbard, Rochester, NY

PENNYWISE CASSEROLE

1 pound lean stewing beef, cut into 1" cubes
(Lamb or pork can also be used for this recipe)
Salt and pepper
1/3 cup vegetable oil
2 medium onions, sliced
2 teaspoons honey
1/2 teaspoon ground cinnamon
1/2 teaspoon ground nutmeg
1/2 teaspoon parsley
1/2 teaspoon basil
8 ounce can tomatoes
4 slices wheat (or white) bread, buttered and quartered

Lightly salt and pepper beef. In skillet over moderate heat, fry beef cubes until browned. Transfer meat to ovenproof dish. In the same skillet, fry onions for 5 minutes until soft, but not browned. Stir in remaining ingredients (except bread); bring to a boil. Pour over meat; cover. Bake in a 350 degree oven for 1 hour. Taste and adjust seasonings, if necessary. Arrange bread slices neatly on top; return to oven for 30 minutes (or until the bread is golden and crisp).

Gwen Campbell, Sterling, VA

MEXICAN COMBO

1 pound ground beef
1 medium onion, diced
1 medium green pepper, diced
2 tablespoons chili powder
1-1/2 cups hot water
1/2 pound sharp cheese, diced
1 can red kidney beans
Salt & pepper to taste

Brown ground beef, onion, and pepper in a large skillet, using fork to break up meat. Mix chili powder and hot water; pour over meat mixture. Simmer 5 to 10 minutes. Add cheese, beans with juice, salt, and pepper. Simmer until cheese melts. Be careful not to let it burn.

Kathy Rankins, Woodford, VA

DYNASTY CASEROLE

Serves 4-6

1 (8-ounce) can water chestnuts sliced
1 (3-ounce) can chow mein noodles
1 carrot sliced
1 can bean sprouts, drained
1 can cream of mushroom soup
1 cup half-and-half cream
1 cup chopped celery (cut on the diagonal)
Dash of hot–pepper sauce and black pepper
2 tablespoons soy sauce
1-1/2 cups cooked chicken chunks or strips
1/4 cup minced green onion
3/4 cup chopped cashew nuts
Hot cooked rice

Preheat oven to 350 degrees and set aside 1/2 cup of crisp chow mein noodles. Mix all other ingredients (except rice) in a large buttered 2-quart casserole or long baking dish. Bake, uncovered, for about 30 minutes. Sprinkle remaining chow mein noodles on top of casserole and bake 10 minutes longer. Serve casserole over hot cooked rice. Pass the soy sauce at the table.

Donna Holter, West Middlesex, Pa.

BAKED BEANS WITH SAUSAGE

Serves 6

1/4 cup molasses
2 tablespoons prepared mustard
2 tablespoons vinegar
2 teaspoons Worcestershire sauce
1/4 teaspoon Tabasco sauce
2 (1-pound) cans baked beans
1 (20-ounce) can apple slices
1 pound pork sausage links, cooked

Mix all ingredients, except sausages, and place in a bean pot. Bake at 350 degrees for 40 minutes. Top with hot sausages and serve.

This is a complete meal with French or garlic bread and a crisp salad.

Mrs. H.W. Walker, Richmond, Va.

CHILI RELLENOS CASSEROLE

16 ounces Ortega whole green chilies
12 ounces Cheddar cheese, grated
12 ounces Monterey Jack cheese, grated
2 eggs, separated
2 egg whites
3 tablespoons flour
12 ounces evaporated milk
14 ounces Ortega green chili salsa

Remove seeds from chilies; flatten and drain. In a greased 9x9-inch pan, layer half the chilies and top with Cheddar cheese. Cover with rest of chilies and top with Monterey Jack cheese. Mix egg yolks, flour, and milk. Whip the 4 egg whites until stiff, then fold into yolk mixture. Pour the whole mixture over chilies and cheese. Bake in a 325 degree oven for 45 minutes. Pour green chili salsa over the top and return to oven for 30 minutes. After baking, allow to sit for 10 minutes. Cut into squares.

Mrs. S. R. Burt, Winnemucca, Nev.

SHRIMP CASSEROLE

Serves 4-5

1 can condensed mushroom soup
1/2 cup milk
2 tablespoons minced parsley
1 tablespoon instant minced onion
1/2 teaspoon salt
2-3 dashes Tabasco sauce
2-1/2 cups cooked rice
2 cups cooked shrimp
1 cup corn flakes
2 tablespoons melted butter
2 tablespoons toasted slivered almonds (optional)

Combine soup, milk, parsley, onions and seasonings. Add rice and shrimp; mix thoroughly. Pour into greased 10x6x2-inch baking dish. Slightly crush corn flakes; combine with melted butter and almonds; sprinkle over top of casserole. Bake at 375 degrees for about 20 minutes or until bubbly.

Agnes Ward, Erie, Pa.

BACON MACARONI 'N CHEESE

Serves 4-6

3/4 pound bacon, diced
1 cup onions, chopped
1 quart milk
2 teaspoons celery salt
1/2 teaspoon pepper
1/4 teaspoon Tabasco sauce
2 cups elbow macaroni
1 cup cheese, grated
1/2 cup pimiento, chopped

In large skillet, cook bacon and onion over low heat for 15 minutes. Drain drippings. Add milk, celery salt, pepper, and Tabasco. Heat to boiling; gradually add macaroni, so that milk continues to boil. Simmer, uncovered, for 20 minutes, stirring often. Add cheese and pimiento; stir until cheese melts. Serve hot.

Agnes Ward, Erie, Pa.

QUICK CHILI-RICE DINNER

Serves 4

3/4 pound ground beef
1/3 cup chopped onion
1 tablespoon chili powder
1/2 teaspoon dry mustard
1 (10-ounce) package whole-kernel corn
1 cup diced green pepper
1 (15-ounce) can tomato sauce
1/2 cup water
1 cup Minute Rice
1/2 cup shredded cheddar cheese

Brown beef and onion in skillet. Add spices, corn, green pepper, tomato sauce, and water. Cover and bring to a full boil, stirring occasionally. Stir in rice; reduce heat; cover and simmer for 5 minutes. Sprinkle with cheese.

Good for when time is limited; takes only 20 minutes to prepare.

Mrs. George Franks, Millerton, Pa.

VEGETABLE CASSEROLE

1 can French-style green beans, drained
1/2 cup chopped celery
1/2 cup chopped green pepper
1/2 cup sour cream
1 can white shoepeg corn, drained
1/2 cup chopped onion
1/4 cup grated sharp cheese
1-1/2 cups crushed cheese crackers
1 can cream of mushroom soup
1/4 cup margarine
1/2 cup sliced almonds

Mix drained beans, corn, celery, green pepper, and onion. Alternate one layer vegetables with a layer of soup, grated cheese, then sour cream. Bake 25 minutes at 350 degrees.

Melt margarine and stir in crackers and almonds. Spread this on top of casserole and cook for 10 more minutes.

Connie Matthes, Florence, SC

CORN AND SAUSAGE CASSEROLE

1 pound sausage
1/4 cup bell pepper, chopped
1 can whole kernel corn, drained
1 large can evaporated milk
2 tablespoons flour
1/4 teaspoons salt
1-1/2 cups grated cheese

Brown sausage and pepper until sausage is cooked. Drain and save 2 tablespoons sausage drippings. Add sausage to casserole dish with corn. Blend sausage drippings with flour in skillet over medium heat. Add milk and salt; simmer 2-3 minutes until thickened, stirring constantly. Pour over sausage and corn mixture; stir together. Top with grated cheese. Bake in a 350 degree oven for 25-30 minutes until bubbly.

Mary M. West, Columbia, IN

SPAGHETTI RING

1/2 pound spaghetti
2 cups hot milk
1/4 cup butter
2 cups shredded Cheddar cheese
2 cups soft bread crumbs
2 eggs, well beaten
2 tablespoons minced onions
2 tablespoons minced parsley
2 tablespoons minced pimento
1 teaspoon salt
1/4 teaspoon pepper

Cook and drain spaghetti. Combine remaining ingredients. Mix thoroughly. Pour into well-greased 10-inch ring mold. Set in pan of hot water 1-inch deep. Bake at 350 degrees until set, about 30 minutes. Unmold on hot platter. Fill center with choice of creamed chicken, creamed seafood or any combination of creamed vegetables.

Hyacinth Rizzo, Snyder, NY

HASH BROWN POTATO CASSEROLE

1 (32-ounce) package frozen hash brown potatoes
1/2 cup melted margarine
8 ounces shredded Cheddar cheese
1 cup onions, chopped
1 pint sour cream
1 can cream of chicken soup
1 teaspoon salt
1/2 teaspoon garlic salt
1 cup corn flakes
1/4 cup melted margarine

Partially defrost hash browns. Mix potatoes, 1/2 cup margarine, cheese, onions, sour cream, soup, and spices. Put into greased 9 x 13-inch dish. Sprinkle corn flakes on top of potatoes; pour the 1/4 cup margarine over corn flakes. Bake uncovered in 350 degree oven for 1 hour and 15 minutes.

Edna Mae Seelos, Niles, Ill.

LAZY DAY LIMA BEAN CASSEROLE

2 cups grated American cheese
2/3 cup undiluted evaporated milk
1/2 teaspoon prepared mustard
2 cups cooked, large lima beans
2 medium tomatoes
Salt and pepper to taste

Combine cheese, milk and mustard. Cook and stir over hot water until cheese melts and sauce is smooth. Put lima beans into ovenproof casserole. Cover with 3/4 of sauce. Top casserole with tomato slices, salt and pepper and the remaining sauce. Bake in a 375 degree oven for 25 minutes or until lightly browned and bubbly on top.

Mrs. Gwen Campbell, Sterling, VA

SKILLET MACARONI AND CHEESE

Serves 6 to 8

1/4 cup butter or margarine
1 cup chopped onion
1 tablespoon all-purpose flour
1-1/2 teaspoons salt
1/4 teaspoon oregano
7 or 8 ounce package elbow macaroni
3-1/2 cups milk
2 cups shredded Cheddar cheese

Melt butter in skillet; add onion and saute until tender. Stir in flour, salt and oregano; add macaroni and milk. Cover and bring to boil; reduce heat and simmer 15 minutes or until macaroni is tender, stirring occasionally. Add cheese and stir until cheese is melted (do not boil).

Barbara Beauregard-Smith, South Australia

STEAK AND POTATO CASSEROLE

2-1/2 pounds round steak, 1/2 - 3/4 inch thick
1/4 cup flour
4 teaspoons salt
1/2 teaspoon pepper
1/4 cup oil
3-1/2 cups water
8 medium carrots, thinly sliced diagonally
8 medium potatoes, thinly sliced
1-3/8-ounce envelope onion soup mix
Chopped parsley for garnish

Preheat oven to 325 degrees. Cut meat into 6 - 8 serving pieces, trimming fat and bone. On wooden board or waxed paper, using meat mallet or edge of heavy saucer, pound mixture of flour, salt and pepper into meat.

In heavy skillet over medium heat, brown meat well on both sides in hot oil. Do not crowd pieces. Arrange browned meat in 3-quart casserole. Place carrots and potato slices on top. Sprinkle with onion soup mix and pour over 3-1/2 cups water. Bake, covered 2 hours or until tender. Skim excess fat. If you wish, thicken with 2 tablespoons flour mixed with 1 tablespoon butter; form into balls and drop into casserole. Return to oven 10 minutes. Sprinkle with parsley and serve.

Eleanor V. Craycraft, Santa Monica, CA

CHINESE TUNA CASSEROLE

Serves 4

14 ounce can Chinese vegetables, drained
10 3/4 ounce can cream of mushroom soup
9 1/4 ounce can tuna fish, drained and flaked
3/4 cup celery, thinly sliced
1 tablespoon soy sauce
1/4 teaspoon pepper
3 ounce can Chinese noodles

Preheat oven to 350 degrees. Mix all ingredients, except noodles, in ungreased 1-1/2 quart casserole. Sprinkle with noodles. Bake uncovered until contents are bubbly and noodles golden brown, about 40 to 45 minutes. Serve with hot rolls and salad. **Judy M. Sax, San Antonio, TX**

SHRIMP AND ASPARAGUS CASSEROLE

Serves 6 to 8

1 cup rice, cooked
1 pound fresh asparagus, cut up and cooked, (or 1 package frozen cut-up asparagus, cooked)
3 cans (4-1/2 ounces each) shrimp
2 tablespoons butter
2 tablespoons flour
1-1/4 cups milk
1/2 pound sharp Cheddar cheese, grated
Salt and paprika

Heat oven to 350 degrees (moderate). Spread rice in buttered baking dish, 11-1/2 x 7-1/2 x 1-1/2". Spread asparagus over rice. Cover with shrimp. Melt butter, stir in flour; cook over low heat, stirring until mixture is smooth, bubbly. Remove from heat. Stir in milk and cheese. Bring to boil; boil 1 minute, stirring constantly. Season to taste with salt and paprika. Pour sauce over shrimp in baking dish. Sprinkle with paprika. Bake 20 minutes.

CHICKEN AND HAM CASSEROLE

7 slices white meat of chicken, uniform size
3 slices boiled ham, cut same size
1/2 small Bermuda onion, finely minced
1/4 cup butter
1/2 cup sliced mushrooms
1 teaspoon paprika
1 teaspoon salt
1/4 teaspoon nutmeg
3/4 cup cream
3-4 tablespoons grated Parmesan cheese

Cook the onion in butter for 5 minutes, stirring constantly and do not let it brown. Add the sliced mushrooms and seasonings and let simmer for 15 minutes. Turn the mixture into an oblong baking dish and arrange chicken and ham on the top. Add enough hot cream to cover the meat. Let simmer in a hot 400 degree oven for 10 minutes. Cover with Parmesan cheese; let remain in oven until cheese is browned.

Agnes Ward, Erie, PA

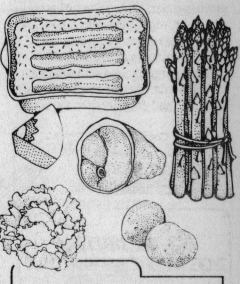

"SOUPER" CHICKEN CASSEROLE

2 cups diced, cooked chicken
1 (16-ounce) bag frozen broccoli, carrots, and cauliflower (thawed and drained)
1 can cream of mushroom soup
1 cup shredded Swiss cheese
1/3 cup sour cream
1/4 teaspoon pepper
1 can French fried onions

Combine all ingredients *except* the cheese and onions. Add one-half of the cheese, and one-half of the onions. Pour into casserole; bake uncovered, in a 350 degree oven for 30 minutes. Top with remaining onions and cheese; bake uncovered 5 minutes longer.

Debbie Vlahoric, Mesa, AZ

TOMATO, BURGER 'N' BEANS
Serves 5

1 pound ground chuck
1 cup water
1 (1 1/2-ounce) package sloppy joe mix
1 (6-ounce) can tomato paste
2 (16-ounce) cans French-style green beans, drained
1 small can mushrooms, drained
1/2 cup shredded cheddar cheese

Brown ground chuck in large skillet; drain off all fat. Stir in sloppy joe seasoning; mix in water until thickened. Add tomato paste. Cover and simmer for 10 minutes. Stir in beans and mushrooms. Turn into a 2-quart casserole; top with cheese. Bake in preheated oven of 350 degrees for 20–30 minutes, or until bubbly.

Hazel Wagener, Carrollton, Ill.

PIZZA CASSEROLE

3 cups all-purpose flour
3 cups instant mashed potatoes
1¼ cups milk
1 cup margarine, melted
1 pound ground beef
1 pound bulk sausage
1 large onion, chopped
1 (8-ounce) can tomato sauce
1 (6-ounce) can pitted ripe olives, drained
1 (6-ounce) can tomato paste
½ package sloppy joe seasoning mix
¼ teaspoon garlic powder
1¼ cups shredded mozzarella cheese

For crust, combine flour, potatoes, milk and margarine. Set aside. For filling, in a 12-inch skillet, cook beef, sausage and onion until onion is tender and meat is no longer pink. Drain off fat. Stir in tomato sauce, olives, tomato paste, seasoning mix and garlic powder.

Press half of crust into 13 x 9 x 2-inch baking pan. Spread filling over crust. Sprinkle with cheese. Roll remaining crust and put on top of filling. Bake at 425 degrees for 30–35 minutes, or until crust is golden. Let stand 5 minutes.

Mrs. A. Curtis, Rector, Ark.

AMISH-STYLE YUM-A-SETTA
Serves 6–8

2 pounds hamburger
Salt and pepper to taste
2 tablespoons brown sugar
¼ cup chopped onion
1 (10¾-ounce) can tomato soup, undiluted
1 (10¾-ounce) can chicken soup, undiluted
1 (16-ounce) package egg noodles
1 (8-ounce) package processed cheese, such as Kraft or Velveeta

Brown hamburger with salt, pepper, brown sugar and onion. Add tomato soup. Cook egg noodles according to package; drain. Add cream of chicken soup. Layer hamburger mixture and noodle mixture in 9 x 12-inch casserole with processed cheese between layers. Bake at 350 degrees for 30 minutes.

This is a great recipe to make for a potluck dinner, for a reunion, or to use up staples around the house. Can easily be made the day before.

Mary C. Canfield, Cuyahoga Falls, Ohio

COUNTRY PIE

Crust:
1 (8-ounce) can tomato sauce (reserve 1/2 cup for filling)
1/2 cup bread crumbs
1/2 teaspoon salt
1/4 cup chopped green pepper
1/4 cup chopped onion
1 pound ground beef
1/8 teaspoon pepper
1/8 teaspoon oregano

Combine these ingredients and mix well. Pat meat mixture into bottom of a greased 9-inch pie plate. Set aside.

Filling:
1-1/3 cups Minute Rice
1-1/2 (8-ounce) cans tomato sauce (plus the reserved 1/2 cup from previous measure)
1-1/2 cups grated cheddar cheese
1 cup water
1/2 teaspoon salt

Combine rice, sauce, salt, water and 1 cup cheese. Spoon rice mixture into meat shell. Cover with foil and bake at 350 degrees for 40 minutes. Uncover and sprinkle remaining cheese on top of pie. Return to oven and bake, uncovered, for 10–15 minutes longer.

Carol Nodoline, Easten, Pa.

FRENCH TUNA BAKE
Serves 4

1 medium eggplant, sliced
1 tomato, peeled and sliced
1 green pepper, cut in strips
1 zucchini, sliced
1 onion, sliced
¼ cup minced fresh parsley
2 tablespoons fresh lemon juice
½ teaspoon salt
⅛ teaspoon black pepper
½ teaspoon dried leaf thyme
2 (6½–7-ounce) cans water-packed tuna, drained
1 cup shredded, low-fat mozzarella cheese

Layer eggplant, tomato, pepper strips, zucchini and onion in buttered (low-calorie margarine) casserole dish. Sprinkle with parsley, lemon juice, salt, pepper and thyme. Bake, uncovered, in preheated 375-degree oven for 45 minutes. Stir in tuna; sprinkle with cheese. Return to oven and bake 15 minutes longer. Aromatic, too! (193 calories per serving)

Judie Betz, Eureka, Calif.

SUNSHINE TORTILLA PIE

Serves 7

1½ pounds ground beef
1 onion, chopped
1 green pepper, chopped
½ cup flour
½ teaspoon salt
1¼ teaspoons chili powder
1 (16-ounce) can tomato sauce
1 cup water
½ cup pimiento-stuffed olives, chopped
12 tortillas
3½ cups sharp cheddar cheese, grated
6 hard-cooked eggs, divided

Sauté meat; add onion and green pepper; cook 5 minutes. Sprinkle vegetables and meat with flour, salt and chili powder. Stir in tomato sauce, water and olives; simmer 5 minutes. In ovenproof dish alternate layers of tortillas, cheese, 3 sliced eggs and sauce over all. Finely chop or sieve remaining 3 eggs; sprinkle on top of sauce.

Gwen Campbell, Sterling, Va.

QUICK AND EASY MACARONI AND CHEESE

1 (7-ounce) package Creamettes macaroni (2 cups)
1 pound lean ground beef
½ cup chopped onion
½ cup sliced celery
2 (8-ounce) cans Hunt's tomato sauce with mushrooms
1 teaspoon salt
¼ teaspoon pepper
1 (8-ounce) package shredded cheddar cheese (2 cups)

Cook macaroni as directed on package; drain. Brown ground beef, onion and celery in skillet. Pour off excess fat. Stir in tomato sauce with mushrooms, salt and pepper. Combine meat mixture with Creamettes macaroni. Pour into a 2-quart casserole and stir in a portion of the cheese; sprinkle top with additional cheese. Bake at 350 degrees for about 25 minutes, or until cheese melts.

Very good with a lettuce salad and Italian bread.

Pat Bianchetta, Coal City, Ill.

MEXICALI CASSEROLE

Serves 8

1/2 cup chopped onion
1 tablespoon shortening, melted
1 (16-ounce) can tomatoes, chopped and drained
1 (17-ounce) can whole-kernel corn, drained
2 (15-ounce) cans chili with beans
1 (8-ounce) package corn muffin mix
1 cup (4 ounces) shredded cheddar cheese

Heat oven to 350 degrees. In skillet, cook onion in shortening for 10 minutes. Add tomatoes, corn and chili; mix until well-blended. Pour into 12 x 8-inch baking dish. Prepare corn muffin mix according to package directions; stir cheese into batter. Spoon batter mixture around edge of baking dish. Bake 30 minutes. This is great with jalapeño pepper cheese, as well as with cheddar cheese.

Leota Baxter, Ingalls, Kan.

LASAGNA-STYLE CASSEROLE

Serves 6

6 ounces large bow-tie pasta (2-1/4 cups)
1 pound ground beef or pork
1 (15-ounce) can pizza sauce
1 teaspoon minced dry onion
1/2 teaspoon dry basil, crushed
1 egg, beaten
1 cup ricotta cheese or cottage cheese
1/4 cup grated Parmesan cheese
1 cup shredded mozzarella cheese

Cook pasta until tender; drain. Fry meat until browned; drain off fat. Add pizza sauce, onion, and basil to meat and mix well. In a bowl, combine egg and cottage cheese or ricotta. In a greased 12x9-1/2x2-inch baking dish, layer half of the pasta.

Spoon cheese mixture over pasta. Sprinkle with Parmesan cheese. Layer remaining pasta, meat, and mozzarella cheese. Bake, covered, at 425 degrees for 15 minutes. Uncover and bake 5-8 minutes longer, or until heated through.

Vickie Vogt, Kewaskum, Wis.

MANDARIN ORANGE CASHEW CASSEROLE

Serves 5

1 pound ground beef
1/4 cup celery, cut diagonally
1/2 cup green onion, cut diagonally in 1-inch pieces
1/4 cup green pepper, chopped
1 1/2 teaspoons garlic, minced
1 cup water
1/4 teaspoon toasted sesame oil
2 tablespoons cornstarch
1 teaspoon sugar
1/4 teaspoon 5-Spice Powder
1/4 teaspoon ginger root, minced
1/4 cup soy sauce
2 tablespoons water
1 (16-ounce) can chop suey vegetables, drained
1 (10-ounce) package frozen peas
1 (3-ounce) can chow mein noodles
1 cup cashew halves

In a skillet cook beef, celery, green onion, green pepper, garlic; drain. Add the water and sesame oil; bring to a boil. Combine cornstarch, sugar, 5-Spice Powder, ginger root, soy sauce and water. Add to beef mixture in skillet; cook until thickened and bubbly. Stir in the drained chop suey vegetables; add frozen peas. Turn into 2-quart casserole; bake, covered, at 375 degrees for 1 1/2 hours; uncover and bake 10 minutes more.

To serve: Sprinkle each individual serving with chow mein noodles; scatter the cashew halves over top surface.

Gwen Campbell, Sterling, Va.

85

SPINACH NOODLE CASSEROLE

serves 10-12

1 pound package noodles
2 (10-ounce) packages frozen chopped spinach
1 pound fresh mushrooms, sliced
1/2 onion, chopped
2-4 tablespoons margarine
1 (10-ounce) can cream of chicken soup
1 (10-ounce) can cream of mushroom soup
1 cup sour cream
2 tablespoons Worcestershire sauce
2 tablespoons margarine
Salt & pepper to taste

Cook noodles and drain. Cook spinach and drain well. Sauté mushrooms and onion in margarine. Mix together all ingredients, except 2 tablespoons margarine. Place in large greased casserole. Dot with margarine. Bake at 350 degrees for 30 minutes or until bubbly.

Note: Recipe may be halved. Omit either can of soup. For a variation you may add 1 (7-ounce) can tuna or 1 pound ground beef, cooked and drained, before baking.

Mrs. George Franks, Millerton, Pa.

MACARONI AND SAUSAGE BAKE

Serves 6

1 pound bulk pork sausage
1/2 cup chopped onion
1 cup elbow macaroni
1 (10-1/2 ounce) can cream of celery soup
2/3 cup milk
3 beaten eggs
1-1/2 cups shredded processed American cheese

Cook macaroni according to package directions. Cook sausage and onion until browned. Drain off excess fat. Combine sausage mixture, macaroni, soup, milk, eggs, and cheese. Place in 2-quart casserole. Bake at 350 degrees for 40-45 minutes.

Sharon M. Crider, Evansville, Wis.

BROCCOLI CASSEROLE

Serves 8

1/4 cup chopped onion
6 tablespoons butter or margarine
1/2 cup water
2 tablespoons flour
8 ounces processed cheese spread
2 packages frozen chopped broccoli, thawed and drained
3 eggs, well beaten
1/2 cup cracker crumbs

Sauté onion in 4 tablespoons butter until soft; stir in flour and add water. Cook over low heat, stirring, until mixture thickens and comes to a boil. Blend in cheese. Combine sauce and broccoli. Add eggs; mix gently until blended. Turn into a 1-1/2 quart casserole; cover with crumbs and dot with remaining butter. Bake at 325 degrees for 30 minutes.

Agnes Ward, Erie, PA

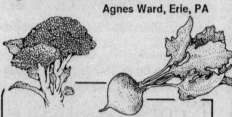

TURNIP CASSEROLE

Serves 4

1 1/2 lbs. turnips, peeled and thinly sliced
2 tablespoons butter
1 onion, thinly sliced
2/3 cup chopped celery
2 tablespoons flour
1 cup milk
1/2 cup grated sharp cheese
Salt and pepper to taste
3 tbsps. bread crumbs

Cook turnips in boiling, salted water to cover until just tender. Drain. Saute in butter the oinion, green pepper, and celery until tender. Sprinkle with flour and cook 1 minute. Add milk and stir until thickened. Stir in cheese, salt and pepper. Combine cheese sauce with turnips, place in baking dish and top with curmbs. Brown under broiler. May be prepared ahead and place-dunder broiler just before serving.

Marcella Swigert, Monroe City, MO

YELLOW SQUASH CASSEROLE

2 pounds yellow squash
1 large onion
1 can cream of chicken soup
1 jar pimientos (optional)
1 cup sour cream
1 teaspoon salt
1/4 teaspoon pepper
1 stick margarine
1 (8-ounce) package Pepperidge Farms herbal dressing

Boil squash until tender; drain and mash. Chop onion, sauté in a half stick margarine until tender. Add soup, chopped pimiento, sour cream, salt, and pepper. Melt the remaining margarine and add to dressing crumbs. Put half of dressing in bottom of baking dish. Mix all ingredients together. Pour on dressing. Spread remaining half of the dressing on top. Bake at 350 degrees for approximately 1 hour.

Mildred Beckham, Edgar, FL

PARSNIP CASSEROLE

2 pounds parsnips
2 tablespoons butter
1/4 teaspoon fresh or dried rosemary
2 tablespoons flour
1/4 cup grated Parmesan cheese
2 cups light cream or half-and-half
1/2 cup cracker crumbs
1/4 cup melted butter

Peel parsnips. Cook in boiling, salted water until tender. Drain; cut each in half lengthwise, or slice in rounds, if parsnips are large. Arrange half the parsnips in bottom of greased 1-1/2 quart baking dish. Dot with half the butter; sprinkle with half the rosemary, flour, and cheese. Drizzle with half the cream. Repeat layers. Mix cracker crumbs with melted butter; sprinkle over casserole. Bake, uncovered, in 400 degree oven for 20 minutes.

Diantha Hibbard, Rochester, NY

CHEESY SPAGHETTI

1 (12-ounce) package thin spaghetti
1/4 pound bacon, cut in small pieces
1 large onion, chopped
1 pound ground beef
2 cups (2 8-ounce cans) tomato
  sauce
1 (4-ounce) can sliced mushrooms,
  drained
1 teaspoon salt
1/2 teaspoon Italian seasoning
1/2 teaspoon garlic salt
1/8 teaspoon pepper
1 cup (4 ounces) shredded cheese
1/2 cup shredded Provolone cheese

Cook spaghetti; drain. Fry bacon slowly until browned. Drain off grease. Add onion and beef; cook until meat is brown; mix in tomato sauce and seasonings. Simmer 15 minutes. In large bowl, combine sauce and spaghetti. Place half of mixture in a buttered 2 quart casserole. Top with half of the Cheddar and half of the Provolone cheese. Repeat layers. Bake in pre-heated 375 degree oven for 20-25 minutes.

Betty L. Perkins, Hot Springs, AR

PORK CHOP CASSEROLE

6 pork chops
1 cup uncooked brown rice
6 slices onion
6 tomato slices
6 green pepper rings
1 teaspoon salt
1/8 teaspoon pepper
2 cups tomato juice

Spray 12-inch skillet with vegetable cooking spray. Brown pork chops on each side. Transfer to plate.

Place rice over bottom of skillet. Arrange chops on top. Stack slices of onion, tomato, and green pepper on top of each chop. Sprinkle with salt and pepper. Pour tomato juice over chops. Cover; simmer 45 minutes or until chops are tender.

Ella Evanicky, Fayetteville, TX

BACON AND RICE CREOLE

1 pound bacon
1 green pepper, diced
3 small onions, chopped
2-1/2 teaspoons salt
1/8 teaspoon pepper
2 cups canned tomatoes
1 cup raw rice (not quick-cooking)

Simmer vegetables and spices in a sauce pan. At the same time, fry the bacon. When bacon is done, remove from pan and crumble into small pieces. Drain off all but 3 tablespoons of fat, to which add the raw rice. Let rice brown lightly. Add the vegetables and bacon; let simmer over very low heat for 30 minutes. Check after 20 minutes to see if it is drying out, if so, add more tomatoes, or some water, or a combination of both.

Linda Taylor, New Lenox, IL

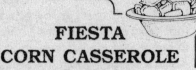

FIESTA CORN CASSEROLE
Serves 4-6

3 tablespoons butter
3 cups corn flakes
1 pound lean ground beef
3/4 teaspoon seasoned salt
1 (8-ounce) can tomato sauce
1 (1-1/4 ounce) package Lawry's
  Taco Seasoning Mix
1 (17-ounce) can whole kernel corn,
  drained (save 1/4 cup liquid)
2 cups grated Cheddar cheese.

Combine butter and 2 cups corn flakes in bottom of a shallow 1-1/2 quart baking dish. Crush remaining corn flakes; set aside. In skillet, brown beef until crumbly; drain. Add seasoned salt, tomato sauce, taco seasoning mix, and reserved liquid from corn; mix well. Layer 1/2 each; corn, meat mixture, and cheese over buttered corn flakes in baking dish; repeat layers. Sprinkle crushed corn flakes over top in diagonal strips.

Agnes Ward, Erie, PA

CHICKEN ALMOND CASSEROLE

5 cups diced, cooked chicken
  breasts
2 cups diced celery
3 cups cooked rice
1 (8-ounce) can sliced water chestnuts
2 cans cream of chicken soup
1/2 cup sour cream
1/2 cup mayonnaise
2 tablespoons chopped onion
2 tablespoons lemon juice
1 tablespoon salt
3/4 teaspoon white pepper
1 cup sliced almonds

Mix above ingredients and put into buttered 9x13 inch baking dish.

Topping:
1/2 cup sliced almonds
3 cups crumbled corn flakes
2/3 cup butter

Mix above ingredients and sprinkle on top of casserole. Bake at 350 degrees for 35-45 minutes. Can be prepared ahead and refrigerated until baking.

Sharon Sisson, Longview, Was

GERMAN SUPPER
Serves 4-5

5-6 potatoes, scrubbed (not peeled)
1/4 cup chopped onion
1/4 teaspoon garlic powder
1/2 teaspoon salt
1/3 teaspoon pepper
3 cups cubed beef Hillshire Farms
  sausage or Eckrich smoked
  sausage
1 (7-ounce) can sauerkraut

Cut potatoes into thumb-size pieces. Add onion, garlic powder, salt, and pepper. Brown in a small amount of oil for 25 minutes until tender. Add sausage; heat; stir occasionally. Drain kraut and spread on top surface. Do not stir. Cover and heat.

Ann Sterzer, Lynch, Neb.

FRESH CORN CASSEROLE

Preheat oven to 350 degrees. Generously butter a 2-quart rectangular baking dish. In blender puree:

1 cup corn (fresh or frozen, thawed)
1/2 cup butter, softened
2 eggs

Pour into bowl; blend in:

1 cup corn
4-ounce can green chilies; drained, seeded, and chopped
1 cup sour cream
1 cup diced Monterey Jack cheese
1/2 cup cornmeal
1-1/2 teaspoons salt

Spread above ingredients in baking dish. Bake 50 - 60 minutes. Serve with sliced tomatoes. This is delicious and very light!

Patricia Staley, Westmont, IL

STUFFED SHELLS
Serves 8-10

1 (12-ounce) package jumbo shells for stuffing
2 tablespoons butter
1 clove garlic, crushed
1/2 cup finely-chopped onion
2 beaten eggs
2 pounds Ricotta cheese
1/2 cup Parmesan and Romano cheese, mixed
1/3 cup parsley flakes
1/8 teaspoon nutmeg
1 cup shredded Mozzarella cheese (4 ounces)
2-3 pounds Italian meat sauce
1/2 cup Parmesan and Romano, mixed for topping

Preheat oven to 350 degrees. Cook shells according to package directions. Rinse with cold water; drain. Melt butter; sauté garlic and onion until soft. Mix together onion, garlic, eggs, ricotta, Parmesan, Romano, parsley, and nutmeg. Stir in Mozzarella, stuff shells with filling. (At this point, the shells may be frozen for future use).

Cover the bottoms of two 13x9x2-inch baking dishes with meat sauce.

Place shells on top of sauce and sprinkle with Parmesan and Romano. Bake, covered with foil, at 350 degrees for 30-40 minutes or until hot and bubbly.

This is a dish that is easy to prepare; and receives many compliments at potluck dinners.

Betty Perkins, Hot Springs, Ark.

DEVILED HAM AND RICE CASSEROLE
Serves 6

1 medium onion, chopped
1/2 medium green pepper, chopped
1/2 cup finely diced celery
2 tablespoons butter or margarine
1 cup raw rice
2 chicken bouillon cubes
2 (4-1/2 ounce) cans deviled ham
3 cups boiling water
Chopped parsley

Sauté first 3 ingredients in butter for 2-3 minutes. Place mixture in 1-1/2 quart casserole with remaining ingredients, except parsley. Mix with fork. Cover and bake for 45 minutes in pre-heated moderate oven at 350 degrees, stirring twice at 15-minute intervals, or until rice is tender. Sprinkle with parsley.

Mrs. Robert Shaffer, Middleburg, PA

ANOTHER HAMBURGER CASSEROLE

1 pound hamburger
1 green pepper, chopped
1 (8-ounce) package of 1/4 inch noodles, cooked
1 can cream of mushroom soup
1 can evaporated milk

Fry hamburger with green pepper, then blend in soup and milk. Combine with cooked noodles and bake 45-60 minutes at 350 degrees. Do not alter any of these ingredients. It takes this combination for the special flavor.

Linda Taylor, New Lenox, IL

CHICKEN LIVER CASSEROLE
Serves 5-6

2 (10-ounce) packages frozen French-style green beans
4 slices bacon, diced
1 pound chicken livers, cut in half
1/2 teaspoon seasoning salt
2 tablespoons sherry
1 (10-ounce) can cream of mushroom soup
1/2 cup sour cream
3/4 cup crushed barbecue potato chips

Cook green beans according to directions. Drain and spread in greased 9x6 or 8x8 inch baking dish. Sauté bacon until crisp; scatter over beans. Stir-fry chicken livers in bacon fat until pinkness disappears. Add next 4 ingredients, as soon as heated; pour over bacon. Top with potato chips. Bake at 375 degrees for 15 minutes, or until bubbly.

This is a very tasty dish and easy to make!

Lillian Smith, Montreal, Que., Canada

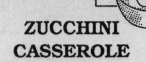

ZUCCHINI CASSEROLE
Serves 12

2 cups bread crumbs
1/4 cup butter or margarine, melted
1/4 teaspoon Italian seasonings
1/4 cup Parmesan cheese
2 pounds zucchini; sliced, parboiled, and drained
1 medium carrot, shredded
10-1/2-ounce can cream of chicken soup
1 cup sour cream
1/4 cup chopped green onion

Combine crumbs, butter, seasonings, and cheese; spread half in bottom of 13 x 9 x 2-inch pan. Combine zucchini and carrot; spread over crumbs. Mix soup, sour cream, and onion; pour over vegetables. Top with remaining crumbs. Bake at 350 degrees for 1 hour.

Lisa Varner, Baton Rouge, LA

HAM, POTATO, AND ONION CASSEROLE

Serves 8-10

6 tablespoons ham drippings or butter
6 tablespoons enriched flour
3 cups milk
2 teaspoons salt
1/4 teaspoon pepper
1/4 pound Cheddar cheese, grated
1 pound diced cooked ham
4 cups cubed cooked potatoes
12 small cooked onions
1/2 cup buttered bread crumbs

Melt drippings or butter. Blend in flour and add milk, stirring constantly. Cook mixture until thickened, boiling about 3 minutes. Add seasonings and grated cheese. Cook slowly until cheese melts. Add cooked ham, potatoes, and onions. Pour mixture into a greased casserole. Sprinkle with buttered bread crumbs. Bake, uncovered, in a 350 degree oven for 30-40 minutes or until crumbs are lightly browned.

Ruby Walsh, West Chicago, Ill.

VEGETABLE CASSEROLE

1 can whole kernel corn, drained
1 can French green beans, drained
1 cup finely chopped celery
1 cup finely chopped onion
1/2 cup green pepper, finely chopped
4 cups grated sharp cheese
1 container sour cream
1 can cream of celery soup

Mix well and pour into a very large casserole.

Topping:
3/4 box Cheese-It crackers, crumbled into 3/4 stick melted margarine. You may add a can of slivered almonds. Bake at 350 degrees for 45 minutes. This makes a large amount. Great for a covered-dish supper!!

Peggy Fowler, Woodruff, SC

CHICKEN-PASTA HOT DISH

Serves 6-8

1/2 pound elbow or spiral pasta (2 cups uncooked)
1/4 cup butter or margarine
1/4 cup finely chopped onion
3 tablespoons all-purpose flour
1-1/2 teaspoons salt
1/8 teaspoon pepper
3 cups milk
3 cups shredded cheddar cheese
2 cups diced cooked chicken or turkey
1 (9-ounce) package frozen Italian-cut green beans, thawed and drained
1 (2-ounce) jar diced pimiento, drained
3 tablespoons cornflake crumbs

Cook pasta according to package directions; drain. In large saucepan, melt butter; add onion and cook until tender. Stir in flour, salt, and pepper. Blend in milk. Cook, stirring constantly, until thickened and bubbly. Add cheese; stir until melted. Combine pasta, cheese sauce, chicken, green beans, and pimiento; mix well. Pour into a 3-quart casserole. Top with cornflake crumbs. Bake in a 350-degree oven until hot, about 30 minutes. Refrigerate leftovers.

**National Pasta Association

ONE-POT TUNA PASTA

Serves 4

3-1/2 cups water
4 chicken bouillon cubes
1/8 teaspoon pepper
1 teaspoon basil leaves
2 cups (8 ounces) elbow pasta or spiral pasta
1 (4-ounce) jar pimiento
1 (9-ounce) package frozen cut green beans
2 cups milk
1 cup (4 ounces) process American cheese
1 (7-ounce) can tuna, drained and broken into chunks

1/4 cup chopped parsley

Bring water, bouillon cubes, pepper and basil leaves to a boil in a 4-quart pot. Gradually add uncooked pasta so that water continues to boil. Cover and simmer for 7 minutes, stirring occasionally.

Meanwhile, dice pimiento. Stir diced pimiento, beans, and milk into pot; cover and simmer 6 to 8 minutes longer or until pasta and beans are tender. Stir in cheese, tuna, and parsley until cheese is melted. Serve from pot or turn into serving dish. Serve immediately.

ONION CASSEROLE

Serves 2

2 large or 3 medium onions
1/4 teaspoon salt
Dash of pepper
2 or 3 tablespoons whipping cream (see directions)
1/3 cup buttered bread crumbs
Garlic powder (optional)

Grease or spray with pan release, a small baking dish, about 2-cup capacity.

Peel onions; cut in half lengthwise; place cut-side down on board; cut in 1/4-inch slices. Use your hands to separate layers. Drop into saucepan of cold salted water. Bring to boil over high heat; boil until onions are transparent but barely fork tender, about 3 minutes. Drain thoroughly. (If doing ahead, set aside.) Return to pan. Sprinkle on salt and pepper. Add 2 tablespoons cream; toss to mix; if onions seem dry, add another tablespoon cream (this depends on how well drained onions were). Spread evenly in prepared dish. Top with crumbs; sprinkle crumbs lightly with garlic powder, if desired.

Bake at 325 or 350 degrees (depending on what else may be cooking in the oven) until heated through and crumbs are golden. 20 to 25 minutes.

WINTER SQUASH CASSEROLE
Serves 2

1 cup mashed squash, thawed if frozen
1 or 2 slices bacon (use two if you can afford the calories)
1/4 cup chopped onion
1/3 cup grated Cheddar cheese
1/4 teaspoon salt
Dash Tabasco or use black pepper
1/4 cup buttered bread crumbs

Grease or spray with pan release a small baking dish, one quart or smaller. Put squash into medium bowl. Fry bacon until crisp; crumble into squash. Leave about 1 tablespoon drippings in skillet. Fry onions in drippings until transparent; add to squash. Add cheese (I grate it directly into the bowl, estimating the measure). Add salt and Tabasco or pepper; mix well. Transfer to prepared baking dish; top with bread crumbs.

Bake at 325 or 350 degrees (depending on what else may be cooking in the oven) until heated through and crumbs begin to brown, 25 to 30 minutes.

TAGLIARINA

1 pound hamburger
1 onion, chopped
2 tablespoons butter
1 (8-ounce) can tomato sauce
1-1/2 cups water
2 cups uncooked noodles
1 (1-cup) can corn
1 large jar whole mushrooms
1 (No. 2) can pitted ripe olives
1 cup Parmesan cheese
Salt to taste

Mince and brown onion in butter in large skillet. Add meat and brown. Add tomato sauce, water and noodles; stir until noodles are tender. Add more water, if needed. Add salt and rest of ingredients. Pour into 11x11x2-inch glass baking dish and sprinkle with Parmesan cheese. Bake 45 minutes in 350 degree oven. Let stand in oven with door open for 15 minutes before serving.

MOCK OYSTER CASSEROLE

1 medium eggplant
1 stick margarine
1-1/2 cups Ritz cracker crumbs
1 egg, beaten
1 (6-1/2 ounce) can minced clams, drained (reserve liquid)
Salt, pepper, Tabasco sauce to taste

Peel eggplant; cut into 1-inch cubes and parboil 3 minutes. Drain well; set aside. Melt margarine and add Ritz crackers; mix well. Reserve 1/3 cup cracker crumb mixture for topping.

Gently mix beaten eggs, drained clams, and eggplant. Add crumbs, salt, pepper, and Tabasco sauce. Then add enough clam liquid to make quite moist, but not soupy. Pour into buttered casserole. Top with remaining crumbs and bake at 350 degrees for 45 minutes.

Rebecca Preston, Weare, N.H.

LUNCHMEAT AND NOODLE CASSEROLE

1/4 cup margarine
1/4 cup all-purpose flour
1/2 teaspoon salt
Dash of pepper
2-1/2 cups milk
1 can lunch meat, cubed
2 cups cooked noodles
1 teaspoon mustard
3/4 cup bread crumbs
2 tablespoons melted margarine
1 (16-ounce) can peas and carrots

Preheat oven to 375 degrees. Melt margarine in a skillet. Blend in flour, salt, pepper, and gradually stir in milk. Cook over medium heat, stirring constantly, until mixture is smooth and thick.

Add meat, noodles, mustard, and peas and carrots. Mix well. Spoon into a greased 1-1/2 quart casserole. Combine crumbs and melted butter; sprinkle over noodles. Bake 25 minutes.

Alpha Wilson, Roswell, N.M.

CORNED BEEF SCALLOP CASSEROLE

1 (3-ounce) package potato soup mix
1-1/2 cups milk
1 cup water
1 cup American cheese, grated
1/2 teaspoon Worcestershire sauce
1 (12-ounce) can corned beef, shredded
3/4 cup carrots, sliced and cooked
1/2 cup celery, sliced and cooked
1/4 cup green peas, cooked
2 tablespoons pimiento, chopped
1 teaspoon parsley, chopped
3/4 cup soft bread crumbs

Empty potato soup mix into saucepan; add milk and water; stir constantly until blended. Cook until mixture comes to a boil; remove from heat. Add cheese and Worcestershire sauce; mix well. Stir in corned beef shreds, carrots, celery, green peas, and pimiento. Turn into a well-greased 1-1/2 quart ovenproof casserole. Sprinkle parsley over the top, then bread crumbs; cover. Bake 350 degrees for 20 minutes; uncover; bake 12 minutes longer until top is golden.

Gwen Campbell, Sterling, Va.

MAIN DISH NOODLES
Serves 2

2-1/2 cups uncooked medium noodles
2 tablespoons butter or margarine
2 tablespoons half-and-half or cream
2 tablespoons Parmesan cheese
1 (6-ounce) can boneless salmon or tuna

Cook noodles in boiling, salted water according to directions on package.

Meanwhile, in a medium saucepan, melt butter. Stir in half-and-half and cheese; leave over low heat. Drain fish; break into lumps; add to butter mixture. Drain cooked noodles; immediately add to saucepan; toss to mix. Serve with additional Parmesan cheese.

LADIES' LUNCHEON LAYERED DISH

1 cup crushed potato chips
4 hard-cooked eggs, sliced
1 onion, sliced thin and separated
  into rings
1/3 cup parsley, chopped
1 (10-1/2-ounce) can cream of
  mushroom soup
1/4 cup sour cream
3/4 cup milk
1/2 teaspoon paprika

Spread 1/3 of potato chips in bottom of a greased 1-1/2 quart ovenproof baking dish. Cover with 1/3 of the egg slices, 1/3 of the onion rings and chopped parsley. Repeat layers until potato chips, egg slices and onion rings are all used. Combine soup with sour cream, milk, and paprika; mix well; pour over all; cover. Bake 350 degrees for 30 minutes; uncover, bake 10 minutes longer until hot, bubbly, and golden.

Gwen Campbell, Sterling, Va.

BAKED RICE WITH HERBS
Serves 4-6

2 tablespoons butter
1 green onion, minced
1/4 cup parsley, chopped fine
1/4 teaspoon thyme
1/4 teaspoon sage
Salt and pepper to taste
1 cup brown rice
2-1/2 cups water
1/2 teaspoon garlic powder

Preheat oven to 350 degrees. Place butter in ovenproof baking dish with lid. Heat butter and sauté green onion until golden. Add parsley, thyme, and sage. Sprinkle with salt and pepper; add rice. Pour 2-1/2 cups water over rice and then stir in garlic powder. Bring to a boil for about 45 minutes or until liquid is absorbed and rice is tender.

This rice goes well with turkey, goose, or duck.

Suzan L. Wiener, Spring Hill, Fla.

LASAGNA SURPRISE
Serves 6-8

3/4 cup chopped onion
2 cloves garlic, finely chopped
2 tablespoons vegetable oil
2 (26-ounce) jars prepared spaghetti/pasta sauce or prepare about 2 quarts of your own tomato-based spaghetti/lasagna sauce recipe (add ground meat or sausage, if desired)
1 (15- or 16-ounce) container ricotta or cottage cheese
1 (10-ounce) package frozen chopped spinach, thawed and well-drained
1 pound mozzarella cheese, shredded
1/2 cup grated Parmesan cheese
2 eggs
1 (1-pound) package lasagna noodles, cooked according to package directions

In a large pan, cook onion and garlic in oil. Add prepared pasta sauce. (If you cook your own sauce, it may not be necessary to add more onion and garlic.) Simmer 15 minutes. In bowl, mix ricotta, spinach, and 1 cup mozzarella, all the Parmesan, and eggs. In 15x9-inch baking dish (or smaller dishes as needed), layer 2 cups sauce, half the lasagna, half the remaining sauce, all the spinach mixture, half the mozzarella, remaining lasagna and sauce. Cover; bake at 350 degrees for 45 minutes or until hot. Uncover; top with remaining mozzarella. Bake 15 minutes. Let stand 15 minutes before serving.

PORK PAGODA

1 cup diced cooked pork
1/2 cup sliced celery
1 cup cooked bean sprouts
1/2 cup sliced mushrooms
1/2 cup sliced carrots
1/4 cup sliced green onions
2 tablespoons oil

1 (10-ounce) can condensed cream of asparagas soup
1/4 cup water
2 teaspoons soy sauce
1 (10-ounce) box frozen chopped spinach, thawed and squeezed dry.

In large skillet, sauté pork and all the vegetables in oil until meat is brown and vegetables are tender. Blend in soup, water, soy sauce, and spinach. Heat, stirring occasionally. Serve hot over chow mein noodles. I have substituted beef for the pork and any other creamed soup, also.

Mrs. Laura Hicks, Troy, Mont.

CROWD PLEASER CASSEROLE
Serves 10-12

1 (20-ounce) package frozen broccoli flowerets
1 (20-ounce) package frozen cauliflower flowerets
4 tablespoons butter or margarine
3 tablespoons flour
3 cups milk
6 ounces (or 1-1/2 cups) shredded cheddar cheese
1 cup Parmesan cheese, shredded or grated
1/2 teaspoon salt
3 cups chopped ham
3 cups fresh bread crumbs tossed with 4 tablespoons butter

Cook broccoli and cauliflower in slightly salted water. Cook slightly underdone. Drain; set aside. Melt 4 tablespoons butter in a 1-quart saucepan; add flour; blend well. Add milk, stirring constantly, until thickened. Add cheddar, Parmesan, and salt. Stir over low heat until cheese melts. Place vegetables in an ungreased 4-quart casserole. Sprinkle with chopped ham. Pour cheese sauce mixture over ham. Make a border of buttered bread crumbs around edge of casserole. Bake uncovered at 350 degrees for 30 minutes.

PASTA PRIMAVERA
Makes 4-6 servings

8 ounces uncooked spaghetti
1 cup tender green beans, cut in
  1-inch pieces
2 small zucchini, sliced
2 small yellow squash, sliced
1 cup thinly sliced carrot
1 cup cauliflower flowerets
1 tablespoon olive oil
2 garlic cloves, minced
1/8 teaspoon crushed red pepper
  flakes
1/4 cup chicken broth
1/4 cup lightly packed fresh basil
  leaves, chopped
1/4 cup oil-packed, sun-dried
  tomatoes
3 tablespoons grated Parmesan
  cheese
1/4 cup chopped fresh parsley

Cook spaghetti according to package directions, drain and set aside. Steam vegetables only until crisp-tender, drain and chill. Sauté garlic in olive oil until light brown. Add crushed red pepper, stir; then add chicken broth and simmer 1 minute. Add chopped basil, spaghetti and vegetables; toss. Arrange on platter. Garnish with sun-dried tomatoes, Parmesan cheese and parsley. Serve at room temperature.
***Recipe provided by the courtesy of the National Pasta Association

BAKED MACARONI AND CHEESE WITH SOUR CREAM
Serves 2

3/4 cup macaroni, uncooked
1/3 cup sour cream
1 cup grated sharp Cheddar cheese
1/3 cup milk
Paprika

Preheat oven to 325 degrees. Cook macaroni in boiling, salted water according to package directions until barely tender. Drain well. Return to saucepan. Add sour cream, cheese, and milk; mix well. Turn into a small greased baking dish; sprinkle on paprika. Bake at 325 degrees for about 25 minutes.

HARVEST SWEET POTATO CASSEROLE
Serves 6

1 (23-ounce) can sweet potatoes or
  yams, drained, *or*
1 (18-ounce) can vacuum-packed
  sweet potatoes
7 tablespoons butter, melted
1 apple, cored and thinly sliced

Topping:
1/4 cup firmly packed brown sugar
1 tablespoon all-purpose flour
1/4 teaspoon cardamom
1 tablespoon cold butter
2 tablespoons chopped pecans

Preheat oven to 350 degrees. In 1-quart round casserole, mash sweet potatoes until smooth. Stir in the 7 tablespoons melted butter. In small bowl cut 1 tablespoon cold butter into brown sugar, flour, and cardamom. Stir in pecans and sprinkle one-half of the mixture over potatoes. Arrange apple slices on top. Sprinkle with remaining mixture. Bake for 35-40 minutes or until apples are crisp/tender.

POTATO AND HAM CASSEROLE
Serves 6-8

1 (5-1/2 ounce) package au gratin
  potatoes
2-1/2 cups diced cooked ham
1 cup canned or frozen peas
1 small onion, chopped
1 small green pepper, chopped
1/3 cup chopped celery
1 cup shredded Cheddar cheese

Preheat oven to 400 degrees. Mix potatoes as directed on package in a 2-quart ovenproof dish. Mix together ham, peas, onion, green pepper, celery, and add to casserole. Sprinkle cheese on top.
Bake 30 minutes and serve hot. This is a great dish for working women who have to cook "hurry-up" dinners.
Mrs. H. W. Walker, Richmond, Va.

REUBEN CASSEROLE

1 can corned beef—or 1 pound deli
1/2 cup thousand island dressing
1 can sauerkraut, drained
6 slices rye bread, cut in cubes or
  crumbled
1/2 pound Swiss cheese, grated
1/2 cup margarine, melted

Crumble corned beef into well-greased 12x8-inch glass dish. Spread dressing, then sauerkraut. Cover with cheese. Toss crumbled bread with melted margarine; sprinkle on top. Bake at 350 degrees for 30 minutes or until hot and bubbly.
Laura Morris, Bunnell, Fla.

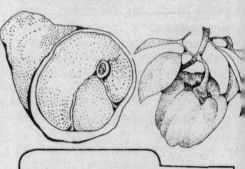

SAUCY SAUSAGE SUPPER
Serves 4

1 (16-ounce) can applesauce (2
  cups)
1 (16-ounce) can sauerkraut,
  drained and snipped (2 cups)
1/3 cup water
2 tablespoons brown sugar, packed
1/2 teaspoon salt
4 small onions, quartered
4 small potatoes, peeled and
  quartered
1 (12-ounce) Polish sausage, cut
  diagonally to desired lengths
Snipped parsley

In a 3-quart saucepan, combine applesauce, sauerkraut, water, brown sugar, and salt; add onions and potatoes. Cover and simmer 20 minutes, stirring occasionally. Add sausage; simmer, covered about 20 minutes longer, stirring occasionally. To serve, spoon sauerkraut mixture onto a platter and top with sausage. Sprinkle with parsley.
Agnes Ward, Erie, Pa.

Cookies
& BARS

ENERGY COOKIES

1/2 cup (1 stick) butter, softened
1 egg
1 teaspoon vanilla
1 cup oatmeal
1/2 cup flour
1 1/4 cups big raisins
1/2 cup walnuts or almonds
2 tablespoons Bran Buds®
1/2 cup chocolate chips

Preheat oven to 350 degrees. Grease an 8-inch square pan.

In large bowl, combine butter, egg and vanilla; beat until well-blended. Add oats and flour, stirring to mix well. Stir in raisins and walnuts. Spread batter evenly over bottom of pan. Sprinkle with bran. Bake for 25 minutes at 350 degrees. Cool in pan. Cut into squares.

Lucy Dowd, Sequim, Wash.

PECAN BUTTERY COOKIES

1 stick butter (1/2 cup)
1/2 stick margarine
1 package butter pecan instant pudding mix
1-1/4 cups all-purpose flour
1 teaspoon vanilla extract
1/4 teaspoon almond extract

Cream together first 3 ingredients. Add flour and extracts; mix well; chill. Shape into 1-inch balls; press down with fork to make an attractive design. Bake at 350 degrees for 10–12 minutes.

Gwen Campbell, Sterling, Va.

PISTACHIO PUDDING COOKIES
Makes 7 dozen

2¼ cups unsifted all-purpose flour
1 teaspoon baking soda
1 cup margarine, well-softened
¼ cup granulated white sugar
¾ cup brownulated light brown sugar
½ teaspoon vanilla
½ teaspoon almond extract
1 (4-ounce) package pistachio instant pudding (used dry)
2 eggs
1 (12-ounce) package butterscotch morsels
1 cup chopped walnuts
Few drops green food coloring, if desired

Mix flour and baking soda in medium bowl. Combine margarine, both sugars, both extracts and instant pudding powder in large mixing bowl. Beat until smooth. Beat in eggs, 1 at a time. Gradually stir in flour mixture. Stir in morsels and nuts. Batter will be very stiff; mix well with floured hands. Cover bowl; chill several hours or overnight for easier shaping. Form into smooth balls by teaspoonfuls. Place 2 inches apart on ungreased cookie sheets. Bake at 375 degrees for 8–10 minutes. Do not overbake. If desired, drizzle with confectioners' sugar icing mixed with a few drops of green food coloring.

These are absolutely delicious. Don't wait for St. Patrick's Day to enjoy them. Have them anytime during the year when you feel like a special cookie treat!!

Hyacinth Rizzo, Snyder, N.Y.

LEMON DROPS
Makes 4 dozen

3 eggs, separated
1 teaspoon grated lemon rind
½ teaspoon lemon extract
½ cup confectioners' sugar
⅓ cup sifted flour

Beat egg yolks until thick and lemon-colored. Stir in rind and extract. Beat egg whites until stiff but not dry. Gradually add confectioners' sugar and beat until stiff. Fold in egg yolk mixture. Gently fold in flour. Drop by teaspoon onto paper-lined baking sheets. Bake in moderate 350-degree oven about 12 minutes, or until golden brown.

Agnes Ward, Erie, Pa.

BASIC BUTTER COOKIES
Makes 30 cookies

1 cup all-purpose flour
1/2 cup cornstarch
1/2 cup powdered sugar
3/4 cup (1-1/2 sticks) real butter, room temperature
1/2 cup coarsely-chopped walnuts

Preheat oven to 300 degrees. Sift first 3 ingredients into large bowl. Add butter and mix well. Stir in walnuts. Drop by teaspoons onto baking sheets. Bake until cookies are lightly golden, about 20-25 minutes.

NOTE: Real butter is the secret of these buttery-tasting cookies.

Agnes Ward, Erie, Pa.

93

SOUR CREAM COOKIES

2 cups sugar
1 cup lard
1 cup sour cream
3 eggs, beaten
1/2 teaspoon salt
1 teaspoon baking soda
1 teaspoon vanilla or lemon flavoring
Enough flour to make a soft dough (2 cups or more as needed)

Combine dry ingredients (except sugar). Beat together sugar and lard; add beaten eggs and sour cream; mix well. Add flavoring. Combine dry ingredients with creamed mixture, blending well. Roll out on a floured surface and cut with cookie cutters. Bake in preheated 400-degree oven until golden brown, about 12 minutes.

Margaret Kudlacik, Rockford, Ill.

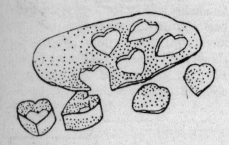

NO-BAKE LEMON GRAHAM SQUARES

Whole graham crackers
1 cup margarine
1/2 cup milk
1 cup sugar
1 egg, slightly beaten
1 cup coconut
1 cup chopped nuts
1 cup graham cracker crumbs

Cover bottom of 9x13-inch pan with whole crackers. Heat to boiling the margarine, milk, sugar, and egg. Add coconut, nuts, and graham cracker crumbs. Spread over the graham crackers in the pan. Chill. Frost with Lemon Icing.

Lemon Icing:
2 cups confectioners' sugar
1 stick margarine
2 tablespoons lemon or to taste

Cut into 1-inch squares. Prepare to have recipe handy when this is served. The recipe is *always* requested. Freezes well, too.

Marjorie McDowell, West Salem, Ill.

RAISIN CRISSCROSS COOKIES
Makes 3 dozen

1/2 cup shortening (part butter *or* margarine)
3/4 cup sugar
1 egg
1/2 teaspoon lemon extract
1 3/4 cups all-purpose flour
3/4 teaspoon cream of tartar
3/4 teaspoon soda
1/4 teaspoon salt
1 cup raisins

Preheat oven to 400 degrees. Mix thoroughly shortening, sugar, egg and extract. Measure flour and sift. Blend flour, cream of tartar, soda and salt. Stir into shortening mixture. Stir in raisins. Roll into 1-inch balls. Place about 3 inches apart on ungreased baking sheet. Flatten with fork dipped in flour, making a crisscross pattern. Bake 8–10 minutes.

Delicious lemon-flavored raisin cookies ... children love them!

Marcella Swigert, Monroe City, Mo.

CRISPY CHOCOLATE CARAMEL BARS
Makes 36

Crust:
1¼ cups all-purpose flour
½ cup margarine *or* butter
½ cup confectioners' sugar

Filling:
1 (14-ounce) package vanilla caramels
⅓ cup half-and-half *or* evaporated milk
¼ cup margarine *or* butter

Topping:
1 (6-ounce) package (1 cup) semisweet chocolate chips
3 tablespoons shortening
¾ cup crisp rice cereal

Heat oven to 350 degrees. Lightly spoon flour into measuring cup. In medium bowl, combine flour and confectioners' sugar. Using pastry blender or fork, cut in ½ cup margarine until crumbly. Lightly press mixture in ungreased 13 x 9-inch pan. Bake at 350 degrees for 10–12 minutes, or until light brown. Meanwhile, in heavy saucepan melt caramels, half-and-half and ¼ cup margarine over low heat, stirring constantly. Spread over baked crust. In medium saucepan over low heat, melt chocolate chips and shortening, stirring constantly. Stir in cereal. Carefully spread over filling. Cool completely; cut into bars.

Grace Moser, Goshen, Ind.

SAND COOKIES
Makes 4 dozen

1/2 pound (2 sticks) margarine, softened
3/4 cup sugar
1 teaspoon baking soda
1 teaspoon vinegar
1 teaspoon vanilla
1 1/2 cups flour
1/2 bag miniature chocolate chips

Beat margarine and sugar for 5 minutes. Dissolve soda in vinegar and add to margarine mixture. Add vanilla; beat in flour. Add chocolate chips.

Drop by teaspoonsful onto ungreased cookie sheets. Bake at 275 degrees for 30 minutes.

Donna Flick, Kalamazoo, Mich.

MINT SWIRL BROWNIES

1 small package (3 ounces) cream cheese, softened
1/4 cup (1/2 stick) margarine, softened
3/4 cup sugar
2 eggs
2/3 cup flour
1/2 teaspoon baking powder
1/2 teaspoon salt
1/3 cup chopped nuts
3 tablespoons cocoa
1/2 teaspoon peppermint extract
Several drops of green food coloring
Chocolate Glaze:
1 tablespoon margarine, melted
1 cup confectioners' sugar, sifted
3 tablespoons cocoa
1/2 teaspoon vanilla
2 tablespoons boiling water

Cream together cream cheese, margarine and sugar; beat in eggs. Stir together flour, baking powder and salt; stir into creamed mixture.

Spoon half the batter into another bowl; stir in nuts and cocoa. Drop chocolate batter by tablespoonsful, checkerboard fashion, into a greased 9-inch square pan.

To remaining batter, add peppermint extract and green food coloring. Spoon green batter into spaces between chocolate batter. Swirl to marbleize, but do not overmix.

Bake in a preheated 350-degree oven for 15-20 minutes. While dough is baking, make *Glaze* by beating together all glaze ingredients until smooth. Remove brownies from oven and pour chocolate glaze over top. Cut at once into bars and cool.

Mrs. Sharon Crider, Evansville, Wis.

BUTTERSCOTCH WHISTLES

1 egg
⅛ teaspoon salt
2 tablespoons flour
½ cup brown sugar
¼ teaspoon vanilla
1 tablespoon chopped nuts

Beat egg; add sugar and salt. Beat thoroughly. Add nuts and flour. Drop mixture from teaspoon onto greased baking sheets. Bake in hot 400-degree oven until brown (1–2 minutes). Remove quickly with spatula. Roll over handle of spoon and cool.

Suzan L. Wiener, Spring Hill, Fla.

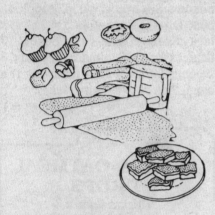

RICH DROP COOKIES

2 cups sifted flour
½ teaspoon baking soda
1½ teaspoons cream of tartar
1 cup white sugar
½ teaspoon salt
1 cup shortening
1 teaspoon vanilla
1 egg

Cream sugar and shortening. Add egg, vanilla and salt. Beat until smooth and fluffy. Sift flour, baking soda and cream of tartar. Add to creamed mixture. Roll into little balls; place on cookie sheet. Decorate with cherry half or colored sprinkles. Bake at 325 degrees for 10–15 minutes.

Rosie O'Connell, Greensburg, Pa.

SUGAR COOKIES

1 cup confectioners' sugar
1 cup white sugar
1 cup butter (do not substitute margarine)
1 cup shortening
2 eggs
1½ teaspoons vanilla
1½ teaspoons salt
1½ teaspoons cream of tartar
1½ teaspoons soda
4¼ cups sifted flour

Blend first 4 ingredients until light and creamy. Add eggs and vanilla. Sift dry ingredients and add to creamed mixture; mix until well-blended. Form into balls. Put on greased cookie sheets. Flatten with glass dipped in sugar. Bake in 350-degree oven for 10 minutes.

Dorothy Pelster, Hastings, Neb.

PEANUT BUTTER ORANGE DATE COOKIES
Makes 6 dozen

3/4 cup butter *or* margarine
1 cup peanut butter, plain or chunky
  style
1 cup granulated sugar
1 cup firmly packed brown sugar
2 eggs
1 1/2 teaspoons grated orange peel
1 teaspoon real vanilla
1 1/2 cups whole-wheat flour
1 cup all-purpose flour
1 teaspoon baking powder
1 teaspoon baking soda
1/2 teaspoon salt
1 cup finely chopped dates

Preheat oven to 350 degrees. Cream butter or margarine; add peanut butter and sugars; beat until light and fluffy. Beat in eggs, orange peel and vanilla. Stir together whole-wheat flour, all-purpose flour, baking powder, baking soda and salt. Sift flour mixture into butter mixture to form a soft dough. Stir in dates. Refrigerate dough for several hours or overnight. Shape dough into walnut-size balls. Place on cookie sheets. Flatten with tines of fork. Bake in 350-degree oven for 10–12 minutes, or until lightly browned. Cool in pan on wire rack; remove from pan and complete cooling. Store in airtight container when cool.

Trenda Leigh, Richmond, Va.

APRICOT-COCONUT BALLS
Makes 5 dozen

2 (6-ounce) packages dried
  apricots, ground
1 cup shredded coconut
⅔ cup sweetened condensed
  milk
  Confectioners' sugar

Combine apricots and coconut; stir to mix. Add condensed milk and mix well. Shape into 1-inch balls and coat with confectioners' sugar.

Mrs. Bruce Fowler, Woodruff, S.C.

GUMDROP JEWELS
Makes 5–6 dozen

1 cup (2 sticks) butter
1 cup firmly packed light
  brown sugar
1 egg
1 teaspoon vanilla extract
1½ cups all-purpose flour
½ teaspoon *each* baking
  soda, baking powder, salt
1 cup quick oats, uncooked
1 cup cut-up gumdrops
½ cup chopped nuts

Preheat oven to 350 degrees. Cream butter. Gradually add sugar and continue beating until blended. Beat in egg and vanilla. Combine flour, soda, baking powder and salt. Gradually add to creamed mixture. Stir in oats, gumdrops and nuts. Drop by rounded teaspoonfuls onto unbuttered cookie sheets. Bake 12–14 minutes. Remove to wire rack to cool.

APPLE BARS

2-1/2 cups flour
1 tablespoon sugar
1 teaspoon salt
1 cup margarine
1 egg yolk and milk to make 2/3 cup

Combine ingredients to make dough. Roll out half of dough; place in 15x10-inch jelly roll pan.

5 cups sliced apples
1 cup sugar
1 teaspoon cinnamon
1 or 2 tablespoons flour
1 egg white

Combine remaining ingredients, except egg white. Put on crust; roll out rest of dough; place on top of apples. Beat the egg white until stiff; spread on top crust. Bake at 400 degrees for 40 minutes. While hot, drizzle glaze over top.

Glaze:
1 cup confectioners' sugar
2 tablespoons milk

Elaine Dodd, Pasco, Wash.

PINEAPPLE-COCONUT COOKIES
Makes 3½ dozen

½ cup sugar
¼ cup brown sugar
¼ cup margarine
¼ cup shortening
1 egg
1 teaspoon vanilla
1¼ cups flour
¾ teaspoon salt
½ teaspoon soda
¼ teaspoon ginger
1 cup coconut
½ cup crushed pineapple, well-
  drained
½ cup chopped nuts

Cream first 6 ingredients together until light and fluffy. Stir dry ingredients together and beat into creamy mixture. Stir in coconut, pineapple and nuts. Drop teaspoonfuls 2 inches apart on a greased cookie sheet. Bake at 375 degrees for 8–10 minutes. Let stand 30 seconds on sheet after removing from oven, then cool on wire racks.

Mrs. A.C. Yoder, Meherrin, Va.

BANANA OATMEAL DROPS
Makes 4 dozen

¾ cup shortening
1 cup sugar
1 egg
1 medium-size banana, mashed
½ teaspoon lemon juice
1½ cups sifted flour
½ teaspoon soda
1 teaspoon salt
¾ teaspoon cinnamon
¼ teaspoon nutmeg
1½ cups quick-cooking oats
½ cup chopped walnuts

Cream together shortening and sugar until light and fluffy. Beat in egg. Stir in banana and lemon juice. Sift together flour, soda, salt, cinnamon and nutmeg. Stir into creamed mixture. Mix in oats and walnuts. Drop from a teaspoon onto greased baking sheets, about 2 inches apart. Bake in a moderate oven of 350 degrees for 12–15 minutes, or until edges turn golden.

Marcella Swigart, Monroe City, Mo.

BRAZIL NUT MELTS

1 cup flour
1/3 cup sugar
1 egg
3 tablespoons orange juice or milk
Confectioners' sugar
1/2 teaspoon salt
1/2 cup shortening
1 teaspoon grated orange peel
3/4 cup chopped Brazil nuts

In large bowl, combine all ingredients except confectioners' sugar. Blend well. Drop by rounded teaspoonsful onto ungreased cookie sheets. Bake at 350 degrees for 10 to 12 minutes.

While still hot, roll in confectioners' sugar.

Mrs. Raymond Weeks, Columbus, Ohio

ORANGE COCONUT REFRIGERATOR COOKIES

Makes 11 dozen

½ cup (1 stick) butter
½ cup firmly packed light brown sugar
¾ cup granulated sugar
1 egg
2 teaspoons grated orange peel
1 teaspoon vanilla extract
1¾ cups all-purpose flour
2 teaspoons baking powder
¼ teaspoon salt
⅓ cup flaked coconut

Cream butter. Add sugars and continue beating until blended. Beat in egg, orange peel and vanilla. Combine flour, baking powder and salt; add to creamed mixture. Blend in coconut. On floured surface form into rolls 1½ inches in diameter. Wrap in waxed paper. Chill several hours. Preheat oven to 400 degrees. Cut rolls into ⅛-inch slices and place on buttered cookie sheets. Bake 5–6 minutes. Remove to wire rack to cool.

Note: The rolls can be placed in wrapping and refrigerated up to 1 week or frozen up to 3 months. If frozen unthaw and bake as directed.

APPLE TREASURE COOKIES

Makes 5–6 dozen

1 cup shortening
1½ cups firmly packed light brown sugar
¼ cup molasses
3 eggs, unbeaten
3½ cups sifted all-purpose flour
½ teaspoon salt
1 teaspoon baking powder
3 teaspoons cinnamon
½ teaspoon nutmeg
½ teaspoon cloves
1 cup roasted peanuts, chopped
1 cup finely chopped apples

Cream shortening with brown sugar until light and fluffy. Add molasses. Add eggs, 1 at a time. In separate bowl sift flour, salt, spices and baking powder; add to sugar-molasses mixture; mix lightly. Stir in peanuts and apples. Drop by spoonfuls onto greased baking sheets. Bake at 350 degrees for 12–15 minutes.

Peggy Fowler, Woodruff, S.C.

GRAHAM CRACKER BARS

Makes 3 dozen

1-1/2 cups graham cracker crumbs
1/4 cup sugar
1/3 cup margarine, melted
1 (8-ounce) package cream cheese, softened
1/2 cup sugar
1 egg
3/4 cup flaked coconut
3/4 cup chopped nuts
1 (6-ounce) package semisweet chocolate pieces

Combine crumbs, sugar, and margarine. Press onto bottom of 13x9-inch baking pan. Bake at 350 degrees for 5 minutes.

Combine cream cheese, sugar, and egg, mixing until well-blended. Spread over crust. Sprinkle with remaining ingredients; press lightly into surface. Bake at 350 degrees for 25-30 minutes, or until lightly browned. Cool and cut into bars.

Ruby Walsh, West Chicago, Ill.

CALIFORNIA TRAIL BARS

Makes 3 dozen

1 cup light corn syrup
1/2 cup packed brown sugar
1/4 teaspoon salt
1-1/2 cups chunk-style peanut butter
1 teaspoon vanilla
1 cup non-fat dry milk
1 cup granola cereal (crush large lumps)
1 cup whole-bran cereal
1 cup raisins
1 (6-ounce) package semisweet chocolate pieces

Line 9x13-inch pan with waxed paper. In heavy saucepan combine syrup, sugar, and salt; bring to boil. Remove from heat; stir in peanut butter and vanilla. Stir in remaining ingredients, except chocolate; cool slightly. Add chocolate; press into prepared pan. Refrigerate 30 minutes; cut into bars. Store in refrigerator.

Sarah Lane, Philadelphia, Pa.

HAWAIIAN OATMEAL COOKIES

Makes 3 dozen

1 cup flour
1 teaspoon baking powder
1 teaspoon baking soda
¾ teaspoon salt
½ cup shortening
½ cup granulated sugar
½ cup brown sugar, packed
1 egg
½ teaspoon vanilla
1 cup rolled oats
1 cup shredded coconut

Sift together flour, baking powder, baking soda and salt; set aside. Cream shortening and sugars until light and fluffy; add egg; mix well. Add vanilla, then flour mixture. Add oats and coconut; mix until well-blended. Shape into small walnut-size balls; place on ungreased cookie sheets. Bake at 350 degrees about 12–15 minutes, or until golden.

Margaret Russo, Winsted, Conn.

CORNFLAKE MACAROONS
Makes 2½ dozen

- 3 egg whites
- 1 cup sugar
- ¼ teaspoon almond extract
- ¼ teaspoon vanilla extract
- 1½ cups flaked coconut
- 3 cups cornflakes

Beat egg whites until stiff but not dry; gradually add sugar. Add flavorings; fold in coconut and cornflakes. Drop by teaspoonfuls onto well-greased cookie sheets. Bake at 300 degrees for about 20 minutes. Remove from cookie sheet as soon as removed from oven.

Sandra Russell, Gainesville, Fla.

FROSTED CHOCOLATE CHIP BARS

- 2½ cups (1 pound) brown sugar
- 3 eggs
- ⅔ cup shortening, melted
- 2¾ cups flour
- 2½ teaspoons baking powder
- ½ teaspoon salt
- 1 cup salted nuts
- 1 (6-ounce) package chocolate chips

Cream sugar and eggs, 1 at a time, beating well after each 1. Add melted shortening, then sifted dry ingredients. Mix well. Add nuts and chocolate chips. Batter will be thick. Grease a 10 x 15½ x ¾-inch pan. Bake at 350 degrees for 25–30 minutes. Frost with recipe which follows. Cut when cool.

Frosting:
- Confectioners' sugar (enough for spreading consistency desired)
- 2 tablespoons butter, melted
- 3 tablespoons milk
- 2 tablespoons cocoa

Blend butter, milk and cocoa; add confectioners' sugar to spreading consistency. Add ½ teaspoon vanilla.

Ilene Ongman, Klamath Falls, Ore.

COCOA BROWNIES
Makes 48-60 bars

- 1 cup flour
- 1 cup sugar
- 1/2 teaspoon salt
- 1/3 cup cocoa
- 1 cup (2 sticks) butter or margarine
- 3 eggs
- 1 1/2 teaspoons vanilla
- 1/2 cup chopped nuts
- 1 box fudge frosting mix

Mix and sift flour, sugar, salt and cocoa into bowl. Work softened butter into dry ingredients. Beat in eggs one at a time; add vanilla, ceasing to beat when blended. Stir in nuts. Turn into greased and floured 9x13x2-inch pan. Level batter with a flat blade to depth of 3/4 inch. Bake in a preheated 325-degree oven for 20 minutes, or until brownies test done.

Cool and frost with prepared frosting mix. Cut into bars.

Mrs. Shirley E. Churchill, Mattawan, Mich.

CREAM CHEESE CHOCOLATE CHIP COOKIES
Makes 4 dozen

- 1 cup margarine
- 1 cup sugar
- 1 (3-ounce) package cream cheese
- 2 eggs
- 1 teaspoon vanilla
- ½ teaspoon lemon extract
- 2½ cups flour
- 1 teaspoon baking powder
- ½ teaspoon baking soda
- 1 cup coarsely chopped pecans or walnuts
- 1 cup semisweet chocolate pieces

Cream margarine, then add sugar, beating until smooth and fluffy. Add cream cheese; blend in eggs, vanilla, and lemon extract. Mix flour, baking powder and baking soda together; stir into cream cheese mixture. Add nuts and chocolate pieces. Drop by teaspoon on lightly greased cookie sheet. Bake at 350 degrees for 12–15 minutes.

D. Villines, Clinton, Mo.

CHOCO DATE BALLS
Makes 3½ dozen

- ½ cup chunky peanut butter
- ¼ cup cocoa or carob powder
- 2 teaspoons vanilla
- 2 cups uncooked oat cereal
- ¼ cup butter or margarine
- ⅔ cup mild-flavored honey
- 1 cup finely snipped dates

In a small mixing bowl, blend peanut butter, cocoa or carob powder and vanilla, using 2 forks. Mix in oats. In a small saucepan bring butter and honey to a boil; stir 1 minute. Remove from heat and add dates. Blend into oat mixture. Shape into bite-size balls. Chill until firm. When firm, store in refrigerator in plastic bags. Best when served chilled.

Peggy Fowler Revels, Woodruff, S.C.

BANANA DROP COOKIES
Makes 4 dozen

- 2 ripe medium bananas, peeled
- 1 cup butter, softened
- 1 cup granulated sugar
- ½ cup brown sugar, packed
- 2 eggs
- 1 teaspoon vanilla extract
- 2 cups flour
- 1 teaspoon ground cinnamon (optional)
- ½ teaspoon baking soda
- ½ teaspoon salt
- 1 cup peanut butter chips
- 1 cup chopped walnuts
- 1 cup raisins

Purée or mash bananas to yield 1 cup; cream together butter and sugars. Beat in bananas, eggs and vanilla; combine flour, cinnamon, soda and salt. Gradually beat dry ingredients into banana mixture. Fold in peanut butter chips, nuts and raisins. Drop by tablespoonfuls onto greased cookie sheets. Bake in a 375-degree oven for 12 minutes until golden brown. Remove to wire rack to cool.

Peggy Fowler Revels, Woodruff, S.C.

HUNKER DUNKER COOKIES

2 cups butter or margarine
2 cups brown sugar
2 cups granulated sugar
4 eggs
2 teaspoons vanilla
2 teaspoons salt
2 teaspoons baking soda
4 cups flour
2 cups oatmeal
2 cups Rice Krispies

Cream butter and sugars together; add eggs and vanilla. Sift dry ingredients together and add to butter mixture. Stir in oatmeal and Rice Krispies. Bake at 350 degrees for 10 minutes.

This recipe is my family's favorite. I sometimes add chocolate chips for variation.

Sharon Sisson, Longview, Wash.

CITRUS SUGAR COOKIES

Makes 5 dozen

½ cup butter *or* margarine
1 cup sugar, divided
2 eggs
1 tablespoon frozen orange juice concentrate, thawed and undiluted
3 tablespoons grated orange rind, divided
2 cups flour
2 teaspoons baking powder

Cream butter and ½ cup sugar until light and fluffy. Add eggs, 1 at a time, beating well after each addition. Blend in orange juice and 1 tablespoon grated orange rind. Combine flour and baking powder; blend into creamed mixture. Wrap dough in waxed paper and refrigerate for 3 hours. Roll out on lightly floured surface to ¼-inch thickness. Cut with a 2-inch cookie cutter. Place in greased cookie sheet. Combine ½ cup sugar and 2 tablespoons grated orange rind; sprinkle mixture over cookies. Bake at 375 degrees for 8–10 minutes.

Barbara Beauregard-Smith, Northfield, South Australia

ICED PEANUT BUTTER COOKIES

½ cup margarine
½ cup sugar
½ cup brown sugar
2 eggs
⅓ cup peanut butter
½ teaspoon baking soda
¼ teaspoon salt
½ teaspoon vanilla
1 cup flour
1 cup rolled oats
1 cup chocolate chips

Mix together margarine, sugar and brown sugar. Blend in eggs, peanut butter, baking soda, vanilla, flour, salt and rolled oats. Spread in a greased 13 x 9 x 2-inch pan and bake at 350 degrees for 20 minutes. As soon as the pan is removed from the oven, sprinkle chocolate bits on the top. Return to oven for a few minutes to melt the chocolate; remove again, spreading chocolate evenly; allow to cool.

Icing:
¼ cup peanut butter
½ cup confectioners' sugar
Milk (2–4 teaspoons)

Combine peanut butter and confectioners' sugar. Moisten with milk until consistency to spread. Ice cooled cookies.

Amelia M. Brown, Pittsburgh, Pa.

OATMEAL FUDGE COOKIES

½ cup milk
½ cup vegetable shortening
6 tablespoons cocoa
¼ teaspoon salt
2 cups sugar
1 teaspoon vanilla
3 cups quick-cooking oatmeal

In saucepan place all ingredients, except oatmeal. Heat and bring to boil, and boil for 1 minute, stirring constantly. Remove from heat and stir in oatmeal. Drop by spoonfuls onto waxed paper. Chill to firm.

Mrs. Thurman White, Troy, N.Y.

BUTTERSCOTCH BARS

1 cup sugar
2 eggs
½ cup butter
2½ cups graham cracker crumbs
1½ cups marshmallows (cut up)
1 cup butterscotch chips
3 tablespoons peanut butter

In saucepan, bring sugar, eggs and butter to a boil, stirring constantly. Remove from heat and cool. Stir in cracker crumbs and marshmallows; press into 9 x 13-inch pan. Melt 1 cup butterscotch chips with peanut butter over hot water. Spread on top of crumbs. Cool. Cut into bars.

Mrs. E.J. Kuchenbecker, Prairie du Chien, Wis.

ORANGE COOKIES

Makes 2-1/2 dozen

1-1/3 cups flour
1/2 teaspoon baking powder
1/4 teaspoon baking soda
1/2 cup sugar
3 tablespoons shortening
3 tablespoons margarine
1 egg
1/3 cup buttermilk
1 teaspoon finely shredded orange peel
2 tablespoons orange juice
Orange Frosting (recipe follows)

Stir together flour, baking powder, and soda; set aside. Beat together sugar, shortening, and margarine. Add egg; beat until fluffy. Beat in buttermilk, orange peel, and orange juice. Add dry ingredients and beat until combined. Drop by teaspoonfuls onto ungreased cookie sheets. Bake at 350 degrees for 10-13 minutes. Cool, then frost.

Orange Frosting:

Beat together 2 cups confectioners' sugar, 3 teaspoons shredded orange peel, and 3 tablespoons orange juice to make a spreadable, thick frosting.

Denise Garcia, Salina, Kans.

RASPBERRY MERINGUE KISSES

3 egg whites
¾ cup sugar
3½ tablespoons raspberry gelatin
1 cup miniature chocolate bits
¼ teaspoon salt
1 teaspoon vinegar

Beat egg whites with salt until foamy. Add raspberry gelatin and sugar gradually. Beat until stiff peaks form and sugar is dissolved. Mix in vinegar and fold in chocolate bits. Drop by teaspoon onto ungreased cookie sheets covered with brown paper. Bake at 250 degrees for 20 minutes. Turn oven off and leave in oven 20 minutes longer.

Note: Too hot an oven may cause the cookies to lose some of their pink coloring, so set temperature at 225–250 degrees according to how your oven heats. For more color, add a few drops of red food coloring.

Wanda J. Harrison, Fremont, Wis.

PECAN BARS

1 stick margarine
1 1/4 cups white flour
2 beaten eggs
1 cup light brown sugar
1/2 cup chopped pecans
1/2 cup shredded coconut
1/2 cup chopped and drained maraschino cherries
1 tablespoon Grape Nuts cereal
2 tablespoons white flour
1/2 teaspoon baking powder
1 teaspoon almond extract

In large mixer bowl, make a crumb mixture of margarine and flour. Pat down firmly into non-stick 9x13-inch pan. Bake for 10 minutes in 350 degree oven. Remove from oven.

Mix together all other ingredients and spread over prepared base. Return to oven and bake at 350 degrees for 20 minutes. Cool in pan, then cut into bars with sharp knife.

Pearle M. Goodwin, South Ryegate, Vt.

CARAMEL-COATED COOKIES
Makes 28–30

Ingredients:
½ cup butter
1 teaspoon vanilla
½ cup confectioners' sugar
½ cup brown sugar, packed firmly
1 egg
2 cups flour

Coating:
36 caramels
6 ounces evaporated milk
Coarsely chopped pecans and shredded coconut

For the dough:

Cream butter with vanilla until soft. Add confectioners' sugar and brown sugar; blend well. Add egg; beat until blended. Mix in flour; blend well; form dough into 1-inch balls. Bake on ungreased cookie sheet in preheated 350-degree oven for 15–18 minutes.

For the coating:

In top of double boiler over simmering water, melt the caramels with evaporated milk, stirring until smooth. Dip cookies, 1 at a time, into caramel mixture; roll lightly into coconut; then roll into nuts. Place each into a small paper liner.

Marie Fusaro, Manasquan, N.J.

SESAME MACAROONS
Makes 3 dozen

½ cup sesame seeds
¼ teaspoon cream of tartar
¼ cup egg whites (about 2)
¼ cup sugar
½ teaspoon almond extract

Toast sesame seeds in 350-degree oven for 15 minutes, or until golden brown. Pulverize seeds in blender. Add cream of tartar to egg whites; beat until stiff. Gradually add sugar, beating well after each addition. Fold in sesame seeds and almond extract. Drop by teaspoonfuls onto lightly greased baking sheet. Bake in 250-degree oven for 30 minutes. Remove at once from baking sheet.

Agnes Ward, Erie, Pa.

SPECIAL SUGAR COOKIES

1/2 cup powdered sugar
1/2 cup white sugar
1 stick butter, softened
1/2 cup vegetable oil
1/2 teaspoon vanilla
2 cups all-purpose flour, plus 2 tablespoons
1 egg, beaten
1/2 teaspoon soda
1/2 teaspoon salt
1/2 teaspoon cream of tartar

Cream two sugars, butter and oil; add beaten egg; beat until fluffy. Sift dry ingredients, add to first mixture. Drop by teaspoonsful onto cookie sheet. Dip a glass bottom into sugar and press cookies down lightly.

Bake at 375 degrees for 10 minutes.

Mrs. Pearl L. Stevenson, Lafayette, Ind.

BANANA DROP COOKIES
Makes 4 dozen

2 ripe bananas, peeled
1 cup butter, softened
1 cup sugar
½ cup brown sugar, packed
2 eggs
1 teaspoon vanilla extract
2 cups flour
1 teaspoon ground cinnamon, optional
1 teaspoon baking soda
½ teaspoon salt
1 cup peanut butter chips
1 cup chopped walnuts
1 cup raisins

Preheat oven to 375 degrees. Mash bananas. Cream together butter and sugars. Beat in bananas, eggs and vanilla. In separate bowl, combine flour, cinnamon, soda and salt. Gradually beat dry ingredients into banana mixture. Fold in peanut butter chips, nuts and raisins. Drop by tablespoonfuls on greased cookie sheets; bake 12 minutes, or until golden brown. Remove wire rack to cool.

Kit Rollins, Cedarburg, W

ANGEL FOOD COOKIES

Makes 4 dozen

1 cup shortening
1/2 cup brown sugar
1/2 cup white sugar
1 egg, beaten
1/4 teaspoon salt
1 teaspoon vanilla flavoring
2 cups flour
1 teaspoon baking soda
1 teaspoon cream of tartar
1 cup Angel Flake coconut

Mix shortening and sugars until creamy. Add egg, then sifted dry ingredients. Stir in flavoring and coconut. Roll dough into small balls. Bake on greased baking sheet for 12-15 minutes at 350 degrees.

Ralph Spencer, Guage, Ky.

JUMBO PEANUT BUTTER APPLE COOKIES

Makes 1½ dozen

1 cup sifted flour
1 cup sifted whole-wheat flour
2 teaspoons baking soda
1 teaspoon cinnamon
¾ teaspoon salt
⅓ cup butter, softened
⅔ cup chunk-style peanut butter
¼ cup sugar
1¾ cups brown sugar
2 eggs
1 teaspoon vanilla
1 cup rolled oats
1 cup peeled, diced apples
½ cup raisins

Mix and sift first 5 ingredients. Cream butter, peanut butter and sugars. Add eggs and vanilla; mix. Add sifted dry ingredients to creamed mixture and mix well. Stir in oats, apples and raisins. Using about ¼ cup of dough for each, shape into balls. Place on ungreased cookie sheet and flatten slightly. Bake in a 350-degree oven for about 12–15 minutes. Let stand on cookie sheet 1 minute before removing to wire cooling rack.

Melba Bellefeuille, Libertyville, Ill.

BUTTERMILK CHOCOLATE CHIP COOKIES

Makes 7 dozen

1 cup shortening
1 cup sugar
1 cup brown sugar, firmly packed
2 eggs
1½ teaspoons vanilla
3 cups sifted flour
1 teaspoon baking soda
½ cup buttermilk
1 (6-ounce) package semisweet chocolate pieces
1 cup chopped pecans

Cream together shortening and sugars until light and fluffy. Beat in eggs, 1 at a time. Blend in vanilla. Sift together flour and baking soda. Add dry ingredients alternately with buttermilk to creamed mixture; mix well. Stir in chocolate pieces and pecans. Drop by teaspoonfuls about 2 inches apart on greased baking sheets. Bake in 350-degree oven for 12–15 minutes, or until done. Remove from baking sheets; cool on racks.

These are my favorite chocolate chip cookies. They are so fabulous!!

Barbara Beauregard-Smith, Northfield, South Australia

ROCKY ROAD S'MORES BARS

½ cup margarine
½ cup packed brown sugar
1 cup flour
½ cup graham cracker crumbs
2 cups miniature marshmallows
1 (6-ounce) package semisweet chocolate pieces
½ cup chopped walnuts (optional)

Beat margarine and brown sugar until light and fluffy. Add combined flour and crumbs; mix well. Press onto bottom of greased 9-inch square pan. Sprinkle with remaining ingredients. Bake at 375 degrees for 15–20 minutes, or until golden brown. Cool; cut into bars.

Loriann Johnson, Gobles, Mich.

BUTTERSCOTCH DATE BARS

1/2 cup margarine
2 cups packed brown sugar
3 eggs
2 teaspoons vanilla
2 cups flour
2 teaspoons baking powder
1 teaspoon salt
1 cup chopped nuts
1 cup chopped dates

Cream margarine and sugar until light and fluffy. Blend in eggs and vanilla. Add combined dry ingredients; mix well. Stir in nuts and dates. Pour into greased 13x9-inch baking pan. Bake at 350 degrees for 30-35 minutes, or until wooden pick inserted in center comes out clean. Cool; cut into bars.

Allie Fields, Pensacola, Fla.

CHERRY PINEAPPLE BARS

Makes 24 bars

1 cup butter
2 cups sifted all-purpose flour
2 egg yolks, beaten
3 tablespoons chopped candied orange peel
2 tablespoons cornstarch
1 cup firmly packed brown sugar
½ teaspoon salt
1 cup crushed pineapple, undrained
½ cup granulated sugar
1 cup maraschino cherries

Combine butter, brown sugar, flour and salt; mix until crumbly. Press about ¾ of crumb mixture on bottom of buttered 13 x 9 x 2-inch baking pan. Bake at 350 degrees for 15 minutes. In a saucepan, combine egg yolks, pineapple, orange peel, granulated sugar and cornstarch. Cook over medium heat, stirring constantly, until thickened. Remove from heat; stir in maraschino cherries. Spoon fruit mixture over baked layer. Sprinkle remaining crumbs over top. Bake at 375 degrees for 40 minutes. Cool before cutting.

Sandra Russell, Gainesville, Fla.

RAISIN JUMBO COOKIES

1 cup water
2 cups raisins
1/2 cup (1 stick) margarine
1 cup brown sugar
3 eggs
1 cup granulated sugar
4 cups flour
1 teaspoon baking powder
2 teaspoons salt
1 1/2 teaspoons cinnamon
1/4 teaspoon cloves
1/4 teaspoon nutmeg
1/4 teaspoon allspice

Boil water and raisins for 5 minutes. Set aside and cool. Mix shortening, both sugars, and eggs. Beat well. Combine dry ingredients and add raisins; mix with creamed mixture. Drop by teaspoonsful onto cookie sheets. Bake at 375 degrees for 12-15 minutes.

Mrs. Marie Popovich, Warren, Mich.

ZUCCHINI COOKIES

1 cup grated zucchini
1 cup sugar
1/2 cup shortening *or* margarine
1 egg
2 cups flour
1 teaspoon ground cinnamon
1/2 teaspoon ground nutmeg
3/4 teaspoon baking powder
1/2 teaspoon baking soda
3/4 cup crushed pineapple, drained
1 cup chopped nuts
1 cup raisins

Cream sugar, shortening and egg. Add grated zucchini and crushed pineapple. Stir in dry ingredients; stir in nuts and raisins. On greased cookie sheet, drop by rounded teaspoonfuls. Bake at 375 degrees for 15 minutes, or until no imprint is left when you press top of cookie lightly. These do not brown on top. While still warm, glaze with a thin confectioners' sugar, canned milk and vanilla frosting.

Note: Dough will keep well for a week if covered and refrigerated.

Mrs. S.R. Burt, Imlay, Nev.

OLD-FASHIONED RAISIN BARS

1 cup raisins
1 cup water
1/2 cup shortening
1/2 teaspoon soda
Pinch of salt
2 cups flour
1 cup sugar
1 teaspoon cinnamon
1/2 teaspoon cloves
1/2 cup nuts (optional)

Boil raisins and water; remove from heat; add shortening and soda to melt. Add dry ingredients and nuts. Spread on cookie sheet and bake 20 minutes at 375 degrees. Top with a thin confectioners' sugar icing. Cut into bars.

Mrs. Melvin Habiger, Spearville, Kan.

WHOLE-WHEAT SNICKERDOODLES
Makes 30

1/2 cup margarine
3/4 cup brown sugar, firmly packed
1 egg
1 teaspoon vanilla
1 1/2 cups whole-wheat flour
1/2 teaspoon baking soda
1/2 teaspoon cream of tartar
1/4 teaspoon salt
2 tablespoons sugar
1/2 teaspoon cinnamon

Preheat oven to 375 degrees. In a small mixer bowl beat margarine with electric mixer on medium speed until softened (about 30 seconds). Add brown sugar and beat until fluffy. Add egg and vanilla. Beat well. In a medium bowl stir together flour, baking soda, cream of tartar and salt. With mixer on low speed, gradually add flour mixture to butter mixture, beating until well-mixed. Stir together sugar and cinnamon. Shape dough into 1-inch balls. Roll the balls in sugar-cinnamon mixture. Place about 2 inches apart on ungreased cookie sheet. Flatten slightly with bottom of drinking glass. Bake in 325-degree oven for 8–10 minutes, or until edges are firm. Cool on rack.

Sharon McClatchey, Muskogee, Okla.

BUTTER PECAN TURTLE BARS

Crust:
2 cups flour
1 cup firmly packed brown sugar
1/2 cup butter, softened

In a 3-quart bowl, combine crust ingredients and mix at medium speed for 2-3 minutes or until particles are fine. Pat firmly into ungreased 13x9x2-inch pan. Sprinkle pecans evenly over unbaked crust.

Caramel layer:
2/3 cup butter
1/2 cup firmly packed brown sugar
1 cup pecan halves
1 cup milk chocolate chips

Preheat oven to 350 degrees. Prepare caramel layer by combining brown sugar and butter in a heavy 1-quart saucepan. Cook over medium heat until entire surface of mixture begins to boil. Boil 1/2-1 minute, stirring constantly. Pour caramel evenly over pecans and crust. Bake at center of oven for 18-22 minutes, or until entire caramel layer is bubbly and crust is light golden brown. Remove from oven. Immediately sprinkle with chips. Let chips melt slightly (2-3 minutes) and slightly swirl them as they melt. Leave some whole for a marbled effect. *Do not spread* them. Cool completely and cut into bars.

ETHEL'S FRUIT COOKIES

3 egg whites
1/2 cup sugar
1/2 cup flour
1 pound chopped dates
3 slices candied pineapple, chopped
2 cups pecans, chopped
1 teaspoon vanilla

Beat egg whites until stiff. Gradually add sugar, flour, fruit and nuts. Stir in vanilla. Drop by teaspoonsful onto greased, foil-lined baking sheet. Bake in a 275-degree oven for about 40 minutes.

Jean Baker, Chula Vista, Calif.

102

MOCHA NUT BUTTERBALLS
Makes 6 dozen

1 cup butter or margarine, softened
1/2 cup granulated sugar
2 teaspoons vanilla
2 teaspoons instant coffee powder
1/4 cup unsweetened cocoa
1 3/4 cups flour
1/2 teaspoon salt
2 cups finely chopped pecans
Confectioners' sugar

Cream first 3 ingredients together until light. Add next 4 ingredients, mixing well. Add nuts. Shape into 1-inch balls and place on greased cookie sheets. Bake in a preheated 325-degree oven for about 15 minutes. Cool on racks. Roll in confectioners' sugar.

These are delicious buttery, nutty cookies!

Mrs. Agnes Ward, Erie, Penn.

JAM SANDWICH COOKIES
Makes 24 filled cookies

½ cup butter
½ cup packed brown sugar
¼ cup honey
1 egg
½ teaspoon vanilla
1¾ cups all-purpose flour
1 teaspoon baking soda
¼ teaspoon salt
Raspberry or other jam

Cream together butter, brown sugar and honey. Beat in egg and vanilla. Combine flour, baking soda and salt. Blend flour mixture into creamed mixture. Chill dough for 30 minutes. Shape dough into small balls (about 1 inch in diameter). Place on lightly greased baking sheets. Flatten balls slightly with bottom of glass dipped in flour. Bake at 350 degrees for 8–10 minutes, or until golden. Cool on baking sheet for few minutes; remove to wire racks to cool completely. When cool, put together in pairs filled with jam. If desired, squeeze filled cookies slightly until jam is visible on edges. Roll edges in coconut. Especially pretty with red jam and coconut.

Donna Bilyk, Alberta, Canada

BLOND BROWNIES

1 cup (2 sticks) butter
1 cup packed brown sugar
4 eggs
1 teaspoon vanilla
1 3/4 cups flour
1/2 teaspoon baking powder
1/2 teaspoon salt
3/4 cup chopped walnuts

Cream butter with brown sugar until fluffy; add eggs, one at a time, beating well after each addition. Sift dry ingredients together. Add to egg mixture, beating until smooth. Stir in nuts.

Bake in preheated 375-degree oven in a greased and floured 9x13-inch pan for about 30 minutes. Cool and cut into squares. Top with spoonsfuls of *Brown Sugar Meringue*, *Tart Lemon Glaze* (recipes follow), or frost as desired.

Brown Sugar Meringue:

Beat *1 egg white* until frothy. Gradually beat in *1/2 cup packed brown sugar* until stiff peaks form. Top squares of Blond Brownies with spoonsful and broil a few minutes to brown meringue.

Tart Lemon Glaze:

Gradually add *1 tablespoon lemon juice* to *2/3 cup confectioners' sugar*. Mix until smooth. Stir in 1 *teaspoon grated lemon rind*. Drizzle over brownies. Chill before cutting into squares.

Hedi Johnson, Great Falls, Mont.

CARROT RAISIN BROWNIES
Makes about 55

1 1/2 cups light brown sugar, packed
1/2 cup (1 stick) butter
2 eggs
1 teaspoon vanilla
1 1/2 cups flour, unsifted
1/2 teaspoon salt
1/2 teaspoon baking soda
1/2 teaspoon baking powder
1/2 cup finely chopped raisins
1 1/2 cups finely grated carrots
1/2 cup finely chopped walnuts

Preheat oven to 350 degrees. Grease and flour a 9x13-inch pan.

Mix sugar and butter; add eggs and vanilla; beat well. Stir in all dry ingredients; add raisins and carrots. Blend to mix well. Spread into a baking pan; sprinkle with chopped walnuts.

Bake at 350 degrees for 40 minutes or until a toothpick inserted in the center comes out clean. Cool. Cut into 1x2-inch rectangles.

Charlotte Adams, Detroit, Mich.

TRILBIES
Makes 8 dozen

1 cup shortening
1 cup butter *or* margarine, softened
3 cups brown sugar
1 teaspoon vanilla
6 cups all-purpose flour
4 cups rolled oats
1 teaspoon salt
2 teaspoons baking soda
1 cup buttermilk
Date Filling (recipe follows)

Preheat oven to 375 degrees. In a large bowl, cream shortening, butter or margarine, and sugar together; add vanilla.

In a large bowl, sift flour; add oats, salt and baking soda; mix together. Add dry ingredients, alternately, with buttermilk to shortening mixture. Mix thoroughly; chill in refrigerator several hours.

Turn out dough onto a lightly floured board and roll out to ⅛-inch thickness. Cut with round cookie cutter and place 1 inch apart on greased baking sheet. Bake until golden brown, 10–12 minutes. Cool on wire racks.

Date Filling:

2 cups finely chopped dates
1 cup water
1 cup sugar
2 tablespoons flour

In a large saucepan, mix ingredients together and cook over medium heat until thick. Let cool. Spread on half the cookies and top with remaining cookies.

Mrs. H.W. Walker, Richmond, Va.

CRISPY CHOCOLATE CHIP COOKIES

3 sticks margarine
2 cups white sugar
2 eggs
2 teaspoons baking powder (mixed with)
2 teaspoons vinegar
1 teaspoon vanilla flavoring
1 teaspoon almond flavoring
3–3 1/4 cups flour
1 (12-ounce) bag chocolate chips *or* M&M candies

Cream margarine and sugar until fluffy (at least 5 minutes). Add eggs, 1 at a time; beat well. Add baking powder-and-vinegar mixture, then flavorings. Add flour gradually. Fold in chocolate chips.

Chocolate mint chips are very good, or M & M's. I often put 2 or 3 M & M's on top of chocolate chip cookies. Store in refrigerator or freezer. Kids love them!!

Mary Jeanne Maas, Rochester, N.Y.

BLACK WALNUT CHOCOLATE DROP COOKIES

Makes 4 dozen

1-3/4 cups sifted flour
1/2 teaspoon baking soda
1 teaspoon baking powder
1/4 teaspoon salt
1 cup chopped black walnuts
1/2 cup butter
1-1/4 cups brown sugar, sifted and packed
1 egg
2 ounces unsweetened chocolate, melted and cooled
1 teaspoon vanilla extract
1/2 cup milk

Mix and sift flour, soda, baking powder, and salt; add nuts and mix. Cream butter; add sugar gradually and cream until fluffy. Add well-beaten egg and chocolate. Add extract to milk. Add dry mixture alternately with milk to creamed mixture, mixing just enough after each addition to combine ingredients. Drop by

spoonfuls on ungreased baking sheets. Bake in preheated 375-degree oven for about 12 minutes. When cool, spread with Chocolate Frosting.

Chocolate Frosting:

1-1/2 ounces unsweetened chocolate, melted
1 egg yolk
3 tablespoons light cream
1-1/4 cups sifted confectioners' sugar

Combine chocolate, slightly beaten egg yolk, and cream; add sugar and mix well.

Kit Rollins, Cedarburg, Wis.

BANANA BROWNIES
Makes 2 dozen bars

1 cup all-purpose flour
1 cup light brown sugar, firmly packed
1/3 cup margarine
1-1/2 teaspoons baking powder
1 egg, lightly beaten
1 cup coarsely mashed bananas
1 (6-ounce) package semisweet chocolate pieces
2 teaspoons grated lemon rind
Milk, if needed

Preheat oven to 350 degrees. Grease an 8-inch square baking pan. In a large bowl, with a mixer set at low speed, blend flour, sugar, and margarine until mixture resembles coarse cornmeal. Blend in baking powder. Stir in egg and bananas. Gently fold in chocolate pieces and lemon rind (add a little milk, if batter is stiff). Spread mixture in baking pan. Bake 25-30 minutes, or until cake tester or wooden toothpick inserted in center comes out clean. Set pan on wire rack to cool. Cut into 1-1/2-inch squares.

Suzan L. Wiener, Spring Hill, Fla.

CREAM CHEESE LEMON BARS
Makes 24

1 (18½-ounce) package lemon cake mix
½ cup butter *or* margarine
3 eggs, divided

2 cups canned lemon frosting
1 (8-ounce) package cream cheese, softened

Grease 9 x 13-inch pan. Combi[ne] cake mix, butter and 1 egg. Stir un[til] moist. Press into pan. Blend frosti[ng] into cream cheese. Reserve ½ cup m[ix]-ture to frost bars. Preheat oven to 3[50] degrees.

Add remaining eggs to remain[ing] frosting mixture. Beat 3–5 minutes [at] high speed. Spread over base. Ba[ke] about 30 minutes. Cool slightly a[nd] frost with reserved frosting. Cut in[to] bars.

Kit Rollins, Cedarburg, W[is.]

BRAN BLONDIES
Makes 36 squares

3/4 cup flour, spooned lightly into cup
1/2 teaspoon baking powder
1/4 teaspoon soda
1/4 teaspoon salt
1/2 cup All-bran cereal
1/2 cup chopped walnuts *or* pecans
1 cup semisweet chocolate morsels
1/2 cup (1 stick) margarine
1 cup brown sugar (use part granulated, if desired)
1 large egg
1 teaspoon vanilla

Prepare a 9-inch square baking pan—spray with pan release, or grease and flour. (I foil-line and spray with pan release.)

Preheat oven to 350 degrees.

Into a small bowl measure flour, baking powder, soda, salt, All-bran, nuts, and chocolate morsels; stir together; set aside. In a medium-size saucepan barely melt margarine. Remove from heat; stir in sugar. Add egg and vanilla; whisk or beat with fork to blend well. With a rubber spatula, stir in dry ingredients. Spread in prepared pan. Bake until cake tester comes out dry, about 20 minutes.

Especially good warm, while chocolate is still soft. Freeze extras; warm in microwave oven.

Note: For chocolate bars, combine only 2/3 cup chocolate morsels with dry ingredients. Melt remaining 1/[3] cup morsels with margarine. Procee[d] as directed.

104

CHOCOLATE PECAN PIE BARS

Makes 36 bars

1-1/4 cups all-purpose flour
1/4 cup sugar
1/2 teaspoon baking powder
1/2 teaspoon cinnamon
1/2 cup margarine
1 cup finely chopped pecans
1/4 cup butter
1 square (1-ounce) semisweet chocolate
3 eggs, beaten
1-1/4 cups packed brown sugar
2 tablespoons water
1 teaspoon vanilla

In mixing bowl, stir together flour, sugar, baking powder and cinnamon. Cut in 1/2 cup margarine until mixture resembles coarse crumbs; stir in pecans. Press into bottom of ungreased 13 x 9-inch pan. Bake in 350 degree oven for 10 minutes. Meanwhile, in a small saucepan, combine 1/4 cup butter and chocolate; heat; stir over low heat until chocolate is melted. In a small mixing bowl, combine eggs, brown sugar, water and vanilla. Stir mixture until well blended; pour over crust. Return to oven. Bake 20 minutes more or until set. Cool on wire rack. Cut into bars.

Patricia Habiger, Spearville, KS

PEANUT BUTTER COOKIES

Makes 100 cookies

3-1/3 cups peanut butter
2-2/3 cups shortening
6 eggs
3/4 teaspoon salt
3/4 teaspoon baking soda
2-1/2 cups brown sugar
3 cups white sugar
4-1/2 cups flour
1 tablespoon vanilla

Cream the sugars, peanut butter,

and shortening all together. Add well beaten eggs and vanilla. Add dry ingredients sifted together. Roll mixture in balls and place on greased sheets. Flatten with fork dipped in granulated sugar. Bake in preheated oven at 375 degrees for 8 or 9 minutes.

This is a large recipe, but it can be adjusted to needs. I usually make the full amount - some to use right away, some to freeze, and some to give away. I am a head cook at our Chichester School and everyone who has eaten these cookies loves them.

Natalie Henshaw, Pittsfield, NH

MOIST OATMEAL COOKIES

Boil gently for 10 minutes:

1 cup water
1 cup sugar
1 cup shortening
1 cup golden raisins
1/2 teaspoon cinnamon
1/2 teaspoon nutmeg
1/2 teaspoon salt

Set aside to cool. Then add:

2 eggs
1 teaspoon vanilla
2 cups flour
1/2 cup nut meats
2 cups oatmeal

Drop by spoonfuls on greased cookie sheet. Bake 10-12 minutes at 350 degrees. Check bottom of cookie—if evenly browned, it's done and not too crispy.

O. Elizabeth Todd, Minneapolis, Minn.

HAWAIIAN OATMEAL COOKIES

Makes 3 dozen

1 cup flour
1 teaspoon baking powder
1 teaspoon baking soda
3/4 teaspoon salt

1/2 cup shortening
1/2 cup granulated sugar
1/2 cup packed brown sugar
1 egg
1/2 teaspoon vanilla
1 cup rolled oats
1 cup shredded coconut

Sift together flour, baking powder, baking soda and salt; set aside. Cream shortening and sugars until light and fluffy; add egg; mix well. Add vanilla, then flour mixture. Add oats and coconut; mix until well blended. Shape into small walnut size balls, place on ungreased cookie sheets. Bake at 350 degrees about 12 to 15 minutes or until golden.

Margaret Russo, Winsted, CT

OATMEAL-CARROT COOKIES

Makes 24 bars

1/2 cup brown sugar
1 tablespoon honey
1/3 cup margarine, melted
1 egg
1-1/2 teaspoon vanilla
3/4 cup shredded carrots
1 cup whole wheat flour
1 teaspoon baking powder
1 teaspoon cinnamon
1/2 teaspoon ground cloves. (optional)
1/2 cup oatmeal
1/4 cup wheat germ
1/2 cup raisins

In a small bowl, cream together sugar, honey, margarine, egg and vanilla until light and fluffy. Add carrots and mix well.

In another bowl, thoroughly stir together flour, baking powder, cinnamon, cloves (if used), oatmeal and wheat germ. Stir in the dry ingredients into the creamed mixture; fold in the raisins. Pour mixture into a 9 x 2 x 2 inch pan sprayed with vegetable oil. Bake at 350 degrees for 30 minutes. Let cool in pan on wire rack. Cut into bars or squares.

Let cookies set overnight so flavors can blend.

Trenda Leigh, Richmond, VA

PUMPKIN CANDY COOKIES

Makes 2 dozen

1/2 cup sugar
1/2 cup firmly-packed brown sugar
1 cup margarine or butter, softened
1 teaspoon vanilla
1 egg
1 cup canned or smoothly-mashed, cooked pumpkin
2 cups flour
1 teaspoon baking soda
1/2 teaspoon salt
1-1/2 teaspoons cinnamon
1/2 teaspoon ginger
1 cup candy-coated chocolate-covered peanuts

Heat oven to 350 degrees. In large bowl, beat sugar, brown sugar, and margarine until light and fluffy. Add vanilla, egg, and pumpkin; blend well. Lightly spoon flour into measuring cup; level off. Stir in flour, baking soda, salt, ginger, and cinnamon; mix well. Stir in candy. Drop by rounded tablespoonfuls, 3 inches apart, onto ungreased cookie sheet. Using metal spoon, flatten into 3-inch circles. Bake 14-17 minutes or until edges are light golden brown. Cool 1 minute; remove from cookie sheets.

FRENCH CHOCOLATE MERINGUES

Makes 4 dozen

1 (6 ounce) package (1 cup) semi-sweet chocolate morsels
3 egg whites (room temperature)
1/2 teaspoon vanilla
1 cup sugar
1 cup finely crushed saltines

Preheat oven 350 degrees. Melt chocolate morsels in top of double boiler over hot water (not boiling). Remove from water; let cool 5 minutes. Combine egg whites and vanilla; beat until stiff, but not dry. Add sugar gradually; beat until very stiff.

Fold in crackers and melted chocolate. Drop by teaspoons on greased cookie sheets. Bake in 350 degree oven for about 10 minutes. Remove from cookie sheets; cool on rack.

Mary A. Grills, New London, Conn.

CHOCOLATE CHIPPER CHAMPS

Makes 2-1/2 dozen

1-1/3 cups packed brown sugar
3/4 cup margarine or butter, softened
1 teaspoon vanilla
2 eggs
2-1/4 cups all purpose flour
1 cup M&M's plain chocolate candies
1/2 cup chopped nuts
1 teaspoon baking soda
1/2 teaspoon salt

Mix brown sugar, margarine, vanilla and eggs in large bowl until well blended. Stir in remaining ingredients. Drop dough by rounded tablespoons about 3 inches apart onto lightly greased cookie sheet. Press 3 or 4 additional candies on top of cookie if desired. Bake until light brown, in a 350 degree oven for 10-12 minutes. Cool slightly; remove to wire rack.

CHOCOLATE PUDDING COOKIES

2-1/4 cups unsifted all-purpose flour
1 teaspoon baking soda
1 cup margarine, well-softened
1/4 cup granulated white sugar
3/4 cup brownulated light brown sugar (or regular brown sugar, packed)
1 teaspoon vanilla
1 (4-serving size) package chocolate instant pudding and pie filling, used dry
2 eggs
1 (12 ounce) package chocolate chips
1 cup chopped walnuts

Combine flour and baking soda in medium bowl. In large bowl combine margarine, both sugars, vanilla, and instant pudding powder. Beat until

smooth and creamy. Beat in eggs. Gradually, stir in flour mixture. Stir in chips and nuts. Batter will be very stiff. Mix well, using your hands to combine all ingredients. Cover bowl; refrigerate several hours or overnight for easier handling. Shape into smooth balls by rounded *teaspoonfuls* (make them very small). They may be rolled around in your hands, making sure at least one of the nuts is in each one. Place 2 inches apart on ungreased cookie sheets. Bake at 375 degrees 8-10 minutes. Do not overbake. Cool on rack.

Frosting:

1 stiffly-beaten egg white
2-1/2 cups sifted confectioners' sugar
2 teaspoons hot water
1 teaspoon vanilla

Add 1/2 cup of the sugar to egg whites. Beat thoroughly. Add remaining sugar alternately with hot water until right spreading consistency. Beat in vanilla. If preferred, a simple confectioners' sugar-milk glaze may be substituted, or just a sifting of the sugar.

Hyacinth Rizzo, Snyder, N.Y.

CHOCOLATE HERMITS

1/2 cup butter
2/3 cup sugar
2 eggs
1/4 cup grated chocolate
2 tablespoons hot water
1/2 cup raisins
1/4 teaspoon salt
2 teaspoons baking powder
1-3/4 cups flour
1 teaspoon cinnamon

Cream butter; add sugar, eggs, raisins, and flour into which the baking powder has been sifted. Add chocolate melted in water, salt, and cinnamon. Mix well and drop from spoon onto greased cookie sheet. Put a raisin in middle of each cookie. Bake in 350 degree oven for 8-10 minutes.

LEMON DROP COOKIES

1/2 cup margarine or butter, softened
1-1/3 cups sugar
1/3 cup lemon juice from concentrate
1 (8-ounce) container sour cream
2-1/2 cups unsifted flour
1 teaspoon baking soda
1 teaspoon salt
1/4 teaspoon nutmeg
Lemon Icing (recipe follows)

Preheat oven to 350 degrees. In large mixer bowl, cream together butter and sugar. Blend in sour cream and lemon juice. Blend dry ingredients together and add to butter mixture. Mix well. Drop by rounded teaspoonfuls, 2 inches apart, on greased baking sheet. Bake 13-15 minutes, or until edges are lightly browned. Cool. Frost with Lemon Icing.

Lemon Icing: (Makes 1/2 cup)
1-1/2 cups confectioners' sugar
2 tablespoons water
1 teaspoon lemon juice from concentrate
1/8 teaspoon nutmeg

Combine all ingredients and mix well. Spread on cooled cookies.
Leota Baxter, Ingalls, Kans.

WRAP-AROUND CHERRY COOKIES

2 tablespoons white sugar
5 tablespoons confectioners' sugar
1/2 cup butter
1 cup all-purpose flour
Maraschino cherries

Mix together all ingredients, except cherries; wrap small amount of dough around well-drained maraschino cherries. Bake at 350 degrees for 12–15 minutes. Remove from pan; cool on rack. Use cherry juice to make confectioners' sugar icing or glaze.
Gwen Campbell, Sterling, Va.

APPLE-OATMEAL-HONEY GOODIES
Makes 5 dozen

1/2 cup shortening
1/2 cup brown sugar
1/2 cup honey
2 eggs, beaten
1 cup chopped apples
1/2 cup oatmeal (uncooked, quick)
1 3/4 cups sifted flour
1/2 teaspoon soda
1/2 teaspoon baking powder
1/4 teaspoon salt
2/3 teaspoon cinnamon
1/4 teaspoon cloves
1 1/2 cups chopped nuts
1 cup raisins

Cream shortening and brown sugar; gradually add honey, beating well. Add eggs and beat. Add chopped apples and oatmeal. Sift dry ingredients together and add. Stir in nuts and raisins. Drop by teaspoonfuls onto greased cookie sheet. Bake at 350 degrees for 10 minutes, or until done.
Brenda Peery, Tannersville, Va.

WALDORF SALAD COOKIES

2 3/4 cups flour
1/2 teaspoon baking soda
1/4 teaspoon salt
1 teaspoon cinnamon
1 1/2 cups brown sugar, packed
3/4 cup mayonnaise
2 large eggs
1 teaspoon vanilla
1 1/2 cups coarsely chopped apples
1 cup coarsely chopped nuts
1/4 cup finely chopped celery

In medium bow, stir together flour, baking soda, sslt and cinnamon. In a large bowl, beat together sugar, mayonnaise, eggs and vanilla until smooth. Add flour mixture and beat at low speed until smooth. Stir in apples, nuts and celery.

Drop by level tablespoonsful onto ungreased cookie sheets. Bake at 350 degrees 10-12 minutes, until lightly browned. Cool on racks completely before storing in tightly covered container.
Shirley Viscosi, Worcester, Mass.

LEMON SQUARES

1 cup sifted flour
1/4 cup confectioners' sugar
1/2 cup melted butter

Mix and press into 8-inch square pan; bake at 350 degrees for 20 minutes.

Then mix:
2 beaten eggs
3 generous tablespoons lemon juice
1 cup sugar
1/2 teaspoon baking powder
2 tablespoons flour

Pour on top of first mixture. Return to oven for 25 minutes. Cut into small squares (very rich) and sprinkle with confectioners' sugar while still hot.
Agnes Ward, Erie, Pa.

CHEWY CHOCOLATE COOKIES
Makes 4½ dozen

1¼ cups butter *or* margarine, softened
1¾–2 cups sugar
2 eggs
2 teaspoons vanilla
2 cups all-purpose flour
¾ cup unsweetened cocoa
1 teaspoon baking soda
Dash salt
1 cup chopped nuts, optional

Cream butter or margarine and sugar in large bowl. Add eggs and vanilla; blend well. Combine flour, cocoa, soda and salt; gradually blend into creamed mixture. Stir in nuts, if desired. Drop by teaspoonfuls onto ungreased cookie sheet. Bake at 350 degrees for 8–9 minutes. *Do not overbake.* Cookies will be soft. Cool on sheets until set, about 1 minute. Remove to wire rack to cool completely. Store in airtight container.
Marcella Swigert, Monroe City, Mo.

107

EASY NO-BAKE BROWNIES

Makes 2 dozen

1 cup finely chopped nuts
1 can sweetened condensed milk
2 (1-ounce) squares unsweetened chocolate
2 to 2-1/2 cups vanilla wafer crumbs (about 48-60 wafers)

In buttered 9-inch square pan, sprinkle 1/4 cup nuts. In saucepan, over low heat, melt chocolate with sweetened condensed milk. Cook and stir until mixture thickens, about 10 minutes. Remove from heat; stir in crumbs and 1/2 cup nuts. Spread evenly in prepared pan. Top with remaining 1/4 cup nuts. Chill 4 hours, or until firm. Cut into 24 squares. Store covered at room temperature.

Dawn Counsil, Williamsport, Pa.

DATE-NUT SQUARES

Makes 2 dozen

3   cups (1 pound) cut-up dates
1   cup water
½   cup *each* granulated sugar, chopped walnuts
¾   cup (1½ sticks) butter
1   cup firmly packed light brown sugar
1¼   cups all-purpose flour
¼   teaspoon salt
1¼   cups quick oats, uncooked

Combine dates, water and granulated sugar; boil 5 minutes, or until thickened. Cool slightly; add nuts; set aside. Preheat oven to 350 degrees. Cream butter. Gradually add brown sugar and continue beating until blended. Add flour, salt and oats. (Mixture will be crumbly.) Pack two-thirds of mixture evenly and firmly on bottom of buttered 13 x 9-inch baking pan; spread with date mixture. Sprinkle remaining crumb mixture over top; press down lightly. Bake 30 minutes. Cool in pan on wire rack. Cut into squares.

BROWN SUGAR CHEWS

1 egg
1 cup brown sugar, packed
1 teaspoon vanilla
½ cup flour
¼ teaspoon salt
¼ teaspoon soda
1 cup coarsely chopped walnuts

Stir together egg, brown sugar and vanilla. Add ½ cup flour sifted with salt and soda. Stir in nuts. Turn into a greased 8 x 8 x 2-inch baking pan and bake at 350 degrees for 18–20 minutes. Cool in pan and cut into squares.

Joy Shamway, Freeport, Ill.

CHICAGO CRUNCHY CHOCOLATE CHIP COOKIES

3-1/2 cups flour
3 teaspoons baking soda
1 teaspoon salt
1/2 cup butter
1/2 cup margarine
1 cup light brown sugar
1 cup granulated sugar
1 egg
1 tablespoon milk
2 teaspoons vanilla
1 cup vegetable oil
1 cup Special K cereal
1 cup quick-cook oats
1 (12-ounce) package semisweet chocolate chips

Mix flour, baking soda, and salt in a small bowl. Cream butter, margarine, and sugars. Add egg; beat well. Add milk, vanilla, and oil. Mix well. Add dry ingredients and mix well. Add Special K, oatmeal, and chocolate chips. Drop by teaspoonfuls on greased cookie sheets. Bake at 350 degrees for 12 minutes, or until lightly browned.

My family loves chocolate chip cookies and these are by far our favorite! I make a double batch and they don't last long.

Phyliss Dixon, Fairbanks, Alaska

CHERRY NUT COOKIES

Makes 4½ dozen

½ cup soft butter *or* margarine
1 cup light brown sugar, packed
1 egg, slightly beaten
1 teaspoon vanilla
2 cups all-purpose flour
½ teaspoon baking soda
¼ teaspoon salt
1 cup chopped walnuts
⅓ cup chopped maraschino cherries

Cream together the butter and sugar. Beat in egg and vanilla until smooth. Blend in flour, baking soda and salt. Stir in walnuts and cherries. Shape dough into a roll about 14 inches long. Wrap in foil or plastic wrap and refrigerate overnight. With a sharp knife, cut dough into ¼-inch slices. Place on ungreased cookie sheets. Bake at 375 degrees for about 10 minutes, or until just golden brown. Remove from cookie sheets while warm. Cool on rack. Store in airtight containers.

Make the dough for these cookies the day before baking, so it can firm up in the refrigerator for thin slicing. The chunks of cherries and nuts make it a good choice to serve during February.

Ella Evanicky, Fayetteville, Texas

POTATO CHIP COOKIES

Makes 2 dozen

1 cup margarine (2 sticks)
½ cup sugar
1 teaspoon vanilla
1 cup crushed potato chips
1 cup all-purpose flour

Preheat oven to 350 degrees. Mix margarine, sugar and vanilla together; blend well. Add potato chips and stir in flour. Form small balls from mixture and place on an ungreased cookie sheet. Press balls flat with the bottom of a glass that has been dipped in sugar. Bake 16–18 minutes, or until lightly browned.

Trenda Leigh, Richmond, Va.

HAWAIIAN BARS

3/4 cup margarine
1 1/2 cups flour
1/2 cup sugar
1/2 teaspoon salt
1 can pineapple pie filling
1 cup flaked coconut

Cut margarine into mixture of flour, sugar and salt until fine particles are formed. Reserve 2 tablespoons of crumb mixture and press remainder into bottom of a 13x9-inch pan. Bake in a preheated 375-degree oven for 15-20 minutes.

Spread pineapple pie filling over partly baked crust. Combine coconut with reserved crumbs and sprinkle over pineapple. Bake 25-30 minutes longer. Cool before cutting into bars.

Mrs. Sharon Crider, Evansville, Wis.

QUICK 'N' EASY COOKIES

1 stick (1/4 pound) margarine
1 cup molasses
1 cup sugar
2 eggs
4 cups flour
1 teaspoon baking soda
2 teaspoons cinnamon
2 teaspoons ginger
1/2 teaspoon ground cloves
1 teaspoon vanilla
3/4 canned milk
1 cup seedless raisins (optional)
1 cup nuts (optional)

Melt margarine and molasses together over low heat. In large mixer bowl, place sugar, eggs and vanilla. Beat at high speed until mixture is light and lemon-colored. Add melted margarine and molasses and beat hard again.

Sift together all dry ingredients. Alternately add flour mixture and milk to molasses batter. Beat until smooth. Stir in raisins and nuts by hand. Drop by teaspoonsful 2 inches apart onto lightly greased cookie sheets. Bake at 350 degrees, 10 minutes for small cookies, 12 minutes for larger cookies. Cool on rack and store in covered jar.

Pearle M. Goodwin, South Ryegate, Vt.

PECAN PIE SURPRISE BARS

1 package Pillsbury yellow cake mix
½ cup butter *or* margarine melted
1 egg
1 cup chopped pecans

Grease bottom and sides of 13 x 9-inch baking pan. Reserve ⅔ cup dry cake mix for filling. In large mixing bowl, combine remaining dry cake mix, butter and 1 egg; mix until crumbly. Press into prepared pan. Bake at 350 degrees for 15–20 minutes until light golden brown. Meanwhile, prepare filling (recipe follows). Pour filling over partially baked crust; sprinkle with pecans. Return to oven, bake for 30–35 minutes until filling is set. Cool; cut into 36 bars.

Filling:
⅔ cup reserved cake mix
½ cup firmly packed brown sugar
1½ cups dark brown syrup
1 teaspoon vanilla
3 eggs

In large mixer bowl, combine all ingredients; beat at medium speed 1–2 minutes.

Mrs. Jerry Gibson, St. Ann, Mo.

GREAT GOOBER BARS

1 (5½-ounce) package instant chocolate pudding and pie filling
1⅓ cups buttermilk biscuit mix
⅓ cup sugar
1 cup milk
1 teaspoon vanilla extract
3 tablespoons vegetable oil
¾ cup salted peanuts, chopped

Combine pudding, biscuit mix and sugar. Add milk, vanilla and oil; mix well. Turn into a greased 8-inch square baking pan. Sprinkle peanuts on top. Bake at 350 degrees, 25–30 minutes; cut into bars.

Gwen Campbell, Sterling, Va.

ALMOND BARS

2 cups brown sugar
1 cup white sugar
¾ cup melted butter
¾ cup melted lard
4½ cups sifted flour
1 cup almonds, sliced
3 eggs, well-beaten
1 teaspoon soda
1 scant teaspoon salt

Cream butter and lard; add sugars and well-beaten eggs. Sift flour with soda and salt. Combine with creamed mixture; add almonds. Pack into bread pan. (I roll in waxed paper.) Chill in refrigerator 24 hours. Slice and bake until brown at 350 degrees. (I substitute margarine for both butter and lard.) This recipe has been passed down through the family for years.

J.P. Hart, Stoughton, Wis.

PUMPKIN SQUARES
Makes 12 servings

1 cup canned pumpkin
3 1/2 cups miniature marshmallows
1/2 teaspoon cinnamon
1/4 teaspoon ginger
1 cup crushed graham crackers (about 14 crackers)
1/4 cup (1/2 stick) margarine, melted
1 envelope whipped topping mix or 2 cups frozen prepared whipped topping

In large saucepan, melt marshmallows with pumpkin and spices over low heat, stirring until smooth. Cool about 15 minutes. Meanwhile, combine crushed graham crackers with melted margarine; reserve 1/4 cup for topping. Pat remaining crumbs firmly into the bottom of an 8-inch square baking dish.

If using dry whipped topping mix, prepare according to package directions. Fold prepared topping into cooled marshmallow mixture and spread over crust. Top with reserved crumbs and chill several hours or overnight.

Cut into squares to serve.

Mrs. Emily Dougherty, Montpelier, Ind.

CINNAMON SQUARES

Makes about 75 2-inch squares

1/2 cup margarine
3/4 cup sugar
1 egg yolk
2 teaspoons vanilla
2 cups flour
3 teaspoons cinnamon
1 egg white
Chocolate chips, chopped walnuts, or coconut

Cream margarine with sugar until fluffy; add egg yolk and vanilla; blend; add flour and cinnamon. Mix well. Divide dough between two greased 15x10x1-inch jelly roll pans. Flatten down with heels of hands in pans. Lightly beat the egg white; brush over batter, and mark batter into squares.

Place chocolate chips, nuts or coconut on top. Bake at 350 degrees 20-30 minutes.

Mrs. Bess Notkin, Chelsea, Mass.

BOBBIE'S APPLE CAKE BARS

Makes 12 bars

2 cups whole-wheat flour
1/4 cup toasted wheat germ
2 teaspoons baking soda
1 teaspoon cinnamon
1/2 teaspoon salt
1/2 teaspoon nutmeg
4 cups diced, peeled, tart cooking apples (4 large)
1 cup sugar
1 cup packed brown sugar
1/2 cup oil
1 cup chopped walnuts
2 eggs, beaten well
1 teaspoon vanilla

Stir together flour, wheat germ, soda, cinnamon, salt and nutmeg; set aside. In large bowl, combine apples, sugars, oil, walnuts, eggs and vanilla. Add flour mixture; stir gently with wooden spoon to blend well. Turn into a greased 9x13x2-inch pan.

Bake in a preheated oven at 350 degrees for 50 minutes until cake tests done (pulls away form sides of pan). Cool in pan on rack. If desired, sprinkle with confectioners' sugar. Cut into 12 bars.

Bobbie Mae Cooley, Bowen, Ill.

GINGERSNAPS

2 cups flour
1 tablespoon ground ginger
2 teaspoons baking soda
1 teaspoon cinnamon
½ teaspoon salt
¾ cup shortening
1 cup sugar
1 egg
¼ cup molasses

Measure flour, ginger, soda, cinnamon and salt; put aside. Cream shortening until soft. Gradually add sugar, creaming until light and fluffy. Beat in egg and molasses. Add dry ingredients over creamed mixture; blend well. Form teaspoonfuls of dough into small balls by rolling them lightly between palms of hands. Roll dough balls in granulated sugar to cover entire surface. Place 2 inches apart on ungreased cookie sheet. Bake at 350 degrees for 12–15 minutes until tops are crackly and cookies are brown.

A good, old-fashioned cookie!

Mrs. George Franks, Millerton, Pa.

CRANBERRY DROPS

About 1-1/2 dozen

1/2 cup butter
1 cup granulated sugar
3/4 cup brown sugar, packed
1/4 cup milk
2 tablespoons orange juice
1 egg
3 cups flour
1 teaspoon baking powder
1/2 teaspoon salt
1/4 teaspoon soda
1 cup chopped nuts
2-1/2 cups coarsely chopped cranberries

Preheat oven to 375 degrees. Cream butter and sugars together. Beat in milk, orange juice and egg. Measure flour before sifting. Stir together flour, baking powder, salt and soda. Blend well with sugar mixture. Stir in chopped nuts and cranberries. Drop dough by teaspoonfuls on greased baking sheet. Bake 10-15 minutes.

P. J. Leikness, Stoughton, Wis.

PEANUT BUTTER DROP COOKIES

1/2 cup sugar
2 tablespoons butter
1 egg
2 tablespoon milk
2 teaspoons baking powder
1/8 teaspoon salt
3/4 cup peanut butter
1 cup flour
1/2 cup nuts, chopped

Cream sugar and butter. Add egg and beat. Add milk and flour, sifted with salt and baking powder. Add peanut butter. Stir in nuts. Drop on greased baking sheet and bake 15 minutes in 400-degree oven.

Suzan L. Wiener, Spring Hill, Fla.

OLD FAMILY FAVORITE TOFFEE SQUARES

1 cup margarine *or* half margarine and half butter
1 cup brown sugar
1 egg yolk
1 teaspoon vanilla
2 cups flour
1 cup chocolate chips
¼ teaspoon Crisco
Ground walnuts

Cream shortening and sugar. Add egg yolk and vanilla; blend together. Add flour, mix together again. Spread this mixture onto a cookie sheet by pinching pieces of dough and pressing dough to cover the cookie sheet, working with your fingers. Bake 15 minutes at 325 degrees.

Melt chocolate chips. Add ¼ teaspoon Crisco to chocolate to keep it soft.

After dough is baked, spread with chocolate, while warm. Thinly spread chocolate with your fingers instead of a knife. While chocolate is still warm, sprinkle with ground walnuts. After chocolate is set, cut cookies into 1½-inch squares.

Luscious!!

Sally Simpson, Detroit, Mich.

SPRITZ
Makes 7–8 dozen

- 1 cup (2 sticks) butter
- ½ cup sugar
- 1 egg
- ½ teaspoon almond extract
- 2¼ cups all-purpose flour
  Food coloring
  Decorative candies

Preheat oven to 350 degrees. Cream butter. Gradually add sugar and continue beating until blended. Beat in egg and almond extract. Gradually blend in flour. Add food coloring, if desired. Fill cookie press. Using star attachment, form circles on unbuttered cookie sheets ... or use other press designs. Decorate with sugar crystals, other candies or nuts. Bake 8–10 minutes. Remove to wire rack to cool.

MISSISSIPPI MUD BARS

- 2 cups sugar
- 1 cup margarine
- 3 tablespoons cocoa
- 4 eggs
- 1½ cups flour
- 1¼ cups coconut
- 1½ cups chopped nuts
- 1 (7-ounce) jar marshmallow creme

Cream together sugar, margarine and cocoa. Add eggs and mix well. Add flour, coconut and nuts. Blend thoroughly.

Bake in greased 12 x 15-inch cookie sheet at 350 degrees for 25–30 minutes. Remove from oven and spread with marshmallow creme.

Frosting:
- 1 pound confectioners' sugar
- ½ cup evaporated milk
- ½ cup cocoa
- ½ cup soft margarine
- 1 teaspoon vanilla

Cream together frosting ingredients, blending well. When bars are cool, frost.
Mrs. L. Mayer, Richmond, Va.

APPLE-BUTTER BARS

Makes 3 dozen

- 1½ cups flour
- 1 teaspoon baking soda
- 1 teaspoon salt
- 1½ cups quick-cooking oats, uncooked
- 1½ cups sugar
- 1 cup butter *or* margarine, melted
- 1½ cups apple butter
- 1 cup chopped pecans *or* walnuts

Combine flour, baking soda and salt in a large mixing bowl. Mix in oats and sugar. Pour in melted butter and mix well.

Press half of this mixture into a greased 13 x 9 x 2-inch baking pan. Mix apple butter and nuts together; spread over mixture in pan. Sprinkle with remaining crumbly mixture.

Bake at 350 degrees for 50–60 minutes, or until brown. Cool before cutting into bars.
Mary Williams, Columbus, Ohio

HERMITS
Makes 4 dozen

- 1 cup light brown sugar
- ¼ cup margarine, softened
- ¼ cup shortening
- ¼ cup cold coffee
- 1 egg
- 1 teaspoon ground cinnamon
- ½ teaspoon ground nutmeg
- 1¾ cups all-purpose flour
- ½ teaspoon baking soda
- 1¼ cups seedless raisins
- ¾ cup chopped walnuts

In large bowl, mix together brown sugar, margarine, shortening, coffee, egg, cinnamon and nutmeg. Stir in remaining ingredients. Drop dough by rounded teaspoonfuls, 2 inches apart, onto ungreased cookie sheet.

Bake in preheated 375-degree oven for 10 minutes. Immediately remove from cookie sheet.
June Harding, Royal Oak, Mich.

STIR 'N DROP COOKIES
Makes 5 dozen
(A new version of old-fashioned sugar cookies)

- 2 eggs
- 2/3 cup cooking oil
- 2 teaspoons vanilla
- 1 teaspoon grated lemon peel
- 3/4 cup sugar
- 2 cups sifted all-purpose flour
- 2 teaspoons baking powder
- 1/2 teaspoon salt

Heat oven to 400 degrees. Beat eggs with fork. Stir in oil, vanilla, lemon peel. Blend in sugar (reserve 1 tablespoonful).

Sift together flour, baking powder, salt; add to egg mixture. Drop by teaspoonfuls about 2 inches apart onto ungreased cookie sheets. Stamp each cookie flat with bottom of glass dipped in sugar. (Lightly oil glass, then dip in reserved sugar — continue dipping sugar). Bake 8 to 10 minutes. Remove at once from cookie sheet. If you bake the cookies one sheet at a time, stir the mixture between each batch. (50 calories per cookie)

Note: When dipping glass in sugar, cookies can be decorated with colored candy bits (not counted in calories). Cookies bake in perfect rounds; come out shiny with sugar and fragrant with homemade flavor!
Claire Marie J. Heroux, Linwood, Mass.

BANANA COOKIES (DIABETIC)
Makes 2 dozen

- 3 medium bananas, mashed
- ⅓ cup oil
- 1 teaspoon vanilla extract
- 2 cups old-fashioned rolled oats
- 1¼ cups chopped walnuts
- ¼ cup raisins

Combine bananas, oil and vanilla. Stir in oats, walnuts and raisins. Drop by tablespoonfuls onto greased cookie sheets. Press down lightly with fork. Preheat oven to 350 degrees. Bake 10–12 minutes until golden brown.
Kit Rollins, Cedarburg, Wis.

MAPLE BARS

1 1/2 cups milk
1/2 cup shortening
4 tablespoons sugar
2 teaspoons salt
2 yeast cakes
4 tablespoons warm water
4 3/4 cups flour
3 eggs, beaten well
Frosting (recipe follows)

Bring milk to boiling point and pour over shortening, sugar and salt in a large bowl. Cool to lukewarm. Dissolve yeast in warm water, and add to lukewarm mixture in bowl along with flour and eggs. Mix well.

Grease bowl and add dough, turning to grease top. Cover and let rise in a warm place until doubled. Turn out onto a well-floured board, and roll 1/2 inch thick. Cut into 2x4-inch pieces. Let rise again in warm place until double.

Deep-fry in oil heated to 375 degrees in deep skillet or fryer until golden on all sides. Remove to paper towels to drain. Make *Frosting*, and frost bars while still warm.

Frosting:
1 1/2 cups confectioners' sugar
3 tablespoons butter
Milk
Maple syrup

Cream sugar and butter, adding a little milk and maple syrup to form an icing of spreading consistency.

Laura Kinzler, Camano Island, Wash.

HEAVENLY CRUNCH

1 package from a box of graham crackers
2 sticks margarine
1/2 cup sugar
2/3 cup chopped pecans

Spread crackers in large jelly roll pan. Chop pecans and sprinkle over crackers. Melt margarine in saucepan. Add sugar; boil 3 minutes. Pour over crackers. Bake in 350-degree oven for 10–15 minutes. Remove from pan before they cool completely. Break into sections. These are delicious!

Joni Bowen, Belen, Miss.

PRIDE OF OHIO COOKIES

1 cup brown sugar
1 cup white sugar
1 cup shortening
1 cup flour
2 eggs
1 cup coconut
1 cup nut meats, chopped
1 teaspoon vanilla
1 teaspoon soda
1 teaspoon baking powder
1/2 teaspoon salt
3 cups quick rolled oats

Beat eggs in mixing bowl; add sugars and softened shortening. Blend well. Stir in coconut, nuts and vanilla. Sift flour and measure, then add soda, baking powder and salt, then sift again. Combine with other mixture. Stir in rolled oats; mix thoroughly by hand. Roll in small balls the size of a walnut and place on ungreased cookie sheet. Bake at 375 degrees for about 9 minutes, or until nicely browned.

Marjorie Baxla, Greenfield, Ohio

CHOCOLATE FUDGE COOKIES

1 1/4 cups brown sugar
1/2 cup butter
1 egg
1/2 cup milk
2 teaspoons baking powder
2 cups flour
1 teaspoon vanilla
1/4 teaspoon salt
2 1/2 squares chocolate, melted

Cream butter and add sugar gradually. Add egg and beat. Mix baking powder with salt and flour, then add vanilla to milk. Add liquid and dry ingredients alternately to egg mixture. Add dry ingredients first and last. Add melted chocolate. Drop from teaspoon onto greased baking sheets and bake 10 minutes in a moderately hot 375-degree oven.

These cookies are delicious plain or iced with chocolate frosting!

Suzan L. Wiener, Spring Hill, Fla.

PEANUT JEWELS

1 cup creamy peanut butter
1 cup seedless raisins
1/2 cup honey
1 teaspoon vanilla
1 cup coconut, flaked or shredded

Mix peanut butter and honey; add raisins and vanilla. Spread coconut on waxed paper or cookie sheet. Drop mixture on coconut, in teaspoonfuls. Roll to coat. Chill.

Suzan L. Wiener, Spring Hill, Fla.

ICED MOLASSES BARS

1 cup butter
1/2 cup sugar
1 cup light molasses
1 egg
3-1/2 cups cake flour, sifted
1 teaspoon soda
1 teaspoon ginger
1 teaspoon cinnamon
1 teaspoon salt
1/2 cup sour cream

Cream butter and sugar until light. Beat in molasses and egg. Add sifted flour, soda, seasonings, and sour cream. Beat until smooth. Spread in greased jelly roll pan. Bake in a moderate oven of 350 degrees for 30 minutes. Cool in pan.

Sour Cream Frosting:
1 cup sour cream
2 cups sugar
Dash of salt
1 teaspoon vanilla

Blend sour cream, sugar, and salt in heavy saucepan. Put over high heat and cook, stirring rapidly, for about 10 minutes, or until smooth and mixture forms a soft ball when tested in cold water. Add vanilla. Spread on top of baked layer and cut into bars. (If preferred, the molasses bars may be iced with your favorite chocolate frosting.)

Trenda Leigh, Richmond, Va.

SOFT GINGER COOKIES

1/2 cup shortening
1 cup sugar
1 egg
1/3 cup molasses
1 1/2 teaspoons cinnamon
1 1/2 teaspoons cloves
1 1/2 teaspoons nutmeg
1/4 teaspoon salt
1 teaspoon ginger
1/2 cup milk
2 1/2 cups flour
1 teaspoon baking powder
1 teaspoon baking soda

Cream together first four ingredients. Stir in spices, salt and milk. Add dry ingredients, and mix well. With teaspoon heap on dough and dip in sugar. Slide off onto cookie sheet. Bake in a 350-degree oven for 8-10 minutes.

These are soft cookies and very good.

Emma B. Walters, Dayton, Wyo.

CRUNCHY OATMEAL COOKIES

Makes 4 dozen

1 cup flour
2 teaspoons baking soda
1 teaspoon baking powder
½ teaspoon salt
1 cup shortening
2 cups cornflakes
1 cup sugar
1 cup brown sugar, packed
2 eggs
1 teaspoon vanilla extract
2 cups uncooked, quick-cooking oats

Combine flour, soda, baking powder and salt. Set aside. In large bowl, cream shortening and sugars; beat in eggs and vanilla. Add flour mixture, mixing well. Stir in oats and cornflakes. Drop by heaping tablespoonfuls onto lightly greased cookie sheets. Bake at 325 degrees for 12–14 minutes.

Cool for 2 minutes on cookie sheet; remove to wire racks and cool completely.

Fran Sievers, Atlanta, Ga.

FORGOTTEN COOKIES

1 large egg white
1/8 teaspoon salt
1/3 cup sugar
1/2 cup chopped pecans
1/2 cup miniature chocolate chips

Beat egg white and salt to soft peaks. Add sugar, 1 tablespoon at a time, beating until stiff and glossy. Stir in chips and nuts. Drop by teaspoon onto foil-covered cookie sheet. Preheat oven to 350 degrees. Place cookies in oven and then turn oven temperature dial off. Do not open the door; leave in oven overnight.

Sharon McClatchey, Muskogee, Okla.

LEMON SUGAR COOKIES

Makes 4 dozen

2¾ cups flour
2 teaspoons baking powder
¼ teaspoon salt
1 cup butter
2 cups sugar
2 eggs
2 teaspoons grated lemon rind
3 tablespoons lemon juice
1 cup quick oats

Sift together flour, baking powder and salt. In large bowl, cream butter and sugar. Add eggs, beating well. Beat in lemon rind and juice. Gradually add flour mixture, then stir in oats. Chill dough thoroughly (at least 2 hours). Roll level tablespoons dough into balls and place on greased cookie sheets, allowing room for cookies to spread. Using a flat-bottom glass or custard cup that has been greased and dipped in sugar, flatten each ball to ¼-inch thickness (dip glass in sugar each time). Bake at 375 degrees until lightly browned around edges, about 8–10 minutes. Cool for 1 minute, then carefully remove from cookie sheets; cool on racks. These cookies are delicate and delicious.

Barbara Beauregard-Smith, Northfield, South Australia

CRUNCHY PEANUT BUTTER COOKIES

Makes 3 - 3-1/2 dozen

1/2 cup margarine (softened)
1/2 cup brown sugar
1/2 cup granulated sugar
1/4 cup peanut butter
1 egg
1/2 teaspoon vanilla
1 cup flour
1/2 teaspoon baking powder
1/2 teaspoon soda
1/2 teaspoon salt
1 cup corn flakes
1 cup rolled oats

Preheat oven to 375 degrees. Cream margarine and both sugars. Beat in peanut butter, egg, and vanilla. Stir in remaining ingredients until well-blended. Drop by teaspoonfuls, 2 inches apart, on lightly greased cookie sheets. Bake 10-12 minutes, or until golden brown.

Jodie McCoy, Tulsa, Okla.

BUTTER CRISPS

Makes 7 dozen

1 cup (2 sticks) butter
1 (3-ounce) package cream cheese, softened
1 cup sugar
1 egg yolk
1 teaspoon vanilla extract
2 cups all-purpose flour
¼ teaspoon *each* salt, baking powder

Preheat oven to 350 degrees. Cream together butter and cream cheese. Gradually add sugar and continue beating until blended. Beat in egg yolk and vanilla. Combine flour, salt and baking powder; gradually add to creamed mixture. Fill cookie press. Use attachments to form cookie designs on unbuttered cookie sheets. Bake 12–15 minutes. Remove to wire rack to cool.

Note: Before baking, dough may be tinted, sprinkled with colored sugar or a cinnamon-sugar mixture, or decorate cookies with a tinted frosting after baking.

COWBOY COOKIES

Makes 6 dozen

1 1/2 cups sugar
1 1/2 cups brown sugar
3/4 cup shortening
3/4 cup margarine
3 eggs
1 teaspoon vanilla
3 cups flour
1 1/2 teaspoons baking soda
3/4 teaspoon baking powder
3/4 teaspoon salt
3 cups oatmeal
1 package (6 ounces) chocolate or
  butterscotch morsels

Cream shortening and margarine; add both sugars, eggs and vanilla. Mix in flour and other dry ingredients. Add chocolate chips.

Drop by well-rounded teaspoonsful onto ungreased cookie sheets. Bake at 350 degrees for 12-15 minutes.

Mrs. Cleo Brown, Shelby, Ohio

BUTTER PECAN TURTLE BARS

Makes 2 dozen

Crust:
2 cups flour
2 cups firmly packed brown
  sugar
1/2 cup soft butter

Combine all ingredients. Mix at medium speed with mixer, 2–3 minutes, or until particles are fine. Pat into ungreased 9 x 12-inch pan.

Filling:
1 cup pecan halves or hickory
  nuts
2/3 cup butter
1/2 cup firmly packed brown sugar
1 cup milk chocolate chips

Spread nuts over crust. Cook, stirring constantly, the butter and brown sugar over medium heat until entire surface of mixture begins to boil, about 1 minute. Pour over pecans. Bake for 20 minutes at 350 degrees. Remove from oven; sprinkle with chocolate chips. Marble chips after they have melted.

Ida Bloedow, Madison, Wis.

OLD-FASHIONED SOFT MOLASSES COOKIES

Makes 2 dozen

2½ cups sifted all-purpose flour
2 teaspoons soda
1 teaspoon cinnamon
1 teaspoon ginger
1 egg, unbeaten
½ cup water
¼ teaspoon salt
½ cup shortening
½ cup sugar
½ cup molasses

Sift together flour, soda, cinnamon, ginger and salt. Cream shortening and sugar until light and fluffy. Add egg and molasses; mix well.

Add dry ingredients to the mixture alternately with water, beginning and ending with dry ingredients.

Drop heaping teaspoonfuls on ungreased baking sheet. Bake in moderate 350-degree oven for about 8 minutes.

Elinor Mesch, Collins, N.Y.

OATMEAL BARS

Makes 5 dozen

1 cup (2 sticks) butter
1-1/3 cups dark brown sugar, firmly
  packed
3/4 cup light corn syrup
5-1/3 cups quick-cooking oats
2 teaspoons vanilla extract

Glaze:
1 (12-ounce) package semisweet
  chocolate chips
1 cup peanut butter

Preheat oven to 350 degrees and position oven rack near the center of the oven. Coat 9x13-inch pan with butter or vegetable shortening. Cream butter and sugar. Mix in syrup, oats, and vanilla. Spread in pan and bake 16 minutes. Cool until lukewarm.

Glaze: Put chips and peanut butter in pan. Stir over low heat until mixture is smooth. Spread over warm bars. Cool and refrigerate. When cool cut into bars.

Kit Rollins, Cedarburg, Wis.

WHOLE-WHEAT GINGERSNAPS

3/4 cup brown sugar
3/4 cup margarine
1 egg
1-1/3 cups white flour
1-1/3 cups whole-wheat flour
2 teaspoons baking soda
1-1/4 teaspoons ground ginger
1 teaspoon cinnamon
1/2 teaspoon salt
1/2 teaspoon ground cloves

Cream brown sugar, margarine, and egg. Add remaining ingredients. Roll dough into walnut-size balls. Flatten these on ungreased baking sheet with a glass dipped in sugar. Bake for 8-10 minutes at 375 degrees.

Marcella Swigert, Monroe City, Mo.

PUMPKIN-FILLED COOKIES

Filling:
1 cup pumpkin
½ cup sugar
½ teaspoon cinnamon
½ teaspoon ginger
¼ teaspoon nutmeg
¼ teaspoon salt

Blend ingredients together. Set aside.

Cookies:
3 cups flour
1 teaspoon salt
½ teaspoon baking soda
½ cup brown sugar
¾ cup soft shortening
1 egg
¼ cup molasses
1 cup rolled oats

Mix and sift together flour, salt and baking soda. Combine sugar, shortening, egg and molasses; mix well. Add dry ingredients to molasses mixture. Add oats. Chill 30 minutes. Roll out ⅛ inch thick; place 1 tablespoon filling on 1 cookie and cover with second cookie. Press together; slit top. Bake 375 degrees for 15 minutes.

Agnes Ward, Erie, Pa.

ANGEL COOKIES

1½ cups bread crumbs
½ cup chopped nuts
½ teaspoon vanilla or almond
     extract
⅔ cup sweetened condensed
     milk
3 drops red food coloring
30 nut halves (walnut or pecan)

Soak bread crumbs in condensed milk to which the extract and coloring have been added. Add chopped nuts. Drop by spoonfuls onto greased cookie sheets. Top each with a nut half; bake at 350 degrees for 12 minutes.
Fun for children to make!

Mrs. Don Shamway, Freeport, Ill.

REESE'S CUP TARTS
Makes 4–5 dozen

½ cup butter
½ cup peanut butter
½ cup granulated sugar
½ cup brown sugar
1 egg
1 teaspoon vanilla
1½ cups all-purpose flour
1 teaspoon soda
½ teaspoon salt
     Reese's miniature peanut-
     butter cups—foil removed

Cream butters and sugars thoroughly. Add egg and vanilla. Beat well. Combine flour, soda and salt. Add to creamed mixture. Take rounded teaspoons of dough and place in greased miniature muffin pans. Bake at 350 degrees for 8–10 minutes, or until cookie puffs up and is barely done. Remove from oven and immediately push a peanut-butter cup into each cookie-filled muffin cup. The cookies will deflate and form a tart shell around the peanut butter cup. Let cool in pan, then refrigerate until shine leaves the chocolate. Gently lift each tart out with tip of sharp knife.

These are easy to prepare and are very elegant. I make them for lots of school parties, showers and special occasions.

Brenda K. Peery, Tannersville, Va.

SHORTBREAD COOKIES
Makes 4 dozen

1 cup butter *or* margarine,
     softened
½ cup sugar
1 teaspoon vanilla
2¼ cups flour

Preheat oven to 325 degrees. Cream together the butter and sugar, then add vanilla and blend until light and fluffy. Stir in flour until well-mixed. Place dough on a floured surface and knead until smooth (do not overwork). Place dough in refrigerator until chilled.

Remove a small portion of dough at a time so the rest will remain chilled. Roll the dough to ¼-inch thickness and cut with cookie cutters. Place cookies on an ungreased cookie sheet and bake for 12–15 minutes, or until the cookies are light brown. Remove cookies to a flat surface to cool. Sprinkle cinnamon/sugar or colored sugars on top of cookies before baking, if desired.

Marg Hale, Tulsa, Okla.

CHEWY NUT SQUARES
Makes 16

1 cup unsifted flour
1/2 cup firmly packed brown sugar
1/2 cup (1 stick) margarine
1/4 cup flour
1/2 cup brown sugar
2 eggs, slightly beaten
1/2 cup dark corn syrup
1 teaspoon vanilla
1/4 teaspoon salt
1/2 cup chopped pecans
1/2 cup flaked coconut

Combine 1 cup unsifted flour with 1/2 cup brown sugar; cut in margarine until fine crumbs form; pat into greased 8-inch square pan. Bake in preheated 325-degree oven for 20 minutes or until lightly browned. Remove from oven.

Mix remaining ingredients. Pour over crust; bake 30 more minutes, or until top is set. Cool. Cut into squares.

Mrs. Ben Winter, Altamont, Ill.

GRANOLA BARS

6 eggs
3 cups granola cereal
1 cup raisins, chopped
1/2 cup almonds, finely chopped
1/2 cup sesame seeds
1/4 cup sunflower seeds

Beat eggs in medium-size bowl. Add remaining ingredients; mix well with spoon. Batter will be thick. Let mixture stand 15 minutes. Pour mixture into well-oiled 9-inch square pan. Press mixture into pan and smooth top. Bake at 350 degrees for 25-30 minutes, until done (lightly browned and firm). Remove from oven and cut into 1x2-inch bars while still hot. Remove from pan by loosening edges gently with a spatula. Cool. Store in an airtight container.

Mrs. L. Mayer, Richmond, Va.

CHERRY POM PONS
Makes 4½ dozen

½ cup cooking oil
2 egg yolks, beaten
3 tablespoons milk
½ teaspoon almond
     extract
3 tablespoons cherry-
     flavored gelatin
1 small package instant
     vanilla pudding
1 cup sifted flour
½ teaspoon baking
     powder
¾ cup chopped pecans
⅔ cup flaked coconut
2 egg whites
1 teaspoon water
1 cup flaked coconut

Combine oil, egg yolks, milk, extract, gelatin, pudding, flour and baking powder in mixing bowl; mix well. Blend in pecans and ⅔ cup coconut. Shape a teaspoonful of dough into balls; dip into combined egg whites and water. Roll in remaining coconut. Place on an ungreased cookie sheet. Bake at 350 degrees for about 12 minutes.

Shari Crider, Stoughton, Wis.

BUTTERSCOTCH REFRIGERATOR COOKIES

Makes 5 dozen

- ½ cup soft butter or shortening
- 1 cup light brown sugar (firmly packed)
- 1 egg, well-beaten
- 1½ cups sifted flour
- 1½ teaspoons baking powder
- ¼ teaspoon salt
- ½ cup chopped nuts
- 1 teaspoon vanilla

Blend all ingredients in a mixing bowl until dough can be handled with your hands. Form into 1 longer or 2 shorter rolls; wrap in plastic wrap or aluminum foil. Chill several hours or overnight in refrigerator. Slice into ⅛-inch-thick slices. Place on lightly greased cookie sheet and bake in 375–400-degree oven for 8–10 minutes.

Marjorie Baxla, Greenfield, Ohio

ITALIAN BOW KNOT COOKIES

Makes 6 dozen medium cookies

- 4 cups flour
- 4 teaspoons baking powder
- 2 teaspoons salt
- 6 eggs, beaten
- 1 cup sugar
- ½ cup oil
- 1½ teaspoons lemon extract

Blend beaten eggs into dry ingredients, following with all other ingredients. Knead until smooth. Roll into pencil lengths and tie in bow knots. Bake on greased cookie sheets in a 400-degree oven for 15 minutes.

Lemon Icing:

- ¼ cup butter
- 1 pound confectioners' sugar
  Juice of 2 lemons

Cream butter; add remaining ingredients. Stir until well-blended. If too thin, add more sugar—too thick, add more lemon juice.

Mrs. Dan Crisia, Fennville, Mich.

SOUR CREAM NUTMEG COOKIES

Makes 3 dozen

- 2 cups sifted flour
- 1 teaspoon nutmeg
- ½ teaspoon baking soda
- 2 teaspoons baking powder
- ¼ teaspoon salt
- ½ cup shortening
- 1 cup sugar
- 1 egg
- ½ cup sour cream
- ½ cup chopped nuts

Sift flour, nutmeg, baking soda, baking powder and salt together. Cream shortening and sugar until light and fluffy. Add egg; beat well. Add sour cream and sifted dry ingredients alternately, beating well after each addition. Add nuts. Drop by teaspoonfuls 2 inches apart onto well-greased baking sheets.

Bake in moderate oven 375 degrees for 10–12 minutes.

Betty Slavin, Omaha, Neb.

SOUR CREAM COCONUT COOKIES

Makes 2½ dozen

- ½ cup shortening
- ½ cup dairy sour cream
- 1 cup sugar
- 1 egg
- 1 egg yolk
- 1 teaspoon vanilla
- 2¾ cups sifted flour
- ¾ teaspoon salt
- ½ teaspoon baking powder
- ½ teaspoon baking soda
- ½ cup flaked coconut

Cream shortening, sour cream and sugar well. Beat in egg, egg yolk and vanilla. Gradually blend in dry ingredients which have been sifted together; add coconut. Chill the dough. Roll to ⅛- to ¼-inch thickness on a lightly floured surface. Cut cookies with floured cookie cutters. Bake on ungreased cookie sheets at 375 degrees for 8–10 minutes. Frost, if desired.

Lisa Boryszewski, Middleport, N.Y.

SOFT CHOCOLATE CHIP COOKIES

- 2-1/4 cups flour
- 3/4 cup sugar
- 1 cup whipped margarine
- 2 eggs
- 1 teaspoon vanilla
- 2 cups chocolate chips
- 1 teaspoon salt
- 1 teaspoon baking soda
- 3/4 cup brown sugar, packed

Preheat oven to 375 degrees. Lightly grease cookie sheets. Mix dry ingredients together and set aside. In a larger bowl combine margarine and both sugars; beat well. Add eggs and vanilla; mix well. Gradually add flour mixture. Stir in chocolate chips. Mixture should be sticky, not stiff. Drop by spoonfuls onto cookie sheet. Bake 15 minutes at 375 degrees.

Juanita Tate, Bloomington, Ind.

WALNUT MERINGUE BARS

Makes 4 dozen

- 2½ cups all-purpose flour
- 5 eggs, separated
- 6 tablespoons sugar
- 1 cup sweet butter
- 2 teaspoons vanilla
- 2 cups apricot jam
- 1 cup sugar
- 3 cups ground walnuts
  Confectioners' sugar

In a bowl, combine flour, egg yolks, sugar, butter and vanilla. Blend with fork until dough comes away from sides of bowl. Press dough into an 11 x 16-inch pan. Spread with jam. Beat egg whites until stiff, gradually beating in 1 cup sugar. Fold in nuts. Spread over dough. Bake at 350 degrees for 40 minutes. Sprinkle with confectioners' sugar. Cool and cut into bars.

Any kind of jam can be substituted for the apricot. The cookie is very rich, so make the bars small.

Ella Evanisky, Fayetteville, Texas

ALMOND MACAROONS

Makes 1½ dozen

- 1 egg white
- ¼ teaspoon salt
- ¾ cup confectioners' sugar
- 1 cup finely minced almonds **or**
- 1 cup finely grated coconut
- ½ teaspoon almond extract

Lightly grease a cookie sheet. Preheat oven to 250 degrees. Beat egg white with salt until stiff. Gradually add ⅔ cup sugar, beating well. Fold in remaining sugar, nuts or coconut. Add flavoring, folding in. Beat well. Drop by teaspoonfuls on prepared sheet and bake for 25 minutes in 250-degree oven. Store in a covered container for 1 week to develop best flavor.

Agnes Ward, Erie, Pa.

BUTTERSCOTCH COCONUT COOKIES

- 2 cups flour
- ½ teaspoon soda
- ½ teaspoon salt
- ½ cup margarine, softened
- ½ cup granulated sugar
- ½ cup packed brown sugar
- 2 eggs
- 1 teaspoon vanilla
- 1 cup butterscotch chips
- ½ cup chopped pecans
- 2½ cups coconut
  Pecan halves (if desired)
  Candied cherry halves (if desired)

Preheat oven to 375 degrees. Combine in a small bowl the flour, soda and salt; set aside. Using larger bowl, combine softened margarine and both sugars; beat until very light and fluffy. Beat in eggs (one at a time) and vanilla. Add flour mixture; mix well. Stir in butterscotch chips and nuts. Drop dough into coconut. With lightly floured or greased hand, roll to coat with coconut. Form into balls. Bake at 375 degrees on ungreased cookie sheet for 10–12 minutes. Garnish each cookie with pecan half before baking if desired or place

half candied cherry on each cookie as you remove from oven. Remove to cooling rack and allow to cool.

Jodie McCoy, Tulsa, Okla.

SOFT SUGAR COOKIES

- ½ cup butter **or** margarine
- 1½ cups white sugar
- 2 eggs
- 1 teaspoon vanilla
- 3 cups unsifted enriched flour
- 1 teaspoon salt
- ½ teaspoon baking powder
- ½ teaspoon baking soda
- 1 cup dairy sour cream

Cream butter or margarine with sugar; add vanilla. Add eggs and beat well. Mix flour, salt, baking powder and baking soda. Add to creamed mixture alternately with sour cream. You may add chocolate chips or raisins, or sprinkle with colored sugar, or sugar and cinnamon before baking. Drop on greased and floured cookie sheets. Bake at 400 degrees for 10–12 minutes.

I have made these cookies for a number of years for my children, and now grandchildren. The recipe is fast and easy.

Doris Mustard, Xenia, Ohio

TOFFEE COOKIES

Makes 3 dozen

- 1½ cups flour
- 1 teaspoon baking powder
- ½ teaspoon salt
- ½ cup margarine
- ¾ cup packed brown sugar
- 1 egg
- 1 teaspoon vanilla
- 1 cup finely chopped Heath bars
- ⅓ cup coarsely chopped pecans

Mix egg, sugar, margarine and vanilla until smooth and creamy. Stir in dry ingredients. Blend in chopped candy bars and nuts. Drop by spoonfuls, 2 inches apart, on greased cookie sheet. Bake at 350 degrees for 12–15 minutes. Remove from cookie sheet. A great crunchy cookie!!

Jodie McCoy, Tulsa, Okla.

CARROT CHEDDAR COOKIES

- 1½ cups oats (quick **or** old-fashioned), uncooked
- 1 cup mild cheddar cheese (4 ounces), shredded
- 1 cup shredded carrots (or canned, no juice)
- ¾ cup all-purpose flour
- ⅔ cup soft butter **or** margarine
- ⅓ cup firmly packed brown sugar
- 1 egg, beaten
- ½ cup small raisins **or** chopped dates
- 1 teaspoon cinnamon
- 1 teaspoon vanilla
- ½ teaspoon salt
- ¼ teaspoon soda
- ⅛ teaspoon cloves

Combine all ingredients and mix well. Drop by rounded tablespoonfuls onto ungreased cookie sheet and flatten. Bake for 16–18 minutes at 350–375 degrees. Store tightly covered.

The small amount of sugar is more nutritious and permits those on low-calorie diets to enjoy.

Mabel E. Holsted, Stanton, Mich.

RICH PEOPLE COOKIES

Makes large batch

- 1-1/2 cups sugar
- 1 cup butter
- 3 eggs
- 1-1/2 teaspoons vanilla
- 2-1/2 cups sifted flour
- 1/2 teaspoon salt
- 1 teaspoon baking soda
- 1 teaspoon cinnamon
- 2 pounds dates, cut up
- 1/2 cup candied cherries
- 1/2 cup candied pineapple
- 1 pound walnuts, in pieces
- 1/2 pound Brazil nuts, cut up
- 1/2 pound almonds, cut up

Cream sugar, butter, eggs and vanilla. Add sifted dry ingredients to creamed mixture. Add all fruits and nuts. Bake at 325 degrees for 12 minutes.

Lucy Dowd, Sequim, Wash.

JEWELED COOKIE BARS

2 eggs
1 cup sugar
1 teaspoon vanilla
1 cup sifted flour
½ teaspoon salt
½ cup chopped, toasted blanched almonds
½ cup cut-up gumdrops
½ cup gumdrops for topping, cut up

Beat eggs until foamy; beat in sugar and vanilla. Sift together flour and salt; stir into creamed mixture. Fold in almonds and gumdrops. Spread in well-greased and floured 9-inch square pan. Sprinkle extra gumdrops over top of batter. Bake in 350-degree oven for 30–35 minutes until top has a dull crust. Cut into squares while still warm, then cool before removing from pan.

Mrs. W.T. Gore, Aztec, N.M.

OATMEAL-RAISIN COOKIES

3 eggs, well-beaten
1 cup raisins
1 teaspoon vanilla
1 cup shortening
1 cup brown sugar
1 cup granulated sugar
2½ cups flour
1 teaspoon salt
2 teaspoons soda
1 teaspoon cinnamon
2 cups oatmeal
½ cup chopped nuts

Combine eggs, raisins and vanilla. Let mixture stand for 1 hour or more. Thoroughly cream together shortening, brown and white sugars. Sift flour, salt, soda and cinnamon. Mix well; blend in egg/raisin mixture, oats and nuts. (Dough will be very stiff.) Roll the dough into balls, the size of a large walnut; roll the balls in a cinnamon-sugar mixture (1 teaspoon cinnamon mixed with 1 cup sugar). Place on cookie sheet about 3 inches apart. Bake at 350

degrees for 10–12 minutes, or until lightly browned. Remove from oven and let cool a few minutes before removing from cookie sheet. These will keep several weeks, stored in a tightly covered container. Put waxed paper between layers of cookies. Let cool *completely* before closing container.

Jean Vincent, Grand Blanc, Mich.

CLOUD 9 COOKIES
Makes 3 dozen

2 egg whites, stiffly beaten
⅔ cup sugar
⅛ teaspoon salt
1 cup chopped almonds
1 cup miniature chocolate chips

Preheat oven to 350 degrees for 15 minutes; turn off when putting cookies in oven. Fold sugar, salt, nuts and chips into stiffly beaten egg whites. Drop by teaspoonfuls onto a well-greased cookie sheet. Leave in oven 2½ hours or overnight, but do not open oven door until time to remove cookies. A good lunch-box or after-school snack.

Joy Shamway, Freeport, Ill.

ROLLED GINGER COOKIES
Makes 5 dozen

1 cup shortening
1 cup sugar
1 egg
1 cup molasses
2 tablespoons vinegar
5 cups sifted all-purpose flour
1½ teaspoons soda
½ teaspoon salt
2–3 teaspoons ground ginger
1 teaspoon cinnamon
1 teaspoon cloves

Cream shortening and sugar. Beat in egg, molasses and vinegar. Sift together dry ingredients; blend in. Chill 3 hours. Roll dough ⅛-inch thick on lightly floured board. Cut in shapes. Place 1 inch apart on greased cookie sheet. Bake at 375 degrees for 5–6 minutes. Cool slightly; remove to rack to cool completely.

Agnes Ward, Erie, Pa.

SCOTTISH BANANA COOKIES
Makes 5 dozen

⅔ cup butter
1 cup sugar
2 eggs
1 teaspoon almond flavoring
2¼ cups flour
2 tablespoons cornstarch
1 teaspoon baking powder
½ teaspoon baking soda
½ teaspoon salt
1½ cups mashed bananas

Cream together butter and sugar until light and fluffy. Add eggs, 1 at a time, and beat well after each addition. Add almond flavoring. Sift together flour, cornstarch, baking powder, baking soda and salt. Add alternately with mashed bananas.

Drop by teaspoonfuls onto greased cookie sheets. Bake in a 400-degree oven for 15 minutes.

Agnes Ward, Erie, Pa.

PECAN CRESCENT COOKIES

1 cup (2 sticks) butter, softened
¼ cup sugar
1 tablespoon cold water
1 teaspoon vanilla extract
2 cups unsifted all-purpose flour
1 cup finely chopped pecans
½ teaspoon salt
½ cup confectioners' sugar

In large bowl, with electric mixer or wooden spoon, blend butter, ¼ cup sugar, water and vanilla. Gradually stir in flour, pecans and salt until well-blended. Form dough into a ball; flatten to 1 inch thick. Wrap in plastic wrap; refrigerate 2 hours. Preheat oven to 375 degrees. Roll dough between palms, a tablespoon at a time, to make 2-inch rolls. Place rolls 2 inches apart on ungreased baking sheets; curve each to make a crescent. Bake 15 minutes to lightly golden. Cool slightly; roll in ½ cup confectioners' sugar. Serve with sherbet, if desired.

Edith Ruth Muldoon, Baldwin, N.Y.

ZEBRA COOKIES
Makes 4–5 dozen

1½ cups sugar
½ cup vegetable oil
1¼ teaspoons vanilla extract
3 eggs
1⅔ cups all-purpose flour
½ cup cocoa
½ tablespoon cinnamon
1½ teaspoons baking powder
¼ teaspoon salt
1 cup confectioners' sugar

In a mixing bowl combine sugar, oil and vanilla. Add eggs, 1 at a time; mix well. Stir in flour, cocoa, cinnamon, baking powder and salt. Cover; refrigerate 2 hours. Lightly grease baking sheet; set aside. Place confectioners' sugar in a shallow dish. Shape dough into 1-inch balls; roll in confectioners' sugar. Place 2 inches apart on baking sheet. Bake at 350 degrees for 11 minutes; cool on rack. (These cookies crack on top as they bake; thus the striped zebra look).

Gwen Campbell, Sterling, Va.

MRS. FIELD'S COOKIES

2 cups butter
2 cups granulated sugar
2 cups brown sugar
4 eggs
2 tablespoons vanilla
4 cups flour
5 cups oatmeal
1 teaspoon salt
2 teaspoons baking powder
2 teaspoons baking soda
1 (24-ounce) package chocolate chips *plus* 8-ounce Hershey bar
3 cups chopped nuts

Cream butter and sugars; add eggs and vanilla. Combine dry ingredients and add to creamed mixture. Add chips and grated Hershey bar. Add chopped nuts. Put on cookie sheet about 2 inches apart. Bake at 375 degrees for about 6 minutes.

Kit Rollins, Cedarburg, Wis.

DATE BARS

1 pound dates
1 cup walnut meats
½ cup flour
¼ teaspoon baking powder
¼ teaspoon salt
1 cup sugar
2 eggs
¼ cup melted butter
Confectioners' sugar

Pit dates and cut into quarters. Mix together flour, baking powder, salt and sugar. Add dates and nuts to flour mixture. Beat eggs. Add melted butter and combine mixtures. Bake in 8 x 12-inch pan for 30 minutes in moderate oven of 350 degrees. When slightly cool, cut into bars. Roll each bar in confectioners' sugar.

Suzan L. Wiener, Spring Hill, Fla.

CANDIED ORANGE PEEL COOKIES
Makes 3 dozen

2 eggs
⅔ cup shortening
1 cup sugar
⅔ cup sour cream
½ cup candied orange peel
2⅓ cups all-purpose flour
2 teaspoons baking powder
¼ teaspoon salt
½ teaspoon baking soda

Beat together first 5 ingredients. Sift together dry ingredients; add to liquid ingredients. Drop by teaspoonfuls onto greased cookie sheet; press small piece of candied peel into top of each cookie. Bake at 375 degrees for 12 minutes, or until lightly browned.

Gwen Campbell, Sterling, Va.

UNBAKED COOKIES

Mix together in a mixing bowl:
3 cups oatmeal
1/2 cup coconut
1/2 cup chopped nuts
4 tablespoons cocoa
1 (6-ounce) package chocolate chips
1 teaspoon vanilla
Dash of salt

Then boil together for 3 minutes the following:
2 cups sugar
1 cup margarine
1/2 cup milk

Pour over the dry mixture; mix well. Drop by teaspoonfuls on waxed paper.

Ilene Ongman, Klamath Falls, Okla.

CHEWY WALNUT SQUARES

1 egg, beaten
1 cup brown sugar
1 teaspoon vanilla
½ cup flour
¼ teaspoon soda
¼ teaspoon salt
1 cup chopped walnuts

Grease an 8-inch square pan. Stir together egg, brown sugar and vanilla. Quickly stir in flour, baking soda and salt. Add walnuts. Spread in pan and bake at 350 degrees for 18 minutes. Cookies should be soft in center when taken from the oven. Leave in pan to cool. Cut into 2-inch squares.

Brenda Peery, Tannersville, Va.

PECAN SANDIES
Makes 4 dozen

¼ cup soft margarine
1 (8-ounce) package softened cream cheese
1 egg
1 teaspoon pecan nut flavoring
1 (2-layer size) package dry cake mix
1 cup chopped pecans

Cream softened margarine and cream cheese. Add egg and flavoring. Beat well. Add dry cake mix; then add chopped pecans. Drop by teaspoonfuls onto greased cookie sheet. Bake in preheated 350-degree oven for 12 minutes, or until browned and done.

Marcia Mitchell, St. Joseph, Mo.

APPLESAUCE CHOCOLATE CHIP COOKIES

2 cups flour
1 teaspoon baking soda
1/2 teaspoon salt
3/4 cup margarine
1 cup light brown sugar
1 egg
1-1/2 teaspoons vanilla
1 cup applesauce
1 cup chocolate chips
1/2 cup chopped pecans

Combine dry ingredients together. Cream margarine and brown sugar until well-blended. Beat egg into mixture; add vanilla. Gradually add dry ingredients to creamed mixture and blend; fold in applesauce, chocolate chips and nuts. Drop by teaspoonfuls onto greased cookie sheets and bake in 375-degree oven for 10–12 minutes.

Jodie McCoy, Tulsa, Okla.

GRANDMA'S SUGAR-RAISIN COOKIES

Makes 6 dozen

1½ cups seedless raisins
1½ cups sugar
1 cup shortening
2 eggs
1 teaspoon vanilla
3 cups flour
1 teaspoon baking powder
1 teaspoon baking soda
½ teaspoon salt
½ teaspoon nutmeg
Sugar

Simmer raisins in water to barely cover, until water is all absorbed. Set aside to cool. Cream sugar and shortening; add eggs and vanilla; beat thoroughly. Sift together the dry ingredients, except last sugar, and add to creamed mixture. Stir in raisins. Roll dough into 1-inch balls; roll in sugar. Place balls 2 inches apart on greased cookie sheets; flatten with bottom of sugar-dipped glass. Bake at 400 degrees for 10 minutes until lightly browned.

Agnes Ward, Erie, Pa.

HALFWAY BARS

1 cup shortening
½ cup brown sugar
½ cup white sugar
2 egg yolks
1 tablespoon cold water
½ teaspoon baking soda
2 cups flour
2 egg whites
1 (6-ounce) package chocolate chips
1 cup brown sugar

Mix first 7 ingredients and pat into 13 x 9-inch pan. Sprinkle with chocolate chips; push chips into mixture. Beat egg whites until stiff and add 1 cup brown sugar. Spread over top of mixture. Do not touch sides of pan. Bake at 325 degrees until golden brown, about 35 minutes.

Mrs. George Brown, Lee, Fla.

DATE DAINTIES

1 cup chopped dates
1 stick margarine
1 egg
1 cup sugar
½ cup chopped pecans
Rice Krispies (2 or more cups)
Shredded coconut

Boil together dates, margarine, egg and sugar for 6–8 minutes, stirring constantly. Add nuts and Rice Krispies. Form into small balls. Roll in coconut.

Chris Bryant, Johnson City, Ind.

ORANGE SUGAR COOKIES

Makes 6 dozen

¾ cup shortening
1 cup sugar
2 eggs, beaten
2 teaspoons grated fresh orange peel
3½ cups flour
3 teaspoons baking powder
¼ teaspoon salt
½ teaspoon vanilla
⅓ cup milk

Cream shortening and sugar; add eggs. Combine sifted flour, baking powder and salt; sift together. Mix into the creamed mixture; add orange peel, vanilla and milk. Chill dough until easy to roll out. Cut out cookies into your desired shapes and bake at 375 degrees for 8–10 minutes.

Jodie McCoy, Tulsa, Okla.

LEMON-PINEAPPLE DROPS

Makes 4 dozen

½ cup shortening
2 eggs
1 (3-ounce) package lemon-flavored gelatin
1 (1-pound) package cake mix
1 (8¼-ounce) can crushed pineapple, well-drained

In mixing bowl, combine shortening and eggs. Blend in dry gelatin. Add half of dry cake mix. Beat at medium speed of mixer until fluffy. Add remaining cake mix. Blend on low speed, scraping sides of bowl constantly. Stir in pineapple. Drop rounded teaspoonfuls 2 inches apart on ungreased cookie sheet. Bake at 375 degrees for 10–12 minutes. Cool 1 minute on cookie sheet. Remove; cool on rack.

Shirley Viscosi, Worcester, Mass.

BASIC BUTTER COOKIES

Makes 30 cookies

1 cup all-purpose flour
½ cup cornstarch
½ cup confectioners' sugar
¾ cup (1½ sticks) real butter, room temperature
½ cup coarsely chopped walnuts

Preheat oven to 300 degrees. Sift first 3 ingredients into large bowl. Add butter and mix well. Stir in walnuts. Drop by teaspoonfuls onto baking sheets. Bake until cookies are lightly golden, about 20–25 minutes.

Note: Real butter is the secret of these buttery-tasting cookies.

Agnes Ward, Erie, Pa.

PUMPKIN CAKE BARS

Makes 24

4 eggs, well-beaten
2 cups cooked pumpkin or 1 (1-pound) can
1-1/2 cups sugar
1/4 teaspoon salt
1 teaspoon ginger
1 teaspoon cinnamon
1/2 teaspoon cloves
1 box yellow cake mix
1/2 cup butter, melted
1 cup chopped pecans

Mix eggs, pumpkin, sugar, salt, ginger, cinnamon and cloves together; pour into a 13 x 9-inch pan. Sprinkle dry cake mix on top. Drizzle melted butter over mix; spread chopped nuts over all. Bake at 325 degrees for 1 hour and 20 minutes. (Cover with foil loosely to keep from browning too soon for the first half of cooking time.) Cut into squares.

Marcella Swigert, Monroe City, Mo.

CHEWY PEANUT BARS

Crust:
  1 cup flour
  ½ cup brown sugar, packed
  ½ cup butter

Topping:
  1 cup brown sugar, packed
  2 eggs
  3 tablespoons flour
  1 teaspoon baking powder
  1 teaspoon vanilla extract
  2 cups salted peanuts, whole or coarsely chopped

Crust: Put flour and sugar in a bowl; mix well. With a pastry blender cut in butter until mixture resembles coarse crumbs. Spread evenly in a greased 13 x 9-inch pan. Bake at 375 degrees for 8–10 minutes, or until crust appears slightly firm in center. Cool.

Topping: Mix sugar and eggs until smooth. Stir in flour, baking powder and vanilla until well-blended. Stir in peanuts. Pour over crust. Bake at 375 degrees for 18–20 minutes, or until browned and edges are firm. (Center may be somewhat soft, but crusted over.) Cool; cut into bars.

Vickie Vogt, Kewaskum, Wis.

CHEESECAKE BARS

1 box Duncan Hines Golden Butter Recipe cake mix
1 egg
1 stick margarine
1 (8-ounce) package cream cheese
2 eggs
1 (1-pound) box confectioners' sugar

Blend together the first 3 ingredients. Crumble and press into greased oblong pan. Then mix next 3 ingredients together and spread on top of bottom layer. Bake at 350 degrees for 35–40 minutes, or until golden brown. Cool completely and cut into bars.

Sue Hibbard, Rochester, N.Y.

CASHEW DROPS

Makes 6–7 dozen

Cookies:
  ½ cup (1 stick) butter
  1 cup firmly packed light brown sugar
  1 egg
  1 teaspoon vanilla extract
  1¾ cups all-purpose flour
  1 teaspoon baking powder
  ½ teaspoon baking soda
  ½ cup dairy sour cream
  1 cup chopped salted cashews

Frosting:
  ¼ cup (½ stick) butter
  2 cups confectioners' sugar
  3 to 3½ tablespoons milk

Preheat oven to 375 degrees. For cookies, cream butter. Gradually add sugar; continue beating until blended. Beat in egg and vanilla. Combine flour, baking powder and soda. Add to creamed mixture alternately with sour cream; fold in cashews. Drop by rounded teaspoonfuls onto buttered cookie sheets. Bake 8–10 minutes. Remove to wire rack to cool. When cool, frost. For frosting, heat butter over low heat until light amber color. Remove from heat and stir in sugar and milk.

WALNUT MACAROONS

1 egg white
⅔ cup white sugar
⅛ teaspoon salt
¼ teaspoon almond extract
⅓ cup very finely chopped walnuts

Beat egg white very stiff, adding sugar slowly. Add salt very gradually while beating; still beating, add extract and chopped nuts. Drop by teaspoonfuls onto cookie sheet (Teflon or nonstick sheet if possible). Bake at 325 degrees for 15 minutes. Cool on rack.

Pearle M. Goodwin, South Ryegate, Vt.

CRISPY CORNFLAKES COOKIES

3 cups cornflakes cereal
1 cup sugar
1 cup walnuts, coarsely chopped
¼ teaspoon almond extract
2 egg yolks, beaten
2 egg whites

Combine first 5 ingredients. Beat egg whites until stiff; fold into cornflakes mixture. Drop by tablespoonfuls onto a well-greased baking sheet. Bake at 350 degrees until pale amber. Allow to cool before removing from cookie sheet.

Gwen Campbell, Sterling, Va.

AGGRESSION COOKIES

6 cups oatmeal
3 cups brown sugar
3 cups (6 sticks) margarine
3 cups flour
3 teaspoons baking soda

Combine all ingredients and beat the daylights out of them! Drop onto ungreased cookie sheets and bake at 350 degrees for about 10 minutes.

Genevieve Gilham, Royal, Ark.

CHOCOLATE MACAROONS

Makes 6 dozen

1 (18.5-ounce) package devil's food cake mix with pudding
1 cup flaked coconut, toasted
½ cup regular oats, uncooked and toasted
¾ cup butter *or* margarine melted
2 teaspoons vanilla
2 eggs, slightly beaten
6 (1.45-ounce) milk chocolate candy bars
¾ cup flaked coconut

Combine first 6 ingredients; chill 30 minutes. Drop by heaping teaspoonfuls 2 inches apart on ungreased cookie sheets. Bake at 350 degrees for 10 minutes. Immediately top each cookie with 1 chocolate square; spread to front; sprinkle cookies with coconut.

Mrs. Robert T. Shaffer, Middleburg, Pa.

PECAN BALLS

Makes 5 dozen

1 cup soft butter
½ cup granulated sugar *or* ½ cup confectioners' sugar
¼ teaspoon salt
1 teaspoon vanilla
2¼ cups flour
1 cup chopped pecans

Mix butter, sugar, salt and vanilla. Work in flour. The last bit of flour may be worked in with hands. Add nuts.

Chill dough. Roll into 1-inch balls. Place on ungreased baking sheet and bake at 350 degrees for 10–12 minutes, until set, but not browned. Roll in sifted confectioners' sugar while warm. Cool; roll again.

Betty Slavin, Omaha, Neb.

WALNUT CLUSTERS

Makes 50

¼ cup butter
½ cup sugar
1 egg, unbeaten
1¼ teaspoons vanilla
1½ squares unsweetened chocolate, melted
½ cup flour
¼ teaspoon baking powder
½ teaspoon salt
2 cups unbroken walnuts

Cream butter and sugar until fluffy. Add egg and vanilla; blend well. Stir in chocolate, then flour sifted with baking powder and salt. Add walnuts. Drop by teaspoonfuls onto greased baking sheet. Bake at 350 degrees for 10 minutes. Cookies should be soft, almost like candy.

Elizabeth S. Lawson, Delbarton, W.Va.

CHOCO SURPRISE COOKIES

Makes 8 dozen

1 cup all-purpose flour
1 teaspoon baking powder
1 teaspoon cinnamon
1 cup peanut butter (creamy)
½ cup margarine, softened
1 cup firmly packed brown sugar
2 eggs, well-beaten
1 (16-ounce) package milk chocolate stars (or Hershey Kisses with tips cut off)
Confectioners' sugar

Combine first 3 ingredients and set aside. Combine and cream until fluffy, the peanut butter, margarine, brown sugar and eggs. Add dry ingredients. Cover dough; chill 1 hour or overnight.

Shape 1 teaspoon dough around star; place on lightly greased cookie sheet or

on Teflon cookie sheet. Bake at 350 degrees for 9–11 minutes, or until lightly browned. Cool slightly on wire racks; then roll in confectioners' sugar. Cool completely before storing.

Mrs. Hobert Howell, Waco, Texas

STARLIGHT MINT SURPRISE COOKIES

Makes 4½ dozen

3 cups flour
1 teaspoon soda
½ teaspoon salt
1 cup butter
1 cup sugar
½ cup brown sugar
2 eggs
1 teaspoon vanilla
1 package chocolate mint wafers

Mix first 3 ingredients; set aside. Cream butter, sugars, eggs and vanilla. Add flour mixture. Cover and chill 2 hours. Enclose each chocolate mint wafer in 1 tablespoon dough. Place on greased cookie sheet, 2 inches apart. Top with pecan half. Bake for 10 minutes in a 375-degree oven.

Ann Sterzer, Lincoln, Neb.

CHERRY WINKS

Makes 2½ dozen

1 cup confectioners' sugar
1 cup butter, softened
1 teaspoon vanilla
1 egg
2 cups flour
2 tablespoons poppy seeds
½ teaspoon salt
Cherry preserves (⅓–½ cup)

Heat oven to 300 degrees. Beat confectioners' sugar and butter until fluffy. Add vanilla and egg; blend well. Stir in flour, poppy seeds, salt; mix well. Drop by rounded teaspoonfuls onto ungreased cookie sheets. With finger make imprint in center of each cookie. Fill with ½ teaspoon preserves. Bake at 300 degrees for 20–25 minutes, or until edges are light golden brown. Remove from cookie sheet immediately.

This is a very light and buttery cookie.

Vickie Vogt, Kewaskum, Wis.

122

BUTTERSCOTCH BARS

Makes about 4 dozen

4 eggs
6-ounce package brown sugar
2 cups buttermilk biscuit mix
2 cups chopped pecans
1 small package (6 ounces) butterscotch morsels
1 teaspoon vanilla

Beat eggs at medium speed of mixer until frothy. Gradually add sugar, beating until thick. Add remaining ingredients, stirring well. Spread batter in a greased and floured 13x9x2-inch pan. Bake in a preheated 325-degree oven for 45 minutes. Cool and cut into bars.

Mrs. Bruce Fowler, Woodruff, S.C.

FIG SQUARES

3 eggs
¾ cup sugar
1 teaspoon vanilla
1 cup flour
⅛ teaspoon salt
2 teaspoons baking powder
1 (8-ounce) package (1½ cups)
   figs, chopped
1 cup walnuts, chopped

Beat eggs until light. Add sugar and vanilla; mix well. Add sifted dry ingredients and mix well. Fold in figs and walnuts. Bake in greased 9-inch square pan at 350 degrees for 30 minutes. Cool; cut in squares; sprinkle with sifted confectioners' sugar. Serve these with hot spiced tea!

Eleanor V. Craycraft, Santa Monica, Calif.

SOUR CREAM DATE DREAMS

¼ cup shortening
¾ cup brown sugar
½ teaspoon vanilla
1 egg, beaten
1¼ cups flour
½ teaspoon soda
¼ teaspoon baking powder
⅔ cup dates, chopped
Walnut halves

¼ teaspoon salt
¼ teaspoon cinnamon
⅛ teaspoon nutmeg
½ cup sour cream

Cream together shortening, sugar and vanilla. Add egg; mix well. Sift together dry ingredients and add to shortening mixture alternately with sour cream. Stir in dates.

Drop by teaspoonfuls onto greased cookie sheet. Top each with a walnut half and bake at 400 degrees for about 8–10 minutes.

Eleanor V. Craycraft, Santa Monica, Calif.

RICH SHORTBREAD COOKIES

2 cups butter
1½ cups confectioners' sugar
2 teaspoons vanilla
4 cups flour
1 teaspoon salt
Candied cherries, if desired

Cream butter thoroughly. Add confectioners' sugar and vanilla; beat well. Add flour and salt; blend together. Form into several rolls and wrap each roll in waxed paper. Refrigerate overnight. Slice and put on ungreased baking sheets. At this point, you may decorate with red cherries. Bake for 20 minutes at 300 degrees.

Great for Valentine's Day festivities!!

Lillian Smith, Montreal, Quebec, Canada

COCONUT CREAM COOKIES

Makes 4¼–5 dozen

1 cup margarine
2 (3-ounce) packages cream
   cheese
1 cup sugar
¼ teaspoon salt
1 teaspoon vanilla
1 egg
2 tablespoons milk
2 cups flour
½ cup coconut
Pecan or walnut halves

Cream together first 7 ingredients

until fluffy. Stir in flour and coconut. Mix well. Drop by small spoonfuls onto greased cookie sheets. Top each cookie with nut half. Bake 20 minutes in 325-degree oven.

Jodie McCoy, Tulsa, Okla.

BUTTERFINGER COOKIES

2⅔ cups flour
1 teaspoon baking soda
⅔ cup Crisco
½ teaspoon salt
1½ cups sugar
2 eggs
4 Butterfinger candy bars,
   chopped

Cream Crisco and sugar; beat in eggs. Sift dry ingredients and sprinkle over candy pieces. Mix well. Stir into egg mixture. Shape dough into rolls. Cover with foil or plastic wrap. Chill rolls. Cut into thin slices. Place slices on greased cookie sheet; bake at 375 degrees for 12 minutes. Remove from pan immediately.

Sue Thomas, Casa Grande, Ariz.

FRUIT-N-HONEY COOKIES

¼ cup brown sugar
½ cup honey
½ cup butter *or* margarine
2 eggs
1½ cups flour
½ teaspoon salt
½ teaspoon baking soda
1 teaspoon cinnamon
½ cup milk
½ cup raisins
½ cup ground nuts
¼ cup coconut

Cream brown sugar, honey and butter together in a mixing bowl. Add eggs. Sift together dry ingredients. Add to creamed mixture alternately with milk. Mix well. Stir in raisins, nuts and coconut. Drop by teaspoonfuls onto greased cookie sheet. Bake at 400 degrees for 6–8 minutes.

Mrs. E. O'Brien, Richmond, Va.

Cooking
FOR TWO

PIZZA SAUCE
Makes 1 cup

2 tablespoons oil
1/2 medium onion, chopped (about 1/3 cup)
1/4 cup chopped green pepper
1 (8-ounce) can tomato sauce
2 teaspoons dried oregano
1 teaspoon vinegar
1/8 teaspoon pepper
Pinch sugar

In a medium saucepan or skillet heat oil; add onion; cook until transparent; stir in green pepper; cook just until wilted. Add tomato sauce, oregano (rub in palm of hand to release flavor), vinegar, pepper and sugar. Stir until boiling; reduce heat to low; simmer about 5 minutes to blend flavors.

Timesaver: Chopped onion and green pepper are available frozen.

THE WORLD'S BEST WATERMELON
Serves 2

2 servings of cubed, seeded watermelon
8 fresh mint leaves
2 wedges of fresh lime

Prepare melon—it's easy to cut into cubes if bought in slices. Remove visible seeds with knife tip; pile into dessert dishes. With scissors snip on slivers of fresh mint. Just before serving squeeze lime juice over melon.

BAKED BROWN BREAD
Makes 12 slices

Especially good spread with cream cheese or served with cheddar cheese.

1 cup All-bran cereal
1 cup buttermilk
2 tablespoons molasses
1 cup flour, spooned lightly into cup
1/3 cup sugar
1 teaspoon soda
1/2 teaspoon salt
1/3 cup chopped walnuts

In a medium-size bowl stir together cereal, buttermilk, and molasses. Set aside for cereal to absorb liquid.

Preheat oven to 350 degrees. Prepare 2 (16-ounce) cans (or an 8x4-inch loaf pan). Spray with pan release, or grease and flour.

Into a small bowl measure flour, sugar, soda, and salt. Whisk thoroughly; whisk in nuts. Stir dry ingredients into cereal just until blended. Spoon into cans (or pan).

Bake until cake tester comes out dry, about 40 minutes. Let cool 5 minutes, rolling cans on counter now and then to loosen bread. Turn out onto rack to cool. Store in refrigerator or freeze, sliced, so it can be thawed as needed.

POTATO SALAD FOR TWO
Serves 2

2 cups cold, boiled potatoes, cubed
2 tablespoons French dressing
1 hard-cooked egg, cut up
1/2 cup finely diced celery
1/2 cucumber, finely diced
1/2 teaspoon celery seeds
1/2 cup grated carrots, optional
1/4 cup mayonnaise

Marinate potatoes in French dressing for 2 hours. Add remaining ingredients. Season with salt and pepper. Garnish with parsley or minced pimiento or olives.

Flo Burtnett, Gage, Okla.

SOY BARBECUE SAUCE
Makes 1/2 cup

This unusual sauce combines with either meatballs or hot dogs to make good sandwiches. Don't be put off by the soy sauce. If it's good-quality it will add a delicate flavor. (I also spoon this sauce over baking pork chops, spare ribs, or whole pork tenderloin.)

1/4 cup water
1/4 cup ketchup
1 tablespoon brown sugar
1 tablespoon soy sauce (I use Kikkoman's)
1 clove garlic, split or 1/8 teaspoon garlic powder

Measure water in liquid measuring cup; add ketchup to the 1/2 cup mark. Add brown sugar, soy sauce, garlic clove or powder. Stir to mix well. Simmer in microwave oven about 2 minutes or transfer to a small saucepan; stir over medium heat until boiling; reduce heat; simmer about 2 minutes.

124

LOUIS DRESSING
Serves 2

Good dressing to spoon over cooked fresh shrimp, crabmeat or chunks of canned salmon on a bed of lettuce.

1/4 cup mayonnaise
1 tablespoon sweet pickle relish
2 tablespoons chili sauce
1 teaspoon lemon juice
1/2 teaspoon horseradish
1/4 teaspoon salt
1 shake or grinding black pepper
1 green onion

In a small bowl combine all ingredients, except green onion. Snip in onion with scissors. Mix well. Cover; chill.

MEATBALL SANDWICHES
Serves 2

Generous 1/2 pound lean ground beef
tablespoons chopped onion
/4 teaspoon salt
inch pepper
oy Barbecue Sauce (recipe follows)
pita bread rounds or buns

Combine beef, onion, salt, and epper. Shape lightly into balls — I ake small ones for sandwiches. Cook a non-stick skillet over medium eat until brown, stirring as necessary. When fully cooked remove all drippings from skillet. Pour barbecue sauce over meatballs; stir to cook; cook on low a few minutes. These can be made ahead and reheated. Serve in warm pita or on toasted buns.

*Meat loaf mixture is a flavorful change for meatballs. It contains pork, so be sure to fully cook.

CHICKEN SALAD-FILLED JUMBO SHELLS
Serves 2

If you don't have cooked chicken on hand follow this work schedule: Cook 2 large chicken breast halves. In a saucepan, cover rinsed chicken with cold water; add 2 split garlic cloves and salt. Bring quickly to boiling; reduce heat; cover; simmer until fork tender, 30 to 40 minutes. Remove to a plate. Discard garlic.

Return chicken broth to boiling (add more water and salt, if necessary). Add pasta shells; cook until fork tender. Cool and drain as directed above. Meanwhile, cook bacon; chop celery; prepare dressing.

When chicken is cool enough to handle remove skin and bones; dice finely. Assemble according to following directions.

Filling:
1/3 cup mayonnaise
2 teaspoons water
1/3 cup celery, finely chopped
1 green onion
2 cups finely diced, cooked chicken
1/4 to 1/2 teaspoon salt (I like plenty of salt, so I use 1/2 teaspoon)
4 strips bacon, cooked until crisp and drained
6-8 jumbo shells, cooked and cooled
Chives for garnish, if available

Into a medium bowl measure mayonnaise and water. (The water prevents salad from being pasty.) Whisk until smooth. Stir in celery; snip in onion with scissors. Add chicken; sprinkle on salt; mix well. Crumble in bacon; mix.

Spoon chicken salad into pasta shells; sprinkle with chopped chives if using. Cover and refrigerate. To serve, arrange on a bed of lettuce.

SOFT PEACH ICE CREAM
Serves 2

Blender-quick and so refreshing.

1 large or 2 small peaches (*or* nectarines)
4 large scoops ice cream (vanilla, almond, butter pecan or whatever sounds good to you)
1/4 teaspoon almond flavoring

Chill 2 small-stemmed dessert or wine glasses.

Peel and pit peaches; slice into blender container. Place ice cream on top; dribble in almond flavoring. Let sit in refrigerator during meal. When ready to serve blend just long enough to combine thoroughly, scraping down as necessary. It's a very thick liquid. Pour into chilled glasses and serve immediately.

SHORTCAKE
Serves 2

1/2 cup flour, spooned lightly into cup
3/4 teaspoon baking powder
1/8 teaspoon salt
1 tablespoon sugar
2 tablespoons shortening (I use half butter)
3 tablespoons milk (I add a few drops vanilla)

Preheat oven to 425 degrees.

Measure flour, baking powder, salt, and sugar into a small bowl; mix. Add shortening; cut in with pastry blender. When like fine crumbs add milk; mix lightly with fork until it comes together (it will be a sticky ball). Drop into two mounds on a small ungreased baking sheet. Use a fork to gently flatten and shape to a thick 3-inch biscuit. Sprinkle with sugar. Bake until beginning to brown, 10 to 12 minutes. Transfer to cooling rack. Split as soon as cool enough to handle. Serve warm or cold.

To assemble strawberry shortcake spread bottom of biscuit with sweetened whipped cream; spoon on sliced berries; cover with biscuit top, berries, and then remaining whipped cream.

PLUM TORTE
Serves 4

3 large red or 4 purple plums
1/2 cup flour, spooned lightly into cup
1/2 teaspoon baking powder
1/8 teaspoon salt
1/4 cup butter, softened
1/2 cup sugar
1 large egg
1/2 teaspoon vanilla (optional)
Sugar and cinnamon

Spray with pan release or grease and flour an 8-inch pie plate.

Wash plums; cut in half; remove seeds; cut red plums into quarters; leave purple ones in halves. Set aside.

Preheat oven to 350 degrees.

Combine flour, baking powder, and salt. To do this, measure baking powder and salt into one-half cup dry measure; add a spoonful of flour; mix well with spoon; lightly spoon in flour to over fill; scrape to level. Set aside.

Measure butter and sugar into medium mixing bowl; beat about 1 minute. Add egg; beat until light and fluffy, several minutes. Beat in flavoring, if using. On low speed beat in dry ingredients, just until blended in. Spread in prepared pie plate. Arrange plum pieces on top, cut side down. Sprinkle lightly with sugar and cinnamon.

Bake until cake tester comes out dry, 30-35 minutes. Let cool on cake rack 5 minutes; turn out. Turn again so crispy sugar crust is on top. Serve plain or with whipped cream.

Freeze leftovers, cut in serving-size pieces. Reheat to warm before serving.

CHOCOLATE BREAD PUDDING
Two large servings

1 tablespoon butter or margarine
1-1/2 cups loosely packed 1/2-inch bread cubes (use French, Italian or Vienna bread)
Scant 1 cup half-and-half or milk
1 envelope or square (1 oz.) unsweetened chocolate
1 large egg
1/3 cup sugar
1/8 teaspoon salt
1 teaspoon vanilla

Preheat oven to 350 degrees. For this pudding, use a small flat-bottom casserole, or a 6-inch souffle dish. Melt butter in dish while preheating oven. Add bread cubes; toss with a fork to mix; set aside.

In small saucepan, combine half-and-half or milk with chocolate. Whisk over low heat until mixture is hot and thoroughly blended. In a small bowl, combine egg, sugar, salt and vanilla; whisk to blend. Add hot chocolate mixture slowly, while whisking. Pour over bread cubes; mix gently, but thoroughly.

Set dish in pan containing 1/2 inch warm tap water. Bake until a rinsed knife inserted half way to center comes out clean, not milky, 25-30 minutes. Remove dish from hot water; cool about 20 minutes before serving. Serve warm with Hard Sauce or serve cool with whipped cream.

Hard Sauce:
2 tablespoons butter, softened
1/3 cup confectioners' sugar
1-2 teaspoons brandy or dark rum

In a small bowl beat butter and sugar with a fork until light. Gradually beat in brandy or rum until no more liquid can be absorbed. Spoon into two mounds; cover and chill. Set out about 20 minutes before serving on warm bread pudding.

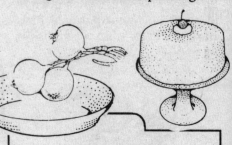

ONION PIE
Serves 2

2 medium onions
3 tablespoons butter or margarine, divided
1/2 cup milk
1 large egg
1 tablespoon Parmesan cheese*
1/2 cup crushed saltine crackers

Preheat oven to 325 degrees. Grease or spray with pan release a 7-inch pie plate. Cut onions in half lengthwise; place cut side down on cutting board and slice thinly. In a small skillet melt 1 tablespoon butter; sauté onions until transparent. Spread in prepared pie plate; set skillet aside.

In pint pitcher measure milk; add egg and cheese; whisk or beat well with a fork. Pour over onions. Bake 15 minutes. Meanwhile, melt remaining 2 tablespoons butter in skillet; add cracker crumbs; toss well; toast lightly over low heat. Sprinkle over pie. Bake just until set, 5-10 minutes longer. Good with any leftover sliced meat.
*Use 1/2 cup grated Cheddar cheese instead of Parmesan cheese, if you prefer.

CORN PUDDING
Serves 2

(A soft creamy pudding)

1 large egg
1/4 teaspoon salt
Pinch pepper
1 teaspoon sugar
1 tablespoon flour
1/3 cup milk
1 (8-ounce) can cream-style corn

Preheat oven to 350 degrees.
Grease or spray with pan release a small baking dish (flat-bottomed, if possible; I use a 6-inch soufflé dish). In a small bowl whisk egg to blend. Whisk in salt, pepper, sugar, flour, and milk. When smooth, whisk in corn. Pour into prepared dish. Bake until set—firm when dish is jiggled—35-40 minutes.

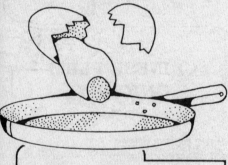

PUFFY FRENCH TOAST
Serves 2

4 slices bread
1/2 cup milk
1 egg
3/4 cup biscuit mix
2 tablespoons sugar
1/2 teaspoon cinnamon
1/2 cup margarine

Melt margarine in skillet on medium heat. With electric mixer, combine milk, egg, biscuit mix, sugar and cinnamon. Cut each slice of bread in half diagonally. Dip in batter; coating completely. Fry four pieces at a time until golden brown and puffy. (About 3 minutes on each side). Sprinkle with confectioners sugar and cinnamon. Serve with warm syrup. (Blueberry syrup is delicious.)

Helen Weissinger, Levittown, PA

GLAZED PARSNIPS
Serves 2

1/2 pound parsnips
1 tablespoon butter or margarine
2 tablespoons brown sugar
Salt and pepper
Pinch nutmeg
1 tablespoon whipping cream
1 tablespoon dry white wine, dry vermouth or sherry

Half-fill a medium saucepan with water; add salt; bring to boiling.
Meanwhile trim top and root ends from parsnips; pare with vegetable peeler. Cut in half lengthwise then crosswise; cut into lengthwise strips to make uniform pieces so they will cook evenly. Drop into boiling water; cover; cook until barely tender, 4 to 5 minutes. Drain; rinse under cold water to stop the cooking; drain well. If done ahead cover and refrigerate; drain again before using.
Melt butter in shallow baking dish in oven with roasting hens. Add parsnips; toss to coat with butter. Sprinkle on brown sugar, salt, pepper, and nutmeg. Dribble on cream and wine. Bake at 350 degrees (with hens) about 20 minutes, stirring once to baste.

THOUSAND ISLAND SALAD
Serves 2

A main–dish salad.

Dressing:
1/4 cup mayonnaise
1-1/2 tablespoons ketchup
1-1/2 teaspoons sweet pickle relish
1/2 green onion

Salad:
Lettuce
1/4 pound ham in bite-size pieces (I add salami if I have it)
3 hard-cooked eggs

Prepare dressing; combine mayonnaise, ketchup, and relish. With scissors, snip in green onion; mix well.
Cover plates with chunks and leaves of lettuce. Top with ham; slice on eggs; spoon on dressing.

CHILI CHEDDAR OMELET
Serves 2

4 eggs
1 tablespoon water
1/4 teaspoon seasoned salt
Butter
1 cup chili
1/4 cup grated Cheddar cheese
1/2 avocado, peeled and sliced

In small bowl, beat eggs, water and seasoned salt together. Pour mixture into well-buttered 10-inch skillet.
Cook omelet over medium heat, letting liquid egg run to edges when eggs are set; slide omelet onto serving plate. Place chili, grated cheese and avocado slices on half of omelet; fold over other half.

Susan L. Wiener, Spring Hill, Fl

CHOCOLATE SAUCE
Serves 2

So good over coffee ice cream!

1/4 cup light cream
1/4 cup sugar
1 square (or envelope) unsweetened chocolate
1 teaspoon butter
1/4 teaspoon vanilla

Measure cream; add sugar to cream in measuring cup; stir to partially dissolve sugar. Set aside.
In a small saucepan combine chocolate and butter. Stir over low heat until melted and smooth. Add cream; stir sauce over medium heat until it thickens, just as it begins to boil. Remove from heat; stir in vanilla. Serve warm or at room temperature.

HOLIDAY CORNISH HENS
Serves 2

Sometimes 22-ounce hens are the smallest available. They are too large for us but the leftover meat makes good sandwiches.

2 Rock Cornish game hens
2 juice oranges
1 large clove garlic
1/4 teaspoon salt
Pinch black pepper
2 tablespoons brown sugar

Line a shallow baking pan with foil. Place two pieces of crushed foil on pan as racks for hens (without racks hens will stick and burn on the bottom due to sugar in the glaze).

Preheat oven to 450 degrees.

Rinse cavity and outside of hens; pat dry with paper towel. Thickly slice one orange; cut slices in half; reserve several center slices for serving decoration. Stuff half of remaining orange slices and half of garlic clove into the cavity of each hen. Place hens breast side up on prepared pan.

Squeeze remaining orange. Combine orange juice (about 1/3 cup), salt, pepper, and brown sugar; stir until sugar dissolves. Brush hens all over with orange sauce. Roast at 450 degrees for 15 minutes, brushing once with sauce. Reduce oven temperature to 350 degrees; roast 50 minutes longer, brushing several times with remaining sauce. Remove orange slices and garlic from cavity. Serve with reserved orange slices on the side.

SWISS VEAL
Serves 2

3/4 pound veal cutlet (or 2 boned and skinned chicken breasts)
3 tablespoons butter
Salt and pepper
Flour
2 thin slices onion, chopped
1/8 teaspoon dried tarragon
1/4 cup dry white wine (use chicken broth if you do not have wine)
1-1/2 teaspoons lemon juice
1/4 cup sour cream

Trim away fat and bone from veal. Cut veal (or chicken) into narrow strips about one inch long. Sprinkle with salt, pepper, and a light dusting of flour.

In a medium skillet heat butter until bubbly. Over medium heat cook meat until evenly brown. Add onions; cook just until soft. Add tarragon and wine; cover; cook on low heat 4 to 5 minutes, until meat tests done with a fork. Drizzle on lemon juice; toss to mix. Stir in sour cream; cook just until sour cream is hot, not boiling.

Serve with buttered noodles.

VEAL IN CREAM
Serves 2

1/2 pound veal scallops (or 2 boned and skinned chicken breasts)
2 tablespoons flour
1/2 teaspoon salt
1/4 teaspoon pepper
1/4 teaspoon paprika
1 tablespoon butter or margarine
1/2 tablespoon cooking oil
1/4 cup whipping cream

Pound veal (or chicken) until very thin according to directions given above.

Mix flour, salt, pepper and paprika; spread on waxed paper or large plate. Coat meat on both sides with mixture; leave on paper in a single layer until needed.

In a large skillet heat butter and oil until bubbly. Add meat, single layer, and cook over medium heat until brown on both sides. Reduce heat to low; cover skillet; cook until tender, 3 to 5 minutes. Add cream; cook uncovered a few minutes until cream has thickened to sauce consistency.

Serve with mashed potatoes or buttered noodles.

LEMON CHICKEN WINGS
Serves 2

3 tablespoons oil
1/2 teaspoon grated lemon peel
1 tablespoon lemon juice
1/2 teaspoon dried oregano leaves
1/2 teaspoon garlic salt
8 chicken wings, tips removed

Measure oil into a medium bowl. Grate lemon peel onto foil; add 1/2 teaspoon to oil; store remaining peel in foil; freeze for later use. Squeeze lemon; add 1 tablespoon juice to oil; chill or freeze remaining juice for another use. Add oregano and garlic salt to oil; whisk until blended. Add chicken wings, toss well; cover and refrigerate up to 24 hours.

Preheat oven to 425 degrees. Place chicken wings, skin-side down, on rack on pan prepared as directed in italics at beginning of this article. Reserve marinade. Bake 20 minutes; brush with marinade, turn; brush other side. Bake until brown and tender, about 30 minutes longer.

CHINESE PLUM CHICKEN
Serves 2

3 red plums, rinsed
2 tablespoons sugar
2 tablespoons orange juice
1/2 teaspoon lemon juice
1/2 teaspoon salt
1 teaspoon flour
1 whole chicken breast, halved

Preheat oven to 350 degrees.

Slice plums into small bowl. Mix in sugar, orange juice, lemon juice, salt, and flour. Spread in center of a square of foil (Use 18-inch heavy-duty foil for this).

Remove skin from chicken and score (make long shallow cuts in a diamond pattern in the flesh). Place cut side down on plum mixture. Fold foil to make a secure package. Place foil package on shallow baking pan (just in case). Bake until fork tender, about 45 minutes. Flip the package over and back, once during baking, to distribute the juices.

To serve, spoon plum sauce over chicken.

OVEN BARBECUED CHICKEN WINGS

Serves 2

4 tablespoons ketchup
2 tablespoons vinegar
2 tablespoons water
1 teaspoon Worcestershire sauce
1 teaspoon sugar
1/2 teaspoon salt
1/4 teaspoon dry mustard
1/4 teaspoon chili powder
1/8 teaspoon pepper or dash
    Tabasco sauce
8 chicken wings, tips removed

Measure all ingredients, except chicken wings, into medium size bowl; whisk until well blended. To do ahead, add chicken wings; toss well; cover and refrigerate up to 24 hours.

For last-minute preparation, dip chicken wings in sauce to coat; place skin-side down on rack on pan prepared as directed in italics at beginning of this article. Bake at 425 degrees for 20 minutes. Brush with sauce; turn; brush other side; bake until brown and tender, about 30 minutes longer.

BEEF PAPRIKA

Serves 4

Freeze half for another meal.
1-1/2 pounds boneless round
    steak
1/4 cup flour
1 teaspoon salt
1/4 teaspoon black pepper
1 medium onion
1 clove garlic
4 tablespoons oil
1 cup beef broth (Swanson's works
    well)
3 drops Tabasco sauce
1 teaspoon paprika
1 tablespoon sour cream

Trim meat; cut into four serving-size pieces. Place meat on cutting board; pound with a mallet on both sides until about 3/8 inch thick. Measure flour, salt, and pepper onto a plate; mix with a fork; coat meat on both sides with flour; set aside.

Slice onion thinly; mince garlic. Heat 1 tablespoon oil in a 12-inch skillet. Cook onions and garlic until transparent. Remove from skillet. Add remaining 3 tablespoons oil to skillet; when hot add meat in single layer. Brown on both sides. Add onions, garlic, broth, Tabasco sauce, and paprika. Stir; bring to boiling; partially cover; cook on low heat until meat is tender, 10 to 15 minutes.

Remove half of meat and sauce to freeze. Stir sour cream into remaining sauce. Set over low heat until sauce is warm.

Serve with noodles. (I cook 2 cups dry noodles for us. Drain cooked noodles; return to warm pan; stir in a large spoonful of paprika sauce to flavor noodles and to prevent them from sticking together.)

For another meal thaw frozen beef in refrigerator. Reheat; stir in 1 tablespoon sour cream just before serving

SUMMER SPAGHETTI

Serves 2

1 large or 2 medium ripe tomatoes
1-1/2 tablespoons olive oil
1 small clove garlic, crushed
5 fresh basil leaves, slivered (or
    1/2 teaspoon crushed dried basil)
1 tablespoon minced parsley
Dash hot pepper sauce
Grinding or pinch black pepper
1/4 teaspoon salt
3 black olives, slivered (optional,
    but a real flavor boost)
2 to 3 ounces thin spaghetti

Peel tomato. Cut in half crosswise; remove and discard juicy seed sections (I use my thumb to scoop them out). Cut tomato into small chunks; set aside in strainer to drain.

In a small bowl combine oil, garlic, basil, parsley, hot sauce, pepper, salt, and olives if using. Add tomato chunks; mix well. Cover; set aside up to two hours on counter. Refrigerate for longer storage, but set out to warm to room temperature before serving.

Cook spaghetti according to package directions (I snap it in half before cooking). Quickly drain in a strainer; return to hot cooking pan; add tomato mixture; toss well. Serve immediately—with slotted spoon to drain, if necessary.

TOMATO-CHEESE BULGUR*

2 servings

A hearty Tex-Mex-flavored side dish to serve with beef or lamb patties, sausage links, roast pork, or lamb.

1-1/2 tablespoons margarine
1/2 onion, chopped
1 clove garlic, minced
1/4 green pepper, chopped
1/2 cup bulgur wheat
1/4 teaspoon dried basil
1/4 teaspoon chili powder
1/4 teaspoon salt
1/2 teaspoon sugar
1 cup tomato juice
1/2 cup shredded sharp Cheddar
    cheese

In medium skillet melt margarine on low heat. Add onion, garlic, and green pepper as you chop them. Cook until onion and green pepper are soft. Add bulgur. Cook one minute, stirring, on medium heat. Remove from heat. Measure in oregano, basil, chili powder, salt, and sugar, then stir in tomato juice. (If skillet is too hot when tomato juice is added, the dish will have a burned taste.) Over medium heat, stir to mix well. Bring to boiling; cover; reduce heat; simmer until all liquid is absorbed, about 20 minutes. Remove from heat; add cheese; stir until melted and serve.

BULGUR SALAD

2 servings

This do-ahead salad is an American version of Tabouli (or Tabbouleh). The mint leaves are optional, but an especially good addition if served with lamb.

1/3 cup bulgur wheat
Water
1 clove garlic
2 tablespoons olive oil
1 tablespoon lemon juice
1/2 teaspoon salt
Dash black pepper
2 sprigs parsley
1 green onion
4 mint leaves (optional)
1 large tomato

Measure bulgur into a small bowl; add hot tap water to cover. Split garlic clove; push down into bulgur; let stand about 20 minutes.

Meanwhile, in a medium bowl, whisk together oil, lemon juice, salt, and pepper. With scissors snip in parsley, green onion, and mint, if using. Chop tomato (on a plate to save juice); add tomato and juice to dressing.

Remove garlic from bulgur; drain in a strainer; press out excess water with back of spoon; add to tomato mixture. Mix well; cover; refrigerate several hours to overnight. (I usually make it in the morning for the evening meal.)

BULGUR PILAF

2 Servings

1 tablespoon butter
1 green onion
1/3 cup bulgur wheat
3/4 cup chicken or beef broth

In medium saucepan melt butter. With scissors snip in onion; cook until soft. Add bulgur; stir over medium heat about one minute. Remove from heat; stir in broth; bring to boiling over high heat; cover; reduce heat; simmer until all liquid is absorbed, 15 to 20 minutes. Taste for salt. Lighten with a fork. Sprinkle with chopped parsley, chives, or other fresh herb if desired. Try adding cooked (or leftover) peas just before serving.

If cooked ahead, add a little water to reheat.

PIEROGI ONE-DISH

12 potatoes, boiled and mashed
1 cup shredded cheddar cheese
1-1/2 cups butter (or margarine)
1 onion, minced
2 cups cooked noodles

Mash potatoes and mix in cheddar cheese. Sauté onions in margarine. Cook noodles and allow to cool. In a well-greased casserole, place a layer of noodles, potatoes, then onions. Repeat with second layer. Cover and bake at 325 degrees for 25 minutes.

FILLING

CHEESE 'N CHIVE

1/2 cup cottage cheese
3 eggs, beaten
1 teaspoon sugar
2 tablespoons chives

Combine all ingredients and mix well. Place by small teaspoonsful on pierogies and seal edges well.

FILLING

CABBAGE 'N BACON

1/2 head cabbage, chopped
1/2 pound bacon
1 small onion, minced

Steam cabbage and place in a meat grinder, cutting until very fine. Meanwhile, fry bacon and crumble. Add bacon and onion to cabbage and blend well.

FILLING

MUSHROOMS

1 cup mushrooms, chopped
2 tablespoons butter
2 egg yolks

Melt butter and sauté mushrooms. Remove from heat and add egg yolks for firmness. Mix well.

BLENDER PIEROGI DOUGH

2 cups cottage cheese
1 tablespoon butter
3 eggs, separated
1 teaspoon salt
1 teaspoon sugar
2-1/2 cups flour

In a blender, mix cottage cheese until smooth. Add egg yolks, salt, sugar and flour. Beat until light. Add egg whites and fold in. Knead on a floured board for about 15 minutes. Roll out as thin as possible and cut with biscuit cutter. Place filling in center of dough and fold. Moisten with water. Carefully place in boiling water until they rise to the top.

PIEROGI DOUGH

3 cups sifted flour
1 teaspoon salt
1/3 cup butter
2 eggs, beaten
3/4 cup warm water

Sift flour and salt together. Use a fork to work in butter (batter will be lumpy). Add eggs and water; stir until smooth. Place dough on well-floured board and knead until smooth, about 15 minutes. Set aside for 15 minutes.

Roll out dough as thin as possible. Cut dough with biscuit cutter. Spoon a small teaspoon of filling onto the center of each piece of pierogi dough.

Fold dough in half and pinch edges together by sealing with water. Carefully place in salted boiling water, cooking about 7 minutes, *or until they rise to the top*. Drain and serve with melted butter.

DESSERT PLUM SAUCE

Plenty for 2 sundaes

2 tablespoons sugar
1/2 teaspoon cornstarch
Pinch salt
2 large red plums
1/2 teaspoon lemon juice, if you have it
Few drops almond flavoring (optional)

In a small dry saucepan mix sugar, cornstarch, and salt until cornstarch disappears using a small whisk. Slice plums into saucepan. Stir gently over medium heat until boiling; reduce heat; simmer until sauce is thickened and clear, about 4 minutes. Stir in lemon juice and almond flavoring, if using. Set aside to cool completely. Serve over vanilla ice cream.

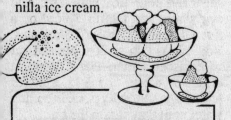

PINEAPPLE BUTTERMILK SHERBET

There is nothing more refreshing on a blistering hot day.

2 cups buttermilk
1/3 cup sugar
1 teaspoon vanilla
1 (8-ounce) can crushed pineapple, undrained (preferably in heavy syrup)

Measure buttermilk into a medium bowl. (I use a stainless steel bowl so that I can put it into the freezer.) Whisk in sugar and vanilla; stir in pineapple. Freeze until mushy. This takes about 2 hours. Whisk well; return bowl to freezer for about 2 hours, stirring now and then for a creamy sherbet.

Leftover sherbet will freeze solid—transfer to refrigerator to soften before serving.

LIME SORBET

Serves 2

A cool lime-flavored ice.

1/3 cup sugar
2/3 cup water
1 lime
Few grains salt

Place a one-quart freezer-safe bowl in freezer.

Combine sugar and water in a small saucepan. Stir over medium heat until sugar dissolves. When it comes to a boil, reduce heat and simmer for 6 minutes.

Roll lime on counter top to release juice; squeeze lime; add juice and salt to sweet syrup. Transfer to chilled bowl and freeze until mushy. It usually takes about 2 hours. Whisk thoroughly; freeze until barely firm. Serve in chilled dishes.

SHORTCAKE

(Two servings)

1/2 cup flour, spoon lightly into cup
3/4 teaspoon baking powder
1/8 teaspoon salt
1 tablespoons sugar
2 tablespoon shortening (I use half butter)
3 tablespoons milk

Preheat oven to 425-degrees. Measure flour, baking powder, salt and sugar into small bowl. Mix with pastry blender. Add shortening; cut in with pastry blender. When like fine crumbs, add milk; mix lightly with fork until it comes together (it will be a sticky ball). Drop into two mounds on small ungreased baking sheet. Use a fork to gently flatten and shape to a thick 3-inch biscuit. Sprinkle with sugar. Bake until beginning to brown, 10 to 12 minutes. Transfer to cooling rack. Split as soon as cool enough to handle, Serve warm or cold.

To assemble strawberry shortcake, spread bottom of shortcake with sweetened whipped cream; spoon on sliced, sweetened strawberries; cover with biscuit top, remaining whipped cream and berries.

SHORTCUT BREAD PUDDING WITH BOURBON SAUCE

Serves 2

Using cinnamon raisin bread is the shortcut. Expect a firm pudding because it is served with sauce.

1 tablespoon butter or margarine
2-1/2 slices cinnamon raisin bread
1 large egg
3/4 cup half-and-half or milk
1/4 cup sugar
1/8 teaspoon salt
1/2 teaspoon vanilla

Preheat oven to 350 degrees. Grease or spray a 1-quart casserole or souffle dish with pan release. Spread butter on one side of bread; cut into 1-inch squares. (1-1/2 cups loosely packed).

In a medium bowl, whisk egg to blend; whisk in half-and-half or milk, sugar, salt and vanilla. Add bread squares; stir until coated. (Let set a few minutes.) Pour into prepared dish. Set dish in pan containing 1/2 inch warm tap water. Bake until a rinsed knife inserted half way to center comes out clean, not milky, 35-40 minutes. Remove dish from hot water; cool at least 20 minutes before serving. Spoon into dessert dishes; pour on Bourbon Sauce.

Bourbon Sauce:
1/4 cup light brown sugar
1-1/2 teaspoons cornstarch
Few grains salt
1/3 cup water
1 to 2 tablespoons bourbon
1 tablespoon butter
1/4 teaspoon vanilla

Use brandy or dark rum instead of bourbon, if you prefer—one tablespoon for a mild-flavored sauce, two tablespoons for a powerful flavor.

In a small saucepan mix brown sugar, cornstarch, and salt. Stir in water; mix until smooth. With a rubber spatula stir over medium heat until boiling. Cook over low heat about 4 minutes, stirring often. Remove from heat; add bourbon; stir 1 minute over high heat (to evaporate the alcohol—empty calories); take off heat; stir in butter and vanilla. If made ahead, cover when cool and leave on counter. Serve sauce warm, or at room temperature, if dessert is hot.

SWEET MILK WAFFLES

An alternative mixing method — folding in beaten egg white — is also given. It makes a somewhat lighter waffle

3 tablespoons butter or margarine (see Note)
1 cup flour, lightly spooned into cup
2 teaspoons baking powder
1 teaspoon sugar
1/4 teaspoon salt
1 large egg
1 cup milk
1/4 teaspoon vanilla

Yield: 2 cups batter; two and one-half 10 by 6-inch waffles.

Spray waffle iron with Pam, release; preheat.

Melt butter in a custard cup in microwave oven or in small saucepan on stove; set aside.

Into pitcher or medium bowl measure flour, baking powder, sugar, and salt. Blend with mixer on lowest speed; set aside.

In a small bowl beat egg until light. On low speed beat in milk, vanilla, and melted butter. Add to dry ingredients; mix to blend well on low speed.

Pour over center three-fourths of preheated waffle iron. Cook until steam is no longer escaping around edge of waffle iron.

Note: If using 2% milk increase butter to 4 tablespoons.

Alternative mixing method: Melt butter. Separate egg putting white into a very clean small bowl and yolk into pitcher or medium bowl. Add milk to egg yolk. Measure flour, baking powder, sugar, and salt into small bowl; whisk to blend. Beat egg white until it will just hold stiff peaks. Transfer beater to yolk-milk mixture; beat until smooth. Add dry ingredients; beat smooth. With rubber spatula stir in melted butter, then fold in beaten egg white. This batter thickens a bit on standing, so refrigerate one hour before using if possible.

RICH BUTTERMILK WAFFLES

1/3 cup butter or margarine
1 cup flour, lightly spooned into cup
1/4 teaspoon salt
1/2 teaspoon soda
1 teaspoon baking powder
1 teaspoon sugar
2 eggs
1 cup buttermilk
1/4 teaspoon vanilla

Yield: 2-1/2 cups batter; three 10 by 6-inch waffles. Spray waffle iron with pan release; preheat.

Melt butter in a custard cup in microwave oven or in small saucepan on stove; set aside.

Measure flour, salt, soda, baking powder, and sugar into a small bowl. Blend with mixer on lowest speed; set aside.

In a pitcher or medium bowl beat eggs until light. On low speed add dry ingredients in three additions alternating with buttermilk in two additions. Blend in melted butter and vanilla.

Pour over center three-fourths of preheated waffle iron. Cook until steam is no longer escaping around edge of waffle iron.

DESSERT SOUFFLE
Two servings

Use one tablespoon dark rum, brandy or a liqueur instead of vanilla if desired.

2 large eggs
1-1/2 tablespoons butter
1-1/2 tablespoons flour
1/8 teaspoon salt
1/2 cup milk
1 teaspoon vanilla
1/4 cup sugar, divided

Separate eggs, whites into very clean medium mixing bowl, yolks into another medium bowl.

Grease or spray with pan release a one-quart straight-sided baking dish. Coat with sugar; set aside.

Preheat oven to 325 degrees.

In a small saucepan melt butter; whisk in flour and salt; cook, whisking, until boiling and bubbly. Whisk in milk; whisk over medium heat until smooth and thick. Remove from heat; whisk in vanilla or other flavoring; set aside to cool.

Beat egg whites just until peaks are soft (tips roll over) when beater is lifted. Gradually beat in half of sugar (2 tablespoons). Beat until stiff and glossy. Transfer beaters to yolks; tilt bowl so beaters are in yolks; beat about 1 minute; gradually beat in remaining sugar (2 tablespoons). On low speed beat in sauce. With a rubber spatula gently fold in egg whites. Pour into prepared dish. Bake until set—cake tester comes out dry— about 25 minutes. Immediately spoon into dessert dishes; pour on chocolate sauce.

ORANGE-FLAVORED APPLES
Serves 2

2 large cooking apples
1 tablespoon butter or margarine
1/4 cup brown sugar
1/4 cup orange juice
Pinch nutmeg

Peel; core and cut apples into eighths.

In medium-size skillet melt butter; swirl to coat bottom of skillet. Add apples. Sprinkle on sugar. Pour orange juice over apples. Cook on high heat until juice begins to boil. Stir; cover with lid ajar; reduce heat to low; cook until apples are barely tender, stirring now and then, about 8 minutes. Remove apples with slotted spoon to bowl. Add nutmeg to sauce; boil over high heat to reduce and thicken, about 1 minute; pour over apples.

Serve over vanilla ice cream, or plain, if you prefer a simple dessert.

Coffee
TIME

PEANUT BUTTER SQUARES
Makes 16-24

1 cup graham cracker crumbs
2 cups confectioners' sugar
1/2 cup butter, melted
1 cup peanut butter
1 small bag (6 ounces) semisweet
    chocolate chips, melted

Mix together first four ingredients. Spread in 8- or 9-inch square pan. Spread melted chocolate chips over mixture; refrigerate until set. Cut into squares to serve.

Kim Schuluchter, Racine, Wis.

APPLE SCHMARREN

¼ cup flour
2 teaspoons sugar
⅜ teaspoon salt
⅔ cup milk
2 eggs

1 medium tart apple,
    peeled and thinly sliced
1½ teaspoons raisins,
    optional
    Cinnamon and confec-
    tioners' sugar
3 tablespoons butter

Combine first 3 ingredients. Whisk in milk and eggs. Peel the apple; slice into batter. Add raisins; fry batter in the butter. I use an 8-inch non-stick fry pan. It should be nicely browned on all sides, so don't stir too often. Serve with cinnamon and confectioners' sugar sprinkled over the top.

Linda Taylor, Gravois Mills, Mo.

VIENNESE RAISIN NUT COFFEE CAKE
1 large coffee cake

2/3 cup milk
1/2 cup (1 stick) butter or margarine
1/4 teaspoon salt
1/2 cup granulated sugar
1 envelope active dry yeast
1 teaspoon sugar
1/4 cup very warm water
3 eggs
4 teaspoons grated lemon rind
3-1/4 cups sifted all-purpose flour
1 cup golden raisins
1/2 cup sliced blanched almonds
Confectioners' sugar

Stir milk, butter, salt and 1/2 cup sugar in small saucepan over very low heat just until butter is melted. Pour mixture into large bowl, cool to lukewarm.

Sprinkle yeast and 1 teaspoon sugar over very warm water in 1 cup glass measure. (Very warm water should feel comfortably warm when dropped on wrist). Stir in dissolved yeast. Let stand until bubbly, about 10 minutes. Stir eggs, yeast mixture, lemon rind and 2 cups flour into cooled milk mixture. Beat with electric mixer at low speed until blended. Increase speed to medium, beat 3 minutes longer. By hand, beat in remaining flour until batter is smooth, beat 1 minute longer. Stir in raisins. Cover with buttered wax paper and a towel. Let rise in warm place, away from drafts, until doubled in volume, about 50 minutes.

While batter is rising, butter 10-inch bundt pan. Sprinkle bottom and sides evenly with almonds. Stir batter

vigorously about 30 seconds. Turn into prepared pan. Cover with buttered wax paper and towel. Let rise in warm place, away from drafts, until almost doubled in volume, about 45 minutes. Bake in preheated oven 350 degrees for 30 minutes or until golden brown and cake sounds hollow when tapped with fingers. Remove from pan to wire rack, cool. Sprinkle lightly with confectioners' sugar.

Leona Teodori, Warren, Mich.

P.D.Q. COFFEE CAKE

1 compressed yeast cake
2-1/2 cups lukewarm milk
1/2 cup shortening (part butter adds
    flavor)
1/2 cup sugar
1 egg
2 teaspoons salt
5 cups flour
1 stick butter or margarine, melted
Cinnamon and sugar mixture

Crumble yeast cake into a bowl and add milk. Stir until dissolved. In separate bowl combine shortening, sugar, egg, and salt. Combine the two mixtures. Add 1 cup of flour at a time to combined yeast mixture; beat after each addition. Beat dough until smooth and blended. Cover bowl and let rise until double. Punch dough down by giving it a stir with a spoon. Divide dough into 3 layer cake pans. Melt 1 stick of butter or margarine. Drizzle on top of cakes. Sprinkle mixture of sugar and cinnamon over cakes. Let rise again. Bake 20 minutes in a 450-degree oven.

Jane Williams, Columbus, Ohio

133

BANANA DATE COFFEE CAKE
Serves 8-10

1/3 cup mashed bananas
1/2 cup butter, softened
3 large eggs
1 teaspoon vanilla
1-1/4 teaspoons water
3 cups flour
1 teaspoon baking soda
2 teaspoons baking powder
1-1/2 cups chopped dates

Topping:
1/3 cup chopped dates
1/3 cup chopped nuts
1/3 cup flaked coconut

Beat together mashed bananas and butter until creamy. Add eggs, vanilla, and water; beat well. Blend in flour, baking soda, and baking powder, and beat well stir in 1-1/2 cups chopped dates. Spoon batter into a greased and floured 9x13-inch baking pan. Combine topping ingredients and sprinkle over batter. Bake in a 350-degree oven for 20-25 minutes, or until knife inserted comes out clean. Cool on rack.

Mrs. D. Garms, Anaheim, Calif.

CINNAMON PUFFS

1-1/4 cups scalded milk
1 package yeast
1 cup quick oatmeal
1/2 cup butter
1/4 cup sugar
1-1/2 teaspoons salt
1 egg
3 cups flour

Dissolve yeast in 1/4 cup milk, cooled. Pour 1 cup hot milk over oatmeal, butter, sugar, and salt. Mix; add 1 egg and yeast. Add 2 cups flour and mix. Add 1 cup flour, more or less. (I use 3-1/2 cups flour). Don't make it too stiff. Let rise 1 hour. Knead down. Let rest for 15-20 minutes. Form into 1 large ball. Divide into quarters, then divide each quarter into 8 parts. Form into balls and put on cookie sheet. Let rise. Bake at 350 degrees for 20-25 minutes. Melt 1 cup margarine. Roll balls in melted margarine and in cinnamon-sugar. (1 cup sugar to 2 teaspoons cinnamon) Roll in mixture while they are still warm.

Sharon Crider, Evansville, Wis.

BLUEBERRY COFFEE CAKE
Serves 10-12

2 cups sifted cake flour
1 teaspoon baking powder
1 teaspoon baking soda
1 cup sugar
2 sticks (1/2 pound) margarine
2 eggs
1 cup cultured sour cream
1 teaspoon vanilla
1 can blueberry pie filling

Preheat oven to 375 degrees. Sift flour, baking powder, soda, and sugar together into a large bowl. Cut in margarine as you would for pie crust. Beat together eggs, sour cream, vanilla, and combine with flour mixture, blending well. Spread half the batter in a greased 13x9x2-inch baking pan. Spoon pie filling over batter and spread evenly. Spread remaining batter over blueberry filling. Sprinkle with the following topping:

Blend together as for pie crust 1/4 cup cake flour, 3 tablespoons margarine, and 1/4 cup sugar. Sprinkle over top of batter in pan. Bake in a moderately hot oven of 375 degrees for 40 minutes, or until lightly browned. Serve warm or cold.

Trenda Leigh, Richmond, Va.

PUMPKIN BREAD
Makes 2 loaves

4 cups flour
3 cups sugar
2 teaspoons baking soda
1 1/2 teaspoons salt
1 teaspoon baking powder
1 teaspoon cinnamon
1 teaspoon nutmeg
1/2 teaspoon cloves
1/4 teaspoon ginger
1 can (16 ounces) pumpkin
1 cup oil
4 eggs
2/3 cup water

Preheat oven to 350 degrees. Grease two 9x5x3-inch loaf pans.

Mix dry ingredients well. Beat pumpkin, oil, eggs and water together; add to dry ingredients. Stir just until moistened; do not overmix.

Divide batter between the two prepared pans. Bake at 350 degrees for 1 hour to 1 hour 15 minutes, or until toothpick inserted in center comes out clean. Cool on rack, removing loaves from pans after 10 minutes.

Charlotte Adams, Detroit, Mich.

NO-FRY DOUGHNUTS
Makes 1½–2 dozen

2 packages yeast
1½ cups lukewarm milk
(scalded then cooled)
½ cup sugar
1 teaspoon nutmeg
2 eggs
4½ cups flour
¼ cup warm water
1 teaspoon salt
¼ teaspoon cinnamon
⅓ cup shortening
¼ cup margarine, melted
Cinnamon and sugar

In large mixer bowl, dissolve yeast in warm water. Add milk, sugar, salt, spices, eggs, shortening and 2 cups flour. Blend ½ minute on top speed, scraping bowl occasionally. Stir in remaining flour, until smooth, scraping sides of bowl. Cover. Let rise in warm place until double, 50–60 minutes. Turn dough onto well-floured, cloth-covered board; roll around lightly to coat with flour (dough will be soft to handle). Roll dough to about ½-inch thickness. Cut with a 2½-inch doughnut cutter. Place 2 inches apart on baking sheet; brush doughnuts with melted margarine. Cover; let rise until double, about 20 minutes. Heat oven to 425 degrees. Bake 8–10 minutes, or until golden brown. Immediately brush with melted margarine and shake in sugar and cinnamon or use doughnut glaze.

Sharon Crider, Evansville, Wis.

CINNAMON TOAST COFFEE CAKE
Serves 10-12

2 cups flour
1 cup sugar
2 teaspoons baking powder
1 teaspoon salt
1 cup milk
2 tablespoons melted butter
1 teaspoon vanilla
1/4 teaspoon cinnamon
1/4 teaspoon nutmeg
1/2 cup seedless raisins

Topping:
1/2 cup melted butter
1/2 cup sugar
1-1/2 tablespoons cinnamon

Combine dry ingredients; stir in milk, 2 tablespoons butter, and vanilla until batter is smooth. Add raisins. Spread evenly into well-greased and lightly floured 15x10x1-inch jelly roll pan or sheet cake pan. Bake at 350 degrees for 20-25 minutes until lightly browned. While coffee cake is baking, combine 1/2 cup sugar and cinnamon. Remove cake from oven after 10 minutes of baking; drizzle 1/2 cup melted butter evenly over top of hot cake; sprinkle with sugar-cinnamon topping mixture and return to oven. Bake 10-15 minutes more. Serve warm.

Dee L. Getchell, Old Lyme, Conn.

DEARBORN INN SWEET BLUEBERRY MUFFINS
Makes 1 dozen

1 egg
1/2 cup milk
1/4 cup salad oil
1 1/2 cups flour
1/2 cup sugar
2 teaspoons baking powder
1/2 teaspoon salt
1 cup fresh blueberries or canned blueberries, drained

Beat egg in bowl and stir in milk and oil. Combine dry ingredients and quickly mix into liquid mixture just until flour is moistened. Do not over-mix; there will be lumps in the batter. Fold in blueberries. Line muffin tins with 12 paper liners and fill each two-thirds full.

Bake in a preheated 400-degree oven for 20-25 minutes or until muffins are golden brown. Remove from muffin pan immediately.

Note: In place of the blueberries, you can use fresh cherries, or fresh peaches cut into cubes, if you wish.

Harriet Blair, Milwaukee, Wis

ORANGE MARMA-LADE COFFEE CAKE
Serves 6-8

1 package dry yeast
2 tablespoons water
1/2 cup milk
2 tablespoons sugar
1/2 teaspoon salt
4 tablespoons margarine
1-1/2 cups flour
1 egg
1/2 cup orange marmalade
1/4 cup sugar
1/4 teaspoon cinnamon

Sprinkle yeast in warm water. Heat milk until film forms over surface. Pour into mixing bowl. Add sugar, salt, and margarine. Stir. Beat in 1/2 cup flour into milk mixture. Beat egg slightly. Stir into milk mixture with yeast. Add remaining 1 cup flour and beat briskly. If a little more flour is needed, beat in additional amount. It should not be more than 2 tablespoons extra. Grease a large bowl. Turn dough into it. Turn dough around once to grease its surface. Grease top lightly with softened margarine. Cover bowl. Let stand in warm place about 1 hour, or until doubled in bulk. Grease 9-inch cake pan. Punch dough down in bowl and turn it out into prepared cake pan. Spread dough lightly. Drop spoonfuls of jam on top and swirl it into dough with spoon. Sprinkle top with sugar and cinnamon. Cover pan. Let rise until doubled. Preheat oven to 375 degrees. Bake for 20-30 minutes, until lightly browned around edges. Remove from pan. Let cool slightly. Serve warm or cool.

Sharon Crider, Evansville, Wis.

PEACH (LOW-CHOLESTEROL) COFFEE CAKE
Serves 16

3 cups flour
2 cups sugar
1/4 teaspoon salt
2 teaspoons baking powder
1 cup margarine (2 sticks)
4 egg whites
1/2 cup egg substitute
1 cup skim milk
2 teaspoons vanilla
1 (10-ounce) can sliced peaches, drained

Preheat oven to 300 degrees. Sift together dry ingredients. Cut in margarine. Reserve 1 cup of the mixture to be used as a topping. In separate bowl, blend in egg substitute, milk, and vanilla; add to remaining dry ingredients. Fold in beaten egg whites. Pour into 9-inch tube pan and top with peach slices, then reserved topping. Bake 40-50 minutes.

Ida Bloedow, Madison, Wis

POTATO DOUGHNUTS

1/4 cup sugar
2 eggs
1 cup mashed potatoes
1/2 cup milk
1 tablespoon baking powder
2-1/2 cups flour
1-1/2 tablespoons shortening
1/2 teaspoon salt
1/4 teaspoon nutmeg
Confectioners' sugar
Cinnamon-sugar

Beat mashed potatoes; add melted shortening, beaten eggs, and milk. Sift dry ingredients together and add to liquid. Dough should be soft enough to roll. Separate and roll out to 3/4-inch thickness. Cut with doughnut cutter and cook in deep fat (365 degrees); fry to golden brown. Drain on absorbent paper and dust with powdered sugar or sugar-cinnamon mixture.

Elizabeth Dunn, Harrisonville, NY

CINNAMON RAISIN BATTER BREAD

1 package active dry yeast
1-1/2 cups warm water (105-115 degrees)
2 tablespoons honey
2 tablespoons butter
1 teaspoon salt
3 cups flour, divided
1 tablespoon cinnamon
1 cup raisins

In a large bowl, dissolve yeast in warm water. Stir in honey. Add butter, salt, and 2 cups of the flour. Beat with electric mixer on low speed until blended. Beat 1 minute on high speed. Stir in remaining flour with a wooden spoon. Cover and let rise in a warm place until doubled in size. Punch down by stirring with a heavy spoon. Add cinnamon and raisins. Spoon batter into a loaf pan. Let rise again until batter reaches the top of the pan (not over!). Bake in preheated 350-degree oven for about 40 minutes or until loaf sounds hollow when lightly tapped. Cool on wire rack.

This batter bread is a wonderful treat for breakfast or in the "munchkin's" lunch sack as a peanut-butter-and-jelly sandwich.

Phyliss Dixon, Fairbanks, Alaska

CRANBERRY COFFEE CAKE

1/2 cup margarine
1 cup sugar
2 eggs
1/2 pint sour cream
1 teaspoon baking soda
1 teaspoon baking powder
2 cups flour
1/2 teaspoon salt
3/4 teaspoon almond extract
1 can whole cranberry sauce
1/2 cup broken walnuts

Cream margarine and sugar. Add eggs, mix medium speed. Reduce speed and add dry ingredients, alternating with sour cream. Add almond extract. Grease 9x13-inch pan. Put half batter in pan and spread evenly. Swirl half the can of cranberry sauce over batter in pan. Add rest of batter to pan. Top with remaining cranberry sauce. Sprinkle on nuts. Bake 350 degrees 50 minutes. Frost while warm.

Icing:
3/4 cup powdered sugar
1 tablespoon warm water
1/4 teaspoon almond extract

Mix together. Drizzle over cake.

Sherri Crider, Stoughton, Wis.

HEATH BAR COFFEE CAKE

2 cups flour
1/4 cup brown sugar
1/4 pound butter or margarine
6 chilled Heath candy bars
1 egg
1 cup milk
1 teaspoon vanilla
1 teaspoon baking soda
1-1/2 teaspoons salt
1-1/2 cups nuts, chopped

Grease and flour a 9x13-inch pan. Mix together flour, sugar, soda, salt, and butter to the consistency of pie dough (reserve 1 cup for topping).

Beat together egg, vanilla, and milk; add to first mixture. Pour into prepared pan. Break up Heath bars into small pieces, using a rolling pin. Add Heath bars and chopped nuts to reserved cup of first mixture; sprinkle on top of cake. Bake at 350 degrees for 40 minutes.

Agnes Ward, Erie, Pa.

CHOCOLATE CHIP STREUSEL COFFEE CAKE

Streusel:
1/2 cup brown sugar
1/2 cup flour
1/4 cup margarine
1/4 cup chopped walnuts
1 cup chocolate chips

Cake:
1 (8-ounce) package cream cheese
1-1/2 cups sugar
3/4 cups margarine
3 eggs
3/4 teaspoon vanilla
2-1/2 cups flour
1-1/2 teaspoons baking powder
3/4 teaspoon baking soda
1/4 teaspoon salt
3/4 cup milk

For streusel, combine brown sugar and flour. Cut in margarine until mixture resembles coarse crumbs. Stir in walnuts and chocolate chips. Set aside. Grease and flour a 13x9x2-inch pan. Combine cream cheese, sugar, and margarine, mixing at medium speed until well-blended. Blend in eggs and vanilla. Add combined dry ingredients alternately with milk, mixing well after each addition. Spoon batter into prepared pan. Sprinkle with crumb mixture. Bake at 350 degrees for 40 minutes. Cool.

Great for large crowds! If you like cheese filling, you'll love it!

Mrs. George Franks, Millerton, Pa.

MINCEMEAT COFFEE RING

1¾ cups sifted flour
2 teaspoons baking powder
½ teaspoon salt
¼ cup sugar
⅓ cup shortening
1 egg
¼ cup milk
¾ cup prepared mincemeat

Into bowl sift flour, baking powder, salt and sugar. Cut in shortening using pastry blender. Beat egg. Add milk and mincemeat. Make a depression in flour mixture and pour liquid in. Mix quickly. Do not overmix. Pour into greased ring mold or tube pan. Bake at 400 degrees for 30–40 minutes. Ice while warm with thin confectioners' sugar icing, tinted green, letting it trickle down from the top over the sides of the ring. Decorate with candied cherries and chopped nuts.

Crockpot
CLASSICS

CORNED BEEF AND CABBAGE

2 medium onions, sliced
1 (2 1/2-to 3-pound) corned beef brisket
1 cup apple juice
1/4 cup packed brown sugar
2 teaspoons orange peel, finely shredded
2 teaspoons prepared mustard
6 whole cloves
6 cabbage wedges

Place onions in crockpot. Trim away any fat that might be present on the corned beef brisket. If needed, cut brisket to fit into Crockpot; place on top of onions. In a bowl combine apple juice, sugar, orange peel, mustard, and cloves; pour over brisket. Place cabbage on top of brisket. Cover; cook on *low* setting for 10-12 hours or on *high* setting for 5-6 hours.

CROCK-STYLE BARBECUE BEANS
Serves 10-12

These beans are great additions to a meal or for take-alongs to potlucks. Fast and easy, these beans stay hot for travel.

8 cups water
3 cans pork and beans
1/4 teaspoon salt
1/4 teaspoon pepper
1/4 teaspoon minced onion
1 small onion, chopped
1/2 cup brown sugar

2/3 cup syrup
3 tablespoons white sugar

Combine water, pork and beans. Add remaining ingredients and stir well. Cook on *low* for six hours, *high* for less than six hours. Stir before serving.

COUNTRY ROAST AND VEGETABLES
Serves 6-8

1 roast, thawed
Several potatoes, canned sliced or whole
Several carrots
Green beans, corn (optional)
1 onion, sliced
1 cup water
1/4 teaspoon salt
1/4 teaspoon pepper
3 tablespoons butter or margarine
1/4 cup flour (optional)

Place roast in Crockpot. Add peeled potatoes, carrots, beans, corn, sliced onion, and butter. Add water and flour for gravy. Sprinkle with salt and pepper. Cook on *low* for 6-12 hours, *high* for less than 6 hours.

CHERRY PORK CHOPS
Serves 6

6 pork chops, cut 3/4-inch thick
1/4 teaspoon salt
1/4 teaspoon pepper
1/2 can cherry pie filling (1 cup)
2 teaspoons lemon juice

1/2 teaspoon instant chicken bouillon granules
1/8 teaspoon ground mace

Trim excess fat from pork chops. Brown pork chops in hot skillet with butter or oil. Sprinkle each chop with salt and pepper. Combine cherry pie filling, lemon juice, chicken bouillon granules, and ground mace in cooker. Stir well. Place pork chops in Crockpot. Cover. Cook on *low* for 4-5 hours. Place chops on platter. Pour cherry sauce over meat.

VEGETABLE BEEF SOUP
Serves 8

This meal-in-one is more than nutritious, it's delicious! Cook for dinner and keep it for lunches, weekends snacks, and light, late-night brunches.

1 pound ground beef
1 large can tomatoes, whole
1 can tomato soup
1 small onion, chopped
2 cups water
1 can lima beans, drained
1 can whole-kernel corn, undrained
1 cup sliced carrots
1 cup potatoes, cut up
1 cup diced celery
1/4 teaspoon salt
1/4 teaspoon pepper

Combine beef, tomatoes, soup, and onion in cooker. Add water, beans, and vegetables. Add salt, pepper, and other spices of preference. Stir well. Cook at lowest setting, 4 to 6 hours.

137

TENDER MEATBALLS IN MUSHROOM GRAVY
Serves 4-6

No running to the store for any of these ingredients; hamburger and mushroom soup are found in every kitchen. Simple and delicious; everyone likes meatballs.

1 pound hamburger
4 slices soft white bread
1 teaspoon salt
1/4 teaspoon pepper
1 tablespoon minced onion
1 can mushroom soup
1/3 cup water

Pull apart bread into small, dime-size pieces. Combine hamburger, bread, salt, pepper, and minced onion in large mixing bowl. Using a spoon, scoop out rounds of meat, or shape into several round, 2-inch balls by hand.

Brown meatballs in a hot skillet using a small amount of butter or oil. Turn them occasionally so all sides are browned. Place meat in cooker. Add soup and water. Cook on *low* for 6 to 12 hours, *high* for up to 6 hours.

CLASSIC SWISS STEAK
Serves 4-6

Super good, super simple, super anytime—for a family lunch, dinner, or for guests.

1 round steak
2 cups flour
1/4 teaspoon salt and pepper
2 tablespoons butter or shortening
1 (4-ounce) can tomato sauce
1 sliced onion
1 sliced green pepper

Cut steak into serving portions. Combine flour, salt, and pepper in medium-size bowl. Roll cut steaks in flour mixture, coating both sides. Melt shortening or butter in hot skillet. Brown meat on both sides, but do not cook. Place browned meat in Crockpot. Add tomato sauce, onion, and green pepper. Cook on *low* for 6 to 12 hours, or on *high* for up to 6 hours.

MINESTRONE SOUP
Serves 6–8

Minestrone soup bean mix*
1 onion, chopped
1 garlic clove
6–8 cups water
1 can tomatoes (about 2 cups)
Italian seasonings to taste (such as oregano, basil, rosemary, thyme, marjoram)
1 meaty ham bone
Spaghetti

Soak bean mix overnight. Rinse. Put in pot with all the other ingredients except spaghetti. Cook in Crockpot for about 6–8 hours on medium; on stove, simmer until beans are soft—several hours. About 15 minutes before serving, add a handful of uncooked spaghetti. Serve with Parmesan cheese.

*If minestrone soup mix is not available in your area, mix your own using several kinds of dried beans, barley and split peas. Use about 2 cups for the soup.

CINDY'S STUFFED PEPPERS

6 to 8 green peppers, or number of servings desired
1 to 2 pounds hamburger
1 onion, sliced
1/4 teaspoon salt
1/4 teaspoon pepper
1 egg
1 slice white bread
1 can tomatoes, whole

Combine hamburger, onion, salt, pepper, and egg in large mixing bowl. Pull apart bread into small pieces. Add to hamburger mixture. Clean and remove seeds and white membrane from green peppers. Stuff peppers with hamburger mixture.

For meat loaf, combine remaining meat into oblong ball. Place meat loaf and peppers in Crockpot. Pour tomatoes, undrained, over meat. Cook on *low* for 6 to 12 hours, *high* for less than 6 hours.

APPLE-RAISIN-TOPPED HAM
Serves 6

This recipe gives ham a new taste and look. Great for dinner, sandwiches, and leftovers.

1 (21-ounce) can apple pie filling
1/3 cup light raisins
1-1/2 pounds fully cooked ham, sliced about 2-3/4 inches thick
1/3 cup orange juice
2 tablespoons water
1 tablespoon lemon juice
1/4 teaspoon ground cinnamon

Combine pie filling, raisins, orange juice, water, lemon juice and cinnamon. Cut ham slice into six equal pieces. Place meat and apple mixture in crockery cooker by alternating layers of each, and ending with the apple mixture. Cover and cook on *low* for 4-5 hours. Serve with rice, if desired.

CROCKPOT APPLE BUTTER

8 cups cooked apples
4 cups sugar
½ cup vinegar
2 teaspoons cinnamon

Place in Crockpot and cook 6 hours on HIGH. This is a great recipe and smells great in the kitchen while cooking.

Thelma Hervey, Hedrick, Iowa

Desserts
DELICIOUS

CHOCOLATE NUT CRUNCH

2 cups vanilla wafer crumbs
1 cup chopped walnuts
1/2 cup butter or margarine
1 cup confectioners' sugar
3 egg yolks, well-beaten
1-1/2 (1-ounce) squares unsweetened chocolate, melted
1/2 teaspoon vanilla
3 egg whites, stiffly beaten

Combine crumbs and nuts; line bottom of 9-inch square pan with half of the crumb mixture. Thoroughly cream butter and sugar; add egg yolks. Add chocolate and vanilla. Mix well. Fold in stiffly beaten egg whites. Spread over crumb mixture. Top with remaining crumb mixture. Chill in refrigerator overnight. Cut in squares.
Ida Bloedow, Madison, Wis.

PEAR CRISP

2 (1-pound) cans pear halves with
  syrup
1/2 cup golden raisins
3/4 cup rolled oats
3/4 cup flour
1/2 cup brown sugar
1/4 cup melted butter
1 teaspoon cinnamon
1/2 teaspoon ground nutmeg

Place pears and raisins in 8 x 8-inch baking dish. Combine remaining ingredients; mix until crumbly. Sprinkle evenly over pears. Bake at 350 degrees until golden brown.
Leota Baxter, Ingalls, Kan.

MARBLE-TOP CHOCOLATE TARTLET

Crust:
1/3 cup margarine
1 cup sifted flour
1 (1-ounce) bar dark chocolate,
  grated
3-4 tablespoons water
Pinch of salt

Cut margarine into flour. Add salt. Stir in chocolate and sprinkle with water. Mix lightly until it holds together. Roll out and place in muffin tins; flute edges. Bake at 450 degrees for about 12 minutes.

Filling:
1 cup sugar
1 tablespoon unflavored gelatin
1 cup milk
2 egg yolks, beaten
1 cup chocolate chips
2 egg whites
1/4 cup sugar
1 cup heavy cream
2 tablespoons confectioners' sugar
1 teaspoon vanilla
Pinch of salt

Combine the sugar, gelatin, and salt; stir in milk and egg yolks. Add chocolate chips and stir over medium heat until it begins to boil. *Do not* boil. Stir until melted; cool; chill until set. Beat egg whites until foamy and gradually add confectioners' sugar. Whip cream, gradually adding 1/4 cup sugar until stiff. Fold beaten egg whites into cooled gelatin; alternately add this and a layer of whipped cream into baked pie crust. Swirl knife through to give a marbled effect. Chill until firm before serving. This makes a wonderful centerpiece.

DATE PUDDING

¾ cup sugar
1 (8-ounce) package
  pitted dates
1 cup chopped nuts
2 eggs
¼ cup milk
1 teaspoon baking
  powder
⅓ cup flour
  Pinch salt
½ teaspoon vanilla
  Butter

Note: Have all ingredients at room temperature.

In a mixing bowl, place chopped dates and nuts. Then add sugar, flour, salt and baking powder. Mix and add beaten eggs, milk and vanilla. Mix well again and spread evenly in a well-greased and floured aluminum baking pan, 7 x 11-inch. Dot all over the top with butter. Bake in 325-degree oven for 30–35 minutes. Do not overbake. Cool overnight in refrigerator, or can be frozen until ready to use.

Before serving cover with whipped cream (or topping). Cut into desired number of squares. Place a red maraschino cherry in center of green-tinted whipped cream for Christmas. Any other time, you can serve with plain whipped cream and walnut or pecan half in center.
Opal Hamer, St. Petersburg, Fla.

139

CRANBERRY DELIGHT

Serves 8

1 cup graham cracker crumbs
1/4 cup margarine, melted
1 cup cranberries
3/4 cup sugar
1/2 cup water
1/4 cup chopped nuts
2 tablespoons orange marmalade (optional)
1 (8 ounce) package cream cheese
1/3 cup confectioners' sugar
1 tablespoon milk
1 teaspoon vanilla
1 cup heavy cream, whipped

Combine graham cracker crumbs and margarine. Press into 8-inch square pan. In saucepan, combine cranberries, sugar and water. Simmer 20 minutes. Stir in nuts and marmalade. Chill in refrigerator; set aside.

Mix cream cheese, confectioners' sugar, milk and vanilla. Fold in whipped cream; spoon over crust. Top with cranberry mixture. Chill overnight.

Deborah M. Mucháy, Cleveland, Ohio

BETHEL GROVE'S ICE CREAM SOCIAL

Makes 1 gallon

1-3/4 cups sugar
6 eggs
1 (3-ounce) package instant vanilla pudding
1/2 cup light corn syrup
1 tablespoon real vanilla

1/4 teaspoon lemon extract
1 quart half-and-half

Beat all ingredients in the order listed until smooth. Pour into cylinder. Add milk to fill line or to 3 inches from top of container. Freeze in freezer (hand-cranked or electric).

ANGELIC PEACH TRIFLE

Makes 10 servings

1 (13-ounce) angel food cake
1 (16-ounce) can Lite sliced peaches, drained (reserve syrup)
1/4 teaspoon almond extract
1-1/2 cups cold skim milk
1 (4-serving-size) package sugar-free vanilla instant pudding and pie filling
1 envelope whipped topping mix (2-cup size)
1 (8-ounce) container low-fat peach yogurt
3 tablespoons natural sliced almonds

Cube cake and arrange 1/3 of the cubes in a 2-quart serving dish. Coarsely chop peaches. Measure 6 tablespoons reserved syrup. Add to peaches with almond extract. Pour milk into deep, narrow bowl. Add pudding and pie filling mix, along with whipped topping mix. Beat until thickened. Fold in yogurt.

Spoon 1/3 peach mixture over layer cake cubes in dish and 1/3 pudding mixture over peaches. Repeat layers, ending with pudding. Sprinkle top with almonds. Chill 4 hours, or overnight. (216 calories per serving)

Anna Y. Bodisch, Coplay, Pa.

GRAHAM CRACKER PUDDING

1 cup brown sugar
2 heaping tablespoons flour
1 teaspoon vanilla
2 cups milk
1 or 2 bananas

Cook sugar, flour, vanilla and milk until thick. Crush 10 graham crackers to very fine crumbs; stir into pudding, along with sliced bananas.

Nancy Mathias, Kokomo, Ind.

DELUXE FUDGY BROWNIES

4 squares unsweetened chocolate
½ cup butter *or* margarine
4 eggs
2 cups sugar
1 cup sifted flour
1 teaspoon vanilla
1 cup coarsely chopped nuts

Melt chocolate and butter together over hot water. Cool slightly. Beat eggs until foamy; gradually add sugar, beating thoroughly after each addition. Add chocolate mixture and blend. Stir in flour. Then add vanilla and nuts. Spread in greased 9 x 9 x 2-inch pan. Bake at 325 degrees for 40–50 minutes. Cool in pan, then cut into squares or bars. Will have crunchy top and bottom crust with a center almost like chocolate cream. Delicious served straight from the freezer.

Ruth Morris, Bradenton, Fla

MOCHA FLUFF
Serves 4

1 envelope gelatin
¼ cup water
¼ cup sugar
¼ teaspoon salt
1½ cups hot, strong coffee
2 tablespoons lemon juice
2 egg whites, stiffly beaten

Soften gelatin in cold water. Add sugar, salt and hot coffee, stirring thoroughly to dissolve. Add lemon juice and cool. When nearly set, beat until stiff. Add egg whites and continue beating until mixture holds its shape. Turn into molds and chill.

Suzan L. Wiener, Spring Hill, Fla.

GOLD RUSH BROWNIES

2 cups graham cracker crumbs
1 can sweetened condensed milk
1 (6-ounce) package chocolate chips
½ cup chopped pecans

Mix together and put into an 8 x 8-inch pan (well-greased). Bake at 350 degrees for 30 minutes. Let brownies cool 10 minutes. Cut into squares and remove from pan.

Norma L. Farrar, Sullivan, Mo.

MILK DUD DESSERT

6 egg yolks
1 cup sugar
1 cup rusk crumbs
½ cup chopped walnuts
1 teaspoon vanilla
1 teaspoon baking powder
6 egg whites
4 small packages Milk Duds
1/2 cup milk

1 cup confectioners' sugar
2 tablespoons butter
½ pint whipping cream

Beat egg yolks; add sugar and beat again.

Mix together rusk crumbs, nuts, vanilla and baking powder. Add to egg mixture. Fold in stiffly beaten egg whites. Bake in 9 x 13-inch greased pan at 350 degrees for 30 minutes. Cool. Melt Milk Duds, milk, confectioners' sugar and butter until smooth, stirring constantly. Let stand until cool and creamy. Whip the cream; spread over baked portion. Pour sauce on top and refrigerate overnight.

FROZEN DESSERT

23 Ritz crackers
1 large box pistachio instant pudding
1 pint vanilla ice cream, softened
1/2 stick melted margarine
3/4 cup milk
1 small carton Cool Whip

Combine Ritz crackers and the margarine and press into a 9-inch pie plate and bake at 350 degrees for 8–10 minutes. Allow to cool. Combine pudding with milk and blend in softened ice cream. Pour into crust. Spread Cool Whip on top surface and freeze. Garnish with chopped nuts.

Jodie McCoy, Tulsa, Okla.

BABY RUTH CANDY BROWNIES

⅔ cup margarine
1 cup brown sugar
¼ cup light corn syrup
¼ cup smooth peanut butter
1 teaspoon vanilla
1 cup quick oatmeal

Topping:
1 (12-ounce) package chocolate

chips
1 (6-ounce) package butter-scotch chips
⅔ cup smooth peanut butter
1 cup salted Spanish peanuts

Combine margarine, sugar and syrup in saucepan. Stir over low heat until margarine melts and sugar dissolves. Add peanut butter and vanilla. Pour over oatmeal; mix well. Press into a greased 13 x 9-inch pan and bake at 375 degrees for 12 minutes. Melt chocolate and butterscotch bits. Add peanut butter and peanuts. Pour over baked mixture. Cool and cut into squares.

Shirley Viscosi, Worcester, Mass.

PECAN BUTTER-SCOTCH BROWNIES
Makes 24 squares

¼ cup vegetable oil
1 tablespoon dark molasses
½ cup brown sugar, firmly packed
½ cup pecans, chopped
2 cups all-purpose flour
2 eggs
2 teaspoons vanilla
¼ teaspoon salt
½ cup milk
½ teaspoon baking powder

Combine all ingredients; spread in a greased 8 x 8 x 2-inch pan. Bake at 350 degrees for 30 minutes; turn out of pan; cut into squares or bars while hot; place a whole pecan on each square.

Gwen Campbell, Sterling, Va.

HULA SALAD

2 packages lime gelatin
2 cups boiling water
1 (16-ounce) can crushed pineapple with syrup
1 pint sour cream
1 cup maraschino cherries
1/2 cup chopped Macadamia nuts
1/2 cup coconut

Dissolve gelatin in boiling water and allow to cool. Add pineapple and sour cream. Fold in cherries and nuts. Pour into serving dish and sprinkle with coconut. Refrigerate.

QUICK APPLE KUCHEN

1 cup flour
1 teaspoon baking powder
1 egg
½ cup sugar
⅓ cup milk
¼ cup butter, melted
2 cups sliced apples
¼ cup sugar
½ teaspoon cinnamon

Sift together flour and baking powder; set aside. Beat egg; add sugar. Add half of dry ingredients; mix well; add milk; add remaining dry ingredients. Mix well and stir in butter.

Turn into well-greased 9 x 9-inch pan. Arrange apple slices on top of batter. Sprinkle with mixture of sugar and cinnamon. Bake at 375 degrees for 30–35 minutes.

June Harding, Ferndale, Mich.

CUSTARD
Serves 4

1-1/2 cups sweet milk (see below)
3 large eggs
1/2 teaspoon vanilla
1/8 teaspoon nutmeg
1/8 teaspoon salt
Nutmeg, garnish

Beat or blend all ingredients until thoroughly combined. Pour into 4 custard cups and sprinkle with additional nutmeg. Set the custard cups in a pan of hot water. The water should come within 1 inch of the tops of the cups. Bake on oven shelf that is just below the oven center. Bake at 300 degrees for 1 hour, or until knife inserted in center comes out clean. Cool 20 minutes. Serve warm or cool to room temperature before serving, or chill in refrigerator and serve cold.

Sweet Milk:
2 cups reconstituted nonfat milk
2/3 cup raisins

Combine milk and raisins in a jar;
cover and refrigerate at least overnight. Before using, shake the jar vigorously. Milk should be an ivory color. Strain the milk to remove the raisins, which will be mushy. Use milk as directed.
Note: It should be made at least one day in advance, but reaches peak sweetness after two or three days. (105 calories per serving)

EASY CHERRY COBBLER

2 cans tart cherries, undrained
1 package white cake mix
1 stick margarine, melted
1 cup nuts

Pour cherries in bottom of 9 x 13-inch pan, then sprinkle dry cake mix over cherries and *do not stir*. Pour melted margarine over cake mix; sprinkle nuts on top. *Do not mix.* Bake at 400 degrees for 30 minutes, or until set. Delicious topped with ice cream.

Denise Garcia, Salina, Kan.

LEMON REFRIGERATED DESSERT

Crust:
1 cup flour
1/2 cup margarine
1 cup finely chopped pecans

Mix flour, margarine and pecans together. Press into a 9 x 13-inch glass dish. Bake 20 minutes at 350 degrees. Cool.

Filling:
8 ounces cream cheese (room temperature)
1 cup confectioners' sugar
1 medium-size container Cool Whip
2 (1 1/2-ounce) packages instant lemon pudding
3 cups milk

Cream sugar and cream cheese. Fold in half of the Cool Whip and
spread mixture over cooled crust. Blend pudding with milk until pudding begins to thicken. Spread on top of cheese mixture. Spread remaining Cool Whip over pudding mixture. Refrigerate until completely cooled and firm.

This can be prepared in advance. I often make it for family gatherings and reunions.

Flo Burtnett, Gage, Okla.

SIMPLY DELICIOUS EASY BROWNIES
Makes 25–30 bars

Grease a 9 x 13-inch baking pan. In large bowl, combine in order given:

1 cup butter *or* margarine
2 cups sugar
4 eggs (beating after each addition)
2 teaspoons vanilla
1½ cups all-purpose flour
½ cup plus 1 tablespoon cocoa
1 teaspoon salt

Mix well and add 1 cup chopped nuts, if desired. Put in pan; bake at 350 degrees for 30 minutes. Check at 25 minutes, if you like brownies chewy. Frost, if desired.

Audrey Reynolds, Lumberport, W.Va.

PASTEL BAVARIAN
Serves 7

1 (4-serving) package sugar-free gelatin, any flavor
3/4 cup boiling water
1/2 cup cold water
Ice cubes
1 (4-ounce) container Cool Whip topping, thawed

Dissolve gelatin in boiling water. Combine cold water and ice cubes to make 1-1/4 cups. Add to gelatin and stir until slightly thickened; remove any unmelted ice. Fold into whipped topping, blending well. Chill in individual dessert dishes or bowl until set, about 2 hours. (50 calories per serving)

Ida Bloedow, Madison, Wis.

CHERRY FRAPPÉ

1 small box cherry-flavored gelatin
1/2 cup boiling water
15 maraschino cherries
2 1/2 cups crushed ice
1 tablespoon maraschino cherry
  syrup

Put gelatin and boiling water in blender. Blend until gelatin is dissolved. Add cherries and syrup; continue to blend until mixture is fluffy. Add crushed ice and blend until mixture is the consistency of ice cream, about 3–4 minutes. Serve immediately in a cup or glass, or pour into 6-ounce paper cups and freeze for future use. Remove frozen frappés from freezer 15 minutes before serving. Top with mint, if desired.

This is a delicious treat for company, as well as your family.

Suzan L. Wiener, Spring Hill, Fla.

BRAN BLONDIES
Makes 36 squares

¾ cup flour, spooned lightly into
  cup
½ teaspoon baking powder
¼ teaspoon soda
¼ teaspoon salt
½ cup All-bran cereal
½ cup chopped walnuts *or*
  pecans
1 cup semisweet chocolate
  morsels
½ cup (1 stick) margarine
1 cup brown sugar (use part
  granulated, if desired)
1 large egg
1 teaspoon vanilla

Prepare a 9-inch square baking pan—spray with pan release, or grease and flour. (I foil-line and spray with pan release.)

Preheat oven to 350 degrees.

Into a small bowl measure flour, baking powder, soda, salt, All-bran, nuts and chocolate morsels; stir together; set aside. In a medium-size saucepan barely melt margarine. Remove from heat; stir in sugar. Add egg and vanilla; whisk or beat with fork to blend well. With a rubber spatula, stir in dry ingredients. Spread in prepared pan. Bake until cake tester comes out dry, about 20 minutes.

Especially good warm, while chocolate is still soft. Freeze extras; warm in microwave oven.

Note: For chocolate bars, combine only ⅔ cup chocolate morsels with dry ingredients. Melt remaining ⅓ cup morsels with margarine. Proceed as directed.

Mary Pledge Peterson, Cincinnati, Ohio

BLUEBERRY CHEESECAKE

1 stick butter or margarine
1 (1-pound) package graham
  crackers, crushed
1 (8-ounce) package cream cheese
1 large container Cool Whip
1 can Eagle Brand milk
1/3 cup lemon juice
2 cups prepared blueberries *or*
  1 (1-pound 5-ounce) can blueberry
  pie filling

Preheat oven to 350 degrees. Mix butter and graham crackers; press in bottom of oblong 9-inch glass dish to form crust. Bake 8-10 minutes until light brown. Cool. In large bowl combine cream cheese, Cool Whip, Eagle Brand milk and lemon juice; blend well. Pour into pie shell. Put blueberries on top. Refrigerate 3-4 hours before serving.

PUMPKIN FLAN
Serves 8

1/2 cup sugar
8 eggs
Sugar
1/4 teaspoon salt
2 (13 ounce) cans evaporated milk
2 teaspoons vanilla
1 cup canned pumpkin (not pie
  filling)
1 (8 ounce) can jellied cranberry
  sauce

Heat 1/2 cup sugar in heavy saucepan over medium heat until caramelized, stirring constantly. Pour caramel into 9x5-inch loaf pan; set aside. Beat eggs, 2/3 cup sugar, salt, evaporated milk, vanilla and pumpkin with wire whisk in large bowl until just blended but not frothy. Carefully pour pumpkin mixture into pan over caramel layer. Set pan inside large shallow baking pan. Place pans on oven rack and pour boiling water in outer pan to 1 inch. Bake at 350 degrees 1 hour or until knife inserted in center comes out clean. Cool on wire rack. Chill.

Just before serving, blend or process cranberry sauce until smooth. Loosen flan from sides of pan and invert onto serving plate. Cover top of flan with cranberry purée.

Bea Comas, Portland, Maine

CHOCOLATE BROWNIES

2 cups sugar
2 cups flour
1 teaspoon soda
2 eggs, beaten
1 cup buttermilk
¼ pound margarine *or* butter
½ cup shortening
¼ cup cocoa
1 cup water

Sift flour, sugar and soda together in large bowl. Bring margarine, water, cocoa and shortening to a boil. Pour over flour and sugar, mix well. Add remaining ingredients. Pour into greased 15½ x 10½ x 1-inch pan. Bake at 350 degrees for 20–30 minutes, or until done.

Brownie Icing:
1 stick margarine *or* butter
¼ cup cocoa
6 tablespoons milk
4 cups confectioners' sugar,
  sifted
1 teaspoon vanilla
1 cup nuts, chopped

Mix first 5 ingredients well with mixer; fold in chopped nuts, and spread on brownies while hot. The icing melts a bit, but firms up again as it all cools. Brownies stay moist and are delicious!!

Dolores Warner, Thomasboro, Ill.

CHERRY BREAD AND BUTTER PUDDING

Serves 6

12 slices white bread
Butter
Cinnamon
1 (10 ounce) jar cherry preserves
4 eggs
2-2/3 cups milk
2 tablespoons sugar
1/4 teaspoon almond extract

Cut crusts from bread. Spread butter on one side of each slice. Arrange four slices in bottom of baking dish 8x8x2-inches. Sprinkle lightly with cinnamon. Spread about 2 teaspoons of preserves on each slice. Repeat, making two more layers. In medium bowl, beat eggs; add milk, sugar and extract and stir well until mixed. Pour over bread. Bake in preheated 325 degree oven for 1 hour. Refrigerate.

If preferred, serve warm from the oven.

Kit Rollins, Cedarburg, Wis.

CHICAGO PUMPKIN SLICES

1 large (2-pie) can pumpkin
1 (12-ounce) can evaporated milk
1 cup sugar
3 eggs
1 teaspoon cinnamon
½ teaspoon ginger
¼ teaspoon cloves
½ teaspoon salt
1 package Jiffy yellow cake mix
1½ sticks margarine, melted
1 cup coarsely ground nuts

Mix together first 8 ingredients; blend well. Put mixture into a 9 x 13 x 2-inch baking pan. Sprinkle top with package of Jiffy cake mix. Melt margarine and pour on top of mixture; sprinkle with ground nuts. Bake in a 350-degree oven for 50–60 minutes.

Joy Shamway, Freeport, Ill.

QUICK AND EASY BROWNIES

½ cup shortening
2 eggs
2 squares bitter chocolate
½ teaspoon baking powder
1 cup sugar
½ teaspoon salt
1 cup nuts, chopped
¼ cup flour
1 teaspoon vanilla

Melt chocolate and shortening together over hot water. Add sugar and eggs; beat thoroughly. Add vanilla and nuts. Mix baking powder and salt with the flour. Add to first mixture. Mix thoroughly. Pour into a greased 8 x 12-inch baking pan and bake 25 minutes in a moderate 350-degree oven.

Suzan L. Wiener, Spring Hill, Fla.

FROZEN FRUIT-MALLOW SQUARES

2 (3-ounce) packages cream cheese, softened
1 cup mayonnaise
1 (30-ounce) can fruit cocktail, drained
2 1/2 cups miniature marshmallows
1 cup chilled whipping cream
1/4 cup pecans, finely chopped

Combine cream cheese and mayonnaise; beat with an electric mixer, blending thoroughly. Stir in fruit cocktail, marshmallows and pecans. In a separate bowl, whip cream until soft peaks form; fold in fruit mixture. Pour into 12 x 7 1/2 x 2-inch glass dish or refrigerator tray. Cover and store in freezer until firm. Ten minutes before serving time, remove from freezer and allow to stand at room temperature. Cut into squares; serve at once.

Gwen Campbell, Sterling, Va.

COOKIES AND CREAM

1 egg, well-beaten with mixer
2/3 cup–1 cup (as desired) confectioners' sugar
1 (8-ounce) container Cool Whip
8 ounces sour cream
*3/4 to 1 (1-pound) package Oreo cookies (crushed, with some pieces)

Add confectioners' sugar to egg; mix until smooth. Beat in sour cream. Fold in Cool Whip. Mix well. Add crushed cookies and stir well to combine. Cover and refrigerate overnight to soften cookie crumbs.

This is the same as that found in the dessert sections of the delis in stores. Any cream-filled sandwich cookie could be used.

*Using three-quarters of the cookies is my preference. Cookies swell when they set. It's all up to the individual's taste.

Lisa Hayden, Fostoria, Ohio

ORANGE-CREAM DESSERT

Serves 10–12

1 teaspoon shredded orange peel
1/2 cup orange juice
1/2 cup sugar
1 cup orange juice
1 prepared 10-inch sponge cake
1 cup whipping cream
1/4 cup sugar
1 teaspoon shredded orange peel
1 cup dairy sour cream

Combine 1 teaspoon peel, 1/2 cup orange juice and 1/2 cup sugar. Heat and stir until sugar dissolves. Add 1 cup orange juice; cool. Drizzle over top, bottom and sides of cake.

Combine whipping cream with 1/4 cup sugar and 1 teaspoon orange peel; beat until stiff peaks form. Fold into the sour cream until blended. Spread evenly over top and sides of cake. Chill several hours. (Sour cream in the frosting gives an unusual tang.)

Margaret Hamfeldt, Louisville, Ky.

APPLE ROLY POLY
Serves 6-8

2 cups prepared baking mix
1/2 cup honey
3/4 teaspoon cinnamon
1/4 teaspoon nutmeg
1/4 teaspoon cloves
3 tablespoons sugar
5 large tart apples, peeled, cored,
  finely chopped
2 tablespoons butter or margarine

Prepare biscuit mix as directed on package. On lightly floured board, roll dough into 1/4 inch oblong (about 10x12 inches). Spread with honey to within 1 inch of the edges of dough. Combine spices and sugar. Toss with apples. Spread apples evenly over the honey, and dot apples with butter. Roll up like a jelly roll and seal well. Bake in greased pan with sides at 350 degrees for 40 minutes. Slice and serve hot with whipped cream, hot lemon, or vanilla sauce.

COLONIAL
BAKED APPLES
Serves 8

3 medium sweet potatoes
1/2 teaspoon finely shredded orange
  peel
2 tablespoons orange juice
1 tablespoon brown sugar
1 tablespoon butter or margarine
1/4 teaspoon nutmeg, ground
1/4 teaspoon salt
1 beaten egg
2 tablespoons milk
8 large cooking apples, peeled and
  cored
1/2 cup corn syrup
2 tablespoons lemon juice

Cook sweet potatoes, covered in enough boiling salted water to cover, for 25 to 35 minutes or until tender. Drain, peel, dice and mash with electric mixer on low speed until smooth. Should have about 1-3/4 cups mashed potatoes. Add orange peel, orange juice, sugar butter, nutmeg and salt. Add egg and milk; set aside. Remove

a slice from top of each apple. Score apple by going around the outside surface with tines of a fork in circular pattern. Using pastry bag fitted with star tip, fill apples with sweet potato mixture. Place apples in 12 x 7-1/2 x 2-inch baking dish. Stir corn syrup and lemon juice together and pour over apples. Bake uncovered in 325 degree oven for 45 minutes or until tender, basting several times with the corn syrup mixture. Serve hot.

Leona Teodori, Warren, MI

BOILED
APPLE DUMPLINGS

3 cups flour
4 teaspoons baking powder
1/2 teaspoon salt
2 tablespoons sugar
2 tablespoons vegetable shortening
1/4 cup milk
3 large tart apples
6 teaspoons sugar
Milk
Sugar

Sift baking powder, salt, and sugar with flour into bowl. Cut in shortening until mixture is in crumbs the size of peas. Stir in 1/4 cup milk. On floured board, roll dough to 1-1/2 inch thickness. Cut into six squares. Pare and core apples and cut in half. Place a half on each square of dough and sprinkle with 1 teaspoon sugar.

Pull the four corners of the dough together, dampen slightly, and press edges to seal. Tie each dumpling in a clean piece of white muslin. Drop dumplings into a large kettle of boiling water. Cook 20-25 minutes depending on size of apple. Serve with milk, cinnamon, and sugar, if desired.

Mrs. A. Dettmer, Canfield, OH

MAPLE APPLE
BROWN BETTY
Serves 4

1-1/2 cups fine bread crumbs,
  toasted lightly
3/4 stick (6 tablespoons) unsalted
  butter
4 apples, peeled and diced
1/2 cup maple syrup
3/4 teaspoon cinnamon
Vanilla ice cream, as an accompaniment

Sprinkle bottom of well-buttered baking dish with one fourth of the crumbs; dot the crumbs with one fourth of the butter. Spread one third of apples over the crumbs. In a small bowl combine the syrup and cinnamon; drizzle one third of mixture over apples. Layer the remaining crumbs, butter, apples and syrup mixture, ending with a layer of crumbs and butter. Bake in a preheated 375 degree oven for 40 minutes or until apples are tender. Serve the dessert with ice cream, if desired.

Peggy Fowler Revels, Woodruff, S. C.

MARSHMALLOW
APPLE CRISP
Serves 6

4 cups peeled, sliced apples
1/4 cup water
3/4 cup flour
1/2 cup sugar
1 teaspoon cinnamon
1/4 teaspoon salt
1/2 cup margarine
1/2 cup miniature marshmallows

Place apples and water in 8-inch square baking dish. Combine flour, sugar, cinnamon, and salt; cut in margarine until mixture is like coarse crumbs. Sprinkle over apples. Bake at 350 degrees for 35 to 40 minutes or until apples are tender. Sprinkle with marshmallows. Broil until lightly browned.

**Barbara Beauregard-Smith, South
Australia**

STRAWBERRY MERINGUE TORTE

3 egg whites
1/2 teaspoon baking powder
1 cup sugar
10 squares or 10 soda crackers
  rolled fine
1/2 cup pecans, rolled fine
3 cups sliced strawberries
Cool Whip

Beat egg whites and baking powder until frothy. Gradually beat in sugar until whites are stiff. Fold in crackers and pecans. Spread in 9-inch pie pan, which has been greased thoroughly with butter. Bake 30 minutes in 300 degree oven.

Fill meringue tart with strawberries; top with Cool Whip when ready to serve.

Ruth Arnett, Fort Recovery, Ohio

STRAWBERRY ALMOND BUTTER

1/2 pound margarine
1 pound powdered sugar
1 pound strawberries
1/2 cup finely ground almonds

Cream butter with powdered sugar and work in the pound of hulled strawberries that have been forced through a colander. When well mixed, stir in almonds and pinch of salt, if desired.

For a change-of-pace dessert, strawberries with sour cream custard is a "conversation piece." This recipe will serve 6 and it looks delightful in a glass bowl that has been chilled.

FROZEN STRAWBERRY DESSERT

24 large marshmallows
1 (10-ounce) package frozen
  strawberries (thawed)
1 cup sifted flour
1/2 cup milk
1 envelope Dream Whip
1 stick margarine

Have margarine at room temperature. Cut margarine into flour to make crumbs. Press into bottom of 7x11-inch pan. Bake at 400 degrees until brown. Cool. Melt marshmallows in milk. Add strawberries and let cool. When cool, add prepared Dream Whip. Pour into crust and freeze. Best when eaten partially frozen.

I keep this dessert in the freezer for unexpected guests.

Charlene Stark, Riceville, Iowa

STRAWBERRY ALMOND FRITTERS

Strawberries
1 cup apricot jam
1 cup toasted almonds
1 cup cracker crumbs
2 eggs

Wash, hull, and dry strawberries on paper towel. Force apricot jam through coarse strainer. Finely chop toasted almonds and crush salted crackers until you have a cupful. Beat eggs slightly. Dip each berry in jam and roll in almonds. When all are coated, dip, two at a time, in egg and then crumbs. Chill. Before serving time, heat deep fat to 360 degrees and cook berries until they are golden brown. Serve at once, passing powdered sugar, if desired. These may be fried in skillet also.

Strawberries are not only for royalty, nor do we have to "sew a fine seam" to enjoy them. We are fortunate enough to have these delectable goodies available to us all year long. Whichever recipe you choose, it will add a noble note to your table.

STRAWBERRY GERMAN CREAM

Serves 6-8

1 (10-ounce) box frozen sliced
  strawberries, thawed
1 cup boiling water
1 (3-ounce) package strawberry
  gelatin
1 envelope dessert topping mix

Drain strawberries, reserving syrup. **Pour boiling water over gelatin in** bowl, stirring until gelatin is dissolved. Add enough cold water to reserved syrup to measure 1 cup; stir into dissolved gelatin. Chill until almost set. Prepare dessert topping mix as package directs. Beat gelatin until foamy. Fold gelatin and strawberries into topping mix. Pour into 1-quart mold. Chill until firm; unmold. Serve with sweetened whipped cream and garnish with strawberries.

Sharon M. Crider, Evansville, Wis.

FROSTY STRAWBERRY SUPREME

Serves 9-12

1 cup all-purpose flour
1/4 cup finely chopped pecans
1/4 cup brown sugar, packed
1/2 cup melted margarine
2 cups egg whites
1 (10-ounce) package frozen
  strawberries, partially thawed
2/3 cup white granulated sugar
2 tablespoons lemon juice
1 cup whipped cream or non-dairy
  whipped topping.

Combine flour, nuts, brown sugar, and melted margarine. Mix well and spread into 13x9-inch pan. Bake at 350 degrees for about 20 to 25 minutes, stirring to crumble. Combine egg whites, sugar, strawberries, and lemon juice in a large deep mixing bowl. Beat with electric mixer at high speed for 15 minutes. Fold in whipped cream or whipped topping. Place one-half the crumbs in bottom of the pan. Pour in strawberry mixture, then top with remaining crumbs. Freeze until firm. Cut into squares to serve. Top each serving with whipped topping, if desired. This is really a "Supreme" dessert.

Note: Use blueberries for a change of pace, adjusting to suit your own taste in regard to sugar.

Shirley Ann Crist, Marion, Ind.

CARAMEL CORN
Serves 6-8

6 toffee bars, (1-1/8 ounce each)
1/4 cup light corn syrup
8 cups popped popcorn
1 cup unsalted roasted peanuts

In heavy saucepan, heat toffee bars and corn syrup over low heat until melted, stirring often. Pour popcorn into large, deep pan. Add warm toffee mixture and peanuts. Toss well until popcorn is coated. Cool; break into chunks.

Children and adults all enjoy caramel corn.

Dorothy Garms, Anaheim, Calif.

CARAMEL CRUNCH

1 cup light brown sugar, firmly packed
1/2 cup butter or margarine
1 (6 ounce) package chocolate chips
1 cup coarsely chopped nuts

Combine sugar and butter in saucepan; boil 7 minutes. Melt chocolate chips in saucepan over low heat. Spread nuts over bottom of buttered 8x8 inch pan. Pour butter and sugar mixture slowly over nuts. Pour melted chocolate over top. Cool. Cut into pieces.

Sharon M. Crider, Evansville, Wis.

DATE NUT BALLS

Cook together for 5 minutes:
1 stick margarine
1 cup sugar
1 egg, beaten
1 (8 ounce) package dates, cut up
Pinch of salt

Remove from heat and cool.
Add:
1 cup chopped nuts
2 cups Rice Krispies
1 teaspoon vanilla

Stir well and shape in small balls. Roll in flaked coconut.

Jean Baker, Chula Vista, Calif.

EASTER EGG CANDY

1 cup hot mashed potatoes
2 tablespoons butter
1 cup shredded coconut
1 teaspoon vanilla
3 - 1 pound boxes confectioners' sugar
1 - 8 ounce package of chocolate chips
1/8 cake paraffin

Combine potatoes and butter; stir in coconut and vanilla. Add sugar gradually, mixing well after each addition. Form into egg shapes, using 1 tablespoon mixture for each egg; place on waxed paper. Let harden for 1-3 days. Melt chocolate over hot water; dip eggs into chocolate, using 2 spoons. Place on waxed paper to harden. Chopped nuts, candied fruits, or peanut butter may be used instead of coconut.

Allie Fields, Pensacola, FL

EASTER PEANUT BUTTER EGGS

2 eggs, well beaten
1/8 teaspoon salt
1-1/2 to 2 cups peanut butter
4-5 cups powdered sugar
1 teaspoon vanilla
1 Hershey chocolate bar
1 - 6 ounce package chocolate chips

Mix the eggs, salt, peanut butter, sugar, and vanilla in order listed. Form dough into egg shapes. Melt the chocolate bar and the chocolate chips in a double boiler. Dip egg shapes into chocolate mixture. Arrange on waxed paper until set.

Sally Thompson, Louisville, KY

ICE CREAM SANDWICHES
Makes 15

32 graham cracker squares
2 tablespoons milk
1 tablespoon cornstarch
1 tub Creamy Deluxe ready to spread frosting (any flavor)
1-1/2 cups chilled whipping cream.

Line 13x9x2 inch pan with aluminum foil. Arrange 16 graham crackers on foil, cutting about 6 of the squares to completely cover foil. Mix milk and cornstarch in large bowl; stir in frosting and whipping cream. Beat on medium speed, scraping bowl constantly, 2 minutes. Beat on high speed until thick and creamy; scrape bowl occasionally. Beat about 3 minutes. Spread over graham crackers in pan. Arrange remaining graham crackers over frosting mixture, cutting about 6 of the squares to completely cover mixture. Cover and freeze until firm, about 8 hours. Cut into 2-1/2 inch squares.

Agnes Ward, Erie, PA

HOMEMADE MARSHMALLOWS

2 cups granulated sugar
3/4 cup water
2 tablespoons gelatin
1/2 cup cold water
1 teaspoon vanilla
1/2 teaspoon salt
Cornstarch
Confectioners' sugar

Mix granulated sugar with 3/4 cup water. Simmer to soft ball stage. Remove from fire. Soften gelatin in cold water. Place on large platter. Pour hot syrup over softened gelatin. Stir until dissolved. Let stand until partially cooled; whip until thick and white, and mixture will nearly hold its shape. Add vanilla and salt. Pour into straight sided pans lined with equal parts of cornstarch and confectioners' sugar, mixed together. Let stand in cool place until firm (not in ice box). Cut into squares with scissors and dust with confectioners' sugar.

Jennie Lien, Stoughton, WI

147

OLD-FASHIONED RICE PUDDING

Serves 6

1 quart skim milk
1 teaspoon Sweet 'N Low sugar
    substitute
1/4 cup raw white rice
1 tablespoon butter
1/4 teaspoon salt
1/4 teaspoon nutmeg
1 teaspoon vanilla

Preheat oven at 325 degrees. In a lightly greased 1-1/2 quart casserole, combine all ingredients. Bake uncovered, stirring frequently, for the first hour. The complete cooking time is 2-1/2 hours. This may be served topped with low-calorie whipped cream or crushed fruit. (115 calories per serving)

Judy Codenys, LaGrange, Texas

FIGGY PUDDING

Serves 8-10

1-1/2 cups all-purpose flour
1 teaspoon baking powder
1/2 teaspoon baking soda
1/2 teaspoon cinnamon
1/2 teaspoon nutmeg
1/2 teaspoon ginger
1 cup chopped cranberries
1 cup shredded carrots
1 cup packed brown sugar
1/2 cup cooking oil
1/2 cup honey
2 beaten eggs

In a large bowl, combine dry ingredients. In a bowl, combine carrots, cranberries, brown sugar, oil, honey, and eggs. Add carrot mixture to dry ingredients. Pour into greased 7-cup mold. Bake in a 325-degree oven for 30 to 40 minutes or until it tests done. Serve with Orange Hard Sauce (recipe follows).

Orange Hard Sauce:

Makes 1/2 cup

1/4 cup butter, softened
1 cup sifted confectioners' sugar
1/4 teaspoon shredded orange peel
1 tablespoon orange juice

Beat butter and sugar together in a small bowl. Beat in peel and juice until well-blended. Spoon into small serving bowl. Chill.

Marcella Swigert, Monroe City, Mo.

PARTY PUNCH BOWL DESSERT

1 box yellow cake mix
2 large boxes strawberry gelatin
2 large containers Cool Whip
2 large (10-ounce) packages frozen
    sliced strawberries
2 large packages regular vanilla
    pudding (*not* instant)
Fresh strawberries for garnish

Use 2 (8-inch) round layer cake pans and a clear glass punch bowl. Make cake according to box directions. Cool; cut layers horizontally by pulling string through so you have 4 layers. Make vanilla pudding according to package directions and let cool. Mix 2-1/2 cups boiling water with 2 packages strawberry gelatin to dissolve. Add the 2 packages of partially thawed berries. Put in refrigerator until mixture thickens—but do not let it get too firm.

To assemble:

In the punch bowl add 1/4 of the gelatin mixture.

First layer of cake, 1/4 more gelatin, spread a layer of Cool Whip, then a layer of pudding.

Second layer of cake, gelatin, Cool Whip, pudding

Third layer of cake, gelatin, Cool Whip, pudding

Fourth layer of cake only, topped with thick layer of Cool Whip. Garnish with fresh, sliced berries. You can make this the night before but *do not* put last layer of Cool Whip on until an hour or so before serving. Use large serving spoon to scoop out servings. Prepare for raving reviews on appearance and taste!

Mary Fuller, Warren, Ohio

CARAMEL TOPPED RICE CUSTARD

Serves 6

12 caramel candies
2-1/4 cups milk, divided
2 cups cooked rice, cooled
4 eggs
1/3 cup packed brown sugar
1 teaspoon vanilla extract
1/4 teaspoon salt

Combine caramels and 1/4 cup milk in small saucepan. Cook, stirring, over medium-low heat until caramels melt. Pour equal amounts into 6 buttered, 3/4-cup custard cups. Spoon 1/3 cup rice into each cup. Blend remaining ingredients; pour evenly into each cup. Place cups in shallow pan, containing 1 inch water. Bake at 350 degrees for 45 minutes, or until custard is set. Loosen custard with knife and invert onto dessert plates. Garnish with chopped nuts or coconut, if desired. Serve warm.

STRAWBERRIES WITH SOUR CREAM CUSTARD

1/2 cup sugar
2-1/2 tablespoons cornstarch
1-1/2 cups milk
4 eggs, beaten
1/2 cup sour cream
1-1/2 teaspoons vanilla
1-2 pints fresh strawberries
    (washed, hulled and halved)

Combine sugar and cornstarch in medium saucepan. Gradually, stir in milk and cook over medium heat, stirring constantly until it boils. Boil and stir 1 minute. Remove from heat. Blend milk mixture *into egg mixture* in saucepan. Add sour cream and vanilla; beat with whisk until well blended. Cool *immediately* by placing in a bowl of ice cold water for a few minutes. Cover and chill thoroughly. To serve, spoon custard sauce over strawberries. Will literally melt in your mouth.

Strawberry Almond Fritters are also completely different from the usual.

CHOCOLATE DELIGHT

Crust:

1/2 cup chopped pecans
1-1/2 cups flour
1-1/4 sticks margarine

Melt margarine; add flour, nuts, and mix well. Pat into 9x13-inch pan. Bake 20-25 minutes at 350 degrees until slightly brown.

First layer:

1 cup powdered sugar
1 medium size Cool Whip
1 (8 ounce) cream cheese

Mix powdered sugar and cream cheese; blend well. Add 1 cup of Cool Whip; spread over crust.

Second layer:

2 (6 ounce) boxes instant chocolate
  pudding mix
3 cups milk

Combine pudding mix and milk. Pour mixture over first layer.

Third layer:

Spread remaining Cool Whip over top. Make dessert 24 hours before serving and refrigerate, but do not freeze.

Beulah Schwallie, Cincinnati, Ohio

LEMON DELIGHT

Serves 12-15

1-1/2 cups flour, sifted
1-1/2 sticks margarine
1/2 cup chopped pecans
1 - 8 ounce package cream cheese
1 cup sifted powdered sugar
1 - 9 ounce container frozen whipped
  topping
2 - 6 ounce packages instant lemon
  pudding mix
2 tablespoons lemon juice
3 cups milk
1/2 cup chopped pecans

Blend together flour, margarine and 1/2 cup pecans. Press into a 13 x 9 inch pan. Bake 20 minutes at 350 degrees. Cool.

Blend together cream cheese, powdered sugar, and 1/2 of 9 ounce carton of whipped topping. Spread over crust. Combine 2 packages instant lemon pudding mix with 2 tablespoons lemon juice and 3 cups milk. Pour over previous layer. When firm, top with remainder of whipped topping. Sprinkle with 1/2 cup pecans. Chill overnight and keep in refrigerator. A delightful tasting dessert.

Barbara Beauregard-Smith, Northfield, South Australia

APPLE DUMPLING DESSERT

1 can (10) country-style refrigerator
  biscuits
2 cups thinly sliced peeled apples
1/2 cup packed brown sugar
1/2 cup evaporated milk
1/2 cup dark corn syrup
1/4 cup margarine

Preheat oven to 375 degrees.

Grease an 8-inch square baking dish. Separate biscuits into 10 individual ones. Place on bottom of buttered baking dish. Arrange apple slices over top.

In small saucepan combine all remaining ingredients and bring to a boil, stirring constantly. Pour hot syrup mixture over apples and biscuits. Bake at 375 degrees for 25-35 minutes or until golden brown and biscuits are done in the center. Serve warm.

For extra goodness, top with whipped cream.

Jodie McCoy, Tulsa, OK

APPLE DESSERT

1 box yellow cake mix
1/2 cup margarine

1/2 cup coconut
2-1/2 cups sliced apples
1/2 cup sugar
1 teaspoon cinnamon
1 cup sour cream
1 egg

Put yellow cake mix, margarine and coconut in bowl and mix like you would for pie crust. Pat into ungreased 13 x 9 inch pan. Bake 10 minutes at 350 degrees. Mix sugar, cinnamon, and apples and put over baked crust. Blend the sour cream and egg; drizzle over top. Bake at 350 degrees for 25 minutes. You can use any flavor cake mix or any kind of fruit. This is a really delicious dessert you will enjoy.

Barbara Smith, Northfield, South Australia

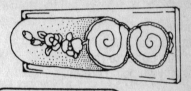

BANANA SPLIT DESSERT

First layer:

2 cups graham cracker crumbs
1/2 cup sugar
1 stick melted margarine
Mix and spread in bottom of 11 x 14-inch casserole.

Second layer:

2 egg whites, stiffly beaten
1 stick softened margarine
1 (1-pound) box powdered sugar

Beat with mixer for 10 minutes, spread over crumbs.

Third layer:

Slice 2-3 bananas over sugar mixture.

Fourth layer:

Spread 1 large can crushed pineapple, drained, over banana layer.

Fifth layer:

Spread 1 large or 2 small cartons Cool Whip over pineapple.

Sixth layer:

Sprinkle chopped pecans and maraschino cherries over all.

Marcella Swigert, Monroe City, MO

CRANBERRY CAKE DESSERT

1 cup sugar
2 cups flour
2 teaspoons baking powder
1/4 teaspoon salt
1 cup milk
3 tablespoons melted butter
2 cups whole cranberries (fresh or frozen)

Sift dry ingredients. Add milk and butter; mix. Add cranberries. Bake in greased 9x13-inch pan at 350 degrees for 30 minutes or until lightly browned. Serve with sauce.

Sauce:
1 cup sugar
1/2 cup butter or margarine
1/2 pint whipping cream

Bring ingredients to gentle boil for about 8 minutes. Spoon warm over cake.

Phyllis Lien, Stoughton, Wis.

DATE AND ALMOND BROWNIES
Makes 16–20 bars

2/3 cup flour
1/2 teaspoon baking powder
1/4 teaspoon salt
1/4 cup butter *or* margarine
2 squares baking chocolate
1 cup sugar
2 eggs, beaten
1/2 cup chopped almonds
1/2 cup chopped dates*
1 teaspoon vanilla extract

Preheat oven to 350 degrees. Grease an 8-inch square pan. Sift flour, baking powder and salt together. Melt butter and chocolate in top of double boiler. Add sugar to eggs; beat well. Add butter and chocolate; stir in flour and add almonds, dates and vanilla. Turn into pan. Bake 25 minutes. Cool in pan; cut into squares or bars. Decorate with dates or almonds, if desired.
*Chopped, uncooked prunes may be substituted for dates, if desired.

Mrs. A. Mayer, Richmond, Va.

FRUIT-COCKTAIL DESSERT
Serves 6

2 eggs
1 can fruit cocktail
1-1/2 cups sugar
2 cups flour
2 teaspoons baking soda
1 teaspoon vanilla
1/2 cup brown sugar
1 cup dry flaked coconut

Mix together eggs and fruit cocktail. Add sugar; mix well. Sift together flour and soda. Add egg mixture; mix. Add vanilla. Put into 9 x 13-inch baking pan. Sprinkle with brown sugar and coconut. Bake at 350 degrees for 30 minutes.

June Harding, Ferndale, Mich.

LIGHT 'N' LUSCIOUS CHILLED TORTE
Serves 5

1/2 cup fructose
2 tablespoons cornstarch
1-1/3 cups skim milk
1/3 cup water
1 egg, well-beaten
1 teaspoon vanilla
1-1/2 squares unsweetened chocolate, melted
1 (10-ounce) angel food loaf cake
1 tablespoon finely chopped nuts

In a saucepan combine fructose and cornstarch; mix to blend. Stir in skim milk and water. Cook, stirring constantly, until mixture begins to thicken. Stir small amount of hot mixture into egg; return egg mixture to pan. Continue cooking until mixture just comes to a boil and thickens. Stir in vanilla and chocolate. Cover surface with waxed paper; chill. Slice cake horizontally, making 3 layers. Fill and frost cake layers. Sprinkle nuts over top of cake. Chill several hours before serving. (150 calories per slice)

Gwen Campbell, Sterling, Va.

MANDARIN ORANGE DESSERT

Make any crumb crust you wish. I make this recipe with Ritz or Hi-Ho crackers.

Crust:
60 Ritz crackers, crushed (2 packages)
1/4 cup sugar
1/4 pound butter or margarine, melted

Mix and press in bottom of 9x13-inch pan.

Filling:
2 small boxes instant coconut pudding mix
2 cups cold milk
1 (8-ounce) Cool Whip
2 cans mandarin oranges, drained

Mix pudding with cold milk until stiff (I use egg beater for 2 minutes). Add Cool Whip. Stir in mandarin oranges; combine carefully. Chill 4–5 hours, or overnight before serving.

Ruth Daklin, St. Charles, Ill.

OLD-FASHIONED RICE PUDDING

2 cups rice
Cover rice with water
2 sticks margarine
1-1/2 cups sugar
1-1/2 cups raisins
2 teaspoons vanilla
4 eggs
4 cups milk (milk may be adjusted to your liking)

Cook rice until tender. Add margarine, sugar and raisins; stir; remove from heat. Mix together in a bowl, well-beaten eggs, milk and vanilla; stir well. Add to rice mixture and bake 30 minutes, covered, and 30 minutes, uncovered at 350 degrees. Do not let rice brown, but bake until fairly firm. Sprinkle cinnamon or nutmeg on individual servings when serving.

Georgia Jarman, Mt. Pleasant, Mich.

150

COBBLER TOPPING

2 cups flour
2 teaspoons baking powder
1/2 teaspoon salt
1 tablespoon sugar
1/4 cup (1/2 stick) butter
2/3 cup milk

Sift dry ingredients into a mixing bowl. Grate in butter, mixing well, rubbing between fingers.

Stir in milk gradually, until the dough holds its shape, adding another tablespoonful or two of milk, if necessary. Turn out onto a floured surface. Divide dough. Pat into 2 (9-inch) rounds or squares. Cut into wedges or squares. Use half to top the cobbler. Bake the other half separately. Rewarm the extras for breakfast.

This topping recipe also makes a good shortcake. Try it with frozen berries or with canned fruit and whipped cream.

APPLE COBBLER WITH HAZEL NUTS

7 tart apples
1/2 cup brown sugar, or to taste
1/3 to 1/2 cup shelled hazel nuts (filberts)
1 teaspoon cinnamon
1 tablespoon flour
Cobbler Topping (recipe follows)

Peel and slice apples. Mix them in a deep baking dish with nuts, sugar, cinnamon, and flour. Spoon biscuit-topping dough onto apples. Bake at 425 degrees for about 30 minutes, until topping is brown and apples are tender.

APPLE NUT TORTE

Serves 8–10

1-1/2 cups sugar
4 eggs, well-beaten
2/3 cup flour
1 teaspoon baking powder

1/2 teaspoon salt
2 cups peeled, chopped apples
1 cup chopped walnuts

Add sugar to eggs; beat until thick and light. Sift together flour, baking powder and salt; fold into egg mixture. Lightly stir in apples and nuts. Grease bottom of 13 x 9 x 2-inch pan. Pour in batter and bake in 350-degree oven for 40–45 minutes. Cool.

Shari Crider, Stoughton, Wis.

MINT BROWNIES

¾ cup plus 2 tablespoons sifted cake flour
1 cup sugar
7 tablespoons cocoa
½ teaspoon baking powder
¾ teaspoon salt
⅔ cup shortening
2 eggs
1 teaspoon vanilla
1 tablespoon light corn syrup
1 cup walnuts, coarsely chopped

In large bowl, beat all ingredients together at low speed, except walnuts; stir in walnuts with spoon. Pour battter into greased 8-inch square pan. Bake at 350 degrees about 40 minutes or until toothpick inserted near center comes out clean. Cool and frost.

Mint Frosting:
1 tablespoon shortening
1 tablespoon butter
2½ tablespoons scalded hot cream
2 cups powdered sugar
¼ teaspoon salt
½ teaspoon vanilla
¼ teaspoon peppermint extract
Green food coloring
1 ounce semisweet chocolate
1 teaspoon shortening

Melt 1 tablespoon shortening and 1 tablespoon butter in hot cream. Pour over powdered sugar and salt; stir well. Add vanilla and peppermint extract, beat until thick enough to spread. Add enough food coloring to tint a pastel mint green. Spread brownies with frosting. Melt chocolate and shortening together. Cool and drizzle over frosting in thin stream from teaspoon. Cut into squares.

Judy Haffner, Auke Bay, Alaska

CREAM CHEESE AND CHERRY DESSERT

Serves 18–20

Crust:
2 cups crushed pretzels
1 cup melted butter *or* margarine
¾ cup sugar

Filling:
1 (8-ounce) package cream cheese, softened
1 cup confectioners' sugar
1 (8-ounce) container whipped topping

Topping:
1 (30-ounce) can cherry pie filling

For crust: Combine ingredients and press into a 9 x 13-inch pan, reserving some for garnish.

For filling: Combine and beat cream cheese with confectioners' sugar. Add whipped topping to the cheese mixture, ½ cup at a time, mixing gently. Spread over crust.

Spread pie filling over top and sprinkle with reserved pretzel mixture. Refrigerate 2–3 hours.

Kit Rollins, Cedarburg, Wis.

APPLE BROWNIES

½ cup butter
¼ teaspoon salt
1 egg, beaten
1 cup sugar
3 medium apples, pared and diced *or* ½ cup applesauce
½ cup chopped walnuts
1 cup flour
½ teaspoon baking powder
½ teaspoon baking soda
½ teaspoon cinnamon

Preheat oven to 350 degrees. Cream together butter and salt, then add the egg and sugar; beat well. Stir in apples, nuts and dry ingredients. Blend well. Pour mixture into a greased and floured 8-inch square pan. Bake for 40 minutes. When cool, cut into squares.

Julie Cassat, Colorado Springs, Colo.

SWEET CHERRY FLAN

(10-inch)

1 cup all-purpose flour
1/2 teaspoon salt
1 (3 ounce) package cream cheese
1/4 cup butter or margarine
1/4 cup shortening
1 cup sour cream
1 cup milk
1 (3-3/4 ounce) package instant vanilla pudding mix
2 cups pitted fresh sweet cherries or 1 can (1 pound) sweet pitted cherries, drained
1 (8 ounce) jar red currant jelly
2 tablespoons lemon juice
1 tablespoon cornstarch

In medium bowl, sift together flour and salt. Cut in cream cheese, butter or margarine and shortening. Mix dough and chill several hours or overnight.

Preheat oven to 450 degrees. Roll out chilled dough to 1/8-inch thickness and line a 10-inch flan pan or pie plate. Prick bottom and sides with fork. Bake 12-15 minutes or until golden brown. Let cool.

In medium mixer bowl, combine sour cream and milk; beat until smooth. Add pudding mix; continue beating until blended and slightly thickened. Pour into baked pastry shell and chill until firm, about 1 hour. Arrange cherries on top of filling.

In small saucepan, combine jelly, lemon juice, and cornstarch. Cook over medium heat until thickened and clear. Cool slightly and pour over cherries.

Bobbie Mae Cooley, Bowen, Ill.

DOUBLE DELICIOUS FUDGIES

Serves 6-9

1 cup chocolate syrup
1 cup water
8 marshmallows, cut into quarters
1/2 cup chopped nuts
1 (18.25 ounce) package chocolate cake mix

Preheat oven to 350 degrees. Blend chocolate syrup and water together; pour into 8x8x2-inch pan. Sprinkle marshmallows and nuts over top of chocolate mixture. Prepare cake batter according to package directions. Pour half the batter over syrup, marshmallows and nut mixture. Bake 35-45 minutes. Cut into squares and serve warm, topped with whipped cream or ice cream.

NOTE: Remaining batter can be made into cupcakes or 1 layer cake.

Agnes Ward, Erie, Pa.

LINCOLN LOG

Serves 5

Cake:
5 eggs, separated
6 tablespoons sugar
½ cup all-purpose flour
½ teaspoon vanilla extract

Mocha Cream Filling and Frosting:
1 cup butter *or* margarine, softened
4½ tablespoons confectioners' sugar
2 tablespoons unsweetened cocoa
2 tablespoons strong, cooled coffee
2 cups whipping cream, whipped

Beat egg yolks with sugar; mix in flour and vanilla. Fold in stiffly beaten egg whites; spread mixture on a buttered waxed-paper–lined jelly roll pan. Bake at 350 degrees for 15 minutes; transfer to a dampened cloth dusted with confectioners' sugar. Roll cake in cloth; cool. Beat butter and confectioners' sugar; stir in cocoa and coffee. Unroll pastry; cover with a thin layer of mocha cream and whipped cream. Reroll cake (without cloth); cut off 2 ends diagonally; reserve. Cover cake and 2 slices with remaining mocha cream; place 1 slice on top of cake, the other slice on the side of cake (to resemble branches). With a fork, trace lines into the cream to simulate the bark.

Gwen Campbell, Sterling, Va.

FLUFFY CHIFFON DESSERT

Serves 4

1 cup hot water
1 cup cold water
1 (3-ounce) package fruit-flavored gelatin
½ cup non-fat dry milk

Prepare gelatin according to package directions. Chill until partially set. Using blender or mixer, whip non-fat dry milk in gelatin until fluffy. Serve immediately, or allow it to reset in refrigerator. (112 calories per serving)

Ann L. Garey, Columbus, Neb.

GELATIN RIBBON SQUARES

Serves 8

1 (3 ounce) package strawberry flavor gelatin
1 (3 ounce) package lemon flavored gelatin
1 (3-ounce) package lime flavored gelatin
3 cups boiling water
1 cup miniature marshmallows
2 medium bananas, diced
1/2 cup mayonnaise
1 (3 ounce) package cream cheese
1-1/2 cups halved seedless green grapes

Place 1 package gelatin in each of 3 bowls. Dissolve each gelatin using 1 cup of boiling water. Add 1/2 cup cold water to each. Chill strawberry gelatin until thick and syrupy. (Let remaining gelatin stand at room temperature). Fold marshmallows and bananas into strawberry gelatin. Pour into lightly-oiled 11x7x1-1/2-inch baking dish. Chill until set. Place mayonnaise and cream cheese in blender. Add lemon gelatin, blend until smooth, pour over strawberry layer. Chill until set. Chill lime gelatin until thick and syrupy. Fold in green grapes, pour over cream cheese layer. Chill until set. Cut into squares.

Melba Bellefeuille, Libertyville, Ill.

MARSHMALLOW POPS

1 (6 ounce) package semi-sweet
  chocolate morsels
1 teaspoon shortening
Regular sized marshmallows
Toothpicks

Melt chocolate and shortening in
the top of a double boiler. Put a toothpick into each marshmallow. Dip
marshmallows into the chocolate
mixture, coating well.

Roll in colored coconut, sugar,
candy "shot", crushed peppermint
stick candy or peanut brittle, cookie
crumbs or chopped nuts. These can
also be decorated with colored gumdrops or colored frosting.

Banana, apple or orange chunks on
toothpicks can be used instead of
marshmallows.

Sue Hibbard, Rochester, NY

MIDNIGHT MINTS
Makes 36

Bottom layer:

1/2 cup margarine
5 tablespoons cocoa
1/4 cup sugar
1 egg, beaten
2 cups graham wafer crumbs
1/2 cup chopped nuts
1 cup coconut

Combine margarine, cocoa, and
sugar in saucepan. Bring slowly to a
boil. Stir in egg to thicken. Remove
from heat; add crumbs, nuts, and
coconut. Pack firmly into greased 9x9
inch pan.

Middle layer:

1/4 cup margarine
3 tablespoons milk
1 teaspoon peppermint extract
2 cups powdered sugar
Green food coloring

Combine all ingredients in bowl.
Mix well, adding a few drops more
liquid, if needed, for easy spreading.
Tint a pretty green. Spread over first
layer; chill until firm.

Top layer:
1 cup chocolate chips
2 tablespoons margarine

Melt chips and margarine in saucepan over low heat. Spread over
chilled second layer. Chill and cut
into squares. Keep stored in refrigerator. These squares are simply delicious and freeze well.

Gay Polier, Spillimacheen, B.C. Canada

MILLIONAIRE CANDY
Makes 4 dozen

1 package German sweet chocolate
1 package peanut butter chips
1 package butterscotch chips
1/4 bar paraffin
1 cup chopped pecans or 1 cup
  shredded coconut

Melt chocolate, peanut butter
chips, butterscotch chips, and paraffin
in top of double boiler. Add nuts; drop
by spoonfuls on waxed paper; chill.
When firm, may be packaged or
served.

Sue Hibbard, Rochester, N.Y.

PEANUT BRITTLE
Makes 1-3/4 pounds

1-1/4 cups sugar
3/4 cup butter or margarine
1-1/2 teaspoons salt
1/4 cup Dr. Pepper
2 cups raw peanuts, shelled
1/2 teaspoon soda

Place all ingredients except soda
into heavy saucepan. Boil, stirring
often until temperature of 290 degrees is reached. Remove from heat;
stir in soda. Pour into 15 x 10-inch
pan. Cool and break into pieces.

Mrs. Bruce Fowler, Woodruff, SC

PEANUT BUTTER SWIRL CANDY

1 pound confectioners' sugar
1 stick margarine
2 tablespoons sweetened condensed milk
1 teaspoon vanilla flavoring
Peanut butter

Mix all ingredients (except peanut
butter) together into a well-combined
mixture and roll out on wax paper
using some confectioners' sugar to
keep from sticking. Spread peanut
butter over dough and roll up in jelly
roll fashion. Let sit 3 hours in refrigerator, then cut into 1/4 inch slices.

Peggy Fowler Revels, Woodruff, S.C.

PRALINES
Makes 20

2 cups sugar
1 teaspoon soda
1 cup buttermilk
1/8 teaspoon salt
2 tablespoons butter or margarine
2-1/2 cups (8 ounce package)
  pecan halves

In large (3-1/2 quart) heavy saucepan (Dutch oven) combine sugar,
soda, buttermilk, and salt. Cook over
high heat about 5 minutes (or to 210
degrees on candy thermometer); stir
often; scrape bottom of pan. Mixture
will foam up. Add butter or margarine and pecans. Over medium heat,
continue cooking, stirring constantly
and scraping bottom and sides of pan
until candy reaches soft ball stage,
(234 degrees on candy thermometer)
about 6 minutes.

Remove from heat; cool slightly,
about 2 minutes. Beat with spoon
until thick and creamy. Drop from tablespoon onto sheet of aluminum foil
or wax paper.

Check on pralines within a minute
or so, should be hard enough to remove up. Do not leave on wax paper
for too long as they could stick to
countertop.

Jo Ann Harris, Dallas, Texas

PUDDING POPS

Serves 6

1 - 4 ounce package instant pudding mix (any flavor)
2 cups milk
6 paper cups
6 wooden sticks or plastic spoons

Pour cold milk into bowl. Add pudding mix. Beat slowly with hand rotary beater until mixture is well blended and creamy. Pour into 6 paper cups. Put a wooden stick or plastic spoon into each cup. Press a square of foil or waxed paper onto the top of the cup to cover. The handle or the stick will poke through the foil.

Freeze until firm, at least 5 hours. To serve, press firmly on the bottom of the cup to pop out.

Molly Baker, Killbuck, OH

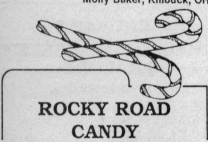

ROCKY ROAD CANDY

1 can sweetened condensed milk
1 (12 ounce) package chocolate chips
2 cups dry roasted peanuts (salted)
1 (10-1/2 ounce) bag mini marshmallows
2 tablespoons butter

On low heat melt together milk, chocolate chips, and butter. Pour into bowl with peanuts and marshmallows; blend well. Pour into 9 x 11 inch pan; refrigerate. Cut into squares and serve. If bottom of pan is covered with wax paper, candy is easier to remove.

Judy Fisk, Aberdeen, Wash.

SHAGGY DOGS

Makes 30

6 bars (1.45 ounces each) milk chocolate candy
1/3 cup milk

2-1/2 cups flaked coconut
1 (10 ounce) bag large marshmallows

In small saucepan, over low heat, melt chocolate. Stir in milk to make thin syrup. Put coconut in shallow dish. Using toothpicks, dip marshmallows into chocolate syrup, then roll in coconut. Allow to sit on wax paper.

Leona Teodori, Warren, Mich.

SWEDISH ROSETTES

(Makes 6 dozen)

1 egg
2 teaspoons sugar
1 cup milk
1 cup all-purpose flour
1/2 teaspoon salt
1 tablespoon lemon extract
Salad oil
Confectioners' sugar

Beat egg slightly; add sugar; add milk. Sift flour and salt. Stir into egg mixture; beat until smooth, about consistency of heavy cream. Add lemon extract. Put enough salad oil in a 1-quart saucepan to fill about 2/3 full. Heat to 400 degrees. Dip rosette forms into hot oil to heat them. Drain excess oil on paper towel. Dip heated forms into batter to not more than 3/4 of their depth. If only a thin layer of batter adheres to the forms, dip them again until a smooth layer adheres. Plunge batter coated forms into hot oil. Cook to desired brown-ness. With fork, ease rosettes off forms onto paper towels to drain. While still warm, dip into confectioners' sugar.

SWEETHEARTS

3/4 cup butter
1 egg yolk
1/2 cup sugar
1-1/2 cup flour

Pinch of salt
Raspberry jam

Cream butter; add sugar gradually, egg yolk, flour and salt. Knead together. Cool in refrigerator for 1 hour. Break off walnut-size pieces; roll in palm of hand; place on cookie sheet. Make indentation by pressing with the thumb. Fill hollow with jam. Bake in moderate 350 degree oven until a light brown. Remove from oven; sprinkle with confectioners' sugar.

Karen Shea Fedders, Dameron, MD

TURTLES

1 pound whole pecans (arranged in clusters of 3)
1 cup white syrup
1 can Eagle Brand condensed milk

Cook syrup and milk to 248 degrees. Stir to keep from scorching. Remove from heat. Put about 1 teaspoon mixture over each cluster of pecans. Place 1 small square of Hershey chocolate bar over each cluster. When melted, smooth out chocolate.

Note: May use melted milk chocolate chips with a little paraffin wax added, in place of chocolate bar squares. Very luscious and easy to make.

Janeen Winchell, Pleasant Hill, Ill.

VALENTINE HEART TARTS

Prepare your own recipe for pastry; roll very thin. Cut with 3-inch heart-shaped cookie cutter. Cut same amount again; cut hole in center. Prick all hearts with fork tines; bake at 350 degrees for 12 to 15 minutes. Cool. To assemble: spread strawberry jelly over uncut hearts. Place the cut-out pastry heart on the top; lightly dust with confectioners' sugar.

Mrs. Gwen Campbell, Sterling, VA

154

BLUEBERRY CREAM DESSERT

Serves 8

Crust:
1-1/4 cups graham cracker crumbs
1/4 cup sugar
6 tablespoons margarine, melted

Filling:
1/2 cup sugar
1 envelope unflavored gelatin
3/4 cup cold water
1 cup sour cream
1 cup blueberry yogurt
1 cup whipped topping
1 cup blueberries

In a small bowl combine crumbs, 1/4 cup sugar, and butter until crumbly. Reserve 1/4 cup crumbs for topping. Press remaining crumbs into bottom of an 8 x 8-inch dish. Bake at 375 degrees for 8-10 minutes until set. Cool. In a small saucepan mix 1/2 cup sugar, unflavored gelatin, and water. Heat mixture and stir until gelatin and sugar are dissolved. Set aside. In a small bowl, combine sour cream and yogurt. Blend into gelatin mixture. Chill until partially set. Fold whipped topping into yogurt mixture. Stir in blueberries. Spoon into crust. Sprinkle with reserved crumbs. Refrigerate until set, about 3 hours.

COCONUT DESSERT CRUST

1 stick butter
1 cup flour
2 tablespoons sugar
1/2 cup pecans

Mix flour, sugar, and butter. Add nuts and pat into 9x13-inch pan. Bake about 10 minutes at 350 degrees. Cool.

1st Layer:
1 package (8 ounce) cream cheese
1 cup powdered sugar
1 small Cool Whip

Mix all together.

2nd layer:
2 packages coconut cream instant pudding

Mix with 3 cups milk (like package says).

3rd layer:
Small container Cool Whip
1 small can coconut flakes, toasted

Place coconut flakes on top of Cool Whip or whipped cream.

Ruth Rueter, Madison, IN

ECLAIR DESSERT

2 (3 ounce) packages instant French vanilla pudding
3-1/2 cups milk
1 (12 ounce) container whipped topping
Graham crackers

Mix pudding and milk at low speed, 1-2 minutes. Fold in whipped topping. Layer graham crackers in bottom of 9x13-inch pan. Pour 1/2 of the pudding mixture over crackers. Layer graham crackers again. Pour remaining pudding mixture, and layer again with crackers.

Chocolate topping:
1-1/2 cups powdered sugar
1 teaspoon vanilla
2 envelopes Nestle Choco Bake (soften by kneading envelopes before opening)
1/4 cup milk

Mix above ingredients until well blended; pour over Eclair Dessert; smooth surface, and refrigerate.

Mary Spencer, Sandusky, Ohio

LEMON CAKE DESSERT

Serves 12

1 (3-ounce) package lemon flavored gelatin
1-1/2 cups sugar
3 cups packaged biscuit mix
4 eggs
3/4 cups salad oil
3/4 cup water
1-1/2 cups sifted powdered sugar
1/2 cup lemon juice

In large mixing bowl place gelatin, 1-1/2 cups sugar, biscuit mix, egg, salad oil, and water. Beat at slow speed until ingredients are combined, then beat at medium speed for 5 minutes. Pour into greased, floured 9-inch baking pan and bake at 350 degrees for 35-40 minutes or until cake tests done. Combine powdered sugar and lemon juice. Remove cake from oven; cool 5 minutes; then pierce cake all over with fork. Pour lemon mixture evenly over top. Cool and serve with whipped cream or ice cream.

Agnes Ward, Erie, PA

RHUBARB MERINGUE DESSERT

Serves 9

1/2 cup margarine, softened
1 cup flour
1 tablespoon sugar
3 eggs, separated
1 cup sugar
2 tablespoons flour
1/4 teaspoon salt
1/2 cup half and half or light cream
2-1/2 cups cut-up rhubarb
1/3 cup sugar
1 teaspoon vanilla
1/4 cup flaked coconut

Heat oven to 350 degrees. Mix margarine, 1 cup flour and 1 tablespoon sugar. Press into ungreased 9x9x2-inch baking pan. Bake 10 minutes at 350.

Mix egg yolks, 1 cup sugar, 2 tablespoons flour, salt and half and half. Stir in rhubarb. Pour over baked layer. Bake 45 minutes.

Beat egg whites until foamy. Beat in 1/3 cup sugar, 1 tablespoon at a time, continuing to beat egg whites until stiff and glossy. Do not underbeat. Beat in vanilla. Spread over rhubarb mixture; sprinkle with coconut. Bake until light brown, about 10 minutes.

A favorite for rhubarb lovers.

Marie Franks, Millerton, PA

CORN PUDDING

Mix together:
1 can creamed style corn
1 stick margarine (melted)
1 box corn bread mix
2 eggs (beaten)
1 (8 ounce) container sour cream

Pour into a casserole dish. Bake at 350 degrees for 45 minutes.

Diane Votaw, Decatur, Ind.

NOODLE PUDDING
Serves 6

8-ounces noodles, cooked
1/2 cup sour cream
1/4 cup granulated sugar
Pinch salt
2 eggs, beaten
1/2 cup creamed cottage cheese
1/2 teaspoon vanilla
Cinnamon to taste
1/4 cup raisins
Glaze:
1/4 cup oleo or butter
1/2 cup brown sugar
1/2 cup whole pecans

Rinse noodles in cold water; drain; add remaining ingredients, mix well. Pour into baking pan, Melt oleo; sprinkle with brown sugar. Press in pecans. Bake at 350 degrees for 1 hour or until done. Let cool 10 minutes,

Edna May Jenks, Chenango Forks, NY

CREAMY RICE PUDDING
(Use 3-quart pot)

1 quart milk
3/4 cup sugar
1/2 cup rice
Salt
1 egg
1 teaspoon cornstarch
1 teaspoon vanilla
1-1/2 cups milk

To milk, add sugar, pinch of salt and rice. Bring to boil; simmer slowly for 1 hour, stirring frequently. Beat egg with cornstarch and vanilla; add 1-1/2 cups milk and mix well. Add egg-milk mixture to rice mixture; stir constantly to prevent scorching. As soon as it thickens some, remove from heat and let stand 10 minutes. (The last addition of milk makes this creamy.)

Mrs. I. T. DeHart, Middletown, PA

GRANDMA'S RICE PUDDING

1/2 cup rice (not instant)
2 cups boiling water
3 cups milk
1/2 cup sugar
1/2 teaspoon salt
1 teaspoon vanilla
Cinnamon

Cook rice in water for about 20 minutes. Add milk and simmer for 20 more minutes. Add sugar and salt and continue simmering until creamy. Do not give up, it may take awhile. Remove from heat and add vanilla. Sprinkle cinnamon over top and serve either warm or at room temperature. Very delicious!

Bernice Streed, Waukegan, IL

QUICK GLORIOUS RICE PUDDING
Serves 6

1 cup pre-cooked quick rice
1 (3 ounce) package vanilla pudding mix (not instant)
1/4 cup raisins (optional)
3 cups milk
1 egg, beaten
1/4 cup sugar
1/4 teaspoon vanilla
Cinnamon sugar

Mix all of the ingredients except vanilla. Cook over medium heat, stirring constantly, until mixture comes to a boil. Remove from heat and cool slightly. Add vanilla. Spoon into individual dessert dishes and sprinkle cinnamon sugar on top. Chill and serve cold.

Hannah V. Ismiel, Chicago, IL

SUET PUDDING
Serves 10-12
About 90 years old

1 cup suet (pressed down and run through a coarse food chopper)
1 cup raisins
1 cup dark syrup
1 cup buttermilk
1/2 cup currants (optional)
2 even teaspoons soda
Pinch salt
Flour

Add flour enough to make stiff dough. Place into greased 2-quart baking dish and steam in steamer on top of stove for at least 1-1/2 hours or until done. Serve with lemon sauce or plain cream. Re-heat by re-steaming.
Lemon Sauce:
1 cup sugar
2 tablespoons cornstarch
Pinch of salt
2 cups cold water
2 tablespoons butter or margarine
1 teaspoon lemon extract

Mix sugar, cornstarch and salt in saucepan. Stir until cornstarch is blended. Add cold water gradually, stirring well. Place on stove and bring to boil, stirring constantly until mixture thickens. Add lemon extract and butter or margarine. Serve hot over pudding.

Mrs. Opal Hamer, St. Petersburg, FL

TOMATO PUDDING
Serves 4 to 6

10-ounce can tomato puree
1/2 cup boiling water
1/2 cup brown sugar
1/2 teaspoon salt
2 cups fresh bread, cut in 1" cubes
1/3 cup butter, melted

Add sugar and salt to puree. Add water; simmer 5 minutes. Add melted butter.

Place bread in greased casserole; cover with tomato butter. Cover, or if extra crispness is desired, bake uncovered at 350 degrees for 30 minutes.

Kit Rollins, Cedarburg, WI

SWEET POTATO PUDDING

4 cups grated raw sweet potatoes
1 cup molasses (or honey)
3/4 cup milk
1 teaspoon nutmeg
1/2 cup margarine, melted
1/2 teaspoon cloves
1/2 cup chopped nuts
1/2 teaspoon salt
2 eggs, well beaten

Mix all ingredients together, except eggs. Add eggs; stir until well blended. Pour into 1-1/2 quart baking dish sprayed with non-stick spray. Bake at 375 degrees for 50-60 minutes or until done (see testing note below).

Note: You may use 1/2 cup granulated sugar and 1/2 cup syrup in place of molasses or honey.

Testing custard for doneness: Insert tip of knife blade in pie/custard/pudding about halfway between edge and center of pie. If blade comes out clean, custard will be firm all the way through when it cools. If you insert knife in center, the filling should cling like a thick cream sauce.

BLUEBERRY TORTE

Crust:
1/4 pound margarine, plus 1 tablespoon
1 cup flour
2 tablespoons sugar

Combine and press into 9-inch square pan. Bake in preheated 375 degree oven about 20 minutes, or until browned.

Filling:
1 envelope Dream Whip, prepared according to package directions
1 (8 ounce) package cream cheese, softened
1 cup powdered sugar

1 can blueberry pie filling

Allow crust to cool. Meanwhile beat prepared Dream Whip with softened cream cheese and powdered sugar. Pour over cooled crust. Top with 1 can blueberry pie filling. Chill well.

Marie Popovich, Warren, MI

CHOCOLATE TORTE
Serves 20

1 (15-ounce) package Oreo cookies, crushed
1/3 cup melted butter
2 (3-ounce) packages instant chocolate pudding
1-1/2 cups milk
1 (9-ounce) carton Cool Whip
1 quart vanilla ice cream, softened

Mix together cookie crumbs and butter. Pat 2/3 of crumbs into a 9 x 13-inch pan. Reserve remaining 1/3 of crumbs for top. Beat together pudding and milk until very thick. Add the softened ice cream and beat together until well blended. Pour pudding mixture over the crumbs. Spread Cool Whip over the pudding mixture and top with remaining crumbs. Refrigerate overnight.

Ida Bloedow, Madison, WI

ELEGANT FINALE TORTE
Serves 12

2 cups sifted flour
2 teaspoons baking powder
1 teaspoon baking soda
1/4 teaspoon salt
1-1/2 teaspoons ground cinnamon
1/2 teaspoon ground cloves
1/8 teaspoon ground ginger
1/2 teaspoon pumpkin pie spice
2 cups firmly packed brown sugar
4 eggs
1 (1 pound) can pumpkin
1 cup finely ground graham crackers
1 cup vegetable oil
1 (6 ounce) package butterscotch morsels
1 cup chopped walnuts

Whipped cream:
1-1/2 cups heavy cream
1/2 teaspoon vanilla
2 tablespoons sugar

Into a large bowl, sift together first 8 ingredients and 2 cups sugar; set aside. In large bowl of mixer, beat eggs at high speed until foamy. Slowly mix in pumpkin, graham cracker crumbs, and oil. By hand, stir in butterscotch morsels and walnuts. Spread batter in 3 greased and waxed paper-lined, 9-inch round cake pans. Bake at 350 degrees for 25-30 minutes. Cool in pans; remove to racks. In chilled bowl beat cream, vanilla, and 2 tablespoons sugar at high speed until soft peaks form. Spread whipped cream on top of each cake layer. Stack layers, frosting-side up. Refrigerate 2-3 hours before serving.

Gwen Campbell, Sterling, Va.

STRAWBERRY REFRIGERATOR TORTE
Serves 8-12

3/4 pound "Nabisco Wafers"
3/4 cup butter
2 eggs, beaten
1 cup confectioners' sugar
1-1/2 cups whipping cream
1 quart fresh strawberries, quartered

Put "Nabiscos" thru a food chopper or crush to crumbs. Reserve 1/4 cup crumbs for topping. Stand additional whole "Nabiscos" wafers upright around and lay on bottom of torte pan. Press the crumbled "Nabiscos" in bottom of torte pan. Cream butter until light. Add eggs and sugar; beat well. Fold in whipped cream and strawberries. Pour into torte pan. Sprinkle with the remaining reserved crumbs Chill in refrigerator 6-8 hours.

This is a very elegant dessert that could be served at a luncheon, surrounded with fresh whole strawberries for garnish.

Mrs. Edward Prinsen, Cedarburg, WI

157

APPLE DUMPLINGS

2 cups flour
2-1/2 teaspoons baking powder
1/2 teaspoon salt
1/2 cup shortening
1/4 cup milk
8 apples
8 tablespoons sugar
4 tablespoons butter
Cinnamon and sugar mixed

Sift flour, salt, and baking powder. Cut in shortening. Add milk and stir. Knead lightly on a floured board. Roll 1/8-inch thick. Divide dough into 8 parts. Peel and core apples. Place one apple on each section of dough. Fill hollow of apple with 1 tablespoon of sugar and 1 teaspoon of butter. Fold dough over apple, pressing edges together. Place in a shallow baking pan. Sprinkle with sugar-cinnamon mixture and dot with remaining butter. Bake at 400 degrees for 30-40 minutes. Serve with cream or half-and-half.

Joy B. Shamway, Freeport, Ill.

GOURMET ORANGE BAKED ALASKA

Serves 6

1 pint orange sherbet
3 large oranges
3 egg whites, stiffly beaten
1/4 teaspoon cream of tartar
1/4 cup plus 2 tablespoons sugar

Scoop sherbet into 6 balls; freeze at least 4 hours until very firm. Cut oranges crosswise in half; cut thin slice from bottom of each half. Cut around edges and membranes; remove fruit and membrane from orange shells. Line bottom of each shell with fruit; refrigerate. Beat egg whites and cream of tartar. Beat in sugar, 1 tablespoon at a time; beat until stiff and glossy. Place orange shells on ungreased baking sheet; fill each with a frozen sherbet ball. Completely cover sherbet ball with meringue, sealing it to the edge of the shell. Bake at 400 degrees for 4-5 minutes, or until meringue is light golden brown. Serve immediately.

Gwen Campbell, Sterling, Va.

BLACK FOREST TRIFLE

1 (9-ounce) package chocolate cake mix
1/4 cup rum or brandy (optional)
1 can cherry pie filling
1 package instant chocolate pudding
1 medium Cool Whip

Bake cake as package directs. Cool and cut in cubes. Prepare pudding as package directs. Arrange one half cake cubes in glass bowl. Sprinkle 1 ounce rum or brandy. Layer one half of pudding, then one half of cherry pie filling; next, one half of Cool Whip. Repeat layering in order given.

Chill at least 3 hours before serving. Looks very pretty in a tall stemmed bowl.

Helen Harlos, Ethel, Miss.

PUMPKIN DESSERT

1-1/3 cups graham cracker crumbs
1/4 cup sugar
1/4 cup soft butter
60 marshmallows
2 cups pumpkin
1 teaspoon cinnamon
1/2 teaspoon ginger
1/2 teaspoon salt
2 packages whipped topping mix, prepared according to package directions
1 cup sweetened whipped cream
Toasted coconut

Mix graham cracker crumbs with sugar and soft butter. Press into a 9x13-inch pan. Bake at 375 degrees for 8 to 10 minutes. Let cool. Melt marshmallows, pumpkin, spices, and salt in a double boiler or other large pan. Fold in whipped topping and spread the mixture over graham cracker crust. Spread the whipped cream over top of pumpkin mixture. Top with toasted coconut. Chill in refrigerator before serving.

Mrs. James Williams, Brainerd, Minn.

OLD-FASHIONED BLUEBERRY BUCKLE

Serves 6

2 cups flour
3 teaspoons baking powder
1/2 cup margarine
1/2 cup sugar
1 egg, beaten
1/2 cup milk
1/2 teaspoon almond flavoring

Topping:
2 cups fresh or frozen blueberries
2 teaspoons lemon juice
1/4 cup sugar
1/3 cup flour
1/2 teaspoon cinnamon
1/4 cup margarine

Sift flour with baking powder. Set aside. In mixing bowl cream margarine and sugar. Add egg; beat until creamy. Combine milk and almond flavoring; add to creamed mixture alternately with flour; beat until smooth. Pour into buttered 9-inch square pan. Sprinkle lemon juice over blueberries and spread over batter. Mix sugar, flour, cinnamon and margarine thoroughly with fingers until crumbly. Spread over blueberries. Bake at 350 degrees for 45-50 minutes, or until it tests done. Serve warm or cold, with cream, if desired.

Holiday
DESSERTS

HOLIDAY DESSERT TORTE
Serves 8–10

1 (10¾-ounce) frozen pound cake, thawed
1 (8-ounce) package cream cheese, softened
2 cups whipped topping with real cream, thawed
⅓ cup semisweet chocolate pieces, melted
½ cup diced, mixed candied fruit

Split pound cake lengthwise into 3 layers. Combine cream cheese and whipped topping. Reserve ⅔ cup of cream cheese mixture. Stir in chocolate. Fold fruit into remaining cream cheese mixture. Spread 2 layers with fruit mixture. Stack. Top with remaining layer. Frost with chocolate mixture. Chill.

Note: This can be made ahead, wrapped securely and frozen. When ready to serve, thaw, wrapped, in refrigerator.

Joy Shamway, Freeport, Ill.

YANKEE DOODLE APPLE PIE

4 cups flour
1 tablespoon sugar
1 teaspoon salt
1 3/4 cups whipped shortening (Crisco)
1 tablespoon cider vinegar
1 egg
1/2 cup water

Mix flour, sugar and salt together. Cut in shortening with fork. In a separate bowl combine vinegar, egg and water. Combine mixtures and stir well. Divide into 5 portions and wrap in waxed paper. Chill in refrigerator for 1 hour. Shape into pie plate.

4 baking apples, cut up
1/2 cup sugar for filling
2 tablespoons flour for filling
1/2 teaspoon nutmeg
1/4 cup lemon juice
1/2 cup sugar for topping
1/4 cup butter for topping
1/2 cup flour for topping

Combine filling and mix with apples. Toss lightly. Spoon into pastry shell. Drizzle with lemon juice. Combine topping ingredients and place on pie. Bake for 1 hour at 425 degrees.

CHOCOLATE SPIDERS
Makes 3 dozen

1½ cups semisweet chocolate morsels
1 (5-ounce) can chow mein noodles
1 cup salted peanuts

Place chocolate morsels in top of double boiler; bring water to a boil. Reduce heat to low; cook until chocolate melts. Add noodles and peanuts, stirring well. Drop chocolate mixture by teaspoonfuls onto greased baking sheets. Refrigerate 8 hours or overnight. Keep chilled until ready to serve.

Mary Mitchell, Cleveland, Ohio

CUSTARD CRUNCH MINCEMEAT PIE

1 unbaked 9-inch pie shell
1 cup sugar
2 tablespoons flour
1/8 teaspoon salt
3 eggs, slightly beaten
1/4 cup butter or margarine, melted
1/2 cup chopped walnuts
1 cup prepared mincemeat

Blend dry ingredients and slowly add to eggs. Add remaining ingredients. Mix well. Pour into pastry shell and bake in a 400-degree oven 15 minutes. Reduce heat to 350 degrees and bake 30 minutes longer.

CRANBERRY CHEWS
Makes 45 bars

1-1/2 cups sifted flour
1-1/2 teaspoons baking powder
1/2 teaspoon salt
2 eggs
1 cup sugar
1 tablespoon lemon juice
3/4 cup jellied cranberry sauce
1 cup chopped pecans

Mix and sift flour, baking powder and salt. Beat eggs well. Add lemon juice, mix. Add sifted dry ingredients, mix. Beat sauce gently with fork. Add sauce and nuts to egg mixture, mix. Spread mixture in greased 9x13-inch pan. Bake in preheated 350 degree oven about 40 minutes. Cool 5 minutes; remove to cooling rack. Cool and cut into bars. Sprinkle with confectioners' sugar, if desired.

Jenni Lien, Stoughton, Wis.

CHRISTMAS APPLE BREAD PUDDING
Serves 4

4 slices stale bread
2 tablespoons butter
3 eggs, well-beaten
⅔ teaspoon cinnamon
½ teaspoon nutmeg
½ teaspoon cloves
½ teaspoon allspice
6 tablespoons brown sugar
Pinch salt
2 cups apple juice
½ teaspoon vanilla

Butter the bread slightly and cut in ½-inch cubes. Place in buttered baking dish. Mix sugar, salt, eggs, apple juice, vanilla and spices. Pour mixture over bread cubes. Bake in a pan of water. Bake at 350 degrees for 40 minutes, or until a knife comes out clean. Sprinkle cinnamon over top, if desired.

Carmen Bickert, Dubuque, Iowa

NORTH POLE LIME-NUT PIE
Serves 6–8

1 (3-ounce) package lime-flavored gelatin
1 teaspoon lime peel, finely shredded
¼ cup lime juice
1 cup evaporated milk
½ cup chopped pecans
1 (4½-ounce) container frozen whipped topping, thawed
1 purchased chocolate-flavored crumb pie shell

Dissolve gelatin in ½ cup boiling water. Stir in lime peel and lime juice. Stir in evaporated milk. Chill until partially set. Fold thawed dessert topping and nuts into mixture. Chill until mixture mounds when spooned. Turn into pie shell. Refrigerate for 3 hours.

Joy Shamway, Freeport, Ill.

SNOW PUDDING
Serves 4

1 tablespoon (envelope) unflavored gelatin
2 cups low-fat milk
1 tablespoon instant coffee
1 (3¾-ounce) package vanilla instant pudding
2 egg whites
4 tablespoons low-fat whipped cream topping

Sprinkle gelatin over 1 cup milk in small pan; heat over low heat, stirring until gelatin is dissolved. Set aside.

Stir together pudding, remaining milk and coffee powder in bowl; add gelatin mixture and beat according to pudding package instructions. Beat egg whites until stiff but not dry; fold into pudding mixture. Turn into 3-cup mold; chill until set. When ready to serve, top with dollops of whipped cream topping. Very rich for the few calories involved! (200 calories per serving)

Judie Betz, Eureka, Calif.

FROZEN CHRISTMAS PUDDING

1-1/2 cups vanilla wafer crumbs
1/2 cup chopped walnuts or pecans
1/2 cup chopped dates
1/2 cup chopped candied fruit peel
Grated rind of 1/2 lemon
1/4 teaspoon cinnamon
1/4 teaspoon nutmeg
8 marshmallows, quartered
1/4 cup hot orange juice
1/4 cup sugar
1 cup heavy cream, whipped

Combine crumbs, nuts, fruit, rind, and spices. Dissolve marshmallows in hot orange juice, add sugar and combine this mixture with first mixture. Fold in whipped cream. Place in refrigerator tray and freeze until firm. May be garnished with holly wreaths made of red cinnamon candies and bits of green gumdrops.

Mrs. Carmen J. Bickert, Dubuque, Iowa

FROSTY THE SNOWMAN'S PUMPKIN SQUARES
Serves 9

1½ cups graham cracker crumbs
¼ cup sugar
¼ cup butter, melted
1½ cups pumpkin
½ cup brown sugar
½ teaspoon salt
1 teaspoon cinnamon
¼ teaspoon ginger
⅛ teaspoon cloves
1 quart vanilla ice cream, softened
Whipped cream
Pecans

Mix graham cracker crumbs with sugar and melted butter. Press into the bottom of a 9-inch square pan. Combine pumpkin with sugar, salt and spices. Fold in the softened ice cream. Pour into crumb-lined pan. Cover and freeze until firm. Cut into squares and top with whipped cream and pecans.

Judy Haffner, Auke Bay, Alaska

CRANBERRIES IN THE SNOW
Serves 12

12 unfrosted cupcakes
1 cup fresh cranberries
1 cup sugar
1/2 cup water
6 egg whites
1/4 teaspoon cream of tartar
3/4 cup sugar

Combine fresh cranberries, sugar and water in saucepan; bring to boil. Cook 5-8 minutes; cool. Beat egg whites and cream of tartar until foamy; add sugar gradually; beat until glossy, stiff peaks form. Place cupcakes on cookie sheet; frost each with meringue. Bake 5 minutes at 400 degrees or until meringue is lightly browned; cool. Top each meringue-frosted cupcake with a dollop of the cooked cooled cranberries.

Gwen Campbell, Sterling, Va.

CHRISTMAS PIE

Serves 6–8

1 envelope unflavored
  gelatin
½ cup sugar
⅛ teaspoon salt
2 eggs, separated
1¼ cups milk
½ teaspoon peppermint
  flavoring
1 cup heavy cream
  whipped
  Green food coloring
1 (9-inch) chocolate
  cookie crust

Mix gelatin, ¼ cup sugar and salt in medium saucepan. Beat together egg yolks and milk. Stir into gelatin mixture. Place over low heat; stir until gelatin dissolves and mixture thickens slightly, about 5 minutes. Remove from heat; stir in peppermint. Chill, stirring occasionally, until mixture mounds slightly when dropped from spoon. Beat egg whites until stiff but not dry. Gradually add ¼ cup sugar; beat until very stiff. Fold into gelatin mixture; fold in whipped cream. Add enough green food coloring to make nice green shade. Pour into pie shell. Chill until firm. Garnish with cherries.

Mrs. Michael D. Carl, Fowlerville, Mich.

FILBERT CAKE

Serves 10

1/2 pound (3 cups) shelled but
  blanched filberts (3 pounds
  unshelled nuts)
10 egg yolks
1/4 teaspoon salt
1 cup sugar
1 teaspoon vanilla
6 egg whites
Whipped cream or butter icing

Finely grind shelled filberts and beat egg yolks until very light. Add salt, sugar and vanilla, mix well. Fold in filbert meat lightly. Beat egg whites until stiff and fold into the mixture. Pour into buttered and lightly-floured 10-inch angel cake pan. Bake at 325 degrees for 1 hour. Cool slowly and remove from pan. Serve as is or with whipped cream or butter icing.

Susan Wiener, Spring Hill, Fla.

FROZEN PUMPKIN SQUARES

Serves 9–12

1¼ cups fine gingersnap
  cookie crumbs
¼ cup sugar
¼ cup butter *or* marga-
  rine, melted
1 (16-ounce) can pump-
  kin
1½ teaspoons pumpkin pie
  spice
¼ cup sugar
1 pint vanilla ice cream,
  softened
2 tablespoons lemon juice
1 (12-ounce) container
  frozen whipped topping,
  thawed

Combine crumbs and sugar. Mix in butter. Press firmly on bottom of 9-inch square pan and set aside. Combine pumpkin, spice and sugar in bowl. Spoon in ice cream and blend well. Fold in lemon juice and 4 cups of the whipped topping. Blend well. Pour over crust. Freeze about 4 hours. Garnish with remaining whipped topping.

Shari Crider, Stoughton, Wis.

CREAM PUFF HEART

1 cup water
½ cup butter
1 cup sifted flour
4 eggs
  Cream Filling (recipe
  follows)
2 (10-ounce) packages
  frozen strawberries,
  drained
  Confectioners' sugar

Fold a 9 x 8½-inch piece of paper in half lengthwise. Sketch half of a heart on it; cut out. Open paper to full heart. Grease baking sheet lightly, and trace with greased pencil on baking sheet.

Heat water and butter in pan to boiling; reduce heat. Add flour. Stir vigorously over low heat until mixture forms a ball (about 1 minute). Remove from heat. Beat in eggs, 1 at a time; beat until smooth after each addition. Drop mixture by spoonfuls, with sides touching, along edge and entire surface of heart outline positioned on the baking sheet. Bake at 400 degrees for 45 minutes. Cool on rack. Cut off top. Fill shell with filling; top with strawberries. Replace top. Dust with confectioners' sugar. Chill until serving.

Cream Filling:

Combine 1 (3-ounce) package vanilla pudding with 1½ cups milk. Follow package directions for cooking. Cool, then fold in 1 cup heavy cream, whipped, and 1 teaspoon vanilla.

This can be refrigerated overnight. Then just dust with confectioners' sugar before serving. This is a wonderful valentine dessert.

Vickie Vogt, Kewaskum, Wis.

FRUIT CAKE PUDDING

Serves 6-8

2 cups cubed fruitcake (aged or
  leftovers)
Sugar to taste
3 eggs or egg substitute, well
  beaten
Milk
1 teaspoon vanilla
1/4 cup coconut

Place cubed fruitcake into 1-1/2 quart casserole. In 2-cup measuring cup, beat eggs with fork or wire whisk. Add enough milk to fill cup; add vanilla. Pour over fruitcake; sprinkle coconut on top. Let sit out while oven preheats to 350 degrees. Bake, uncovered, for 45 minutes or until silver knife inserted into center comes out clean. Serve with whipped cream or whipped topping, if desired.

Agnes Ward, Erie, Pa.

Foreign & EXOTIC

SOPAPILLAS

1 package dry yeast
1 cup warm water
1 egg
1 cup milk
5 teaspoons baking
  powder (1 for each cup
  of flour)
½ cup sugar
1 teaspoon salt
5 cups flour

In large bowl, add yeast to water and dissolve. Add egg, milk and sugar. Mix until mixture starts to foam. Add flour, salt and baking powder, a little at a time; mix to thick dough. Let sit for 15 minutes. Put dough on floured board and roll to ¼-inch thickness. Cut in 2-inch squares or triangles. Fry in hot oil until brown, as you would doughnuts. Serve warm with melted honey.

Mrs. W.T. Gore, Aztec, N.M.

RUSSIAN MEATLOAF
Serves 4

As in most Russian recipes, potatoes and vegetables are added to stretch the meat portions of the dish. Russian foods are usually very filling and satisfying. This one is no exception.

2 pounds hamburger
3 eggs
1 medium potato, grated
2 carrots, grated

1 medium onion, diced
1/2 teaspoon salt
Pepper to taste
1/2 tablespoon parsley
1/2 teaspoon dill
2 slices dry bread, crushed
1 cup tomato sauce

Put all ingredients in large mixing bowl and mix with hands until thoroughly combined. Mold into loaf and place in an 8x12-inch casserole. Cover with foil and bake in a 350-degree oven for 1-1/2 hours. Remove cover and bake for additional 30 minutes until browned. Remove from baking dish and place on serving platter. Cover with 1 cup tomato sauce.

Roberta Rothwell, Palmdale, Calif.

FINSKA KAKOR
(Finnish cakes)
Makes 4 dozen

Mix together thoroughly:
3/4 cup soft butter
1/4 cup sugar
1 teaspoon almond extract
Stir in:
2 cups sifted flour

Mix thoroughly with hands. Chill dough. Roll out 1/4-inch thick. Cut into strips 2-1/2 inches long and 3/4 inch wide. Brush tops lightly with 1 egg white, slightly beaten. Sprinkle with mixture of 1 tablespoon sugar and 1/2 cup finely chopped, blanched almonds. Carefully transfer to ungreased baking sheet. Bake in a 350-degree oven for about 17-20 minutes, or just until cookies begin to turn a very delicate golden brown.

Leona Teodori, Warren, Mich.

TACO CASSEROLE

1 pound ground beef
1 (1 1/4-ounce) package taco
  seasoning mix
1/4 cup water
3 cups regular corn chips
2 cups (8 ounces) cheddar cheese
1 medium tomato, chopped
1 cup sour cream

Crumble ground beef into a 2-quart casserole; microwave on HIGH for 5–6 minutes; drain. Stir in seasoning mix and water; microwave for 2 minutes. Stir in chips and 1 1/2 cups cheese; microwave for 2 1/2 minutes, or until heated through. Stir; top with tomato and remaining cheese. Microwave for 2 minutes, or until cheese is melted. Top with sour cream.

FINNISH FLAT BREAD (RIESKA)

¼ cup oatmeal
¼ cup whole-wheat flour
3 cups all-purpose flour
¼ cup sugar
3 teaspoons soda
½ cup shortening
2 cups buttermilk

Combine dry ingredients with shortening. Mix well. Add buttermilk. Divide dough in half; shape into round loaves. Place on cookie sheet. Flatten. Bake at 450 degrees for 15–20 minutes.

Faye Hope, Detroit, Mich.

EASY-AS-PIE SHORTCAKE
Serves 4

4 cake-type doughnuts (plain or sugar-dusted)
1 (10-ounce) package frozen strawberries (or berries of your choice)
Whipped topping

Split doughnuts lengthwise. Place 1 doughnut half in dessert dish. Top with whipped topping and 2–3 tablespoons of berries. Place other half of doughnut on top, and repeat layers. Top with whipped topping and berries.

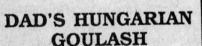

DAD'S HUNGARIAN GOULASH
Serves 6

3 pounds lean beef stew meat
3-4 large onions, chopped
1/2 cup flour to coat meat
Salt to taste
Garlic powder to taste
Pepper to taste
Hungarian sweet paprika to taste
1 tablespoon caraway seeds
Dash soy sauce
Dash Worcestershire sauce
11 ounces of beef stock or consommé
2-3 tablespoons sour cream

In large skillet sauté chopped onions until golden brown in fat or oil on medium-high heat. Season stew meat with salt, pepper, garlic powder, paprika; roll meat in flour. Sauté in same pan with onions over medium-high heat. Add the beef stock with a dash of soy and Worcestershire sauce. Bring to boil and simmer, covered, for 2-1/2-3 hours until meat is fork tender. Add more beef stock, if necessary. Just before serving, stir in caraway seeds and sour cream.

Joan Ross, Amenia, Wyo.

PECENÀ KACHNA (ROAST DUCK)
Serves 4

1 (5-pound) duck
Salt to taste
1 teaspoon caraway seeds
1 cup water

Wash dressed duck and dry thoroughly. Sprinkle with salt and caraway seeds, inside and outside. Pour 1 cup water into roasting pan; put in duck, breast down, cover; roast in a 350-degree oven for 1½ hours. Turn duck and roast, uncovered, for 30 minutes longer, or until duck has been browned.

During the roasting, pierce skin several times, and add water as needed. Serve with dumplings and sauerkraut.

Ella Evanicky, Fayetteville, Texas

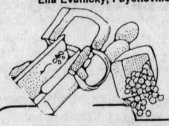

RINDFLEISCH MIT APFELN (BEEF WITH APPLES)
Serves 4

4–6 tart apples, cored and sliced
3–4 tablespoons butter *or* bacon drippings
1 tablespoon sugar (or to taste)
1 cup beef gravy
Few drops lemon juice
Pinch cinnamon
¼ cup raisins *or* dried currants
4 large slices cooked beef (boiled or roasted)

Lightly fry apple slices in the drippings or butter until golden brown. Add sugar, beef gravy, lemon juice and cinnamon. Simmer over low heat until apples are soft. Add raisins or currants and the beef slices; cook just until meat is heated through.

Marguerite Seyse, Buffalo, N.Y.

SWEDISH POTATO SAUSAGE
Serves 12–14

2 pounds ground beef
1 pound ground pork
6 pounds potatoes, ground
2 medium onions, ground
1 cup milk, scalded
1 teaspoon black pepper
3 tablespoons salt
1 teaspoon allspice
2 teaspoons ginger

Mix all ingredients together. Pack into 2 greased angel food cake pans; cover with aluminum foil and steam in a 300-degree oven, over large pan of hot water, for 4–5 hours, using meat thermometer.

Kathy Somerville, Nashville, Ind.

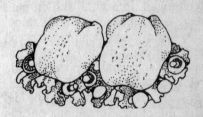

RUSSIAN CREAM
Serves 6–8

3/4 cup sugar
1 envelope unflavored gelatin
1 1/4 cups cold water
1 teaspoon vanilla
1 cup sour cream
1 cup whipped cream *or* Cool Whip
1 (10-ounce) package frozen raspberries, thawed

Dissolve sugar and gelatin in water. Add sour cream and chill until thickened. Add vanilla and whipped cream; pour into 9x13-inch pan. Chill at least 3 hours. Cut into squares and serve topped with raspberries, undrained.

This recipe was given to my mother by the owner of a little restaurant in Vienna.

Jami Shimizo, Spokane, Wash.

RED CABBAGE ROLLS

Makes 8 rolls

1 medium head of red cabbage, with the center core removed
2 tablespoons butter
1 cup bread crumbs
1 egg
3 tablespoons oil
2 cups clear meat stock or bouillon
3 small onions, minced
1 pound ground pork mixed with beef
Salt & pepper to taste
4 tablespoons all-purpose flour
1/3 cup half-and-half

Bring a large pot of salted water to full boil. Plunge the head of red cabbage into the boiling water. Let it cool for 5 minutes, carefully removing outer leaves. Repeat until all leaves are removed. In a small skillet, melt butter. Add onion; sauté until shiny. In a large bowl, combine bread crumbs, ground meats, sautéed onion, egg, salt, and pepper. Divide mixture into 8 portions. Take 2 cabbage leaves at a time, placing one leaf inside the other. Spread one portion of the mixture over surface (be sure to stop short of the edges). Roll up into a roll. Repeat with remaining cabbage and mixture. Heat oil in a large fry pan. Add cabbage rolls; sauté gently.

Dissolve flour in stock or bouillon; add to fry pan. Cover and cook gently over low heat for 40 minutes; stirring occasionally. Add salt and pepper to taste. Add the half-and-half; stir to blend. Place on a warm serving dish. Spoon sauce over cabbage rolls. Serve mashed potatoes or rice, and a tossed salad.

Marie Fusaro, Manasquan, N.J.

CZECH DUMPLINGS

4　cups flour
2　unbeaten eggs
½　teaspoon salt
1½　cups milk

2　or 3 slices dry bread
Additional fried bread crumbs

Sift and measure the flour into a bowl. Make a well and into it put the eggs, salt and milk. Mix until smooth. The dough should be very thick. Cube the dry bread and brown in hot fat. Cool and add to dough. Mix well. Cut off dumplings with a tablespoon and drop into boiling, salted water. Stir once. Cook 15–20 minutes. Remove dumplings immediately and tear each one apart with 2 forks. Sprinkle with melted butter and fried bread crumbs.

Jane Kremenak, Salt Lake City, Utah

CHICKEN WITH DUMPLINGS A LA ITALIANO

Soup:
3 quarts water
1 whole chicken, 2-1/2 to 3 pounds
1 onion
2-3 teaspoons salt
Parsley leaves

Egg Dumpling Mixture:
6 eggs
1/2 cup grated Parmesan cheese
1/2 cup Italian bread crumbs
1/2 teaspoon salt
Pinch black pepper
Few sprigs parsley, chopped
1/2 pound ground chuck

Soup:
Rinse chicken, and put into pan with 3 quarts boiling water; add onion, salt, and parsley; boil for 1-1/2 hours. Let stand awhile, then strain into another pan. Serve chicken separately.

Dumplings:
Blend dumpling mixture well. Put soup on to boil again and drop the dumpling mixture into the boiling soup by tablespoonfuls. Make ground chuck into shape of small marbles and drop into the soup; cook for 10 minutes. Serve hot with extra grated cheese.

Leona Teodori, Warren, Mich.

SOPA RANCHERA (RANCH-STYLE SOUP)

Serves 4

1/4 cup chopped onion
1 tablespoon cooking oil
4 cups chicken broth
1/4 cup long grain rice
1/4 cup tomato purée
1/4 teaspoon salt
Dash pepper
1 cup frozen peas

In saucepan cook onion in hot oil until tender, but not brown. Stir in chicken broth, rice, tomato purée, salt, and pepper. Bring to a boil. Reduce heat; cover and simmer for 25 minutes. Stir in frozen peas; simmer, covered, for 5 minutes longer.

Mrs. Robert Shaffer, Middleburg, Pa.

MEXICAN SOUFFLÉ

3 (4-ounce) cans green chiles (minced)
2 cups grated Monterey cheese
2 cups grated medium-sharp cheddar cheese
6 large eggs
1 cup flour
4 cups milk
Salt and pepper to taste

Butter bottom of 3-quart soufflé dish. Layer chiles and cheeses in bottom. Beat eggs, flour, milk, seasonings, and pour over chiles and cheeses. Bake at 350 degrees for 1 hour. Let stand 5 minutes before serving.

DANISH STUFFED CABBAGE
Serves 6

1   large head leafy green cabbage
1½   pounds ground beef
1   small onion, chopped
¼   cup green pepper, chopped
2   eggs
½   cup cooked rice
1   teaspoon salt
⅛   teaspoon seasoned pepper
⅛   teaspoon marjoram
  Butter *or* margarine
1   (1-pound) can stewed tomatoes
½   cup water
1   tablespoon vinegar

Discard core of cabbage. Remove large leaves; reserve. Working from the bottom, use paring knife to hollow out cabbage, leaving shell and leaves in a large bowl; add boiling water to cover; let stand 10 minutes. Drain. Combine beef, onion, pepper, eggs, rice and seasonings. Fill cabbage shell, mounding mixture on top. Dot with butter. Press softened outside leaves around stuffed cabbage shell. Tie with soft cord or secure with toothpicks to hold shape. Place in Dutch oven. Combine remaining ingredients; pour around cabbage. Cover. Bake at 325 degrees for 2½ hours.

Leona Teodori, Warren, Mich.

ITALIAN FRIED BOW TIES
Makes 15-20 dozen

6 large eggs
1 tablespoon vanilla
1/2 teaspoon salt
6 cups flour
1/2 cup sugar
1/3 cup butter *or* oil
1 tablespoon baking powder

Beat eggs. Add remaining ingredients to make a soft dough. Knead well. Let stand 15 minutes. Knead 5 minutes longer. Place in bowl and keep covered. Roll out small amount of dough at a time, rolling each piece as thin as possible. Cut in narrow strips, about 4 inches long. Form in shapes of a bow tie.

Fry in deep fat, about 360 degrees until delicately browned. Drain on paper towels. Drizzle lightly with thin confectioners' sugar icing or sprinkle with confectioners' sugar. Keeps well in tightly covered container.

Diantha Susan Hibbard, Rochester, N.Y.

RANTOTT CSIRKE (HUNGARIAN OVEN-FRIED CHICKEN)
Serves 4

½   cup butter *or* margarine
½   cup all-purpose flour
1   (2–2½-pound) broiler-fryer, cut up
2   eggs
1   teaspoon salt
1   tablespoon paprika
⅛   teaspoon nutmeg
⅛   teaspoon poultry seasoning
2   tablespoons lime juice
1   cup bread crumbs

Heat oven to 350 degrees. In oven melt butter in a 13 x 9 x 2-inch baking dish. Place flour and chicken pieces in a paper bag; coat thoroughly; set aside. Combine and beat together eggs, salt, paprika, nutmeg, poultry seasoning and lime juice. Dip floured pieces, one at a time, in egg mixture. Dip in crumbs; turn to coat evenly. Place chicken in baking dish skin side down. Bake 50 minutes, or until fork-tender, turning once.

Gwen Campbell, Sterling, Va.

DEEP-FRIED CAULI-FLOWER - KVETAK (CZECHOSLOVAKIA)

1 head cauliflower
2 eggs
1/4 cup milk
Salt to taste
1/2 cup flour
2 cups bread crumbs

Separate cauliflower into flowerets. Beat eggs and milk together. Season cauliflower with salt; roll in flour. Dip in egg mixture; coat with bread crumbs. Heat oil to 400 degrees; fry cauliflower until golden brown. Remove from fryer; place in 1-1/2- or 2-quart casserole. Bake at 350 degrees for about 10 minutes or until tender. Do not overcook.

Yes, this is an old family favorite brought over from Czechoslovakia, although it is a favorite among Americans and Canadians as well.

Mrs. Lewis A. Mason, Bokigo, Canada

BOBOTIE (SOUTH AFRICA HAMBURGER PIE)
Serves 10

2½   tablespoons butter *or* margarine
2   cups onion, chopped
2   cups soft bread crumbs
½   cup milk
3   pounds chuck beef (ground)
1   egg
1½   tablespoons curry powder
¼   teaspoon salt
3   tablespoons plum jam
2   tablespoons lime juice
⅓   cup blanched almonds, ground
4   bay leaves
2   lemons, sliced
4   pimiento strips

In skillet melt butter; sauté onion until golden. Soak bread crumbs in milk. Combine with next 7 ingredients. Place bay leaves on bottom of an ungreased 10-inch pie plate. Pat meat mixture on top; bake at 350 degrees for 1 hour.

To garnish:

Arrange lemon slices in a border around edge of meat pie. On center top lay a lemon slice that has been cut halfway through and twisted. Place a pimiento strip on 4 sides; cut into wedges to serve.

Gwen Campbell, Sterling, Va.

KJOTT PIE (NORWEGIAN MEAT PIE)

Serves 4–6

6 eggs
2 1/2 cups bread cubes
1 tablespoon chopped onion
5 strips bacon
1/2 cup chopped celery
1/4 teaspoon garlic salt
1 1/2 teaspoons–1 tablespoon Worcestershire sauce
3/4–1 pound ground beef
2 1/2 cups milk
1/2 teaspoon lemon juice
1 teaspoon salt
1/4 pound cheese, grated
1/2 teaspoon celery salt

Beat 1 egg with 1/2 cup milk. Add 2 1/2 cups bread cubes; let stand for 5 minutes. Add to ground beef. Also add Worcestershire sauce, lemon juice, salt and chopped onion; mix well. Line bottom and sides of casserole dish (7 x 11 x 2-inch) or large pie pan with mixture.

Fry bacon until crisp. Crumble and sprinkle over meat in dish; add grated cheese over this and then add chopped celery. Beat remaining 5 eggs and 2 cups milk together; add celery salt and garlic salt. Pour over mixture in dish. Bake at 400 degrees for 15 minutes. Then lower temperature to 350 degrees for 30 minutes, or until mixture is firm.

Mary M. West, Columbia, Ind.

CHICKEN SALTIMBOCCA (ITALY)

Serves 6

1½   pounds boneless chicken breasts (3 whole breasts)
¼   teaspoon sage
6   thin slices boiled ham
¼   cup flour
¼   cup butter *or* margarine
½   cup white wine
1   (10¾-ounce) can condensed chicken broth

Flatten chicken breasts with the flat side of a knife; rub with sage. Top each breast with 2 slices of ham. Secure with toothpicks. Dust with flour. Brown in butter or margarine in a skillet. Add wine. Bring to a boil, stirring to loosen browned bits. Add broth and bring to a boil. Reduce heat; simmer 5 minutes, or until sauce thickens slightly.

Kenneth McAdams, El Dorado, Ark.

ORIENTAL CHICKEN BREASTS

Serves 4

1/2 cup soy sauce
1/2 cup water
Juice of 1 lime
2 cloves garlic, crushed
Dash of hot pepper sauce
1/2 teaspoon black pepper
2 tablespoons olive oil
1 tablespoon sugar
4 chicken breasts (skinned and boned)

Mix all ingredients, except chicken, in a glass bowl. Marinate breasts several hours in mixture (refrigerate). Cover grill with heavy aluminum foil. Pierce foil with fork. Grill chicken over hot coals, turning once, for about 15 minutes. Chicken is done when no pink shows after piercing with fork. Garnish with lime slices.

POMMES SOUFFLÉS (Puffed Potato Slices)

Serves 4

From France, this recipe is 150 years old.

2 medium-size potatoes
32 ounces cooking oil

Peel potatoes and trim into the shape of a cylinder. Cut potatoes into 1/4-to 3/8-inch slices. Rinse in cold water and dry well. Pour cooking oil into 2 frying pans (16 ounces in each). Heat 1 pan to 325 degrees and the other to 375 degrees. Drop slices in the 325-degree pan and shake back and forth for 7 minutes. Remove and drain for about 5-6 seconds. Place in 375-degree pan and brown. The potatoes will puff up as they brown. Two medium-size potatoes should yield about 30 slices. Not all slices will puff up. For best results, do not use new potatoes.

Kenneth McAdams, El Dorado, Ark.

ORIENTAL VEGETABLES

Serves 4

1 bell pepper, sliced
6 green onions, split lengthwise
12 snow peas
4 ounces fresh mushrooms, sliced
Few water chestnuts, sliced
1 can Chinese noodles

Cook on foil, alongside chicken. Baste foil generously with vegetable oil. Place pepper on foil, and gently stir-fry, using plastic spatula. When pepper appears half-done, add remaining vegetables, and continue stir-frying until done. Serve atop Chinese noodles, with soy sauce.

FINSKA KAKOR (Finnish cakes)

Makes 4 dozen

Mix together thoroughly:
¾   cup soft butter
¼   cup sugar
1   teaspoon almond extract

Stir in:
2   cups sifted flour

Mix thoroughly with hands. Chill dough. Roll out ¼ inch thick. Cut into strips 2½ inches long and ¾ inch wide. Brush tops lightly with 1 egg white, slightly beaten. Sprinkle with mixture of 1 tablespoon sugar and ½ cup finely chopped, blanched almonds. Carefully transfer to ungreased baking sheet. Bake in a 350-degree oven for about 17–20 minutes, or just until cookies begin to turn a very delicate golden brown.

Leona Teodori, Warren, Mich.

HUNGARIAN NOODLES OR KLUSE

Serves 5

2 cups flour
2 eggs
1 cup water
1 teaspoon salt

Beat all the above ingredients with a wooden spoon until the dough is soft, and bubbles form. Make dough somewhat stiff. Cut with a spoon into boiling salted water. Let noodles boil until they rise to the top and boil for 5 minutes. Drain and serve with chicken.

This recipe was made by my mother-in-law. She used to cool the mixture and then fry them with a pound of side pork and onion, like fried potatoes. She did this to serve a family of 15 at one time. This recipe is about 50 years old. It takes about 20 minutes to prepare.

Theresa Guillaume, Mosinee, WI

HONEY-HAM CHOW MEIN

1 medium green pepper
1 medium onion
2 ribs celery
1 small can mushrooms
2 tablespoons vegetable oil
2 cups cooked ham strips
1 cup chicken bouillon
2 tablespoons honey
1 tablespoon corn starch
1 tablespoon soy sauce
1/4 cup water

Cut green pepper in strips, onion in slices, celery in pieces (for Chinese effect, cut on the bias) and mushrooms in slices. Heat oil; add onions and ham; cook until ham is slightly browned. Add bouillon, pepper, celery and mushrooms; cover tightly; cook slowly for 6 minutes. Mix remaining ingredients; add and cook for 2 minutes, stirring constantly. Serve with crisp noodles, or over a bed of rice.

Mrs. Gwen Campbell, Sterling, VA

ITALIAN VEGETABLE SALAD

1 head cauliflower, cut into pieces
1 bunch broccoli, cut into pieces
3 zucchini, sliced
5 tomatoes, cut into chunks or 1 basket of cherry tomatoes
1 can black pitted olives, sliced
1 (16 ounce) bottle of Seven Seas Italian Dressing
1 teaspoon salt
1/2 teaspoon pepper

Mix all ingredients together and let stand overnight in refrigerator. This is a great recipe for picnics or potlucks.

Edna Mae Seelos, Niles, IL

ENCHILADA CASSEROLE

12 corn tortillas
2 pounds hamburger
2 tablespoons chili powder
1/2 teaspoon garlic powder
1 medium onion, chopped
15 ounce can tomato sauce
Salt and pepper
1 cups grated Colby or Cheddar cheese
1 can cream of chicken soup
3/4 cup milk

Brown meat, garlic and onion. Add tomato sauce, chili powder, salt and pepper. Heat 9 x 13 inch pan. Line bottom with 6 tortillas. Add meat on top. Cover with 6 more tortillas. Spread chicken soup over these and then milk. Cover with cheese. Bake 25 minutes at 350 degrees. A very easy and tasty dish!

Mrs. Carrie Orth, Burlington, IA

QUICK MEXICAN DISH

Serves 6-8

1 can cream of cheese soup
1 can cream of onion soup
16 ounce can tomatoes, chopped and drained
1 pound ground beef
1 package taco seasoning
8 ounce package Cheddar cheese, grated
11 ounce package Doritos, crushed
Onion, chopped
16 ounce can corn, drained
1 can green chilies, chopped

Brown meat and onion; drain. Add seasonings and corn. Mix together. Add soups and tomatoes. Grease an oblong baking dish. In bottom of dish crush Doritos to completely cover the bottom. Add meat mixture, then pour soup mixture over the meat. Top with cheese. Bake 350 degrees for 25 minutes.

Add sour cream on top of baked casserole, and sliced ripe olives. This is quick and easy!

Patricia Staley, Westmont, IL

ENCHILADA SQUARES

1 pound ground beef
1 cup chopped onion
4-ounce can diced green chilies, drained
4 eggs
8-ounce can tomato sauce
5-1/3-ounce can (2/3 cup) evaporated milk
1 (12-ounce) envelope enchilada sauce mix and 1 teaspoon chili powder
1 cup shredded Cheddar cheese
1/2 cup sliced black olives

Brown beef and onion, drain. Spread meat mixture in lightly buttered 10 x 6 x 2-inch baking dish. Sprinkle diced green chilies over meat mixtures. Beat eggs, tomato sauce, evaporated milk, enchilada sauce. Sprinkle sliced black olives over top.

If desired, sprinkle 2 cups corn chips over top.

Bake in a 350 degree oven for 25 minutes or until set. Sprinkle with cheese and bake 5 more minutes. Let set 10 minutes before cutting.

Barbara June Ohde, Atkinson, NE

167

VIENNESE POPPY SEED CAKE

Makes 1 large tube cake

1/2 pound butter, softened
4 beaten egg yolks
4 stiffly beaten egg whites (not dry)
1-1/2 cups sugar
1 teaspoon baking soda
1/2 pint sour cream
2 cups flour
2 teaspoons vanilla
2-1/4 ounces poppy seeds

Cream butter; gradually beat in sugar until fluffy. Stir in poppy seeds and vanilla with beaten egg yolks. Add sour cream that has been mixed with baking soda to creamed mixture, *alternately* with flour, ending with flour. Fold in the stiffly beaten egg whites. Pour into an ungreased 9- or 10-inch tube pan. Bake in a 350-degree oven for 1 hour or until it tests done. Cool on rack 15 minutes. Loosen and remove from pan. Completely cool on rack. This moist cake needs no frosting and freezes well.

Joan Ross, Amenia, N.Y.

RUMANIAN APPLE TORTE

2 eggs
1/2 cup sugar
1/2 cup sifted all-purpose flour
1/2 teaspoon baking powder
1/4 teaspoon salt
1 cup chopped apples
1/2 cup chopped walnuts

Beat eggs until light, gradually add sugar and beat until fluffy. Sift dry ingredients and add to mixture. Add apples and nuts; blend well.

Bake in greased 8x8-inch pan at 325 degrees for 40 minutes. There is no shortening in this recipe. Delicious!

Mildred V. Schuler, Beaver Falls, Pa.

DUTCH TEA CAKES (KLETSKOPPEN)

This recipe is more than 400 years old and originated in the Dutch city of Leyden.

1-1/2 cups brown sugar
2 tablespoons water
1/4 cup butter
1 teaspoon cinnamon
1 cup ground almonds
1 cup flour

Mix sugar and water to make a thick paste. Add butter, cinnamon, almonds, and flour. Shape into small rounds, about 1 inch in diameter, on a baking sheet greased with unsalted fat. Place at least 2 inches apart. Bake about 15 minutes in 350-degree oven. Remove from oven; let stand 30 seconds and lift from baking sheet with spatula. If wafers become too hard to remove easily, return to oven for a minute, then remove.

Agnes Ward, Erie, Pa.

POTATO DUMPLINGS (GERMANY)

Serves 6–8

3 pounds medium potatoes
2 medium eggs
1 cup unsifted all-purpose flour
1/2 cup packaged dry bread crumbs
1/4 teaspoon nutmeg
1/4 cup chopped parsley
Salt
Dash of pepper

Cook unpeeled potatoes, covered, in boiling water just until tender—about 30 minutes. Drain; cool slightly; peel.

Put potatoes through ricer. Spread on paper towels to dry well. Turn potatoes into large bowl. Lightly toss with 2-1/2 teaspoons salt and the dash pepper. Make a well in center; break eggs into it.

Sift 3/4 cup flour over eggs. Then add bread crumbs, nutmeg, and parsley. With hands, work mixture until it is smooth and holds together. Shape into approximately 18 egg-size balls. Roll in remaining flour.

Meanwhile, in large pan, bring about 2 quarts lightly salted water to boiling point; reduce heat. Drop in at one time just enough potato balls to fit comfortably in pan. Boil gently, uncovered, 2 minutes after they rise to surface. With slotted spoon, transfer dumplings to paper towels; drain. Serve hot.

Judie Betz, Eureka, Calif.

PUACKI (POLISH DOUGHNUTS)

2 cups milk
1 scant cup butter
2 packages dry yeast
5 eggs
1-1/4 cups sugar
1-1/2 teaspoons vanilla extract
1/2 teaspoon lemon extract
1/2 teaspoon salt
8-10 cups flour
1 stick butter

Dissolve yeast in 2 tablespoons sugar and a little warm water. Scald milk; add butter to it and let cool. Beat eggs, sugar, salt, and the two extracts until very light in color, at least 7 minutes. Add flour, a little at a time; beat after each addition. This is not a sticky dough. Let rise in bowl until double, then roll out 1/2-inch thick and cut 2-inch rounds with a biscuit cutter. Let rise again, until double. Fry in hot oil (deep-fat fry) until brown on one side; turn and brown on the other; lift out of fat and drain on a brown paper sack. Melt butter; dip doughnuts in butter then shake in a paper sack with some sugar. Doughnuts are ready to eat. These can be frozen before you dip in melted butter and shake in sugar.

Kathleen Dwyer, Saginaw, Minn.

168

MEXICAN PIE

Crust:
2 cups beef broth
1 cup long-grain rice
1 tablespoon margarine
1 teaspoon salt
2 eggs, slightly beaten
2 tablespoons chopped pimiento

Filling:
1 pound ground beef
1 garlic clove, crushed
1 teaspoon cumin
1/2 teaspoon salt
1/2 cup mild taco sauce
1 egg, beaten

Guacamole:
1 large avocado, peeled and quartered
1 tablespoon chopped onion
1 tablespoon mild taco sauce
1/2 teaspoon salt
1/2 teaspoon lemon juice

1 cup sour cream

Crust: Grease a 10-inch pie pan. In medium saucepan, heat broth to boiling. Stir in rice, margarine and salt. Return to a boil. Cover reduce heat; simmer until rice is tender. Remove from heat; let cool slightly; stir in eggs and pimiento. Press against bottom and sides of pie plate.

Filling: Preheat oven to 350 degrees. In skillet, brown beef. Drain. Stir in garlic, cumin and salt; cook 2 more minutes. Remove from heat; stir in taco sauce and egg. Spoon filling into crust. Bake 25 minutes.

Guacamole: In small bowl, mash 3 avocado quarters (reserve 1 quarter for garnish). Stir in remaining ingredients. Cover and set aside.

Remove pie from oven. Spread guacamole over meat. Top with sour cream. Return to oven and bake 5 more minutes. Slice remaining avocado; sprinkle on pie.

Suzanne Dawson, Cypress, TX

CRAB MEAT PIES (BRIKS)

Makes 10 pies

4 tablespoons butter
2 medium sized onions, finely chopped
3 cloves garlic, crushed
1/4 cup finely chopped fresh coriander leaves
1 hot pepper, finely chopped
1 teaspoon salt
1/2 teaspoon pepper
4.5-ounce can crab meat, drained
1/2 cup Parmesan cheese
11 small eggs
10 sheets filo dough
Oil for frying

In frying pan, melt butter. Over medium heat, stir-fry onions, garlic, coriander leaves, hot pepper, salt and pepper for 10 minutes. Remove from heat. Make a filling by stirring in crab meat and cheese; set aside. Beat one of the eggs; set aside. Fold a sheet of filo dough over twice to make a square. Place 1/10 of the filling in center; form into a well. Keep dough soft by placing wet towel over sheets while making pies. Brush edges of square with beaten egg; break an egg into the well; fold over to form a triangle. Press edges together. Turn them in about 1/2"; brush again with egg to make sure they are well sealed. In frying pan, pour oil to 3/4" thickness; heat; gently slide in pies; fry over slightly higher than medium heat for about 2 minutes on each side, or until sides are golden brown. Remove and place on paper towels; drain. When all the pies are finished, serve immediately.

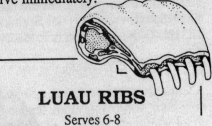

LUAU RIBS

Serves 6-8

1/2 cup brown sugar, firmly packed
2 teaspoons ginger
1/3 cup catsup
1/3 cup vinegar
2 cloves garlic, minced
2 (4-1/2-ounces each) cans apple and apricot baby food

2 tablespoons soy sauce or Worcestershire sauce
6 to 8 pounds meaty spareribs
1 teaspoon salt
Dash of pepper

Mix brown sugar and ginger. Combine with baby food, catsup, vinegar, soy sauce and garlic. Rub ribs with salt and pepper. Place ribs, meat side up, on rack in a shallow pan. Bake at 450 degrees for 15 minutes; pour off fat. Reduce oven temperature to 350 degrees. Baste ribs with sauce and continue baking for 1-1/2 hours (depending on your oven.) While baking, baste with sauce several times.

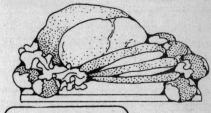

ITALIAN TURKEY LOAF

1-1/4 pounds ground turkey
1 cup egg plant, diced
1 onion, chopped
6-8 mushrooms, chopped
1 egg white, beaten
1/3 teaspoon sage
1/3 teaspoon tarragon
2 tablespoons low sodium tomato sauce
2 cups bran flakes cereal
1 medium pepper, chopped
2 medium tomatoes, peeled and chopped
1 whole egg, beaten
1/3 teaspoon oregano
1 clove garlic
1/4 teaspoon pepper

Place all ingredients, except tomato sauce, in large mixing bowl. Mix until well blended. Press mixture in loaf pan 8x5x3-inches. Spread tomato sauce evenly over top of loaf; bake at 350 degrees for 30 minutes. Remove from oven and drain off excess liquid. Return to oven for additional 45 minutes or until loaf is done. Allow to sit a few minutes before removing from pan and slicing.

Winnie Dettmer, Canfield, Ohio

SLEEK GREEK SALAD
Serves 6

1/2 pound cooked shrimp
1/2 pound feta cheese (rinsed, patted dry, and crumbled)
4 green onions, sliced
2 teaspoons fresh chopped oregano (or 3/4 teaspoon dried)
2 teaspoons fresh chopped basil (or 3/4 teaspoon dried)
1/4 cup sliced ripe olives
3 tomatoes (peeled, cored, and chopped)
1 (12-ounce) package uncooked spaghetti

In a 3-quart bowl combine the shrimp, cheese, onions, seasonings, olives, and tomatoes. Let stand at room temperature for 1 hour. Cook spaghetti in 5 quarts water until tender; drain. Toss the salad ingredients with the hot pasta and serve immediately.

This is a warm main-dish salad that is rich-tasting even though it is low in calories.

Sharon Vircks, Auburn, Wash

ORIENTAL CABBAGE SALAD
Serves 6-8

4 cups shredded cabbage
1/4 cup sliced onion
4 ounces sliced water chestnuts
1 (3-ounce) package oriental noodle soup with chicken flavor
3 tablespoons cider vinegar
2 tablespoons sugar
2 tablespoons salad oil
1/2 teaspoon pepper
1/4 teaspoon salt

Crush noodles to separate. Place in colander. Pour 2 cups boiling water over noodles to soften slightly. Combine drained noodles, cabbage, onions, and water chestnuts in large bowl.

For dressing mix together vinegar, sugar, oil, pepper, salt, and seasoning packet from soup mix. Mix well and pour over cabbage; toss. Chill a few hours before serving.

Loretta M. Brown, Birdsboro, Pa.

GATEAU AUX POIRES (PEAR CAKE)
Serves 8

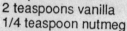

2 eggs, plus 1 yolk
1 cup skim milk
2 teaspoons vanilla
1/4 teaspoon nutmeg
1 cup flour
1/3 cup sugar
1/4 teaspoon salt
1 teaspoon baking powder
3 pears
1/2 tablespoon confectioners' sugar

Preheat oven to 375 degrees. In a mixing bowl, beat together eggs, egg yolk, skim milk, vanilla, and nutmeg. Sift flour with sugar, salt, and baking powder; gradually add liquid ingredients. Pour batter into a deep 9-inch pie dish.

Peel pears; cut in half lengthwise, removing the cores and seeds. Place pears in a circle in the batter, cut sides down and with the stem ends toward center. Do not allow the bottom ends to touch the sides of the dish. The rounded sides of the pears will be above the batter level.

Place in the oven and bake for 35 minutes or until top is a deep golden brown and pears are tender when pierced with a small, sharp knife. The batter will have puffed. Pear Cake should be eaten warm or cool. Sprinkle with confectioners' sugar before serving.

Suzan L. Wiener, Spring Hill, Fla.

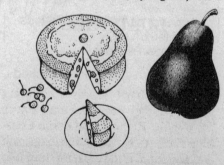

HELADO DE MANGO (MANGO SHERBET)
Serves 6

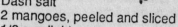

1 cup water
3/4 cup sugar
Dash salt
2 mangoes, peeled and sliced
1/2 cup light cream
1/4 cup lemon juice
2 egg whites

In saucepan combine water, 1/2 cup sugar, and salt. Cook 5 minutes; cool. In blender combine mangoes and cream, blending until smooth. Stir in cooled syrup and lemon juice. Place in freezer until partially frozen. Beat egg whites to soft peaks; gradually add 1/4 cup sugar, beating to stiff peaks. Place partially frozen mixture into chilled mixing bowl; break into chunks. Beat until mixture is smooth. Fold in beaten egg whites. Freeze until firm.

Kenneth McAdams, El Dorado, Ark.

CZECHOSLOVAKIAN COOKIES
Makes 2-1/2 dozen

1 cup butter
1 cup sugar
2 egg yolks
2 cups flour, sifted
1 cup walnuts, chopped
1/2 cup raspberry or strawberry jam

Cream butter until soft. Gradually add the sugar, creaming until light and fluffy. Add egg yolks and blend well. Gradually add flour and mix thoroughly. Then fold in nuts. Spoon half the batter into a buttered 8-inch square cake pan; spread evenly. Top with jam. Cover with remaining cookie dough. Bake in a moderately slow 325-degree oven for 1 hour or until lightly browned. Cool and cut into 1x2-inch bars.

This cookie recipe is over 100 years old and is also called Kolacky.

Ella Evanicky, Fayetteville, Texas

CANTON ALMOND COOKIES
Makes 5 dozen

3 cups all-purpose flour
1 cup sugar
1/4 teaspoon salt
1/2 teaspoon baking soda
1 cup shortening, room temperature
1 egg, lightly beaten
1/4 teaspoon vanilla extract
1/2 teaspoon almond extract
1 cup almonds, blanched and split

Mix flour, sugar, salt, and baking soda. Add shortening; cut in until mixture resembles cornmeal. Add egg; vanilla extract, and almond extract. Mix until egg is absorbed and mixture is smooth. Shape into 3/4-inch balls; place on ungreased baking sheet. Flatten each cookie with a flour-dipped fork; press an almond half into the center. Bake at 350 degrees for 20 minutes or until a pale golden brown. Remove from baking sheet; cool on rack.

Gwen Campbell, Sterling, Va.

SWISS POTATO SOUP
Serves 8

1 large onion, chopped (1 cup)
3 tablespoons butter
3 large potatoes, cut up
1 teaspoon salt
1/4 teaspoon dry mustard
1/8 teaspoon white pepper
3 cups water
2 cups milk
8 ounces sliced Swiss cheese, cut up
2 tablespoons parsley, chopped

Sauté onion in butter until soft; stir in potatoes, salt, mustard, pepper, and water. Heat to boiling; cover. Simmer 30 minutes, or until potatoes are very soft; press through a fine sieve into large bowl; return to soup kettle. Stir in milk; heat slowly just to boiling. Stir in cheese until melted. Ladle into soup bowls or plates; sprinkle with parsley. You can chill several hours and serve cold, if you prefer.

Mrs. Merle Mishler, Hollsopple, Pa.

GRAMMA'S POTATO PANCAKES "KATOFEL PANNE KUCHEN" (GERMAN)

2 pounds peeled, raw potatoes
1 tablespoon salt
2 tablespoons flour
3 eggs, separated
1 cup milk or cream
Fat for frying (I use Crisco)

Grate raw potatoes into a bowl with cold water. Shortly before frying, squeeze through a clean cloth. Add salt, flour, egg yolks, and milk; beat egg whites until stiff and fold into potato mixture. Drop tablespoons of this mixture into hot fat in frying pan. Fry pancakes until crisp and golden. They should be served at once with pot roast or as a main dish with salad, vegetables, and fruit.
Note: 1/2 cup finely grated onion can be added to batter, before adding egg whites.

Agnes Ward, Erie, Pa.

CABBAGE ROLLS

12 cabbage leaves
1 pound lean ground beef
1/2 pound ground pork
1/2 cup rice, long grain
1 onion, chopped
2 eggs, beaten
1 teaspoon salt
1/2 teaspoon pepper
1 large onion, sliced

Sauce (Sweet-Sour):
1 can tomato soup, mixed with 1/4 cup water
1 (1-pound) can stewed tomatoes
1/3 cup lemon juice
1/8 teaspoon pepper
1/4 cup brown sugar

Add cabbage leaves to boiling water. Simmer 4 minutes until leaves are pliable. Remove and drain. Combine beef, pork, rice, onion, eggs, salt and pepper. Divide meat mixture into 12 balls and place in center of cabbage leaves. Fold sides over stuffing and fasten with toothpicks.

Preheat oven to 375 degrees. Place cabbage rolls in a greased 3-quart casserole. Add onion slices and pour sauce over rolls. Sprinkle with brown sugar and cover. Bake, covered, for 11/2–2 hours.

This may be served with a mushroom sauce, regular tomato sauce or sour cream, instead of the sweet-sour sauce. Reheated, they are even more delicious!

Betty L. Perkins, Hot Springs, Ark.

ITALIAN CHEESECAKE
Serves 6–8

Crust:
2 cups sifted flour
1/2 teaspoon salt
2/3 cup butter
2 tablespoons dry sherry
1 teaspoon water

Filling:
1-1/2 pounds ricotta cheese
1/3 cup toasted, chopped almonds
1 pound chopped citron
1 pound diced candied orange peel
1 pound diced candied cherries
1 teaspoon vanilla
4 eggs, slightly beaten
1/3 cup sugar

Sift flour and salt together. Cut in butter. Add sherry and water, stirring with a fork. Wrap dough in waxed paper and chill for 1 hour.

Mix the ricotta cheese, almonds, citron, orange peel, cherries and vanilla. Combine eggs and sugar, then add to cheese mixture, stirring until blended. Roll two-thirds of dough between 2 floured sheets of waxed paper in a circle to fit a 9-inch, loose-bottom cake pan or a 10-inch pie plate. Fit rolled dough in pan. Fill with cheese mixture. Roll remaining dough and cut into 1/2-inch strips. Arrange strips in a lattice pattern on top of filling. Crimp edges. Bake at 350 degrees for 45 minutes, or until lightly browned and crust is golden. Cool.

Leona Teodori, Warren, Mich.

RASPBERRY OATCAKE ROUNDS
Makes 18

½ cup hydrogenated shortening
1 cup oats *or* quick-cooking oats
1 cup all-purpose flour
⅓ cup granulated sugar
½ teaspoon baking soda
¼ teaspoon salt
2–3 tablespoons cold water
½ cup red raspberry jam
⅓ cup confectioners' sugar

Cut shortening into oats, flour, sugar, baking soda and salt until mixture resembles fine crumbs. Add cold water, 1 tablespoon at a time, until mixture forms a stiff dough. Roll until ½ inch thick on lightly floured surface. Cut 9 (2½-inch) rounds with a biscuit cutter and 9 (2½-inch) rounds with a doughnut cutter. Place on ungreased baking sheet. Bake in 375-degree oven until oatcakes start to brown, 12–15 minutes. Cool on wire rack. Spread raspberry jam on oatcakes cut with biscuit cutter; place oatcake cut with doughnut cutter on top. Fill center with raspberry jam. Dust top of oatcake with confectioners' sugar.

This recipe originated from Scotland. It is an old family recipe that was altered to be even more tasty and colorful by the addition of red raspberry jam and confectioners' sugar.

Tillie Minarik, Verdigre, Neb.

GREEK PASTITSIO BAKE
Serves 8

Pasta Layer:
2 cups cooked, drained elbow macaroni
2 eggs, beaten
1/3 cup grated Parmesan cheese
1 tablespoon butter, melted

In large bowl stir together above ingredients and spoon evenly into a 13x9-inch shallow baking dish.

Meat Layer:
1 pound ground beef, lean
1/2 cup onion, finely chopped
1 clove garlic, finely chopped
1 (8-ounce) can tomato sauce
1/8 teaspoon pepper
1/4 teaspoon ground allspice
1/4 teaspoon cinnamon
1/4 teaspoon nutmeg
2 teaspoons instant beef bouillon granules *or* 2 beef bouillon cubes

In large skillet, brown meat; pour off fat. Stir in onion and garlic; cook and stir until onion is tender. Add tomato sauce, spices, bouillon, and pepper. Mix well and simmer for 10 minutes. Spoon evenly over macaroni mixture.

Cream Sauce:
3 tablespoons butter or margarine
2 tablespoons flour
1 teaspoon chicken-flavored bouillon (instant) *or* 1 bouillon cube
1/8 teaspoon pepper
1/4 cup grated Parmesan cheese
2 cups milk

Melt butter or margarine; stir in flour, chicken bouillon, and pepper. Gradually stir in milk. Cook and stir over medium heat until slightly thickened. Remove from heat and stir in 1/4 cup grated Parmesan cheese. Spoon over the meat layer. Cover; bake at 325 degrees for 30 minutes, or until bubbly. Garnish with parsley. *Really tasty!*

Agnes Ward, Erie, Pa.

CAULIFLOWER ITALIANO
Serves 6

1 tablespoon chopped onion
1 small clove garlic, crushed
2 tablespoons low-calorie Italian salad dressing
3 cups small fresh cauliflowerets
2 tablespoons green pepper, chopped
1 cup cherry tomatoes, halved
1/2 teaspoon salt
1/8 teaspoon dried basil leaves, crushed

In an 8-inch skillet cook onion and garlic in salad dressing until tender; add cauliflowerets and 1/4 cup water. Cook, covered, over low heat for 10 minutes. Add green pepper; cook until cauliflower is tender, about 5 minutes. Stir in remaining ingredients; heat thoroughly. (35 calories per serving)

Charlotte Forney, Bellevue, Ohio

SHORTCUT CASSOULET
Serves 6

2 tablespoons oil
1 pound ground lamb
1 onion, chopped
4 cloves garlic, minced
6 cups white beans, cooked

3 cups sliced turnips
3 cups chicken stock
2 tablespoons rosemary
4 teaspoons oregano
2 tablespoons cornstarch
2 tablespoons cold water
4 scallions, thinly sliced

In a 10-inch Dutch oven or 5-quart heavy-bottom pan, heat oil and brown lamb with onions and garlic. Add cooked beans, turnips, stock, rosemary and oregano. Cover pan and simmer until turnips are tender. Dissolve cornstarch in cold water and add to the simmering mixture. Stir until thickened. Garnish with scallions before serving.

Leona Teodori, Warren, Mich.

ITALIAN BROCCOLI
Serves 4–6

1 bunch of broccoli
½ cup olive oil (any oil can be used)
2 tablespoons lemon juice
2 cloves garlic, crushed
¼ teaspoon oregano
Salt and pepper to taste

Cook broccoli in 1 inch of boiling water for 10–12 minutes, or until tender. Drain. Meanwhile, mix together remaining ingredients and pour over drained broccoli. Serve hot or cold.

Harriet Silverman, Plainview, N.Y.

DUTCH APPLE CAKE

3 cups flour
2 cups sugar
1 cup oil
2 teaspoons vanilla
3 teaspoons baking powder
1/2 cup orange juice
4 eggs

Mix all above ingredients together in bowl with electric mixer. Pour half of batter into greased and floured tube pan. Layer half of apple mixture into batter, and then spread on rest of batter. Pour rest of apple mixture on top. Bake in preheated 350 degree oven for 1 hour and 10 minutes until golden brown. Cool 1 hour in pan before removing.

Apple Mixture:

4 or 5 apples, thinly sliced
2 teaspoons cinnamon
5 tablespoons sugar

Toss together in bowl until apples are coated.

Mrs. Joseph E. Yokitis,
Sinking Spring, PA

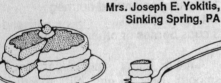

PALACINKY (THIN PANCAKES)

2 eggs
Pinch of salt
3 tablespoons sugar
2 cups milk
2 cups flour
1/4 cup butter for pan
Jam

Beat together eggs, salt, sugar, milk, and flour until smooth. Heat a frying pan; brush with butter. Pour in a thin layer of batter and spread by tilting the pan. Pancakes must be very thin, almost transparent. Fry on both sides to a golden brown. Spread with jam, roll up, and dust with vanilla bean flavored powdered sugar.

Palacinky is the name for thin pancakes, usually served around the holidays—very similar to crepe suzettes.

BUCHE DE NOEL (FRENCH YULE LOG)

Serves 8

Spongecake:

4 eggs
2 egg yolks
3/4 cup granulated sugar
1 teaspoon vanilla
1 cup sifted all-purpose flour
1/2 teaspoon baking powder
3 tablespoons unsalted butter, melted
Confectioners' sugar
Raspberry preserves

Mocha Butter Cream Frosting:

1/4 cup butter or margarine
2 cups confectioners' sugar (divided)
1 teaspoon vanilla extract
1-1/2 tablespoons instant coffee powder
2 ounces bittersweet chocolate, melted
2 to 4 tablespoons heavy cream

To make cake, line greased jelly roll pan (15-1/2x10-1/2) with wax paper. Grease and dust lightly with flour. Set aside. In large bowl, put eggs, egg yolks, sugar, and vanilla. Beat at high speed for 8 minutes. Mixture will triple in volume and be creamy. Fold in sifted flour and baking powder gently with slotted spoon, lifting to aerate. Fold in melted butter. Do not over-fold. Pour batter into prepared pan. Bake at 350 degrees for 20-25 minutes. Remove from oven.

While cake is still in pan, cut off crisp edges. Invert pan on towel dusted with confectioners' sugar. Remove wax paper at once. Roll both cake and towel together. Cool on rack, seam side down. Unroll carefully and fill with preserves. Roll again. Frost.

To make frosting, blend butter, 1 cup confectioners' sugar. Add coffee, dissolved in vanilla. Add chocolate and heavy cream. Add remaining 1 cup confectioners' sugar until desired consistency.

ENCHILADAS

1 pound ground beef
1 onion, chopped
2 teaspoons salt
1/4 teaspoon pepper
2 teaspoons chili powder
1 dozen corn tortillas
2 cups sauce (recipe follows)
1-1/2 cups sharp grated cheese

Brown meat and onion; add seasonings. Dip each tortilla in warm oil. On each one, spoon 2 tablespoons sauce, a generous tablespoon of filling and a sprinkling of cheese; roll up and place close together in large pan. Pour remaining sauce and cheese over top. Bake at 350 degrees for 15-20 minutes.

Sauce:

1 (No. 2-1/2) can tomatoes
1 medium onion, chopped
2 teaspoons chili powder
1/8 teaspoon oregano
1 (6-ounce) can tomato paste
1 garlic clove, minced
1/2 teaspoon salt
1/4 teaspoon cayenne pepper

Combine above ingredients. Simmer about 1 hour until slightly thickened.

Jean Baker, Chula Vista, Calif.

SWEDISH TOAST

1 cup margarine
1-1/2 cups sugar
1 cup commercial sour cream
1/2 cup ground almonds
1/4 teaspoon salt
2 eggs
3-3/4 cups flour
1 teaspoon soda

Mix all ingredients and pour into two greased and floured loaf pans. Bake in 350-degree oven for 45 minutes. Cool. Slice and place slices on cookie sheet. Place in oven again for 13-15 minutes until lightly browned, or slice as you want and use your toaster. Then spread the toast with butter and eat. Delicious!

Sandra Young, Victoria, Texas

GERMAN-STYLE BEANS
Serves 6

 4   slices bacon
 ½   cup onion, chopped
1½   tablespoons sugar
1½   tablespoons flour
 ¼   teaspoon celery seed
 ½   teaspoon salt
 2   (15½-ounce) cans green and shelled beans
 ⅓   cup vinegar

Cook bacon until crisp; remove and drain bacon. Add onion to bacon drippings. Cook until tender. Add sugar, flour, celery seed and salt. Cook until bubbly. Drain beans; reserve ⅓ cup liquid. Add bean liquid and vinegar to flour mixture. Stir; add beans. Simmer about 10–15 minutes, or until slightly thickened and thoroughly heated. Crumble bacon and add to beans.

Leota Baxter, Ingalls, Kan.

APPLE STRUDEL (GERMANY)
Serves 8

2 cups sifted flour
3 teaspoons baking powder
1/2 teaspoon salt
3 tablespoons sugar
1/4 cup shortening
2/3-3/4 cup milk
Butter, melted
1 teaspoon cinnamon
3/4 cup apples, chopped
1/2 cup brown sugar
1 tablespoon cream *or* half-and-half
Confectioners' sugar
1/2 teaspoon vanilla

Sift flour with the baking powder, salt, and 3 tablespoons of sugar. Cut shortening into the dry ingredients until evenly distributed; add milk to make soft dough. Turn onto a lightly floured board and knead gently. Roll dough into a rectangular shape, which is 1/4-inch thick. Brush melted butter over the top surface of rectangle. Combine the cinnamon, 1/2 cup sugar, and apples. Cover the dough's surface with apple-cinnamon mixture. Roll in jelly roll fashion to enclose the fruit filling. Place on a greased cookie sheet; shape the roll into the form of a semicircle. Bake at 400 degrees for 30 minutes. Sprinkle brown sugar over the top during the last 15 minutes of baking time. Combine remaining ingredients for icing. Frost strudel and sprinkle with nuts, if desired.

Zenana Warren, Bloomville, Ohio

EUROPEAN TORTE SQUARES

 ½   pound butter (2 sticks)
 1   cup sugar
 6   egg yolks
 2   cups flour
 1   teaspoon salt
 1   teaspoon baking powder
     Grape jelly

Cream butter and sugar. Add the 6 egg yolks and cream well. Sift flour, salt and baking powder; add to creamed mixture. Pat this mixture on a cookie sheet and spread top surface with grape jelly. Top this with icing (recipe follows).

Icing:
 6   egg whites
 1   cup ground nuts
 1   cup sugar

Beat egg whites until they hold peaks. Add nuts and sugar; blend well. Use this on top of torte. Cut in squares and bake for 30 minutes at 375 degrees.

Jen Lien, Stoughton, Wis.

MEXICAN STUFFED GREEN PEPPERS

6–8 large green peppers
1 pound bulk sausage, *or* 1 pound ground beef
1/2 cup green onion, chopped
1 can chili beef soup
1/2 cup tomato juice
1/2 cup Monterey Jack cheese, grated
1 (12-ounce) can Mexicorn, drained
1 cup cooked rice
1 cup tortilla chips, crushed

Slice off tops of peppers; remove seeds; rinse insides of peppers. Place peppers in a 2-quart casserole; cover and microwave on HIGH for 7–10 minutes. Let stand 4 minutes.

Place sausage and onion in a 2-quart casserole; microwave on HIGH for 4–6 minutes; stir twice. Drain and break up meat. Stir in soup, tomato juice, cheese, Mexicorn and rice. Mix well and spoon into peppers; cover and microwave on (70 percent) MEDIUM HIGH for 7–9 minutes, or until hot. Sprinkle with tortilla chips.

ENGLISH STEAMED FRUIT PUDDING
Serves 8

1/4 pound (1 stick) butter
1/2 cup sugar
1 egg
1 1/2 cups flour
1/2 teaspoon baking soda
1/4 teaspoon ground nutmeg
1/4 cup buttermilk
3 cups berries or other diced fruit

Cream butter and sugar until smooth. Beat in egg. Sift together flour, baking soda and nutmeg. Add to butter mixture, along with buttermilk. (Batter should be firm, but still a little sticky.) With floured hands line a 4-cup mold with 2/3 of the dough. Fill with the fruit. Top with the rest of dough and smooth with a spatula. Cover mold tightly with foil. Place on a steamer rack. Cover and steam over medium heat, 2 1/2–3 hours, or until pastry is done. Cool 15 minutes, then unmold onto a serving platter. Slice to serve and accompany with heavy cream or whipped cream.

I acquired this recipe several years ago from an Englishman, who said this was his favorite dessert. It has brought rave reviews every time I have served it. I've used various fruits but raspberries, apricots and blueberries are my favorites. It freezes well.

Roxanne E. Chan, Albany, Calif.

174

Fantastic FRUITS

BLUEBERRY BUTTER

Makes 8 pints

8 cups blueberries, fresh or dry-
    pack frozen (rinsed and drained)
8 large green cooking apples,
    peeled, cored and sliced
8 cups sugar
4 cups water
1 teaspoon ground allspice
1 teaspoon ground mace
1 teaspoon ground nutmeg

Combine all ingredients in large saucepan or kettle. Bring to a boil; lower heat and simmer 1 hour, stirring occasionally. Cook until mixture is thick. Spoon hot mixture into sterilized glasses. Seal, cool and store in cool, dry place.

APRICOT-APPLE COMPOTE

Serves 3-4

10 dried apricot halves, soaked
4 medium apples
Lemon juice to taste
1/8 teaspoon grated lemon rind
Cinnamon to taste

Pare, quarter, and core apples. Cut into eighths. Place apples in saucepan; add apricots and a few tablespoons of water in which apricots have soaked. Cover and simmer until apples are tender, about 20 minutes. While hot, add cinnamon, lemon juice, and grated rind. Serve hot or cold. (70 calories per serving)

Suzan L. Wiener, Spring Hill, Fla.

FRUIT WHIP

1   (8-ounce) package
    cream cheese
1   can sweetened con-
    densed milk
1   (8-ounce) container
    Cool Whip
1   (No. 2) can fruit cock-
    tail, drained
1   (No. 2) can mandarin
    oranges, drained
1   (No. 2) can chunk
    pineapple, drained
    Any fruits or nuts
    desired

Beat cream cheese and milk until smooth. Add Cool Whip. Fold in drained fruit. Chill and serve in attractive bowl.

Pat Habiger, Spearville, Kan.

FRESH PEACH MUFFINS

1 cup chopped peaches
1 teaspoon lemon juice
1 cup milk
1 egg
1/4 cup margarine
2/3 cup sugar
1/4 teaspoon cinnamon
3 teaspoons baking powder
2 cups unsifted flour

Sprinkle peaches with lemon juice and set aside. Mix remaining ingredients, adding flour last. Fold in fruit. Fill greased muffin tins 2/3 full. Bake at 450 degrees for 20 minutes.

CHEESE-FILLED PEARS

Serves 4

4 pears, halved, peeled, and cored
1 (8-ounce) package of cream
    cheese, softened
1/4 cup honey
1/4 cup vanilla wafer crumbs
1/2 cup crushed pecans

Combine cream cheese, crushed pecans, and honey. Beat until well-blended. Fill pear halves with mixture. Place in shallow baking pan. Sprinkle with vanilla wafer crumbs. Bake 30 minutes at 350 degrees, or until tender.

June Harding, Ferndale, Mich.

BLUEBERRY SALAD

2 packages blackberry gelatin
2 cups blueberries, fresh or frozen
1 (8-1/2-ounce) can crushed
    pineapple, drained
1/2 cup sugar
1 (8-ounce) package cream cheese
1 cup sour cream
1/2 teaspoon vanilla

In large bowl, prepare gelatin as directed on package. Thicken. In medium bowl mix together blueberries and pineapple. Add fruit to gelatin when thickened. In small bowl, cream sugar, cream cheese, sour cream, and vanilla. Spread on gelatin mixture after it congeals. Chopped pecans may be sprinkled on top, if desired.

FRESH STRAWBERRY TAPIOCA

Serves 6-8

1 pint sliced, hulled fresh strawberries
1/2 cup granulated sugar
1/4 cup quick-cooking tapioca
1/4 teaspoon salt
2 tablespoons lemon juice
1/3 cup heavy cream, whipped

Sprinkle berries with 1/4 cup sugar and let stand 30 minutes. Drain and add enough water to juice to make 2 cups. In saucepan, combine juice with rest of sugar, tapioca, and salt. Cook over medium heat, stirring until mixture comes to boil. Cool and stir occasionally. Add berries, lemon juice, and refrigerate. Just before serving, fold in cream.

Suzan L. Wiener, Spring Hill, Fla.

RHUBARB-PINEAPPLE COBBLER

Serves 8-9

1 cup granulated sugar
1 cup water
1 (20-ounce) can crushed pineapple, undrained
3 cups rhubarb, finely cut

Topping:
1 (9-ounce) package white or yellow Jiffy Cake Mix, prepared according to directions
1 (3-ounce) package strawberry gelatin

In a saucepan, combine the first 3 ingredients. Bring to a boil and boil 1 minute, stirring constantly. Set aside. Grease a 9x13-inch pan; put rhubarb on the bottom and pour sauce over all. Place in a 350-degree oven while making cake topping. For topping, prepare cake mix according to directions. Pour this evenly over rhubarb and sauce. Sprinkle dry gelatin over batter and cut in with knife. Return to the oven for 25 to 30 minutes, or until lightly browned.

RHUBARB AND STRAWBERRY PUDDING

4 cups rhubarb
3 cups sugar
1 egg
1/4 teaspoon salt
1/2 cup crushed strawberries

Make a biscuit dough of the following:
2 cups flour
1 teaspoon salt
1 tablespoon sugar
4 teaspoons baking powder
4 tablespoons shortening
3/4 cup milk

Cut the rhubarb into 1-inch pieces. Cook until tender. Add strawberries. Add the sugar, salt, and slightly beaten egg. Pour into a buttered baking dish. Drop the biscuit dough by spoonfuls on top of the rhubarb. Bake 25 minutes in a moderately hot, 375-degree oven. Serve warm, topped with whipped cream.

This is the best pudding ever. You can use ice cream instead of the whipped cream, and strawberries may be omitted, if desired. My family really loves it; so will yours!

Suzan L. Wiener, Spring Hill, Fla.

EASY APPLE TARTS

4 cups peeled, sliced cooking apples
1/2 cup sugar
3 tablespoons flour
1 teaspoon cinnamon
1 teaspoon nutmeg
1 (8-ounce) can Quick Crescent Dinner Rolls

Topping:
1/2 cup brown sugar
1 teaspoon cinnamon
2 tablespoons margarine, melted

Combine first 5 ingredients. Separate dough into 4 triangles. Press 2 of these over bottom of pan. Spread apple mixture over dough and then place 2 remaining rectangles on top. Combine brown sugar and cinnamon; sprinkle over top; drizzle with margarine. Bake at 375 degrees for 30-40 minutes.

BAKED BANANAS AND COCONUT WITH CUSTARD

4 large, firm bananas
2 tablespoons butter
1/2 cup pineapple juice
1/4 cup packed brown sugar
1/8 teaspoon ground mace or nutmeg
1 cup flaked coconut

Heat oven to 400 degrees. Butter a baking dish about 10x6x2-inches. Peel bananas and cut in half lengthwise, then crosswise. Put bananas in prepared baking dish and dot each piece with some of the butter. Combine pineapple juice, brown sugar, and mace or nutmeg and pour over the bananas, then sprinkle coconut over all. Bake for about 12 minutes, or until coconut is browned and bananas are hot. Serve hot, topped with Custard Sauce.

Custard Sauce:
3/4 cup milk
2 egg yolks
2 tablespoons sugar
Pinch of salt
1/2 teaspoon vanilla extract

Scald milk in top of double boiler, over direct heat. Beat egg yolks; blend in sugar and salt, then gradually stir in milk. Pour back into the top of double boiler and set over simmering water. Cook, stirring, until mixture coats a metal spoon, about 10 minutes. Cool quickly and stir in vanilla. This is a delicious, light dessert.

Lillian Smith, Montreal, Quebec, Canada

FROSTY FRESH FRUIT BOWL
Serves 10

2 cups water
1 cup sugar
1/4 cup lemon juice
1-1/2 tablespoons anise seed
1/4 teaspoon salt
1 small pineapple, cut into bite-size chunks
1 small honeydew melon, cut into bite-size chunks
1 small canteloupe, cut into bite-size chunks
2 oranges, cut into bite-size chunks
1 nectarine, cut into wedges
4 apricots, cut into wedges
1 purple plum, cut into wedges
2 cups seedless green grapes
1 lime, sliced

In a saucepan, combine water with sugar, lemon juice, anise seed, and salt; cook 15 minutes until mixture reaches light-syrup consistency; chill. Prepare and combine all fruit; place in a large bowl; pour chilled syrup through a strainer over fruits. Chill until frosty-cold; stir occasionally.

Gwen Campbell, Sterling, Va.

FRUITED BANANA SPLITS
Serves 2

1 1/2 cups cottage cheese
1/2 cup toasted coconut
1 1/2 cups chopped pineapple, drained
1 cup strawberry halves
2 bananas

Combine 1 1/2 cups cottage cheese and 1/2 cup toasted coconut; mix lightly and chill. Combine pineapple and strawberry halves; mix lightly. Slice bananas in pieces or lengthwise. For each salad, arrange bananas in individual dishes and scoop cottage cheese on top of bananas. Surround with fruit and serve with Kraft French Dressing.

To toast coconut, spread in layer pan and toast in oven at 350 degrees until lightly browned, stirring once or twice, so it will not burn.

Edna Askins, Greenville, Texas

RAISIN-NUT PIE

3 eggs
3/4 cup dark corn syrup
1/2 cup firmly packed light brown sugar
1/4 cup margarine, melted
1/4 teaspoon salt
1 teaspoon pure vanilla extract
1 cup raisins
1/2 cup chopped pecans
1 unbaked 9-inch pastry shell

Using a fork, beat eggs lightly in a bowl. Beat in corn syrup, brown sugar, margarine, salt and vanilla until well-blended. Stir in raisins and nuts. Pour into pastry shell and bake in pre-heated 350-degree oven for 40–50 minutes, or until knife inserted half-way between center and edge comes out clean. Cool and serve.

Suzan L. Wiener, Spring Hill, Fla.

PEAR BREAD
Makes 2 loaves

3/4 cup brown sugar
1/2 cup shortening
2 eggs
1/3 cup peeled, mashed, ripe pears
2 tablespoons lemon juice
1 teaspoon vanilla
2 cups flour
1 1/2 teaspoons ground ginger
1 teaspoon ground mace
1/2 teaspoon ground cinnamon
1 teaspoon baking soda
1 teaspoon salt
2 cups coarsely chopped pears
1/2 cup chopped nuts
Sugar Topping:
1/4 cup sugar
1 1/2 teaspoons soft butter

In large bowl, combine sugar, shortening, eggs, mashed pears, lemon juice and vanilla. Beat until smooth.

Combine next 6 ingredients and stir into creamed mixture. Fold in chopped pears and nuts. Pour into two greased and floured loaf pans.

Mix *Sugar Topping* ingredients to make crunchy mixture and sprinkle atop batter in pans.

Bake in preheated 350-degree oven for about 60 minutes. Cool.

Mrs. Agnes Ward, Erie, Penn.

APPLE GRUNT
Serves 5–6

2¼ cups sliced apples, unpeeled
2 cups flour
1 teaspoon baking powder
½ teaspoon soda
½ teaspoon salt
3 tablespoons soft margarine
½ cup sugar
1 egg
½ cup buttermilk

Butter a 10¼ x 6¼ x 2-inch baking pan. Wash apples; cut in quarters; core and thinly slice quarters. Cover with wet toweling to prevent discoloration. Sift flour; measure and resift 3 times with baking powder, soda and salt. Cream margarine and sugar; beat in egg. Add flour mixture in 2–3 portions alternately with buttermilk; begin and end with flour; beat well. Fold in apples. Turn into prepared pan and sprinkle with topping. Bake 30 minutes at 400 degrees.

Topping:
⅓ cup brown sugar
1 tablespoon flour
½ teaspoon cinnamon
2 tablespoons firm margarine

Combine topping ingredients; sprinkle on cake. Bake 30 minutes.

APPLE PLUMPLINGS

2 cups flour
1 teaspoon baking powder
1 cup milk
1 egg, beaten
6 large apples

Mix all ingredients, except apples. Peel apples and core; cut into 1/2-inch cubes. Add to batter. Drop mixture into deep, hot oil by tablespoonfuls. Be sure that each spoonful has some apple pieces in it. When brown, lift out of oil and drain on paper towels or brown paper. Serve while hot.

Joy Shamway, Freeport, Ill.

APPLE BUTTER

Makes 8 half-pints

6 pounds tart apples
6 cups cider *or* apple juice
1/2 teaspoon ground cloves
3 cups sugar
2 teaspoons ground cinnamon

Core and quarter unpared apples. In 4–6 quart kettle, combine apples and cider. Cook about 30 minutes, or until soft. Pass through food mill. Boil gently for 30 minutes, stirring often. Add sugar and spices. Cook and stir over low heat until sugar dissolves. Boil gently, stirring often, until desired thickness. Ladle hot apple butter into hot jars, leaving 1/2-inch headspace. Adjust lids. Process in boiling water bath for 10 minutes.

Melissa Meckley, Cata Wassa, Pa.

FRUIT TACOS WITH CREAM CHEESE

Serves 10

16 ounces cream cheese, softened
2 tablespoons grated orange rind
2–3 tablespoons sugar
3 tablespoons orange juice
2 oranges, peeled and cubed
1 cup strawberries, halved
1 kiwi, peeled, halved and sliced
1 banana, peeled, halved and sliced
1 (20-ounce) can pineapple chunks, drained
1 cup shredded coconut
1 box taco shells

In medium bowl, blend cream cheese, orange rind, sugar and orange juice; chill. Combine cut-up fruit, pineapple and coconut; chill. Heat taco shells according to package directions. Spread cream cheese mixture on shells; top with fruit mixture. Serve immediately.

Laura Hicks, Troy, Mont.

DESERT ISLAND FRUIT DESSERT

Serves 6

2 cups sliced peaches, coarsely chopped
1 apple, peeled and chopped
1/2 cup dates, chopped
1/4 cup dried apricots, chopped
1 banana, peeled and cut into 1-inch pieces
2 oranges, peeled and chopped coarsely
1 cup green seedless grapes
1 cup shredded coconut
Candied ginger
Lettuce
1 packet whipped topping mix
1/2 cup dairy sour cream

In a large bowl gently mix the first five fruits. Spread the lettuce on a large chilled platter; place the fruits on the lettuce leaves. Make the whipped topping according to package directions; fold in the sour cream. Place the orange pieces around the edge of the platter; scatter the grapes across the fruit. Dollop the whipped cream mixture here and there; sprinkle the coconut and candied ginger on the cream dollops.

Gwen Campbell, Sterling, Va.

FRESH CRANBERRY TARTLETS

6 servings

Quick Cranberry Sauce:
2 cups (1/2 pound) fresh cranberries
1 cup water
1 cup sugar
Cheesecake Filling:
1 small package (3 ounces) cream cheese, softened
1/4 cup sugar
1 egg, slightly beaten
1 tablespoon milk
1 teaspoon lemon juice
1/2 teaspoon vanilla
Coconut Pastry:
1/4 cup finely shredded coconut
6 teaspoons finely crushed cornflake crumbs
Ingredients for your favorite pastry recipe

First, make *Quick Cranberry Sauce*

by heating cranberries with water and sugar to boiling point. Stir until sugar dissolves. Boil rapidly until berries pop open (about 5 minutes). This makes 2 cups sauce. Chill.

Make *Cheesecake Filling* by beating cream cheese with sugar until smooth and creamy. Add remaining filling ingredients and again, beat until smooth.

For *Coconut Pastry*, make your favorite pastry recipe, blending in the shredded coconut. Roll out pastry and cut to fill six medium-size muffin tins, just like small pie crusts, fluting or pinching edge to stand 1/2 inch above top of muffin tin. Sprinkle 1 teaspoon cornflake crumbs in the bottom of each crust, and top each with 2 1/2 tablespoons *Cheesecake Filling* mixture.

Bake in 350-degree oven for 25 minutes; cool. Just before serving, fill each tartlet with *Cranberry Sauce*, and top with additional snips of coconut, if desired.

Mrs. Amelia Brown, Pittsburgh, Penn.

APPLE APRICOT MEDLEY

Serves 4

2 large, tart green apples
1 cup dried apricots, about 25 to 35 halves
1/2 cup water
1/3 cup orange juice
1/4 cup lemon juice
1 teaspoon almond extract
Brown sugar, optional
1/2 cup toasted, slivered almonds

Core and slice apples into wedges approximately 1/3-inch thick. In medium-size saucepan, combine apples with apricot halves. Add water, orange and lemon juices, and almond extract to saucepan. Simmer apples and apricots, covered, for 5 minutes. Remove from heat and let stand, covered, for 5 minutes. Taste for sweetness. Stir in brown sugar to taste, if necessary. Put in serving bowl and chill until serving time. Sprinkle with almonds.

Suzan L. Wiener, Spring Hill, Fla.

PEACH CLAFOUTI
Serves 6

5 tablespoons sugar, divided
3 cups sliced, peeled fresh peaches
1 cup milk
1 cup half-and-half cream
3 eggs
1/4 cup flour
Pinch of salt
1 teaspoon vanilla
Confectioners' sugar or vanilla ice
    cream

Sprinkle a well-buttered 1-1/2-quart shallow, oval baking dish with 2 tablespoons sugar. Distribute peaches over the sugar. In a blender, combine milk, cream, eggs, flour, and salt for 2 minutes. Add vanilla and remaining sugar. Blend mixture for a few seconds; then pour over fruit. Bake in preheated 375-degree oven for 45-50 minutes or until puffed and golden.

Sprinkle the Clafouti with confectioners' sugar or top with vanilla ice cream. Serve immediately.
Marcella Swigert, Monroe City, Mo.

PEACH EASE
Serves 8

1 (29-ounce) can sliced peaches
3 tablespoons quick-cooking tapioca
1/2 teaspoon cinnamon
4 tablespoons butter or margarine,
    melted
1/2 cup flour
1/2 cup sugar
1/3 cup milk
2 teaspoons baking powder
1 teaspoon vanilla

Preheat oven to 400 degrees. Place peaches with juice in a 7x11-inch baking pan. Stir in tapioca and cinnamon. In mixing bowl, combine remaining ingredients. Spoon batter over peaches. Bake 25-30 minutes or until cake tests done.

For an extra crunch, sprinkle 1/4 cup chopped pecans over batter before baking.
Agnes Ward, Erie, Pa.

FRUIT ICE

1/2 cup orange juice or 1/3 cup
    pineapple juice
1 tablespoon lemon juice
1/2 cup water
1 egg white

Combine fruit juices and water; freeze. Stir mixture often while freezing. When almost hard, fold in one stiffly beaten egg white. Place in an individual mold and allow to set by returning to freezer.
Suzan L. Wiener, Spring Hill, Fla.

FRUIT PANCAKE PUFF
Serves 4

1/2 cup butter
1 cup all-purpose flour
1 cup milk
4 eggs
1/4 teaspoon salt
2 (10-ounce) packages frozen
    mixed fruit, thawed and drained
2 tablespoons firmly packed
    brown sugar
Pinch of freshly grated nutmeg

Preheat oven to 425 degrees. Melt 1/4 cup butter in heavy 10-inch skillet in oven, 3 to 5 minutes. Mix flour, milk, eggs, and salt in blender until smooth. Pour batter into hot skillet. Bake until pancake is puffed and golden brown, 20 to 25 minutes.

Meanwhile, combine remaining 1/4 cup butter, fruit, brown sugar and nutmeg in medium saucepan. Stir over low heat until butter is melted and sauce is warm, about 5 minutes. Place pancake on serving platter. Cut into 4 wedges. Top with fruit, using slotted spoon, and serve, passing sauce separately.

CHOCOLATE-COVERED STRAWBERRIES

1/2 cup semi-sweet chocolate chips
1 tablespoon corn syrup
5 tablespoons butter or margarine
36 strawberries

Place chips, syrup, and butter in saucepan. Melt over low heat. Stir until smooth. Remove from heat; place in pan of water. Dip berries into chocolate; place on waxed paper. Chill.
Lisa Varner, Baton Rouge, La.

FRITTURA DIFICHI RUSPOLI—(HOT FRIED FIGS)

8 firm black figs or extra large fresh
    prunes, peeled
1/2 cup dark rum
1/3 cup all-purpose flour
1/4 cup chopped walnuts
1/2 teaspoon vanilla extract
1/2 cup water (Mix vanilla and water
    together)
Vegetable oil for frying
Confectioners' sugar

Soak figs in the rum for 1 hour; turn often to completely even out flavor. In a bowl slowly stir the flour into the water and vanilla mixture. Beat until smooth and creamy. Add walnuts and mix well. Put about 3/4 inch of oil into skillet and set on medium high heat. When oil is hot; dip each fig or prune into the prepared batter and drop into the hot oil. Fry until golden brown on each side (about 3 minutes). Sprinkle confectioners' sugar over top and serve hot.
Marie Fusaro, Manasquan, N.J.

SPICED PINEAPPLE CHUNKS

1 (20 ounce) can juice pack pineapple
    chunks
1 tablespoon sugar
1 tablespoon vinegar
3 (3-inch) sticks cinnamon
6 whole cloves

Drain pineapple, reserve juice, set pineapple aside.

Combine reserved juice, sugar, vinegar, stick cinnamon and whole cloves in 1-quart container. Microwave on **HIGH** for 5 minutes. Add pineapple chunks, microwave for 4-6 minutes on **HIGH** stir once. Cool. Store in covered container. Drain. Serve on picks.

STRAWBERRY SWIRL

2 (10-ounce) boxes frozen strawberries *or* 2 cups sliced fresh strawberries
2 tablespoons sugar
1 (3-ounce) package strawberry gelatin
1 cup water, boiling
34 large marshmallows (1/2 pound)
1/2 cup milk
1 cup whipping cream, whipped, *or* 1 package Dream Whip, whipped
Crumb Crust (recipe follows)

Sprinkle sugar over fresh strawberries; let stand 30 minutes. Dissolve gelatin in boiling water. Drain strawberries, reserving juice. Add water to juice to make 1 cup. Add to gelatin; chill until partially set, 1 hour and 15 minutes. Meanwhile, combine marshmallows and milk in double boiler; heat and stir until marshmallows melt. Cool thoroughly; fold in whipped cream. Add berries to gelatin, then fold in marshmallow mixture to marble. Pour into crumb crust. Chill until set. Cut into squares.

Crumb Crust:
Mix 1 cup graham cracker crumbs, 1 tablespoon sugar and 1/4 cup melted margarine. Press firmly into bottom of 9x9x2-inch baking dish. Chill.

This is nice to serve when you are having friends in for dessert and coffee.

Mrs. Albert H. Foley, Lemoyne, Pa.

RHUBARB CRUNCH

CRUST/TOPPING
1 cup flour
1 cup brown sugar
3/4 cup oatmeal
1/2 cup butter *or* margarine, melted
1 teaspoon cinnamon

Mix crust ingredients until crumbly. Press one-half of the mixture into a 9-inch pan. Cover with 4 cups sliced rhubarb.

1 cup sugar
1 cup water
2 tablespoons cornstarch
1 teaspoon vanilla

Cook over medium heat until thickened and clear. Pour over rhubarb. Crumble remainder of crust /topping mixture over top surface and bake at 350 degrees for 1 hour.

Phyliss Dixon, Fairbanks, Alaska

BLUEBERRY PUDDING
Serves 6

1 quart blueberries
2 cups water
1 cup sugar
1/8 teaspoon salt
Butter
8 slices white sandwich bread
Cool Whip

Stew blueberries in water with sugar and salt for 15 minutes. Butter bread slices. Place alternate layers of bread and blueberries in a deep, buttered baking dish. Bake at 350 degrees for 15–20 minutes. Cool and chill. Serve chilled with Cool Whip.

Joy B. Shamway, Freeport, Ill.

EASY FRUIT COBBLER

4 cups canned *or* fresh fruit
2 teaspoons butter
1 cup flour
1 teaspoon baking powder
1 cup sugar
1 cup sweet milk
1/8 teaspoon salt

Melt butter in baking dish (9x13-inch) allowing it to cover bottom; grease sides of dish well. Prepare a thin batter by stirring sugar and baking powder into flour. Beat in milk and salt. Pour batter into baking dish. Spread fruit over batter. (The batter will rise through the fruit and form a nice crust). Bake in a 350-degree oven for 25-30 minutes, or until light golden brown.

Dovie Lucy, McLoud, Okla.

BANANA TURNOVERS

4 cups flour
2 teaspoons salt
1⅓ cups shortening
⅓ cup cold water
4 bananas
8 tablespoons raisins
8 teaspoons sunflower seeds

Mix flour and salt together. Cut in shortening until mixture resembles coarse meal. Sprinkle with water and mix lightly with fork. Divide into 8 balls. Roll each ball out into an 8-inch square on floured board. Cut bananas into slices and put half on 1 half of the square. Add 1 tablespoon raisins and 1 teaspoon sunflower seeds. Fold dough over to make triangle. Seal edges. Bake at 400 degrees for 15–20 minutes on an ungreased cookie sheet. Remove from sheet and cool slightly.

Laura Hicks, Troy, Mont.

LIGHT—ENDING RAINBOW FRUIT BOWL

1 cantaloupe
1 pineapple
1 pint strawberries
1 pint blueberries
2 cups seedless green grapes
2 cups seedless red grapes
2 cups fresh orange sections, cut in half
1 cup sliced and cut peaches

Cut cantaloupe (rind and seeds removed) into bite-size pieces. Cut pineapple (rind and core removed) into bite-size pieces. Halve or quarter strawberries (depending on their size); add to cantaloupe along with blueberries, green and red grapes, fresh orange sections and cut peaches. Mix well, adding enough orange juice to moisten. Serve, topped with a generous dollop of sour cream.

Gwen Campbell, Sterling, Va.

PEACH COBBLER

Serves 8

3 cups sliced fresh peaches
2 tablespoons lemon juice
2 tablespoons butter
4 teaspoons baking powder
1/3 cup butter
3/4 cup sugar
3 tablespoons flour
1/2 teaspoon salt
1 tablespoon sugar
1 egg, well-beaten
3/4 cup milk
2 cups flour

Put peaches in a greased baking dish. Mix together 1 tablespoon sugar and 3 tablespoons flour. Sprinkle over peaches. Sprinkle with lemon juice and dot with 2 tablespoons butter.

Topping:

Sift dry ingredients (2 cups flour, baking powder, salt and sugar); mix in 1/3 cup butter until mixture is like coarse crumbs. Add egg and milk; mix until just moistened.

Drop dough in mounds over peaches. Bake in 425-degree oven for 30 minutes.

Mrs. Olen Begly, West Salem, Ohio

SAUCY BANANA

Makes 1 serving

1 banana
1/2 cup orange juice
1 teaspoon butter
1 tablespoon brown sugar
Dash cinnamon
Frozen yogurt *or* ice cream

Peel and slice banana lengthwise with a table knife. Place banana in microwave bowl or shallow dish. Pour orange juice over banana and dot with butter and brown sugar. Shake a dash of cinnamon on top. Microwave on HIGH (100 percent) for 1 minute; turn and microwave another 30 seconds. May be served with frozen yogurt or vanilla ice cream.

Toaster-oven method: Assemble as above in a metal pan. Bake 12 minutes at 375 degrees.

Peggy Fowler Revels, Woodruff, S.C.

PEACH PECAN CROWN

1 package spice cake mix
1/4 cup melted margarine
2/3 cup packed brown sugar
1 1/2 cups pecan halves (any nuts)
1 pint heavy cream
1/3 cup confectioners' sugar
1/4 teaspoon nutmeg
6 peaches, peeled, sliced, sprinkled with brown sugar
1 1/2 tablespoons light corn syrup

Preheat oven to 350 degrees. Grease and flour a 9-inch layer cake pan and a 6-cup ring mold. Combine margarine, brown sugar and syrup; blend. Spoon 1/3 of this mixture into ring mold, the remainder into cake pan. Arrange nuts over mixture in both pans. Prepare cake mixture according to directions on package. Gently spoon enough of this batter on the nuts in the ring mold; fill half full. Pour remaining batter into layer-cake pan. Bake at 350 degrees for 30 minutes, or until tests done with toothpick. Invert round layer cake onto serving plate … ring mold on a wire rack. Cool.

Cream confectioners' sugar and nutmeg together with heavy cream. Fold peaches into mixture and spread a layer of cream mixture over round layer. Place ring on top and fill center with remaining cream mixture. Chill several hours before serving. This can also be made with canned peaches that have been thoroughly drained.

ALOHA APPLE ROYALE

5   medium-size apples, peeled and thinly sliced
1/2 cup crushed pineapple
1/2 cup sugar
1/2 teaspoon cinnamon
1/4 teaspoon nutmeg
1/4 cup walnuts, chopped
1/2 cup shredded coconut
1/4 cup shortening
1/4 cup butter *or* margarine, softened

1/2 cup brown sugar, firmly packed
1   egg, beaten
3/4 cup all-purpose flour
1/2 teaspoon vanilla extract

Combine apple slices and crushed pineapple; spread into a 9-inch pie plate. Sprinkle with sugar and spices; top with walnuts and coconut. Cream together shortening and butter; add brown sugar; stir in egg. Add flour and vanilla; mix thoroughly. Spread batter on top of apple/pineapple mixture. Bake at 375 degrees for 35 minutes, or until top is crisp and golden.

Gwen Campbell, Sterling, Va.

CRANBERRY–PEAR CRISP

Serves 6

1 (12-ounce) package fresh *or* frozen cranberries, thawed
2 pears, cored and sliced
2 tablespoons flour
1 cup sugar
1 teaspoon ground cinnamon
1/2 cup brown sugar, packed
1/2 cup flour
1/3 cup butter *or* margarine, softened
3/4 cup old-fashioned oats, uncooked
3/4 cup chopped walnuts
    Whipped cream (optional)

Place cranberries and pear slices into an oblong 2-quart baking dish. Sprinkle with combined 2 tablespoons flour, sugar and cinnamon.

In medium size mixing bowl combine brown sugar and 1/2 cup flour. Cut in butter or margarine until mixture is crumbly. Add oats and walnuts. Mix well; sprinkle over fruit mixture. Bake in a preheated 350-degree oven for 30–35 minutes, or until juice is bubbly. Serve warm topped with whipped cream, if desired..

Quick, easy and delicious dessert!
Anna Y. Bodisch, Coplay, Pa.

Holiday
SPECIALS

LECHERLE
About 70 2-inch cookies

3/4 cup honey
2 tablespoons orange juice
2 eggs
1 cup powdered sugar
3 cups flour
1/2 teaspoon salt
1 teaspoon baking soda
1/3 cup finely-chopped candied citron
2 teaspoons cinnamon
1 teaspoon ground cloves
Clear Glaze (recipe follows)

Put orange juice and honey into small saucepan and bring to boil. Remove from heat and set aside. Beat eggs, continue beating as you slowly add sugar. Stir in flour, salt and baking soda, mix well. Add citron, cinnamon, cloves, reserved honey and orange juice; mix until thoroughly combined. Cover dough, chill for 2 to 3 hours.

Preheat oven to 350 degrees. Place dough on lightly floured surface and sprinkle top of dough with a little flour. Roll to 1/4-inch thickness. Cut into circles, diamonds, squares or any shape you wish, and place about 1 inch apart on ungreased cookie sheets. Bake for 10-12 minutes or until slightly colored around the edges. Remove from oven and transfer cookies to racks to cool. While they are still warm, brush tops with Clear Glaze.

Store airtight for several days to mellow before using.

Clear Glaze:
1 cup powdered sugar
2 tablespoons water

Combine powdered sugar and water, and mix well to dissolve any sugar lumps, making a smooth, runny glaze. Brush or spoon on cookies while still warm.

Leona Teodori, Warren, Mich.

HOLIDAY CRANBERRY BREAD

2¼ cups flour
¾ cup sugar
1 tablespoon baking powder
½ teaspoon salt
1 cup milk
1 egg, beaten
3 tablespoons melted butter *or* margarine
1 teaspoon vanilla
1 cup chopped cranberries
½ cup chopped walnuts

Combine flour, sugar, baking powder and salt. Set aside. Combine milk, egg, butter and vanilla. Add milk mixture to flour mixture. Stir just until mixed. Stir in cranberries and walnuts. Turn into greased 9-inch round pan. Bake in 350-degree oven for 45–50 minutes, or until cake tester inserted in center comes out clean. Let cool in pans 10 minutes. Remove from pan and cool completely. Wrap lightly and store 1 day before serving.

HALLOWEEN PARTY DIP

½ cup pumpkin
½ cup orange marmalade
½ cup plain yogurt
¼ teaspoon cinnamon
⅛ teaspoon nutmeg
⅛ teaspoon cloves, ground
½ cup whipping cream, whipped
¼ cup pecans, coarsely chopped
Banana chunks, apple slices, orange sections, strawberries for dipping

In a bowl combine pumpkin, marmalade, yogurt and spices; mix well. Fold whipped cream into pumpkin mixture; spoon into serving dish placed on a large platter; chill. Before serving, top with nuts; place "dippers" around party dip on platter.

Gwen Campbell, Sterling, Va.

MONSTER HASH

3 cups pumpkin seeds, washed
2 tablespoons margarine
1 teaspoon salt

Melt margarine in frying pan; add salt and pumpkin seeds. Sauté for 5 minutes, coating seeds well. Place on a cookie sheet and bake 20 minutes at 300 degrees.

GOOEY CHOCOLATE CAKE
Serves 16

1 cup buttermilk
1 cup vegetable oil
2 eggs
2 cups flour
2 cups sugar
1 tablespoon baking soda
1/2 teaspoon salt
1/2 cup cocoa
1 cup strong hot coffee

Mix together the buttermilk, oil and eggs. Set aside. In separate bowl, sift together flour, sugar, soda, and salt, if desired. Add cocoa to dry mixture. Combine buttermilk mixture and dry ingredients, beat about 2 minutes. Slowly add the hot coffee, beating well. Bake in greased and floured 9x13-inch baking pan at 350 degrees for 35-40 minutes.

Frosting:
3-4 (1-ounce) squares unsweetened chocolate
3 tablespoons margarine
1 (1-pound) box confectioners' sugar
3-6 tablespoons strong coffee

Over low heat, melt chocolate and margarine (for very dark, use 4 squares). Cool slightly and beat in confectioners' sugar. Add 3 tablespoons coffee and beat; add remaining coffee to make the proper consistency for spreading. Cake may be frosted as a single layer or cut in half and frosted as layer cake.

Another "love token" is a Praline Cake, equally as delicious, and it will serve 12—if cut carefully.

HOLIDAY GARLAND HAM
Serves 20

5 pounds precooked ham
Whole cloves
1 cup brown sugar, firmly packed
½ cup maple-flavored syrup
¼ cup Dijon mustard
1 tablespoon cornstarch
1 (20-ounce) can crushed pineapple with juice
Vegetable Garland (recipe follows)

Score ham; stud with cloves. Place on rack in shallow baking pan; bake at 350 degrees for 2 hours. Combine sugar, maple syrup and mustard; use ¾ cup glaze mixture to baste ham during last 40 minutes of baking. In saucepan, blend remaining glaze mixture, cornstarch and pineapple with juice. Cook until sauce thickens; serve extra glaze as sauce over slices of ham.

Vegetable Garland:
2 (15-ounce) cans whole baby carrots
4 ears corn, quartered
2 acorn squash, cut into serving pieces
1 butternut squash, cut into serving pieces

Cook corn and squash separately in salted, boiling water; cook corn 5 minutes; squash, 15–20 minutes.

To serve: Place ham on large platter; arrange vegetables in a garland around the ham.

Gwen Campbell, Sterling, Va.

EGGNOG COOKIES
Makes 6 dozen

1 cup butter
2 cups sugar
1 cup eggnog
1/2 teaspoon nutmeg
1 teaspoon baking soda
5-1/2 cups sifted flour

Cream butter and sugar until light and fluffy. Add eggnog, nutmeg, and soda; mix well. Add enough flour to make stiff dough. Chill. Roll to 1/8-inch thickness on lightly floured pastry cloth and cut with Christmas cookie cutters. Brush with slightly beaten egg white and decorate with candied fruits or colored sugar. Bake at 375 degrees for 8-10 minutes, or until lightly browned.

Jenni Lien, Stoughton, Wis.

WALNUT MACAROONS

1 egg white
2/3 cup white sugar
1/8 teaspoon salt
1/4 teaspoon almond extract
1/3 cup very finely chopped walnuts

Beat egg whites very stiff, adding sugar slowly. Add salt, very gradually while beating; still beating, add extract and chopped nuts. Drop by teaspoonfuls onto cookie sheet (teflon or non-stick sheet if possible). Bake at 325 degrees for 15 minutes. Cool on rack.

Pearle M. Goodwin, South Ryegate, Vt.

PORTUGUESE FRUIT CAKE

2/3 cup packed brown sugar
2/3 cup shortening
2 eggs
1/3 cup honey
1/3 cup light molasses
1/4 cup apple cider or apple juice
1-1/2 cups all-purpose flour
1/2 teaspoon baking powder
1/2 teaspoon salt
1/4 teaspoon ground cinnamon
1/4 teaspoon ground cloves
2/3 cup pitted dates, chopped
2/3 cup raisins
2/3 cup chopped almonds
1/3 cup chopped candied cherries
1/3 cup chopped candied pineapple
1/3 cup chopped candied citron
2 tablespoons all-purpose flour
1/2 cup powdered sugar
1 slightly beaten egg white

In large mixer bowl, cream brown sugar and shortening. Beat in eggs, honey, molasses, and apple cider or apple juice. Stir together 1-1/2 cups flour, baking powder, salt, cinnamon and cloves. Coat dates, raisins, almonds, cherries, pineapple and citron with remaining 2 tablespoons flour. Stir flour mixture into creamed mixture, fold in fruits and nuts. Grease a 9x9x2-inch baking pan, line bottom with waxed paper. Spread batter evenly in pan. Place pan with batter on the top oven shelf. Place another pan on bottom oven shelf and fill with hot water. Bake at 300 degrees for 1 hour and 25 minutes. Cool cake in pan. Remove from pan. Wrap and store cake overnight. Frost cake with mixture of sifted powdered sugar and egg white.

Leona Teodori, Warren, Mich.

HOLIDAY CRANBERRY MOUSSE

Serves 8

1 (20 ounce) can crushed pineapple in juice

1 (6 ounce) package strawberry gelatin
1 cup water
1 (1 pound) can whole berry cranberry sauce
3 tablespoons fresh lemon juice
1 teaspoon fresh grated lemon peel
1/4 teaspoon ground nutmeg
2 cups dairy sour cream
1/2 cup chopped pecans

Drain pineapple well, reserving all juice. Add juice to gelatin in 2 quart saucepan. Stir in water. Heat to boiling, stirring to dissolve gelatin. Remove from heat. Blend in cranberry sauce. Add lemon juice, lemon peel and nutmeg. Chill until mixture thickens slightly. Blend sour cream into gelatin mixture. Fold in pineapple and pecans, pour into 2-quart mold. Chill until firm. Unmold onto serving plate.

Melba Bellefeuille, Libertyville, Ill.

CRANBERRY SCONES

Serves 16

2-1/2 cups all-purpose flour
2-1/2 teaspoons baking powder
1/2 teaspoon baking soda
3/4 cup cold butter or margarine, cut into small pieces
1 cup coarsely-chopped cranberries
2/3 cup granulated sugar
3/4 cup buttermilk

Preheat oven to 400 degrees. Have an ungreased large cookie sheet ready. Mix flour, baking powder and soda in large bowl. Cut in butter with pastry blender until mixture resembles coarse crumbs. Stir in cranberries and sugar, then buttermilk just until blended. Cut dough in half. On lightly-floured surface with lightly floured finger tips, press half the dough into 8-inch circle about 1/2 inch thick. Cut into 8 wedges. Place on cookie sheet 1/2 inch apart. Bake 12-15 minutes until puffed and lightly brown. Remove to rack, and repeat with remaining dough. Serve warm.

Edna Askins, Greenville, Texas

ALMOND SNOWBALL COOKIES

Makes 5 dozen

½ cup butter or margarine
¼ cup evaporated milk
½ teaspoon grated lemon rind
1¾ cups sifted flour
¾ cup sugar
½ teaspoon salt
1 cup finely chopped almonds
6 tablespoons confectioners' sugar
½ pound candied cherries

Cream butter; beat in milk, a little at a time, until all is blended with butter. Add lemon rind. Sift flour with sugar and salt; gradually add to butter mixture. Add nuts; mix well. Pinch off pieces of dough, about a teaspoon. Flatten dough in palm of hand. Place a cherry on dough; pinch dough up around cherry completely. Roll between palms. Place on lightly greased, floured cookie sheet. Bake at 375 degrees for 12 minutes. Roll in confectioners' sugar while still warm.

Mrs. Don Shamway, Freeport, Ill.

CHILDREN'S CHRISTMAS EVE TREAT

Yield: 12

1 box rainbow colored flat-bottomed ice cream cones
1 (9 ounce) box white cake mix
1/4 cup red cherries, chopped
1/4 cup green cherries, chopped
1/2 box miniature chocolate covered mint patties

Place ice cream cones in a 12-cup muffin tin. Prepare cake mix according to package directions; fold in green and red cherries. Half fill each cone with cake batter. Bake 350 degrees for 25-30 minutes; remove from oven. While still hot, place 3 to 4 mint patties on top of each cupcake. They will melt and run down inside of the cone.

Mrs. Gwen Campbell, Sterling, Va.

MERRY MINT BROWNIES

3/4 cup plus 2 tablespoons sifted
   cake flour
1 cup sugar
7 tablespoons cocoa
1/2 teaspoon baking powder
3/4 teaspoon salt
2/3 cup shortening
2 eggs
1 teaspoon vanilla
1 tablespoon light corn syrup
1 cup walnuts, coarsely chopped

In large bowl, beat all ingredients together at low speed, except walnuts; stir in walnuts with spoon. Pour batter into greased 8-inch square pan. Bake at 350 degrees about 40 minutes or until toothpick inserted near center comes out clean. Cool and frost.

Mint Frosting:
1 tablespoon shortening
1 tablespoon butter
2-1/2 tablespoons scalded hot
   cream
2 cups powdered sugar
1/4 teaspoon salt
1/2 teaspoon vanilla
1/4 teaspoon peppermint extract
Green food coloring
1 ounce semi-sweet chocolate
1 teaspoon shortening

Melt 1 tablespoon shortening and 1 tablespoon butter in hot cream. Pour over powdered sugar and salt; stir well. Add vanilla and peppermint extract, beat until thick enough to spread. Add enough food coloring to tint a Christmas green. Spread brownies with frosting. Melt chocolate and shortening together. Cool and drizzle over frosting in thin stream from teaspoon. Cut into squares.

Judy Haffner, Auke Bay, Alaska

MEXICAN YULETIDE COOKIES

About 6-1/2 dozen

1 cup butter

3/4 cup powdered sugar
1 egg
1-1/2 teaspoons vanilla
1/8 teaspoon salt
2 cups sifted flour
1 cup uncooked oatmeal
1 cup chopped pecans
Powdered sugar for rolling

Cream butter; add sugar gradually; beat in egg and vanilla. Blend in salt, flour, oatmeal and pecans. Shape rounded teaspoonfuls of dough into balls. Place on ungreased cookie sheets. Bake at 325 degrees about 20 minutes. Roll in powdered sugar while warm.

P. J. Leikness, Stoughton, Wis.

CHRISTMAS CRANBERRY DATE SQUARES

Filling:
3 cups fresh cranberries
1 package pitted dates
2 cups water

Crust:
1 cup butter
1 teaspoon vanilla
1-1/2 cups brown sugar
2 cups flour
1/2 teaspoon baking soda
1/2 teaspoon salt
2 cups quick oatmeal

Glaze:
1-1/4 cups powdered sugar
1/2 teaspoon vanilla
2 tablespoons orange juice

Cream butter, adding sugar gradually. Blend in vanilla. Sift flour, soda and salt; add to creamed mixture. Stir in oatmeal. Pat slightly more than half of crust mixture in a buttered 10x15-inch jelly roll pan. Cook filling ingredients in water over medium heat until cranberries pop, stirring constantly. Cool. Spread filling over crust. Sprinkle rest of crust mixture over top. Bake in preheated oven at 350 degrees for 25-30 minutes. Cool in pan on wire rack. Beat glaze ingredients until smooth. When bars are cool, drizzle with glaze. Cut into bars.

Mrs. Carmen J. Bickert, Dubuque, Iowa

CHRISTMAS EGGNOG BREAD

This is delicious for a Christmas brunch.

  3   cups flour
  ¾   cup sugar
  1   tablespoon baking
      powder
  1   teaspoon salt
  ½   teaspoon nutmeg
1½   cups Borden's eggnog
  1   egg, beaten
  ¼   cup margarine, softened
  1   cup white raisins
  ½   cup red cherries
  ½   cup green cherries
  ¾   cup chopped nuts
      (pecans)

In a large bowl put together the dry ingredients. In separate bowl, mix eggnog, egg and softened margarine; add to dry ingredients. Add nuts and fruit. Bake for 60 minutes at 350 degrees in a greased 9x5 inch loaf pan. Let stand 10 minutes and place onto rack; cool.

Esther M. Garback, Gloversville, N.Y.

PATRIOTIC BISCUITS

2 cups sifted flour
2 tablespoons sugar
3 teaspoons baking powder
1/2 teaspoon salt
1/2 cup butter
1 egg, beaten
1/2 cup milk

Sift together flour, sugar, baking powder and salt. Cut in butter with a pastry blender. Add egg and milk. Blend thoroughly. Knead the dough on a lightly floured surface until smooth. Roll to 1/2-inch thickness and cut with biscuit cutter. Place on a greased baking sheet and brush with melted butter. Bake at 450 degrees for about 7 minutes.

CHRISTMAS WREATH
Makes 1 wreath

2-1/4 to 2-3/4 cups flour
1 package active dry yeast
3/4 cup milk
3 tablespoons sugar
3 tablespoons butter or margarine
1/4 teaspoon salt
1 egg
Milk
Pecan halves

In large mixer bowl, combine 1 cup flour and yeast. Heat milk, sugar, butter or margarine and salt just to warm (115-120 degrees) and butter starts to melt, stirring constantly. Add to flour mixture, add egg. Beat on low speed with electric mixer for one-half minute, scraping bowl constantly. Beat for 3 minutes at high speed. Stir in as much remaining flour as you can mix in with a spoon. Turn onto lightly floured surface; knead in enough remaining flour to make moderately-soft dough that is smooth and elastic (3-5 minutes total). Place in lightly-greased bowl, turn once to grease surface. Cover, let rise until double, about 1 hour.

Punch dough down, divide into 3 portions, shape into balls, cover and let rest 10 minutes. Roll each ball to 20-inch rope. Grease outside of a 6-ounce custard cup and invert the dish in the center of greased baking sheet. Starting at center, braid ropes loosely to ends. Wrap braid around custard cup, stretching as necessary to join ends, pinch to seal. Cover, let rise until nearly double, about 30 minutes. Brush carefully with milk, tuck pecan halves in braid. Bake at 375 degrees for 20 minutes. Cool bread on wire rack. Loosen braid from custard cup with narrow spatula, remove cup. If desired, wrap and freeze bread until needed. To thaw, let stand at room temperature.

Leona Teodori, Warren, Mich.

IRISH BROWN SODA BREAD

2 cups stone-ground whole-wheat or barley flour
1 cup unbleached white flour
3/4 teaspoon salt
3/4 teaspoon soda
1-1/4 cups buttermilk or whole milk soured with 1 tablespoon lemon juice or vinegar
1-1/2 tablespoons vegetable oil or melted butter

Preheat oven to 425 degrees. Sift dry ingredients into a big bowl or just stir with clean hands. You'll need them floured for the kneading step. Combine buttermilk or milk mixture and melted butter or oil in a measuring cup and stir into dry ingredients.

Knead dough a few moments until it sticks together nicely in a ball. Place on a greased and floured, or non-stick, baking sheet or in a 10-inch pie pan, and pat the ball into a flat circle 1-1/2 inches high.

Dip a knife into flour and score the giant biscuit with a cross 3/4 inch deep. Bake at 425 degrees for 15 minutes, then at 350 degrees for 15 more minutes. Thump the loaf. If it sounds hollow, it's done. Turn it out onto a rack to cool to lukewarm before serving.

If the crust seems too hard, wrap the bread for a few minutes in a cloth wrung out of warm water. To serve, remove the damp cloth and wrap the bread in a clean, dry cloth and place in a basket.

At the table, each person breaks off his farl (fourth) with his hands. The only knife to touch the bread is the one with the butter on it. Treated so kindly, the warm bread tastes better.

Soda bread goes well with butter and jam and a glass of milk for a snack. It's glorious with an Irish stew, or a seafood chowder, or with Red Flannel Hash that is baked along with the bread. An apple cobbler for dessert shares the oven.

HOLIDAY MERINGUE COOKIES
Makes 3 dozen

2 egg whites
Dash salt
1/8 teaspoon cream of tartar
3/4 cup sugar
1/2 teaspoon vanilla
1 cup miniature chocolate chips
1 cup chopped walnuts
Crushed peppermint candy (3–4 tablespoons)

Beat egg whites in small mixer bowl at high speed until foamy. Add cream of tartar and salt; beat to form soft peaks. Add sugar, 1 tablespoon at a time, beating after each addition. Meringue should be stiff and shiny. Fold in vanilla, chocolate chips and nuts. Drop by teaspoonfuls onto lightly greased cookie sheets, leaving about 1½-inch space between cookies. Sprinkle with candy. Bake 40 minutes at 250 degrees. Cool on wire racks. Store in airtight container.

Deanna Nilvar, Temple, Texas

HARVEST POPCORN
Makes 2½ quarts

2 quarts freshly popped popcorn, unsalted
2 (1½-ounce) cans potato sticks
1 cup salted mixed nuts
½ cup unsalted butter, melted
1 teaspoon lemon-pepper seasoning
1 teaspoon dried whole dill weed
1 teaspoon Worcestershire sauce
½ teaspoon garlic powder
½ teaspoon onion powder

Combine popcorn, potato sticks and nuts in a 15 x 10 x 1-inch jelly roll pan. Combine remaining ingredients; pour over popcorn mixture, stirring until evenly coated. Bake at 350 degrees, for 6–8 minutes, stirring mixture once.

Sharon Case, Chicago, Ill.

CHRISTMAS STOLLEN

3/4 cup warm water
1 package active dry yeast
1/2 cup sugar
1/2 teaspoon salt
3 eggs
1 egg yolk (save egg white)
1/2 cup margarine
3-1/2 cups unsifted flour
1/2 cup chopped blanched almonds
1/4 cup chopped citron
1/4 cup chopped candied cherries
1/4 cup golden raisins
1 tablespoon grated lemon rind
2 tablespoons margarine
1 tablespoon water

Measure warm water into large warm mixing bowl. Sprinkle in yeast; stir to dissolve. Add sugar, salt, 3 whole eggs, egg yolk, 1/2 cup margarine, and half the flour. Beat 10 minutes at medium speed of electric mixer. Blend in remaining flour, almonds, fruits and lemon peel. Cover, let rise in warm place until double in size, about 1 hour and 30 minutes. Stir down batter by beating 25 strokes. Cover tightly and refrigerate overnight.

Turn dough onto well-floured board, divide in half. Press each half into 10x7-inch oval. Spread ovals with 2 tablespoons margarine. Fold each oval in two, lengthwise; firmly pressing folded edges only. Place on greased baking sheets, brush with slightly-beaten egg white, blended with 1 tablespoon water. Let rise in warm place until doubled, about 1 hour. Bake at 375 degrees for 15-20 minutes or until done. Frost with powdered sugar glaze and decorate with blanched almonds, citron and candied cherries.

Judy Haffner, Auke Bay, Alaska

PUMPKIN GINGERBREAD

Serves 8–12

½ cup butter *or* margarine, softened
½ cup sugar
½ cup molasses
1 egg
1½ cups all-purpose flour
¾ teaspoon baking soda
¾ teaspoon ground ginger
¾ teaspoon cinnamon
1 cup canned pumpkin
1 (4-serving size) package *instant* vanilla pudding mix
½ cup milk
½ of a 4½-ounce carton frozen whipped dessert topping, thawed
Pecan halves

Cream together butter *or* margarine and sugar. Beat in molasses and egg. Stir together flour, soda, spices and ¼ teaspoon salt. Add to creamed mixture alternately with ½ cup water (batter may appear curdled). Pour into a greased 9 x 9 x 2-inch baking pan. Bake at 350 degrees for 30–35 minutes. Cool. Stir together pumpkin, pudding mix and milk. Fold in whipped topping. Chill. To serve, cut gingerbread into squares and top with some of the pumpkin mixture. Garnish with pecans.

Diantha Susan Hibbard, Rochester, N.Y.

CHOCOLATE SNOWBALLS

3/4 cup margarine
1/2 cup sugar
2 teaspoons vanilla
1 beaten egg
2 cups flour
1/2 teaspoon salt
1 cup chopped nuts
1 small package (6 ounces) chocolate chips
Confectioners' sugar

Combine all ingredients except confectioners' sugar, mixing well. Shape into 1-inch balls. Place on ungreased cookie sheets. Bake in a preheated 350-degree oven for 15-20 minutes. Cool slightly, then roll in confectioners' sugar. Cool completely and store in a covered tin.

Mrs. Sharon Crider, Evansville, Wis.

FESTIVE CRANBERRY CHEESECAKE

Serves 12

1 cup graham cracker crumbs
3 tablespoons sugar
3 tablespoons margarine, melted
3 (8-ounce) packages cream cheese, softened
¾ cup sugar
2 tablespoons flour
2 teaspoons vanilla
3 eggs
1 cup sour cream

Combine crumbs, sugar and margarine. Press onto bottom of 9-inch springform pan. Bake at 325 degrees for 10 minutes.

Combine cream cheese, sugar, flour and vanilla, mixing at medium speed on electric mixer until well-blended. Add eggs, 1 at a time, mixing well after each addition. Blend in sour cream. Pour over crust. Bake at 325 degrees for 55 minutes. Loosen cake from rim of pan. Cool before removing rim of pan. Chill. Spoon relish over cheesecake. Garnish with whipped cream and orange peel, if desired.

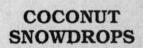

COCONUT SNOWDROPS

2 cups confectioners' sugar
1 cup unsweetened cocoa
2/3 cup sweetened condensed milk
2 teaspoons vanilla extract
3 cups flaked coconut

In medium bowl, combine sugar and cocoa. Add sweetened condensed milk and vanilla. Stir until well-blended. Mixture will be very stiff. Stir in 1 cup coconut. Shape into 1-inch balls and roll in remaining 2 cups coconut. Place in an airtight container and refrigerate.

Leona Teodori, Warren, Mich.

PAINTED COOKIES
About 5 dozen

1 cup butter or margarine
1 cup sugar
2 eggs
1/4 cup milk
2 teaspoons vanilla
4 cups all-purpose flour
1 teaspoon baking powder
3/4 teaspoon baking soda
Egg yolk paint (recipe follows)

Cream butter, gradually add sugar, beating until light and fluffy. Add eggs, one at a time, beating after each addition. Add milk and vanilla, mix well. Combine flour, baking powder and soda, add to creamed mixture, stirring until blended. Shape dough into 2 balls, wrap each in waxed paper and chill 4 hours. Work with half of dough at a time, store remainder in refrigerator. Roll dough to 1/8-inch thickness on floured waxed paper, cut with 2-1/2 to 3-inch cookie cutter, and transfer to lightly-greased cookie sheets. Paint assorted designs on cookies using small art brush and egg yolk paint. Bake at 375 degrees for 6-8 minutes, cool on racks.

Egg Yolk Paint:
1 egg yolk, beaten
1/4 teaspoon water
Paste or liquid food coloring

Combine egg yolk and water, stir well. Divide mixture evenly into 2 custard cups, tint as desired with food coloring. Keep paint covered until ready to use. If paint thickens, add a few drops of water, and stir well.

NOTE: Prepare one recipe egg yolk paint for every 2 colors of paint desired. Makes 1-1/2 tablespoons.

Leona Teodori, Warren, Mich.

ALMOND HOLLY LEAVES
Makes 12 dozen

1 pound butter, softened
1 cup sifted confectioners' sugar
2 eggs, beaten

4 cups all-purpose flour
1 cup almonds, toasted and finely chopped

Cream butter; gradually add confectioners' sugar, beating well. Add eggs; beat well. Stir in flour and almonds. Roll dough to 1/4-inch thickness on a floured surface with a floured rolling pin. Cut into holly-leaf shapes with 1½-inch cookie cutter. Place cookies on ungreased cookie sheets, and bake in 350-degree oven for 10 minutes, or until edges are golden. Cool on wire racks.

Leona Teodori, Warren, Mich.

IRISH PORK CHOP CASSEROLE

4 pork chops
1 pound apples
½ cup brown sugar
Water
4 carrots, chopped
1 onion, cut into small circles
¼ teaspoon sage

Put chops into greased baking dish. Place apples and brown sugar on top of chops. Add a little water, if necessary. Bake at 300 degrees for 2½ hours. With 1 hour of baking time remaining add carrots and onions. Return to oven to continue with baking time. If a thick sauce is necessary, it can be thickened when cooked. Sage can be added before cooking, if desired.

FIREWORKS LEMONADE

1 cup sugar
1 cup hot water
Juice of 7 lemons
1 1/2 lemons, thinly sliced
1 quart cold water
2 cups crushed ice

In a large pitcher combine the sugar and hot water. Add lemon juice, lemon, water and ice. Enjoy!

CHRISTMAS EVE PARTY CANAPÉS
Makes 35

1 cup Swiss cheese, shredded
1 cup mayonnaise
1 (3-ounce) package cream cheese, softened
½ cup sour cream
2 tablespoons mustard
1 tablespoon fresh lemon juice
1 (6-ounce) package frozen crabmeat, thawed and drained
Assorted bite-size breads

Combine Swiss cheese, mayonnaise, cream cheese, mustard, sour cream and lemon juice. Gently fold crabmeat into cheese mixture. Spread generously on bread squares. Place squares on baking sheet. Place into preheated broiler and broil until lightly browned; serve immediately.

Gwen Campbell, Sterling, Va.

GOBLINS' JELLY DOUGHNUTS

1 cup milk
⅓ cup shortening
⅓ cup sugar
½ teaspoon salt
2 packages yeast
¼ cup warm water
3 eggs, beaten
4 teaspoons vanilla
6 cups sifted flour

Scald milk. Add shortening, sugar and salt; set aside to cool. Dissolve yeast in water and add to milk mixture. Mix in eggs, vanilla and half of flour. Beat until smooth, adding more flour slowly. Knead about 7 minutes. Let rise until double in bulk. Punch down and divide into 4 parts. Roll out dough and cut into doughnuts. Let rise until double in bulk. Deep-fry until lightly browned and drain. When doughnuts are slightly cooled garnish with your favorite jelly.

EASTER BONNET COOKIES

You may use commercial, plain round cookies or make the following recipe, using a scalloped, circle cookie cutter.

Rolled Cookies:
- 3½ cups all-purpose flour
- 1 teaspoon baking powder
- ½ teaspoon salt
- 1 cup shortening
- 1½ cups sugar
- 2 eggs, well-beaten
- 1½ teaspoons vanilla

Sift flour, baking powder and salt together. Cream shortening; add sugar gradually; beat until light. Add beaten eggs; blend well; add vanilla. Combine dry ingredients with creamed mixture. Chill. Roll out dough thin; cut with cookie cutter. Grease baking sheet. Bake at 400 degrees for 6–10 minutes. When cool, frost with yellow icing. Use tines of small fork to draw lines around edge of cookies. This simulates the appearance of a straw hat.

Frosting:
- 2 cups confectioners' sugar
- 2 tablespoons hot water *or* milk
- 1 teaspoon vanilla *or* almond flavoring

While frosting is still moist, place a colored marshmallow in center of cookie. May add colored-sugar flowers. Dip underside of flowers in frosting and place on marshmallow crown or straw brim of hat. Sugar flowers can usually be found in a supermarket section where colored sugars and cake decorating icings are displayed.

Dorothy Stranix, Victoria, B.C., Canada

CHRISTMAS ORANGE BREAD

Makes 1 loaf

- ½ cup shortening
- ¾ cup granulated sugar
- 3 eggs
- ½ cup mashed bananas
- ½ cup orange juice
- 2½ cups sifted flour
- 4 teaspoons baking powder
- ¾ teaspoon salt
- 1½ cups mixed candied fruit
- ¼ cup raisins
- ¾ cup chopped nuts

Cream shortening; add sugar and beat until light and fluffy. Add eggs, 1 at a time, beating well after each addition. Combine bananas and orange juice; add to creamed mixture alternately with sifted dry ingredients mixed with fruits and nuts. Pack into greased and waxed-paper–lined loaf pan, 9 x 5 x 3-inch. Bake in a 350-degree oven for 1 hour, or until done. Cool about 20 minutes before turning out onto rack.

Jennie Lien, Stoughton, Wis.

GREEN & WHITE PUDDING SQUARES

Serves 8

- 2 cups grated coconut
- 4 cups boiling water
- 2 cups hot milk
- 6 tablespoons cornstarch
- 1/4 teaspoon salt
- 6 tablespoons sugar

Pour boiling water over coconut in a large bowl. Steep 10 minutes. Process in blender, half at a time, and strain.

Add hot milk to the coconut pulp. Blend 5 seconds. Strain.

Measure 4 cups of liquid. Heat to just boiling.

Combine salt, sugar, and cornstarch. Stir in a little liquid to make a paste. Slowly add to the hot liquid and stir-cook until thick. Pour half the pudding into a shallow buttered pan or platter. Stir 6 drops green food coloring and 1/4 teaspoon mint extract into the remaining pudding.

When the white pudding has set, pour the green pudding on top of it. Chill until completely set. Cut into squares. Serve on small plates.

COLONIAL FRIED CHICKEN

- 3 pounds fryer chicken parts
- 1 cup salad dressing
- 3 tablespoons flour
- 1 teaspoon paprika
- 1/4 teaspoon thyme
- 1 teaspoon salt
- 1/2 teaspoon pepper
- 3 tablespoons oil

Rinse chicken in cool water and pat dry. Pour salad dressing over chicken in a shallow dish, coating each piece. Then mix flour, paprika, thyme, salt and pepper together. Dip chicken into flour mixture. Heat oil and lightly brown chicken in a frying pan for about 3 minutes on each side.

Then place chicken in the shallow dish and cover with foil. Bake for 1 hour at 350 degrees; remove foil and bake an additional 10 minutes at 400 degrees.

IRISH LAMB STEW

Serves 4

- 8 medium-size potatoes
- 2 large onions
- 2 pounds lamb stew meat, bone-in if available

- 2 stalks celery
- 1/3 teaspoon dried thyme leaves
- 1 teaspoon salt, or to taste
- 1/4 teaspoon black pepper, or to taste
- Water to cover

Thinly peel all the potatoes. Slice 4 of them, thinly. In a heavy Dutch oven, layer sliced potatoes, 1 sliced onion, and the lamb. Sprinkle generously with the salt, pepper, and thyme. Add the other sliced onion and the 4 whole potatoes. Pour in the water and bring to boiling. Reduce heat and cover. Simmer 2-1/2 hours, or until the sliced potatoes have melted into the broth, or bake at 350 degrees for 2-1/2 hours.

GALA EGGNOG CAKE

2 cups flour
1-1/2 cups sugar
1 tablespoon baking powder
1 teaspoon salt
1/4 teaspoon nutmeg
3 eggs
1 teaspoon vanilla
1 cup eggnog
1/2 cup soft butter

Grease and flour bottoms of two 9-inch round pans or two 8-inch square pans. Combine all ingredients in large mixing bowl. Blend well on low speed of electric mixer. Then beat 1 minute at low speed. Pour into pans. Bake at 350 degrees for 25-30 minutes or until cake springs back when lightly touched in the middle. Cool; fill and frost.

Eggnog Frosting:
1/4 cup flour
1/4 teaspoon salt
1 cup eggnog
2/3 cup butter
1 cup sugar
1 teaspoon vanilla

Combine flour, salt and eggnog in a small saucepan. Cook over low heat, stirring constantly until very thick. Cool. Cream butter, gradually add sugar; cream well. Add flour mixture, beat until light and fluffy, blend in vanilla.

Joy Shamway, Freeport, Ill.

JINGLE-JAM MERINGUES
Makes 3 dozen

⅔ cup margarine
2 egg yolks, unbeaten
1 teaspoon vanilla
2 teaspoons baking powder
½ cup thick raspberry jam
1 cup sugar
2 tablespoons milk
2½ cups flour, sifted
⅛ teaspoon salt

Meringue Frosting:
2 egg whites
½ cup plus 2 tablespoons sugar

⅔ cup chopped pecans *or* walnuts

Cream together margarine and sugar until light and fluffy. Beat in egg yolks, milk and vanilla. Sift flour, baking powder and salt together and stir into creamed mixture; mix thoroughly. Make balls of heaping teaspoonfuls of mixture. Place on greased baking sheet. Flatten balls to ¼-inch thickness; top each with ½ teaspoon jam. Beat egg whites until stiff, adding sugar gradually; fold in nuts. Spread meringue on cookies, completely covering the jam. Bake at 350 degrees for 15 minutes.

These cookies are a little different and very delicious. Any flavor jam can be used. Instead of the jam, you might like to use peanut butter and jam or jelly mixed for Goobers.

Shirley Anne Crist, Marion, Ind.

CANDY CANE ANGEL CAKE

10 egg whites
1 teaspoon cream of tartar
1-1/4 cups white sugar
1 cup sifted white flour
1/2 teaspoon peppermint extract
1/2 cup finely-crushed peppermint candy canes
1/2 cup finely-chopped walnuts

Beat egg whites and cream of tartar together in large bowl until frothy, and peaks will just hold without tipping over. All other ingredients are mixed by hand until blended. Fold all into egg whites using a rubber spatula and folding over and over until all ingredients are evenly distributed. Gently spoon into ungreased 10-inch tube pan and place in preheated 375 degree oven. Bake for 20 minutes. Reduce heat to 275 degrees and finish baking 15-20 minutes. Remove from oven and invert pan; let cake cool to room temperature. With thin knife work all around edges of cake to remove it from pan. Serve with very lightly-sweetened whipped cream with a garnish of maraschino cherry.

Pearle M. Goodwin, South Ryegate, Vt.

BROWN SUGAR CHRISTMAS CUT-OUT COOKIES

1 pound (2 cups) butter
1 cup brown sugar
1 cup white sugar
1 teaspoon vanilla
2 eggs
1 teaspoon soda
1/2 teaspoon salt
6 cups flour

Cream butter with sugars until well blended; mix in vanilla, eggs, soda and salt. Blend in flour until dough is stiff. Chill dough about 1 hour or store in refrigerator until ready to use. Roll out about 1/4 of the dough at a time and cut into desired shapes. Place on lightly greased cookie sheets and bake in 375 degree oven for 10-12 minutes or until lightly browned around edges. Decorate with powdered sugar icing.

Barbara Beauregard - Smith, Northfield, S. A.. Australia

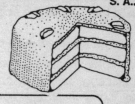

SNOWBALLS
Makes 4 dozen mini-donuts

3-1/2 cups all-purpose flour
1-1/2 cups sugar
1 cup milk
2 eggs
2 teaspoons vanilla
Dash salt
Salad oil
Confectioners' sugar

In large bowl, combine all ingredients except oil and confectioners' sugar, stirring until mixture forms sticky dough.

In deep skillet, heat 1-inch oil to 375 degrees. Drop batter by teaspoonfuls a few at a time, into hot oil. Fry 1 minute or until browned. Drain on paper toweling. Roll in confectioners' sugar.

Bobbie Mae Cooley, Bowen, Ill.

SNOWY WHITE FRUIT CAKE

1 (8 ounce) package cream cheese
1/3 cup shortening
1-3/4 cups sugar
6 egg whites
3 cups sifted flour
4 teaspoons baking powder
3/4 teaspoon salt
3/4 cup milk
1/2 cup water
1 teaspoon vanilla
2 cups candied fruit
1/2 cup candied cherries
1/2 cup chopped nuts
1/2 cup flour

Cream shortening and cream cheese together. Add sugar and cream well. Add egg whites, 2 at a time, beat well after each addition. Sift dry ingredients together. Combine milk, water and flavoring. Add sifted dry ingredients to creamed mixture alternately with liquid. Add 1/2 cup flour to nuts and candied fruit, then fold into cake batter. Bake in two well-greased loaf pans at 275 degrees for one hour.

Mrs. H. W. Walker, Richmond, Va.

POOR MAN'S FRUIT CAKE

4 cups flour
1 teaspoon baking powder
1 teaspoon salt
1 teaspoon ground cloves
1 teaspoon nutmeg
1 teaspoon allspice
1 teaspoon cinnamon
2 teaspoons baking soda
1 cup shortening
2 cups sugar
2 cups raisins
2 cups hot water
1 cup coarsely-cut nut meats (your choice)

Sift together flour, baking powder and salt. Mix in cloves, nutmeg, allspice and cinnamon. Cream sugar and shortening. Add raisins to hot water and bring to boil; cool. Add soda in a little water. Add sugar mixture; mix well. Add dry ingredients, mix well. Add nut meats; mix well. Bake in 13x10-inch cake pan at 350 degrees until done, about 45-50 minutes.

Joy Shamway, Freeport, Ill.

CHRISTMAS CAKE
Serves 20

2 cups flour
3 cups sugar
2 teaspoons baking soda
2 eggs, beaten
2 cups crushed pineapple
1/2 cup butter or margarine
1 small can evaporated milk
1 can coconut
1 teaspoon vanilla
1 cup chopped nuts

Sift flour, 2 cups sugar and soda together into bowl; stir in eggs and pineapple. Mix thoroughly; turn batter into cake pan 9x13x2-inches. Bake at 350 degrees for 30 minutes.

Meanwhile, combine remaining ingredients except coconut, vanilla, and nuts in saucepan and cook over low heat until butter melts, then cook for 2 minutes. Remove from heat and stir in coconut, vanilla and nuts; spread over hot cake.

Agnes Ward, Erie, Pa.

MEXICAN YULETIDE COOKIES
Makes 6½ dozen

1 cup butter
¾ cup confectioners' sugar
1 egg
1½ teaspoons vanilla
⅛ teaspoon salt
2 cups flour
1 cup uncooked oatmeal
1 cup chopped pecans
Confectioners' sugar for rolling

Cream butter; add sugar gradually; beat in egg and vanilla. Blend in salt, flour, oatmeal and pecans. Shape rounded teaspoonfuls of dough into balls. Place on ungreased cookie sheets. Bake at 325 degrees for 20 minutes. Roll in confectioners' sugar while warm.

P.J. Leikness, Stoughton, Wis.

CRANBERRY MINCEMEAT PIE

Pastry for 2-crust (9-inch) pie
2 cups prepared mincemeat
1 can (16 ounces) whole-berry cranberry sauce
1 cup coarsely chopped pecans
2 tablespoons grated orange rind
1 teaspoon tapioca
2 teaspoons rum or rum extract (optional)

Line pie plate with prepared bottom crust. Mix mincemeat, cranberry sauce, pecans, orange rind, tapioca and rum; pour mixture into pie shell and cover with top crust. Seal edges and slash top as a vent. Bake in a 400-degree oven 30-35 minutes, or until brown. Cool before cutting.

CHOCOLATE STARS
Makes 8 dozen

1½ cups sifted flour
1½ cups unblanched almonds, grated
1 teaspoon grated lemon peel
1 cup butter
1½ cups sugar
2 egg yolks
4 (1-ounce) squares unsweetened chocolate, melted and cooled

Mix flour, nuts and rind. Cream butter; add sugar gradually; cream until fluffy. Add egg yolks and chocolate; mix well. Add flour mixture gradually; mix. Roll ⅛-inch thick on floured board and cut with floured 2¾-inch star-shaped cutter. Bake on ungreased cookie sheets in preheated, 350-degree oven for 8 minutes.

Kit Rollins, Cedarburg, Wis.

PUMPKIN BREAD ROLL

Makes 4 1-pound coffee can breads

1 can pumpkin
4 eggs
1 cup oil
2/3 cup water
3 teaspoons cinnamon
3-1/4 cups flour
3 cups sugar
2 teaspoons baking soda
1 cup chopped walnuts
4 (1 pound) coffee cans
Powdered sugar

Grease and flour coffee cans generously. In mixer bowl, combine all ingredients, except powdered sugar, until well blended. Distribute equally in coffee cans. Bake at 350 degrees for 60 minutes or until top tests done. Remove from cans to rack, cool on sides, turning occasionally to keep round. Set upright and sprinkle with powdered sugar. Freezes well.

Agnes Russell, Concord, N.H.

MINCEMEAT COOKIES

2 cups shortening
5 eggs
1 teaspoon salt
6½ cups flour
3 cups mincemeat
3 cups brown sugar
2 teaspoons soda
3 tablespoons hot water
1 cup nuts

Cream shortening. Add brown sugar and mix until well-blended. Add eggs and beat thoroughly. Mix salt and soda with the flour. Add water to first mixture. Add mincemeat and flour mixture alternately to first mixture. Add nuts. Mix thoroughly. Drop with a spoon onto greased baking sheet and bake 10 minutes in a moderately hot 375-degree oven.

These cookies don't last long in my house as they are really extra-delicious!

Suzan L. Wiener, Spring Hill, Fla.

CORN BREAD STUFFING

1 (10-ounce) package corn bread mix
½ cup butter
1 cup chopped onion
1 cup diced celery
2 eggs, beaten
¼ cup chopped parsley
½ teaspoon poultry seasoning
¼ teaspoon black pepper

Mix and bake corn bread mix according to package directions. Cool and cut into ½-inch cubes. In a large skillet cook onion and celery in ¼ cup melted butter over medium heat, stirring occasionally for about 10 minutes. Stir in parsley, poultry seasoning and pepper. Combine with corn bread and ¼ cup butter in a large bowl. Mix well. This stuffing may be prepared one day in advance and kept refrigerated. Do not fill turkey until ready to roast.

Sarah M. Burkett, Centralia, Ill.

WILD RICE STUFFING

2 cups precooked wild rice
½ cup finely chopped onion
½ cup finely chopped celery
½ cup finely chopped mushrooms
2 tablespoons butter
1 teaspoon lemon juice
1 teaspoon tarragon
½ teaspoon thyme
1 egg, beaten
Salt and pepper to taste

Precook washed rice for 10 minutes and drain. In a skillet, melt butter; cook chopped onion and celery until tender, but not brown. Add wild rice. Add mushrooms, lemon juice, tarragon and thyme. Add beaten egg, salt and pepper. Mix well, and stuff your bird.

Lucy Andrews, Sequim, Wash.

SANTA'S WHISKERS

Makes 5 dozen

1 cup butter *or* margarine, softened
1 cup sugar
2 tablespoons milk
1 teaspoon vanilla *or* rum flavoring
2½ cups flour
¾ cup finely chopped red or green candied cherries
½ cup finely chopped pecans
¾ cup flaked coconut

In mixing bowl, cream butter o margarine and sugar; blend in milk and vanilla or rum flavoring. Stir in flour chopped candied cherries and chopped pecans. Form dough into 2 (8-inch) rolls. Roll in flaked coconut to coa outside. Wrap in waxed paper or clea plastic wrap; chill thoroughly.

Cut into ¼-inch slices. Place or ungreased cookie sheet and bake ir 375-degree oven until edges are golden about 12 minutes.

Kit Rollins, Cedarburg, Wis

CRANBERRY COOKIES

Makes 2 dozen

½ cup butter *or* margarine
1 cup sugar
¾ cup brown sugar, packed
¼ cup milk
2 tablespoons orange juice
1 egg
3 cups sifted flour
1 teaspoon baking powder
¼ teaspoon soda
½ teaspoon salt
1 cup chopped nuts
2½ cups (12-ounce package) fresh cranberries, chopped

Preheat oven to 375 degrees. Cream butter and sugars together; beat in milk, orange juice and egg. Sift together flour, baking powder, soda and salt. Combine with creamed mixture; blend well. Stir in cranberries and chopped nuts. Drop by teaspoonfuls on greased cookie sheet. Bake at 375 degrees for 10–15 minutes.

Edna Askins, Greenville, Texas

ELF OVEN-FRIED CHICKEN

Serves 4

10 (24 ounces) chicken breasts
 2 cups dairy sour cream *or* plain yogurt
¼ cup lemon juice.
 4 teaspoons Worcestershire sauce
 2 teaspoons celery salt *or* ground celery seed
 2 teaspoons paprika
 4 garlic cloves, finely chopped *or*
½ teaspoon garlic powder
 2 teaspoons salt
½ teaspoon pepper
 2 teaspoons poultry seasoning
 2 teaspoons parsley
½ cup margarine, melted
    Cornflakes crumbs

Cut chicken breasts in half. Wipe dry; remove skin and excess fat. In large bowl, combine all ingredients except margarine and cornflakes; stir well. Add chicken, making sure each piece is covered well. Let stand overnight in refrigerator. Remove chicken pieces from mixture; blot off excess with dry towel. Dip each piece in melted margarine, then roll in cornflakes crumbs. Place chicken in single layer on shallow pan. Sprinkle with additional parsley. Bake at 375 degrees for 25–30 minutes, or until chicken tests done.

Marcella Swigert, MonroeCity, Mo.

JAPANESE FRUITCAKE

Makes one 3-layer, 8-inch cake

3 cups flour, divided
1 teaspoon cinnamon
1 teaspoon allspice
1 teaspoon nutmeg
1 teaspoon cloves
1 teaspoon baking powder
1 cup butter
2 cups sugar
4 eggs
1 cup milk

1 cup jam
1 cup seedless raisins
1 cup chopped nuts
Frosting (recipe follows)

Sift 2 cups flour with spices and baking powder. Mix remaining 1 cup flour with raisins and nuts.

Cream butter and sugar in another bowl. Add eggs, one at a time, beating well after each addition. Add flour/spice mixture to creamed mixture alternately with milk. Add jam, raisins and nuts to mixture and mix well.

Pour batter into three 8-inch cake pans which have been greased and floured. Bake in a preheated 350-degree oven for 35 minutes. Cool completely before completing cake with *Frosting*.

Frosting:

2 cups flaked coconut
Grated rind and juice of 3 oranges
1 small can crushed pineapple
2 1/2 cups sugar
2 tablespoons flour

Combine all ingredients in a saucepan; mix well. Stirring constantly, cook until thick. Cool. Spread between cooled cake layers and on top and sides of cake.

Margaret Cotton, Franklin, Va.

CHOCOLATE STARS

About 8 dozen

1-1/2 cups sifted flour
1-1/2 cups unblanched almonds, grated
1 teaspoon grated lemon peel
1 cup butter
1-1/2 cups sugar
2 egg yolks
4 squares (1 ounce each) unsweetened chocolate, melted and cooled

Mix flour, nuts and rind. Cream butter, add sugar gradually, cream until fluffy. Add egg yolks, chocolate, and mix well. Add flour mixture gradually, mix. Roll 1/8 inch thick on floured board and cut with floured 2-3/4 inch star-shaped cutter. Bake on ungreased cookie sheets in preheated 350 degree oven about 8 minutes.

Mrs. Kit Rollins, Cedarburg, Wis.

FESTIVE COCOA CARDS

Yield: 12 cookies

1 cup butter or margarine, softened
1/2 cup sugar
3/4 cup molasses or dark corn syrup
1 egg
1 teaspoon vanilla extract
3/4 cup flour
1/2 cup cocoa
1/2 teaspoon baking soda
Tubes of red and green frosting

In large bowl, cream butter and sugar until light and fluffy. Beat in molasses, egg and vanilla. Combine flour, cocoa and baking soda. Stir into butter mixture until well blended. Chill 1 hour. On a lightly floured surface, roll dough into a 12 x 15-inch oblong. Cut into twelve 3 x 5-inch oblongs. Place on greased cookie sheets. Bake in 350 degree oven 10-12 minutes or until firm to the touch. Cool on cookie sheets. Write names or greetings on cookies.

Roberta Wiggin, Mechanicville, N.Y.

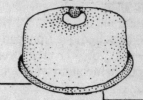

EASY FRUIT CAKE

1 box spice cake mix
1 (8 ounce) jar mixed fruit and peels
1 (4 ounce) jar candied cherries
1 (4 ounce) jar candied pineapple
1 cup golden light raisins
2 eggs
1 cup pecans
1 cup walnuts
Pineapple juice in place of water for cake mix
1/4 cup dates, chopped
1/4 cup prunes, chopped

Mix cake mix with eggs and pineapple juice. Flour fruits and nuts and add to cake batter. Pour into two bread pans that have been buttered and dusted with flour. Fill 3/4 full. Bake at 350 degrees for 1-1/2 hours or until done.

Leona Teodori, Warren, Mich.

MINCEMEAT SQUARES

Makes 24 bars

2-1/2 cups flour
1-1/2 teaspoons baking soda
1/2 teaspoon salt
1-1/2 cups quick cooking rolled oats
1 cup firmly packed dark brown sugar
3/4 cup (1-1/2 sticks) butter or margarine
1 (16 ounce) jar prepared mincemeat

Sift flour, baking soda and salt into large bowl. Stir in rolled oats and brown sugar until blended. Cut in butter or margarine with pastry blender until mixture is crumbly. Pat half the mixture into greased 11x7x1-inch baking pan. Spread mincemeat on top. Sprinkle remaining oat mixture over and press into mincemeat. Bake in moderate oven at 375 degrees for 25 minutes or until topping is golden. Cool in pan on wire rack 15 minutes.

With sharp knife, cut 3 times lengthwise and 5 times crosswise to make 24 bars. Remove from pan with spatula and store, layered between wax paper, in metal tin with tight-fitting lid.

Melba Bellefeuille, Libertyville, Ill.

CHRISTMAS PUDDING SAUCE

Serves 10-12

1 cup sifted powdered sugar
2 egg yolks, well beaten
1/2 cup melted butter
1 teaspoon vanilla or 2 tablespoons sherry
1 cup heavy cream, whipped

Gradually stir powdered sugar into beaten egg yolks. Beat in butter, vanilla or sherry. Fold in whipped cream. Serve with hot pudding.

NOTE: Leftover sauce can be stored, covered in refrigerator. Beat well before using.

Agnes Ward, Erie, Pa.

HALLOWEEN PUMPKIN CHIFFON

Serves 9

1 tablespoon gelatin
1/4 cup cold water
3 eggs, separated
1/4 cup sugar
1 1/4 cups canned or cooked pumpkin
1/2 cup 2 percent milk
1 teaspoon pumpkin pie spice
Dash of salt, if desired
13 packets Equal brand low-calorie sweetener
12 graham cracker squares
1/4 teaspoon cinnamon

Soak gelatin in cold water. Beat egg yolks slightly in an enamel pan or top of double boiler. Add sugar, pumpkin, milk, pumpkin pie spice and salt. Cook over low heat or hot water, but not boiling. Stir in gelatin until dissolved. Chill. When pumpkin mixture is beginning to set, whip egg whites until stiff, but not dry. Add 12 packets of Equal and beat just until mixed. Fold egg whites into pumpkin mixture. Line bottom of 8-inch square baking pan with 9 graham crackers. Spread pumpkin mixture evenly in pan. Make crumbs from the 3 remaining graham crackers; add 1 packet Equal and cinnamon. Mix and spread over top of pumpkin. Chill until firm. Cut into 9 equal squares.

Peggy Fowler, Woodruff, S.C.

WALNUT GLAZE

(for fruit cakes)

2 tablespoons butter, melted (do not substitute)
2 tablespoons honey
1 cup finely-chopped walnuts

Combine honey and butter. Blend. Add walnuts and stir. Chill. Spread onto ripened fruit cake the day of serving. Can also be used as an ice cream topping.

Pearle M. Goodwin, South Reygate, Vt.

CHRISTMAS EGGNOG CHERRY NUT LOAF

2-1/2 cups all-purpose flour
3/4 cup sugar
1 tablespoon baking powder
1 teaspoon salt
1 egg, beaten
1 recipe of homemade eggnog (recipe follows)
1/3 cup oil
1/2 cup chopped walnuts or pecans
1/2 cup chopped maraschino cherries, red and green

In mixing bowl, stir together flour, baking powder and salt. Mix egg, eggnog and oil. Stir in dry ingredients mixing well. Fold in nuts and cherries after they have been coated with flour. Pour into greased and floured 8x4x2-inch loaf pans. Bake at 350 degrees for 40-50 minutes or until tests done. Cool for 10 minutes before removing from pans.

Homemade Eggnog:

1 cup light cream
1/4 cup sugar
1/4 teaspoon ground nutmeg

Beat all ingredients together.

Carmen Bickert, Dubuque, Iowa

IRISH EGGY MASHED POTATOES

Serves 3

2 cups mashed potatoes
1 egg
Salt and pepper to taste
1 teaspoon dried parsley flakes or
1 to 2 tablespoons fresh minced parsley
Paprika

Whip egg and combine with mashed potatoes and a little salt, pepper, and parsley flakes. Put into a baking dish; sprinkle paprika over the top and bake at 350 to 375 degrees for 25 minutes. Serve hot from the baking dish.

WHITE CHRISTMAS PIE

Makes 2 pies

1 tablespoon gelatin
1 cup sugar
4 tablespoons flour
1/2 teaspoon salt
1-1/2 cups milk
3/4 teaspoon vanilla extract
1/4 teaspoon almond extract
1/2 cup whipping cream, whipped
3 egg whites
1/4 teaspoon cream of tartar
1-1/2 cups moist shredded coconut
2 baked 9-inch pie shells

Soften gelatin in 1/4 cup cold water, set aside. Combine 1/2 cup sugar, flour and salt in saucepan, stir in milk, bring to boil over low heat, stirring constantly. Boil 1 minute, remove from heat. Stir in softened gelatin, cool until partially set. Pour into large bowl. Beat with rotary beater until smooth. Blend in vanilla and almond extracts, fold whipped cream into custard. Beat egg whites until soft peaks form, add cream of tartar and 1/2 cup sugar, beating until stiff. Fold into custard mixture. Carefully fold in 1 cup coconut. Spoon into cooled pie shells. Sprinkle with remaining coconut. Chill for 2 hours or until set. Remove from refrigerator 20 minutes before serving.

Melba Bellefeuille, Libertyville, Ill.

CHRISTMAS BRAID BREAD

1-1/2 packages or cakes yeast
1/8 cup water, warm
1/4 teaspoon sugar
1/2 cup milk, scalded
1/4 cup sugar
1 teaspoon salt
1/4 cup margarine, softened
3 cups flour
1 egg
1/2 cup raisins
1/8 teaspoon cinnamon

Dissolve yeast in water, add 1/4 teaspoon sugar. Mix all ingredients. Knead 10 minutes. Let dough rest 10 minutes, covered. Let dough rise to double, then punch down, dividing dough into 3 equal balls. Roll into three strips the same length. Braid loosely, place on cookie sheet. Let rise until double in size. Bake at 350 degrees for 35 minutes. While warm drizzle with glaze.

Glaze:
1/2 cup powdered sugar
1 teaspoon margarine, softened
1 tablespoon water

Mix all ingredients well. Drizzle over bread.

Pearl Stevenson, Lafayette, Ind.

GREEK CHRISTMAS BREAD

1 package dry yeast
1/4 cup warm water
1/3 cup sugar
1 teaspoon ground cardamom
1/4 teaspoon salt
1 egg
1/4 cup milk
1/4 cup vegetable oil
1-1/2 cups whole wheat flour
1 cup all-purpose flour
1/4 cup raisins
1/4 cup walnuts
1/4 cup citron

Dissolve yeast in warm water. Combine sugar, cardamom, salt, egg, milk and oil in large bowl, mix well. Add yeast mixture, flour, raisins, nuts and citron, mix well. Add enough extra flour to make soft dough. Turn dough onto floured surface, knead until smooth and elastic, about 5 minutes. Shape into round loaf. Place round loaf onto lightly-oiled 8-inch round cake pan. Cover with damp towel, let rise in warm draft-free place until doubled, about 1 hour. Bake at 350 degrees for 35-40 minutes or until brown.

Marie Fusaro, Manasquan, N.J.

CHRISTMAS PINWHEEL COOKIES

Makes 3 dozen

¼ cup chopped red candied cherries
¼ cup chopped green candied cherries
½ cup chopped walnuts
½ cup shortening
¾ cup sugar
1 egg
1 tablespoon milk
1 teaspoon vanilla
1¼ cups flour
½ teaspoon baking powder
¼ teaspoon salt

Coarsely grind cherries and walnuts and set aside for filling. Cream shortening and sugar together. Add egg; beat well. Stir in milk and vanilla. Sift together flour, salt and baking powder. Stir into creamed mixture. If necessary, chill dough to handle easier. Roll out on lightly floured board or pastry sheet into a 10-inch square, ¼ inch thick. Sprinkle with cherries and nuts; roll up as for jelly roll; roll in waxed paper; chill thoroughly. Cut into ¼-inch slices and place on greased baking sheets. Bake at 400 degrees for 10–12 minutes.

Judy Haffner, Auke Bay, Alaska

SANTA'S STUFFED CELERY

Makes 15 appetizers

1 (2¼-ounce) can deviled ham
1 (3-ounce) package cream cheese, softened
½ teaspoon prepared mustard
½ teaspoon chili sauce
4 stalks celery, cut into 3-inch pieces
Pickle relish

Blend cream cheese, deviled ham, mustard and chili sauce. Stuff celery with the mixture. Top with pickle relish for garnish.

Judy Haffner, Auke Bay, Alaska

CANDLESTICK BARS

1 (14 ounce) package gingerbread mix
1 (8 ounce) can applesauce
1/2 cup raisins
1 (4 ounce) jar chopped mixed candied fruits and peels
1 (14 ounce) package white creamy frosting mix
2 tablespoons lemon juice

Combine gingerbread mix and apple sauce, beat 2 minutes at medium speed or 2 minutes with spoon. Stir in raisins, fruits and peels. Spread in 15-1/2x10-1/2x1-inch jelly roll pan. Bake 375 degrees for 15 minutes. Prepare frosting and add lemon juice, substituting lemon juice for half the liquid. Spread on cooled bars. Decorate with red and yellow gum drops to look like a candle. Use red candy for candle and yellow candy for flame.

Melba Bellefeuille, Libertyville, Ill.

KRIS CRINKLES

3 ounces unsweetened chocolate
2 cups walnuts, finely ground
1 cup sugar
2 eggs
Dash salt
2 tablespoons flour
1 teaspoon cinnamon
1/4 teaspoon nutmeg
1/2 teaspoon cloves
1/4 cup white bread crumbs, finely crushed
Confectioners' sugar

Preheat oven to 325 degrees. Melt chocolate and add walnuts. Add sugar, eggs, and salt. Remove to mixing bowl and add flour and spices; mix well. Add bread crumbs, mix. Shape into small balls and roll in confectioners' sugar. Bake on greased cookie sheets for about 12 minutes or until tops of cookies crinkle and crack. Remove and roll in confectioners' sugar again and cool.

Suzan L. Wiener, Spring Hill, Fla.

MINCEMEAT PEEK-A-BOOS
Makes 6 dozen

1½ cups butter *or* margarine, softened
¾ cup granulated sugar
¾ cup packed brown sugar
1 egg
¼ cup milk
4½ cups all-purpose flour
¾ teaspoon baking soda
¾ teaspoon salt
1¼ cups prepared mincemeat
¼ cup orange marmalade

Cream butter or margarine and sugars; beat in egg and milk. Stir together flour, soda and salt; stir into creamed mixture. Wrap and chill dough. On floured surface roll *half* the dough at a time, ⅛-inch thick; cut with 2½-inch round cookie cutter. Cut small hole in center of half the rounds (use a thimble if you have one). Combine mincemeat and marmalade. Place 1 teaspoon mincemeat mixture on each plain round; top each with a cut-out round. Seal edges with fork. Place on ungreased baking sheet; bake at 375 degrees for 10–12 minutes. Cool on wire rack. Wrap; label; freeze, if desired.

Diantha Susan Hibbard, Rochester, N.Y.

HERMITS

1 cup sugar
1/2 cup salad oil
2 1/2 cups flour
1/2 teaspoon nutmeg
1 teaspoon baking soda
1 teaspoon cinnamon
1/2 cup milk
1/2 cup molasses
1 cup raisins

Mix in order given. Blend well. Place in greased 9x13-inch pan and bake at 350 degrees for about 25 minutes. Do not overbake. When you remove from the oven, sprinkle with sugar.

Pearle M. Goodwin, South Ryegate, Vt.

CRANBERRY COOKIES
Yield: 2 dozen

1/2 cup butter or margarine
1 cup sugar
3/4 cup brown sugar, packed
1/4 cup milk
2 tablespoons orange juice
1 egg
3 cups sifted flour
1 teaspoon baking powder
1/4 teaspoon soda
1/2 teaspoon salt
1 cup chopped nuts
2-1/2 cups (12 ounce package) fresh cranberries, chopped

Preheat oven to 375 degrees. Cream butter and sugar together, beat in milk, juice and egg. Sift together flour, baking powder, soda and salt. Combine with creamed mixture, blend well. Stir in cranberries and nuts. Drop by teaspoonfuls on greased cookie sheet. Bake at 375 degrees for 10-15 minutes.

Edna Askins, Greenville, Texas

HOLIDAY ANGEL TOWER

1 package angel food cake mix
1 (1 pound 2-1/2 ounce) jar mincemeat
1 (8 ounce) package cream cheese, softened
1/4 cup walnuts, chopped
2 cups heavy cream, whipped and sweetened

Prepare and bake angel food mix as directed on package. Cool. Slice into three layers. Blend mincemeat, cream cheese and nuts. Spread mixture between layers, and put layers together. Cover and refrigerate several hours or overnight. Frost with whipped cream before serving. Store in refrigerator.

Judy Haffner, Auke Bay, Alaska

COOKIES
Makes 150–170 cookies

2 pounds dates
½ pound candied cherries
½ pound candied pineapple
½ pound shelled almonds
½ pound shelled Brazil nuts
2½ cups sifted flour
1 teaspoon baking soda
1 teaspoon salt
1 teaspoon cinnamon
1 cup butter
1½ cups sugar
2 eggs

Discard date pits and cut dates in chunks. Quarter cherries. Slice pineapple in thin slivers. Blanch almonds; chop coarsely and toast until golden. Chop Brazil nuts. Sift flour, baking soda, salt and cinnamon together. Preheat oven to 400 degrees. Work butter until soft and creamy. Add sugar gradually; continue working until smooth. Beat in eggs thoroughly. Stir in sifted flour mixture, all fruits and nuts. Drop by teaspoonfuls on ungreased cookie sheet. Bake 10 minutes; do not overbake. Cookies are best when soft in texture. Remove from sheet.

Leona Teodori, Warren, Mich.

CANDY CANE COOKIES
Makes 30

¾ cup butter *or* margarine, softened
¾ cup sugar
1 egg
½ teaspoon vanilla
½ teaspoon peppermint extract
2 cups flour
½ teaspoon salt
¼ teaspoon baking powder
⅓ cup flaked coconut
1 teaspoon red food coloring

Cream butter and sugar; beat in egg, vanilla and extract. Sift flour with salt and baking powder; stir into creamed mixture. Divide dough in half. Stir coconut into 1 portion; blend food coloring into remaining dough. Cover; chill doughs for 10 minutes.

Divide each dough into 30 balls; keep half of each dough chilled until ready to use. With hands, roll each ball into 5-inch rope. For each cane, pinch together 1 end of red rope and 1 end of white rope; twist ropes together. Pinch together remaining ends. Place on ungreased cookie sheet; curve to form cane. Leave space between canes, as they expand during baking. Repeat with remaining balls. Bake at 375 degrees for 10 minutes.

Kit Rollins, Cedarburg, Wis.

MINCEMEAT SQUARES
Makes 24 bars

2½ cups flour
1½ teaspoons baking soda
½ teaspoon salt
1½ cups quick-cooking rolled oats
1 cup firmly packed dark brown sugar
¾ cup (1½ sticks) butter *or* margarine
1 (16-ounce) jar prepared mincemeat

Sift flour, baking soda and salt into large bowl. Stir in rolled oats and brown sugar until blended. Cut in butter or margarine with pastry blender until mixture is crumbly. Pat half the mixture into greased 11 x 7 x 1-inch baking pan. Spread mincemeat on top. Sprinkle remaining oat mixture over and press into mincemeat. Bake in moderate oven at 375 degrees for 25 minutes, or until topping is golden. Cool in pan on wire rack for 15 minutes.

With sharp knife, cut 3 times lengthwise and 5 times crosswise to make 24 bars. Remove from pan with spatula and store, layered between waxed paper, in metal tin with tight-fitting lid.

Melba Bellefeuille, Libertyville, Ill.

TRADITIONAL PUMPKIN PIE

3 eggs
1/2 teaspoon salt
2/3 cup brown sugar
1/3 cup sugar
1-1/2 cups milk (evaporated milk may be used)
1-1/2 cups cooked pumpkin
2 teaspoons cinnamon
1 teaspoon ginger
1/2 teaspoon nutmeg
1/8 teaspoon allspice
1 unbaked 9-inch pastry shell

Beat eggs; stir in salt, sugar and milk. Add pumpkin and spices. Mix well; pour into pastry shell. Bake at 425 degrees for 35-45 minutes or until center firms up.

Agnes Ward, Erie, Pa.

CHRISTMAS BISCUITS

2 cups butter
4 cups sugar
4 eggs
1 teaspoon baking soda
1 cup sour cream
Sifted flour

Cream butter and sugar; beat in eggs, one at a time. Dissolve soda in sour cream; stir into creamed mixture. Add enough flour to make an easily-handled dough; chill overnight. Roll dough out thin on floured board; cut with round cookie cutter. Place on baking sheet and bake at 350 degrees for 10-12 minutes.

Agnes Ward, Erie, Pa.

SAINT NICHOLAS COOKIES

1 cup butter
2 cups sugar
1 cup shortening
½ cup sour cream
½ teaspoon soda
4 cups flour
½ teaspoon cloves
1 teaspoon cinnamon
½ cup chopped nut meats

Cream together first 3 ingredients. Blend together sour cream and soda. Add to first mixture. Sift remaining ingredients and add. Stir in nut meats. Press into loaf pan and chill overnight. Slice; place on cookie sheet and bake in 350-degree oven for about 10–12 minutes.

Leona Teodori, Warren, Mich.

SPICED BANANA FRUIT CAKE

3-1/2 cups sifted flour
4 teaspoons baking powder
1 teaspoon salt
1/2 teaspoon soda
2 teaspoons cinnamon
2 teaspoons ginger
1 teaspoon nutmeg
1-1/3 cups shortening
1-1/3 cups sugar
4 eggs, beaten
2 cups mashed ripe banana
1-1/2 cups chopped nuts
1 cup raisins
4 cups diced candied fruits

Sift dry ingredients. Cream shortening. Gradually blend in sugar. Beat in eggs. Add flour mixture alternately with banana. Mix raisins, nuts and candied fruits into batter. Turn into two well greased and floured 9-inch bread pans. Bake at 300 degrees for 2 hours or until done.

Judy Haffner, Auke Bay, Alaska

HOLIDAY MINCEMEAT UPSIDE DOWN CAKE

1-1/2 cups sugar
3/4 cup unsalted butter
3-1/2 cups all-purpose flour
1-1/2 cups sweet milk
3-1/2 teaspoons baking powder
3 eggs
1-1/2 cups mincemeat
1-1/2 cups apples, chopped
1/2 cup fresh orange juice
1/2 cup sugar
2 tablespoons melted butter
1/2 cup brown sugar, firmly packed

Cream butter and sugar; beat in eggs. Add milk, flour and baking powder. Set aside. In bottom of baking pan melt butter and brown sugar; place mincemeat mixture over this. Pour cake batter over all. Bake 375 degrees for 40 minutes. On cake plate, turn cake upside down. To serve: cut into squares; serve with whipped cream.

Gwen Campbell, Sterling, Va.

JOLLY GOOD PLUM CAKE

Serves 12

2 cups all-purpose flour
1 teaspoon baking soda
1 teaspoon nutmeg
1/2 teaspoon salt
1-1/2 cups sugar
1 cup salad oil
3 eggs
1 cup buttermilk
1 (7-1/2 ounce) jar junior plums
1 teaspoon vanilla
1 cup chopped walnuts

Preheat oven to 350 degrees. Sift together flour, baking soda, nutmeg and salt. In large bowl, combine sugar and oil. Add eggs and beat well. Alternately add sifted ingredients and buttermilk; mix well. Add plums and vanilla, stirring to blend. Fold in chopped walnuts. Spoon batter into greased 13x9x2-inch baking pan. Bake 45 minutes or until done. Let cool in pan. Cut into squares in pan.

Bobbie Mae Cooley, Bowen, Ill.

WITCHES' ORANGE COOKIES

1 egg
½ cup margarine
½ cup orange juice
2 teaspoons orange rind
2 cups sifted flour
½ teaspoon salt
½ teaspoon baking powder
1 teaspoon cinnamon
½ cup chopped nuts
½ cup raisins

Beat egg well. Add margarine, orange juice and rind; set aside. Sift flour, salt, baking powder and cinnamon together. Combine with egg mixture. Fold in nuts and raisins. Drop by teaspoon on lightly greased cookie sheet. Bake at 375 degrees for 15 minutes, or until lightly browned. Enjoy!

PUMPKIN MUFFINS

1½ cups sifted flour
1 teaspoon salt
2 teaspoons baking powder
½ cup sugar
½ teaspoon nutmeg
½ teaspoon cinnamon
¼ cup margarine, softened
1 egg
½ cup cooked pumpkin
⅓ cup milk
⅓ cup raisins

Sift flour, salt, baking powder, sugar, nutmeg and cinnamon together. Set aside. Combine margarine, egg, pumpkin and milk. Add to flour mixture. Fold in raisins. Fill muffin tins and bake at 400 degrees for 20 minutes.

SNOWFALL CAKE

1 round sponge cake
2 packages instant vanilla custard
Snowfall cream (recipe follows)
Candied fruits
1/2 cup confectioners' sugar, sifted

Cut cake into 3 equal layers; place waxed paper between layers; chill. Prepare custard filling; chill. When chilled, spread 1/2 the custard on first layer; top with second layer and cover with remaining custard; top with last layer. Cover entire cake with Snowfall Cream; gently press candied fruits on sides and in 2 rounds on top of cake. Gently "snowfall" the confectioners' sugar across top of cake and add candied fruits.

Snowfall Cream:
4 cups whipping cream
4-8 tablespoons powdered sugar

Whip cream until soft peaks form; beat in sugar until stiff peaks form.

Gwen Campbell, Sterling, Va.

CHRISTMAS MACAROON PIE

2 dozen macaroons, dried thoroughly
1/2 cup soft butter
1/2 cup milk
2 slightly-beaten eggs
1/3 cup sugar
Pinch of salt
1/2 envelope unflavored gelatin
1/4 cup cold water
1 cup heavy cream, whipped
1/4 cup finely-chopped pecans
4 large marshmallows, cut fine
1 slice canned pineapple, cut fine
2 ounces candied cherries

Make crust from crushed macaroons and butter. Press into 9-inch pie plate. Make custard of next 5 ingredients over low heat. Soak gelatin in cold water and add to hot custard, stirring until gelatin dissolves. Allow to cool, then fold in fruits, nuts and marshmallows. Pour into pie shell and chill.

Julie Habiger, Spearville, Kan.

MINCEMEAT BREAD
Makes 2 loaves

1 (9 ounce) package dry mincemeat
1 cup whole wheat flour
2 cups sifted flour
3/4 cup sugar
4 teaspoons baking powder
1 teaspoon salt
1 egg, beaten
1 cup evaporated milk or half-and-half

Crumble mincemeat into saucepan; add 1/2 cup water. Bring to boil, stirring constantly. Cook about 4 minutes; cool. Blend flours, sugar, salt and baking powder together. Combine egg and evaporated milk; add flour mixture, mixing until smooth. Fold in mincemeat. Place in 2 greased loaf pans. Bake at 350 degrees for about 45 minutes or until it tests done. May be glazed, if desired, after cooling.

Agnes Ward, Erie, Pa.

NOEL ROASTED CHESTNUT BREAD

2 (13-3/4 ounce) packages hot roll mix
1-1/4 cups warm milk
2 eggs
1/4 cup honey
1/2 teaspoon cinnamon
1/2 teaspoon nutmeg
1 cup canned roasted chestnut purée
2 tablespoons honey
2 tablespoons almonds, flaked

Prepare hot roll mix according to package directions; beat in eggs, honey and spices. Let rise 30 minutes. Turn onto floured surface; knead roasted chestnuts gently into dough. Place in round 1-1/2-quart ovenproof casserole; allow to rise until double in volume. Bake at 375 degrees 40-50 minutes until deep golden brown. Loosen from casserole; cool on wire rack. While still warm, brush bread with honey; sprinkle with flaked almonds.

Gwen Campbell, Sterling, Va.

CANDLESTICK BARS

1 (14-ounce) package gingerbread mix
1 (8-ounce) can applesauce
½ cup raisins
1 (4-ounce) jar chopped mixed candied fruits and peels
1 (14-ounce) package white creamy frosting mix
2 tablespoons lemon juice

Combine gingerbread mix and applesauce; beat 2 minutes at medium speed or 2 minutes with spoon. Stir in raisins, fruits and peels. Spread in 15½ x 10½ x 1-inch jelly roll pan. Bake at 375 degrees for 15 minutes. Prepare frosting and add lemon juice, substituting lemon juice for half the liquid. Spread on cooled bars. Decorate with red and yellow gumdrops to look like a candle. Use red candy for candle and yellow candy for flame.

Melba Bellefeuille, Libertyville, Ill.

CHRISTMAS CARROT LOAF
Makes 1 loaf

1-1/4 cups sifted flour
1/2 cup sugar
1/2 teaspoon baking powder
1/2 teaspoon soda
1 teaspoon cinnamon
1/2 teaspoon nutmeg
1/2 teaspoon ginger
1/4 teaspoon salt
2 eggs, beaten
1/4 cup oil
1/4 cup milk
1 cup shredded carrots
3/4 cup coconut
1/4 cup maraschino cherries, chopped and drained
1/4 cup raisins
1/4 cup chopped pecans.

Sift flour, baking powder and soda together with spices in large bowl. Combine eggs, oil and milk in bowl, mix well. Add dry ingredients, beat well. Stir in remaining ingredients. Turn into greased loaf pan. Bake at 350 degrees for 50-60 minutes.

Melba Bellefeuille, Libertyville, Ill.

PUMPKIN COOKIES

1 cup brown sugar
1 cup cooked pumpkin
½ cup Mazola oil
2 cups sifted flour
1 teaspoon vanilla
1 teaspoon baking soda
1 teaspoon baking powder
½ teaspoon salt
½ teaspoon cinnamon
½ teaspoon nutmeg
½ cup raisins
½ cup nuts
⅔ cup orange slices (candy), finely chopped

Mix all ingredients together. Drop by spoonfuls onto greased cookie sheet. Bake at 375 degrees for about 10 minutes.

Marcella Swigert, Monroe City, Mo.

Ice Cream
TREATS

MAPLE ICE CREAM
Makes 1 gallon

6 tablespoons flour
1-1/2 cups brown sugar
2/3 cup white sugar
1/2 and 1/8 teaspoon salt
3 eggs, separated
2-1/2 quarts milk
1 can evaporated milk
1 teaspoon maple flavoring
1/2 teaspoon vanilla flavoring

Mix flour, sugars, salt, egg yolks, and 1-1/2 cups of the milk. Bring 1-1/2 quarts of the milk to a boil; add flour mixture to milk and boil 5 minutes; remove from heat and cool. Add stiffly beaten egg whites, remainder of milk, vanilla, maple, and evaporated milk; freeze.

To freeze: Use a 4-quart hand-crank or electric ice-cream maker. Pour maple mixture into freezer container; insert dasher and cover with lid. Place in bucket; attach the hand crank or motor.

Fill bucket half full with ice. Sprinkle on about 1 cup salt (rock). Continue adding layers of ice and salt in a 4-to-1 proportion to 1 inch below can lid. (As ice melts, add more ice and salt up to this level.) Begin cranking. (For electric ice-cream maker, follow manufacturer's direction.) It takes about 20-25 minutes to freeze.

To serve, remve crank or motor. Drain off water. Wipe off lid before removing. Remove dasher. Serve immediately for best texture. Makes about 1 gallon or 8 (8 ounce) servings.

Mrs. Olen Begly, West Salem, Ohio

DOUBLE BERRY FROST
Serves 5–6

1 pint (2 cups) strawberry ice cream
1 (10-ounce) package frozen strawberries
2 cups milk

Place all ingredients in blender container. Cover; blend until smooth and frothy, about 1 minute. Pour into cups.

Peggy Fowler Revels, Woodruff, S.C.

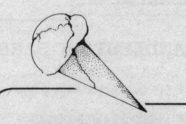

MOM'S BLUE-RIBBON ICE CREAM
Makes 1 gallon

2-1/2 cups sugar
4-6 eggs
1/8 teaspoon salt
1 tablespoon flour
1-1/2 tablespoons vanilla
1/2 teaspoon lemon flavoring
1 quart cream

Beat sugar and eggs until very thick. Mix all remaining ingredients with the creamed sugar and eggs. Pour mixture into chilled gallon freezer cylinder. Pour in milk to reach fill line or 3 inches from top. Freeze by hand-crank or electric freezer until firm or very hard to crank.

LIME MILK SHERBET
Makes 1-1/2 pints

3/4 cup sugar
3/4 cup water
2 cups evaporated milk
1/2 teaspoon vanilla
1/4 - 3/8 cup lime juice

Boil sugar and water to a thin syrup. Cool and put into ice-cream can with the milk. Add vanilla and lime juice. Freeze with 1-to-8 salt-ice mixture. Note: Ice used in the freezing mixture should be finely cracked. For cracking, a heavy sack and a wooden mallet are very useful.

Marcella Swigert, Monroe City, Mo.

PINK BANANA BLIZZARD
Makes 6 cups

1 (6-ounce) can frozen red punch concentrate, undiluted
2 bananas, cut into chunks
2 cups milk
1 pint vanilla ice cream

In electric blender container, combine half of all ingredients. Cover; blend until smooth and frothy, 15 to 20 seconds. Pour into tall glasses. Repeat with remaining ingredients. Serve immediately with straws.

Leota Baxter, Ingalls, Kan.

ORANGE-PINEAPPLE ICE CREAM
Makes 1 gallon

1 (6-ounce) package orange-
   pineapple gelatin
2 cups boiling water
4 eggs
1-1/2 cups sugar
2 tablespoons flour
1/4 teaspoon salt
2 cups half-and-half
1 (20-ounce) can crushed chilled
   pineapple, undrained
1 (14-ounce) can sweetened
   condensed milk, chilled
1 (8-ounce) carton non-dairy frozen
   whipped topping, thawed
1 (12-ounce) can frozen orange-
   pineapple concentrate, thawed
   and undiluted

Dissolve gelatin in boiling water; let cool to room temperature. Set aside. Beat eggs in large bowl on medium speed of electric mixer until frothy. Add sugar, flour, salt, and half-and-half, mixing to blend. Place mixture in heavy saucepan over medium heat, stirring constantly until mixture coats back of a spoon (soft custard), about 10 minutes. (Mixture may also be cooked in a microwave.) Cool; stir in gelatin mixture, pineapple, condensed milk, whipped topping, and concentrate. Chill ingredients thoroughly (overnight is best). Pour into freezer can of a 1-gallon ice cream maker. Freeze according to manufacturer's directions. Allow ice cream flavors to ripen at least 1 hour before serving.

Marcella Swigert, Monroe City, Mo.

PEANUT BUTTER SHAKE
Makes 4 cups

2 cups milk
1 pint vanilla ice cream
1/4 cup creamy peanut butter

Combine all ingredients in container of electric blender; process until smooth. Serve at once.

Bertha Fowler, Woodruff, S.C.

ICE–CREAM TREAT
Serves 12

32 chocolate chip cookies
1/4 cup margarine, melted
1 cup chocolate fudge topping
2 quarts ice cream, any flavor
Prepared whipped topping for
   garnish
Strawberries for garnish

Finely roll or crush 20 cookies. Combine cookie crumbs and margarine. Press onto bottom of pie plate. Stand remaining cookies around edge of pie plate. Spread 3/4 cup fudge topping over prepared crust. Freeze about 15 minutes. Meanwhile, soften 1 quart ice cream. Spread softened ice cream over fudge layer. Freeze for about 30 minutes. Scoop remaining ice cream into balls. Arrange over ice-cream layer. Freeze until firm for about 4 hours, or overnight. Garnish with whipped topping, remaining fudge topping and strawberries.

Suzan L. Wiener, Spring Hill, Fla.

ICED TEA A LA MODE
Serves 3

2 cups double-strength cold tea
1 pint vanilla ice cream

Blend tea and ice cream until smooth and pour into a tall glass.

ICED TEA SODA
Serves 8

4 cups double-strength cold tea
1/2 cup light corn syrup
1 pint vanilla ice cream
Carbonated water

Blend tea and corn syrup. Fill a tall glass half-full with mixture. Add a scoop of ice cream, then fill the glass to the top with carbonated water.

PINEAPPLE BUTTER-MILK SHERBET
Serves 6

2 cups buttermilk
1 cup sugar
1 (9-ounce) can crushed pineapple
1 egg white, stiffly beaten
1 teaspoon vanilla
1/2 teaspoon unflavored gelatin
2 teaspoons cold water

Drain pineapple. Combine buttermilk, sugar, pineapple, and vanilla. Add gelatin which has been soaked in cold water and dissolved over hot water. Fold in egg white.

To freeze in churn-type freezer: Pour into freezer can and freeze according to directions with freezer.

Great as a dessert following a dinner and super with brownies!

Anne S. Moffett, APO, N.Y.

LEMON VELVET ICE CREAM
Serves 6

2 cups (1 pint) heavy cream *or* half-
   and-half
3/4 cup granulated sugar
1/2 cup frozen lemonade concentrate, thawed

Stir heavy cream and sugar in an 8-inch square metal baking pan until sugar is dissolved. Stir in lemon juice until blended. Freeze about 3 hours until firm. Remove from freezer and let stand at room temperature, 5 minutes before serving.

Diantha Susan Hibbard, Rochester, N.Y.

CITRUS ICED TEA A LA MODE
Serves 5

3 cups double-strength cold tea
1/2 cup chilled orange juice
1 pint vanilla ice cream

Blend ingredients until smooth and pour into a tall glass.

Kids
IN THE KITCHEN

MAGIC PUDDING COOKIES

Makes 3 dozen

- 1 cup Bisquick baking mix
- 1 (4-serving) box instant pudding
- ¼ cup salad oil
- 1 egg

Combine baking mix with instant pudding. Add salad oil and egg. When the dough forms a ball, shape a teaspoonful into a ball and place onto an ungreased cookie sheet. Flatten the balls lightly and sprinkle with colored sugar. Bake at 350 degrees for 5–8 minutes.

Whenever I feel like a cookie treat, my mom lets me make this recipe. Each time you make them it's like magic—a new taste treat depending on which instant pudding flavor you use!

Dustan Neyland, Gillette, Wyo.

NO-BAKE ORANGE SLICES

- 1 small can frozen orange juice concentrate
- 1 (17-ounce) package vanilla wafers, crushed
- ¼ pound soft butter (1 stick)
- 1 (1-pound) package confectioners' sugar
- 1 cup chopped nuts
- 2 cups coconut

Mix all ingredients; except coconut, and roll mixture into balls. Roll balls in coconut.

Barbara Hurlocker, Rock Hill, S.C.

WHOOPIE PIES

- 6 tablespoons Crisco shortening
- ½ teaspoon salt
- 1 cup sugar
- 1 egg
- 1 teaspoon vanilla
- 1 cup milk
- 2 cups flour
- 5 tablespoons cocoa
- 1½ teaspoons soda

Cream together first 6 ingredients. Blend flour, cocoa and soda and add to first mixture; blend well. Drop by spoonfuls on an ungreased cookie sheet. Bake at 425 degrees for 10 minutes. Put 2 pies together with this filling:

- ¾ cup Crisco shortening
- ¾ cup confectioners' sugar
- 6 tablespoons marshmallow creme

Combine ingredients and beat well.

Barbara Farren, Addison, Maine

COCONUT BALLS

- ¼ cup shortening
- 1 egg
- 1 teaspoon vanilla
- ¼ pound graham crackers, crushed
- ¼ cup sugar
- ¼ cup coconut

Mix shortening and egg and cook until thickened. Add remainder of ingredients; mix and roll into balls.

Marguerite Myers, Germantown, N.Y.

SAVORY CRACKERS

- ¼ teaspoon garlic powder
- ¼ teaspoon dill weed
- 1 package dry ranch-style dressing mix
- 1 (1-pound) package oyster crackers
- ½ cup salad oil

In container with tight-fitting lid combine garlic powder, dill weed and dry dressing mix; stir to combine. Add oyster crackers; put on lid and shake until crackers are covered with seasoning. Sprinkle oil over all. Cover again and shake until oil is absorbed.

Place crackers on cookie sheet; heat in 350-degree oven for 10 minutes.

Donna K. Gore, Aztec, N.M.

SEVEN-LAYER BARS

- ½ cup butter
- 1½ cups crushed graham crackers
- 1 cup flaked coconut
- 1 (6-ounce) package chocolate chips
- 1 (6-ounce) package butterscotch chips
- 1 cup nuts
- 1 can sweetened condensed milk

Melt butter in bottom of 9 x 13-inch pan. Put all other ingredients in pan in layers in order given, pouring milk over the top of last layer. Bake 15–20 minutes in 350-degree oven.

Mrs. Roger Krueger, Neshkoro, Wis.

PEACH 'N PINEAPPLE SHAKE

- 1 pint vanilla ice cream, softened
- ¾ cup drained, chilled, canned, sliced peaches
- ¾ cup chilled unsweetened pineapple juice
- 1 cup cold milk
- ½ teaspoon vanilla extract
  Fresh mint, if desired

Place ice cream, peaches and pineapple juice in blender and cover. Blend on high speed until smooth. Add milk and vanilla. Blend well again. Serve at once in chilled, tall glasses garnished with fresh mint.

Veronica Gengler, Saukville, Wis.

FRUIT MILK SHAKE
Serves 4

A delicious new way to serve fruit!

- 3 cups ripe fresh fruit in season *or* canned fruit in light syrup *or* natural juice
- ½ cup non-fat dry milk
- 1 cup water or drained juice from can
- 8 ice cubes

Peel fruit if necessary. Cut fruit into pieces; mash through a strainer or in a food mill. Crush ice cubes (one way is to place them in a heavy plastic bag and use a rolling pin or hammer). Blend fruit, milk powder and liquid with a beater. Add crushed ice and blend again.

Mary Linger, Jacksonville, Fla.

ELEPHANT'S JUG

- 1 cup milk
- ¼ cup peanut butter (either crunchy *or* smooth)
- 1 ripe banana
- 2 teaspoons sugar
- 4 ice cubes

Combine all ingredients, except ice cubes, in blender and blend until smooth. Add ice and blend just until ice is crushed.

Pour into 2 glasses and serve immediately.

This makes a good snack for children after school or a quick breakfast when time is short.

Monica W. Cox, Cleveland, Miss.

ORANGE JULIUS
Serves 2

- ⅓ cup frozen orange juice concentrate
- ½ cup milk
- ½ cup water
- ¼ cup sugar (*or* less, depending on taste)
- ½ teaspoon vanilla
  Ice cubes—5 or 6

Combine all ingredients in blender container; cover and blend until smooth, on lowest speed of blender. Serve immediately.

Richard Ferschweiler, Paisley, Ore.

JUICY FRUIT SHAKE
Serves 4

- 1½ cups sweetened pineapple juice
- 2½ cups milk

In blender, blend chilled sweetened pineapple, apricot and strawberry or raspberry juice and milk. Serve over ice.

Leah Seymour, Columbia Cross Roads, Pa.

COTTONTAIL MILK SHAKE
Serves 1

- 1 banana
- 1 egg
- 1 cup cold milk
- 1 tablespoon honey
- 1 tablespoon peanut butter

Put all ingredients in blender and blend on high speed for 30 seconds. Pour into glass and serve.

Mrs. Floyd Morrison, Omaha, Ga.

OATMEAL CRACKERS

- 3 cups rolled oats
- 1 cup wheat germ
- 2 cups flour
- 3 tablespoons sugar
- 1 teaspoon salt
- ¾ cup oil
- 1 cup water

Combine all ingredients and place onto cookie sheets. Cut into squares and sprinkle with salt. Bake for 30 minutes at 300 degrees, or until crisp.

Heather Grauer, Seneca, Kan.

CARAMEL APPLES

- 1 package caramels (10 ounces)
- 4 teaspoons water
- 4–5 medium-size apples

Put caramels and water on top of double boiler. Place over low heat until melted, about 15 minutes, stirring occasionally. Insert sticks into clean apples. Dip into melted caramels; twirl until apples are coated; set on butter-coated waxed paper. Refrigerate until cool.

Mrs. Harold Kramer, Parkersburg, Iowa

YOGURT FRUIT CRUNCH
Serves 4

It's smooth, crunchy and sweet.

- 2 cups plain low-fat yogurt
- 1 cup dry cereal (granola type o dry crunchy cereal)
- 1 cup fruit, fresh or canned in light syrup or natural juices

Spoon layers of cereal, yogurt an fruit into 4 individual bowls.

Betty Poorman, Springfield, I

NO-BAKE CHOCOLATE COOKIES

- 2 cups sugar
- ½ cup butter or margarine
- ½ cup milk
- 5 tablespoons cocoa
- 3 cups quick-cooking oatmeal
- 1 cup walnuts
- ½ teaspoon vanilla

Mix and cook together for 1 minute, the sugar, butter and milk. Remove from heat and add cocoa, oats and nuts. Add vanilla and stir until it can be dropped from a spoon onto waxed paper.

Genevieve Burns, McMinnville, Ore.

QUICK GRAHAM TREATS

- 2 cups confectioners' sugar
- ½ stick margarine or butter, softened
- 1 teaspoon vanilla
  Milk (1 or 2 tablespoons)
  Graham crackers

Combine sugar, margarine or butter, vanilla and 1 tablespoon milk; blend until smooth. If too thick, add more milk. Spread about 1 tablespoon frosting on a graham cracker and top with a second cracker. The number of sandwich cookies this makes depends upon whether you spread the frosting or the children spread it. Kids love this!

Georgia Bender, Kittanning, Pa.

GOOFY BARS

- 1 package white cake mix
- 2 eggs
  Water
- 1 cup brown sugar
- 1 cup chocolate chips
- 1 cup miniature marshmallows

Place dry cake mix in a bowl. Pu eggs in a glass measuring cup and ad enough water to make ⅔ cup; add t cake mix with brown sugar. Beat unti blended and spread in a greased 9 x 13 inch pan. Sprinkle chocolate chips an marshmallows on top. Bake at 35 degrees for 30-40 minutes.

Cheryl Santefort, Thornton, Iow

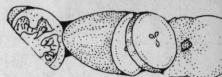

FUDGE BARS

- 1 cup shortening
- 2 cups sugar
- 4 eggs
- ½ teaspoon salt
- 1½ cups flour
- ½ teaspoon baking powder
- 4 tablespoons cocoa
- 2 teaspoons vanilla
- ½ cup nuts

Combine all ingredients and spread in greased and floured 9 x 13-inch pan. Bake at 350 degrees until toothpick comes out clean.

Mrs. Roger Krueger, Neshkoro, Wis.

AMISH HAT

- 4 Ritz crackers
- 1 large marshmallow or 4 small marshmallows
  Peanut butter

Spread peanut butter on crackers and add marshmallows. Place in microwave or under broiler and broil until marshmallow is soft.

Betty Klopfenstein, Waterman, Ill.

FINGER JELL-O

- 1½ cups boiling water
- 1 (3-ounce) package orange Jell-O
- 2 packages Knox unflavored gelatin
- 1½ cups cold orange juice

Dissolve Jell-O and gelatin in boil ing water and add the cold orange juice Pour into a square dish and chill unti set. Cut into squares.

Mary Hale, Tulsa, Okla

EASY PEANUT BUTTER COOKIES

This is a favorite with children!

1 cup peanut butter
1 cup sugar
1 egg
1 teaspoon vanilla

Mix peanut butter and sugar; stir in remaining ingredients. Shape in 1-inch balls and put on ungreased cookie sheets. Press with fork to flatten slightly and bake in a 350-degree oven for 12–15 minutes.
Note: There is no flour in this recipe.
Elizabeth McJunkin, Toronto, Kan.

PEANUT BUTTER S'MORES

Split hamburger buns
Peanut butter
Marshmallow creme *or* marshmallows

Split hamburger buns and spread each half with peanut butter. Top with a big teaspoon of marshmallow creme or marshmallows. Place bun halves on broiler pan and broil until marshmallow top is lightly brown.
Betty Klopfenstein, Waterman, Ill.

WHIZZ BARS

1 (6-ounce) package chocolate chips
1 (6-ounce) package butterscotch chips
½ cup peanut butter
1 (10½-ounce) package miniature marshmallows
1 cup salted peanuts
½ cup Rice Krispies

Combine chips and peanut butter; melt. Pour over remaining ingredients and press into a 9 x 13-inch pan. Refrigerate until set. This makes a quick snack when you don't have time to bake.
Cheryl Santefort, Thornton, Ill.

NO-BAKE MARSHMALLOW COOKIES

1 (12-ounce) package chocolate morsels
2 tablespoons butter
3 eggs
2 cups confectioners' sugar
1 cup chopped walnuts
1 (10½-ounce) bag miniature marshmallows
Coconut

Melt chocolate morsels with butter in heavy pan over low heat, or in double boiler. Cool. Beat eggs; add sugar, walnuts and marshmallows. Mix all together in large bowl. Shape into balls; roll in coconut and refrigerate. Will keep about 1 month. Butterscotch morsels may be substituted for chocolate.
Marg Ondus, Southwest, Pa.

OATMEAL COOKIES

¾ cup flour
1 teaspoon baking powder
½ teaspoon salt
¾ cup oatmeal
½ teaspoon cinnamon
½ cup sugar
¼ cup shortening
½ cup raisins *or* nuts
1 egg
3 tablespoons milk

Sift flour, baking powder, salt and cinnamon. Cream shortening and sugar together until smooth. Add egg and beat until blended. Stir in oatmeal, raisins or nuts, and milk. Mix well. Add flour mixture. Mix. Drop by teaspoonfuls onto a greased cookie sheet. Bake about 12 minutes in a 375-degree oven.
David Andrews, Butler, Pa.

COCONUT MACAROONS
Makes 2½ dozen

2 cups shredded coconut
⅓ cup sweetened condensed milk
½ teaspoon vanilla extract
1 egg white, stiffly beaten

Blend coconut, milk and vanilla thoroughly; stir in egg white. Drop from teaspoon onto greased cookie sheets; bake in 350-degree oven for 15 minutes. Remove from pan while warm.
Elsie Swanson, Bar Harbor, Maine.

LUSCIOUS LIME WHIP

1 (3-ounce) package lime gelatin
1 (13¼-ounce) can crushed pineapple, drained
8 ounces creamed cottage cheese
1 (4¼-ounce) container Cool Whip

Gently combine all ingredients and refrigerate until well-chilled.
Note: Gelatin is used directly from package. It is not dissolved.
Molly Cairnes, Germantown, Wis.

SEASONED CEREAL SNACKS
Makes 4 cups

⅓ cup margarine, melted
½ teaspoon garlic salt
2 teaspoons Worcestershire sauce
2½ cups Kellogg's Most® cereal
1 cup thin pretzel sticks
½ cup salted peanuts

Combine melted margarine, garlic salt and Worcestershire sauce in a 13 x 9-inch pan. Stir in cereal, peanuts and pretzels. Bake in 250-degree oven for 40–45 minutes. Cool and store in airtight container.
Mary Bell, Cincinnati, Ohio

NO-BAKE PEANUT SQUARES

- 1 cup light corn syrup
- 1 cup white sugar
- 1 cup peanut butter
- 4 cups cornflakes
- 4 cups Cheerios
- 1 cup peanuts

In a 2-quart pan melt together just until smooth the first 3 ingredients, stirring constantly. Do not boil. Remove from heat. Measure the last 3 ingredients into a large bowl. Pour over peanut butter mixture. Stir, coating cereal and nuts. Spread in buttered large pan. Cut into squares. Press down.

Travis Williams, Stockton, Kan.

FINGER GELATIN

- 4 (1-ounce) packages unflavored gelatin
  Fruit-flavored diet pop (16 ounces)

Dissolve gelatin in half the pop. Heat the remaining pop slightly. Add to softened gelatin. Pour into square pan. Chill in refrigerator for about 10 minutes. Cut into squares. Eat with your fingers!

Diane Cole, Cleveland, Ohio

CRAB-CHEESE FONDUE

- 1½ sticks butter *or* margarine
- 1 (8-ounce) package Velveeta cheese
- 1 small can crabmeat
  French bread

Melt butter or margarine and cheese over low heat. Stir well until cheese and butter are combined. Stir in crabmeat. Spear French bread with fondue forks and dip in mixture.

Mrs. John Clifford, Grofton, Wis.

NO-BAKE CHOCOLATE BARS

- 1 cup chopped walnuts
- 4 cups graham cracker crumbs
- ½ cup sifted confectioners' sugar
- 1 (12-ounce) package semisweet chocolate chips
- 1 cup evaporated milk
- 1 teaspoon vanilla

Combine nuts, crumbs and sugar in a large bowl. Melt chocolate and evaporated milk over low heat stirring constantly. Blend well. Add vanilla and then set aside ½ cup chocolate mixture. Stir in crumbs mixture and spread in a well-buttered, 9-inch square pan. Spread rest of chocolate mixture over top. Chill and cut into bars.

Lucille Wardlow, Oxnard, Colo.

CANDY COOKIES

- 1 cup white sugar
- 1 cup white Karo
- 1 cup peanut butter
- 2 cups cornflakes
- 1½ cups Cheerios
- 1½ cups Rice Krispies

Combine sugar and syrup; boil until clear. Mix in peanut butter. Combine cereals and mix well. Pour peanut butter-syrup mixture over cereals; drop by spoonfuls onto waxed paper. Store in cool place.

Elva Henderson, Presque Isle, Maine

BUTTERSCOTCH COOKIES

Makes 5 dozen

- 2 cups granulated sugar
- ¾ cup margarine
- ⅔ cup evaporated milk
- 1 (3¾-ounce) box butterscotch instant pudding mix
- 3½ cups quick oatmeal

Mix sugar, margarine and evaporated milk in saucepan and bring to a rolling boil on low heat, stirring constantly. Remove from heat and add pudding mix and oatmeal. Mix thoroughly. Cool 3 minutes; drop by teaspoonfuls onto waxed paper. Let sit until cool. Chocolate, chocolate fudge, lemon, or coconut instant puddings may be substituted.

Mrs. Herman A. Strasser, Evans, Colo.

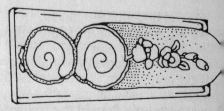

COCOA PEANUT LOGS

- 1 cup semisweet chocolate pieces
- ⅓ cup peanut butter
- 4 cups cocoa-flavored corn puffs cereal

Butter a 9-inch square pan. Melt chocolate with peanut butter in heavy, medium pan over low heat, stirring constantly. When well-blended remove from heat. Stir in cocoa corn puffs to coat well. Press mixture into prepared pan. Cool or refrigerate until mixture is hardened. Cut into log-shaped bars.

Mrs. M. Piccinni, Ozone Park, N.Y.

HOPSCOTCH CRUNCHIES

Makes 1½ dozen

- 1 (6-ounce) package butterscotch morsels
- ½ cup peanut butter
- 1 (3-ounce) can chow mein noodles
- 1 cup miniature marshmallows

Melt over hot water in double boiler 1 package butterscotch morsels and ½ cup peanut butter. Remove from heat; stir in 1 can chow mein noodles and marshmallows. Drop by teaspoonfuls onto waxed paper. Chill until set.

Lisa Bauman, Fort Wayne, Ind.

RICE KRISPY TREATS
Makes 24

No more standing over a double boiler waiting for the marshmallows to melt. This treat can be ready to chill in 10 minutes, and that includes getting out the ingredients. They have been a favorite of kids for years.

- ½ cup butter *or* margarine
- 45 large marshmallows (*or* 4 cups miniature)
- 5 cups rice cereal

Place butter and marshmallows in a 3-quart casserole. Do not cover. Microwave on HIGH for 3 minutes, stirring often. Add cereal. Mix until completely coated with marshmallow mixture. With buttered hands, press into 8 x 12-inch or 9 x 13-inch pan. Cool. Cut into bars.

Mary Fran Williams, Dayton, Ohio

SOFT PRETZELS
Makes 8–10

Fun to twist any way you like!

- 1 loaf frozen bread dough
  Poppy *or* sesame seeds

Thaw covered dough overnight in refrigerator, or for several hours at room temperature, until soft enough to shape. On a floured surface, cut dough the long way into 8 strips. Cover and let rise 10 minutes. Roll each strip on floured surface or between floured hands until ½ inch thick and 18 inches long. Shape strips into pretzel shape and place on greased cookie sheets. Brush with lukewarm water. Sprinkle lightly with sesame or poppy seeds.

Let rise, uncovered, for 15–20 minutes in warm, draft-free place. Place a shallow pan of water on bottom shelf of oven. Preheat to 425 degrees. Bake pretzels on center shelf of oven for 18–20 minutes, or until golden brown.

Mabel Phillips, Dallas, Texas

MIXED DRY CEREAL AND NUTS
Serves 9–10

- 2 tablespoons margarine
- 1¼ cups unsalted roasted peanuts
- 2½ cups assorted unsweetened, ready-to-eat cereals
- 1 teaspoon paprika
- ¼ teaspoon onion powder
- ⅛ teaspoon garlic powder
- 1¼ teaspoons chili powder

Preheat oven to 250 degrees. Melt margarine in large baking pan in oven. Remove pan from oven; stir in nuts and cereals; mix well. Sprinkle with seasonings; stir well. Bake, uncovered, in oven 20–30 minutes, or until light-colored cereals begin to brown. Stir every 10 minutes. Serve warm or cooled. Store cooled cereal snack in tightly closed containers. If snack needs re-crisping, reheat in 250-degree oven for a few minutes.

A crunchy, low-salt treat that is a sure crowd pleaser.

Heather Williams, Dayton, Ohio

CUTOUT COOKIES
Makes 10 dozen

- 3 cups flour
- ¼ teaspoon salt
- ½ teaspoon nutmeg *or* 1 teaspoon vanilla
- 1 cup butter *or* margarine
- ½ cup milk
- 1 cup sugar
- 1 teaspoon soda

Mix first 4 ingredients as you would pie crust. Heat milk, sugar and soda until it foams. Cool mixture; add to flour mixture. Chill dough thoroughly. Roll out on floured board. Cut in various shapes. Bake on greased cookie sheet at 375 degrees for 3–5 minutes, or until lightly browned.

The dough is very easy to roll out so the recipe is ideal for the young cook.

I make the cookies all year long using the shape cutters according to what special day is coming up.

Phyllis Last, Green Bay, Wis.

SAVORY SUNFLOWER SNACK
Makes 2 cups

- 3¾ cups sunflower seeds
- 3 tablespoons oil
- ¼ teaspoon cayenne
- 3 tablespoons soy sauce
- ½ teaspoon ground celery seed
- ¼ teaspoon paprika

Combine sunflower seeds with other seasonings in a shallow baking pan. Stir well. Bake in preheated 350-degree oven for 20 minutes, stirring after 10 minutes.

Remove pan from oven. Drain on paper towels to blot excess oil. Cool and store in tightly covered container.

To double recipe, bake about 30 minutes.

Mary Bell, Cincinnati, Ohio

STRAWBERRY SPREAD

- 1 jar strawberry jam
- 1 pint marshmallow creme

Combine ingredients and mix well. Use on hot rolls, toast or as an ice-cream topping.

Rebbie Baker, Killbuck, Ohio

SNOW-CONE SYRUP

- 2 cups sugar
- ¾ cup water
- 1 package unsweetened Kool-Aid

Bring sugar and water to a full boil. Remove from heat and stir in Kool-Aid. Chill. It's now ready for the crushed ice.

Sue Hibbard, Rochester, N.Y.

CHOCOLATE PEANUT BUTTER APPLES

Makes 6–8

6–8 medium-size apples
6–8 wooden skewers
1 cup semisweet chocolate mini chips
1 cup peanut butter-flavored chips
1 tablespoon vegetable oil

Wash apples and dry thoroughly. Insert wooden skewer into each apple. Set aside. Melt mini chips and peanut butter chips with oil in top of double boiler or in a heavy 1½-quart saucepan over low heat; stir constantly until smooth. Remove from heat; dip apples in mixture (tilting pan as needed). Twirl to remove excess coating; place apples on waxed-paper–covered cookie sheet. Refrigerate until firm.

Peggy Fowler Revels, Woodruff, S.C.

LEMONADE COOKIES

1 cup margarine
1 cup sugar
2 eggs
1 (6-ounce) can lemonade concentrate, thawed
1 (3¼-ounce) size (French's or McCormicks) yellow decorator's sugar
3 cups flour
1 teaspoon soda

Cream margarine and sugar; add eggs and mix well. Add flour and soda alternately with ½ cup lemonade concentrate. Drop by teaspoonfuls on ungreased cookie sheet. Bake at 400 degrees for 8–10 minutes. Paint with remaining lemonade and sprinkle with sugar. Remove to rack and cool. Sugar sticks better if you brush 1 or 2 at a time with pastry brush and then sprinkle sugar on them immediately.

Diane Cole. Cleveland. Ohio

WHIPPER-SNAPPERS

1 (18½-ounce) package lemon cake mix
2 cups frozen whipped topping, thawed
1 egg, beaten
1 teaspoon lemon flavoring Confectioners' sugar

Combine dry cake mix, whipped topping, egg and flavoring. Stir together until well-mixed. With hands dusted with confectioners' sugar, shape dough into small balls and roll in confectioners' sugar.

Bake in preheated 350-degree oven on greased cookie sheets for 10 minutes. These will puff up, and when they begin to settle down they are done. They should be slightly soft when you take them from the oven. Do not overbake.

These freeze well. Vary the recipe with a chocolate cake mix and vanilla flavoring.

Florence Satterfield, Greenfield, Ohio

JIFFY RAISIN SQUARES

1 (8-ounce) package cake mix, spice *or* vanilla
1 (3½-ounce) package butterscotch pudding
2 eggs
½ cup milk
1 cup seedless raisins

Beat in bowl, the cake mix, pudding mix, eggs and milk until smooth. Add raisins and pour into jelly roll pan. Bake at 350 degrees for 20 minutes. Cut into squares. Makes squares ½–¾-inch thick. Two may be spread with jelly or jam and put together as a "sandwich" for easy packing in a lunch box.

STRAWBERRY GEMS

1 cup margarine
1 (3-ounce) package strawberry gelatin
¼ cup sugar
2 cups flour

Cream margarine with gelatin and sugar. Beat until well-mixed. Blend in flour with wooden spoon or pastry blender until dough forms. Press into an 8-inch square on ungreased cookie sheet. Cut into 1-inch squares. Do not separate.

Bake in preheated 325-degree oven for 25 minutes. Cool 5 minutes. Recut. Roll in confectioners' sugar.

Sharon Crider, Evansville, Wis.

ROCKY ROAD BROWNIES

Makes 48 bars

You may begin with your favorite brownie recipe, but it is easier to start with a mix.

1 (22-ounce) package brownie mix
2 cups miniature marshmallows
1 (1-ounce) square unsweetened chocolate
2 tablespoons margarine
1 teaspoon vanilla
Dash salt
2 cups confectioners' sugar
¼ cup water

Prepare brownie mix according to package directions. Spoon into an 8 x 12-inch pan and smooth the top. Microwave on HIGH for 6 minutes. Remove from the oven. Sprinkle marshmallows over the top. Cool. Put chocolate and margarine into a glass bowl. Microwave on HIGH for 1 minute to melt. Add remaining ingredients and beat. Carefully spread frosting over the marshmallows. Cut into bars when cool.

Mabel Phillips, Dallas, Texas

LEMON REFRIGERATOR PUDDING
Serves 10

1 (21-ounce) can lemon pie filling
2 (11-ounce) cans mandarin oranges, drained
½ cup flaked coconut
2 cups miniature marshmallows
1 cup dairy sour cream
Cocktail cherries

Combine all ingredients, except cocktail cherries. Chill in refrigerator until needed; then serve decorated with cherries.

Marie D. Robinson, Largo, Fla.

SHERBET DESSERT

1 teaspoon vanilla
1 pint whipping cream *or* Dream Whip
18 soft coconut macaroons, crumbled
½ cup nuts
1 quart lime sherbet
1 quart raspberry sherbet

Combine vanilla and whipping cream or Dream Whip. Beat on high speed with electric mixer until creamy and fluffy. Mix macaroons and nuts in whipping cream. Take half the mixture and spread in pan. Spoon lime sherbet and raspberry sherbet over this, then top with remaining cream mixture. Place in freezer. Makes enough for one 9 x 13-inch pan or two 8 x 8-inch pans.

Mrs. Andrew L. Asaro, El Cajon, Calif.

PUDDING TORTONI
Serves 8

1 (4-serving size) package coconut cream pudding and pie filling, not instant
1¼ cups milk
⅓ cup sugar
½ teaspoon almond *or* rum extract

2 cups whipped cream *or* prepared Dream Whip topping
¼ cup coconut, toasted

Combine pudding mix, milk and sugar in a saucepan; cook as directed on package. Cover surface with waxed paper; chill. Beat until creamy. Add almond extract; then fold in whipped cream. Pour into individual soufflé cups. Sprinkle with toasted coconut. Freeze until firm, about 3 hours. Remove from freezer 15 minutes before serving.

Agnes E. Verska, Upper Marlboro, Md.

WAFFLE SUNDAES

2 frozen blueberry waffles (jumbo size), toasted
2 scoops strawberry *or* vanilla ice cream
Banana slices
Strawberry preserves
Whipped topping

For each serving, top 1 waffle with 1 scoop ice cream. Arrange banana slices around ice cream. Spoon preserves over ice cream. Garnish with whipped topping. Serve immediately.

Quick and easy to fix.

Mrs. Bruce Fowler, Woodruff, S.C.

CHOCOLATE MARSHMALLOW CUPS

3 cups miniature marshmallows
1 (12-ounce) package semisweet chocolate bits
1 cup crunchy peanut butter
1 stick butter
24 (1¾-inch) paper-lined muffin cups *or* 48 miniature muffin papers

Place 4 marshmallows in each cup. Combine chocolate bits, peanut butter and butter in a 2-quart saucepan. Cook over low heat, stirring often, until mixture is melted and smooth; remove from heat. Spoon chocolate mixture over marshmallows, using 3 or 4 table-

spoons for each cup. Cover and refrigerate. Store in refrigerator.

Jane Weimann, Woodstock, Conn.

STRAWBERRY YOGURT PIE

1 graham cracker pie shell
1 (8-ounce) carton strawberry yogurt
1 (8-ounce) carton Cool Whip
1 (10-ounce) package frozen strawberries (thawed)

Combine yogurt, Cool Whip and thawed strawberries; pour into pie shell. Freeze. Before serving, thaw pie for about 30 minutes. Garnish with additional Cool Whip and strawberries.

Jodie McCoy, Tulsa, Okla.

ICE-CREAM DELIGHT
Serves 2–3

1 (3-ounce) package gelatin, any flavor
1 cup boiling water
1 pint vanilla ice cream
Lime juice, if available

Dissolve gelatin in boiling water. Add softened ice cream and stir well. Add a squeeze of lime juice, if desired. Mix lightly and well. Pour into dessert dishes and refrigerate until set.

Miss Bald, Montserrat, West Indies

ANGEL FOOD CAKE WITH FLUFFY FROSTING

1 (already prepared) angel food cake
1 envelope Dream Whip
1 (4-serving) package any flavor instant pudding
1½ cups cold milk

Combine Dream Whip, pudding mix and cold milk. Beat at high speed to soft peaks (4–6 minutes). Frost angel food cake. Store in refrigerator.

Mary Lou C. Hendrickson, Deer River, Minn.

PAPER CUP FROZEN SALAD

2 cups sour cream
2 tablespoons lemon juice
⅛ teaspoon salt
½ cup sugar
1 (8-ounce) can crushed, drained pineapple
1 banana, diced
4 drops red food coloring
¼ cup chopped nuts
1 (1-pound) can pitted bing cherries, drained

Combine sour cream, lemon juice, sugar, salt and red food coloring. Add fruit and nuts. Put in paper cups and freeze. Muffin tins can be used.

Barbara G. Swain, England, Ark.

SCRUMPTIOUS SALAD MOLD

1 (30-ounce) can fruit cocktail, drained
1 (9-ounce) carton whipped topping
1 (1-pound) container cottage cheese
1 (3-ounce) package gelatin, any flavor
½ cup chopped nuts

Drain fruit cocktail. Fold together whipped topping, cottage cheese and dry gelatin. Fold in fruit cocktail and nuts.

This is a delicious salad—no effort to make.

Amelia Gydus, Trumbull, Conn.

SUMMER FRUIT SALAD
Serves 4

Change the fruit depending on the season.

½ cup cubed melon or watermelon

½ cup fresh or canned pineapple in natural juice or light syrup
1 cup diced fruit: pears, apples, peaches, etc.
¼ cup orange juice

Cut up fruit. Combine fruits and orange juice. Stir. Chill 1 hour or more. *Variation:* When in season, try seedless grape halves or other fruits as a change.

Mary Hale, Tulsa, Okla.

BEST DEVILED EGGS

6 hard-cooked eggs
¼ cup mayonnaise or salad dressing
2 tablespoons finely chopped onion
1 tablespoon finely chopped green olives
1 teaspoon vinegar
1 teaspoon prepared mustard
Dash of salt and pepper
Paprika

Slice eggs in half lengthwise and remove yolks. Mash yolks with mayonnaise or salad dressing. Add the remaining ingredients and stir all together well. Stuff egg white with yolk mixture. Sprinkle paprika lightly on top.

Jodie McCoy, Tulsa, Okla.

PISTACHIO DESSERT

1 medium-size can crushed pineapple (do not drain)
1 (3½-ounce) box pistachio instant pudding
1 large container Cool Whip

Empty can of pineapple into bowl. Sprinkle pudding mix over the pineapple, and stir by hand until mixture thickens. Add the Cool Whip and stir until all is blended. Spread in flat container to chill. For a shortcut, chill for 15 minutes in freezer. Serve with Ritz crackers.

Bea Nagy, Natrona Heights, Pa.

ORANGE DELIGHT

1 package orange gelatin
½ pint vanilla ice cream
½ pint whipped cream

Prepare gelatin according to package directions. When gelatin is partially set, add ice cream and beat well. Stir in whipped cream and allow to set again. Put in sherbet glasses to serve and top with whipped cream and chopped nuts.

Ellen A. Johnson, Payette, Idaho

SCALLOPED APPLES

4 medium (1–1¼ pounds) tart apples, peeled, cored and sliced
½ cup sugar
¼ teaspoon cinnamon
¼ teaspoon cloves
½ cup butter or margarine
2 cups fresh bread crumbs (4 slices bread)

Toss apples with sugar and spices. In skillet, melt butter; add crumbs and toss lightly, stirring. In greased 8-inch square baking pan, layer half the apples, then half the crumbs. Top with layers of remaining apples and crumbs. Bake in preheated 350-degree oven for 45 minutes, or until tender. Serve warm as a side dish with pork or ham, or as a dessert topped with vanilla ice cream.

Eleanor Swift, Commack, N.Y.

RICE AND CHERRY SUPREME

1 cup whipping cream
½ cup sugar
3 cups cold cooked rice
½ teaspoon vanilla
1 can cherry pie filling

Beat cream and sugar together. Gently fold in rice, vanilla and cherry pie filling.

Sharon M. Crider, Evansville, Wis.

EASY MARSHMALLOW FUDGE

⅔ cup evaporated milk
1½ cups sugar
½ teaspoon salt
32 marshmallows (½ pound)
1 (12-ounce) package sem-
    isweet chocolate chips
1 teaspoon vanilla extract
½ teaspoon peppermint extract

Combine evaporated milk, sugar, salt
and marshmallows in a saucepan. Cook
over low heat, stirring constantly, until
marshmallows melt. Blend in chocolate chips; stir until smooth. Add both
extracts. Pour into buttered 8-inch
square pan. Chill. Cut into squares.

Patty Ross, Trenton, Ohio

BANANA PEANUT BUTTER SALAD

6 bananas
⅓ cup peanut butter
4 red apples, diced, unpeeled
⅓ cup chopped nuts
½ teaspoon salt
¼ cup lemon juice
Mayonnaise
Lettuce leaves

Cut bananas lengthwise. Spread with
peanut butter. Place on lettuce. Toss
together the apples, nuts, salt and lemon
juice. Sprinkle over bananas, accompa-
nied by mayonnaise.

Margaret Lewis, Dubuque, Iowa

RICH-N-COOL SALAD

1 large package lemon gelatin
1 large container Cool Whip
1 (8-ounce) package cream
    cheese

Make gelatin according to directions
on package. Soften cream cheese. Just
before gelatin sets, add Cool Whip and
cream cheese. Beat with hand mixer
until smooth. Chill and serve.

Mrs. John Pyle, Burbank, Ill.

TUNA-APPLE SALAD
Serves 4

Try as a crunchy salad or in a sandwich.

1 (6½ - or 7-ounce) can tuna
    (packed in water)
1 unpeeled, diced apple
1 stalk celery, chopped
2 tablespoons mayonnaise
1 tablespoon lemon juice
Lettuce, as desired

Rinse and drain tuna. Mix tuna and
other ingredients, except lettuce, in
bowl. Use immediately or chill 1–2
hours. Serve on a bed of lettuce leaves.
Variations: Oil-packed instead of water-packed tuna may be used. Pour oil
from tuna can; rinse tuna with cold
water, and drain well.

Jane Martin, Van Wert, Ohio

5-CUP SALAD

1 cup mandarin oranges, drained
1 cup shredded coconut
1 cup miniature marshmallows
1 cup crushed pineapple,
    drained
1 cup sour cream

Combine all of the ingredients in a
bowl and chill until serving time.
This may be used as a fruit salad or
as a dessert.

Martha Short, Bloomington, Ind.

EASY FRUIT SALAD

1 large can pineapple, reserve
    juice
1 can mandarin oranges, drained
3 bananas, sliced
1 package instant coconut
    pudding

Mix pudding with pineapple juice;
add mandarin oranges and bananas.
Stir. Ready to serve.

Nene Jordon, Rome, Ga.

EGG AND BAKED BEAN SALAD
Serves 4–5

2½ cups (No. 2 can) baked beans,
    well-drained
4 hard-cooked eggs, chopped
½ cup sliced celery
¼ cup chopped parsley
½ cup finely chopped onion
1 tablespoon mayonnaise
1 teaspoon prepared mustard
    Prepared horseradish (1–2
    teaspoons, or as desired)
½ teaspoon salt
⅛ teaspoon pepper
    Several leaves lettuce
3 slices bacon, cooked and
    crumbled

Combine beans, eggs, celery, parsley and onion in a bowl. Blend mayonnaise with the seasonings. Stir into bean
and egg mixture. Chill at least 1 hour.
Serve in bowls lined with crisp lettuce.
Garnish with crumbled bacon.

Esther Baumler, Decorah, Iowa

GREEN BEAN SALAD

2 cups chopped green beans
½ cup chopped green pepper
¼ cup radishes, chopped
½ medium onion, diced
½ medium pickle, diced
    Salt and pepper to taste
    Creamy Italian dressing,
    enough to hold salad together

Chop vegetables together and mix
well. Add dressing. Chill and serve.

B.J. Nall, New Mexico

APPLESAUCE DELIGHT
Serves 6

1 (3-ounce) package red gelatin
1 cup boiling water
1½ cups applesauce (15 ounces)

Dissolve gelatin in water; blend in
applesauce. Pour into mold or serving
dish and chill until firm. Makes 2½
cups.

Mrs. Charles Coburn, Chicago, Ill.

CANDY CHEESE GEMS

8 ounces cream cheese, softened
7 ounces flaked coconut
1 (3-ounce) package lemon-flavored gelatin
1 tablespoon sugar
1 cup chopped pecans

Combine first 4 ingredients. Chill until firm. Roll into 1-inch balls. Coat balls with chopped nuts. Chill until firm.

Bonnie Broton, Dodge Center, Minn.

RICE KRISPIE DATE BALLS
(No-Bake)

1 cup margarine
1½ cups sugar
2 tablespoons milk
2 cups chopped dates
1 teaspoon salt
1 cup chopped nuts
2 teaspoons vanilla
4½ cups Rice Krispies
Coconut

Mix first 5 ingredients and bring to a boil. Boil for 2 minutes. Add next 3 ingredients. Shape into balls and roll in coconut.

Mrs. Beryl Becker, Cressona, Pa.

FRUIT-FLAVORED SYRUP
Makes 1 pint

1 envelope unsweetened Kool-Aid, any flavor
½ cup water
1¾ cups light corn syrup

In a tightly covered jar, shake Kool-Aid and water. Add corn syrup and shake until thoroughly blended. Keep covered and store in refrigerator. Children will love this on pancakes.

Mrs. S.R. Burt, Imlay, Nev.

PEANUT BUTTER CRUNCH

1½ sticks margarine
2 cups peanut butter
1 (1-pound) box confectioners sugar
3 cups crushed Rice Krispies

Melt margarine and peanut butter together. Add confectioners' sugar and cereal. Mix with hands and shape into 1-inch balls. Refrigerate 1 hour.

Dip:
1 (12-ounce) package chocolate chips
½ cake of paraffin (make sure Mom supervises!)

Melt together in double boiler. Remove from heat and dip in balls. Refrigerate 1 hour.

Terry Hasty, Mackinaw, Ill.

CHOCO-PEANUT BUTTER BALLS
Makes 4 dozen

¾ cup margarine
1½ cups peanut butter
1 pound confectioners' sugar

Melt margarine and peanut butter in a saucepan on low heat. Stir well and remove from heat. Add confectioners' sugar and beat until well-blended. Roll mixture into small balls. Refrigerate on waxed paper for at least 30 minutes.

Chocolate Covering:
½ bar of paraffin wax
1 (12-ounce) package chocolate bits

Melt wax and chocolate bits in a double boiler. Dip shaped peanut butter balls into chocolate. Place on waxed paper and let chocolate become hardened. Store in refrigerator or a cool place.

Ruth Pratt, Greensburg, Pa.

LAYER FUDGE

12 ounces butterscotch-flavor pieces
1 (15-ounce) can sweetened condensed milk
2 teaspoons vanilla
2 cups miniature marshmallows
1 cup chopped pecans
12 ounces semisweet chocolate pieces

Line a 10 x 6 x 2-inch loaf pan with foil; butter foil. Melt butterscotch pieces; remove from heat. Stir in ⅔ cup sweetened condensed milk and 1 teaspoon vanilla. Spread in pan; sprinkle evenly with marshmallows and pecans, pressing lightly into candy layer. Melt chocolate pieces; remove from heat; stir in remaining milk and vanilla. Spread evenly over marshmallow layer. Chill 3 hours, or until firm. Lift candy out by lifting foil out; peel off. Cut in 1-inch squares. Makes about 3 pounds.

Mrs. Phil Hamilton, Tucson, Ariz.

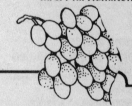

FRUIT AND JUICE GELATIN
Serves 4

A low-sugar salad or dessert for all the family.

1 tablespoon unflavored gelatin
2 cups unsweetened fruit juice (do not use fresh or frozen pineapple juice; it will not gel)
1 cup sliced fruit such as peaches, pears, apples, bananas, berries, etc.

Mix together ¼ cup juice and gelatin in a bowl. Measure another ¼ cup juice; boil it, then add hot juice to the above mixture and stir until gelatin is dissolved. Add remaining juice and stir. Put in refrigerator to set. After the gelatin begins to set a little, add the sliced fruit and return gelatin to refrigerator until firm.

Sally Simpson, Detroit, Mich.

CHOCOLATE YUMMIES

Tube of saltine crackers
2 sticks butter
1 cup brown sugar
12 ounces chocolate chips

Grease a jelly roll pan. Single layer saltines on the bottom of pan and set aside. Melt butter and mix in brown sugar; bring to a boil, stirring constantly, for 3 minutes. Remove from burner and pour evenly over crackers. Bake at 350 degrees for 7 minutes on middle rack of oven. Remove from oven and pour chocolate chips over hot topping; spread evenly to make thin coating. Refrigerate. Break up into chunks or separate the crackers.

Easy candy for the children to make. Freezes well.

Jane and Shirley Weimann, Woodstock, Conn.

CHOCOLATE CARAMEL TURTLES

1 (1-pound) package caramels
2 tablespoons water
¾ pound salted cashews
1 (6-ounce) package semisweet chocolate pieces

Heat caramels and water in top part of double boiler over boiling water, about 5 minutes. Stir occasionally until evenly melted. Grease baking sheet. Arrange 36 groups of 4 cashews each, about 2 inches apart on sheet. Drop melted caramels by teaspoonfuls on each group of nuts. Let turtles cool 15 minutes. Melt chocolate pieces over hot water, not boiling water. Drop by teaspoonful on top of each caramel turtle; spread chocolate if necessary with spatula. Set in cool, dry place until firm. All children love to make and eat these.

Beverly Brannon, Vidor, Texas

MARSHMALLOW WALNUT FUDGE

½ pound butter (2 sticks)
8 squares (8 ounces) unsweetened chocolate
1 cup coarsely chopped walnuts
1 pound sifted confectioners' sugar
1 teaspoon vanilla extract
32 marshmallows

Combine butter and chocolate in saucepan. Melt over low heat. Pour into large bowl. Add nuts, sugar and vanilla. Knead until well-blended. Pat into greased 8 x 8-inch pan. Cut marshmallows in half crosswise. Place cut side down at 1-inch intervals so marshmallows will be in center of each piece. Chill several hours. Cut between the marshmallows in 1-inch squares.

Heather Williams, Dayton, Ohio

RAISIN CANDY

1½ cups seeded raisins, chopped
½ cup coconut
½ cup chopped nuts
¼ cup confectioners' sugar

Combine all ingredients. Roll into balls.

Ann Albritton, Salem, Ore.

GRAND GRAHAM CRACKERS

2 tablespoons butter *or* margarine
½ teaspoon vanilla
⅛ teaspoon salt
1 cup confectioners' sugar
Half-and-half (3–4 tablespoons)
Graham crackers

Melt butter or margarine; add remaining ingredients and blend until spreading consistency. If necessary, thin with additional half-and-half. Spread mixture between graham crackers.

Alice McNamara, Eucha, Okla.

NO-COOK COCONUT CANDY

1 (6-ounce) can frozen orange juice, unsweetened
1 (12-ounce) box vanilla wafers, crushed
1 (1-pound) box confectioners' sugar
½ cup melted margarine
1 cup chopped nuts
1 cup coconut
Additional coconut for garnish

Thaw orange juice until slushy. Combine all ingredients in a large bowl and mix thoroughly. Mixture will be stiff. Sprinkle a layer of coconut into a 9 x 13-inch pan. Pour in candy and press down evenly with your hands. Be sure to cover the entire layer of coconut. Sprinkle more coconut over the top and press down gently. Cut into bars of the desired size and refrigerate.

Jodie McCoy, Tulsa, Okla.

NOODLE DROP CANDY

1 (12-ounce) package chocolate chips
1 small can chow mein noodles
1 (12-ounce) package butterscotch chips
1 small can peanuts

Melt chips in double boiler. Add noodles and peanuts. Drop on waxed paper by spoonfuls. Let cool and then enjoy.

Cheryl Brooks, San Jose, Calif.

CARAMEL NUGGETS

36 caramels
4 tablespoons milk
1 cup Rice Krispies
1 cup coconut
1 cup chopped nuts

Melt caramels and milk in top of double boiler. Add Rice Krispies, coconut and nuts. Mix well; form into 1-inch balls. Roll in confectioners' sugar.

Brent Habiger, Spearville, Kan.

213

STUFFED FRANKS
Serves 4

Mashed potato buds
2 tablespoons grated onion
2 tablespoons chopped parsley
1 teaspoon prepared mustard
8 frankfurters

Prepare mashed potato buds as directed on package. Mix potatoes, onion, parsley and mustard. Cut the franks lengthwise, being careful not to cut completely through. Flatten frank and spread with potato mixture. Set oven control at broil; broil franks 5 inches from heat for 5–8 minutes, or until potatoes are brown.

Cary L. Woods, Bellevue, Mich.

GRILLED TURKEY SANDWICH
Makes 8 sandwiches

8 slices bread
1 (4½-ounce) can deviled ham
Slices cooked turkey (8–12)
1 (8-ounce) package American cheese (8 slices)

Toast bread under broiler on 1 side. Turn over and spread untoasted side with deviled ham. Cover with turkey and top with cheese slice. Broil until cheese is browned and bubbly. Serve hot.

Mrs. Henry Wettach, Springwater, N.Y.

HAMBURGER

Place one ¼-pound hamburger patty on microwave roasting rack. Cover with waxed paper. Microwave at HIGH 1 minute. Turn over; cover. Microwave 30 seconds to 1½ minutes, or until meat is no longer pink. Let stand 1–2 minutes.

For 2 patties, microwave first side 1½ minutes; turn. Microwave second side 1–2½ minutes.

Mary Hale, Tulsa, Okla.

PIZZA BURGERS

¼ cup onion, chopped
1 pound ground beef
1 can tomato soup (regular size)
⅛ cup shredded cheese (longhorn may be used)
½ teaspoon oregano
Pepper
Buns (8–10)

Brown onion and ground beef. Add remaining ingredients and simmer 30 minutes. Fill buns with meat mixture and serve with tossed salad.

Mrs. James Schwan, Aberdeen, S.D.

PINK POPCORN BALLS

7 cups popped corn
3 cups miniature marshmallows
2 tablespoons butter
¼ teaspoon salt
Few drops red food coloring

Place popped corn in large buttered bowl. In bottom of double boiler, heat about 1 inch of water to boiling. Combine butter, marshmallows and salt in top of double boiler, over hot water. Stir until melted together. Stir in food coloring to desired shade. Pour over popcorn. Stir gently to coat.

Grease hands with butter and quickly shape popcorn into 10 medium-size balls.

Sharon Crider, Evansville, Wis.

WHITE CHOCOLATE CLUSTERS

3 pounds white chocolate
6 cups Rice Krispies
1 pound Spanish peanuts

Melt chocolate in top of double boiler and combine with Rice Krispies and nuts. Drop by tablespoonfuls onto a cookie sheet and refrigerate.

Mrs. William Wiedenhoeft, Sullivan, Wis.

PEANUT BUTTER FUDGE

2 cups creamy *or* chunky peanut butter
2 sticks (½ pound) margarine
1 pound confectioners' sugar

Melt peanut butter and margarine together. Stir in confectioners' sugar and mix well. Pour into greased 9 x 13 inch pan. Chill. Cut in squares.

Jean Ginnetty, Weymouth, Mass.

PEANUT BUTTER GRAHAMS
Makes 3 dozen

1 cup peanut butter, smooth *or* chunky
1 cup raisins
1 cup quick-cooking oatmeal
3 tablespoons butter *or* margarine
½ cup chopped nuts
¼ cup brown sugar or honey
½ cup graham cracker crumbs
½ cup graham cracker crumbs, reserved to roll balls in

Combine all ingredients and roll into 1-inch balls. Roll balls in graham cracker crumbs. Refrigerate.

Jeanette Schneider, Oceanside, Calif.

BONBONS

Easy enough for a young child. They love to work the dough.

½ cup butter
2½ cups confectioners' sugar
1 teaspoon vanilla
½ cup nuts, if desired

Mix thoroughly with a fork. Add nuts last. Roll into small balls. If desired, cover with melted chocolate.

Ryan Sykes, Monmouth, Ill.

DEVILED CHEESE

Serves 6

Children like to make this for after-school snacks or after the game.

1½ cups (6 ounces) grated cheese
1 teaspoon dry mustard
½ teaspoon salt
⅛ teaspoon cayenne
2 tablespoons melted butter
1 teaspoon vinegar
   Toast

Blend cheese, mustard, salt, cayenne and butter; gradually stir in vinegar. Spread on hot toast; bake in hot oven at 400 degrees for about 5 minutes. Serve with hot chocolate.

Elsie Swanson, Ellsworth, Maine

CLUB SANDWICH

3 slices bread (for each sandwich)
   Ham
   Mustard
   Swiss cheese
   Mayonnaise
   Lettuce
   Turkey
   Tomatoes
   Bacon, cooked crisp

Toast 3 slices of bread for each sandwich. Between 2 slices, place layers of ham (can use boiled), mustard, Swiss cheese, mayonnaise and lettuce. Top with turkey, mayonnaise, lettuce, tomato, bacon (3 or 4 slices per sandwich) and third slice of bread. Hold together with frilled toothpicks. Cut diagonally in quarters and stand on plate with points upward.

Mrs. Charles L. Savy, Secane, Pa.

CRAZY CRUST PIZZA

1 cup flour
3 eggs
⅔ cup milk
½ pound ground beef
½ cup onions
   Pizza sauce
   Cheese
   Pepperoni
   Mushrooms
   Peppers
   Onion

Mix flour, eggs and milk. Beat 2–3 minutes. Brown ground beef and onions. Grease baking sheet; pour flour mixture onto sheet. Add meat and onions. Bake 25 minutes in 425-degree oven. Take out of oven; add sauce, cheese and rest of ingredients. Bake 10 additional minutes.

Lorraine Ritchey, Mars, Pa.

JIFFY JOES

Makes 6 sandwiches

1 pound ground beef
½ cup chopped green pepper
½ cup Kraft barbecue sauce
1 (8-ounce) jar Cheez Whiz pasteurized process cheese spread
6 hamburger buns, split

Crumble meat into 1-quart casserole; stir in peppers. Microwave on HIGH for 5–6 minutes, or until meat loses pink color when stirred; drain. Add barbecue sauce to meat mixture; mix lightly. Microwave Cheez Whiz according to label directions; stir into meat mixture. Microwave 2 minutes, or until thoroughly heated. Fill buns with meat mixture. A saucy, super sandwich.

Heather Williams, Dayton, Ohio

SUNBEAMS

1 cup non-fat dry milk powder
½ cup honey
½ cup peanut butter
½ cup granola-type cereal crushed

Mix dry milk, honey and peanut butter together; chill. Form into balls the size of marbles. Roll in crushed cereal.

These are easy to make, good and nutritious.

Kimberly Slavin, Fort Calhoun, Neb.

CONEY ISLAND DOGS

Serves 5–6

1 (15-ounce) can chili with beans
1 package hot dogs
8 hot-dog buns, split
½ cup grated cheese

Place chili in glass bowl. Microwave 2 minutes on HIGH power. Stir. Microwave another minute, or until hot and bubbly. Set aside. Place hot dogs on open buns on a paper plate. Microwave 1½–2 minutes or until warm. Spoon chili over hot dogs. Sprinkle cheese on top.

Shirley Jones, Indianapolis, Ind.

BEEF BACON CHEESEBURGERS

Makes 6–8 patties

2½ pounds ground beef
2 onions, chopped
2 tablespoons A-1 Sauce
1 pound bacon
   Cheese slices (6–8)

In a large bowl, mix together ground beef, onions and A-1 Sauce. Fry bacon until done. Remove from pan and place on paper towel and set aside. Cook hamburgers until done. Place a slice of cheese on hamburger and bacon, as desired. Continue to cook hamburgers until cheese melts.

Christina Cooper, New Castle, Ind.

HOT DOGS

Place hot dog in a split hot-dog bun. Wrap loosely in paper towel to prevent the bun from becoming soggy. Place hot dog in the microwave. Follow the chart below for the plain hot dog or any of the other hot-dog recipes.

1 hot dog	30–45 seconds
2 hot dogs	45–50 seconds
3 hot dogs	1–1½ minutes
4 hot dogs	1½–2 minutes
5 hot dogs	2–2½ minutes

Defrost hot dog first, if frozen.

Mary Hale, Tulsa, Okla.

CORNFLAKES CRUNCHIES

1 cup dark corn syrup
1 cup sugar
1 teaspoon vanilla
2 cups peanut butter
5 cups cornflakes

Bring syrup, sugar and vanilla to a boil in small saucepan. Remove from heat. Add peanut butter and stir until mixture is smooth. Pour over cornflakes in large bowl. Mix well. Drop by spoonfuls onto waxed paper. Chill. Store in tightly covered container.

Marla Weech, Hoisington, Kan.

BACON-WRAPPED HOT DOGS

Hot dogs
Yellow cheese
Breakfast bacon
Prepared mustard
Worcestershire sauce

Cook hot dogs in boiling water about 8 minutes. Drain water off and let cool. When hot dogs are cold, slice lengthwise almost through in the center. Now put a piece of cheese in each hot dog and a little prepared mustard. Wrap breakfast bacon around each hot dog. Put hot dogs in casserole and sprinkle Worcestershire sauce over all. Cover casserole with foil and bake until bacon is cooked. If not brown enough, take foil off and cook a little longer.

Eunice Roscher, Waco, Texas

HOT DOG ON A STICK
Serves 1

Insert wooden ice-cream stick in hot dog lengthwise 1½–2 inches. Microwave on paper plate 30–45 seconds on HIGH power. Serve with mustard, ketchup or relish.

Mary Hale, Tulsa, Okla.

MINI-BURGERS

1 (10-count) can biscuits
1 pound ground beef *or* pork (make into 10 small patties)
3 slices cheese (cut each slice into 4 pieces)
   Tomato slices
   Lettuce
   Pickles
   Salad dressing

Bake biscuits as directed on can; remove from oven and cool. Fry patties until done. Remove from pan and place a slice of cheese on each. Break each biscuit apart and spread with salad dressing. Stack like a hamburger to each child's taste with tomato slices, lettuce and pickle. These are just the right size for children's hands. Serve them with carrot sticks, radishes and celery.

Mella Smith, Blossom, Texas

PIZZA HOT DOGS

4 hot-dog buns
4 hot dogs
12 slices mozzarella cheese
   Pizza sauce
   Parmesan cheese, grated

Split hot-dog buns and hot dogs lengthwise. Place layer of cheese on buns. Add hot-dog slices to each bun. Top with pizza sauce. Sprinkle with Parmesan cheese. Place on broiler pan. Broil until brown and bubbly.

Betty Klopfenstein, Waterman, Ill.

CHEESY HOT DOG
Serves 1

Slash hot dog lengthwise, but not completely through. Place in bun. Fill hot dog center with ¼-inch slice of cheese. Microwave on HIGH power on paper plate or towel 30–45 seconds.

Mary Hale, Tulsa, Okla.

HURRY-UP TACOS
Serves 8

1 pound ground beef
½ cup chopped onion
1 (8-ounce) jar Cheez Whiz pasteurized process cheese spread
   Shredded lettuce
   Chopped tomato
   Pitted ripe olive slices
8 taco shells

Crumble meat into 1-quart casserole; stir in onions. Microwave on HIGH 5–6 minutes, or until meat loses pink color when stirred; drain. Microwave Cheez Whiz according to label directions. Wrap taco shells in paper towels. Microwave 1 minute, rearranging shells after 30 seconds. Fill shells with meat mixture. Top with remaining ingredients.

Mary Linger, Jacksonville, Fla

SPEEDY MACARONI AND CHEESE
Serves 3–4

1 cup uncooked macaroni
2 tablespoons flour
1 tablespoon instant minced onion
1 teaspoon salt
   Dash Tabasco sauce
1 cup milk
1 cup water
2 tablespoons margarine
1 cup shredded cheddar cheese

In 2-quart glass casserole combine macaroni, flour, onion, salt and Tabasco sauce. Stir in milk and water. Dot with margarine and cover. Microwave on HIGH for 5 minutes, then on SIMMER (MEDIUM) for an additional 10 minutes, or until macaroni is almost tender. Stir about 3 times during cooking. Stir in cheese. Let stand 5 minutes before serving.

Mary Bell, Cincinnati, Ohio

CHOCOLATE FLUFF AND STUFF

- ¾ cup water
- 2 envelopes unflavored gelatin
- ⅔ cup sugar
- ¼ cup cocoa
- ½ cup milk
- ½ teaspoon vanilla
- 2 cups frozen whipped dessert topping, thawed

Place water in 1-cup measure; cover. Microwave on HIGH, 2–2½ minutes, or until boiling. Add gelatin; stir to dissolve. Set aside.

In small bowl combine sugar and cocoa. Slowly blend in milk, stirring to dissolve sugar and cocoa. Stir in vanilla. Blend in dissolved gelatin. Skim off any foam. Pour ½ cup of chocolate-gelatin mixture into small bowl. Blend in whipped topping. Pour remaining gelatin mixture into an 8 x 8-inch baking dish. Spoon chocolate-whipped topping mixture over and spread evenly with spatula.

Refrigerate until firm, about 1 hour. Cut into 16 squares.

Shirley Jones, Indianapolis, Ind.

MAGIC MARSHMALLOW PUFFS

- 1 can crescent refrigerator rolls
  Several large marshmallows
- ¼ cup melted butter
- ¼ cup sugar
- 1 teaspoon cinnamon

Separate rolls into triangles. Dip 1 marshmallow at a time into the melted butter. Then roll marshmallow in a mixture of sugar and cinnamon. Wrap the dough triangle around marshmallow; completely cover it and squeeze edges of dough tightly to seal. Dip into melted butter again and place buttered side down in muffin tin. Place muffin tin on sheet of foil (to prevent gooey drippings in the oven) and bake in a 375-degree oven for 10–12 minutes, or until golden brown. As they bake, the marshmallows melt and leave a hollow puff in the center. Immediately remove from the muffin cups when done and, if desired, drizzle with a glaze made of confectioners' sugar and water.

Carol Wallace, Hastings, Mich.

GRAHAM CRACKER SNACKS

Graham crackers
- ½ cup margarine
- ½ cup butter
- ½ cup sugar
  Almonds *or* pecans, sliced

Line jelly roll pan with graham crackers, with sides touching. (Keebler's are best since they don't get soggy.)

Melt together margarine, butter and sugar. Bring to boil; boil for 2 minutes. Pour over graham crackers. Sprinkle with sliced almonds or pecans.

Bake at 350 degrees for 10 minutes. Remove from pan while still warm. Place on cooling racks.

Marilyn Holmer, Belvidere, Ill.

PIZZA DOG
Serves 1

Slash hot dog lengthwise, but not completely through. Place in bun. Spread center of hot dog with pizza sauce, ketchup or tomato sauce. Sprinkle with Italian seasoning and mozzarella cheese. Microwave on HIGH power on paper plate or towel 30–45 seconds.

May Hale, Tulsa, Okla.

CRUNCHOLA MIX

- 4 cups cereal (Cheerios, Corn Chex, etc., *or* any combination)
- 1 cup peanuts *or* mixed nuts
- 1 cup pretzel sticks, the smallest size
- 1 cup seasoned croutons
- ½ cup salad oil *or* 6 tablespoons melted butter
- 2 teaspoons Worcestershire sauce
- ¼ teaspoon garlic powder

In a large shallow pan coat crunch ingredients with the combined oil and seasonings. Heat in oven at 250 degrees for about 45 minutes, stirring every 15 minutes. Spread on absorbent paper to cool.

Fran Sievers, Atlanta, Ga.

SPICY SNACKIN' CORN
Makes 4 cups

- 4 cups popped popcorn
- ¼ teaspoon instant minced garlic
- 1 tablespoon imitation bacon bits
- ½ cup sliced almonds
- ¼ teaspoon lemon pepper
- 4 slices processed cheese

Spoon popcorn, garlic, bacon and almonds into 8-inch round glass cake dish. Sprinkle with pepper. Mix well. Lay cheese slices on top of mixture. Bake at 350 degrees until cheese melts, 5–10 minutes. Blend well with spoon. Cool. Break up into pieces.

Jean Fulgham, Eureka, Calif.

CRISPY PIZZA POTATO SKINS
Makes 16 wedges

- 4 baking potatoes
- 1 cup spicy pizza sauce
- ¼ cup grated Parmesan cheese
- 1 cup shredded mozzarella cheese

Bake potatoes as usual. Cut each potato into wedge-shaped quarters. Scrape out most of the pulp (save potato to make patties).

Brush or spread pizza sauce over each wedge. Sprinkle with Parmesan cheese, then with mozzarella cheese. Bake 8–10 minutes in 450-degree oven, or until cheese melts. Serve very hot.

Winter Eve Gore, Aztec, N.M.

Meat
DISHES

ROAST DUCK WITH CHERRIES AND MADEIRA
Serves 4

1 (5-pound) duckling
Salt

Lemon juice
1 clove garlic, cut
1 (1-pound) can bing cherries, pitted
2 tablespoons Madeira wine
2 tablespoons sugar
2½ cups Brown Sauce (recipe follows)

Rub duck with salt, lemon juice and garlic. Roast at 350 degrees on 1 side for 30 minutes; turn duck on other side; roast 30 minutes more. Pour off fat; turn duck breast side up; roast another 1½ hours: continue to pour off fat. Drain liquid from cherries; simmer juice and Madeira wine for 10–15 minutes. Return cherries to liquid; add sugar; simmer. Add Brown Sauce, cherries and liquid; bring to a gentle boil. To serve, pass Cherry-Madeira Sauce with carved slices of roast duck.

Brown Sauce:
2 tablespoons butter or margarine
3 tablespoons flour
1½ cups boiling water
2 tablespoons beef bouillon granules
½ teaspoon brown gravy coloring

Melt butter in a saucepan; let brown. Add flour; cook until browned. Stir in 1½ cups boiling water; add bouillon granules and gravy coloring; simmer until hot and bubbling.

Gwen Cambpell, Sterling, Va.

DIFFERENT PIZZA

3/4 cup spaghetti or pizza sauce
1/2 pound pork sausage
4-ounce package refrigerated crescent rolls
1 cup cooked brown rice
1/4 cup shredded mild cheddar cheese
1/2 cup shredded mozzarella cheese
4 eggs
1/4 cup milk
1/2 teaspoon salt
1/8 teaspoon pepper
2 tablespoons grated Parmesan cheese

Brown sausage and drain. Mix with cooked brown rice. Place crescent rolls in lightly greased electric skillet. Spoon sauce and rice mixture over rolls. Top with cheddar and mozarella cheese. Pour beaten eggs, milk and salt and pepper mixture over this. Sprinkle with Parmesan cheese and bake in 300-degree skillet for 30 minutes.

Cut into wedges and serve.

Monica W. Cox, Cleveland, Miss.

SUNDAY NIGHT SCRAMBLED EGGS

1/2 pound bulk sausage (or smoked, summer)
1 onion, chopped
1/2 bell pepper, chopped
1 (17-ounce) can cream-style corn
1 cup grated Velveeta cheese
4 beaten eggs
1/4 cup milk

Brown sausage; pour off any grease. Add remaining ingredients and stir until eggs are set and cheese melted. If desired, sauté onion and pepper before adding other ingredients. Just the thing to have after Sunday's "honey-do chores."

BARBECUED RIB CHOPS
Serves 8

1 (5/8-ounce) package Italian salad dressing mix
1 (6-ounce) can tomato paste
8 lamb-rib chops, 3/4-inch thickness

Combine salad dressing mix and tomato paste; spread in thin layer over top side of chops. Broil 3 to 4 inches from source of heat, or cook on outdoor grill, 5-7 minutes. Turn; brush second side with sauce; cook 5 minutes longer, or until desired degree of doneness.

Marcella Swigert, Monroe City, Mo.

218

SAUSAGE-APPLE LOAF

2 eggs
½ teaspoon rosemary, crushed
½ teaspoon salt
¼ teaspoon ground sage
¼ teaspoon pepper
¼ teaspoon dry mustard
1 cup dry bread crumbs
1 cup thick applesauce
1 onion, finely chopped
2 pounds sausage meat

Preheat oven to 350 degrees. Lightly grease a 9 x 5 x 3-inch pan and line the bottom with greased waxed paper. In a large bowl beat eggs with seasonings and mustard. Stir in bread crumbs, applesauce and onion. Add half the sausage meat and work with your hands, or a fork, until evenly mixed. Work in remaining meat and firmly press into pan with palm of your hand. Lay a sheet of foil over top and bake in center of oven for 1 hour. Remove foil and drain off fat. Continue baking, uncovered, for 45 minutes more. Let cool in pan 5 minutes before turning out. This is excellent hot or cold.

Lillian Smith, Montreal, Quebec, Canada

HAMBURGER ROYAL
Serves 6

1 pound lean ground beef
1 medium onion, chopped
1 medium bell pepper, chopped
12-ounce can vacuum-packed corn with pimientos and peppers (Mexican-style)
15-ounce can tomato sauce

Cook hamburger, onion and green pepper until hamburger is brown and onion and green pepper are limp. Add corn and tomato sauce. Simmer for 15 minutes until heated through. Serve over hamburger buns.

Mary F. Speece, Lakeland, Fla.

SOUR CREAM TUNA LOAF

1 (13-ounce) can tuna, drained
6 slices white bread, crumbled
2 tablespoons instant minced onion
1 (2-ounce) jar chopped pimiento
2 cans cream of mushroom soup
½ cup grated cheddar cheese
3 eggs
1 tablespoon lemon juice
½ teaspoon salt
¼ teaspoon pepper
1 (16-ounce) carton sour cream

In large bowl, mix tuna, bread, eggs, onion, lemon juice, salt, pepper, pimiento and only 8 ounces (half) of the sour cream. Mix well; place in greased loaf pan. Bake at 350 degrees for 45 minutes until set.

Sour Cream Sauce:

Heat mushroom soup and desired amount of cheese (½ cup or more) until bubbly. Remove from heat and blend in remaining sour cream. Slice loaf and spoon over each serving.

J.L. Rede, Tucumcari, N.M.

BUTTER CRUST CHICKEN

1 frying chicken, cut up or parts
2 sticks margarine
1-1/2 teaspoons salt
1/2 cup flour
Paprika

Melt margarine; add salt and flour to make a medium-thick paste. Dip chicken and place on a cookie sheet. Sprinkle with paprika. Bake at 350 degrees for 1 hour, or until chicken is brown and tender. The chicken does not have to be turned while baking.

Marilyn Thomas, Carlisle, Ind.

SPARERIBS L'ORANGE
Serves 4

3 pounds spareribs, cut into serving pieces
3 tablespoons water

Basting sauce:
1 (6-ounce) can frozen orange juice
2 tablespoons water
1/2 cup brown sugar, firmly packed
1 tablespoon liquid smoke
2 tablespoons fresh lime juice
1 tablespoon white vinegar
1/2 cup honey
1 tablespoon Dijon mustard
1/4 teaspoon salt
1/8 teaspoon pepper
3 green onions, sliced, for garnish
Orange slices for garnish

In a baking pan, place ribs meaty side up; sprinkle with 3 tablespoons water. Bake 375 degrees for 30 minutes; drain off fat. In a saucepan combine all basting ingredients. Simmer 5 minutes; pour over ribs. Reduce heat to 350 degrees; bake 50 minutes; baste occasionally. To serve, sprinkle with sliced green onions; place orange slices around ribs.

Gwen Campbell, Sterling, Va.

CHICKEN CHOW MEIN

1 or 2 onions, chopped
1 green pepper, chopped
2 cups chicken
2 cups soup or bouillon
3 tablespoons soy sauce
2 or 3 tablespoons cornstarch

Sauté vegetables for 5 minutes. Add chicken. Add cornstarch to the soup or bouillon; then add to vegetables and chicken. Add soy sauce. Cook until thick and clear. Serve over rice. Garnish with tomatoes and serve with Chinese noodles.

Karen Donchez, Bethlehem, Pa.

GOLDEN GLAZED CHICKEN
Serves 4

2 chicken breasts, split and skinned
Salt and pepper
Paprika
1 tablespoon diet margarine
4 slices onion
4 slices orange
2 tablespoons cornstarch
1 teaspoon instant chicken bouillon
1 tablespoon orange juice *or* water
Snipped parsley

Arrange chicken breasts in 8- or 9-inch round glass baking dish with thicker portion toward edge of dish. Sprinkle with salt, pepper and paprika. Divide margarine into fourths; place pieces atop each breast. Top each with onion and orange slices. Cover with waxed paper. Microwave on HIGH for 10–12 minutes, or until chicken is done, rotating dish once. Let stand 5 minutes. Combine cornstarch, bouillon and orange juice in 1-cup glass measure. Drain juice from chicken into cornstarch mixture; mix well. Microwave on HIGH, uncovered, 45 seconds to 1 minute, or until mixture boils and thickens, stirring once. Spoon onto chicken breasts. Garnish with parsley. (170 calories per serving)

Mrs. Olen Begley, West Salem, Ohio

MARINATED PORK CHOPS
Serves 6

6 pork chops
3/4 cup honey
1/2 cup white vinegar
1/4 cup soy sauce
1/2 teaspoon ginger
1/4 teaspoon or less garlic powder

Place pork chops in 13x9-inch baking dish. Combine remaining ingredients; pour over pork chops. Cover and refrigerate for about 8 hours.

Remove from refrigerator; let stand 30 minutes. Bake in marinade, covered, at 350 degrees for 1 hour, or until meat is tender.

Flo Burtnett, Gage, Okla.

BEEF ROLL-UPS
Serves 6

2 pounds ground beef
1 cup shredded cheddar cheese
2/3 cup chopped onion
1/4 cup ketchup
2 tablespoons Parmesan cheese
2 tablespoons Worcestershire sauce
1/4 teaspoon pepper
1 teaspoon salt
2 eggs
12 strips bacon

Combine beef, cheese, onion, ketchup, Parmesan cheese, Worcestershire sauce, salt, pepper, and eggs. Mix well and divide in half. Shape each half into an 11-inch roll. Place beef roll on one end of bacon strips. Roll up, using waxed paper as an aid so that roll is wrapped with bacon. Cut into 6 patties. Secure bacon ends with toothpicks. Place on broiler rack; repeat with other roll. Broil 7 inches from source of heat.

Whole beef rolls can be baked, if you wish. Bake at 375 degrees for 40 minutes.

Diantha Susan Hibbard, Rochester, N.Y.

HAWAIIAN CHICKEN

5 deboned chicken breasts, diced
1 (16-ounce) can crushed pineapple
2 cups fresh pineapple chunks
1 green pepper, diced
1-1/2 cups brown sugar
1/2 cup lemon juice
2 tablespoons cornstarch

In a saucepan, combine pineapple including syrup, peppers, and brown sugar. Bring to a boil. Remove from heat and add lemon juice and corn starch. Mix well. Add diced chicken and heat throughly.

FOIL-WRAPPED PICNIC DINNERS
Serves 4

1-1/2 pounds round steak
2 packages frozen peas and carrots
4 medium potatoes, pared
1 package frozen broccoli, tops only
Salt and pepper to taste
1 (10-1/2-ounce) can cream of mushroom soup
1 envelope dry onion soup mix
8 cherry tomatoes

Cut meat into 1-inch pieces. Place frozen peas, carrots, and broccoli in colander; run cold water over all just until separated; drain. Tear off 4 pieces of heavy-duty aluminum foil, each 18 x 15 inches. On center of each piece, place meat, peas, carrots, potatoes, and broccoli tops. Sprinkle with salt and pepper to taste. Stir together mushroom soup and onion soup mix; spoon soup mixture over meat and vegetables. Place cherry tomatoes on top of mixture; wrap securely in foil; place on hot coals. Cook 50-55 minutes, or until meat is tender.

Gwen Campbell, Sterling, Va.

NO-FRILLS HENS ON THE GRILL
Serves 4

Marinade:
1/2 cup olive oil
1/2 cup fresh orange juice
2-1/4 tablespoons soy sauce
1/2 cup wine vinegar
1/4 teaspoon liquid hot sauce
1/2 teaspoon Worcestershire sauce
1/4 teaspoon thyme
1/4 teaspoon salt
1/4 teaspoon pepper
4 Cornish game hens

Combine marinade ingredients; pour into oblong glass dish. Place hens in marinade; marinade 4 to 5 hours; turn occasionally. Place hens on grill over hot coals; baste with marinade frequently. Cook about 1 hour.

Gwen Campbell, Sterling, Va.

SALMON LOAF FOR TWO
Serves 4

2 cups canned salmon, boned and flaked
1 egg
Liquid from salmon, plus milk to make ¾ cup
1½ cups cracker crumbs
1 tablespoon lemon juice
1 teaspoon chopped onion
⅛ teaspoon salt
⅛ teaspoon pepper

Heat oven to 350 degrees. Grease a 9 x 5 x 3-inch loaf pan. Blend egg into flaked salmon. Stir in remaining ingredients. Spoon into pan. Bake 45 minutes, or until top is brown and crisp.

Flo Burtnett, Gage, Okla.

CHICKEN RICE POCKETS
Serves 8–10

1/3 cup long-grain rice
1/2 teaspoon instant chicken bouillon granules
1-1/2 cups cooked chicken, chopped
2 or 3 small tomatoes, seeded and chopped
1 avocado, peeled, seeded and chopped
1 cup frozen chopped broccoli, cooked and drained
1 hard-cooked egg, chopped
1/2 cup shreddid cheddar cheese
1/4 cup sliced olives
1/2 cup mayonnaise
1 tablespoon Dijon-style mustard
2 teaspoons honey
1/4 teaspoon celery salt
1/8 teaspoon pepper
4 or 5 large pita bread rounds, halves

In saucepan bring 2/3 cup water to boiling. Stir in rice and bouillon granules. Reduce heat. Cover and simmer for 20 minutes, or until tender and water is absorbed. Meanwhile, combine chicken, tomatoes, avocado, broccoli, egg, cheese and olives. Add cooked rice. Stir together mayonnaise, mustard, honey, celery salt and pepper. Pour over rice mixture; toss to coat. Cover and chill. Spoon about 1/2 cup into each pita bread half.

Laura Hicks, Troy, Mont.

OVEN STEAK DINNER

1-1/2 pounds round steak, 1/2-inch thick
4 medium carrots
4 medium potatoes, pared and cut in half
1 can cream of mushroom soup
1 envelope dry onion soup mix
1 package frozen peas

Heat oven to 450 degrees. Cut meat into pieces. Place peas in colander; run cold water over them until they break apart. Drain. Tear off 4 pieces heavy-duty aluminum foil, each 18 x 15 inches. On center of each piece place 1 carrot thinly sliced, 1 potato cut into quarters, and 1/4 of the meat. Stir together soup and soup mix; spoon over meat and top with peas. Wrap securely; place on ungreased baking sheet. Bake 50-60 minutes, or until tender.

Donna Holter, West Middlesex, Pa.

HAM BEANS
Serves 6

1 pound navy beans
½ cup onions, chopped
1 meaty ham bone
3 cups water
Salt and pepper to taste

Soak beans in water to cover overnight. Rinse and put into Crockpot or other pan along with other ingredients. Celery and carrots may be added, if desired. Simmer 6–8 hours in a Crockpot on medium, or for a shorter length of time on the stove. When beans are soft, they are done. Serve with chopped raw onions and corn bread.

QUICK-BAKE PORK CHOPS
Serves 6

6 pork chops
2 teaspoons salt
3 tablespoons melted shortening
1 cup uncooked long-grain rice
3/4 teaspoon chili powder
1/2 cup chopped green pepper
1/2 cup tomatoes
6 green pepper rings
3/4 cup shredded processed American cheese

In a large skillet, brown pork chops in shortening for 20 minutes. Drain off excess fat. Add chili powder, salt, and pepper; sprinkle over meat. Add rice and chopped green pepper; spoon canned tomatoes over chops and rice. Cover skillet and cook over low heat for 30-35 minutes, stirring occasionally. Add in pepper rings; cover and cook for 5 minutes longer. Sprinkle top with cheese and cover until cheese melts.

Suzan L. Wiener, Spring Hill, Fla.

BARBECUED CHICKEN

Boil cut-up fryers 15 minutes in water seasoned with bay leaves. Drain off water, and combine with sauce.

Sauce:
1-1/2 tablespoons oil
1 stick margarine
4 tablespoons soy sauce
3 tablespoons lemon juice
2 tablespoons Worcestershire sauce
1/4 to 1 teaspoon liquid smoke
1 clove crushed garlic
1-1/2 teaspoons vinegar
Dash salt and pepper

Combine and simmer 5 minutes. Pour sauce over chicken, and marinate 1 hour to overnight. Cook on barbecue grill for 10-12 minutes, or until brown, basting with sauce. (The marinade will become jellied if chilled overnight.) This method saves time in barbecuing and chicken is absolutely delicious!!

Rose Pickens, Eugene, Ore.

SPRINGTIME CASSOULET OF LAMB
Serves 6

4 cups lamb shoulder, cubed
1 tablespoon vegetable oil
1 clove garlic, minced
4 cups beef broth (bouillon)
3 1/4 cups water, divided
4 carrots, sliced
3 ribs celery, sliced
1 parsnip, sliced
1 bay leaf
1 1/2 tablespoons paprika
2 ounces medium noodles
1 1/2 cups frozen Italian green
  beans
1 cup frozen green peas
1 jar small white onions, with liquid
1 can Great Northern beans
1 tablespoon all-purpose flour

Cut lamb into 1/2-inch cubes. In Dutch oven heat oil. Add lamb and brown on all sides; add garlic; cook 5 minutes. Add broth, 3 cups water and next 5 ingredients. Bring to a boil; reduce heat; cover and simmer for 35 minutes. Discard bay leaf. Add noodles; simmer 5 minutes. Add green beans and peas. Bring to a boil; simmer 5 minutes, or until vegetables and noodles are tender. Gently stir in the small onions and beans. In a small bowl, blend together flour and remaining 1/4 cup water. Add to the cassoulet, stirring until thickened.

Gwen Campbell, Sterling, Va.

SWISS STEAK
Serves 4

1½ pounds round steak
  (about 1 inch thick)
¼ cup all-purpose flour
  Salt and pepper to taste
3 tablespoons vegetable
  oil
1 large (6-ounce) onion,
  sliced
1 large rib celery, sliced

½ pound mushrooms,
  sliced
1 clove garlic, finely
  chopped
1 (8-ounce) can stewed
  tomatoes
¼ teaspoon dried, crushed
  basil
¼ teaspoon dried, crushed
  oregano
¼ teaspoon dried, crushed
  thyme

Trim excess fat from steak. With the edge of a heavy saucer or a meat mallet pound flour into both sides of steak. Sprinkle with salt and pepper. In a large skillet heat oil; add steak. With medium-high heat brown meat well on both sides. Place steak in a baking dish (12 x 8 x 2-inch). In the drippings in the skillet, lightly cook onion, celery, garlic and mushrooms. Stir in tomatoes, basil, oregano and thyme. Pour over steak; cover lightly with foil. Bake at 300 degrees for 1¼–1½ hours, or until tender.

Marion A. Jones, Pottsville, Pa.

SHISH KABOBS

1 pound lamb steak, 3/4-inch
  thickness
4 slices canned pineapple
Water-pack tomato wedges
Green pepper wedges
Onion
1/4 pound mushrooms
1-1/2 tablespoons cooking oil
2 tablespoons minced onion
3 tablespoons lemon juice
1/2 teaspoon salt

Cut lamb into 1-inch squares and marinate for several hours in oil, lemon juice, minced onion, and salt. Drain lamb and alternate on 4 metal skewers with mushroom caps, 1-inch pieces of pineapple, as well as tomato and green pepper wedges. Broil 4 inches from broiler for about 12-15 minutes turning several times, or place on barbecue grill and cook until desired doneness.

Suzan L. Wiener, Spring Hill, Fla.

SUMMER SUPPER ON A SKEWER
Serves 6

1 (6-ounce) can frozen orange juice
  concentrate
1/2 cup honey
1/4 cup crystallized ginger, finely
  chopped
1/4 teaspoon marjoram leaves
2 pounds chicken, veal, beef, or
  pork, cut into 1-inch cubes
1 acorn squash, cut into 2-inch
  pieces
4 apples, unpeeled and quartered
12 plump prunes

Mix orange juice concentrate, honey, ginger, and marjoram. Place meat in shallow glass dish; pour orange juice mixture over meat. Cover; refrigerate several hours; turn meat occasionally. Cook squash in boiling, salted water 10 minutes; drain. Remove meat from marinade; reserve marinade. On 6 skewers, alternate meat, squash, apples, and prunes. Place on grill 3 inches from coals. Cook 30 minutes, or until meat is brown, and squash, apples, and prunes are tender. Turn and baste frequently with reserved marinade. Can be served over hot fluffy rice, if desired.

Gwen Campbell, Sterling, Va.

BUDGET CHICKEN AMERICANA
Serves 4

2 pounds chicken parts
1/4 cup margarine
1 (10-1/2-ounce) can cream of
  mushroom soup
1/4 teaspoon thyme
1/4 teaspoon rosemary
1/4 teaspoon ground sage
1/2 cup water
12 small pearl onions

Brown chicken in margarine. Stir in soup, thyme, rosemary, sage and water. Bring to a boil; reduce heat; simmer 10 minutes. Add onions; simmer gently for 40 minutes, or until chicken is fork tender.

Gwen Campbell, Sterling, Va.

CHICKEN SUPREME

4 split chicken breasts *or* 8 chicken filets
6 tablespoons margarine
1/2 cup diced onions
1/2 cup diced green peppers
1/2 cup diced celery
8 ounces sharp, grated cheddar cheese
1 can cream of chicken soup
1 can cream of celery soup

Brown chicken in melted margarine in frying pan. Put chicken in a 9 x 13-inch pan. Sauté celery, green pepper and onion in margarine. Add cream of celery and cream of chicken soup. Dilute with 2 cans water. Let come to boil and pour over chicken. Cover and bake at 375 degrees for 2 hours. With 30 minutes of baking time remaining, sprinkle cheddar cheese over chicken and continue baking, uncovered.

Elizabeth Svitek, Canonsburg, Pa.

SALMON LOAF
Serves 5–6

1 (1-pound) can salmon
2 tablespoons melted butter
2 egg yolks
1 teaspoon Worcestershire sauce
½ teaspoon salt
½ cup milk
½ cup soft bread crumbs
1 teaspoon lemon juice
2 egg whites, stiffly beaten

Remove bones from salmon; add all ingredients, except egg whites. Fold in egg whites carefully. Place in greased loaf pan (8½ x 4½ x 2½-inch) and bake in a 350-degree oven until brown. Serve with cream of mushroom sauce made by heating 1 can cream of mushroom soup with 1 teaspoon Worcestershire sauce.

Shari Crider, Stoughton, Wis.

BROILED FISH DINNER

4 haddock fillets (1 pound total)
4 tomatoes
2 medium potatoes, boiled and sliced
2 tablespoons melted butter *or* margarine
1 tablespoon melted fat
Salt and pepper

Place a piece of waxed paper in broiler pan. Place fish, skin side down, on paper. Brush with melted fat; sprinkle with salt and pepper. Set broiler pan in oven so that fish is 3 inches from heat. Cut tomatoes in halves; spread melted butter over each half; sprinkle with salt and pepper. After fish has broiled 10 minutes, put tomatoes and potatoes around fish; broil 10 minutes more.

Diane Holmes, Brooksville, Fla.

HAM LOAF
Serves 12

3 pounds smoked ham
2 pounds lean fresh pork
3 eggs
1½ cans tomato soup
1 teaspoon paprika

Have ham and pork ground at the market or store. Beat eggs; add tomato soup and paprika; mix with ground meat. Place mixture in a loaf pan and bake in a 350-degree oven for 1½ hours.

Place baking pan in hot water to bake.

Ham Sauce:
1 cup mayonnaise
1 cup whipped cream
⅓ cup prepared mustard

Add mustard to mayonnaise. Fold in whipped cream just before serving.

Lucy Dowd, Sequim, Wash.

ORANGE PORK STEAKS
Serves 6

6 blade *or* arm bone pork steaks (2½ pounds)
2 tablespoons cooking oil
4 medium sweet potatoes, peeled and cut in ½-inch-thick slices
2 medium oranges
½ cup brown sugar
½ teaspoon salt
Dash ground nutmeg
Dash ground cinnamon

Cook steaks in skillet with cooking oil until browned. Sprinkle with salt. In a 9 x 13-inch baking dish arrange sweet potatoes. Thinly slice one of the oranges; place on top of potatoes; cover with steaks. Squeeze remaining orange; add water to juice to measure ½ cup. Combine juice, brown sugar, salt and spices. Pour over steaks. Bake, covered, at 350 degrees for 45 minutes. Uncover; bake 30 minutes more.

Leota Baxter, Ingalls, Kan.

POOR MAN'S LOBSTER

1 (1-pound) package frozen cod fillets (unthawed)
2 tablespoons salt
2 tablespoons white vinegar
Water to cover
Melted butter and lemon

Place frozen fillets and salt in saucepan with cold water to just cover. Bring to boil; lower heat and cook 10 minutes. Drain. Cover again with cold water and white vinegar. Bring to boil. Lower heat and cook 10 minutes more. Drain.

Serve, dipping each bite into melted butter and lemon. Tastes just like lobster with no salt or vinegar taste.

I squeeze lemon juice directly into the hot melted butter.

Madeline Darrow, Warren, Mich.

PEPPER STEAK WITH RICE
Serves 4

1 pound lean beef steak, 1/2-inch thickness
2 tablespoons margarine
Garlic powder
1 (10-ounce) can beef broth
1 cup sliced green onions, including tops
2 green peppers, cut into strips
2 tablespoons cornstarch
1/4 cup water
1/4 cup soy sauce
2 large, fresh tomatoes (cut into wedges)

Cut meat into 1/4-inch-wide strips. In large skillet, brown meat in melted margarine. Add garlic powder and beef broth. Cover and simmer 20 minutes. Stir in onions and green peppers. Cover and simmer 15 minutes.

Blend cornstarch, water and soy sauce. Stir into meat mixture. Cook and stir until thickened.

Add tomatoes and stir until heated; serve over rice. (This recipe earlier won a third prize in Illinois Beef Cook-off.)

Barbara Lindholm, Pekin, Ill.

BUTTER-HERB BAKED FISH

½ cup butter *or* margarine
⅔ cup crushed saltine crackers
¼ cup grated Parmesan cheese
½ teaspoon *each* basil leaves, oregano leaves and salt
¼ teaspoon garlic powder
1 pound frozen sole, perch *or* flounder fillets, thawed and drained (Fresh fish may be used.)

Preheat oven to 350 degrees. In 13 x 9-inch baking pan, melt butter in preheated oven, 5–7 minutes. Meanwhile, in a 9-inch pie pan combine cracker crumbs, Parmesan cheese, basil, oregano, salt and garlic powder. Dip fish fillets in melted butter, and then in crumb mixture. Arrange fillets in baking pan. Bake near center of 350-degree oven for 25–30 minutes, or until fish is tender and flakes with a fork. Serve immediately.

Peggy Fowler Revels, Woodruff, S.C.

SEAFOOD QUICHE

1 quart heavy cream
5 eggs
1 clove of garlic, crushed
1 teaspoon celery seed
¾ cup cheddar cheese (chopped)
¼ pound *each* of shrimp, crabmeat and scallops Butter
¼ cup Parmesan cheese Paprika
1 (9-inch) unbaked pie shell

Pour heavy cream in saucepan and heat to simmer or tiny bubbles. Remove from heat. In a large bowl whisk together eggs, garlic and celery seed; add to heavy cream. Place cheddar cheese in bottom of pie crust; set aside. Sauté all seafood in a large skillet or saucepan with butter. When seafood has cooked about 8 minutes, place over cheese. Then pour cream mixture over all ingredients in the pie crust. Sprinkle with Parmesan cheese and paprika. Bake at 350 degrees for approximately 30 minutes, or until knife comes out clean.

Sheila Symonowicz, Loganville, Pa.

STEAK ROLLS

4 cubed steaks
1/2 cup finely diced celery
1/2 cup mushrooms, chopped and drained

Place celery and mushrooms in center of cubed steaks. Roll up and fasten with 4 toothpicks. Roll in flour and brown slowly in oil in skillet.
Combine:
1 package onion soup mix
1/2 cup ketchup
1/4 teaspoon garlic powder
1/4 teaspoon Worcestershire sauce
1 1/2 cups water

Take steaks out of skillet. Arrange in a baking dish; pour sauce over top surface of steaks. Bake at 350 degrees for about 1 to 1 1/2 hours, or until done.

Dorothy Dayle Hare, Fremont, Neb.

LIVER KABOBS
Serves 4

4 slices bacon
12 ounces calves liver
1/2 pound mushrooms
4 tomatoes
2 tablespoons oil for broiling
Salt
Freshly ground black pepper

Cut bacon slices in half and flatten with the edge of a knife and roll up. Trim liver and cut into cubes. Trim mushrooms and slice tomatoes in half. Thread 4 skewers with alternate liver cubes, bacon rolls, mushroom caps and halved tomatoes. Brush kabobs with oil and season with salt and pepper. Put under a moderately hot broiler and cook for 10–15 minutes, turning occasionally.

Suzan Wiener, Spring Hill, Fla.

HAM LOAF
Serves 6

2 cups ground ham
1 cup bread crumbs *or* crushed cornflakes
1 egg
1 cup shredded carrots
1 cup milk

Grind ham coarsely in a meat grinder, then mix with other ingredients. Form into loaf and bake in a loaf-pan at 350 degrees for 45 minutes. Pineapple slices sprinkled with brown sugar may be added as a garnish and baked with the loaf for the last 15 minutes.

ATLANTIC COAST CRABMEAT BAKE

Serves 3

1½ cups light cream
½ pound crabmeat
1 teaspoon prepared mustard
1 cup onion, minced
1 teaspoon liquid hot sauce
1¼ tablespoons butter or margarine
1 cup bread crumbs
1 egg, beaten
2 teaspoons fresh lemon juice
¼ teaspoon salt
¼ teaspoon pepper
Cracker crumbs for topping
Butter or margarine for topping

In a large saucepan heat the cream and the next 10 ingredients. Place mixture in an ovenproof casserole; cover with cracker crumbs; dot with butter. Bake 400 degrees, 15 minutes until crumbs are golden and crispy.

Gwen Campbell, Sterling, Va.

HAWAIIAN HAM CUBES

Makes 10–12 servings

1 (10-ounce) jar orange marmalade
1 tablespoon soy sauce
1 pound ham, cut into 1/2-inch cubes
1 (8-ounce) can pineapple chunks, drained
1 large green pepper, cut into 1/2-inch squares

Mix marmalade and soy sauce in a 2-quart casserole. Stir in remaining ingredients until well-coated. Cover with a tight-fitting lid or plastic wrap.

Microwave on HIGH, 100 percent power, for 10 minutes, or until hot and bubbly. Stir halfway through the cooking time.

If desired, prepare recipe right in a dish to fit a chafing dish. Remove from microwave oven and elegantly serve at a party.

Marie Fusaro, Manasquan, N.J.

MEDITERRANEAN BAKED FISH

Serves 4

2 pounds tomatoes
1 tablespoon vegetable oil
3/4 cup chopped onion
1/2 cup diced green pepper
1 garlic clove, crushed
1 teaspoon salt
1 teaspoon grated orange peel
1/2 teaspoon thyme leaves, crushed
1/4 teaspoon fennel seed
1/16 teaspoon ground black pepper
1-1/2 pounds fish fillets

Use tomatoes held at room temperature until fully ripe. Preheat oven to 350 degrees. Cut tomatoes into 1/4-inch cubes (makes about 4 cups); set aside. In a medium saucepan heat oil until hot. Add onion, green pepper, and garlic. Sauté until onion is transparent, about 5 minutes. Add salt, orange peel, thyme, fennel, black pepper, and reserved tomato. Simmer, uncovered, stirring frequently for 15 minutes. Spoon half of the tomato mixture into a 13x9x2-inch baking pan. Arrange fish in a single layer over sauce. Spoon remaining tomato mixture on fish. Cover and bake until fish flakes easily with a fork, about 20 minutes. (209 calories per serving)

Sally Jones, Indianapolis, Ind.

CLAM CAKES

1 pint of clams, chopped
1 teaspoon baking powder
1 cup milk
2 eggs
2 cups flour
½ teaspoon salt
½ cup clam juice
Fat for frying

Mix flour, baking powder and salt; set aside. Beat eggs; add milk and clam juice. Add chopped clams, then flour mixture. Mix well. Drop by large spoonfuls into hot fat (or onto grill). When browned remove from fat and drain on paper towel or brown paper. Serve hot.

Mrs. Stanley Thims, Falmouth, Maine

PINEAPPLE HAM

3 ounces ground or finely chopped ham
¼ teaspoon mustard
1 tablespoon mayonnaise
1 tablespoon pineapple juice
3 slices canned pineapple, drained
Cauliflower sprigs for garnish

Mix together chopped ham, mustard, mayonnaise and pineapple juice. Then arrange the 3 pineapple slices on a baking tray and cover with ham mixture. Bake in 350-degree oven for 15 minutes.

This is a delicious recipe which my whole family loves!

Suzan L. Wiener, Spring Hill, Fla.

SCALLOPED POTATOES AND HAM

Serves 4

4 medium-size potatoes
Slices of leftover ham
Flour
Margarine
1 to 1½ cups milk
Salt and pepper to taste

Peel potatoes and cover with cold water. Heat oven to 350 degrees. Grease 2-quart baking dish. Layer ham slices in bottom of dish. Slice potatoes in thin slices to cover ham. Sprinkle potato layer with 1 tablespoon flour, salt and pepper to taste, and dot layer with 1 tablespoon margarine. Repeat, making 2 more layers. Pour milk over potatoes until it can be seen through the top layer. Bake covered for 45 minutes. Uncover and bake for 20–30 minutes more until top has browned.

225

BEEF ROULADEN

8 slices round steak (6 x 3 x ¼ inch)
Salt and pepper to taste
8 strips bacon, uncooked
Mustard
8 lengthwise slices carrots
8 lengthwise slices pickle
8 tablespoons chopped onion
2 tablespoons flour
¼ cup sour cream

Season meat with salt and pepper. On each slice of round steak lay 1 strip bacon, a little mustard, 1 slice carrot and 1 slice pickle. Sprinkle 1 tablespoon onion along length. Roll up and fasten with toothpicks or skewers. Fry in fat until brown. Cover with water and simmer 1½–2 hours, covered. Test for doneness with fork. To make gravy, add flour, sour cream and a little water to juices in pan. Season to taste.

June Harding, Ferndale, Mich.

MOLDED SHRIMP RING

1 (3-ounce) package lemon gelatin
1½ cups boiling water
½ cup ketchup
1 small can shrimp
1 cup chopped celery
1 teaspoon grated onion
1 cup cooked peas
10 stuffed olives, sliced

Dissolve gelatin in boiling water. Add ketchup and let set until slightly congealed. Then add remaining ingredients. Mix well and pour into mold. Let set until firm. Serve with the following:

Dressing:
½ cup mayonnaise
2 tablespoons cream
1 hard-cooked egg, cut up fine

Mix all ingredients together.
Mrs. Roy G. Carlson, Sycamore, Ill.

BAKED YOGURT CHICKEN
Serves 4

2-1/2–3 pounds chicken, cut up
Salt and pepper
6 tablespoons butter *or* margarine
2 tablespoons flour
1 tablespoon paprika
2 cups plain yogurt
1/4 pound fresh mushrooms, sliced
2 tablespoons fresh lemon juice
2 tablespoons chopped fresh dill or parsley

Wash chicken pieces and wipe dry. Add salt and pepper. In a large pan, melt 4 tablespoons butter; fry chicken until golden brown. Remove to buttered, shallow baking dish. Sprinkle flour and paprika into pan juices and cook, stirring for 1 minute. Stir in yogurt and mix well. Spoon over chicken. Sauté mushrooms in remaining 2 tablespoons butter and lemon juice for 1 minute and spoon over chicken. Sprinkle with dill. Bake, covered, at 325 degrees for about 1-1/4 hours, or until chicken is tender.

Laura Hicks, Troy, Mont.

BOILED HAM DINNER
Serves 4–6

1 ham bone with chunks of meat
3–4 carrots
4–6 small whole onions
3–4 potatoes
1 bay leaf
6 peppercorns and cloves
Water to cover
1 small head of cabbage

Cook ham in large pot with carrots and potatoes (peeled and cut into chunks), peeled onions, bay leaf, peppercorns, cloves and water. Simmer until carrots are tender. On the stove, that would be about 1½ hours; in a slow cooker on medium setting, about 6. Add cabbage, cut into wedges, and cook for 20 more minutes.

BAKED HAM IN A BLANKET
Serves 12-15

1 (12-to 15-pound) ham
4 cups flour
1 cup brown sugar
2 tablespoons ground cloves
2 tablespoons cinnamon
2 tablespoons mustard
1 teaspoon black pepper
Water or cider

Have a butcher cut off small end of ham. Trim off rind and excess fat. Place in open roasting pan with fat side up. Combine remaining ingredients, adding enough liquid to make stiff dough. Roll into sheet to cover ham over top, ends, and sides. It is not necessary to add water to pan in which ham is baked. Place in cold oven. Bake at 300 degrees, allowing 25 minutes per pound of ham.

HAM AND CORN CROQUETTES
Serves 4

1 cup cream-style corn
2 tablespoons green pepper, chopped
1 cup ground ham
½ cup dried bread crumbs
1 egg, beaten

Mix all ingredients in saucepan. Heat to boiling. Cook for a minute or 2 to let the egg thicken. Remove from heat and chill.

When mixture is cold, shape into patties and dip into more dried bread crumbs, then in 1 egg beaten with 2 tablespoons water, then in crumbs again. They may be put back into the refrigerator until you are ready to fry them, or fry at once. Fry 2 at a time in deep fat until brown. Serve with a sauce made from canned mushroom soup diluted with a little milk and heated.

FILET MIGNON TETA-A-TETA

Valentine's Dinner for 2

4 tablespoons butter
2 tablespoons shallots, minced
1 clove garlic, whole
1 tablespoon Worcestershire sauce
1 teaspoon soy sauce
2 (6-ounce each) Filets Mignons
3 ounces brandy
1 tablespoon cashew nuts, coarsely
   chopped

Heat 2 tablespoons butter in skillet; add shallots and garlic; sauté over medium heat for 5 minutes. Remove and discard garlic. Increase heat to high, add Worcestershire sauce and soy sauce; place filets in pan. Let cook 3 minutes on each side, turning once for slightly rare. Transfer filets to warm dish. Deglaze pan with brandy and then ignite with a match (be careful of flames). Remove pan from heat, swirl in remaining butter to thicken sauce. Pour over filets and top with cashew nuts. Serve immediately.

Marie Fusaro, Manasquan, NJ

SPANISH RICE STEAKS

Serves 4

4 cube steaks
1 cup all-purpose flour
1/2 cup vegetable oil
Salt and pepper to taste
1 onion, sliced
1 (5 ounce) can Spanish rice
1/4 teaspoon sugar
2 teaspoons parsley flakes

Coat steaks with flour. In skillet, brown steaks in oil. Transfer to lightly greased 9 inch square baking dish. Season with salt and pepper; set aside. Saute onions slices; add Spanish rice and sugar; mix well. Spoon rice mixture over steaks; sprinkle with parsley flakes.

Gwen Campbell, Sterling, VA

FRUITED POT ROAST

4 pounds chuck roast or pot roast
2 tablespoons margarine
1-1/2 teaspoons salt
1/8 teaspoon pepper
1 cup apple juice
1 cup dried apricots
1 cup pitted prunes
1 cup tart apples, pared and sliced
2 cinnamon sticks, or 1/4 teaspoon
   ground cinnamon

Brown meat in margarine. Pour off the drippings. Season with salt and pepper. Cover and simmer in Dutch oven (or bake at 350 degrees) for 2-2-1/2 hours, or until tender.

Turn meat over and add fruit. Continue cooking for 30 minutes or until apples are tender. Serve on a warm platter, surrounded by the fruit.

Mrs. L.W. Mayer, Richmond, VA

MOCK STROGANOFF

Serves 6

1/4 cup onion, chopped
1 tablespoon margarine, melted
2 tablespoons oil, any kind (except
   olive oil)
Salt to taste
3 cups cubed, cooked beef
1 can (10-3/4 ounces) condensed
   tomato soup
1 can (3 or 4 ounces) chopped mushrooms
1 (8 ounce) can peas, drained
1 teaspoon sugar
1 cup dairy sour cream
Hot cooked and buttered noodles of
   your choice

Saute onion in oil and margarine in a large frying pan; add beef and brown lightly. Stir in tomato soup, mushrooms, peas, sugar, and salt. Cover mixture, simmer 20 minutes to blend flavors. Stir in sour cream; heat just to boiling point (Don't let sauce boil, as sour cream may curdle). Serve over buttered hot noodles.

Marie Fusaro, NJ

GLAZED BEEF PINWHEEL ROLL

1 pound lean ground beef
1/4 teaspoon salt
1/4 teaspoon pepper
1 onion, chopped fine
1 egg
1 tablespoon milk
1 cup soft bread crumbs
1-1/2 cups raw carrots, shredded
2 tablespoons fresh parsley, minced
Chili Glaze (recipe follows)

Mix all ingredients, except carrots and parsley. Wet rolling pin; roll beef mixture on a sheet of wax paper to make a rectangle 6 inches wide and 1/2 inch thick. Spread with mixture of carrots and parsley. Roll as for jelly roll. Place in a shallow baking pan, uncovered. Spread top of roll with chili glaze. Bake at 350 degrees for 1 hour.

Chili Glaze:

Combine 1/2 cup chili sauce with 1/2 cup water, 1 tablespoon corn syrup, and 1 tablespoon Worcestershire sauce.

Gwen Campbell, Sterling, Va.

BEEF BEER BALLS

1 pound ground beef
1/4 to 1 teaspoon ground cloves, depending upon taste
1/2 teaspoon salt
1/4 teaspoon black pepper
1/2 teaspoon Accent seasoning
1/2 cup catsup
2 tablespoons Worcestershire sauce
12 ounces of beer

Mix ground beef, ground cloves, salt, pepper and Accent. Form into small balls about the size of walnuts. Brown well. Mix catsup, Worcestershire sauce and beer in separate pan. Simmer for 10 minutes. Drain fat from meatballs, add sauce. Cover; simmer 2 hours. Serve on toothpicks.

Ruby Jo Keplin

Micro- MAGIC

ORANGE YOGURT CAKE
Serves 8–10

1 egg, slightly beaten
1 (8-ounce) carton orange yogurt
1 (9-ounce) package yellow *or* white
   cake mix (Jiffy cake mix)
1/2 teaspoon grated orange peel
   (optional)

Grease an 8-inch round baking dish lightly; line with waxed paper. Combine egg, yogurt and orange peel; add cake mix and blend. Beat 2 minutes. Pour into baking dish. Place in microwave on inverted pie plate. Microwave on SLOW-COOK (30 percent power) for 6 minutes; make 1/2 turn. Microwave on HIGH (100 percent power) for 6 minutes. Let stand flat on counter to cool for 5–10 minutes. Turn onto serving place and frost when completely cooled.
Note: Try chocolate cake mix with vanilla or cherry yogurt, or spice cake mix with apple or peach yogurt.
   Karen Blunt, Mason City, Iowa

CHILLED FRUIT AMBROSIA
Serves 6–8

1 (10-ounce) package frozen strawberries, thawed
1 (8-1/4-ounce) can pineapple chunks
5 tablespoons brown sugar
1 tablespoon cornstarch
1 (11-ounce) can sliced mandarin
   oranges, drained

1/2 cup thinly sliced apples
1/4 cup green seedless grapes
1/4 cup shredded coconut
1/4 cup quick-cooking oats
2 tablespoons flour
1/4 teaspoon cinnamon
2 tablespoons butter *or* margarine

Drain strawberries and pineapple; reserve syrup; combine to make 1 cup liquid. In a 10 x 6-inch microwave-safe dish mix 2 tablespoons of the sugar with cornstarch; blend in juices. Microwave, uncovered, 3–4 minutes on HIGH; stir after each minute; add fruits and coconut. Mix remaining sugar, oats, flour and cinnamon. Cut in butter; sprinkle over fruits. Microwave, uncovered, 3 minutes on HIGH; turn dish 1/2 turn after 1-1/2 minutes. Chill well before serving.
   Gwen Campbell, Sterling, Va.

PASTA AND TUNA SALAD
Serves 6

1 (7-ounce) package pasta shells or
   elbow macaroni, cooked
1 (10-ounce) package frozen peas,
   prepared as directed
1 (6-ounce) can tuna, drained
1 cup creamy ranch dressing
3 green onions, sliced
10 cherry tomatoes, halved (optional)

Combine pasta and peas with tuna, dressing, onions, and tomatoes in serving bowl; mix gently to coat evenly. Cover and refrigerate.

CIDER SNAP
Serves 2

2 cups apple cider *or* apple juice
4 teaspoons red cinnamon candies
Thin apple slices, optional

In a 4-cup measure combine apple cider and cinnamon candies. Microwave, uncovered, on 100 percent power or HIGH for 4–5 minutes or until candies dissolve and the cider is steaming hot, stirring once. Serve in mugs. Garnish with apple slices, if desired.
   Laura Hicks, Troy, Mont.

SALMON CASSEROLE
Serves 2-3

1 small can salmon
1/2 cup fresh bread crumbs
1/4 cup minced celery
1 tablespoon minced onion
1 tablespoon parsley
1 tablespoon margarine
2 cheese slices

Rinse salmon in cold water to remove as much salt as possible. Drain; flake in a 3-quart bowl. Blend in bread crumbs, celery, onion, parsley, and margarine; mix together. Press into a small tube pan or shape into a ring in a small dish. Decorate top with cheese slices, cut into strips. Microwave on HIGH for 10 minutes. For the last 3 minutes of cooking time, fill center of ring with peas.

HONEY AND LEMON MICROWAVE ENGLISH MUFFIN BREAD

Makes 2 loaves

cups flour
packages dry yeast
teaspoon salt
/4 teaspoon soda
2 tablespoons grated lemon rind
-3/4 cups milk
/2 cup water
/3 cup honey
Cornmeal

In a large bowl combine 3 cups flour, dry yeast, salt and soda. Stir in lemon rind. Combine milk, water and honey in a saucepan. Heat until very warm (120–130 degrees). Add to dry ingredients and beat well. Stir in remaining flour to make a stiff batter. Spoon into 2 (8-1/2 x 4-1/2 x 2-1/2-inch) loaf dishes which have been greased and sprinkled with cornmeal. Sprinkle tops with cornmeal. Allow to rise to top of dish. Microwave on HIGH for 6-1/2 minutes. Allow to rest 5 minutes. Surface will be pale. Toast and serve.

Ruth Meinert, Davis, Ill.

PARMESAN-BUTTERED ROLLS

Makes 6–8 rolls

1/4 cup butter *or* margarine, softened
2 tablespoons grated Parmesan cheese
1 teaspoon dried parsley flakes
1/4 teaspoon garlic salt
6–8 dinner rolls

Combine margarine, cheese, parsley flakes and garlic salt. Cut each roll crosswise, two-thirds of the way to the bottom. Spoon or spread about 1 rounded teaspoon margarine mixture on cut surface of each roll. Microwave, uncovered, on HIGH (100 percent) until warm, 30 seconds to 1 minute.

Sharon M. Crider, Stoughton, Wis.

CHOCOLATE CRACKLES

Makes 4 dozen

1/2 cup plus 2 tablespoons Butter Flavor Crisco
6 tablespoons cocoa
1 cup sugar
2 teaspoons baking powder
1/2 teaspoon salt
2 eggs
1 teaspoon vanilla
2 cups flour
1/2 cup chopped nuts
1/2 cup confectioners' sugar in sifter

In medium bowl microwave Butter Flavor Crisco on HIGH power for 45–60 seconds or until melted. Add cocoa, blend. Beat in sugar, baking powder, salt, eggs and vanilla. Stir in flour and nuts. Mix well. Cover and refrigerate until firm. Shape dough into 1-inch balls; roll in confectioners' sugar. Arrange 8 balls, 2 inches apart, in a circle on waxed-paper-lined plate.

Microwave at MEDIUM power for 1-1/2–2 minutes or until cookies are puffed and surface is dry, but cookies should be soft to touch. Cool on waxed paper on countertop. Before serving, sprinkle with confectioners' sugar, if desired.

Sue Thomas, Casa Grande, Ariz.

ANYTIME CRUNCH BARS

Makes 16 bars

6 ounces (1 cup) semisweet chocolate chips
1/2 cup peanut butter chips
1/3 cup margarine
1 teaspoon vanilla
2 cups crisp rice cereal
1 cup quick-cooking rolled oats

Glaze:
1/4 cup peanut butter chips
1 teaspoon oil

Grease 9-inch square or round pan. In medium, microwave-safe bowl, combine chocolate chips, 1/2 cup peanut butter chips and margarine. Micro-

wave on MEDIUM for 2–3 minutes, stirring once halfway through cooking. Stir until smooth. Remove from heat; stir in vanilla. Add cereal and oats; stir until well-coated. Press in greased pan.

To prepare glaze, in small, microwave-safe bowl, combine glaze ingredients. Microwave on MEDIUM for 1–2 minutes; stir until smooth. Drizzle over bars. If desired, refrigerate until set. Cut into bars.

Barbara Nowakowski, North Tonawanda, N.Y.

CARAMEL CHEERIOS BARS

14–16 ounces caramel candies
1/4 cup water
1/2 cup peanut butter
4 cups Cheerios
1 cup salted peanuts

Topping:
1 cup chocolate chips
1/4 cup peanut butter
2 tablespoons margarine

Combine caramels, water and peanut butter in large mixing bowl. Microwave on HIGH for 3–5 minutes until melted; stir every minute. Stir in cereal and peanuts; press into buttered 13 x 9-inch pan. Melt topping ingredients in a 2-cup glass measure by microwaving them for 2 minutes on 50 percent power or MEDIUM. Stir, then microwave 2 more minutes on MEDIUM; blend well. Spread over bars. Cool before cutting.

Mrs. Merle Mishler, Hollsopple, Pa.

ORANGE TEA

1 cup orange juice
2 cups water
1 tablespoon sugar
2 tea bags
4 orange slices

In a 2-quart measure, microwave the orange juice, water and sugar for 7–9 minutes. Stir; add tea bags and let stand, covered, for about 5 minutes. Serve with an orange slice.

CRUNCHY-TOPPED PUMPKIN CAKE

Serves 12

2 eggs
1 (16-ounce) can *or* 2 cups cooked
   and mashed pumpkin
3/4 cup evaporated milk
1/2 cup firmly packed brown sugar
1 teaspoon cinnamon
1/4 teaspoon nutmeg
1 (9-ounce) package yellow cake mix
1/2 cup margarine

In 2-quart microwave-proof bowl or casserole, whisk 2 eggs. Blend in pumpkin, milk, sugar, cinnamon and nutmeg. Microwave on HIGH, uncovered, 4 minutes, or until hot and slightly thickened, stirring once halfway through. Pour into microwave-proof 8-inch square baking dish. Sprinkle with dry cake mix.

Microwave margarine in a microwave-proof small bowl on HIGH for 1 minute, or until melted. Drizzle evenly over cake mix. Microwave, uncovered, on HIGH for 8 minutes, or until top is set, rotating dish twice. Place dish under conventional broiler for 2 minutes, or until lightly browned. Cool and refrigerate. Cut in squares.

June Harding, Ferndale, Mich.

APPLE CAKE

Serves 8

1-1/2 cups flour
1 teaspoon baking powder
1 teaspoon cinnamon
1/4 teaspoon salt
1/2 cup butter *or* margarine
3/4 cup sugar
2 eggs
1/4 cup vegetable oil
1 large tart apple (1-1/2 cups),
   peeled, cored and chopped
1/2 cup chopped walnuts
1/2 teaspoon vanilla

Glaze:
1/2 cup confectioners' sugar
2 teaspoons milk

Mix flour, baking powder, cinnamon and salt. Melt butter in an 8-inch square glass baking dish. Add sugar, eggs and oil. Mix with fork until blended. Stir in flour mixture, then apple, walnuts and vanilla; smooth top. Place on inverted plate. Microwave on HIGH for 8–10 minutes turning twice, until pick inserted comes out clean. Cool 30 minutes. Mix glaze ingredients and drizzle over cake.

Ruth Meinert, Davis, Ill.

PINEAPPLE DREAM CAKE

Serves 10–12

1-1/2 cups shredded coconut
1 package yellow cake mix (without
   pudding)
1 (3-ounce) package instant vanilla
   pudding
1 (8-ounce) can crushed pineapple,
   undrained
1 cup sour cream
2 eggs

In a pie plate, spread coconut; microwave 5–7 minutes on HIGH; stir 3–4 times until golden. Cool. Grease bundt pan, coat with the toasted coconut. In a large mixing bowl, place cake mix, pudding, undrained pineapple, sour cream and eggs. Blend well; pour into greased bundt pan, on top of coconut. Microwave on 70 percent power for 14–17 minutes. Let stand 10 minutes. Cakes in the microwave will not brown, but the toasted coconut adds some color.

Mrs. Merle Mishler, Hollsopple, Pa.

CARAMEL COFFEE RING

Serves 8

1/2 cup packed brown sugar
1/4 cup butter

1 tablespoon water
1/2 cup chopped nuts
1 (10- *or* 12-ounce) can refrigerated
   buttermilk biscuits

In a ring-shaped microwave baking dish put the sugar, butter and water. Microwave on HIGH for 1–1-1/2 minutes until melted; stir to blend. Sprinkle nuts around ring; arrange biscuits on top, slightly overlapping. Microwave on MEDIUM for 4–6 minutes, turning dish after half the time, until dough springs back when lightly touched and top looks dry. Invert on a serving plate. Let stand 2 minutes before removing pan. Serve warm.

Ruth Meinert, Davis, Ill.

POPEYE'S FRENCH BREAD

Serves 6

4 cups fresh spinach leaves
1 small onion, chopped
1 clove garlic, minced
3 tablespoons butter *or* margarine
1 teaspoon Worcestershire sauce
1 (8-ounce) loaf French bread
1 tomato, thinly sliced
1 cup shredded mozzarella *or* Monterey Jack cheese

Wash spinach well and remove thick stems. Place in a 1-quart microwave-safe casserole and cover with lid. Cook on HIGH 2–2-1/2 minutes, or until wilted. Drain well and squeeze to remove excess liquid. Chop coarsely and return to casserole. Place onion, garlic and butter in 1-cup glass measure. Cook on HIGH for 1-1/2–2 minutes or until tender. Add to spinach along with Worcestershire sauce; mix well. Cut bread almost in half lengthwise. Open up and spread spinach mixture over bottom half. Top with tomato slices; sprinkle with cheese. Close bread and wrap in paper towels. Microwave on HIGH for 1-1/2 minutes or until cheese starts to melt, rotating loaf once. Cut into 6 slices and serve at once.

Mrs. A.S. Warren, Charlotte, N.C.

230

MISSISSIPPI MUD CAKE

Serves 16

Cake:

1 cup butter *or* margarine
2 cups granulated sugar
1/2 cup unsweetened cocoa powder
4 large eggs
2 teaspoons vanilla extract
1-1/2 cups all-purpose flour
3/4 cup walnut pieces, chopped coarsely
1/4 teaspoon salt
1/2 cup miniature marshmallows

Frosting:

1/2 cup butter *or* margarine
1/3 cup milk
1/4 cup unsweetened cocoa powder
1/2 teaspoon vanilla extract
1 (16-ounce) box confectioners' sugar

To make cake, put butter in large mixing bowl. Microwave on HIGH for 1–1-1/2 minutes until melted. Stir in sugar and cocoa powder. Add eggs and vanilla; beat vigorously until well-blended. Stir in flour, walnuts and salt. Let batter rest 10 minutes. Pour into an 11-3/4 x 7-1/2-inch baking dish. Place on a plastic trivet or inverted saucer in microwave oven. Microwave on MEDIUM for 9 minutes, rotating dish 1/2 turn after 3 minutes. Shield the corners of the dish with small triangles of foil (don't let triangles touch each other or sides of oven). Microwave on HIGH for 3–5 minutes, rotating dish 1/2 turn once, until top is mostly dry with a few moist spots and pick inserted near center comes out clean. Sprinkle marshmallows evenly over top of cake. Let stand about 5 minutes until marshmallows are slightly melted.

Meanwhile to make frosting, put butter in a large bowl. Microwave on HIGH for 30–60 seconds until melted. Stir in milk, cocoa powder and vanilla. Add sugar and beat vigorously until smooth. Spread evenly over marshmallows (cake will be warm). Let stand on flat, heatproof surface for 30 minutes until slightly warm, or cool completely and serve at room temperature.

Karen Waido, Mendota, Ill.

BREAKFAST RING

Serves 4

1/2 cup brown sugar
1 teaspoon cinnamon
1/4 cup maple syrup
1/2 cup chopped nuts
1 package (8- *or* 10-count size) refrigerator biscuits

Put nuts in bottom of small microwave bundt pan. Mix together cinnamon and brown sugar. Dip each biscuit in maple syrup and then in sugar mixture. Arrange in pan sideways. Microwave at power level 4, MEDIUM, for 9 minutes.

Sue Thomas, Casa Grande, Ariz.

CHOCOLATE SHEET CAKE

1 cup margarine
1/2 cup unsweetened cocoa
2 cups granulated sugar
4 eggs
1 teaspoon baking powder
1/4 teaspoon salt
1-1/2 cups flour
2 teaspoons vanilla
1/2 cup pecan pieces
1-1/4 cups miniature marshmallows

Place margarine in a 2-quart casserole. Microwave on HIGH for 1-1/2–2 minutes. Beat in cocoa with wooden spoon with sugar; then add eggs. Blend in baking powder, salt and flour; stir in vanilla and pecans. Spread batter in a 2-quart dish. Microwave on MEDIUM-HIGH (70 percent) for 11–12 minutes. Rotate, if necessary, every 3 minutes. Leave cake in pan; layer the marshmallows over hot cake. Cover with plastic wrap; let stand 5 minutes. Uncover; spread over top of cake; let cool.

Frosting:

2 tablespoons margarine
2 tablespoons unsweetened cocoa
2 tablespoons milk
2 cups confectioners' sugar
1 teaspoon vanilla

Place margarine in a 4-cup measure; microwave on HIGH for 30–40 seconds. Stir in cocoa, then milk; blend in sugar and vanilla. Spread on top of sheet cake.

CHEESY MICROWAVE LASAGNA
Serves 6–8

1/2 pound lasagna noodles
2 (8-ounce) cans tomato sauce
1 (6-ounce) can tomato paste
1 tablespoon oregano
2 teaspoons basil
1/4 teaspoon garlic powder
1 pound ground beef, cooked and drained
2 cups cottage cheese
1 egg
1 tablespoon parsley flakes
1 (6-ounce) package sliced mozzarella cheese
1 (6-ounce) package cheddar cheese
1/2 cup grated Parmesan cheese

In the bottom of baking dish place 1 tablespoon oil, noodles and water to cover. Microwave on HIGH for 8 minutes. Drain noodles. In large bowl mix tomato sauce, paste, oregano, basil, 1/2 teaspoon salt and garlic powder. Spread 1/2 cup sauce over bottom of baking dish. Mix beef with remaining sauce. In small bowl mix cottage cheese, egg and parsley. Layer 3 noodles, half of cottage cheese mixture, half of mozzarella and cheddar cheese, half of sauce in baking dish. Repeat layers. Sprinkle Parmesan cheese over top. Cover with waxed paper, microwave on HIGH for 20–26 minutes, rotating dish 1/4 turn every 8 minutes. Let stand 10 minutes before cutting. Can be made ahead and refrigerated. Add 4–6 minutes to cooking time.

Mrs. Merle Mishler, Hollsopple, Pa.

CHICKEN KIEV
Serves 4–6

2/3 cup melted butter
3/4 cup dry bread crumbs *or* crushed cornflakes
3 tablespoons grated Parmesan cheese
1 teaspoon basil
1 teaspoon oregano
1/2 teaspoon garlic salt
1/4 teaspoon salt
4 chicken breasts, deboned and skinned
Pepper to taste

Sauce:
1/2 cup apple juice *or* white wine
1/2 cup chopped green onion
1/4 cup chopped fresh parsley
Reserved butter

Melt butter in glass mixing bowl in microwave for 40 seconds on HIGH. Dip chicken breasts in melted butter. Set aside melted butter after dipping chicken.

Combine bread crumbs, cheese, spices, salt and pepper. Dip chicken in crumb mixture to coat. Arrange chicken in 13 x 9 x 2-inch glass baking dish. Microwave on HIGH for 9 minutes. Rotate dish 1/2 turn; cook approximately 9 minutes longer, or until fork-tender.

Combine sauce ingredients, including reserved butter, and pour over chicken. Cover with waxed paper and microwave for 3–5 minutes on 70 percent power *or* 1-1/2–2 minutes on HIGH. Let stand, covered, for 5–6 minutes. Spoon sauce over chicken and serve hot. Garnish with paprika and parsley.

Carolyn Griffin, Macon, Ga.

CAULIFLOWER AND CARROT MEDLEY
Serves 8

1 head cauliflower *or* 1 (20-ounce) package frozen cauliflower florets
4 cups carrot slices, 1/4 inch thick
2 tablespoons water
1/4 teaspoon Dijon-style mustard
1 cup chicken broth
1/2 cup sour cream
3 tablespoons flour
1-1/4 cups grated cheddar cheese, divided
2 green onions, sliced

Place cauliflower, carrots and onions in a 3-quart casserole. Add 2 tablespoons water. (If using frozen vegetables, do not add water.) Cover and cook with HIGH power, 14–15 minutes. Let stand for 8–10 minutes without removing cover

In large blender jar mix broth, mustard, sour cream and flour until smooth. Pour into a 4-cup measure and microwave with HIGH power, 4–5 minutes, until thick, stirring twice. Add 1 cup cheese and stir until melted.

Drain vegetables and add sauce; stir to coat vegetables with sauce. Sprinkle remaining cheese on top. Microwave with HIGH power, 4–5 minutes, until cheese melts and vegetables are heated through.

Yvonne Schilling, Wauwatosa, Wis.

SOUTH-OF-THE-BORDER CHOCOLATE CAKE
Sérves 8

package microwave chocolate cake
  mix with round pan
1/3 cup water
1/3 cup vegetable oil
egg
teaspoon cinnamon

Topping:
cup semisweet chocolate chips
2 teaspoons almond extract mixed
  with 2 tablespoons water
1/2 cup whipping cream
2-1/2 teaspoons confectioners' sugar
1/2 teaspoon vanilla extract
1/4 cup almonds

Using solid shortening grease round pan provided with mix. In medium bowl, combine all cake ingredients. Beat with spoon about 1 minute or until well-blended. Pour into pan. Microwave on HIGH for 6-1/2 minutes; if microwave oven is under 600 watts microwave on HIGH for 8 minutes. Cake is done when top no longer has any wet spots and it pulls away from sides of pan. If cake is not done, add additional time in 30-second intervals. Immediately invert cake onto serving plate. Cool completely.

In microwave-safe bowl, combine chocolate chips, almond extract and the 2 tablespoons water; microwave on MEDIUM for 1-1/2–2-1/2 minutes or until chocolate chips are melted, stirring once halfway through cooking. Beat until smooth. Cool 20 minutes, or until slightly thickened. Spread onto top of cake.

In small bowl, beat whipping cream until soft peaks form. Blend in confectioners' sugar and vanilla; beat until stiff peaks form. Spread over chocolate icing on cake. Stick almonds into whipped cream. Store in refrigerator.

Frances Allen, Mount Juliet, Tenn.

TOFFEE COFFEE CAKE
Serves 8–10

1/2 cup butter *or* margarine
1 cup sugar
2 eggs
1 teaspoon vanilla
1 cup sour cream
1-1/2 cups sifted all-purpose flour
1/2 teaspoon baking powder
1/2 teaspoon baking soda
1/4 teaspoon salt
3 tablespoons sugar
3/4 teaspoon cinnamon
1/2 cup almond brickle chips *or*
  crushed Heath bars
Almond Glaze (recipe follows)
1 tablespoon sliced almonds

Place butter in 2-quart glass measure and cook on HIGH for 20–30 seconds, or until softened. Cream in 1 cup sugar. Add eggs, 1 at a time, beating well after each. Blend in vanilla and sour cream. Add flour, baking powder, soda and salt; beat until smooth. Grease a 10–12 cup microwave-safe tube pan. Combine 3 tablespoons sugar with cinnamon; sprinkle pan with 1 tablespoon of mixture. Spoon half of batter into pan; sprinkle with brickle chips and remaining cinnamon-sugar. Spoon remaining batter on top, spreading evenly. Cook on MEDIUM (50 percent), uncovered, for 13–14 minutes, or until edges are set, rotating pan once. Then cook on HIGH 1-1/2–2-1/2 minutes, or until no longer doughy, rotating pan once. Let stand 10 minutes; invert onto serving plate and let cool. Spoon Almond Glaze over cake; sprinkle with almonds.

Almond Glaze:
2 tablespoons butter *or* margarine
1 cup unsifted confectioners' sugar
1–2 tablespoons hot water
1/4 teaspoon almond extract

Place butter in a 2-cup glass measure; cook on HIGH for 10–20 seconds, or until softened. Mix in sugar; add hot water until of drizzling consistency. Stir in almond extract.

Mrs. A.S. Warren, Charlotte, N.C.

BARK COOKIES
Makes 4 dozen

2 pounds almond bark
1 cup peanut butter
2 cups dry roasted peanuts
3 cups Rice Krispies
2 cups miniature marshmallows

In an 8-cup microwave-safe dish melt almond bark on MEDIUM heat. Add rest of ingredients, 1 at a time, stirring well after each addition.

Drop by spoonfuls onto waxed paper.

Sue Thomas, Casa Grande, Ariz.

BROWNIE NUT CUPCAKES
Makes 1-1/2 dozen

1 cup milk
1/2 cup cocoa
1/2 cup shortening
1-1/2 cups flour
1 cup sugar
1 teaspoon baking powder
1/2 teaspoon baking soda
1 egg
1/2 cup semisweet chocolate chips
1/2 cup chopped walnuts

Line 6 medium muffin cups, 2 x 2 x 1-1/4 inches, or 6 (6-ounce) custard cups with paper baking cups. Arrange cups in circle on 12-inch plate.

Put milk and cocoa in 2-1/2-quart bowl; add shortening. Microwave, uncovered, on HIGH for 2 minutes; stir until shortening is melted. Stir in flour, sugar, baking powder, baking soda and egg. Add chocolate chips and walnuts; mix until smooth. (Mixture will be thick.) Fill muffin cups half full. Sprinkle with additional chocolate chips and walnuts, if desired.

Microwave, uncovered, on HIGH for 2–3 minutes, rotating plate 1/4 turn after 1 minute, until wooden pick inserted in center comes out clean. (Parts of cupcakes will appear moist, but will continue to cook while standing.) Let stand, uncovered, for 1 minute; remove to rack. Repeat with remaining batter.

Barbara Nowakowski, North Tonawanda, N.Y.

233

STEAK-VEGETABLE POCKETS

Serves 2

1/2 pound beef top round steak
2 tablespoons cold water
1 tablespoon soy sauce
1 teaspoon cornstarch
1 small carrot, thinly sliced
1 tablespoon water
1/2 cup broccoli buds
6 fresh mushrooms, sliced
2 tablespoons green onion sliced
1 tablespoon cooking oil
1 small tomato, chopped
2 pita bread rounds

Partially freeze meat. With a sharp knife thinly slice meat across the grain, into bite-size strips. In a small bowl stir together 2 tablespoons water, soy sauce and cornstarch; set aside. Place carrots in shallow baking dish; sprinkle with 1 tablespoon water. Cover with vented plastic wrap. Microwave on 100 percent power on HIGH for 2 minutes. Stir in broccoli, mushrooms and green onion. Microwave, covered, on 100 percent power or HIGH for 1–2 minutes more, or until crisp-tender. Drain; cover and set aside.

Preheat a 10-inch microwave browning dish on 100 percent power or HIGH for 3 minutes. Add oil; swirl to coat dish. Add beef. Microwave, uncovered, on 100 percent power or HIGH for 2–3 minutes or until meat is done, stirring twice. Stir the soy sauce mixture. Stir into beef. Microwave, uncovered, on 100 percent power or HIGH for 1–2 minutes or until mixture is thick and bubbly, stirring every 30 seconds. Gently toss the beef mixture with broccoli mixture and chopped tomato. Halve the pita bread. Carefully spoon some of the mixture into each of the 4 pita bread halves.

Laura Hicks, Troy, Mont.

FISH CREOLE

1 pound sole or orange roughy fillets

1 (8-ounce) can tomato sauce
1 (2.5-ounce) jar sliced mushrooms
1/2 green pepper, diced
1/4 teaspoon garlic powder
1/4 teaspoon oregano
3 green onions, sliced
1 stalk celery, diagonally sliced
3 tablespoons water
1 teaspoon instant chicken bouillon

Rinse fish and pat dry. Arrange in 3-quart oblong baking dish with thicker portions toward outside of dish. Combine remaining ingredients in a 4-cup glass measure; pour evenly over fish. Cover with plastic wrap; microwave on HIGH for 8–10 minutes, or until fish flakes easily. Let stand 5 minutes.

FLORENTINE NOODLES

1/2 cup chopped onion
1 (10-ounce) package frozen chopped spinach
1 (10-ounce) can cream of celery soup
1/2 cup sour cream

1/2 cup grated Parmesan cheese
1/8 teaspoon pepper
1/8 teaspoon ground nutmeg
Dash of cayenne pepper
2 cups cooked wide egg noodles (6 ounces uncooked)

Place onion in 2-quart casserole; cover with lid; microwave on HIGH for 3 minutes; stir once. Add spinach; cover and microwave on HIGH about 5 minutes; stir once. Stir in soup, sour cream, cheese, pepper, nutmeg, and cayenne. Cover and microwave on 50% power for about 8 minutes; stir once. Add hot noodles. Toss to coat.
Suggestion: Add 2 cups cooked ham or sausage to make a complete meal.

SAUCY GINGER CHICKEN

Serves 4

4 chicken breasts, skinned and deboned
1/4 teaspoon onion powder
1/2 teaspoon garlic powder
1/8 teaspoon ground ginger
2 eggs, beaten lightly
2 tablespoons apple juice
1/4 cup Parmesan cheese
2 cups seasoned bread crumbs
1/2 stick butter *or* margarine

Season chicken breasts with spices. Mix eggs and apple juice; dip breasts in egg mixture. Combine cheese and bread crumbs; roll breasts in crumb mixture. Place chicken in 8 x 8 x 2-inch square, microwave-safe baking dish; pour butter over all. Cover; cook on HIGH for 25 minutes, rotating dish twice during cooking. Remove chicken to warmed platter; pour sauce over chicken breasts.

Gwen Campbell, Sterling, Va.

SHORTCUT SEAFOOD AND CHICKEN CASSEROLE

Serves 6

1 (16-ounce) can whole tomatoes, undrained
1 (10-ounce) package frozen green peas
1 (6-1/2-ounce) can minced clams, undrained
1 (5-ounce) can chunk chicken, drained
1 (4-1/4-ounce) can broken shrimp, rinsed and drained
2 cups uncooked instant rice
2 tablespoons instant minced onion
1 teaspoon chicken bouillon granules
1 teaspoon paprika
1/4 teaspoon turmeric
1/4 teaspoon ground red pepper

Mix all ingredients in 3-quart casserole, breaking up tomatoes with fork. Cover tightly and microwave on HIGH for 11–14 minutes, stirring after 5 minutes, until liquid is absorbed.

Barbara Nowakowski, North Tonawanda, N.Y.

HOT CHICKEN SALAD IN CHEESE TARTS
Serves 6

2 cups coarsely cut up cooked
   chicken *or* turkey
1 cup celery, thinly sliced
2 tablespoons lemon juice
1 tablespoon onion, finely chopped
1/2 teaspoon salt
1/4 teaspoon pepper
3/4 cup mayonnaise
1 cup seedless green grapes, halved
1/2 cup slivered almonds, toasted

Cheese Tarts:
1/4 cup plus 2 tablespoons margarine
1 cup flour
1/2 teaspoon salt
1/2 cup (2 ounces) finely shredded
   cheddar cheese
2–3 tablespoons cold water

Prepare Cheese Tarts. Toss chicken, celery, lemon juice, onion, salt and pepper in 1-1/2-quart bowl. Stir in mayonnaise. Fold in grapes and 1/4 cup of the almonds carefully. Cover loosely and microwave on MEDIUM (50 percent) for 6–7 minutes, stirring after 3 minutes, until hot. Spoon chicken mixture into tarts. Sprinkle with remaining almonds.

Cheese Tarts: Cut margarine into flour and salt until particles are size of small peas. Stir in cheese. Sprinkle in water, 1 tablespoon at a time, tossing with fork until all flour is moistened and pastry cleans side of bowl (1–2 teaspoons water may be added, if necessary).

Gather pastry into a ball; shape into flattened round on lightly floured surface. Roll into 13-inch circle about 1/8-inch thick. Cut into 6 (4-1/2-inch) circles. Shape pastry circles over backs of 6 (6-ounce) custard cups, making pleats so pastry will fit closely. Prick with fork to prevent puffing.

Arrange custard cups in circle on 12-inch plate. Microwave, uncovered, on HIGH about 5 minutes, rotating plate 1/2 turn after 3 minutes, until tart shells are dry and flaky. Let stand, uncovered, 5 minutes. Loosen edge of each tart with tip of knife; remove each tart from cup carefully. Let cool on rack.

Barbara Nowakowski, North Tonawanda, N.Y.

MAKE-AHEAD MASHED POTATOES
Serves 6

6 medium potatoes (about 2 pounds)
1-1/2 cups creamed cottage cheese
1/2 cup sour cream *or* Lite sour
   cream
1/8 teaspoon garlic powder
1/2 teaspoon salt
2 teaspoons dried chopped chives
Pepper to taste
Butter
Parmesan cheese
Paprika

Peel and quarter potatoes. In a 1-1/2-quart casserole combine potatoes and 1/2 cup water. Cover casserole and microwave on HIGH (100 percent power) for 15–20 minutes, or until very tender, stirring once. Drain. Transfer potatoes to a large bowl. Beat with electric mixer on low speed. Add cottage cheese, sour cream, garlic powder, salt, pepper and chives and beat until smooth and fluffy. Turn into a greased 1-1/2-quart casserole. Brush with butter and sprinkle with Parmesan cheese and paprika. Chill up to 24 hours. Cover and microwave on HIGH (100 percent power) for 8–10 minutes, or until heated through.

Karen Blunt, Mason City, Iowa

PORK CHOW MEIN
Serves 6–8

1 pound pork, cut in 1/2-inch cubes
2 cups celery, thinly sliced
1 cup onion, chopped
2 tablespoons cornstarch
1/4 cup water
1 (16-ounce) can Chinese vegetables, drained and rinsed
1 tablespoon brown sauce *or* molasses
2 tablespoons soy sauce
1/4 teaspoon ginger, ground
1 tablespoon cornstarch
1 cup beef broth

Place pork cubes in covered 3-quart casserole dish. Microwave on HIGH for 4 minutes, stirring once. Add celery and onion; cover; cook on HIGH for 3 minutes. Blend 2 tablespoons cornstarch and 1/4 cup water; stir into meat mixture. Add Chinese vegetables, brown sauce or molasses, 2 tablespoons of soy sauce and 1/4 teaspoon ginger.

Blend 1 tablespoon cornstarch with 1/4 cup beef broth. Add the rest of the beef broth to the casserole. Heat on LOW for 20–25 minutes, stirring twice. Mix in cornstarch and beef broth mixture, stirring well. Cook for 2–3 minutes more.

Kathleen Dwyer, Saginaw, Minn.

HOT GERMAN POTATO SALAD
Serves 8–10

8 medium potatoes
8 strips lean bacon
1 medium onion, finely chopped
3 tablespoons flour
1/4 cup sugar
1 teaspoon salt
1/2 teaspoon celery seed
1 cup water
1/3 cup vinegar

Pierce potatoes and microwave in a circle for 12–15 minutes on HIGH. Turn over and rearrange after 5 minutes. Be sure they are cooked through. Peel and slice. Cut bacon in pieces and put in casserole with onion. Cover with paper towel and microwave on HIGH for 8 minutes, or until crisp. Stir after 4 minutes. Remove bacon and drain. Stir flour, sugar, salt and celery seed into bacon fat until smooth. Microwave on HIGH for 1–2 minutes until bubbly. Stir in water and vinegar. Microwave on HIGH 5 minutes. Stir after 1 minute. Cook until it boils and thickens. Stir until smooth. Add potatoes and bacon; stir. May be made ahead and reheated.

Mrs. Merle Mishler, Hollsopple, Pa.

235

CHEESEBURGER-VEGETABLE CASSEROLE

Serves 4–6

1 pound ground beef
1/2 cup chopped onion
1/4 cup butter *or* margarine
1/4 cup flour
1 teaspoon salt
Dash pepper

1-1/2 cups milk

1-1/2 cups shredded sharp American cheese
1 teaspoon Worcestershire sauce
1 (10-ounce) package frozen mixed vegetables
1/4 cup chopped canned pimiento
Packaged instant mashed potatoes, enough for 4 servings

In a large bowl crumble the beef. Add onion. Microwave, covered, until meat is brown, about 5 minutes, stirring several times to break up meat. Drain off fat. In a 4-cup measure, melt butter about 45 seconds. Stir in flour, salt and pepper. Gradually stir in milk. Microwave, uncovered, 1 minute; stir. Microwave until thick and bubbly, about 3 minutes, stirring every 30 seconds. Stir in 1 cup of the cheese and Worcestershire sauce. Add to meat mixture. Break up frozen vegetables. Stir vegetables and pimiento into meat mixture. Turn into an 8 x 8 x 2-inch baking dish. Microwave, covered, 10 minutes, turning after 5 minutes.

Prepare the instant potatoes according to package directions, except decrease water by 1/4 cup. Spoon the prepared potatoes around the edge of the casserole. Sprinkle remaining cheese over potatoes. Microwave, uncovered, until cheese is melted, about 1 minute.

Laura Hicks, Troy, Mont.

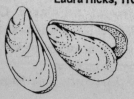

CHICKEN AND BEAN CASSEROLE

1 pound chicken cutlets (no thicker than 1/4 inch)
2 eggs, beaten
1 cup bread crumbs
1 (8-ounce) can tomato sauce
1 small onion, chopped
1 clove garlic, minced
1 teaspoon mustard
1 teaspoon Worcestershire sauce
Dash pepper
1 (8-ounce) box frozen Italian beans, thawed

If cutlets are thicker than 1/4 inch, just flatten with a rolling pin. Dip each cutlet into beaten eggs and then in bread crumbs. Place chicken cutlets in 2-quart microwave dish and cook, covered, on HIGH for 5 minutes. While chicken is cooking combine tomato sauce, onion, garlic, mustard, Worcestershire sauce and pepper. Remove chicken from baking dish. Place thawed beans in bottom of baking dish. Top beans with chicken. Then top all with tomato sauce mixture. Cover and cook for 10 minutes on HIGH.

Marla Balaklaw, Cortland, N.Y.

CHICKEN CORDON BLEU

Serves 6

3 large chicken breasts, deboned, skinned and halved lengthwise (about 1-1/2 pounds)
6 thin slices boiled ham
6 thin slices Swiss cheese
2 tablespoons butter
1 (10-3/4-ounce) can cream of mushroom soup
2 tablespoons milk *or* white wine
1 (2-1/2–3-ounce) can sliced mushrooms, drained
1 tablespoon minced parsley

Pound chicken breasts with mallet until 1/4-inch thickness. Place 1 slice ham and 1 slice cheese on each. Tuck in sides and roll up, jelly-roll fashion. Skewer with 2 toothpicks; set aside. Melt butter in 8 x 12-inch glass baking dish, in microwave. Microwave breasts in melted butter on HIGH for 3 minutes, uncovered. Turn chicken over so seam side is down; microwave on HIGH for 3 minutes. Combine soup with milk and mushrooms. Pour over chicken. Cover with waxed paper. Microwave on HIGH for 7 minutes, rotating dish after 3-1/2 minutes. Garnish with minced parsley.

Mrs. Merle Mishler, Hollsopple, Pa.

CHEESY ENCHILADA CASSEROLE

Serves 6–8

1 pound ground chuck
1 teaspoon garlic salt
1 teaspoon onion salt
1 tablespoon chili powder
2 cups shredded Velveeta cheese
1 (10-3/4-ounce) can mushroom soup
1 (10-ounce) can enchilada sauce (mild)
2/3 cup evaporated milk
8 large corn tortillas

Preheat an 8-1/4-inch browning skillet for 5 minutes on HIGH. Turn after 2-1/2 minutes. Place ground chuck in skillet and microwave on HIGH for 3 minutes. Add garlic salt, onion salt and chili powder, and cook for 1-1/2 minutes; turn skillet. Add enchilada sauce, mushroom soup and evaporated milk. Stir well. Cook for 1-1/2 minutes; stir; turn skillet and cook for 1-1/2 minutes.

Remove from oven. Tear 8 corn tortillas into fourths. Place in 9 x 13-inch glass microwave dish. Spoon mixture over tortillas until all are covered. Return to oven and cook for 4 minutes on MEDIUM. After 2 minutes, turn skillet; do not stir. Add 2 cups shredded Velveeta cheese and cook for 1-1/2 minutes, or until cheese is melted. Remove from oven and serve with tossed salad and your favorite beverage.

Joan D. Sisk, Warner Robins, Ga.

236

DOUBLE CHOCOLATE BARS

Makes 2 dozen

First Layer:
1/2 cup butter *or* margarine
1/4 cup sugar
2 eggs
1 teaspoon vanilla
3/4 cup flour
4 tablespoons cocoa
1/4 teaspoon baking powder
1/4 teaspoon salt
1/2 cup pecans

Second Layer:
2 cups miniature marshmallows

Topping:
6 ounces chocolate chips
1 cup peanut butter
1-1/2 cups Rice Krispies

Mix all first-layer ingredients together. Pour into an 11 x 9-inch dish. Microwave on SIMMER (50 percent) power for 6 minutes, then on HIGH power for 3 minutes.

Spread 2 cups miniature marshmallows on top and put in microwave on HIGH for 1-1/4 minutes. Spread the melted marshmallows, let cool.

Melt 6 ounces chocolate chips and 1 cup peanut butter; stir in Rice Krispies. Microwave on HIGH for 1–1/4 minutes. Spread on bars, let cool.

Mary Ann Donlan, Waterloo, Iowa

APPLE NUT TORTE

4 eggs
1 cup sugar
¾ cup flour
1 teaspoon baking powder
½ teaspoon salt
4 cups sliced apples
½ teaspoon cinnamon
1 cup chopped nuts
½ teaspoon vanilla

Beat eggs at high speed until frothy,

about 1 minute. Gradually add sugar; beat until mixture forms soft mounds, about 5 minutes. Fold in flour, baking powder, cinnamon and salt. Fold in apples, nuts and vanilla. Grease only bottom of 12 x 8-inch pan; spoon batter into dish; spread evenly. Cover with waxed paper. Microwave 8–9 minutes. Preheat broiler. Broil about 3 inches from heat for 2–3 minutes.

CHOCOLATE CHIP BARS

1/2 cup butter or margarine
3/4 cup brown sugar
1 egg
1 tablespoon milk
1 teaspoon vanilla
1-1/4 cups flour
1/2 teaspoon baking powder
1/8 teaspoon salt
6 ounces chocolate chips (1 cup)
1/2 cup nuts (optional)

Mix all ingredients together, except the chips, but use only 1/2 cup in the mixture; the other half, place on top of batter. Microwave in an 8- or 9-inch glass pan, for 6-1/2 minutes.

POPCORN BALLS

1/4 cup (1/2 stick) butter or margarine
1 (10-1/2-ounce) bag miniature marshmallows
1 package (4-serving-size) Jell-O Brand gelatin, any flavor
3 quarts (12 cups) popped popcorn

Heat butter and marshmallows in large microwave bowl at HIGH 1-1/2 to 2 minutes or until marshmallows are puffed. Add gelatin; stir to blend. Pour marshmallow mixture over popcorn and stir to coat. Shape into balls or other shapes with buttered hands.

APPLE MUFFINS

1/3 cup melted shortening
1/2 cup sugar
1 egg, beaten
1/2 cup milk
1 1/2 cups flour
1 tablespoon baking powder
1 teaspoon cinnamon
1 cup finely chopped apples
1/4 cup sugar
1/2 teaspoon cinnamon

In a large bowl, beat shortening and sugar; stir in egg and milk. Add flour, baking powder, cinnamon and apples; stir until just blended. Fill 6 paper-lined muffin cups, 1/2 full. Sprinkle tops with sugar-cinnamon mixture and microwave for 2 1/2 minutes; turn once, if necessary.

LOUISIANA POPCORN

Makes 2 quarts

3 tablespoons butter
1/2 teaspoon salt
1/4 teaspoon garlic powder
1/4 teaspoon chili powder
1/4 teaspoon crushed thyme
1/8 teaspoon ground red pepper
2 tablespoons grated cheddar cheese
2 quarts popped popcorn

In a 1-cup glass measure, combine butter, salt, garlic and chili powders, thyme, pepper and cheese. Cook on MEDIUM, 1-1/2–2 minutes, or until melted. Stir well and pour over popped corn. Toss to coat evenly.

Cecilia Rooney, Point Pleasant, N.J.

SWISS FILLET ROLLS
Serves 4

1 small onion, chopped
2 cups (8 ounces) sliced fresh mushrooms
2 tablespoons butter *or* margarine
1 cup herb-seasoned stuffing mix
1 pound white fish fillets (flounder, sole, etc.)
Salt and pepper

Sauce:
1 tablespoon butter *or* margarine
1 tablespoon flour
1/8 teaspoon salt
1/2 cup milk
1/4 cup shredded Swiss cheese
1 tablespoon dry white wine
Snipped fresh parsley, if desired

Combine onion, mushrooms and butter in 1-quart glass measure. Cook on HIGH for 2-1/2–3 minutes, or until tender. Mix in stuffing mix; set aside. Place fillets on flat surface; sprinkle with salt and pepper. Divide stuffing evenly among fillets. Roll up with stuffing inside; place seam side down in shallow glass baking dish (1-1/2-quart) and cover with vented plastic wrap. Cook on HIGH for 4–4-1/2 minutes, or until fish flakes easily with fork. Set aside. Place butter in 2-cup glass measure; microwave on HIGH for 30-40 seconds, or until melted. Blend in flour and salt; stir in milk. Cook on HIGH for 1–1-1/2 minutes, or until mixture boils and thickens, stirring once. Stir in cheese and wine. Spoon sauce over fillets; garnish with parsley.

Mrs. A.S. Warren, Charlotte, N.C.

MEXICAN BEEF AND RICE

1 pound ground beef
Salt and pepper to taste
8 whole green onions, sliced
1 (15-ounce) can tomato sauce
1 cup water
1/4 cup sliced, pitted ripe olives
1 tablespoon chili powder
1-1/2 cups Minute Rice
Hot peppers, if desired
Tortilla chips

Combine all ingredients except tortilla chips in a microwave dish. Cover and cook on HIGH for 5 minutes. Stir and cook for 5 minutes longer. Let stand 5 minutes; fluff with a fork.

Serve with tortilla chips. Salt and pepper to taste.

Mrs. W.O. Tucker, Jonesboro, Ark

CRUSTLESS QUICHE LORRAINE
Serves 6

10 slices bacon
1/4 cup finely chopped onion *or* 1 tablespoon instant minced onion
1 cup shredded cheddar cheese
4 eggs
1 (13-ounce) can evaporated milk
3/4 teaspoon salt
1/4 teaspoon sugar
1/8 teaspoon cayenne pepper

Cook bacon between layers of paper towels for about 8–10 minutes on HIGH. Crumble bacon. Sprinkle cheese, bacon and onion in 9-inch glass pie plate. Beat remaining ingredients with rotary beater until well-blended. Pour over bacon mixture. Microwave on HIGH for 9 minutes. Turn dish, 1/4 turn, every 3 minutes of cooking time. Let stand 10 minutes for center to finish cooking.

Mary Ann Donlan, Waterloo, Iowa

BARBECUED PORK CHOPS
Serves 4

6 pork chops, 1/2-inch thick
1 cup barbecue sauce
1/2 cup chopped onion
1/8 teaspoon minced garlic
1/2 teaspoon salt
1/8 teaspoon pepper

Arrange chops in a 12 x 8-inch dish. Combine remaining ingredients. Pour over chops. Cover with plastic wr and microwave on HIGH for 5 minute Let stand, covered, for 5 minutes. Rep 2 more times, basting with sauce duri rest times. If need be, chops can cooked 5 minutes more after the la standing time. Turn the dish 1/4 tu after each rest period.

Shari Crider, Stoughton, W

TACO MAIN DISH
Serves 2–4

1 pound ground beef
1 medium onion, diced
1 (1-pound) can kidney beans, drained
1/2 package dry taco seasoning mix
1 can olives (black *or* green)
1 package frozen corn *or* 1 can whole-kernel corn
1 cup Doritos, crushed
1 (8-ounce) can tomato sauce

Brown first 2 ingredients in 1-1/2 quart baking dish in microwave o HIGH for 5 minutes. Add remainin ingredients. Heat through. Cover wit grated cheese. Microwave on HIGH, o until cheese melts and bubbles.

Sue Thomas, Casa Grande, Ari

SALAMI
Serves 6–8

2 pounds lean ground beef
1/4 teaspoon salt
1/4 teaspoon pepper
1/8 teaspoon garlic powder
1 tablespoon mustard seed
2 tablespoons Morton Tender Quick salt
1 tablespoon Liquid Smoke
3/4 cup water

Mix all ingredients well. Divide in 2 rolls; wrap in plastic wrap and twi ends securely. Cook on MEDIU HIGH for 34 minutes. Let stand minutes. Refrigerate. If microwave not equipped with turntable, turn 2 or times during cooking time.

Ann Elsie Schmetzer, Madisonville, K

MILLION-DOLLAR CHEESECAKE
Serves 8–10

Crust:
(1)0 chocolate sandwich cookies with
   filling, crushed
(t)ablespoons margarine, melted

Combine crushed cookies and margarine. Press on the bottom of a 9-inch round glass dish. Rotating pan midway through cooking, microwave on HIGH for 2 minutes.

Cheesecake Filling:
(3) (8-ounce) packages cream cheese
(1/)2 pound white chocolate, cut into
   small pieces
(4) large eggs
(3/)4 cup plus 1 tablespoon sugar
(1-)1/2 tablespoons white creme de
   cacao
(3/)4 cup sour cream
(1) (8-ounce) container non-dairy
   whipped topping
(D)ark chocolate shavings for garnish

Put cream cheese and white chocolate into a large glass mixing bowl. Stirring midway through cooking time, microwave on MEDIUM for 4 minutes, or until cheese is softened and chocolate is melted. Add eggs and beat with mixer or whisk. Add 3/4 cup sugar and 1 tablespoon creme de cacao; mix well. Pour over prepared crust. Rotating pan 1/4 turn after 3 minutes, microwave on MEDIUM HIGH for 10–12 minutes, or until center jiggles only slightly. Combine sour cream with remaining sugar and liqueur; spread over top of cheesecake. Microwave on MEDIUM HIGH for 1 minute. Let cool and refrigerate. Spread whipped topping over top and garnish with dark chocolate shavings before serving.

LEMON BARS
Makes 15

Crust:
(1)/2 cup butter *or* margarine, at room
   temperature
(1)/4 cup confectioners' sugar

1 cup all-purpose flour
1/8 teaspoon salt

Topping:
2 large eggs
1 cup granulated sugar
1 teaspoon freshly grated lemon peel
1/4 cup fresh lemon juice
2 tablespoons all-purpose flour
1/4 teaspoon baking powder

Spray bottom of an 8-inch square glass baking dish with vegetable cooking spray. To make crust, beat butter and sugar in a medium-size bowl with electric mixer or wooden spoon until blended. Stir in flour and salt until well-blended. With lightly floured fingertips press mixture evenly in bottom of prepared dish. Place dish on plastic trivet or inverted saucer in microwave oven. Microwave, uncovered, on HIGH 3–5 minutes, rotating dish 1/2 turn once. Crust will look dry on top with some wet spots on bottom (lift dish to check) and will not be browned. Let stand 15 minutes or until slightly cooled.

To make topping, slightly beat eggs in small bowl. Stir in remaining ingredients until blended. Pour over crust. Microwave, uncovered, on HIGH 3–5 minutes, rotating dish 1/2 turn once, until edges are set. Top will have some foamy spots and center will be slightly loose. It will set on standing. Cool completely in baking dish on flat heat-proof surface. Cut into 2-1/2 x 1-1/2-inch bars. Remove carefully with narrow metal spatula.

Karen Waldo, Mendota, Ill.

RAISIN-NUT DROPS
Makes 2 dozen

1 (6-ounce) package semisweet
   chocolate chips
1 cup jumbo peanuts
1 cup seedless raisins

Place chocolate, peanuts and raisins in a 2-1/2-quart casserole dish. Place in microwave and cook 1–3 minutes on HIGH until chocolate chips melt. Stir to cover peanuts and raisins completely. Drop by teaspoonfuls onto waxed paper. Place in refrigerator to set.

Barbara Penland, Goshen, Ind.

PECAN SPREAD
Serves 12

1 (8-ounce) package cream cheese
2 tablespoons milk
1/4 cup chopped green pepper
1/2 teaspoon garlic salt
1/4 teaspoon pepper
2 tablespoons dry onion flakes
1/2 cup sour cream
1 tablespoon melted butter *or* margarine
1/3 cup chopped pecans
1/2 teaspoon salt

Place cream cheese in a medium, micro-safe bowl; microwave on HIGH power for 30–45 seconds. Add milk, green pepper, garlic salt, pepper, onion flakes and sour cream; mix well.

Microwave butter *or* margarine in small micro-safe dish for 15 seconds on HIGH power to melt; stir in pecans and salt. Microwave 1 minute on HIGH power to toast pecans. Sprinkle buttered pecans over cheese mixture in serving dish. Serve with crackers or crisp vegetables.

Yvonne Schilling, Wauwatosa, Wis.

CHUNKY GRANOLA

6 cups rolled oats
1/2 cup sunflower seeds *or* nuts
1/2 cup coconut
1/2 cup wheat germ
1/2 cup powdered milk
2/3 cup honey
2/3 cup oil
1 teaspoon vanilla

In microwave heat rolled oats 3 minutes on HIGH. Stir together vanilla, oil and honey; add to dry ingredients. Heat on HIGH for 6 minutes, stirring 3 times.

Raisins, dates or dried fruit may be added with nuts, etc. Spread to cool.

Sue Thomas, Casa Grande, Ariz.

STRAWBERRY MOUSSE

Serves 4–6

1 (10-ounce) package frozen strawberries, defrosted
1 envelope unflavored gelatin
1/4 cup granulated sugar

1/2 teaspoon lemon juice
1/4 teaspoon lemon peel
2 egg whites
1/4 teaspoon cream of tartar
1 cup frozen whipped topping, thawed

Mash strawberries; press through
sieve *or* blend in an electric blender
until smooth (puréed). Sprinkle gelatin
over puréed fruit. Microwave on HIGH
(100 percent) for 2–3 minutes, or until
the gelatin dissolves. Stir in 2 tablespoons sugar, lemon juice and lemon
peel. Chill for 20 minutes, or until thickened, but not set.

Beat egg whites and cream of tartar
until foamy. Gradually add remaining
sugar. Beat until stiff, but not dry. Fold
beaten egg whites into strawberry
mixture. Then fold in whipped topping.
Pour into a 1-quart serving dish or 4
individual serving dishes. Refrigerate
for 4 hours, or until set. Garnish with
whipped topping and a dab of orange
marmalade, if desired.

Marie Fusaro, Manasquan, N.J.

FROSTED MEAT LOAF DINNER

Serves 4

This makes a very attractive and
complete meal on one plate.

2 cups bread crumbs
1/2 cup chopped onion
Salt and pepper to taste
1/2 cup milk
2 pounds ground beef
2 eggs, beaten
4 cups mashed potatoes
1-1/2 cups cheese, shredded
Paprika
1 or 2 packages frozen mixed vegetables, cooked

Mix all ingredients together, except
the last 4. Shape and form into a ring
loaf. Bake in microwave according to
directions of your oven. Remove loaf
from microwave and invert onto a platter. Frost loaf ring with mashed potatoes. Sprinkle cheese over top. Return
to oven to melt cheese. Sprinkle with
paprika and fill center of ring with
mixed vegetables.

Ann Elsie Schmetzer, Madisonville, Ky.

CHEESY ASPARAGUS

Serves 3–4

2 (14-1/2-ounce) cans cut, well-
drained asparagus
1/4 teaspoon salt
1/8 teaspoon pepper
2 hard-cooked eggs, sliced
1 (4-ounce) can mushrooms, drained
1 (10-1/2-ounce) can cheddar cheese
soup
5 crushed soda crackers
2 ounces slivered almonds
1/2 cup cheddar cheese
Pinch of paprika

Place half of asparagus in 1-1/2-
quart casserole. Sprinkle with half of
salt and pepper. Top with half of egg
slices. Add half of mushrooms. Beat
cheese soup with fork. Spoon half of
soup over mushrooms. Top with half of
crackers. Sprinkle almonds over all.
Repeat layers. Microwave 8–10 minutes at 70 percent power, MEDIUM;
should be hot and bubbly. Top with
cheese and paprika. Microwave at 50
percent power, 4–6 minutes until cheese
melts. Let sit, covered, 10 minutes
before serving.

Sue Thomas, Casa Grande, Ariz.

SOUR CREAM BURGERS

Serves 2

1/4 cup sour cream
2 tablespoons sliced green onion
4 teaspoons fine dry bread crumbs

1/4 teaspoon salt
Dash of pepper
1/2 pound ground beef
2 hamburger buns, toasted
Lettuce leaves
Sliced tomatoes

Stir together sour cream, green o
ion, bread crumbs, salt and pepper. A
ground beef, mixing well. Shape mi
ture into 2 (3/4-inch-thick) patties. Pla
patties in a small baking dish. Loose
cover with plastic wrap or waxed p
per. Microwave on 100 percent pow
or HIGH for 3 minutes. Turn patti
over; rotate baking dish 1/2 turn. Micr
wave on 100 percent power or HIG
for 2–3 minutes more, or until don
Drain off fat. Serve patties on toaste
buns with lettuce and tomato. Dollo
with additional sour cream, if desire

Laura Hicks, Troy, Mo

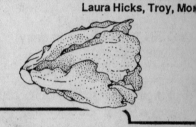

SCALLOPED CHEESE POTATOES

Serves 5–6

1/4 cup margarine
3 tablespoons flour
2 teaspoons dried chives *or* green
onion
1/2 teaspoon salt
1/2 teaspoon dry mustard
1/8 teaspoon pepper
1-3/4 cups milk
4 medium potatoes, peeled and slice
1 cup grated cheese

Microwave margarine in 2-quart ca
serole for 45 seconds, or until melte
Stir in flour, chives, salt, dry mustar
and pepper. Blend in milk. Microwav
on HIGH 6–7 minutes, or until thick
ened, stirring often. Mix in potatoe
and cheese; cover. Microwave on HIG
for 15–20 minutes until potatoes ar
tender, stirring 2–3 times.

Mrs. Warren G. Anderson, Fremont, Ne